Management

St. Clair Press Titles
In Management and Organizations

ORGANIZATIONAL BEHAVIOR AND MANAGEMENT:
A Contingency Approach
    Henry L. Tosi and W. Clay Hamner

CONTEMPORARY PROBLEMS IN PERSONNEL
    W. Clay Hamner and Frank L. Schmidt

MANAGEMENT, Second Edition
    Henry L. Tosi and Stephen J. Carroll

READINGS IN MANAGEMENT: Contingencies, Structure, and Process
    Henry L. Tosi

EXPERIENCES IN MANAGEMENT AND ORGANIZATIONAL BEHAVIOR,
Second Edition
    Douglas T. Hall, Roy J. Lewicki, Donald D. Bowen,
    and Francine S. Hall

THEORIES OF ORGANIZATION
    Henry L. Tosi

Management
SECOND EDITION

Henry L. Tosi
University of Florida

Stephen J. Carroll
University of Maryland

1807 1982

John Wiley & Sons

New York   Chichester   Brisbane   Toronto

Library of Congress Cataloging in Publication Data:

Tosi, Henry L.
  Management.

  Bibliography: p.
  Includes index.
  1. Management. 2. Organization. I. Carroll,
Stephen J., 1930–   joint author. II. Title.
HD31.T645 1982   658.4   80-28875
ISBN 0-471-07884-0

Printed in the United States of America

10 9 8 7 6 5 4 3 2 1

To Robert G. St. Clair

PREFACE TO THE SECOND EDITION

Much of what we said in the first edition is still relevant in this new edition. In that sense the book is very much the same. We have tried to write a book based on contingency theory—the idea that the best way to manage "all depends on the situation."

As in the first edition, we have remained as prescriptive as we could be because we believe that such an approach is necessary. Managers make decisions; they prescribe. We think a textbook on management should do likewise, though the prescriptions can be based on theory and research. To do this, we have had to make some choices about which particular theoretical approach to favor, then and now. We made the choices and they appear in the book. There are no apologies for what we have selected to cover—or to omit. Before judging our posture too harshly, the reader, we hope, will take the time to consider how the pieces fit together and criticize the whole view we present, not some relatively small piece of the concept. As we said in the preface to the first edition, "Sometimes our fabric is smooth and at other times—we hope not too often—it may be rough, but we hope that the ideas are developed with reasonableness and logical consistency."

We have made some important changes, however, changes that are substantial enough to amount to a major revision, rather than a cosmetic alteration of the first edition. First, we have restructured the chapters in a very important way. In the first edition we included chapters that were directly aimed at how to manage different types of organizations. We tried to integrate organizational behavior, organization theory, and management theory in what we thought to be a unique approach. The chapters on managing bureaucratic organizations included topics such as motivation, leadership, and control. The chapters on organic organizations contained similar material, but with specific reference to organic types. In this edition we have unbundled those chapters and now include in the topic chapters (e.g., leadership) the concepts relevant for organic and mechanistic organizations. We hope this will be a pedagogical improvement.

Second, we have emphasized management process more in this edition. There are new chapters on strategic planning, departmentation, coordination, control, and applications of motivation.

Third, we have not dodged the issue of sexism in our writing style. We have far more examples of female managers than in the first edition. We hope we have been fair in our treatment of both sexes. Where we have failed, we hope to do better in the future.

Fourth, we have included cases, both in the text and at chapter ends. With a single exception, these are based on actual events. The cases were prepared by us or by some of our students.

Many of these changes, which we think will make this book better, were suggested by Bob St. Clair. He was most instrumental in the first edition and, with the second edition, as the principle of St. Clair Press (the publisher of the first edition), he was again very supportive. He died in 1979 and we lost not only a professional colleague without parallel but also a very good friend. Thus we have dedicated this second edition to him. Those who knew him will understand our decision.

There are others who were very helpful to us. Several reviewers have made many useful suggestions: Delf Dodge of the University of Michigan, Debbie Schellenberg and Ann Smith at Indiana University, Allan Bludhorn of Penn State, Tom Martin of Southern Illinois, among others.

Still others helped in the preparation of the manuscript: Barbara Washington, Tanya Davis, Diane Johnson, Heidi Middleton, Kandy Kidd, and Vicki La Placa. Nancy Geiger and Jan Zahrly deserve a very special mention because of their very close support and assistance in putting the pieces of the book together. They tried very hard to keep things such as references, footnotes, figures, and cases organized. We are grateful for what they did, though we take responsibility for all errors of logic, omission, or commission.

With these changes, as we said in the earlier edition, "We hope the book works."

Henry L. Tosi
Stephen J. Carroll

PREFACE TO THE FIRST EDITION

The basic structure of this book is drawn from a wide range of ideas that are part of management and organization literature. The "contingency" theme is of course not a new one. We all know that "it all depends." In this book we try to tell the reader what it depends upon, and what to do when he knows.

There is a reason for this prescriptive approach. In recent years organization and management theorists have moved away from such an approach. Because of the belief that "there is no one best way," an excessive amount of work in the field is descriptive. But managing requires prescription. In this book we take a very prescriptive position.

We would like to thank all of the creators of the good books of the past—the sources of the ideas that form the substance of our field—but there are so many that it is an impossible task. It is of course upon their ideas that our text is built. What we have sought to do is to draw out essential ideas and weave them into "managerial process contingency theory," a perhaps elaborate way of saying that what a manager should do does indeed "all depend." Sometimes our fabric is smooth, and at other times—we hope not too often—it may be rough, but we hope that the ideas are always developed with reasonableness and logical consistency.

• • •

We would also like to say a word about our collaboration. The conceptual model underlying this book is Henry Tosi's, but each of us regards the other, not simply as a co-author, but as a collaborator without equal.

Finally, a word about our approach to the question of the social responsibility of managers. Much of the substance of a text in this subject, because it deals with widely applicable techniques of management, is not directly related to the treatment of various social ills. Do we think women and minorities should have equal opportunity as managers? Our position is simply that they should. In this book, however, we have generally used the convention of the masculine pronoun because, as many authors have discovered, there is no effective English-language singular that includes both sexes. We have also opted occasionally for female examples, simply to underscore our view that good management is nondiscriminatory.

Students should bear in mind that many management techniques discussed in this book can be applied effectively to various areas of social responsibility, including that of advancing the employment of women and minorities in management positions. Chapter 19, which deals with contemporary management problems, has precisely the purpose of encouraging analysis for that type of application.

It remains to be said that we take responsibility for all errors of logic, omission, or commission. We hope the book works.

Henry L. Tosi
Stephen J. Carroll

CONTENTS

Management

Introduction

This book presents a "management process contingency theory" approach to studying managing, managers, and the organizations in which they work. The general idea of the theory is quite simple. It is that some managerial strategies are more important than others in certain circumstances. But to make such a statement is not very useful unless the "managerial strategies" and the nature of the "certain circumstances" are defined and the manner in which circumstances affect strategies is clearly specified. That is what we will do in this book.

In this first part, we outline in some detail the basic elements of management process contingency theory. Chapter 1 describes the fundamental ideas in this theory, along with a discussion of what managers do.

Chapter 2 shows where the ideas come from. The conventional, though quite incorrect, view is that management thinking and writing began around the turn of the twentieth century with Frederick Taylor; management practice actually began when human beings formed groups to do things collectively. In Chapter 2 we present an historical perspective that tells how we arrived at the state of the field today.

CHAPTER ONE

The Nature of Managerial Work

Item 1.1

In 1971 Ed Johnson left college after two years of studying liberal arts. He did not know what to do with himself. He disliked formal study. He was not trained for a particular field although he had superior mechanical skills and intelligence. One night Ed discussed his uncertain future with some relatives at a family gathering. These relatives owned a chain of variety goods discount houses. Ed's uncle suggested that he might start a business of his own and recommended the television antenna business. In fact, his uncle said that given the chain store's difficulties in finding a reliable supplier of this product, they might consider providing him with financial backing if he would agree to supply them with this product.

Ed enthusiastically went out and purchased several television antennas so that he could determine how they were designed and manufactured. He also read some electrical engineering books on antenna design.

Ed went into business to manufacture television antennas and to supply his relatives' stores. He obtained the loan from his family, purchased an old warehouse, converted it to a factory, hired a worker to help him design some machines for use in manufacturing, and hired an accountant on a part-time basis to keep the company books.

By 1973 he had produced enough profit to repay part of his relatives' loan and to expand to a larger building. He hired more workers, established an organizational system, appointed his first worker as foreman and developed plans to produce several types of television antennas.

By 1978 he had reached his production capacity and sales goals. Ed decided to move to a larger factory so that he could also serve as a distributor for television sets and radios. In the new factory Ed found he had to spend more time on the road selling his products. He became less involved in the day-to-day operation of his production facilities largely because he was selling to others as well as to his relatives. He could no longer talk to his workers face to face, to show sympathy for their concerns, or to help them with production problems. He missed the warm relationship he had had with his workers.

He had other problems as well. His family felt he was favoring his new customers over his own relatives with respect to delivery schedules and product pricing. He was having great trouble keeping track of his costs, revenues, and profits. His accountant complained about the way accounting records were kept. Ed was not sure about how to best utilize his time.

Pam Hall was a computer project manager for the Division of Social Services in Florida. Her job was to supervise a project team designing and implementing a computer system for disbursing Medicare and Social Security funds to nursing home patients in the state. Different state departments provided specialists from their groups to work part time on Hall's project team. There were representatives from the computer programming department, the systems analysis department, and the accounting department in her group. The project had several definite, different stages, with deadlines for each stage and a very firm deadline for project completion. If the project was not completed on time, an outside organization would have to be hired to perform these check disbursement activities.

**Item
1.2**

Hall's project was falling behind schedule. One of her problems was the refusal of the head of the programming department to free up enough time for the programmer who was assigned to Hall's group. This made it impossible to get the programming done for the project. Some representatives from other groups also were not working sufficiently long on their project team assignments. Since they were evaluated for pay increases by the regular supervisor rather than by Hall, they were reluctant to reject extra work assignments given them from their regular department.

Hall met with the heads of the programming, systems analysis, and accounting departments. She pleaded her case for the need of their personnel. There was some improvement. There was slightly more time allocated to her project but things are still out of hand.

Hall met with her group and told them that the project was getting too far behind schedule. She pounded the table and shouted, "You better decide right now if you are going to give this project your best or not. If you are not, get off this project team right now. I'm telling you to shape up or ship out!"

Afterwards, when her assistant, Bill Ward, mentioned her strong stance in a joking manner, Hall replied, "Listen! I first try the considerate approach. When that doesn't work, I get tough. I'm going to reach my deadline no matter what I have to do."

Things improved for a while. When a programming problem arose later, though, Hall complained about the lack of cooperation she was receiving to the Head of the Division of Human Services. She then received all the time she needed from the various specialists. The project was completed on time and the system checked out in good order.

**Item
1.3**

In the spring of 1976, Dean John Lemon of the College of Business, Winthrop University, was having some difficulties. The associate dean had just resigned, and the college was experiencing a great deal of stress due to an unprecedented growth in the number of students majoring in business administration. Classes were very large, the college was being pressured to expand its popular graduate programs, the secretarial work force was inadequate for the increased burden of work, and the faculty's morale was low, as evidenced by a number of resignations and a large amount of griping.

Dean Lemon persuaded Professor Reed Garvey to take the position of associate dean for one year. Professor Garvey almost immediately started a number of activities. He surveyed the faculty of the College to identify the faculty's perception of all their present and future problems. Garvey summarized this information and presented it to the College's executive committee. He had the executive committee establish a set of long-term and short-term goals for the college. Every faculty member was assigned to various task forces to investigate the problems identified in the survey and to develop a set of recommendations for each problem. The reports from the task forces were presented to the executive committee.

Garvey led a series of negotiations with higher level administrators in the university, which resulted in a significant increase in staff, faculty, and budget to the college. Several statistical reporting systems were instituted to insure that all faculty and units within the college were treated equitably with respect to such matters as number of students taught, number of course preparations developed, pay received as compared to contribution to the college, and various privileges such as payments for the expenses of attending meetings. One year later, although the college operated on a much more formal and structured basis than before, faculty morale had significantly improved and there were far fewer problems for the dean to resolve.

**Item
1.4**

Dr. John Harris, an oral surgeon located in a suburb of Washington, D.C., has a very large and unusually efficient dental practice. This practice came to the attention of Professor Joan Jackson of the State University College of Business and Management when she was referred to Dr. Harris for a tooth extraction.

When she arrived for her first appointment with Harris, Jackson checked in with a receptionist behind a closed window at the front of the building. She then entered a large waiting room filled with many patients. She was routed to various work stations where information was collected, the fee paid in advance, anesthesia administered, and the tooth extracted. Jackson was later awakened on a bed in another room. She was then taken to a room at the rear of the building where she was given strong black coffee. A little later, she was picked up by her husband as previously arranged.

Impressed with the size of the staff, the efficiency of the layout and procedures employed, and the low fees charged, Professor Jackson met with Dr. Harris to discuss his management philosophy and approach. Jackson learned that Dr. Harris had taken two years to plan the layout and type of practice he would have. Patients were moved through the building on an assembly line basis.

Dr. Harris and his two salaried dentists each used three operatories at the same time. Patients were prepared and set up so that they were immediately available for treatment. Whenever one patient's operation was completed a dentist simply went from one operatory to another. The sleeping patient was then moved by wheelchair to one of nine recovery rooms and a timer was set so the patient could be awakened at the proper time.

Dr. Harris developed a very precise set of job duties for all fifteen dental auxiliaries employed in the practice. Because of these job specifications and careful training, Dr. Harris did very little supervision and motivation on a face-to-face basis. Dr. Harris took great pride in processing such a large number of patients and charging low fees.

Ed, Pam, Reed, and John are managers. All four plan, organize, lead, and control people and resources to achieve some objective. The resources of an organization must be allocated effectively to achieve organization goals. Managing becomes especially important when resources become more costly and/or more scarce.

Good management can have a significant economic and psychological impact on a society. As this book is being written, one of the world's largest firms, Chrysler, is facing bankruptcy. Many commentators attribute Chrysler's difficulties to "bad management." Indeed, the present management admits past decisions had a significant effect on the present difficulties. What are the consequences if Chrysler does go bankrupt? There is speculation that 140,000 Chrysler employees will be out of work and there may be as many as 200,000 jobs lost in firms of suppliers. Along with the unemployment and economic losses, there are accompanying psychological costs. Individuals lose self-respect and marital conflict increases, as do alcoholism and suicide.

The Chrysler incident is a very obvious example of bad management, but thousands of other organizations that are poorly operated cause similar, though admittedly less exaggerated, effects. In hospitals the effects of bad management are high costs and patient deaths; in armies, bad management loses wars; in universities, bad management leads to wasted funds and lost learning opportunities.

Good management can lead to better results in any kind of organization—hospitals, churches, schools, government agencies, sports teams, and business enterprises—so it makes sense to try to improve management skills. If we want better management, then we must understand what it is. Only when we understand something can we improve it. It is only when there is a body of knowledge in a discipline that the discipline can be taught to others. Otherwise, doing something well depends upon either intuition or self-teaching. A person who is "intuitive," or a "natural," at anything, whether it be management, music, or athletics, cannot easily pass the skill on to others. An effective golf teacher knows the components of a good swing and can convey them to a student, but when the intuitive golfer is asked how to hit a particular shot, he or she is likely to say, "Just swing through the ball." That has little meaning to someone trying to learn how to play. The senior buyer of women's fashions in a large department store who has a "sense of the market" can train a new buyer only when the premises on which buying decisions are made can be communicated to the new buyer. Unless the senior buyer is aware of which data were used to make decisions and knows how these data are evaluated, training another person to be a buyer is impossible.

This is an important point to remember. Unless we understand that the manager's job is very complex, we will fall into the trap of assuming that management is nothing more than "common sense." But common sense is common sense only when we know the important factors that affect a situation, when we are able to divine what must be done. Certainly we can learn to do anything by experience. Analysis and understanding can be facilitated by systematic study. Yet, because all of us manage something—for example, our personal finances, a family, or a baseball team—we have a tendency to believe that management is an intuitive skill, or just a matter of common sense.

As we observe effective managers, it is easy for us to assume mistakenly that these are easy skills to master. Like anyone who is very good at anything, effective managers make the work look easy; they seem to do their jobs effortlessly and their results are usually good. Also, if we ask several different managers how they do their job, and what is important to their success on the job, often we get very different answers. One will tell you that intelligence is important. Another will emphasize initiative. Another may point out the importance of technical skills. Does this mean that there are no underlying basic concepts that are applicable to management? We do not think so.

Management is a process and an activity that in its basics can be learned. Experience and intuition based on experience are both brought to bear by the seasoned manager, as they are by a professional athlete or the senior buyer with a sense of the market. Prospective managers can equip themselves with a knowledge of certain basic techniques—for example, of decision making or financial planning—and to these ultimately add the wisdom and intuition that are the products of experience. Similarly, managers can learn to understand how humans respond, and how these responses will occur in particular situations. Again, they can bring the depth of experience to bear ultimately on how well these basic tools are used.

There are differences in the way outstanding individuals perform in any field—art, music, sports, and business—yet in every field there are some principles, basic guides, approaches, or theories which give some direction to a novice and to which the expert must return when his or her performance levels begin to deteriorate. These theories, or guides, can be translated into instructions that are used to teach others how to act in a particular situation. Such a body of principles, ideas, and concepts from which appropriate instructions can be derived exist in most areas of human endeavor, and they also exist for management.

MANAGERS—A DEFINITION

The president of General Electric is a manager. So is the afternoon shift supervisor at McDonald's. There are, of course, some important differences in what they do, how they do it, and the kinds of decisions they make. However, there are some things that are common to their jobs.

Frederick Taylor (we will have more to say about him in Chapter 2) popularized the idea of scientific management around the early 1900s. One of his basic premises was that it is important to separate the activities of managing a task from its execution. Taylor reasoned that it would be easier to use resources more efficiently by making this distinction and using it as a basis for the analysis of both managerial and other types of work.

Operative Employees

Those people in an organization who are involved in the work, not planning or managing it, are operative employees. In an automobile plant, they work on an assembly line. In an airline maintenance facility, they may be highly trained machinists. In a research laboratory, they might have doctoral degrees in science. Operative personnel work at the lines in steel-rolling mills and behind the counters in department stores. Their primary task is making the product or providing the service.

Specialists

People with high skill levels in a particular kind of job are specialists, a particular class of employees. Typically, their education and experience make it relatively difficult for them to move about from one type of job to another. A specialist generally is extensively trained in a very narrow area of competence. A long apprenticeship, many years of training, and an intense personal investment of time and resources may be required before one is characterized as a specialist. A specialist may often be a professional. Computer programmers, doctors, teachers, personnel technicians, and engineers are specialists who may also be performing operative activities.

Managers

Managers in organizations are in positions which have at least two characteristics:

1. *They make decisions about how other people, primarily subordinates, use resources.* Managers usually are delegated the right to decide how those who work for them can use resources needed to accomplish the operative tasks, the execution of work. Managers make resource allocation decisions that other people must implement. For example, a manager may decide whether to spend available funds on new office equipment such as typewriters or on new office furniture. In some firms managers make decisions about how millions of dollars will be spent for new plants. These decisions, of course, have wide implications not only for company employees but also for the regions where these new plants might be located. A product manager of a cosmetics firm may have to decide whether the advertising program should be directed at women over forty or at women under forty. Once such decisions are made and methods formulated to carry them out, the actual work is done by the operative employees.

2. They are responsible to a higher superior for the supervision of sub-ordinates. Most people who work in organizations have a person to whom they are accountable for how well they do their jobs. Perhaps what most sharply distinguishes a manager's job from that of others in an organization is that managers not only make decisions about what resources others can use to achieve objectives, but they are also responsible for insuring that it is done well. This means that they must be concerned with the effective use of human resources as well as physical resources such as plant and equipment. Managers are responsible for the work of other people. Some are responsible for operative employees or specialists, whereas others manage managers.

MANAGEMENT PROCESSES

In this book we focus on what managers do in all types of organizations—educational, economic, government, therapeutic, and social. To be sure, we will use more examples from industrial organizations because these have been more extensively studied than the other types. The fact that we use such a broad set of examples is purposeful; it is to show that the basic managerial processes that must be carried out are similar regardless of the type of organization. Basically, all managers carry out the following processes in their job:

1. Planning. Planning involves the establishment of goals and the determination of ways to achieve them.

2. Organizing. Organizing is the process of insuring that there are necessary human and physical resources to accomplish the plan. It also involves defining the tasks of individuals and groups and specifying authority relationships between groups and between individuals.

3. Leading. Leading is the managerial process of motivating and influencing others to obtain compliance from them, so that they contribute to the achievement of organizational goals.

4. Controlling. Controlling includes those activities designed to insure that actual performance conforms to the plan. Another phase of control is coordinating, that is, developing and maintaining proper relationships between activities, whether physical or mental, in the organization.

These basic processes are evident in the descriptions of the managers at the beginning of this chapter. All four managers had to develop plans, organize, lead, and control. They each went about it in different ways, of course. Ed Johnson's planning was a little less formal than the planning of John Harris and Reed Garvey. The other processes differed in importance among the managers. Pam Hall spent much of her time coordinating, since implementing the new system requires the right sequencing of activities of many different and independent groups. Ed Johnson had the most difficult organizing problem because he started a new organization from scratch and because he had to reorganize due to rapid growth. Control is also performed differently by these managers. Reed Garvey's programs will be evaluated based on faculty satisfaction and the absence of complaints and grievances about faculty assignments. Each manager had different problems of leading. Ed Johnson's workers were engaged in routine and, perhaps, boring work and were probably much more difficult to motivate than those who worked for Garvey or Harris.

DECISION MAKING AND MANAGERIAL PROCESSES

Each manager planned, organized, led, and controlled differently from the others. This is because there are different ways to perform each of these managerial processes and managers must decide which approach they will use. **Decision making cuts across all the management processes.** Decision making is a basic skill required in every aspect of managerial work.

HOW MANAGERIAL WORK DIFFERS BY ORGANIZATIONAL LEVEL

In all but the smallest organization there are several levels of management. In a factory, workers are managed by supervisors, supervisors report to department managers, and the plant superintendent supervises the department managers. In universities, presidents supervise provosts, provosts are responsible for deans, deans for department chairpersons, and department chairpersons for faculty.

The emphasis on the different managerial processes varies depending on where the manager's job is located in the organization hierarchy. Some managers spend more time planning while others spend more time in controlling. The types of decisions made at the top levels are different from the types made at lower levels. Figure 1.1 shows how the managerial processes will vary by level. Managers at the upper levels spend more time planning than those at lower levels. The percentage of time spent in controlling decreases steadily as one moves from lower to higher organization levels.

Lower or Supervisory Management

This level is the only one at which a manager does not supervise other managers. A lower-level manager usually has responsibility for operative employees or specialists. Plant foremen, heads of secretarial pools, or a supervisor of data processing fall into the supervisory management category. At this level the primary work is control and supervision. Managers spend little time in planning. What planning efforts there are tend to be routine planning activities, such as scheduling.

The organizing process is somewhat limited at this supervisory management level, usually involving little more than simple reassignment of duties of employees. Often organizing entails insuring that operative employees have the appropriate raw materials and equipment to perform their jobs. Coordination of activities of people within the supervisory unit, as well as working out smooth relationships with other units, is a major activity of this level.

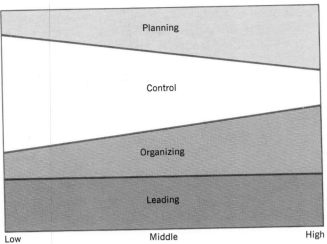

FIGURE 1.1 Managerial processes and organization level. (*Source:* Mahoney, Thomas A., Thomas H. Jerdee, and Stephen J. Carroll, "The Job(s) of Management," *Industrial Relations,* vol. 4, no. 2, Feb. 1965, pp. 97–110.)

Under normal working conditions the leadership role of the lower-level manager will be to insure that the workers have the necessary resources to do their jobs and that interpersonal and intergroup problems do not get in the way of effective personnel.

Middle Management

Middle managers supervise other managers as well as operative employees. Middle managers do more planning than those at lower levels. The primary planning activity is the translation of broad organization objectives into specific product or service plans.

Organizing will require the design of authority and responsibility relationships consistent with the general type of organization structure chosen by top management. For example, a top-level decision may be made to organize a firm on a regional basis. Middle-level managers will design and implement the specific details of this organization structure. The specific departmental configurations will be determined by middle management. For example, where the personnel department is located to best serve the regional executives would be a question dealt with at this level of management.

Control processes focus on the design of monitoring systems and the determination of specific performance criteria. These criteria, or performance standards, will be used to judge how well managers at lower levels perform.

Managers at this level must be well versed in the technological aspects of their organizations. They make decisions about production techniques, marketing and distribution methods, and other technical business functions for which they are responsible.

At middle-management levels, the leadership role is to influence other managers. The leadership role is to provide guidance, to clarify, and to interpret policies and decisions made at higher management levels to the supervisory group.

Top Management

Top management is the small group of employees at the highest level of the organization. It includes the board of directors, president or chief executive officer, and the immediate groups that make decisions about organization objectives and how to get there.

Top management assesses market conditions and translates them into general action steps or policies. This is the planning function of top management, the function in which it spends most of its time. These managers interpret the environment in which the organization operates and attempts to ease the adjustment of the organization to it. The long-run success of the firm depends upon how accurately the environment is assessed and translated into policies that insure the product or service of the firm in sufficient quantity, of good quality, and in time.

The organizing process is directed at determining the general structural form and the general philosophy of decentralization of authority. Top management must decide whether the firm should be organized by product line, geographic region, or some other approach. The decentralization issue has to do with the point in the organization at which certain decisions are made. In a decentralized firm, important decisions are made by lower-level managers. With high centralization, more decisions are reserved for top management.

Top management decision making will focus largely on policy questions, i.e., general directions and strategies, rather than specific problems. For instance, top management may decide after an appropriate staff analysis that a merger may be financially attractive. They will leave to middle levels the details of carrying out the merger.

The leadership role of top management is very complex. While this group will have to deal effectively with their immediate subordinates, they also have a major effect on those at lower levels. People at lower levels develop confidence in and commitment and loyalty to an organization on the basis of the assessment of the role and operation of the top management. When those at lower levels believe that top managers are making decisions and implementing policies in their own *personal* interest to the exclusion of the rest of the organization or other groups, confidence and support will be eroded. Dissatisfaction will increase and personnel, particularly the good ones, are likely to leave the organization.

MANAGEMENT PROCESS CONTINGENCY THEORY

All managers plan, but planning is done differently in different organizations. Planning methods appropriate in one situation will not be so for another. The same can be said for the other managerial processes—organizing, leading, and controlling.

Over the past several years, research has indicated that the factors that seem to be the most important determinants of which approach will be most effective are:
1. The structure of the organization
2. The personnel

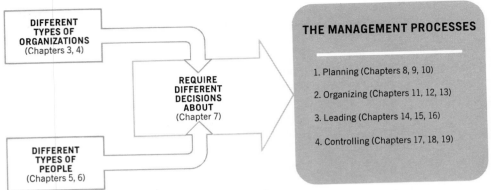

FIGURE 1.2 Management process contingency theory.

The tasks that people perform in John Harris' organization do not change very much from one period to another. The structure of this organization is very stable. People come in to this dental practice regularly with the same problems day in and day out, so John Harris can develop a fairly routine method of handling them. This is quite different from the work of Pam Hall, whose work cuts across many departmental lines in The Division of Social Services.

The personnel that work in these organizations are also quite a bit different. The workers in the TV antenna plant are not likely to be highly interested in their job because it is repetitive and boring. They will probably be most interested in the financial aspects of work and not the work itself. It is unlikely that they will have any advanced education. On the other hand, those who work for Reed Garvey, Ed Johnson, and Pam Hall have had much education and training. They probably have a good deal of interest in their work since it is challenging and "professional." Differences such as these between the various groups of workers will require different approaches to leading.

This book is based on management process contingency theory. It is a theory that takes into account such variations to provide prescriptions about how to manage. The three basic components in management process contingency theory are:

1. The type of organization
2. The types of personnel
3. The management processes

Figure 1.2 illustrates the structure of management process contingency theory as well as the way this book is organized. The core of this approach is the management process. As we have said, this includes planning, organizing, leading, and controlling. These processes are discussed in Chapters 7 through 19.

The important point about these processes is that they are carried out in a different way depending on the organization and the type of people in it. We discuss several different types of organizations in Chapters 3 and 4. Organizations are different because the environment in which they exist is very different. Some organizations are very bureaucratic because the external environment is very predictable. Other organizations are more loosely structured because the external environment is very unstable and unpredictable.

Individuals and groups are different, also. Some people are highly committed to where they work and others are less so. The human factors in management process contingency theory are discussed in Chapters 5 and 6.

The final major aspect of this approach is organizational and individual change. Organizations must change to keep pace with their environment, and people must change to become and remain more effective. How these change processes should operate is discussed in Chapters 17 and 18.

SUMMARY

In this chapter we have shown that the processes of planning, organizing, leading, and controlling are performed by all managers. Yet they are done differently in different types of organizations. This is the basic concept that underlies management process contingency theory—that different types of people require different management methods.

Bob Shack

Case 1.1

Bob Shack wondered what he should do. Bob is a carpenter who, with one helper, has earned a reputation as a very skilled tradesman. He was happy in his work. He had control over his workday, which he liked because he could attend the various sports events in his hometown of Boston. Two days ago, Kathy Mondlak called Bob to ask him if he wished to purchase Cambridge Home Builders, Incorporated. Bill Mondlak, the owner of Cambridge Homes, dropped dead from a heart attack last week. Mrs. Mondlak thought the business was perfect for Bob.

Bob knew that Cambridge Home Builders with its twenty-two workers, four trucks, and several buildings was a going and thriving business. The offer came at a lucky time for him. He could afford to buy the business because his wife had recently inherited a large sum of money. But he worried about what this new job might require of him. He wondered if he would be happy in this new role. Could he get out to the Celtics and Red Sox games as he did before? Certainly Bill Mondlak had never had time to really enjoy life.

1. If Bob accepts this offer, how will his work change?
2. What are some of the more important advantages and disadvantages in buying this business?
3. What factors should Bob consider when making this decision?

DISCUSSION QUESTIONS

1. Managers perform numerous jobs. Discuss the importance of these different areas.
2. What differentiates a manager's job from a worker's?
3. Is there a difference between managers and decision makers? If so, what is it?
4. Do you believe that a good manager of, say, a marketing sales staff could manage a research laboratory as well? What is the reason for your answer?

5. What are the basic differences in how managerial work varies as a function of organization level?
6. Think about the following statements:
   (a) Management is common sense.
   (b) Management is an intuitive skill.
   True or false or some of both?
7. What is your understanding of managerial process contingency theory?
8. Of what utility are "principles" to any area of study? Can you think of a field where "principles" are *extremely* important? Another where they are of no significance whatever?

CHAPTER TWO

A Short History of Management Thinking

Appointment of Minor Judges

The next day Moses took his seat to serve as judge for the people, and they stood around him from morning till evening. When his father-in-law saw all that Moses was doing for the people, he said, "What is this you are doing for the people? Why do you alone sit as judge, while all these people stand around you from morning till evening?"

Moses answered him, "Because the people come to me to seek God's will. Whenever they have a dispute, it is brought to me, and I decide between the parties and inform them of God's decrees and laws."

Moses' father-in-law replied, "What you are doing is not good. You and these people who come to you will only wear yourselves out. The work is too heavy for you; you cannot handle it alone. Listen now to me and I will give you some advice, and may God be with you. You must be the people's representative before God and bring their disputes to him. Teach them the decrees and laws, and show them the way to live and the duties they are to perform. But select capable men from all the people—men who fear God, trustworthy men who hate dishonest gain—and appoint them as officials over thousands, hundreds, fifties and tens. Have them serve as judges for the people at all times, but have them bring every difficult case to you; the simple cases they can decide themselves. That will make your load lighter, because they will share it with you. If you do this and God so commands, you will be able to stand the strain, and all these people will go home satisfied."

Moses listened to his father-in-law and did everything he said. He chose capable men from all Israel and made them leaders of the people, officials over thousands, hundreds, fifties and tens. They served as judges for the people at all times. The difficult cases they brought to Moses, but the simple ones they decided themselves.

Source: Exodus 18:13–26.

Since men first grouped together, they have tried to organize their activities so that they can be more efficient. The selection which opens this chapter describes how Moses was advised to, and did, organize the tribes of Israel so that his time was better used. Concern with management and management problems is as old as the human race. Even those modern management writers to whom great influence is attributed have roots reaching back into time.

Hoagland, for example, shows how a famous study by Frederick Taylor (who is called the "father of scientific management," because his writings at the turn of the century were seminal to the contemporary study of management problems) can be traced back at least to the Renaissance:[1] One of Taylor's most famous studies centered on the task of "shoveling." Concerned with increasing the productivity of common laborers, Taylor conducted research to determine the most efficient way to perform this task. Hoagland, through historical documents, traces the genesis of this study back to Taylor's teachers in the mid-nineteenth century and farther back to work on the same problem by many others, including Leonardo da Vinci. In this chapter, we present some of the more important historical antecedents of modern management theory.

SOME ANTECEDENTS OF MODERN MANAGEMENT THINKING

In the ancient world, management techniques were used to achieve religious, military, and political goals. (Much of this discussion follows George.[2]) It was in organizations of this type that management thinking originated, and writing on the art of management, as well as the development of various managerial tools and procedures, was about and for such organizations. There were few, if any, economic organizations of the kind we know today. Manufacturing, retailing, and distribution organizations of the size we know did not exist.

In ancient Egypt, the pyramids, built for religious and political purposes, were constructed primarily with human labor and crude equipment. One great pyramid contains more than 2 million stones, each weighing about 2½ tons. The individual stones were cut in a quarry, moved by water and land to the pyramid site, and then placed precisely into their assigned positions, often very high. The construction required the labor of 100,000 men working for twenty years, and the problems of planning the work, organizing the work teams, and maintaining such a large work force, as well as the motivation and supervision problems, were obviously tremendous. Egyptian writings surviving from this period make it clear that the pyramid builders thought about these problems and developed management advice for future generations.

Egypt governed a large geographic territory, and the rulers tried various methods of managing their empire until finally settling upon a system which gave local areas autonomy so long as certain key directives from the central government were followed. The Egyptians also invented methods of record keeping, methods they found especially useful in tax collecting, and established rules regulating the activities of individuals engaged in various specialized trades. Similar laws and rules governing economic relationships were developed and written about in Babylonia, China, Greece, and India. Military operations also required managerial skills of a high order, and the ancient Persians and Romans developed elaborate management techniques for conducting their vast military undertakings.

THE MIDDLE AGES AND THE RENAISSANCE

Complex economic organizations first began to develop during the Middle Ages. Organizations quite modern in character originated in Italy during this period, and became especially advanced in Venice by the fifteenth century. Many merchants of Venice formed partnerships, joint ventures, and trading companies. There were some obvious advantages to this form of economic ownership. Since much business was in sea trade, losses were often very substantial when ships were lost. Financing a particular expedition by several families, rather than by only one, reduced the risks involved in such an undertaking. The profits were also reduced by spreading the risk, of course, but joint financing made possible far more extensive undertakings than would otherwise have been the case.

The Venetians were adept not only in the financing but also in the operation of large-scale manufacturing enterprises. The famous Arsenal of Venice, for example, which was put into operation in 1436 to manufacture arms needed to protect the trade of the city used many modern production methods and inventory techniques. A form of assembly-line process was used in outfitting ships. Warehouses were arrayed on the sides of a canal so that when the ships were towed along it, parts and supplies from the warehouses were placed on ships in their proper sequence. Standard parts and an emphasis on efficiency also characterized the production system. Finally, the Arsenal employed many artisans and manual workers and used many personnel techniques, such as performance rating and incentive wage systems, similar to those used today.

For the most part, however, until the Industrial Revolution economic organizations were primarily involved in trade and finance. Very little activity centered on the manufacturing processes as we know them today. Most production, especially that of consumer goods, was carried on in the home. True, there were craftsmen in metals, woods, leather, and so forth, but one factor which severely limited the growth of manufacturing was the difficulty of harnessing power.

THE INDUSTRIAL REVOLUTION

The Industrial Revolution came to different parts of the world at different times. In the late 1700s it may be said to have begun in England with the invention of the steam engine. This provided a simple, flexible means of converting natural materials such as coal into energy to drive belts, turn wheels, and provide other forms of mechanical motion. Since the steam engine provided such energy anywhere, factories of considerable size could be located in many different places. About the same time came new methods of smelting iron, which also facilitated industrial growth.

The factory system became widespread during the Industrial Revolution. During the early eighteenth century the domestic system prevailed. To use textiles as an example, with this method of production a farmer and his family would produce cloth on their own loom and sell their finished products at the local fair for whatever they could get. The type of production that succeeded this system was the putting-out system. Entrepreneurs, acting as brokers, contracted for a family's output at a fixed price and supplied the family with raw materials. This turned the farmer into an employee of the broker. When it then became obvious that it would be more efficient to have all of the manpower and the equipment under direct supervision in one building, the factory system began to emerge.

Development and widespread use of power to run machines made the factory possible. A factory, as we know it, requires equipment to be at a particular location, rather than spread through the countryside. Since transportation in the early nineteenth century was limited and workers had to live close to their jobs, the population started to move from the farm into the cities, where the factories were located. This movement created rapid urban growth, industrial slums, and health and other social problems, some of which are still with us.

The corporate form of ownership also stimulated the growth of the factory system. Investors or owners of a corporation are liable only for the amount of their respective investments and can thus spread their risks with minimal liability. In addition, the corporate form of ownership is an excellent way to accumulate the capital needed to build and equip a large factory.

But harnessing power with a steam engine was only part of the impetus to economic growth during the Industrial Revolution. About the same time that Watt invented the steam engine, another important event took place that shaped thinking about how economic affairs should be arranged. Adam Smith, an economic philosopher, published *The Wealth of Nations*.

This book, along with other ideas about industrial freedom and liberty that were gaining acceptance at this time, spurred a change in thinking that was to have a profound impact on the economic sectors of society. Prior to the late 1700s, it was generally held that economic decisions should be made by the state. Resource allocations were decided by a small cadre of men around the king, or simply by the king himself. Smith believed that these decisions were better made by individuals acting in their own self-interest. Under these conditions, he asserted, the common good would be enhanced. This concept forms the basic assumptions underlying classic economic theory of markets, especially the competitive model.

The concept is based on the conviction that men and institutions must be free to compete, because competition is in accord with natural law. Men, institutions, and ideas, through competition, prove their fitness for survival. Free competition and free markets lead to the maximum benefit for mankind. The self-interests of various segments of the economy striving to maximize their own well-being will lead to a self-regulation of the economic system. There is no need for political interference. The economy will be guided by the "invisible hand," not the heavy hand of the sovereign. As Smith put it:

Every individual endeavors to employ his capital so that its produce may be of greatest value. He generally neither intends to promote the public interest, nor knows how much he is promoting it. He intends only his own security, only his own gain. And he is in this led by an *invisible hand* to promote an end which was no part of his intention. By pursuing his own interest he frequently promotes that of society more effectively than when he really intends to promote it.

Smith also convincingly argued that the wealth of a nation did not rest in the quantities of gold it held. The idea that it did had led to wars and explorations in which the primary purpose was to increase a nation's storehouse of gold. Smith showed how the wealth of a nation could be advanced by increasing the productivity of the capital and productive components of society.

The new economic philosophy, coupled with advancing technology, shifted the wealth in the society. A new class emerged in England and in the other countries where similar developments took place. The new class came into conflict (still not fully resolved) with the old, landed class for political and economic supremacy. The new industrialists had a different set of ideas about "right," "wrong," and "importance" than did the old, landed class. The new class emphasized individual initiative and individual responsibility. The old, landed class felt more responsibility for their workers than did the new class. The newer class had a much stronger work orientation than did the landed class, and it did not emphasize intellectual, cultural, and recreational pursuits to the same degree as the landed gentry.

THE GROWTH OF INDUSTRY IN THE UNITED STATES

Before the American Revolution there was little industry in the Colonies, largely because of the sparse population, the lack of capital, and restrictive legislation from England which hindered manufacturing. The Revolution gave some impetus to industry, however, and manufacturing grew slowly until the 1820s, when a number of inventions and technical advances stimulated its growth. In the first half of the nineteenth century, most U.S. factories were small, and corporate ownership was not nearly as popular as individual or partnership forms. Labor was scarce. In fact, about half of all factory workers were children. In the 1840s and 1850s the construction of new roads, railroads, and canals stimulated industrial growth. About the same time, increased immigration furnished the large labor force necessary for work in factories, railroads, and coal mines.

The Civil War increased the rate of U.S. industrial growth even further, especially in steel, textiles, leather, meat packing, and prepared foods. The railroads opened the West, stimulating demand for many products manufactured in the East, and new inventions and developments also fostered increased industrialization. Two new methods of producing steel, for example, the Bessemer and the open hearth process, were developed in Europe. These were imported to the United States, and the steel industry began its growth to the gigantic size it has today. The oil industry was started when George Bissell was informed by a chemistry professor at Yale that crude oil from western Pennsylvania could be converted into an excellent illuminant, with valuable by-products resulting from the production process. John D. Rockefeller and others created an oil industry that became one of the world's strongest economic forces.

The steel and oil industries depended on the railroads to transport their products, while the railroads were major purchasers of steel for their tracks. The network of railroads that eventually spanned the country also made it possible to consolidate smaller factories geared to the needs of particular regions, and efficiencies of size became possible.

As in England, the spirit of laissez-faire capitalism characterized U.S. economic life. The owners of large firms became known as "robber barons" and were accused of having little concern for anything except wealth and power. A flaw was becoming apparent in the theory of competition. Adam Smith's argument had been that if individuals were left alone to compete freely, the general well-being would be served, but this conclusion was based on the assumption that there would be a *large* number of buyers and a *large* number of sellers. As huge fortunes were accumulated in the United States, many smaller sellers were consolidated into fewer larger ones, and the **monopoly**—a case in which a single firm has almost complete control of the quality and price of its goods and services—emerged. When goods or services such as oil, steel, and rail transportation are vital to the society, those who control them have enormous power and can misuse it. In time, U.S. monopolies were accused of practices harmful to society: fixing prices, rather than having them result from competitive market forces, and forcing raw material producers to accept the monopolist's price, since there were few other customers.

The Sherman Anti-Trust Act was passed in 1890 as a response to these practices. It prohibited monopoly or tendency toward monopoly. While it is considered by many to be the beginning of a too extensive government regulation of business, the Sherman Act was designed to produce the same result as laissez-faire capitalism—increased social benefits, since the economy, unregulated, was not working as intended in theory. In any event, the Sherman Act significantly affected what an industrialist could do. With its enactment there was no longer unbridled freedom to act only in the best interests of a given firm. There were now some things that a businessman could not do, and these constraints made it more difficult to maximize profit. For instance, the Act made it illegal to form a trust to raise prices arbitrarily. As a result, owners had to begin to focus more sharply on managing the resources of the business.

Just as U.S. industry grew after the Civil War, so did the unrest of U.S. labor. By the mid-1870s, workers were beginning to react against extremely difficult and often unreasonable working conditions. Because of increased immigration after the war, there was a vast labor supply available to industry. Because workers had both better working conditions in the United States than they had in Europe and the promise and hope of more, they tended to be somewhat more tolerant of difficult working conditions. But by the 1880s poor working conditions, low wages, and an almost total lack of job security were stimulating intensive union activity, especially in the coal-mining industry. Unions were not widely successful in obtaining contracts, but they were instrumental in bringing about legislation covering working conditions. Like the Sherman Act, these laws were a constraint on the decisions that a businessman could make. Industry was powerful, but abrasive; growing, but inefficient. It drew recklessly on the vast human and physical resources available to it.

It was in this societal and economic milieu of a growing economy, increased regulation, and advancing unionism that the scientific management movement began.

CONTEMPORARY MANAGEMENT MOVEMENTS

The times were ripe, then, for the emergence of people such a Frederick W. Taylor and his colleagues in scientific management. Around 1900 managers began to experiment with ways to use raw materials, workers, and equipment more efficiently. When their experiments met with success, their ideas were sought out by others who had similar problems. Since that time, numerous practitioners and theorists have contributed to the present state of the modern art and practice of management. They came from diverse backgrounds, ranging from engineering to journalism, and in a short history it is impossible to give all of them the kind of treatment they deserve. As George[2] has noted, to "write a history of management is to write a history of man." In this section, we want to point out the *major* approaches and *some* of the important contributors to each.

There are five major schools of thought about management: (1) scientific management, (2) administrative theory, (3) the behavioral approach, (4) management science, and (5) the contingency approach. We discuss some of the major ideas of and contributions to each school of thought in this section. Figure 2.1 depicts the development of management thinking since 1900. The primary thrust comes from the **scientific management** movement and the work of Taylor.

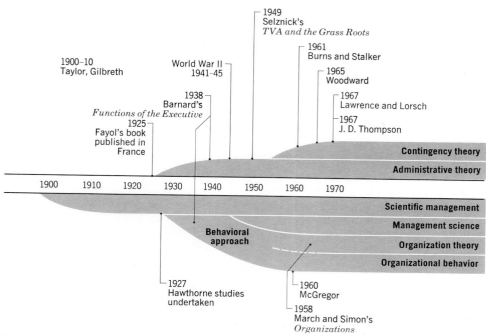

FIGURE 2.1   Sources of modern management ideas.

The year 1925, with the publication of Henri Fayol's *General and Industrial Management* in France, marked the beginning of the **administrative theory** era. The **behavioral approach** to management (also called the "human relations" approach) is generally acknowledged to have begun around 1927, with the advent of the Hawthorne studies, while World War II saw the birth of operations research or **management science.** Interdisciplinary teams were brought together to solve major war problems. Psychologists, economists, but especially engineers and mathematicians, contributed to this line of thinking.

The **contingency approach** can be traced back to at least 1949 and Selznick's study, *TVA and the Grass Roots.* Later studies and theory development in this area provided a basis for potential integration of the varied strains of thought from the other approaches.

The major ideas from the five different points of view are discussed here. The reader will note the divergencies. By the mid-1960s, there was a great deal of confusion in management thinking because of the many schools of thought. Perhaps we are closer today to achieving a degree of integration of them.

THE SCIENTIFIC MANAGEMENT APPROACH

Scientific management was focused on the lowest level of the organization: the worker and the boss. The basic question to which most scientific management research was addressed was: "How can the job be designed most efficiently?" Taylor, who was born to a well-to-do Philadelphia family but who was unable to complete college because of poor eyesight, was the best known of these researchers. He took a job in industry as an apprentice at the Midvale Steel Company in 1878 and quickly rose through the ranks to become chief engineer in 1884, at the age of 28.

Based on his experiences and studies, Taylor developed many ideas to increase management efficiency, and he became widely sought as a consultant to other firms. His ideas, when applied, met with considerable success. He presented papers reporting his results to professional engineering societies and later in several books.[3] There are some, however, who believe that Taylor did not originate most of the ideas, nor did he write his books alone. Hoagland, for example, has shown how Taylor was influenced by previously developed ideas.[1] Others have shown that a good deal of his book *Scientific Management* was written by a colleague named Morris Cooke.[4]

Henry L. Gantt was a colleague of Taylor's and worked with him on several consulting projects. Frank and Lillian Gilbreth were also leaders in the scientific management movement. Together the Gilbreths worked to develop scientific approaches to measuring work and designing efficient work practices. Scientific management is a collection of ideas on management by these and other writers. Some of the more important ideas of scientific management are these:

1. Current management practice was inefficient. Most scientific management writers believed that the way management was practiced in their time was inefficient. This view, of course, was a necessary justification for their own work. Taylor argued that the economic success of a firm was not indicative of its efficiency. A firm could be successful, even though inefficient, if it had a patent, a location advantage, or if its competitors were equally inefficient. Gantt felt that the abundance of natural resources in the nation, rather than the quality of its management, accounted for its high standard of living.

2. *Management must adopt the scientific method in industry.* A tenet of Taylor and his colleagues was the use of "scientific method." The scientific method involves solving problems by research, rather than relying on experience or intuition. It required evaluation of alternatives by making systematic and objective comparisons among them to see which is best. One example was Taylor's famous metal-cutting experiments, which started in 1880 and lasted 26 years. The purpose was to find the optimum method for cutting metal through the use of science rather than to continue to rely upon experience as in the past. Initially, locomotive wheels were cut, since they were of a uniform hardness and quality. Later other materials were used. More than 800,000 pounds of steel were cut in the study. Twelve variables affecting the cutting process were identified. The relationship of these variables to the cutting of metal were converted to mathematical equations. They were then converted to special slide rules so that this knowledge could be applied by the worker on the job.

3. *Specialization should be practiced.* Taylor and his colleagues believed that each individual in an organization should be a specialist. This would insure that a person knew his job well and would make it easier to train and select employees. Taylor believed in specialization for management as well. For example, he advocated the use of "functional foremanship," where each employee would be supervised by several different foremen, each with distinct responsibilities. One foreman would be in charge of machine speeds, another of discipline, another of planning, and so on.

4. *Planning and scheduling were essential.* In scientific management there was a very strong emphasis on planning. It was considered to be the essence of management. Everything was to be done according to a plan. Yearly plans were to be broken down into monthly, weekly, and daily plans. Plans for a whole organization were to be broken down into plans for smaller units, and even further to individuals.

Planning techniques were devised. Gantt devised the "Gantt Chart," which not only helped a manager to make optimum use of his resources by carefully scheduling jobs among available equipment, but helped to ascertain at a glance whether certain jobs were behind schedule or not.

Planning and scheduling meant obtaining materials at the right time, at the right place, and in the right condition for efficient use. Frank Gilbreth especially was concerned with this problem. He invented the movable scaffold so that the bricks could be delivered at the most efficient height for a bricklayer. Gilbreth even had the bricks placed on the scaffold with the good side of the brick facing upward so that the bricklayer could place it without first inspecting it, increasing speed but not sacrificing quality.

5. *Proper selection should be done.* It was important that the right man be selected for each job. Taylor believed there were first-class men, second-class men, and so on, depending upon their qualifications for a task. Just as a draft horse and a race horse were fitted for particular types of work, in Taylor's view so were people best fitted for some jobs but unsuited for others. Taylor advised the use of tests to identify whether or not a person had the critical attributes for a particular job. For example, he devised a test for measuring the perceptual speed and reaction time of quality inspectors.

6. *The standard method should be found.* Scientific management emphasized finding through research the best way to perform a given task. Those assigned to that task would then be required to carry it out in the prescribed manner. This standard method was to be used until a better one was developed. To improve methods, workers were studied by observers, or by motion pictures, making it possible to analyze a task in slow motion. A work method was carefully studied to see whether certain motions could be combined, shifted to another part of the body, or eliminated or whether the work place could be redesigned for greater efficiency.

7. *Standard times for each task should be established.* Taylor believed a primary barrier to greater efficiency was management's lack of knowledge about what constituted a fair performance level for an employee. Believing that the output of most workers was below their capability, he did not think that historical productivity records used by management could be accurate indicators of how long it should take to complete a task.

Taylor believed that scientific methods should be used to establish performance standards for each task and devised a procedure for establishing them. First, the best way to do a task would be developed through work analysis and simplification procedures. Then workers would be trained to do it in this best way. Next, the workers would be observed and timed with a stopwatch while performing the task several times. Then an average time for each task would be calculated. Each worker would then be rated as to effort and skill. These effort and skill ratings then were used to adjust the average time, resulting in a time that reflected what the average qualified worker could do. Thus, for each task in the organization, a standard time would be established. This could serve as a means of evaluating an employee's performance, motivating an employee to perform at a higher level, and predicting output levels. It could be used in planning a work system. Standard times would be especially useful in assembly-line operations, since timing is of the utmost importance when work is interdependent. A part on one line must meet another part coming down another line at just the right time for the work to flow smoothly through the system.

8. *Wage incentives should be utilized.* A basic premise of most scientific management pioneers was that a man should be paid on the basis of what he does, rather than the amount of time he puts into the job. Many wage incentive plans were devised and implemented. These wage incentive plans generally paid workers a bonus if they reached or surpassed the standard time established by time-study procedures.

Results under Scientific Management

The application of these scientific management action principles resulted in significant productivity increases. In his most famous case, Taylor significantly improved productivity of the loading of pig iron bars into railroad cars. Working at the time for Bethlehem Steel Company, Taylor observed that about seventy-five laborers were each handling about 12½ tons of iron a day. He chose a worker, Schmidt—strong, energetic, and known to have a money orientation. He promised Schmidt a raise from $1.15 to $1.85 a day if he would perform the job exactly as Taylor wanted. Taylor's analysis of that job indicated that productivity was highest when the worker was resting almost half of the time. Schmidt picked up the bars, carried them, put them down, and rested *exactly* as Taylor told him. His productivity rate reached 47½ tons a day, a rate he maintained for three years. (Interestingly, no other worker similarly trained on this job was able to reach Schmidt's productivity rate.)

In the well-known shoveling experiment, Taylor found through experimentation that the optimum size shovel for handling material carried about 21½ pounds of material. This meant that big shovels should be used for light material, such as cinders, and a small shovel for heavy material, such as sand. By varying the shovel to fit the material, careful training of workers in the best method to shovel the material, and the use of incentive wage systems, Taylor was able to increase productivity from 16 to 59 tons of material shoveled per day, while the number of shovelers needed per day was decreased from 500 to 140.

The Gilbreths, in a number of applications of their work redesign methods, also demonstrated spectacular increases in productivity. Frank Gilbreth was able to increase the average productivity of bricklayers from 120 to 350 bricks per hour. This was accomplished in part by decreasing the number of motions used in bricklaying from eighteen to five. While in London at a Japanese–British exposition, Gilbreth observed a female worker in an exhibition booth who was acknowledged to be extremely productive at attaching labels to boxes. She worked at the rate of 24 boxes in 40 seconds. Gilbreth suggested some changes in her methods, and in her first attempt with the new method she disposed of 24 boxes in 26 seconds. In her second attempt, the time was reduced to 20 seconds.

Such results were typical when scientific management was applied, and they led to a strong advocacy of scientific management methods. The analysis and redesign of work was widely applied in industry. As Daniel Bell[5] says of this movement:

> . . . The prophet of modern work was Frederick W. Taylor, and the stop watch was his rod. If any social upheaval can ever be attributed to one man, the logic of efficiency as a mode of life is due to Taylor. With "scientific management," as formulated by Taylor in 1893, we pass far beyond the old, rough computations of the division of labor and more into the division of time itself. . . .

> There is no little irony in the fact that one of Taylor's chief admirers was Lenin. In a notable speech in June 1919, Lenin urged "the study and teaching of the Taylor system and its systematic trial and adaptation." The logic of efficiency knows no social boundaries.

ADMINISTRATIVE THEORY

By the late 1920s a group of managers had begun to write about the job of the administrator. They began to analyze the basic task of management. They were also concerned with the development of principles of management—guides for designing and managing an organization. Most of these writers worked independently of the others but nevertheless came to similar conclusions about management. Two of the more prominent earlier contributors were Henri Fayol[6] and Chester Barnard.[7]

Henri Fayol

Fayol (see item 2.2) distinguished management activities from technical activities, pointing out that managerial activities increased in importance and technical activities decreased in importance as we move from the lowest to the highest level of an organization. He felt that management could, and should, be taught at all educational levels. Only the lack of a management theory, which he would help create, prevented this from occurring.

Fayol proposed fourteen principles of management. He stressed the importance of specialization of labor to make the best use of human resources, although he warned that this could be carried too far. Fayol also proposed that responsibility must increase as authority increases, that discipline or obedience is essential in any prosperous enterprise, and that organizational members should receive orders from only one superior. He stressed the importance of determining the proper organization level at which managerial decisions are made.

Fayol was concerned about the use of human resources as well. Equality of treatment was to him very important. To facilitate motivation, the wage payment system, he believed, must fit the type of job and situation and supervisors must encourage initiative among their subordinates.

Item 2.2 Henri Fayol

A BUSINESS SCIENTIST

From his practical experience Fayol developed a framework for a unifying doctrine of administration that might hold good wherever the art of government had to be exercised. He originated the symbol of formal organization, the organization chart, which, with his organization manual of job descriptions, remains the chief instrument of business management. He produced ideas on human relationships. . . . Not least, he was a firm advocate of the view that management can and should be taught. This was a revolutionary idea when he first propounded it in 1908.

Fayol's first paper on management theory was read to the *Congrès des Mines et de la Métallurgie* in 1900. He followed this with his "Discourse on the General Principles of Administration" at the Jubilee Congress of the *Société de l'Industrie Minérale* in 1908, a paper which appeared in the third number of the *Bulletin de la Société de l'Industrie Minérale* for 1916 and was published as a book by Dunod of Paris. This was translated into English by Conbrough in 1929, and again by Constance Storrs in 1949. It is the latter translation which is in widespread use under the title *General and Industrial Management,* and by which Fayol is primarily known to the British and American reader.

Fayol was born in 1841 of the French *petite bourgeoisie.* . . .

His working life fell into four periods. For twelve years from 1860 he was a junior executive interesting himself in the problems of mining engineering, especially fire hazards. Promoted to Manager of a group of pits in 1872, he became concerned chiefly with the factors determining the economic life of the pits in his charge. This not only stimulated him to write a geological monograph but aroused his interest in thinking and planning ahead. In 1888 he was appointed Managing Director of the combine, taking over when the undertaking was on the verge of bankruptcy. He closed uneconomic metallurgical works, replaced exhausted mines with rich acquisitions and expanded the whole organization. When he retired in 1918 the financial position of the combine was impregnable. It had made a contribution of the greatest value to the Allied cause in the First World War, and it had an administrative, technical, and scientific staff famous throughout France.

In his retirement Fayol devoted his time to the popularization of his own views on management and to the development of theoretical studies. He immediately founded the Centre for Administrative Studies, which had a profound influence on business, the Army, and the Navy in France, and attempted to persuade the French government to pay attention to principles of administration. By invitation of the Under-Secretary of State for Posts and Telegraphs he undertook an investigation of this department. At the time of his death in 1925 he was engaged in investigating the organization of the French tobacco industry. . . .

FAYOL'S CONTRIBUTION   Henri Fayol was an able man whose talents had a fertile field for development in the social and economic environment of France between 1860 and 1925. His abilities placed him in the élite comprised of those who had attended the *grandes écoles,* the most senior administrators in business, government, the armed forces, and in other fields. At the time he commenced his business career the French economy had "taken off" and was passing through [a] period of rapid growth [in which] there was a sense in which French business needed a theory of management, as did American business in a similar stage of development. Fayol's work in France, a country with a long tradition of administration, was complementary to that of Taylor in the U.S.A., a nation which revered the principle of "coming up the hard way." That Taylor worked primarily on the operative level, from the bottom of the hierarchy upwards, while Fayol concentrated on the senior manager and worked downwards, was not merely a reflection of their different careers; it was also a reflection of the political and social history of the two nations.

Fayol's views on management theory contain some weaknesses of analysis and assessment. His principles, elements, and duties overlap; he confused structure and process; and there is a vagueness and superficiality about some of his terms and definitions. He hinted at, but did not elaborate, the limitations of his view that management can and should be taught. Senior managers and administrators he imagined as an intellectual élite, a view which could not be supported universally although true of his own circle and still largely obtaining in France today. He placed a higher value on management theory than it could be expected to support, in 1924 addressing a conference on the importance of administrative doctrine as a contribution to peace.

Nevertheless Fayol's contribution to management theory is unique and valuable. He was a generation ahead of his time in proclaiming its significance and he propounded many views which have been attributed to others who followed. While acclaimed for originating the organization chart, the job specification, and the concept of management education and training, he has been underestimated. His views on human relationships at work anticipated many of the basic findings of industrial psychology. His idea of flexible planning at all levels lies behind the development of the *Commissariat du Plan* which has played such a significant part in the recent expansion of the French economy.

Although it is clear that he was exceptionally gifted, Fayol maintained that his phenomenal business success was due primarily not to his personal qualities but to the application of simple principles which could be taught and learned. These constituted his theory of management. It exercised, and continues to exercise, a profound influence on efforts to clarify thinking on organization, and is one of the foundations of organization theory. His emphasis on unremitting effort has the flavor of Samuel Smiles of latter nineteenth century Britain, but it is probable that his biological model could only have been produced by a Frenchman. . . .—Norman H. Cuthbert

Source: *Scientific Business,* February 1964.

Chester Barnard

Barnard,[7] another important management theorist, perceived the organization differently than Fayol, who stressed designing an organization in a rational and systematic way and then fitting individuals to it. Barnard paid more attention to human factors. He saw organizations evolving out of the attempt to reconcile organizational needs with individual needs.

Organizations, to Barnard, are systems of cooperative effort and coordinated activities. They are formed, or develop, to overcome the inherent limitations of an individual's capacity; that is, when the task to be done requires more than one person, organized effort is necessary.

Like Fayol, Barnard was aware of the formal, designated structure of organization—but he recognized that what really occurred in the context of any organization was different from the charts, job specifications, and procedures specified by management. He made it clear in his analysis that there were informal organizations that existed side by side with the formal. These resulted from different human needs that could not be dealt with by the formal system.

Barnard, in his exposition of this concept, provided groundwork for later analysis that examined the interrelationship of individuals and groups with organizations. Much of what transpires at work can be accounted for by the formal organization. Much, however, can be understood only if the psychological and sociological aspects of organizational life are more fully considered.

He also examined the structure of organization in terms of decision making. Top-level management set objectives. The next management level established plans to achieve them. Then the next lower level developed more detailed plans, until the operating level was reached.

Barnard, like Fayol, also described what executives must do to manage an organization efficiently. The executive functions, according to Barnard, are:

1. *Maintaining organization communication.* This involves integrating managers and their jobs in the system. Competent managers, compatible to the needs of the organization, should be able to communicate effectively to achieve organization purpose.

2. *Securing the essential services of individuals.* Managers are responsible for recruiting, or inducing individuals to join an organization, as well as seeing to it that they produce once they join.

3. *Formulating purpose and objectives.* Managers are responsible for stating, in operational terms, the goals of the organization, then breaking them down into subgoals to be assigned to lower-level units.

The Administrative Point of View

Some of the major ideas that flow from the administrative approach to management are the treatment of authority, management functions, principles of management, organization structure, and emphasis on objectives.

In the administrative approach, **authority** and **responsibility** are seen as rights and obligations of employees and managers. Authority is the right of a manager to decide about resource allocation. Responsibility is the obligation to perform according to job requirements. Authority and responsibility are associated with a position and should be co-equal; that is, a person should not be responsible for those things about which he has no authority. Line authority flows down, according to the administrative school, from the top of the hierarchy to the lowest managerial level.

An **emphasis on objectives** is required to develop a rational relationship among activities. When goals are clearly defined and stated, other resources can be arranged in such a way as to maximize the possibility of attainment. Managers, the administrative theorists believed, would be able to select the best alternative from those available only when goals are known.

One of the more important contributions of the administrative school to management theory is **organization structure,** or guidance on how to design an organization. Many principles of management deal with this problem. Davis, for example, states the principle of **functional homogeneity.**[8] "Duties should be grouped in a manner which will provide the greatest functional similarity." Such grouping would result in lower costs and better performance. Relationships **between** activities, he said, should be governed by the principle of **complementary functions:** "The functions involved in the completion of a project, and their performance factors, must be related in a manner that will facilitate the cumulation of results into the effective, economical accomplishment of the final objectives." Davis then goes on to detail the things that make functions complementary. This design aspect of administrative theory helps a great deal in defining an organization system.

Principles of management are both a strength and a weakness of the administrative approach. Principles were seen by the administrative school as guides to action for managers. Drawn from real-world experiences, they were meant to facilitate high performance. The message from the administrative school was, "Follow the principles, and success will very likely come."

Yet many critics, such as March and Simon,[9] attacked these principles because they were based on observation, not research, and they were "proverbs." But many of the principles have extremely sound bases. For instance the **unity of command** principle states that a person should receive orders from only one superior. This "proverb," based on the experience of the administrative theorists, has a more glamorous conceptual formulation by the social scientist; he calls it avoiding *role conflict.* Role conflict occurs when a person receives inconsistent demands from two or more others so that complying with one of the demands precludes compliance with another. Research has shown the negative effects on individuals of high role conflict.[10,11] It was said another way 2,000 years ago: "No man can serve two masters: for either he will hate the one and love the other; or else he will hold to the one, and despise the other."

Management functions are those activities that all executives perform in whole or part. The administrative theorists did the most extensive early analysis of what these functions are. Managerial functions are planning, organizing, and controlling. *Planning* is the determining, in advance of activity execution, what factors are required to achieve goals. The planning function includes defining the objective and determining what resources are necessary. *Organizing* is the function of acquiring and assembling resources in proper relationship to each other to achieve objectives. *Controlling* is insuring that activities, when carried out, conform to plans to achieve objectives.

The administrative theory school, then, stresses a rational approach to management: If we define our objective, then it is possible to organize resources to achieve it. This is what scientific management was concerned with also.

THE BEHAVIORAL APPROACH

The scientific management movement analyzed the activities of workers; the administrative management writers focused on the activities of managers. The behavioral approach to management sought to understand how human psychological processes—such as motivation and attitude—interact with what one does—activities—to affect performance.

The behavioral approach is probably more fragmented than either the scientific management or the administrative management approach. Behavioralists come from many different social science disciplines (political science, sociology, psychology, and anthropology), and while there are varying emphases among them, they can be generally grouped into two categories. The first category studies *organizational behavior* and considers as a point of focus the individual. Much of the work in this area stems from the Hawthorne studies (discussed below). The second category studies *organizational theory* and tends to consider the organization as a focal point. Much of the theoretical base for this area derives from the work of social psychologists and sociologists.

Organizational Behavior

In the early years of the scientific management movement, behavioral scientists were deeply involved. Their concern was with problems such as worker fatigue, boredom, and job design. Quite a different perspective emerged after the Hawthorne experiment at Western Electric in the late 1920s, which gave rise to the "human relations" approach.[12]

The Hawthorne experiment was carried out in the Hawthorne plant of Western

Electric, an AT&T subsidiary in Cicero, Illinois. The Hawthorne studies (started in 1927) were prompted by an experiment that was carried out by the company's engineers between 1924 and 1927. The engineers, in the best tradition of scientific management, were seeking the answers to industrial questions through research. They studied two groups to determine the effects of different levels of illumination on worker performance. In one group the level of illumination was changed while in the other it was not. They found that when illumination was increased, the level of performance increased. But productivity also increased when the level of illumination *decreased*, even down to the level of moonlight. Moreover, productivity also increased in the control group. These results seemed contrary to reason, and so the engineers examined other factors that might have affected the results. The workers in the experiment were the center of attention. They appeared to react as they thought they should react.

The researchers concluded that the way people were treated made an important difference in performance. Obviously, the subjects were responding, *not* to the level of light, but to the experiment itself and to their involvement in it. They were responding in a way that they thought the experimenters wanted and because they were the center of attention. Since that time this effect in research has been known as the "Hawthorne Effect."

The Hawthorne studies that followed the experiment were conducted by a team of researchers headed by Elton Mayo and F. J. Roethlisberger, from Harvard. The results of these studies are summarized here.

1. *The First Relay Assembly Group.* The first study investigated the effects on worker output of variations in the physical conditions of work, such as rest pauses, hours of work, temperature, and humidity. The study group consisted of six experienced female operators who assembled telephone relays. When each relay was assembled it was dropped down a chute, at which time a mechanism punched a hole in a piece of moving tape. Productivity could be accurately measured by counting the number of holes in the tape and, since it moved at a constant speed, one could later determine productivity levels for any particular time period.

Over a two-year period many changes were made in the working conditions, especially with respect to rest pauses. Two five-minute, then two ten-minute, then six five-minute rest pauses were tried. Food was served with the rest pauses. The work day and the work week were shortened, first by one-half hour a day, then by one hour, then to a five-day instead of a six-day week. Each change in the physical working conditions was made separately and lasted several weeks.

In addition to these changes, the task was simplified somewhat. Workers in the room were put on an incentive wage plan that enabled them to earn more money if the performance level of the group increased. The approach to supervision in the room was different from that in the previous work location. In the relay assembly room, much more attention, interest, and consideration were shown to the workers than on their previous jobs.

In addition, records were kept on temperature, humidity, hours of sleep, food eaten, and so on. The data amassed in this study were extensive and detailed.

Over the two-year period, productivity *generally* went up steadily, no matter what changes in working conditions were made. At the end of the study the investigators formulated five hypotheses to account for the increased production: (1) improved methods of work, (2) reduction in fatigue with changes in rest pauses and shorter hours, (3) reduction in monotony due to rest pauses and hour changes, (4) effect of a wage incentive plan, and (5) effect of the new method of supervision. The first three hypotheses were rejected by the investigators, leaving wage incentives and the method of supervision to be tested in further studies.

2. The Second Relay Assembly Group. To test the effects of wage incentives, a group of workers was selected who remained in the regular work department, but were taken off the regular wage plan and put on a group incentive plan. Productivity increased in the study group by 13 percent, as did their earnings. But the study was terminated after nine weeks because of the resentment of other workers in the department. The investigators concluded, perhaps unwisely, that group rivalry was the cause of the increased production rather than the incentive wage plan.

3. The Mica-splitting Test Room. To examine the effects of different supervision, another group of workers already on piecework was studied. The change in supervision seemed, at first, to make a difference in performance. But with worsening of economic conditions accompanying the Depression, productivity declined and remained stable for a long period of time.

4. The Interviewing Program. The investigators had rejected all their hypotheses about a single cause of the increased productivity. They decided that employee behavior was the result of a reaction to a complex social system made up of several interdependent elements. An interviewing program was initiated in 1928 which lasted several years and which involved more than 21,000 interviews with workers to try to understand some of these complex interrelationships. In this study, several conclusions were reached:

(a) Morale is improved when individuals have a chance to air their grievances.

(b) Complaints are not objective statements of fact.

(c) Workers are influenced in their job demands by experiences outside the work situation.

(d) Worker satisfaction is influenced by how the employee views his social status relative to others.

5. The Bank Wiring Observation Room. In this study, fourteen male workers were formed into a work group and closely observed for seven months. The researchers, in observing the group, saw the emergence of a social system when these workers were placed together. The social system influenced worker behavior considerably. This study will be described in detail in Chapter 9 because it highlights concepts useful to understanding how and why groups affect the behavior of individuals.

The Hawthorne studies seemed to point up the importance of leadership practices and work-group pressures on employee satisfaction and performance. They downgraded the importance of economic incentives in worker motivation. They also stressed the importance of examining the effect of any one factor, such as pay, in terms of a whole social system, pointing out that employees react to a whole complex of forces together, rather than to one factor alone.

While the Hawthorne studies represent the main point of departure for the behavioral approach, both the research methods and the conclusions have been questioned.[13-16] (see case 2.1). For instance, it is said that the research had a management bias, striving to increase productivity without regard to the welfare of workers. Criticism has also been leveled at the research method; for example, that samples were too small, the questions vague. Others criticize the fact that the results were misinterpreted. For example, in the second relay assembly study, production increased with incentives, yet the researchers concluded that group rivalry was the cause. Some questioned the conclusion that management and workers have similar rather than contradictory objectives.

In 1978 Richard Franke and James Kaul reanalyzed the data from the Hawthorne studies. Their reanalysis showed that in some of the experiments, higher productivity occurred because management imposed discipline, there was a threat of unemployment, and rest pauses were used quite effectively.[17] Of course, these conclusions are quite different from those of the original researchers. Regardless of the merit of the criticisms, the research had a significant impact on thinking about management problems. It provided the impetus for critics of the scientific management movement to argue that any effort to develop a science of management without taking the human factor into account would be fruitless.

World War II intensified the interest of the federal government in management problems research, and it funded literally thousands of studies on leadership, job satisfaction, and small-group problems. Psychologists and sociologists gained increased credibility with all groups concerned with management problems. More recent areas of research from the behavioral approach have been in the areas of motivation and job design, much of which, in fact, forms the basis for the content of this book.

Organizational Theory

The administrative theorists were concerned with describing primarily what managers do and proposing "rules" or principles of organization, such as the principle of unity of command. They were concerned with the question of how an organization could be designed to operate more effectively to achieve objectives in a "rational" way. They looked at organization problems rather than at human problems. This broad view could also be found in the behavioral schools, largely based on the work of Max Weber. This German sociologist, whose emphasis was on bureaucracy, was an important influence on writing and theory about the study of organization.

Max Weber's analysis considered organizations as part of broader society.[18] He described the characteristics of the bureaucracy, which he viewed as the most efficient form for large complex organizations such as business, government, and the military. The bureaucratic form of organization, as described by Weber, uses extensive formal rules and procedures to govern the job behavior of organization members. Organizational positions are arrayed in a hierarchy, each with a particular established amount of authority and responsibility. Promotion to higher positions is based on technical competence, objectively judged. Weber felt that this type of organization emphasized predictability of behavior and results and showed great stability over time. He suggested that organizations naturally evolved toward this rational form.

Chester Barnard, as we mentioned earlier, was identified with the administrative theory school. However, much of his work had a significant effect on the behavioral approach, especially in the area of organization theory. He added much to the thinking about organization with such concepts as "the linking pin," "the zone of indifference," and "the acceptance theory of authority."

The "linking pin" concept was a way of considering organizational relationships between superiors and subordinates in organizations.

> The executives of several unit organizations, as a group, usually with at least one other person as a superior, form an executive organization. Accordingly, persons specializing in executive functions . . . are "members of" or contributors to, two units of organization in one complex organization—first, the so-called "working" unit and second, the executive unit.

The "zone of indifference" and the "acceptance theory of authority" contributed substantially to the view of how compliance was obtained. In the administrative school's view, authority was seen as the right of a superior. Barnard maintained that authority works when it is accepted, and that it is accepted often because a communication from a superior falls within the recipient's "zone of indifference," which means substantially that the person is willing to comply.

Using concepts from Barnard, March and Simon surveyed a wide range of empirical work in psychology and sociology, as well as economic theory, to write the book *Organizations*.[9] This book was stimulated by feelings that the existing research and theory about organization and management were inadequate. The classical principles of management as formulated by Fayol and others were attacked, as we noted earlier; March and Simon contended that such principles were not only logically inconsistent, but oversimplified. They extended the Barnard view of the organization as a social system. Following Barnard, they presented a more elaborate motivational theory for organizational members than the classical writers. They emphasized individual decision making as a basis for understanding behavior in organizations. One of the salient points they developed was that of "bounded rationality." To make the optimal decisions suggested by the administrative theorists, they said, the manager would have to select the best of *all* possible alternatives. But the executive, as an "administrative man," is limited by his own perceptions. He has limited knowledge in making organizational decisions and cannot, therefore, make optimal decisions.

CRITICS OF "STRUCTURE."   March and Simon were not the only ones who felt that the principles of management and organization defined by the scientific and administrative schools were limited. There was developing a feeling that the bureaucratic structure was a limited form of organization that would work under some but not all circumstances. In fact, critics of this persuasion argued that rigid job specifications, rules, and policies stifled the creativity, growth, development, and general effectivensss of the human side of the organization.

Douglas McGregor, in *The Human Side of Enterprise*,[19] said that most managers made a set of incorrect assumptions about those who worked for them. He called these assumptions, collectively, Theory X. Theory X assumed that man was lazy, his personal goals ran counter to the organization's, and that, because of this, man had to be controlled externally. In a work context, this meant close supervision and guidance so that management would insure high performance. Theory Y assumptions, on the other hand, were based on greater trust in others. Man was more mature, self-motivated, and self-controlled than Theory X gave him credit for. McGregor suggested that there was little need for either rigid organization or inter-personal controls.

Chris Argyris[20] also made a strong case for reducing the amount of organiza-tional control. He believed that many constraints placed by organization structure on human beings were self-defeating to organizational goals of effectiveness and efficiency. The basic thrust of this argument, along with McGregor's, is that the bureaucratic form of organization is incongruent with the basic needs of the healthy individual. Argyris maintains that the bureaucratic form of organization treats lower organizational members like children. This fosters dependence and leads to the frustration of higher-order human needs. This frustration expresses itself in lack of work involvement and antiorganizational activities such as sabotage.

A concept that embodies these ideas in the management of work organization is the **human resource approach.** It assumes that the job, or task itself, is the primary source of satisfaction and motivation for employees. Tasks, and the orga-nization, should be designed in such a way that individuals have the opportunity to satisfy their higher-level needs through the work itself. This strategy rests heavily on behavioral science techniques to fuse the interests of the organization and the individual. The emphasis in the human resource approach is on individual involve-ment in the decisions made in the organization.

THE MANAGEMENT SCIENCE MOVEMENT

Management science, or operations research, grew out of World War II research on the application of quantitative methods to military and logistical problems. Some of the earliest projects were to increase bombing accuracy, to develop search meth-ods for submarines, to minimize ship loss due to submarine attacks, and to improve methods for loading and unloading ships. This approach to problem solving is interdisciplinary. Problems are attacked by teams, and team members come from a wide variety of fields, though for the most part they are engineers, mathematicians, statisticians, economists, and psychologists.

Miller and Starr[21] consider operations research to be applied decision theory. It uses "any scientific, mathematical, or logical means to attempt to cope with problems that confront the executive when he tries to achieve a thoroughgoing rationality in dealing with his decision problems." But how does this differ from some of the other points of view of the scientific management and administrative theory schools? Miller and Starr offer this way of distinguishing operations research approaches from these others:

> Management Science differs from Taylor's scientific management in many ways. It is not concerned primarily with production tasks and the efficiency of men and machines. Rather, the efficiency is a secondary achievement which should follow adequate planning. In other words, poor decisions can be implemented in an effi-cient way.

Thus, the operations research movement tries to marry the concern of the scientific management school with production and efficiency with the planning approach and the emphasis on objectives of the administrative theory school. This is attempted, however, with an eye toward integrating several fields of knowledge and using systematic analytical techniques, especially quantitative methods, to deal with problems facing managers and organizations. Management scientists use models (representations of real life) with computers to make the necessary and often quite complex mathematical computations to optimize the attainment of a given set of objectives. Today, basic techniques such as linear programming, game theory, queuing theory, and statistical decision theory are being applied to many business problems.

However, managment science does not eliminate from consideration the effects of behavioral problems. Miller and Starr note that "management science is essentially quantitative; however, the important problems that cannot be quantified are handled qualitatively. Whether quantitative or qualitative methods are applied, operations research is used to produce rational decisions and logical plans of action."

CONTINGENCY THEORIES OF MANAGEMENT

At the point we have now reached in our short history, the field of management was in a state of turmoil and confusion. Advocates of one point of view criticized, often mistakenly, other approaches. The administrative theorists argued that the behavioral approach proponents did not understand the realities of the world of business and administration. Critics of "principles" said principles were limited because there were many ways to organize and be successful. Every approach and everyone involved with them were wrong; psychologists were too narrow, sociologists too broad, principles inapplicable, and management science approaches capable of dealing only with trivial problems.

All the critics were right, of course, and all were wrong. The major problem was that critics tended to disparage other contributions without really understanding them. No one took the time to develop an integrated approach to fit together the pieces of the puzzle in a systematic way.

This sorting, sifting, and reformulation of ideas, bringing threads from all the contributing areas and weaving them into a more general approach is what contingency theories of management seek to do. Critics of the administrative and scientific management theorists were correct. There *is* no one best way to manage. But the critics never really told anyone how to proceed to develop a proper managerial strategy. It *did* all depend—but on what?

Some of the answers began to emerge, though in a very seminal way, from a study of the Tennessee Valley Authority by Selznick, *TVA and the Grass Roots*.[22] He showed how various other organizations and interest groups in the outside environment of the TVA affected managerial decisions. The structure of any organization is subjected to many such outside restraints, he claimed, so the organization develops both formal and informal systems that help it to adapt to the outside environment and thus to survive. Selznick made it clear on what the formal structure depended. Not only that, but he described how and through what kind of strategy the adjustment took place. James D. Thompson,[23] an important organization scholar in this tradition, suggests that the basic task of an administrator is the co-alignment of environmental factors with the internal technology, organizational structure, and human resources.

In 1961 Burns and Stalker published a study of British industry. They found differences in the structures of the firms they studied and traced these differences to the nature of the technology used and the markets served. When the technological and market environments were uncertain, a loose organization was found. When the environment was more predictable, a more traditional bureaucracy seemed to be most effective. Burns and Stalker not only saw the environment effect as important but specified more precisely than had been done before what the internal structure should look like, given a certain kind of environment.

Another English study reported by Woodward, following the Burns and Stalker model, showed that the type of organizational structure used was related to a firm's economic performance when type of technology was taken into account.

Lawrence and Lorsch[24] studied a highly effective and a less effective organization in three different industries: plastics, food, and container. These industries were chosen because they operated in environments that differed with respect to rate of technological change for the products they produced and the production methods used. The industries also differed with respect to the type of competitive situation they were in. These factors led to differences in the amount of environmental uncertainty. Lawrence and Lorsch found that in the plastics and food industries, companies were faced with much change and uncertainty, while the container industry was much more stable and predictable. They concluded that the closer the organizational structure matched the requirements imposed on it by the environment, the more successful was the firm. The effective organization had, for example, a high degree of coordinated effort when the environment required it. And a high degree of task specialization was present in high-performance firms when the environment demanded this. In general, they concluded that organizations in a stable environment are more effective if they have more detailed procedures and more centralization of the decision-making process, while organizations in an unstable environment have decentralization, participation, and less emphasis on rules and standard procedures.

Charles Perrow[25] another well-known behavioral scientist, has examined this research and other case studies of many large U.S. companies and has concluded that it is very important that a proper fit exist between an organization and its environment and that one organization's structure and style of management may be effective in one type of environment, quite ineffective in another.

SUMMARY

The insights of the contingency view have had a marked impact on the writing of this book. We believe that the studies by Selznick, Burns and Stalker, Woodward, and Lawrence and Lorsch, along with the work of James Thompson, enable the manager to see fairly clearly how the environment affects the structure of an organization. At the same time, the manager must be aware that ideas from the administrative school can be put to good use in management structure and strategy. Planning is important, but it can only be as effective as the amount of information

available. Additionally, operations research and decision theory can provide both methods for dealing with certain environments—such as the stable environment faced by the bureaucratic organization—and decision approaches for dealing with greater uncertainty, which may characterize the environment of an organic, or flexible, organization. Finally, motivation theories, developed by the behavioral approach, describe what kind of internal psychological factors seem related to high performance in different types of organizations, and this information, too, can be of great value to the manager. These concepts are all brought into our analysis, and because they are, the approach in this book is termed the "managerial process contingency approach." All of the studies reviewed in this book reveal facets of the problem of managing. We have tried to synthesize the constructs, ideas, and principles that seem to emerge as most effective from these studies (that is, from what is known about organizations, individuals, and managing) and show how this synthesis (from all of the schools of thought on managers and managing) can be effectively applied in the various circumstances in which organizations and individuals find themselves. To conclude our short history, then, the purpose of this book is to specify, as well as can be done at this stage of the art, how a manager can manage effectively.

Case 2.1 Paine versus Connor

In 1978 a careful reanalysis of the original data from the Hawthorne studies was published in an academic journal. This reanalysis seemed to indicate that the original researchers drew incorrect conclusions about what had caused worker productivity to increase in some of the Hawthorne experiments. The reanalysis of the data appeared to show that fear of management discipline and fear of job loss were the major determinants of worker productivity, not the more humane management that the workers had been exposed to.

A few weeks after the article was published, Professor Jack Paine discussed the reinterpretation of the Hawthorne studies with Professor Terry Connor over coffee in the faculty lounge. They found they disagreed about the meaning of the new perspective. At one point in the heated conversation Dr. Connor said, "I don't care whether the human relations approach increases productivity or not. It should be used in industrial organizations because it is more humane. It doesn't need any more justification that that."

Dr. Paine violently disagreed. He said, "We should try to increase productivity first. High productivity is good for workers as well as for managers. If human relations works, fine. But the emphasis should be on getting good results. Human relations problems will go away with high productivity because wages can be increased, profits will go up and prices will come down. Then everyone will be happy."

1. How can each of these professors justify his position? What are the bases for each position?
2. What do you believe is the best position on this issue? Why?

Gannon Construction Company

Chuck Gannon, owner of Gannon Construction Company, attended a management seminar sponsored by The Capital County Chamber of Commerce. Chuck, who had never formally studied management, was very stimulated by what he heard. He was especially interested in scientific management and in the benefits of using standards and goals in managing work. On a break between meetings, Chuck asked the management consultant teaching the course a question. "In my business, I have trucks that leave every day from my materials plant to go to the job site. But my job site changes every day as the road is built. How can I use standards for my road crews in my business? Is scientific management useful only in a factory setting?"

1. Is scientific management just useful in a factory setting? Why or why not?
2. How could Chuck Gannon set standards for work done by Gannon Construction?

DISCUSSION QUESTIONS

1. Although Fredrick Taylor (1856–1915) and Henri Fayol (1841–1925) lived in the same era, their ideas and contributions followed different paths. Compare and contrast the ideas of these two important figures.
2. Historically, Taylor, Fayol, and Barnard are thought to be major "sources of modern management ideas." Discuss the contributions of each of these men.
3. Discuss the contribution of the Hawthorne experiment to the field of management. What is the Hawthorne effect?
4. Explain Adam Smith's "invisible hand" theory.
5. Why was Adam Smith, the father of economics, so influential in the field of management?
6. What forces influenced management from the time of the Civil War to the early 1900s?
7. If so much thought was given to management problems before the twentieth century, what made the Frederick Taylor era the starting point of scientific management?
8. Think about the points of view of the administrative theorists and the scientific management writers. How are they similar? Different?
9. How do you feel about the basic prescriptions of scientific management outlined in this chapter? Do they make sense to you as a manager? As an employee?
10. What is your opinion of the importance of the behavioral approach? How can an understanding of human behavior facilitate the manager's job?
11. Some have said that managers are concerned with manipulation of people. What schools of thought would contribute the knowledge one needs to "manipulate" others?

REFERENCES

1. Hoagland, J. "Historical antecedents of organization research," in W. W. Cooper et al. (eds.), New perspectives in organization research. New York, Wiley, 1964.

2. George, C. S. The history of management thought. Englewood Cliffs, N.J., Prentice-Hall, 1972.

3. Taylor, F. W. Scientific management. New York, Harper, 1947.

4. Wrege, C. David, and A. M. Stotka. "Cooke creates a classic: The story behind F. W. Taylor's principles of scientific management," Academy of Management Review, 3 (1978): 737–749.

5. Bell, Daniel. Work and its discontents. The cult of efficiency in America. New York, League for Industrial Democracy, 1970.

6. Fayol, H. General and industrial management, C. Storrs (trans.). London, Sir Isaac Pitman and Sons, 1949.

7. Barnard, C. The functions of the executive. Cambridge, Harvard University Press, 1938.

8. Davis, R. C. The fundamentals of top management. New York, Harper, 1951.

9. March, J., and H. Simon. Organizations. New York, Wiley, 1958.

10. Rizzo, J., R. J. House, and S. Lirtzman. "Role conflict and ambiguity in complex organizations," Administrative Science Quarterly, 15 (1970): 150–163.

11. Tosi, H. L. "A reexamination of personality as a determinant of the effects of participation," Personnel Psychology 23 (1970): 91–99.

12. Roethlisberger, F. J., and W. J. Dickson. Management and the worker. Cambridge, Harvard University Press, 1939.

13. Carey, A. "The Hawthorne studies: A radical criticism," American Sociological Review, 32 (1967): 408–16.

14. Sykes, A. J. N. "Economic interest and the Hawthorne researches," Human Relations, 18 (1965): 253–63.

15. Kerr, Clark. "What became of the independent spirit?" Fortune, 48 (1953): 110–11.

16. Bendix, R., and L. N. Fisher. "The perspectives of Elton Mayo," Review of Economics and Statistics, 31 (1949): 312–321.

17. Franke, R., and J. Kaul. "The Hawthorne experiments: First statistical interrelation," American Sociological Review, 43 (1978): 623–643.

18. Weber, Max. The theory of social and economic organization, (T. Parsons, trans.). New York, The Free Press, 1947.

19. McGregor, D. The human side of enterprise. New York, McGraw-Hill, 1960.

20. Argyris, C. Personality and organization. New York, Harper & Bros., 1957.

21. Miller, D., and M. Starr. The structure of human decisions. Englewood Cliffs, N.J., Prentice-Hall, 1967.

22. Selznick, P. TVA and the grass roots. Berkeley, University of California Press, 1949.

23. Thompson, J. D. Organizations in action. New York, McGraw-Hill, 1967.

24. Lawrence, P. R., and J. W. Lorsch. Organization and environment. Managing differentiation and integration. Graduate School of Business Administration, Harvard University, 1967.

25. Perrow, C. Organizational analysis: A sociological view. Wadsworth, 1970.

Organization and Environment

In the introduction to Part I, we said that the basic idea of management process contingency theory is that some managerial strategies are more important than others in certain circumstances. In this section we begin to develop more fully some of those special circumstances, particularly the organization and its relationship with the environment.

Organizations are social systems that interact with general, social, and cultural forces as well as other specific organizations. These forces are outside the boundary of the organization, but they affect it in many ways.

These external forces have much to do with why organizations are different. Organizations are different because they (1) serve different markets, (2) are affected by different government regulations, and (3) use different methods to produce their goods and services. The important difference between organizations is how their internal activities (or subsystems) are affected by the external environment and how these internal subsystems are related to each other. These ideas are examined in Part II.

A critical determinant of an organization's structure is the degree of uncertainty about other segments of society with which it must interact (government, competitors, or labor unions, for example). Chapter 3 examines this environment, especially the market and technological sectors. Chapter 4 describes different forms of organizational adaptation to environments. The mechanistic form interacts effectively with a stable environment, the organic form with a volatile environment, and the mixed organization with both stable and volatile environments.

These different types of organization attract different types of individuals to work in them. We will discuss differences among individuals in Part III. The differences in people interact with the differences in structure such that the way a manager performs the managerial processes must differ if an effective level of performance is to be reached.

CHAPTER THREE

The Organization and The Environment

Item 3.1 Powertec Inc.—An Organic Organization

Powertec Inc. was founded in Houston in 1963. Most of its top-level managers originally worked for one of the electronic divisions of one of the largest multinational companies in the world. Powertec makes advanced electronic equipment. The products vary from solid state motor starters to wave-making machines for swimming pools. Most of its products consist of various power control devices and complete systems for materials melting, precipitator controls, and DC motor control systems. Most of the systems sold are tailored to a customer's unique needs and range in cost from $25,000 to $2.5 million.

Powertec employs approximately 240 persons. Virtually all of them have been trained in engineering or allied technical specialties. All eight of the top company executives have degrees in electrical engineering. Four of these individuals also have at least master's degrees in electrical engineering. The executive group includes the president, vice president of engineering, vice president of marketing, manager of corporate development, engineering manager of motor control systems, group engineering manager of power systems, manager of mechanical engineering and drafting, and product manager of resistance heating. Five of the top managers have at least three patents to their credit.

Since its inception, the company has been very successful, growing at an average rate of 25 percent a year. Recently it doubled its plant capacity at its original location. In addition, it has acquired two subsidiary companies also making sophisticated industrial products. Much of the company's business is obtained as a result of invitations to bid on various power control systems needed by industrial plants and utility companies. Some of the bids are for the company's engineering consulting experience, rather than its products. In this case the customer uses Powertec's managerial and technical personnel in consulting arrangements. Powertec had kept its personnel fully employed; they have never had to lay off a worker for lack of work.

A visitor at Powertec is immediately struck by the appearance of the offices and production area in the plant. The production area consists of a large number of workbenches scattered over the floor of the plant, seemingly in a very haphazard manner. Large coils of wire and piles of sheet metal are everywhere. The production facilities seem much more primitive and chaotic than most manufacturing plants. The benches are all staffed by individuals using rather simple hand tools such as wire cutters, screw drivers, and soldering irons. Simple electronic test devices are also present.

Pat Cahill, a new MBA graduate, was visiting Powertec interviewing for a job. He was surprised at the look of the place, and said so. His host, Tom Frost, replied, "Maybe we do need some more order around the place. We could at least use some storage racks to get the wire off the floor."

Cahill met Powertec's president, who was dressed in a faded sport shirt and slacks. He hardly looked different from all the other workers in the plant. The president was conferring with a technician at his workbench about a technical problem the technician was having. He had stopped the president on the way to the coffee machine.

Later in the day, Cahill went to Frost's office. The office, like that of all the managers, had a very spartan appearance. There was no carpeting and the desks were simple and quite small. Cahill was very curious and he asked Frost some questions.

CAHILL: Are all managers employed by Powertec trained engineers?

FROST: Yes. We only employ engineering personnel here. We want not only engineers in all higher positions, but superior engineers. Not all engineers can do the work we require around here.

CAHILL: Even the marketing personnel are engineers?

FROST: Yes, they are. You must remember also that in this company all of the managers get involved in marketing. Our marketing department receives bids. The senior managers then visit the customers and then develop the bid proposals based on their evaluation of customer needs. Of course, many of our customers know what they want, but we are often able to do things for them that they had not considered.

CAHILL: Do you have any industrial engineering person or unit in this organization? I don't see any on the organization chart.

FROST: No, we don't use any standards or goals or motion study around here. Our business is quality. We stress technical performance here and there's no emphasis on efficiency.

CAHILL: How do you rate your personnel for purposes of pay increases or promotions without any standards to use?

FROST: Oh, we have a form. It rates people on such things as initiative and judgment. We have a couple of people rate each manager, engineer, and technician. As far as promotion goes around here, we feel a man doesn't merit promotion for meeting goals but for learning a lot. We consider what a person has accomplished but in this business a person is expected to keep learning all the time.

CAHILL: Does the company provide this learning?

FROST: We pay people to attend various technical conferences. Our people attend a lot of these. We also pay for various courses at various universities on subjects of concern to us. The company also pays for all the subscriptions we want to technical journals. I must subscribe to more than a dozen journals myself.

CAHILL: Who does the planning for this company?

FROST: The president meets with the vice presidents to discuss business possibilities all of the time. We do set profit objectives each year. We try to meet them. Sometimes we have to change our prices and delivery dates during the year to end up with the profits we want. We, of course, sometimes bid high and sometimes quite low on various jobs depending on how our contracts in hand compare with our capacity.

CAHILL: How about competition? Is it pretty tough?

FROST: I'll say. More and more of the big boys (large multinational firms) are getting into this business because they see some opportunities. We are also getting more competition from foreign firms. We really can never be sure who else is going to bid on a contract against us or whether they need the job or not. One company in Colorado who almost always bids against us was just bought out by a bigger firm. I don't know what's going to happen with them now.

CAHILL: How about product changes? Do you have many of those?

FROST: Of course. We are continuously changing our products. Any new development, and this happens weekly in our business, is scrutinized to see if we can use it to cut costs or improve the performance of our systems.

CAHILL: How do you like it here compared to Melton Electric (large multinational firm) where you worked before?

FROST: It's great. They gave me a piece of the action when I came aboard two years ago for just twenty-five grand. My investment is worth much more than that now. Also we get along so well here. Everybody's so casual here. I really got sick of the petty politics that were always going on at Melton.

Powertec does not fit the stereotype of places where people work. A common notion held about work organizations is that they have very well defined rules and policies, that individuals are often pigeonholed in jobs that are dull and uninteresting, and that these workplaces have rigid hierarchial relationships that determine how a person should act with a superior.

Nothing could be further from the truth. To be sure, many elements of the stereotyped idea of the workplace do exist, otherwise the stereotype itself would not exist. Also, most organizations have some common characteristics that exist in all but the smallest. Some firms are like Powertec; they have few rules and procedures.

The way a person does a job is not very precisely defined. Other organizations, as we have suggested, have more detailed policies, guides, and rules. Yet both might be equally effective and profitable, even though each has a very different managerial approach.

Differences between organizations are very important because they lead to different managerial approaches. In fact, the central theme of this book is to describe how to manage different types of organization.

In this chapter we will show why these differences exist. It is not just because someone decided to manage Powertec this way. One of the important reasons is that Powertec exists in a particular environment setting and this exerts tremendous pressures that Powertec must accept. All organisms—man, animals, and vegetables—must adapt to their environment or perish. Some animals have the physiological characteristics and biological systems for living in the harsh mountain terrain, others do not. Certain fruits thrive in tropical temperatures, and will not grow in cold climates.

Organizations, too, must adapt. They are open systems in relationships with the environment. An organization must either evolve into a form that will function in the environmental demands placed on it, or it must design or shape such a form.

Two major groups of ideas that deal with the how and the why of organization differences are presented in this chapter. The first set has to do with the external environment within which the organization operates and some characteristics of the environment that shape and form the organization's activities. The second set of ideas has to do with a way of describing and categorizing the various activities of the organization.

THE ENVIRONMENT AND THE ORGANIZATION

Organizations exist in an environment made up of other organizations and sectors of the society that affect it in different ways. These external units provide inputs, make use of outputs, exert pressure for certain kinds of decisions, and in general deal in some important way with the organization. Customers of a firm are part of the external environment. Competitors that sell to these same customers are part of the environment. Other parts of the environment may be sources of raw materials and supplies that are transformed into the product.

Viewed in this way, organizations are "open systems," that is, a system that is affected by and absorbs inputs from outside. It transforms those inputs into goods or services and then distributes these goods and services to users outside the organization. Figure 3.1 illustrates the "open system" concept of organization.

FIGURE 3.1 The open systems view—the organization as a transformation element.

THE RELEVANT ENVIRONMENT

Not all external pressures affect an organization. The relevant environment of any organization is made up of groups or institutions beyond its boundaries that provide immediate inputs, exert significant pressure on decisions, or make use of the organization's output. At any one time there are some external organizations that are closer to and have a more significant effect on what goes on in a firm than do others.[1] Any outside force that is able to generate sufficient pressure to lead to changes within organizations, in either the managerial practice, production methods, or marketing and distribution activities, must of necessity be defined as part of the relevant environment because the organization must adapt to it. For instance, customers and suppliers are in the relevant environment of a business organization. A sudden shift in the type or level of consumer demand, for example, can force internal changes, as when a slump in auto sales causes auto firms to lay off managerial, technical, and operative workers.

Conditions could also change that would bring other institutions or organizations into the relevant environment. When new external factors emerge and impose demands that may exert pressure or may threaten the existence of the organization, some accommodation must be made. When equal opportunity laws were passed, for instance, many firms had to change their hiring procedures as well as the criteria used for promotion.

In this book we give special emphasis to the two sectors of the environment that seem to be used most frequently in analyzing management problems in business organizations: **the market** and **the technological environmental** sectors. Of course, the environment of most firms is composed of more segments that these two. Governmental activities, at local, state, and federal levels are of importance. They are more a problem to some firms than others. Different government agencies may be in the relevant environment of different firms, i.e., the Food and Drug Administration will regulate activities of a pharmaceutical firm while the Environmental Protection Agency might be actively involved with power companies and paper manufacturers. Unions are also in the relevant environment for some firms. The auto industry must deal with the UAW, the Teamsters represent transportation workers, and the UMW affects firms in coal mining. While our discussion and analysis will emphasize the market and the technological environments, the reader should always keep in mind that when other external elements exert pressures, the firm will have to adapt.

The Market Environment

Organizations produce some sort of commodity, product, value, or service for a particular set of individuals, the consumers of the output. The output can obviously take many forms such as automobiles, steel, television sets, bread, pencils, books—the list of products consumed by people is virtually endless. The same holds true of services. Advertising agencies sell ideas and services to clients. Welfare agencies provide social services or information. Hospitals provide health care services to patients by having available a wide variety of health care facilities in one location, convenient for both patients and doctors.

The market environment of a firm includes not only an organization's customers but also its competitors. Some industries, such as publishing, contain many different companies each of which may have a small percentage of the total industry sales. The automobile industry in the United States is composed of only a small group of companies, although this is changing somewhat at present due to foreign competition. Some market environments are highly competitive and some much less so.

We might also consider the "market" for services or outputs of departments within a complex organization. The output of the production department, e.g., television sets, furniture, or toys, becomes an input for the marketing unit. Departments in organizations provide some sort of product or service to other units. These may range from specific tangible products such as subassemblies, completed units, memoranda, or reports, to services, ideas, or other, more abstract values. For example, the marketing division is the "market," or user, of the output from the manufacturing division. A shop foreman is a user (the market) of reports produced by the production control department.

The Technological Environment

The technology of an industry includes the machines, procedures, and knowledge used to produce the products or services. Products and services incorporate scientific or technical knowledge. Some companies, such as those in the electronics fields, may have very sophisticated technology, while those in other industries, such as clothing, may have a relatively much simpler technology. The body scan is a very advanced medical device that can be used to x-ray the whole body at one time. This device utilizes the most current scientific knowledge available.

The processes used to produce the product or service also incorporate scientific and technical knowledge. The same product may be produced with technical processes that differ in complexity. A sweater may be made entirely by hand or by a machine. Thus, the technological environment influences the nature of a product itself or the way the product is manufactured.

Other Environmental Sectors

As we said, other sectors of the organization set may be important. Currently, for example, EPA is exerting substantial pressure on electricity-generating public utilities to clean up smoke emmisions to reduce pollutants. This governmental agency with its regulatory activity will have different effects on those firms with which it interacts than, say, the Department of Agriculture may have with private sector firms with which it interacts. Figure 3.2 shows the case of a firm that has the government, the market, and technology in its relevant environment. As the number of relevant factors in the environment increases, environmental complexity grows and makes it more difficult for the firm to adapt.

CHARACTERISTICS OF THE ENVIRONMENT

Two important research studies support the idea that organizations were more successful when they had management systems and organization structures congruent with the state of the external environment. Lawrence and Lorsch found that organizations that were effective in a dynamic or rapidly changing environment had sharper differentiation among the subunits and also had very important coordinating

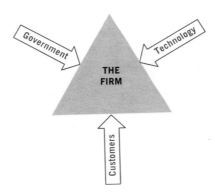

FIGURE 3.2 An organization with a relevant environment comprised of a market sector, the government, and a technological sector.

units.[2] Burns and Stalker found that mechanistic organizations were more effective in stable environments, but organic organizations were more effective in dynamic environments.[3] Change and uncertainty are important characteristics of the environment.

The degree of uncertainty and change in the environment causes the organization to take the form—structure—that it does. The uncertainty of the environment has substantial implications for the internal structure of the organization, the type of individual who is likely to join a particular operation, and the shaping of perceptions, attitudes, and values in the organization. Most important, however, is that the environmental uncertainty has a significant effect on the degree to which internal subsystems of the organization take on highly routine or repetitive characteristics.

The degree of change may be conceived of as a continuum, at the opposite ends of which are (1) stability and (2) volatility (see Figure 3.3). In some environments the degree of change may be moderate. In others it could be more turbulent.

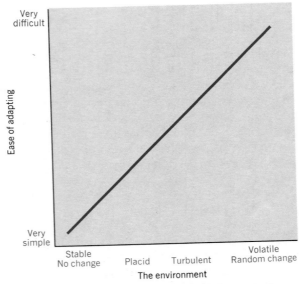

FIGURE 3.3 Degree of environmental change and ease of adapting.

The Stable Environment

The stable environment is one in which changes are relatively small, occurring in small increments, with a minimal impact on the structure, processes, and output of the organization. Changes are likely to be in size of the market (e.g., the amount of beer consumed or insurance sold). For the organization the impact of changes in the stable environment will largely be on the size of the membership of the organization. The product is unlikely to change significantly and there will be little need to alter the production process of the organization with change in the environment.

The stable environment is characterized by high levels of **predictability**. It is very likely that we will be able to make reasonably accurate predictions of the level of the market based on some fairly common set of change measures or indexes. For instance, the level of automobile sales may be predicted from the relatively accurate data available on changes in population and income.

The Volatile Environment

The volatile environment is likely to be turbulent and unstable, with more intense changes than in the stable environment. Changes are also more rapid and random, and prediction is difficult.

When the market is volatile, the customers may change and the level of demand may vary widely. The woman's fashion market is relatively volatile. Product decisions of designers and manufacturers are based on consumer tastes and preferences, and these are highly changeable and difficult to predict. The market for semiconductors (integrated circuits) also displays a great deal of volatility. From 1970 to 1974, industry sales plunged by 25 percent and many small electronics firms founded in the early '70s went out of business.

When the technology is volatile, new concepts and ideas are being rapidly generated. These new ideas affect either the manner in which the production processes are carried out or the nature of the processes themselves. The effects of a volatile technology can be seen in the recent history of the watch industry. Electronic digital watches were introduced in the early 1970s and a timepiece sold for several hundred dollars. These timepieces were operated by battery-powered quartz crystals. These vibrated at very high frequencies that were translated into lighted digits by small integrated electronic circuits. Many firms began manufacturing and marketing these new quartz crystal timepieces and there were some major technological breakthroughs in integrated circuit manufacturing that drove prices down to below $20 for a timepiece by 1975. Competition was extremely fierce among the manufacturers, and many U.S. watch manufacturers have lost their prominence in an industry dominated by K. Hattori, the Japanese manufacturer of Seiko watches.

ORGANIZATION SUBSYSTEMS

An organization is a group of people working together to achieve an objective or set of objectives. To understand how organizations adapt to the environment and how to manage them, we must begin by understanding their basic elements or subsystems. An organization system is a set of interrelated subsystems which absorbs inputs from other systems and transforms them into outputs that are used by other systems, as shown in Figure 3.1. Subsystems are related groups of activities within the organization that must be performed to meet its objectives.

An organization transforms inputs (or resources) into outputs (or goods and services) by means of a **production** subsystem, a technological process—a complex of physical objects, procedures, and knowledge by which a certain result is obtained. Some technologies are composed primarily of physical objects, as when steel, component parts, and other materials are transformed into automobiles on an assembly line in an automobile firm, or as when gasoline is produced by the sophisticated and complex equipment used in a refinery. In other technologies the physical objects may be quite simple but the procedures and the knowledge quite sophisticated, as when a surgeon performs a delicate operation using simple instruments.

There are also *boundary-spanning* activities that transfer inputs into and outputs from an organization. The technology needs raw materials to operate. The products it creates must be sold or otherwise distributed. *External-monitoring* subsystems try to monitor the organization's environment. *Control* and *managerial* subsystems are intended to solve coordination and control problems, resolve conflict, and facilitate decision making.[4]

PRODUCTION SUBSYSTEMS

The production subsystem is the technical core of the organization that produces the product, service, or ideas that are bought, or otherwise consumed, by the public.[5] Organizations are often categorized by their production subsystems. Automotive firms, hospitals, educational institutions are designated as such specifically because of what they do, and how they do it.

Every organization has a production subsystem, whether it is a bank, a manufacturer, a hospital, a department store, or a public service agency. In a business firm the production system is the task-oriented work that creates the product or service—for example, an assembly line, a transaction system for tellers in a bank, or those activities in a retailing outlet that take place after goods are bought but before they are sold. In hospitals, the care facilities, operating rooms, and emergency operations are different parts of the total production subsystem. The minds of creative staffs are part of the production system of an advertising agency. The product is a campaign to sell a product, idea, or person.

The production subsystem is important because it is the "technical core" of the organization (see Figure 3.4). It generally will require large sums to build, create, or otherwise develop it. This large investment produces pressures for effective and efficient utilization, and some mechanisms are designed to protect it from unpredictable fluctuations in the environment. (Some of these mechanisms, such as buffering and smoothing, are discussed later in this chapter.) Production technologies can be classified into these three types: long-linked, mediating, and intensive.[5]

Long-linked Technologies

Long-linked technologies involve serial interdependence of tasks, such as task B, which can be performed only after task A is completed, while task C requires both to be finished. An assembly line is a clear and a striking example of long-linked technology. For instance, in a food processing plant, each step in manufacturing

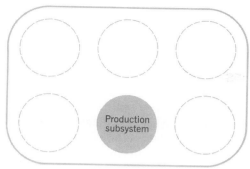

FIGURE 3.4 The production subsystem: task-oriented activities.

must follow sequentially to obtain the correct quality of product. To process tomato juice, the tomatoes must be cleaned, mashed, strained, cooked and the juice sealed in cans, in that sequence.

Mediating Technologies

Mediating technologies are production subsystems that contain activities designed to link clients or customers who are or who wish to be interdependent. The phone company links callers with those called; banks link depositors with borrowers.

Though a mediating technology itself may be standardized, fluctuations in either demand or supply may be very extreme and not easily influenced by the organization. Such variability in demand often requires a substantial investment in the production subsystem to handle peak loads. This means that it is underused in one period, but is overloaded at other times. Long-distance telephone circuits, for example, are extremely busy on Christmas and Mother's Day, while it is virtually certain there will be open lines any weekday at 1:00 A.M., a time of day when there is underutilization of equipment.

Intensive Technologies

Intensive technologies are systems in which a wide range of different techniques can be used "but the selection, combination and order of application are determined by feedback from the object itself."[5] A university is an intensive technology system. From a large number of different courses, certain patterns and sequences are defined for different majors or concentrations. Job-shop manufacturing (where general-purpose equipment is used to manufacture different products), construction firms, and hospitals are all examples of organizations in which the specific techniques and tools used depend on the nature of the problem or project.

Protecting the Production Subsystem

Since there is such a large investment in this system, whether it is made up of expensive equipment or highly trained professionals, it represents the greatest potential area in which operating efficiencies can be obtained. In other words, if we can manage this system well, we have an upper hand on the problem of keeping operating costs in line.

The technical core can be protected against environmental variations by *buff-ering* and *smoothing*.[5] The need for buffering and smoothing is, of course, greatest when there is a substantial degree of volatility in the environment.

Buffering is protecting internal operations by sealing off the production system from external forces. For example, say that a plant has a continuous-assembly operation and therefore needs a steady flow of raw materials, but the supply of raw materials is variable, uncertain, or otherwise not in synchronization with use. The solution, then, is to create an inventory of raw materials that will permit steady production. The same holds true when there is smooth, steady production but variable demand. The firm simply produces to inventory. Inventory acts as a buffer against the environment's variability.

Smoothing is minimizing severe fluctuations of the environment by "offering inducements to those who use . . . services during 'trough' periods, or [charging] premiums to those who contribute to 'peaking.' "[2] Offering discount rates to early-morning callers is a smoothing strategy used by the telephone company. Discounts offered to buyers during off-seasons is another such strategy (e.g., lower hotel rates during the summer months in Florida).

BOUNDARY-SPANNING SUBSYSTEMS

Boundary-spanning subsystems carry on transactions with individuals and organizations in the external environment, procuring inputs, disposing of outputs, or assisting in these functions. They are called "boundary-spanning" because, while the activities themselves are performed within the organization, they connect it with outside organizations, across the boundary so to speak. Selling, procuring raw materials, recruiting personnel, and securing capital are examples of boundary-spanning functions (see Figure 3.5).

EXTERNAL-MONITORING SUBSYSTEMS

Since the major objective of an organization is survival, and it does so in some environment, when the environment changes, the organization must change (see

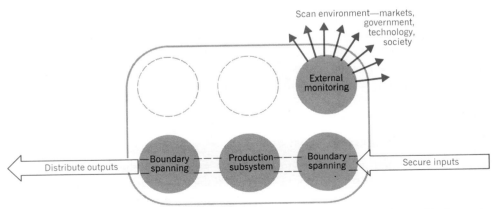

FIGURE 3.5   Boundary-spanning subsystems carry on exchange transactions with the environment.

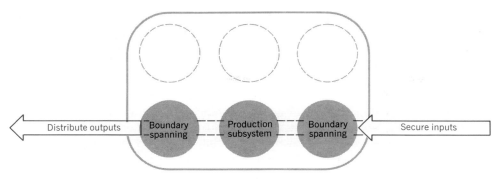

FIGURE 3.6 External-monitoring subsystems scan the environment for changes that affect the organization.

Figure 3.6). Therefore, the environment must be monitored. This is accomplished by the external-monitoring subsystems. Research and development is one kind of external-monitoring subsystem activity. Efforts to keep abreast of current technology and to provide products that are being demanded by the market are organizational attempts to adapt to the world.

Lobbying to influence government policy in areas that might affect the organization is also an external-monitoring activity. Major changes in government requirements on pollution control, for example, could have a serious effect on the level of an organization's survival.

CONTROL SUBSYSTEMS

Control subsystem activities seek to smooth out the problems of operating the other subsystems and to monitor their internal operation. As we use the term *control system* here, it goes far beyond the simple application of accounting and reporting systems, though these are important aspects of it (see Figure 3.7).

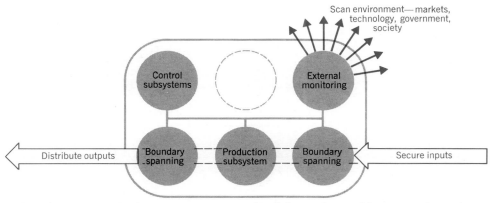

FIGURE 3.7 Control subsystems increase predictability within and between other subsystems.

Control subsystem activities also focus on setting performance standards for tasks, raw materials standards, and product or service quality standards. Evaluation activities are carried out to insure that such standards are met, rules and norms are established, and performance is monitored in the control subsystem. Specialized groups such as industrial engineering or quality control may have responsibility in these activities.

Control subsystems seek to insure the effective operation of the entire system by increasing the level of predictability of the other subsystems. Equipment and machinery require standardized raw material inputs, and thus there must be certain minimum quality standards for such materials. Machinery must be operated in certain ways to protect it and to insure proper coordination with other machinery or the production system will break down or, at best, will operate inefficiently.

Control systems seek to obtain smooth operations by affecting attitudes and behavior of people. One important function of control subsystems is controlling subsystems activities including indoctrination, socialization, maintaining morale, rewarding and punishing of organization members, training activities, and overseeing the compensation system and the performance appraisal system.

MANAGERIAL SUBSYSTEMS

"[Managerial] subsystems," say Katz and Kahn, "comprise the organized activities for [dealing] . . . with coordination of subsystems and adjustment of the total system to its environment."[4] But to differentiate the managerial subsystem from the control subsystem, the managerial subsystem is concerned with general policy questions; the control subsystem is the translation of these general policy and coordination processes into specific actions, standards, and programs. Perhaps the best way to think of the managerial subsystem is to view it as those activities and processes that coordinate the relationship between external monitoring, boundary-spanning, production, and control subsystems. These activities include, at least, the determination of organization structure, the interpretation of market information, and marketing strategic decisions about the place—and placement—of the organization in the environment. Determining general policy and strategy to interact with the environ-

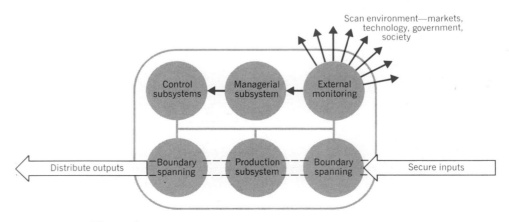

FIGURE 3.8   The total system.

ment with the intent of insuring long-term survival is a function of the managerial subsystem.

The resolution of internal conflict between departments is also one of its functions, as is the use of the authority structure to disseminate directives and to resolve conflict. In essence, then, in the control subsystems, standards and techniques for implementing them are developed. In the managerial systems, the shape and relationships among these control systems are devised. For example, quality standards are determined in the control system, but the determination of where, at what level, and at what position a decision is made about the adequacy of quality levels is a function of the managerial subsystems. Stated another way, the managerial subsystem is the decision-making structure for major decisions. The total organization system is shown in Figure 3.8.

THE STRUCTURE/ENVIRONMENT (S/E) MODEL

In this chapter we have emphasized the idea that organization structure will differ according to the conditions of the environment. That is, the organization's subsystems (production, boundary spanning, etc.) will differ depending on whether or not the technology and/or market is stable or volatile.

TYPES OF ORGANIZATIONS

From these ideas about subsystems, their interface with the environment, and the character of the environment, we can form some specific ideas about the different types of organizations. Figure 3.9 illustrates the basic model we follow in the rest of the book. One axis represents the market environment; the other axis represents the technological sector of the environment. The extreme ends of the stability—volatility continuum are also shown in Figure 3.9.

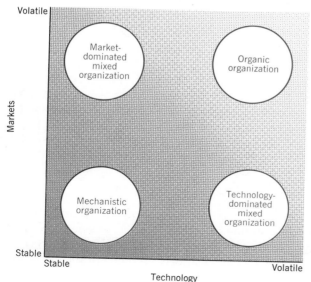

FIGURE 3.9   The environment and type of organization.

Within Figure 3.9 four different types of organizations are represented: (1) the mechanistic organization, (2) the organic organization, (3) the technology-dominated mixed organization, and (4) the market-dominated mixed organization. These four types fall at the extreme ends of the uncertainty continuum in the technology and market environments. We do not mean to suggest that these are the only types; rather they are useful for analytical and prescriptive purposes.

Mechanistic Type

The mechanistic organization develops in response to a stable market and a stable technology. It uses standard production methods and has well-defined, fixed channels of distribution. Tasks in it change slowly. Authority/responsibility relationships are specified. Mechanistic form is the appropriate adjustment to the stable environment.

Organic Type

The important characteristic of an organic organization—which must adapt to a volatile environment—is its ability to change. There is not an intensive investment in plant and equipment, and high skill levels are required of employees. They may be moved from one part of the organization to another as demands change. There is little centralized decision making, and authority is often not well-defined.

Market-dominated (MD) Mixed Type

In the market-dominated mixed (MD-mixed) type of organization, the technology is relatively unchanging, but the markets are in constant flux. Under such conditions, their marketing units are their most influential subsystems. An example of a market-dominated mixed organization would be a women's apparel manufacturer. The technology for making the product has been stable for a long period of time, but the market is extremely volatile because competitors go into and out of business constantly due to price competition, because there are several distinct selling seasons, and because of unpredictable style preferences of customers.

Technology-dominated (TD) Mixed Type

When the market is stable but the technology is constantly changing, then the research and development (R & D) group—the scientists who deal with that technology—will be the dominant force in the organization. This is the technology-dominated mixed organization (TD-mixed). The marketing group will be much like that in a hierarchical organization, but the R & D group will be relatively flexible.

EXTENSIONS OF THE S/E MODEL

There is probably no *pure* organizational type like those shown in Figure 3.9, but many organizations may come close to one of them. There are several ways that organizations might deviate from those we have described. First, a very large organization may have highly autonomous units that exist in different sectors of the grid in Figure 3.9. For example, a conglomerate may have an insurance subsidiary,

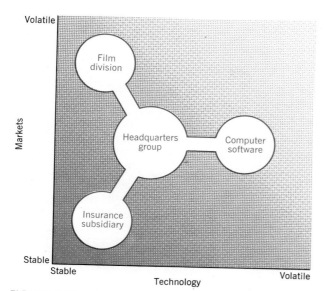

FIGURE 3.10 A conglomerate with major divisions in different environments.

a film-making subsidiary, and a computer-software consulting group. Figure 3.10 would represent such a firm. The management problems are complex, as one might guess. Each one of the four subsidiaries should be organized differently and, yet, there must be an integrative strategy at the headquarters level that can cope with the problems of the very different units.

Figure 3.11 illustrates another possibility of multi-unit organization. This figure indicates that the firm has three divisions, but each one is located in a similar environment. (For example, the major divisions of automobile firms all have relatively similar environments.) Most of these divisions would very likely be organized in a similar fashion. They would face similar problems and it is likely that a corporate management system would be more easily developed than in the case of a corporate management system of the conglomerate in Figure 3.10.

It is obvious that very large organizations like the large governmental agencies and companies such as IBM, AT&T, Westinghouse, and General Electric are actually composed of many separate and different organizations, some of which have relationships with each other and some of which are quite independent of each other. These organizations must carefully differentiate (segregate) their individual units from each other while at the same time providing some sort of integrating mechanism to coordinate them.

ADAPTATION: ACTIVE AND PASSIVE

The preceding discussion could lead to the assumption that organizations are passive, subject to the buffeting of the environment, adapting to it or perishing. It is possible, however, for an organization to do many things that might influence the

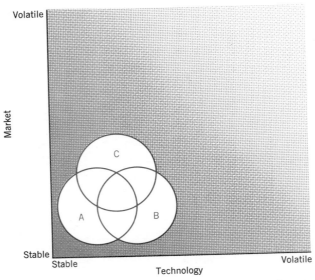

FIGURE 3.11 A firm with major divisions located in a similar environment.

nature of its environment. For example, lobbying to change government regulations or laws can help insure relatively moderate to low government intervention. Or where a stable technology exists, spending large amounts of time and money on research may produce a breakthrough, thus increasing technological volatility. In a later chapter we will discuss how an organization can influence its environment.

SUMMARY

Organizations must adapt to the environment in which they exist. There are many sectors of the environment that may affect organizations, but of interest to us are the market and the technological environments.

The environment affects the various subsystems that make up the organization. Organizations have (1) production, (2) boundary-spanning, (3) external-monitoring, (4) control, and (5) managerial subsystems. The degree of uncertainty or volatility in the environment causes these subsystems to be either fairly rigid or fairly flexible. When the environmental sector is very stable, the subsystems are rigid; when the environment is uncertain, subsystems must be flexible. However, organizations are not passive; it is possible for an organization to do many things that might influence its environment.

Four general types of organizations are suggested. These are shown in Figure 3.9. The mechanistic organization exists when the market and technology are both stable. The organic form exists when the market and technology are both uncertain. When the market is volatile and the technology is stable, the market-dominated mixed organization is the most likely form of accommodating to the environment. The technological-dominated mixed organization exists in environments where the market is stable but the technology is volatile.

American Concrete Association

James Runnels is membership and training director of the American Concrete Association. He is concerned because the membership of ACA is not growing. The American Cement Association consists of 900 members, all of whom are contractors throughout the United States involved in cement construction. There are more than nine thousand potential members in the United States, but membership seems to have reached a peak some three years earlier. Without new members, who make annual contributions of $1,000 to $2,000 a year depending on their size, the association's programs cannot be maintained in the face of increasing costs. These programs include training, lobbying, and information programs. The training programs include both managerial and technical training on various topics relevant to the industry. The lobbying activities are directed at the Federal Highway Agency and various federal and state legislative committees concerned with public construction. The information programs involve the dissemination of technical information on highway construction and on the uses of concrete for various products such as tennis courts, playgrounds, boat piers, barn floors, railroad ties, swimming pools.

1. Why do so many trade associations exist in the United States?
2. What would cause some firms to join and some firms not to join such a trade association?
3. How would you advise James Runnels to handle his problem?

Maine Wood Products

Maine Wood Products was formed in 1975 by Jake Forsgren to produce lobster traps for the independent lobstermen sailing from the northern coast of Maine. Jake was born in Maine, but moved away. At age forty-five he returned to the Northeast and bought a small sawmill in the town where he was born. Jake felt that he could make lobster traps cheaper than the lobstermen themselves because of quantity buying of wood, which was very plentiful in Maine, and through the use of efficient machinery and methods.

The small business prospered and Jake and his sons kept quite busy making the lobster traps. Jake still had, however, excess space and equipment. He decided to expand into other wooden products such as toys and window boxes for flowers. After designing the new products and contacting potential customers, Jake hired seven workers. This was relatively easy because of the high unemployment in the area. He put them to work on the orders he received.

Shortly after the business was in operation, the sawmill was visited by a federal occupational safety official and a staff member from the State's Unemployment Commission. They told Jake that he had to make various changes in his operations and his system of management. In the next two weeks, three more officials of regulatory agencies visited Jake's shop. At the beginning of the next week, Jake gave all of his hired workers notice that they would be terminated in two weeks. He told his sons that Maine Wood Products would never be more than a family business again.

1. What does this case illustrate about the environmental pressures on a business?
2. Evaluate the benefits and costs of some of the regulatory activities described in the case.

DISCUSSION QUESTIONS

1. Both the market and the technological environmental sectors are given special emphasis by the authors. Describe both of these in detail.
2. What are stable and volatile environments? Which organizational structure(s) is best suited for each of these environments?
3. Why would the production subsystem of an organization be presumed to be the most important by some people?
4. Describe the three types of technologies emphasized in the chapter: long-linked, mediating, and intensive.
5. Why are the techniques of buffering and smoothing so critical?
6. Which subsystem of the organization do you deem most important? Why? How would the other subsystems interact with this one?
7. Which type of organization do you feel you would fit into best? Why?
8. Briefly describe the four major types of organizations. Do you feel that organizations can easily be classified into one of these types? Why or why not?
9. What is the production subsystem in a restaurant? The boundary-spanning subsystem?
10. What particular organizational environment is currently volatile for the automotive industry? Fast-food franchisers? Hospitals?
11. Is it easy for you to visualize how a unit may perform boundary-spanning functions at one time, production at another, and maintenance functions at yet another time?
12. How can the different levels of technological environmental volatility affect the reactions of two people similarly trained, but in different conditions—for example, an electrical engineer in a stable technology firm and one in a volatile technology?

REFERENCES

1. Evan, W. M. The Organization-Set: "Toward a theory of interorganizational relations" in J. Thompson (ed.), Approaches to organizational design. Pittsburgh, University of Pittsburgh Press, 1966.
2. Lawrence, P. R., and J. W. Lorsch. Organization and environment: Managing differentiation and integration. Graduate School of Business Administration, Harvard University, 1967.
3. Burns, T., and G. Stalker. The management of innovation. London, Tavistock, 1961.
4. Katz, D., and R. Kahn. The social psychology of organizations, 2nd ed. New York, Wiley, 1978.
5. Thompson, J. Organizations in action. New York, McGraw Hill, 1967.

CHAPTER FOUR

Types of Organizations

International Steel Products Company: A Mechanistic Organization

International Steel Products Company produced buckets, steel drums, and trash cans out of sheet steel in their bucket and drum division. The Syracuse plant was headed by Jim Bell. In 1980 Bell was interviewed by a professor from a nearby university, Dr. Angela Freeman. Dr. Freeman was especially interested in how the different units and individuals at International Steel Products coordinated their activities. In response to her question, Bell told her that the answer was in the manuals on the shelf behind his desk. He then showed her one manual which contained very detailed position descriptions for every manager from foreman to himself. Professor Freeman found that the position descriptions contained a list of the responsibilities of each position in addition to the key reporting relationships for that individual. Looking further, Bell showed Freeman some of the many detailed procedure manuals he had available. Freeman followed up on this information.

FREEMAN: I imagine that budgets are an important management tool in this company?

BELL: You bet! The budget is our guide. It tells us what we are supposed to do for the year. We couldn't get along without it. Our budget tells us how much income the plant is to produce and also what all our expenses should be.

FREEMAN: How is the budget determined? Where do you get your figures?

BELL: Well, we submit the budget based on the statistical sales forecast made by the marketing department. They are rarely off very much. The forecast tells us how many items of different products we will have to deliver and when. We then use performance and cost standards determined by our industrial engineering and accounting departments to establish the figures in all the categories.

FREEMAN: Are these standards based on historical performance and cost figures in this company?

BELL: Well, some of them are. We have been using the same equipment for a long time. Some of them are based on time studies and cost analyses made in this company and some standards are from published information provided by our trade association. Also we are expected every year to cut costs in various expense categories over what they have been in the past.

FREEMAN: What if you don't meet the budget?

BELL: Well, that has never happened yet. The managers make sure we meet it. We have a bonus system here based on how well we do on the budget. If we do better than our plant income goal or if we do better than standard on our output, we get what could be a significant sum of money to distribute among the eligible managers.

FREEMAN: Who are the eligible managers?

BELL: They include all managers whose activities could be expected to have direct impact on plant income or operating expenses.

Professor Freeman also interviewed Dick Polaski, the personnel manager of the plant.

FREEMAN: This seems to be a company that is big on performance standards?

POLASKI: Yes, in this company all product costs are based on standards. We have standards for direct labor and for indirect labor as well as for materials and other expenses. Some of the standards we derive ourselves and some come from other plants of this company with similar equipment and manufacturing processes. Having plants in different parts of the country making the same products is an advantage, since the corporate headquarters people can compare costs and performance among the different plants.

FREEMAN: How about personnel policies and procedures in this plant? What are they like?

POLASKI: Well, we have very specific policies and procedures covering all aspects of personnel from hiring to firing. Here is our personnel policy manual. As you can see, it has become pretty large over the years.

FREEMAN: What about the firing that you mentioned? Do you do that often?

POLASKI: If an employee cannot make the performance standards set for his task within the probationary period, he is let go. Also we sometimes fire workers for repeated violations of some of our plant rules. We use a progressive discipline system here. All rules are published with the penalties that may be imposed for their violation depending on circumstances. Before a worker is fired, usually some lower level of discipline is first imposed such as a written warning, a one day's suspension, or some other punishment. Of course, for very serious offenses such as participating in an illegal strike, the worker may be fired right away.

FREEMAN: How do your employees like working under your standards and rules?

POLASKI: The foremen and the managers seem to be pretty well satisfied. Our turnover rate among them is very low. As for the men, they do their work but most of them don't show very much interest in it. Our foremen have to keep after the men all the time or they will slack off whenever they get a chance. Our quit rate is not bad at all for this area according to the figures that I have collected for corporate and plant management. Our pay is relatively high for this area and I'm sure that our men make more here than they could elsewhere.

FREEMAN: Let me ask about something else. How do the different departments in the company get along?

FREEMAN: Pretty well. After all, our bonus system is based on the whole plant's performance and everybody has to work together or we won't make it. The biggest problem is between sales and production. A customer will sometimes call up sales and ask them if they can get a delivery date that is earlier than scheduled. They go over to production and the manufacturing people blow their top. Naturally, changing the production schedule is going to increase our operating expenses.

FREEMAN: So you never change the production schedule?

POLASKI: I didn't say that! Sometimes they do and sometimes they don't, depending on the circumstances. Once in a while, the plant manager intervenes if the customer calls him directly and is able to convince him that they have a real crisis.

FREEMAN: Thanks for your help. I'm going to have to move on now if I am going to finish my interviews.

In Chapter 3 we stated that an organization can be viewed as a system composed of interrelated subsystems, (production, boundary-spanning, external-monitoring, control, and managerial). The structure of an organization (the relationship between subsystems) is influenced by the demands placed on it by its relevant environment. An organization's market and technology are especially influential environmental factors in the shaping of its structure.

Market and technological factors may take on characteristics ranging from a high degree of stability (infrequent change and thus high predictability) to high levels of volatility (frequent change and thus high unpredictability or uncertainty). Figure 4.1 summarizes the environmental/organization relationship described in Chapter 3. The subsystems, which are in all four organizational types, will take on different characteristics and relate to each other differently in each of the types of organization. The variations are largely determined by the external environment. Such variations are very clear when you compare the International Steel Products Company (Item 4.1) with Powertec, described in Item 3.1.

In this chapter we discuss two major topics. First, we will describe how the five subsystems can be expected to vary within each organization type. Of course these variances can be expressed only as theoretical, general tendencies, not as hard-and-fast rules. Nevertheless, organizations of all types do exhibit certain general structures and characteristics, depending upon their environment. Similarities and differences in structure and characteristics from organization to organization reflect adaptation to the forces and problems presented by their environments. Second, we will show how these subsystems become transformed into the more easily identified unit of most organizations, i.e., departments.

The organic and mechanistic organizations represent extreme ends of a continuum of types. For both of these organizations, the different environments are relatively similar. For the former the market and technological sectors are stable; for the latter they are both volatile. Many organizations interact with environments that have both stable and volatile characteristics. We call organizations that have at least one major subsystem interacting with a volatile environment "mixed-form" organizations. The mixed-form type of organization is probably more prevalent than either the mechanistic or organic types.

There are two mixed types in our analytical framework. The first, called technology-dominated mixed (TD-mixed), has a relatively stable market and a volatile technology. The second, the market-dominated mixed (MD-mixed), has a stable technology and a volatile market.

There are two important points to remember about mixed organizations. The first has to do with a major managerial problem: How can you develop a strategy for integrating the operations of two organizational components that take on very different structural characteristics because they interact with different environments?

The second has to do with power and influence over policy and strategy. As a general rule, the organizational sector that interacts with the most volatile or uncertain sector of the environment will exert the greatest influence in determining what the policy, strategy, and general direction of the total organization will be. It is for that reason that we have classified organizations as market-dominated or technology-dominated according to which subsystem of the organization faces a volatile environment.

FIGURE 4.1   Environmental Characteristics and Organization Type

Market Environment Characteristic	Technology Environment Characteristic	Organization Type
Stable	Stable	Mechanistic
Stable	Volatile	Technology-dominated (TD) Mixed
Volatile	Stable	Market-dominated (MD) Mixed
Volatile	Volatile	Organic

THE MECHANISTIC ORGANIZATION

The mechanistic form of organization is the most appropriate for organizational adaptation when the environment is highly stable.[1] We can expect the mechanistic form to emerge whenever the market and the technology are stable and predictable. This is the case, for example, for many government agencies in which there is little technological change. The client group (market) is fairly well-defined, and there is little competition in the provision of services. The same is true for organizations such as banks, insurance companies, and companies in the container industry, which produce bottles and cans and which have had a very stable technology and market for a number of years.

PRODUCTION SUBSYSTEMS

The mechanistic organization's production subsystem is characterized by a relatively high degree of repetitiveness. That is, a standard way of performing tasks is established and routinized particularly at lower organization levels. Virtually anyone assigned those tasks must perform them in the prescribed way. The assembly line is, of course, a good example of such repetitive tasks, but white-collar work in banks, insurance companies, and government agencies are similarly routine.

In mechanistic organizations the production subsystem may have the extreme division of labor or task specialization. Since the work activities can be standardized, they can be reduced to relatively small work units. As a result, the employees may have only limited knowledge of how their work input contributes to the final result or product.

The workers need only a low-level skill to perform their jobs. This can lead to a high level of dependence of the individual on the organization. It is easy to replace workers, since low skill levels mean that probably a large labor pool is available for the work, and the individual who does the work has little control over how he produces or what he does. This lack of job security gives rise to a need for some sort of protection, which is likely to be an external agent—such as a union or the civil service system—to provide some job security against arbitrary actions of managers.

BOUNDARY-SPANNING SUBSYSTEMS

The two *major* boundary-spanning activities are distributing the product and/or service and procuring the human and material resources required to produce the product or service.

Because the market of the mechanistic organization is relatively unchanging, it is likely that the **channels of distribution**—those organizations through which the product or service flows to the final user—will be fairly well defined and standardized. New distribution channels will arise only if current methods of distribution become extremely inefficient. It is also likely that the organization will have a great deal of influence over the distribution mechanism. The automobile industry, for instance, exerts strong control over its dealers, as do steel manufacturers and petroleum firms.

It is likely that the products manufactured or the services of organizations in an industry that has many mechanistic organizations will be fairly similar in terms of function and use. Therefore, a consumer may use any one of a large number of products from different firms to obtain the kind of satisfaction he or she needs. If this is so, then the marketing strategy is likely to be based on pricing and differentiation through advertising. Witness the automobile industry. A Nissan Motors' product performs the same functions and has the same use as a Chrysler product. It is the "image" of the car that is important. The "better" car is better not because it is a substantially different product. In the U.S. auto industry, one company sells "happiness," another sells "sophisticated beauty," and a third sells "engineering."

The ***procurement function*** is likely to be made up of well-developed and well-defined sources for inputs. In large industries such as the auto industry, firms may have captive suppliers. A captive supplier is a firm that sells a large portion of its product to just one other firm. It depends primarily upon one customer for the bulk of its business. This gives the customer the capacity to influence such things as price and production techniques to such an extent that the supplier may well be considered as a subsidiary.

With a highly repetitive production subsystem and well-defined sources of supply, it is possible to minimize the total production cost if the production subsystems can function at a fairly even rate. Since even in a stable market and with a stable technology there are minor fluctuations, a level rate of production activities may be sustained by maintaining inventories of both raw materials and finished goods.

Other boundary-spanning functions also bring different resources into the organization. ***Recruiting*** by the personnel department, for example, is a boundary-spanning activity. The personnel department must go outside the firm to acquire the human inputs required to maintain a viable organization over time—it must find workers. The recruiting process may be regarded as a boundary-spanning activity, but the other responsibilities of the personnel department, such as the implementation of performance evaluation and compensation (programs designed to stabilize or obtain desired performance), belong in the control subsystem.

EXTERNAL-MONITORING SUBSYSTEMS

In an organization operating in a stable environment, the external monitoring system will be relatively simple in structure, since interpreting the environment is relatively easy. There is a fairly explicit set of rules for interpreting changes in the environment because the organization will learn by experience what parts of the environment it should monitor. It will have a fairly good information base to be used in making decisions. An organization operating in a stable environment may be able to use standard census data, for example, or other similar market research information as a basis for deciding how to make internal adjustments. Collecting this information can be done fairly easily.

Fairly simple ways of adapting to changes in the environment will emerge. For instance, management might determine from experience and research that a sales reduction of 3 percent requires a work force reduction 10 percent in Plant X, 5 percent in Plant Y, and the elimination of all overtime in other plants. In short, it is possible to develop a fairly systematic cutback procedure that can be implemented in a simple way to deal with changes, especially when there is reduced demand in the current market environment.

The stability of the environment facilitates long-range planning. Long-term resource commitments may be made with a great deal more certainty than in less stable environments, in turn facilitating the acquisition of the capital required for investment in plant, equipment, and resources at costs lower than where more risk is involved.

However, when the environment becomes less certain, serious adjustment problems occur because the plant and equipment are not easily shifted to other uses. When the economy turned down in 1979 and the oil shortage pressed harder than many anticipated, Chrysler had some serious problems. It turned to the federal government for assistance. Chrysler illustrates the precarious dependence of a firm with very heavy capital investment on being able to predict accurately the future environment. One executive of that firm noted that if auto sales drop by 1 million cars, it cost Chrysler $150 million.

Since, by definition, technological changes are relatively minimal in a stable environment, engineering and research and development activities in a mechanistic organization are more likely to focus on applications engineering than on advancing the science or state of the art. The engineer in the mechanistic organization will be more concerned with improving the product within the existing technology than with trying to develop a new product. One of the few ways to increase return on investment in such an organization will be through cost reduction, because market potential is relatively limited, precluding substantial sales increases.

CONTROL SUBSYSTEMS

Control activities in a mechanistic organization are likely to be based on historically developed information that has achieved organizational credibility as an acceptable performance measurement. Even in organizations in which no measures of profitability are available, costs that have historically been associated with sets of activities will come to be regarded as acceptable measures. This can be seen in International Steel, where standards play an important role in control.

Often personnel involved in control systems fail to place proper emphasis on the achievement of overall objectives. They are more concerned with control itself. This is called "the inversion of means and ends." The purpose of the control subsystems is to increase internal effectiveness. To do this they should provide support to the organization, not cause problems. This, however, is not generally the situation when a specialist argues insistently that his or her field of specialization must be performed at a high level of proficiency. Thus, auditors who sometimes audit for auditing's sake or personnel executives who collect employment data for no other reason than that it is a "common" personnel practice are not aiding anything other than their own status.

Managerial performance evaluation will be a major control activity. Because there is a great deal of performance information available, it will be simple to collect, making it easy for someone to sit in judgment on the "numbers" that are used as performance measures. Having such information and being involved in the evaluation process gives a department—say, personnel—a great deal of power. Such power can have a significant effect on decisions made in other parts of the firm. Auditing and budgeting units have the same potential power. When information is centralized and controlled, those who have it are extremely influential. Since information is localized in control subsystems, these subsystems have a great deal of organization influence.

Morale is especially difficult to maintain when the work is routine, repetitive, or programmed. Boredom and alienation have been found to be higher for assembly-line workers than for workers with less structured jobs, as would exist in mechanistic organizations.[2] Workers may have a feeling of isolation, of not feeling a sense of identity with the organization and what it does, and a feeling of powerlessness— helpless and controlled by various forces in the organization. Boredom and alientation can lead to high rates of absenteeism and turnover as well as grievances and work stoppages.

But most individuals in the mechanistic organization seem to adjust to the organization's work demands. In fact, some studies show that most employees in repetitive, programmed jobs will not choose more complex jobs when given the opportunity to do so.[3] It is quite possible that work that demands little of the job holder attracts individuals who, because of low self-esteem, lack other job opportunities, or because of some other factor prefer work of this type.

MANAGERIAL SUBSYSTEMS

There will be centralized decision making at the top administrative level in a mechanistic organization. Much performance information can be collected and transmitted easily to the higher levels so that decisions can be made there to change operations at lower levels without requiring a great deal of involvement of managers at those levels.

Lower-level operations will be closely monitored, and this monitoring will be centralized in the hands of a relatively small number of people. The amount of discretion in decisions that lower-level managers have is likely to be relatively small. This is clearly demonstrated in a study by Comstock and Scott.[4] They found that when tasks are highly predictable, as they are in mechanistic organizations, policy decisions can be more easily separated from routine decisions and there is greater centralization of many routine administrative decisions.

The mechanistic organization has a fairly rigid hierarchy. Lines of authority and responsibility will be clear. Jobs will be very well-defined. Much conflict will be settled and many problems will be solved by appealing to executives at higher levels, or using the formal hierarchical system as a problem-resolution mechanism.

One of the major problems with which the managerial subsystem must deal is conflict between the "management" group and employees. In industrial organizations this will take the form of union–management bargaining, and in public organizations by the relationship between the administrative staffs and civil service agencies.

Generally, people will be promoted to top-level managerial positions in a mechanistic organization after fairly long careers in them. There will be a relatively small proportion of managers relative to the number of workers, and the number of positions at higher levels will be relatively small.

This can create a special problem when individuals employed by such a firm have high achievement needs, because they will find promotion opportunities limited and will go elsewhere to satisfy their advancement needs. Because there are a relatively small number of managerial positions and since the managers at the higher levels make promotion decisions, it is likely that there will be a high degree of similarity in point of view, or homogeneity of attitude, among high-level executives. Promotions will come not only for what one can do, but also because one has the "right" point of view.

THE ORGANIC ORGANIZATION

A more flexible, "organic" organization is found where the market and technological sectors are volatile. The organic organization is one in which the structure, relationships, and jobs are loosely defined. This makes the process of adapting to change relatively easy. This is shown in the case of Powertec, in item 3.1. Powertec can easily change its production system to meet the very changing demands of its customers.

PRODUCTION SUBSYSTEMS

In the organic organization, the production subsystem is composed primarily of general-purpose equipment or technology. Essentially, it is a job-shop in which the various production elements can be rearranged, when necessary, to perform the activities necessary to produce outputs as the market or the technology changes. The production subsystem itself will, therefore, be in a fairly constant state of change. The sequencing of operations will vary from project to project so that the development of routine, repetitive production procedures is relatively difficult, if not impossible. An intensive technology is one in which a variety of

> techniques is drawn upon in order to achieve a change in some specific object; but the selection, combination, and order of application are determined by feedback from the object itself. When the object is human, this intensive technology is regarded as "therapeutic," but the same technical logic is found also in the construction industry . . . and in research where the objects of concern are nonhuman. . . . The intensive technology is a custom technology. Its successful employment rests in part on the availability of all the capacities potentially needed, but equally on the appropriate custom of selected capacities as required by the individual case or project.[5]

BOUNDARY-SPANNING SUBSYSTEMS

The method of delivering the product or service will vary from customer to customer. Such variation means, essentially, that the organization will probably have to handle its own marketing. It cannot easily transfer this function to other jobbers, or develop a channel of distribution similar to that which distributes, say, automobiles or groceries.

Since the distribution function cannot be routinized, highly skilled individuals will be needed in the marketing functions. Those involved with the procurement function will also need to be highly skilled in finding different types of raw materials and resources, because both the level and type of raw material inputs will change from time to time.

EXTERNAL-MONITORING SUBSYSTEMS

External-monitoring subsystem activities in the organic organization will be performed by individuals in marketing and distribution functions, procurement, and engineering and research development. Individuals in those subsystems must know how to interpret the environment. For the mechanistic organizations there are fairly well-defined external cues that will trigger internal organizational adjustments. For the organic organization, the external information to cue internal change will probably occur in an unpredictable fashion. Thus, ***individual skill,*** rather than well-defined rules about how to respond to changes, is essential in assessing how the organization must adapt, because it is very difficult to specify in advance what aspect of the environment must be monitored.

Clinical, analytical skill is required of those who must determine how to restructure the organization in response to external changes. In the organic organization the process of organization adjustment and the resulting set of relationships will nearly always vary. This means that the individuals in the external-monitoring subsystem in an organic organization will be very influential in decision making. One study of research activities in volatile environments found that those involved in the research used highly diverse and highly decentralized patterns of communication to transmit information between research groups. Research projects needed more flexible methods of communication than regular organization structure provides.[6]

Those performing environmental monitoring activities must continually update their skills and abilities. In order to maintain an inventory of high skills in these critical areas, the organization may simply hire individuals with the required capability, rather than train members in the skills for necessary adaptation. And since, by definition, these skills may be rapidly changing, there may be a fairly high level of turnover among those involved in the adaptive processes.

The cost of developing skills for monitoring the external environment may be too high for an organization to bear, so the organization will recruit those who have acquired these skills on their own. Those who are hired and work in such a capacity are likely to be more highly trained or more highly skilled than those performing other functions. This affects the compensation levels in organizations. In the organic organization, individuals are as likely to be paid for the level of education and training they bring to the job as for the level of importance of their job within the organization.

Acquiring capital may be difficult since there is high risk involved. With a highly unpredictable environment, investors are less willing to take the long-term risk of lending capital for a fixed return. With the high risk that might go along with the organic organization, the capital structure will be weighted toward equity or self-generated funds.

CONTROL SUBSYSTEMS

In organic organizations historical data are of little use for control purposes, since there may be little history to go by. Therefore, cost standards will come from projected estimates. This means that control, performance, evaluation, and subsequent decisions about what to do will be much more subjective than based on "objective" previous performance measures. In organic organizations it is likely that "end results" will be less frequently used for assessment than in mechanistic organizations. There will be much stronger focus on the manner in which individuals go about performing their work.

The persons or groups most influential in determining company strategy will be either (1) those with expertise in a particular area or (2) those with the greatest financial interest. The expert will have great influence simply because of his or her capabilities. If expertise is the predominant power base, the influence pattern will shift from time to time, depending upon the nature of the project or activity and who is the house expert at a particular time. When policy influence derives from the level of financial interest, the owners or the major stockholders make the decisions. In this case the organization will be an extension of those personal interests.

Personnel in organic organizations are likely to have a short-range commitment to the organization. They will be more interested in their professional area. There may be relatively few long-term projects to provide a basis for lengthy tenure. Individuals with particular skills will be brought into the organization when they are required. When their services are no longer needed, they may be relieved of responsibility or they may move on voluntarily. This makes it unlikely that they will be highly committed to the organization as a place to work.

This uncertainty about one's future may not be a particular problem. It is likely that those who accept employment in such an organization have learned that relatively rapid movement is part of the game. As in the case of the aerospace industry, engineers typically move from firm to firm as the major contracts move. Professionals who work in these types of organizations may be willing to apply their skills in any number of organizations so long as they are able to do what they have been trained to do and what they believe to be important.

MANAGERIAL SUBSYSTEMS

The managerial subsystem in an organic organization will be much less rigid than in other forms of organization. There will be few policy guidelines to use in the decision-making process because the variability of the environment will preclude well-defined, set policies over time. Major policy and strategy must be consistently changed to meet the changing requirements.

The organization structure will be flexible, one in which individuals move from project team to project team as the need for their skills arises, with the authority structure different for each project. When the project is completed and the team disbanded, the individuals may move to different teams. If their skills are no longer required in the organization, they may be terminated, either willingly or unwillingly.

Organic organizations are likely to be relatively small compared to mechanistic organizations. This smallness, in and of itself, facilitates adaptability to the environment. As an organization grows, however, it begins to develop some degree of procedural rigidity and hierarchy, which could make effective adaptation to a changing environment very difficult.

Generally organic organizations will, when possible, seek to move to a more stable environmental sector. This is desirable because it makes planning and control easier. If it can move in such a direction, the organization will be able to make longer-term commitments to its members, perhaps easing recruitment problems, since persons will be willing to join an organization where they can make a "career."

This last point may be an important one, especially when individuals have a high degree of anxiety about their careers. While a person might have a great deal of confidence in his or her own skills and abilities as a professional, the uncertainty of where he or she will be working can pose a problem. This career anxiety is probably related to lower levels of organization commitment, which in turn would make it difficult to obtain high levels of compliance from individuals.

MIXED ORGANIZATIONS

A mixed organization has subsystems that interact with environments that have very different degrees of certainty. We call one type of mixed organization a technology-dominated mixed (TD-mixed) type because of the influence of the technical segment of the organization. The second type is called a market-dominated mixed (MD-mixed) because of the need to have market-dominated policies and strategies.

Figure 4.2 represents the mixed organization. It shows two organization units, one organic and one mechanistic. Manager X of the organic unit will need to operate with a loose structure, make decisions under uncertain conditions, and often must manage highly trained personnel such as engineers or marketing professionals. On

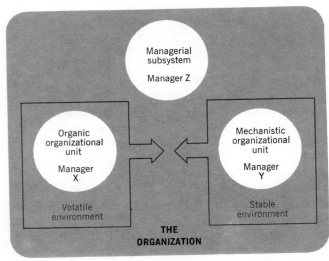

FIGURE 4.2 The interface problem in the mixed organization.

the other hand, manager Y will find that he or she is responsible for a highly routine system with well-defined decision rules and policies. These differences between the organizational units may create problems for manager X and manager Y—and also for manager Z, who must manage the interface between the units.

The difficulty of managing this interface problem depends upon the amount of interdependence between the units. When the work flow requires that two units work closely together, managing will be difficult. Obviously the greater the interdependence, the higher the need for integration and coordination.

Figure 4.3 shows some of the differences between the internal structures of the organic and dynamic units. Such differences have been shown in some research,[7,8] and while it is true that any particular organization may not have exactly these characteristics, they seem to be very prominent generally. Specifically, there will be differences in (1) general structure, (2) objectives, (3) authority, (4) bases for compensation, (5) evaluation criteria, (6) organization climate, and (7) organization status of units.

Objectives

Not only do different organizational groups have different assigned objectives, but the time span for objectives also differs. The mechanistic segment will tend to have short-range objectives, while the organic unit has long-range objectives.

Authority Structure

In the better-performing mechanistic organizations, influence resides at higher management levels, but it resides at lower management levels in the organic organizations or units.[8] Such differences in power may in themselves contribute to conflict. In the mechanistic unit, power and influence are based on position that a person holds or control over resources, while in the organic unit, knowledge of how to do the job is most critical and influence arises out of personal skill and expertise.[8] Thus, at the interface of the organic and mechanistic organizational units of a mixed-type organization, one group may not respond well to the influence attempts of another group because each is using an appeal that is acceptable to its own members, but not to the other.

Compensation Bases

For an organization with components in two different environments, we can expect two different approaches to the determination of pay. When compensation is based on different factors, feelings of inequity may arise. In the organic units the quality of a person's training and experience is important. What one has done, where one has been to school, and achievements in other organizations will be critical in determining the basic pay rate. In addition, increases in compensation may come from an assessment of how well the individual is recognized in a professional area of competence. On the other hand, in the mechanistic sector the level and relative importance of the position held by the individual as determined through job evaluation procedures is more critical. Increases in compensation will be based on merit (which is more likely to be assessed in terms of hard measures of performance), as well as tenure.

FIGURE 4.3   Organizational Differences Between the Organic and Mechanistic Units

Factor	Mechanistic Unit	Dynamic Unit
General Structure	• Emphasis on rules • More formality • Limited autonomy in decisions • Narrow job definition	• Less rigid structure • Fewer rules and policies • Greater discretion in decisions • More job scope
Objectives	• Short-range/cost	• Long-range/development
Bases of authority	• Position power • Commitment to organization • Centralization	• Skill and expert power • Commitment to self and discipline • Decentralization
Bases of compensation	• Level and relative importance of the position • Increases based on "merit" and tenure	• Quality of training and experience • Increases based on experience in area of competence
Evaluation criteria	• Objective measures • Focus on results as outcomes • Short time span between performance and results	• Subjective criteria • Focus on activities rather than results • Long time span between performance and results
Organization climate	• Rules-oriented formalism	• Innovation-oriented
Status	• Lower	• Higher

Performance Evaluation Criteria

Performance evaluation criteria in the mechanistic and organic units of a mixed organization will differ. In organic units, composed of professionals or highly specialized managers, performance evaluation will lean toward the subjective.

Differences in the methods of evaluation used may lead to feelings of inequity, especially when such methods influence pay. They may also lead to feelings of jealousy between groups, especially on the part of those whose performance is rated low, and this can lead to conflict.

Organization Climate

The organization climate refers to how an organization's practices and procedures are perceived by the members, and the relationship of such perceptions to ways of thinking about the organization and subsequent behavior.[9] A more highly structured, formal climate has a tendency to arouse power needs and to reduce achievement and affiliation needs for individuals. Thus, in mechanistic organization units we expect more concerns about power than in the organic units. On the other hand, in organic units where there is informality in structure, high standards of perform-

Mechanistic (low status)	Factor	Organic (high status)
Less years of formal education
Functional training	Education	More years of formal education
Technical training
Greater restrictions, adherence to rules, policies, and procedures	Organizational privileges	More freedom, travel, benefits, autonomy
Individual more dependent on organization	Direction of dependence	Organization more dependent on individual

ance, encouragement of innovation, and toleration of conflicts, the need for achievement is more likely to be aroused.

Status Differences

Within an organization, groups will have different status. Some of the factors that reflect status differences are shown in Figure 4.4 In general, units operating in the more volatile boundary of an organization will have the highest status because they are the units (and individuals) upon whom the organization must depend for adaptation to change.

The organic unit will also tend to have highly educated specialists in it, since such personnel are needed to cope with its environmental uncertainties. This means, often, that the specialist is in a situation where his skills and ability are very important, and he is less dependent on the organization than it is on him. Such persons may enjoy more organizational privileges than others.

Persons with high status, or those from high-status organization units, may seek to dominate lower-status groups. Thus, where the market forces involve much uncertainty, the marketing units will attempt to dominate. When the technology is volatile, the technology or production units will try to exert influence over the more stable units. For example, in a small company manufacturing soaps and detergents, the production technology was fairly stable, but competition with other firms in the industry was very keen. Profits of the firm depended, to a considerable extent, on the effectiveness of the advertising and sales promotion programs. In this company the marketing department dominated both the production and the research departments. On the other hand, in a company that manufactured electronic test equipment for industrial customers, successful competition was based on performance characteristics of the equipment as compared to other equipment available in the market. In this company the research department was the highest-ranking organizational unit, and it imposed its desires on all other departments.[10]

TECHNOLOGY-DOMINATED (TD) MIXED ORGANIZATIONS

For technology-dominated mixed (TD-mixed) organizations, the technological environment poses the major problems. The market sector of the environment of these organizations is relatively stable. Scientific breakthroughs or new production technology can provide their creator or early adopter with a significant competitive advantage. Therefore, it is important to monitor the technological environment carefully and to adjust the system when necessary.

The technology-dominated mixed organization will have one major part of its structure with mechanistic characteristics and another part that will be less tightly structured or organic. This combination presents the problem of achieving good relationships between these two parts of the organization. Cole and Wiley, the drug manufacturer described in Item 4.2, illustrates some of these points.

Item 4.2 Cole and Wiley: A Technology-Dominated Mixed Organization

Cole and Wiley is one of the largest drug manufacturers in the world. It has developed some of the most popular drug preparations for a wide variety of diseases and illnesses. In 1979 Ben Watkins, the New England regional sales manager for the company, was interviewed by Mary Paine, a reporter for a nationally distributed marketing and sales magazine, about the company's system for managing the sales force.

PAINE: Let's talk about the situation that your medical representatives typically face in carrying out their job. What basically are they supposed to do?

WATKINS: Well, essentially they must make sure that physicians in their area are acquainted with our products and are aware of our product's advantages. They should call on all of the physicians in their area at least once a month. During a visit to a physician, the medical salesperson must talk about whatever preparation we are emphasizing at that particular time. We usually require our sales personnel to discuss two or three products on a single visit with one product receiving the greatest emphasis.

PAINE: What do you do to help them convince the physician to prescribe your products?

WATKINS: We have many different selling aids that we provide the medical representatives. Here are some of them. This particular poster summarizes a lot of what we know about cirrhosis of the liver. This little booklet provides a lot of information about epilepsy and an anticonvulsant drug we have developed to deal with it. We also furnish the physician with free samples of our drugs, with articles that report on the use of our products in various research studies, and with other promotional material such as these notepads, or these little flashlights designed to keep the name of a new drug in the physician's mind.

PAINE: What else do you do to help sell your products?

WATKINS: Well, of course we carefully select our personnel. If possible we prefer to hire an individual with a master's degree in business and a science undergraduate degree. We need people who are able to converse effectively with physicians. We also spend an enormous amount of time and money on training. Here is a book we had produced to teach our medical representatives about glaucoma. We recently produced a preparation for the treatment of glaucoma that does not have the side effects of another company's preparation, which was a drug long used for this disease. As you can see, it uses a programmed learning format so that the medical representative can progress at his or her own rate for self-instruction. In addition, we also bring our sales personnel back to Boston for various conferences we run on our new preparations and our current sales programs. We also teach our sales personnel how to make a presentation to a physician.

PAINE: So they are supposed to follow a specific procedure on calling on a physician?

WATKINS: Definitely. We tell them exactly what to say, when to say it, and how to say it. We work out the best way to get a good result and try to get them to do it that way.

PAINE: Do they only call on physicians? Is that the only thing they do?

WATKINS: No, they sometimes run meetings in a particular community where they provide dinner and drinks to physicians and their spouses and show some film or videotape that our marketing department has commissioned. We send these films to various locations around the country. The films generally deal with some medical problem for which we have developed products. Also, our sales personnel staff booths that we set up at state medical association meetings. In addition, they call on drugstores as well as physicians.

PAINE: What do they do at drugstores?

WATKINS: They tell the druggist what drugs the company is promoting in that area at the time so the druggist knows that local physicians may be prescribing them. They also check the druggists' supply of our products to make sure they have an adequate amount on hand and carry out other promotional programs directed at the druggist. We tell our sales staff each month what we want them to do when visiting the various pharmacies in their area.

PAINE: Do you assign them a certain number of physician calls to make in a particular period?

WATKINS: Yes. Our salespeople have a schedule for each day, which they must follow or explain to us why they deviated from it. Of course, the schedule depends on the amount of travel time necessary for a salesperson to reach a certain community. We do expect the salesperson to stay overnight at those locations that are far from his home.

PAINE: How do you evaluate their performances?

WATKINS: Well, we have a management by objectives system in use in this company. Every medical representative is supposed to produce a given amount of sales for each of our drugs in his district. These are the salesperson's goals. We then send him or her these computer sheets that tell the sales for each or our products in his or her district for each three month period. As you can see, this report tells the medical representative how much the sales are above or below those expected in this area.

PAINE: Does he set these goals himself?

WATKINS: No. They are sent to him by this office, but if he thinks they are not possible to attain, and can convince us that they are unrealistic, we might change them.

PAINE: Does the salesperson have any other goals except sales goals for different products?

WATKINS: Yes, I set self-improvement goals for each of my subordinates when we have our yearly performance review interviews. For example, here is one for Bob Wills in Vermont: Increased product knowledge in the non-steroid anti-inflammatory area.

PAINE: Do you pay a bonus for reaching or exceeding sales goals?

WATKINS: No, we don't want our salespeople to become too pushy in dealing with physicians. You must be careful not to offend them. This company believes that sales will be the result of developing high quality products and then providing physicians with accurate information about these products.

PAINE: How well has your research and development division done in providing your sales personnel with high-quality products?

WATKINS: They have done an excellent job. We have far more products coming out than any competitor. Our products are also new and significant, not just a "me too" product that is just a copy of somebody else's.

PAINE: What's your research and development unit like? You must have visited your research labs.

WATKINS: Yes, I have once or twice. They are located in Pennsylvania and are pretty impressive facilities. They seem to be a very pleasant place to work.

PAINE: What types of management procedures do they use? Do they have a management by objectives system too?

WATKINS: Oh no. They are pretty informal. It's sort of like a university atmosphere down there. They are not held accountable for reaching specific goals. They are not told how to carry out their responsibilities.

Polaroid is an example of a TD-mixed company. Cameras are still sold to the same market as they have been for years. Yet there are continual new developments from Polaroid, the latest being the SX-70, a truly instant camera. R & D and technology dominate this firm. Almost everything else in the firm reacts to these segments of Polaroid.

Production Subsystems

The production activities in a TD-mixed organization will likely be an intensive technology in which there are a variety of possible procedures or methods, but only one set that is most appropriate in a given situation. It is unlikely that we would find asembly-line technology requiring large capital investment in this type of environmental setting, though some work may be highly routine and repetetive. Large investment in special-purpose technology or machinery is highly risky; therefore, the tendency would be to use, where possible, general-purpose processes for production.

Boundary-spanning Subsystems

In the TD-mixed organization, the channels of distribution will be fairly well fixed. Products will perhaps change technologically, but they will be sold as they had been before any new developments. For example, Polaroid's SX-70 camera is sold through camera shops, department stores, and discount stores—as were earlier Land cameras.

If a boundary-spanning unit must be in contact with an outside firm in the technological environment, however, it must be able to change as technology changes. New sources of supply will be needed as raw-material requirements change.

In the early stages of technological change, product pricing will take advantage of the innovation and price will be high. However, if competitors enter the market with similar but lower-priced products, there will be some problems in the rigid marketing section. Customers may be reluctant to buy until there is more price stability.

External-monitoring Subsystems

Major policy and strategy influence in a TD-mixed organization comes from those in the technological sector. In this group there is a great reliance on individual skill and ability in assessing the environment. Research and development, rather than applications engineering, is critical to survival and profitability, thus placing more emphasis on advanced knowledge and skills than on pragmatic application of design.

Market research activities, though, will be fairly simple. They will most probably focus on existing, or easily collectible, data that have become fairly widely accepted indicators to be used in decision making. In this external-monitoring activity, there will be a need for individuals not necessarily with experience in the firm or industry, but who know how to apply standard research, or monitoring, techniques.

Control Subsystems

Control subsystems in TD-mixed organizations face a paradoxical problem. The market sector will develop systematic marketing and distribution processes that will result in a somewhat mechanistic marketing unit. By their nature, systematic procedures and rules that accompany the mechanistic structure limit discretion. This will contrast sharply with the organization's technological activities, in which there must be freedom to adjust and react to the changing environment. This can be seen in Cole and Wiley. The sales force is rather tightly managed. The R & D group, on the other hand, is seen as having a good deal of freedom.

For control and evaluation purposes, some special problems exist for the control subsystems. For example, because of the stable market, it may be possible to develop an acceptable set of distribution cost estimates. This could result in quantified, objective "cost" estimates against which actual costs can be compared. A manager will therefore be able to measure marketing efficiency with some accuracy. When "objective" data such as these are available, they become the basis for performance evaluations.

The performance evaluation problem in the technological segment of the organization will be difficult. At the volatile boundary the individual has little control over what outside people and organizations do. In addition, since the determination of a need for change, the internal implementation of the change, and the resulting effect on the performance level of the organization may cover a long period of time, it is difficult to develop performance criteria quite as objective as we can for, say, marketing or production units. This will lead to two obviously different types of criteria used in performance evaluation, one subjective and one objective. This in turn will result in perceived inequities among organization members, because no matter which criteria are used in a part of the organization, members may feel that the other type is better.

In personnel selection emphasis will be on acquiring highly skilled and trained professionals for the technological segments. The level of organization commitment of this group will probably be lower than that of those in the more stable sections of the organization, since they will identify to some extent with their professional group. This identification with other professionals outside the company should be of value to the organization, however, since such contacts are a valuable source of ideas.

Managerial Subsystems

The authority structure of the TD-mixed organization will be somewhat varied. In the marketing sector we would expect to find fairly well-defined job responsibilities, accountability to specific superiors for work, limited discretion for decisions, and centralized decision making. Those in this unit will find themselves subjected to standardized rules, policies, and procedures. On the other hand, in the technological sector, there will be more freedom of action. The production subsystem is likely to be caught in the middle, between pressures from research and engineering to adopt newer production methods and the marketing unit's desire to maintain the product relatively as is.

MARKET-DOMINATED (MD) MIXED ORGANIZATIONS

In the market-dominated form of organization, the significant policy influence group will come from the marketing group because of the need to stay in close touch with a constantly changing, unpredictable consumer or client group. Firms in the record industry and in the fashion industry are often of the type. Item 4.3, which describes the characteristics of Donna Fashions, is an example of a market-dominated mixed organization.

Donna Fashions Inc.:
A Market-Dominated Mixed Organization

Donna Fashions Inc. was begun in the early 1950s in a Midwestern city. The brand has become widely known among women who buy middle-priced clothes in large and medium-sized department stores in the major cities in the United States. The owner, Del Burwell, is a very well-known figure in the industry as an innovator. The firm products are primarily sportswear and coordinates, which women can put together to make various outfits from components with colors that match or go together. The groups of coordinated components may contain skirts (straight or pleated), pants (basic or fashion), jackets (blazer, fashion, etc.) vests, sweaters, or shirts. Donna Fashions attempts to produce color shades that match only with their own other pieces.

This approach has been copied by other manufacturers and there is intense competition within the industry. Donna Fashions must compete with both large and small domestic firms as well as foreign producers in Taiwan, Hong Kong, Korea, and several European countries. New companies are constantly sprouting up to replace old firms that go bankrupt. Price competition is very high in the industry.

There are four distinct selling seasons in the industry. These are early fall, late fall, spring, and summer. These short seasons create very difficult problems in forecasting, producing, and delivering products, as the garments must be ordered, produced, and delivered within a relatively short period of time. Garments that are delivered late must be sold at a lower price, as department stores steadily decrease price between the beginning and end of a particular selling season. Also, it is important to forecast correctly which styles and types of garments will sell in a particular season, since once the bolts of cloth are cut into particular patterns, there is no turning back.

The process for producing garments has not changed in a number of years, except for the addition of faster sewing machines, scissors, and other tools of the trade. Thus, there are usually few difficulties in manufacturing the garments. In garment manufacturing there is an emphasis on efficiency since labor costs are a relatively high proportion of total costs. Performance standards, time study, and motion study are widely used in the industry.

There are, however, many difficulties in scheduling and meeting scheduled delivery dates. If the delivery dates are not met, the garments can only be sold at reduced prices. The use of the coordinate group idea has made the problem of scheduling a difficult one for Donna Fashions because the most efficient way to produce garments is to have each plant specialize in a particular item, such as jackets and vests, pants, skirts, or blouses. The logistics of getting all of these separate items together at the same time to meet its schedule can produce severe problems. If, for example, everything is ready to ship on time except the blouses, the entire order may be canceled since the buyer will not except delivery on coordinate groups with any items missing.

In an attempt to coordinate production and delivery, the company is constructing a new multi-million-dollar central distribution plant at the present home office location, where all administrative and some production functions are performed. All production runs will be shipped to this new facility and then be dispatched by a computer-programmed delivery inventory scheduling method. This facility is planned to help cope with an increasingly serious problem of returned merchandise from customers who refuse acceptance because delivery is later than promised.

To try to increase the accuracy of sales forecasting and to pinpoint specific reasons for late deliveries, Burwell instituted a computer printout of each day's sales, as reported by telephone by field salespeople. Initially this printout was distributed to the president, the vice president of sales, the sales forecast manager, the treasurer, the production manager, and the eight regional sales managers. All of these people were located at the firm's headquarters offices. The printout was voluminous, often running one hundred or more pages.

Burwell relied a great deal on his "feel of the situation" for making decisions. Although he made all final important operating and policy decisions, he said that all department heads should feel free to act as "you see fit"; he said that he would back any decision made without consultation with him. Despite Burwell's exhortations that he need not be consulted, almost all vice presidents and departmental managers conferred daily with him, usually regarding the progress of the then-current fashion season's products. During each fashion season many style modifications and quantity-level changes were made. With rare exceptions Burwell made all important daily decision in these matters.

These daily decision sessions were marked by emotional outbursts by various management personnel. The meetings were informal, and different managers would meet at different times. If one individual felt that a daily printout indicated change "X," regardless of whether or not it affected his department, he would go to the president asking that the change be effected. If another department manager or even a vice president was present and disagreed, inevitably a shouting match developed in the president's office. Usually Burwell remained impassive during these interchanges, making his decision after all participants had finished.

In spite of Burwell's efforts, customer return of goods continued to increase. At one point forty percent of all shipments were being returned for late delivery. Some said the forecasting process took too long. Others argued that it was a coordination problem between the various production plants and the shipping department located at the home office site. Some sales personnel thought customers were returning goods because they were of poor quality.

Burwell added a statistical analyst to the staff to help in forecasting. New reports were generated and circulated to go with the old. Later a computer analyst was hired. He changed the format of the computer printouts given to the company's managers. Some of them complained that the new data breakdowns did not give them the information necessary for their work. The emotional outbursts between company personnel continued. As the problems mounted, Burwell wondered about the desirability of resigning and turning the business over to a professional manager. He had worked his way up in this industry from a long apprenticeship in New York's garment industry and now felt quite insecure about his managerial abilities.

Production Subsystems

The type of environment confronting MD-mixed organizations leads to programmed production tasks performed with a stable technology. Skill requirements for those in this system will be moderately low, and job security will probably result from union protection. The performance of the production system will be measured by relatively objective measures of cost. There will be considerable pressure from the marketing segment to change the product to meet changing consumer preferences.

External-monitoring Subsystem

The relatively placid external technological environment requires little scientific research or development in the MD-mixed organization. Technical engineering functions will probably be of an applied nature. Engineers, for instance, though highly trained, will probably not be engaged in research on new projects. They will probably spend their time trying, say, to find sources for less costly raw materials.

In the marketing segment of the organization there will be very extensive efforts devoted to uncovering new markets. More than likely, those performing this function will rely on a clinical assessment, or judgment, of markets. Experience, intuition, and judgment will be more useful in determining what and where markets will be, rather than extensive research efforts using standard market data sets such as population data, income estimates, or traditional buying patterns. In Donna Fashions, for instance, president Burwell trusted his "feel of the situation."

Boundary-spanning Subsystems

In general, product changes of an MD-mixed firm will be style or design changes, rather than changes in what the product will do. Therefore, in MD-mixed organizations the raw materials acquisition will be most significant when they may directly change the character of the output, or if the market requires a product with different raw material requirements. That is, if market changes require a different type of raw material, then purchasing must seek new sources of supply. For instance, when a dress manufacturer finds that new materials are selling in the market and they must be used in manufacturing, the purchasing staff will have to seek out new sources of supply.

Product pricing will be controlled by the firm's marketing segment, since it must have latitude and discretion in price setting to sell effectively. There will be a great responsiveness to customer orientations. Those in the marketing staff can be characterized as "promoters" rather than as sales managers.

Control Subsystems

The major control problems will exist in the marketing segment of the MD-mixed firm. The flexible and varied nature of the marketing and distribution system will make collection of historical and relevant cost data difficult, since distribution systems may be changing. Some control difficulties are likely to occur because of the applied nature of the required technical activities. The educational experiences of engineers and scientists often teach them to value research activities, yet such jobs in the MD-mixed organizations may be concerned more with mundane applications problems. This can lead to disillusionment, dissatisfaction, and attendant problems of keeping staff adequately interested in work. This may be an especially acute problem because of the higher status of the marketing group in the organization.

Managerial Subsystems

A hierarchical authority structure will prevail in the technical sectors of the market-dominated firm, and a looser authority structure will exist in the marketing and distribution sectors, which will have more individual discretion and freedom in decision making. Methods to monitor changes in and adapt to the environment will be developed in such a way as to be triggered by decisions made in the marketing sector of the firm. It is highly likely that the MD-mixed organization will be headed by someone with marketing or sales background.

As in a technologically dominated firm, there will be problems in relating the organic and mechanistic segments of the organization to each other. The well-defined structure of the technical sector may not only pose adjustment problems for the professional who work in it but also may present difficulties when it is interrelated to the more flexible organization structure in the marketing sector.

DIFFERENTIATION AND INTEGRATION

How does the systems view of organizations that we have outlined relate to the more common view of organizations as groups of departments? One helpful analogy is a clock. Looking at the dials, hands, face, and setting knobs does not give any idea of "what makes it tick." Only after we "take off the cover" and watch the clock while it is running do we see the systems. We see how each part is related to other parts—for example, how the hour and minute dials are linked to the alarm mechanism. Not all parts move at the same speed, but they all move systematically and in a pattern that is discernible as we watch the clockwork.

Organizations also have different systems that operate at different rates and with different degrees of predictability. Just like a clock, in organizations each subsystem operates with its own pattern, but ultimately coordination among them is necessary.

Departments of organizations are created when the activities of these organization subsystems are unbundled, rearranged, regrouped into departments, and linked back together. The process of unbundling and rearranging subsystems is called *differentiation*. The process of regrouping and relinking them is called *integration*. The problem of designing organizations (which we address in Chapter 11) is to decide how to restructure organization subsystems into departments.

DIFFERENTIATION

Differentiation is the process of unbundling the organization systems, separating their activities and regrouping these activities into departments. Let us assume that Figure 4.5 represents the subsystems of a manufacturer of two products, A and B. One way to differentiate the subsystem activities would be to break them down into functional organizational units. Functional departments are departments into which

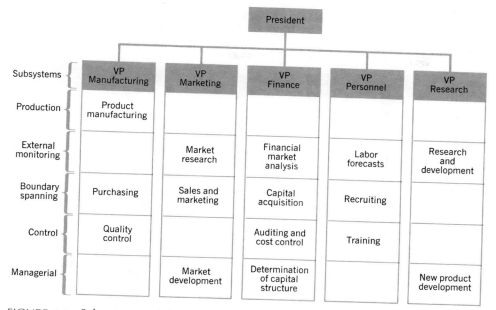

FIGURE 4.5   Subsystems and departments in a hypothetical manufacturing firm.

similar activities are assigned. They may very closely approximate the subsystems. Such an organization is shown in Figure 4.5. The production subsystem is completely housed in The Manufacturing Division (or department). A boundary-spanning function of purchasing is in the Manufacturing Division, while recruitment is in the Personnel Division.

The same subsystems can be differentiated, or separated, in another way. This would be in terms of products. In our example the firm could have two product divisions, Division A and Division B. Figure 4.6 shows this form of organization. In each division all the different subsystems exist but in different product units. General Motors Corporation, which has a Buick Division and a Chevrolet Division, is illustrative of a product organization. Each product division has the major responsibility of manufacturing and marketing its own cars, often competing with each other for sales.

Horizontal and Vertical Differentiation

There are two types of differentiation, horizontal and vertical. Horizontal differentiation refers to the number of different units at a particular organizational level. Figure 4.7 shows a university, with a very high degree of horizontal differentiation. Each of these eight colleges has a head (usually a dean). Each dean has the same amount of authority within the college and the same relationship with the provost as other deans.

Contrast this degree of horizontal differentiation with that shown in the organization illustrated in Figure 4.8. In this there is very little horizontal differentiation. At the organizational level of vice president, there are only three major differentiated units.

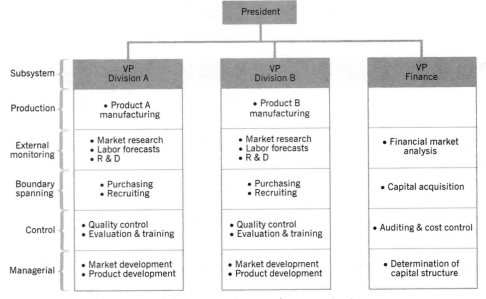

FIGURE 4.6   Subsystems and departments in a product organization.

Vertical differentiation refers to the number of major organization levels that exist. An organization can have a low vertical integration, like a university, or a very high level, such as some major firms, which may have as many as twelve levels. Organizations that have a large number of levels are called "tall" organizations. Those with few levels are called "flat."

INTEGRATION

Whereas differentiation unbundles the subsystems into departments (or subunits), the integration process brings them back together. The integrating process is nec-

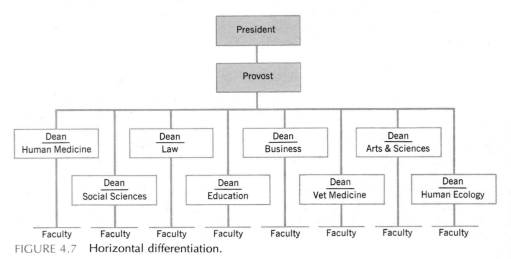

FIGURE 4.7   Horizontal differentiation.

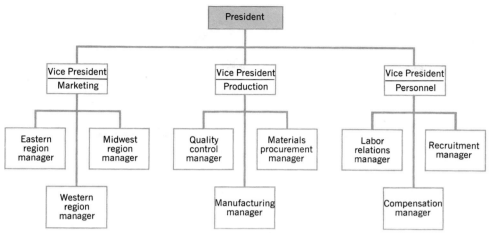

FIGURE 4.8 Vertical differentiation.

essary to keep the organizational components together and is particularly critical when a system overlaps two or more departments as does the boundary-spanning system in Figure 4.6.

   Integrating mechanisms perform this linking process. The primary integrating mechanism is the ***formal authority system,*** which defines who reports to whom and the nature of the reporting relationships. ***Procedures*** are also integrating devices. A procedure links work activities of several different people, often in different departments, to accomplish some project. A procedure outlines each step to complete a project and in which department and/or by whom the step will be performed.

DIFFERENTIATION, INTEGRATION, AND ORGANIZATION EFFECTIVENESS

Differentiation and integration are associated with organization effectiveness.[11] In a study of the chemical processing industry, with a rapidly changing technological environment, the most successful firms were those in which departments were more sharply distinct and separate from each other, but they were also linked strongly together by integrating mechanisms in organization structure. The subunits in the less effective firms were not so well integrated with each other. This research suggests that in more volatile environments, there must be clearer delineations among individual specialists and among departments. There will probably be more organizational units and subspecialists. But they must be strongly linked together. In a more stable environment, organizations seem to be more successful with less differentiation, and consequently, with a lower need for strong integration devices.

SUMMARY

The question that was posed at the beginning of Chapter 3 was, "Why and how are organizations different?" In Chapter 3 and in Chapter 4 we have tried to provide an answer. They are different because they are in different types of environments. The differences in organizations have to do with how the subsystems relate to each

FIGURE 4.9 Summary Table of Differences among Types of Organizations

Organization Subsystem	Type of Organization			
	Mechanistic	Organic	TD-Mixed	MD-Mixed
Production	• Repetitive work • High division of labor • Low skill level • Jobs well defined	• Non-routine work • Intensive technology • Jobs loosely defined	• Intensive and mediating technologies • Highly skilled staff	• Long-linked and/or repetitive technology
Boundary-spanning	• Fixed distribution channels • Well-defined sources of supply	• Varied systems for distribution • Requires highly skilled individuals	• Fixed marketing channels • High prices in early product stages	• Distribution channels influenced by "style" changes • "Promoters" rather than salespersons
External-monitoring	• Simple system • Good information base • Set rules for interpreting environment	• Clinical skill required to judge changes • Very important function	• Extensive R & D • Clinical skills required for technological environment • Simple monitoring of market • R&D most influential	• Clinical skills required in marketing areas • Little R & D • Marketing most influential
Control	• Standardized budgeting • Historical costs and standards • Possible inversion of ends and means	• Evaluation based on projected "best way" • Minimal use of historical data	• Standard historical costs and standards in marketing function • More subjective evaluation in technical areas	• Subjective evaluation in marketing areas • Standard costs in technical and production areas
Managerial	• Centralized decision making • Rigid hierarchy • Conflict between higher and lower levels	• Decentralized decision making • Flexible structure and work assignments • Conflict between professionals	• Decentralized control in technical functions • Hierarchical control in marketing • Interface management problems	• Decentralized control in marketing function • Centralized control in other areas • Interface management problems
Environmental characteristics	• Stable technology • Stable market	• Volatile technology • Volatile market	• Volatile technology • Stable market	• Stable technology • Volatile market

other. Figure 4.9 summarizes the form of the subsystems in the different technolog-

89

Types of
Organizations
ical and market environments.

The reader must remember that in reality the environment of most organizations is exceedingly more complex than we have outlined here. There are more than four types of organizations. These four we have described are useful models, though, and we will discuss how the manager can manage more effectively in each of them.

Mr. Wu

Mungchi Company is a large Chinese company located in Taiwan. The company product line includes many customer durables such as washing machines and refrigerators as well as industrial goods such as large motors. In the past few years the company, under license agreements with several U.S. and Japanese firms, has begun the production of various electronic products. Recently, Mungchi established three separate divisions: a consumer durables division, an industrial goods division, and an electronics division. The company has a very formalized managerial system with many detailed procedures, rules, and policies to guide individual managers throughout all divisions of the company.

Vincent Melnyck, a management consultant, visited Mungchi Company several times in the past several years with his partner to work on various company problems. One of the first problems the consultants encountered was a great deal of friction between the top management group of the electronics division and the company headquarters staff. The management of this subsidiary, which manufactured advanced telecommunications equipment, greatly resented the strong direction and controls imposed by the staff personnel at company headquarters. Relationships between this subsidiary's president and the headquarters finance department were especially cool.

The consultants were asked to conduct a management development seminar for all of the company's top managers including the managers of subsidiary companies. These seminars were held early Saturday mornings over a period of several weeks. During one of the lectures on organizational structure, Mr. Melnyck talked about the importance of taking a "contingency" perspective in structuring an organization. He pointed out that each organization should have the type of structure and system appropriate for the demands placed upon it by its environment and personnel. He went to say that the highly formalized organization, sometimes called *mechanistic,* seemed most appropriate when environmental demands were stable and when organizational members did not identify with outside reference groups. The *organic* organization, on the other hand, seemed more appropriate when the firm's outside environment was more volatile and the organization employed many professionals.

As Melnyck discussed these subjects, he noticed that the president of the telecommunications company became quite excited and agitated in his seat. When Melnyck called for a coffee break, he noticed Mr. Wu, the president of the telecommunication subsidiary, running over to the seat of the corporate vice president of finance. Mr. Wu began to vigorously shake his finger in the face of Mr. Han, finance VP, speaking loudly in Chinese. Although Melnyck did not understand Chinese, he had a pretty good idea of what the conversation was all about.

1. What was upsetting Mr. Wu so much?
2. What types of structure and subsystems would be most appropriate in Mr. Wu's telecommunications company?
3. How should the divisions of the Mungchi Company be related to each other?
4. What are the problems that are likely to develop in a company with divisions that are so different?

CASE 4.2 Crozier Scientific Instruments Corp.

Crozier Scientific Instruments Corp. was started in Orange Grove, California, at the end of World War II by a John Crozier, world-famous professor at a leading U.S. University. Crozier known for his work in the field of optics, obtained a contract to design and build equipment to monitor the effects of nuclear explosions. This equipment worked effectively and the company received other military contracts and later received contracts for equipment to observe and record physical phenomena in space. Some of the company's early inventions were later developed into X-ray scanning devices used in airport security or medical diagnosis. The company has grown over the years until it now consists of about 350 employees, grouped into different product divisions. Most of the employees have engineering degrees.

The space products division has the most highly trained personnel. This division includes several very competent physical scientists, as well as engineers with advanced graduate education and long experience. However, employment in this division fluctuates widely, depending on the contracts the firm is able to obtain. Professionals are hired and terminated in relationship to the company's success in bidding for various government contracts. This source of business provides about three-quarters of the company's income. Fortunately there is a large electronics industry in the state and most professionals who lose their job with one firm find employment with another very shortly.

The government contracts division is set up as a matrix organizational system. Each professional is a member of a project team and a functional organizational unit such as manufacturing, engineering, or quality control. It is not uncommon for the head of a functional unit also to be assigned to a project.

The company production facilities use a job lot system. The unit being assembled is moved from one specialized work station to another until it is completed. The workers are highly skilled and use general purpose equipment. There is little formalization of tasks. There are very few standing plans such as standard operating procedures, standard methods, or performance standards. Some individual managers and supervisors, however, do establish objectives and standards for specific tasks or projects on a more or less subjective basis.

Communications and interpersonal relations in the company are quite informal and open. All employees say what they think and freely give their ideas and suggestions to others. There is a good deal of collaboration in solving technical problems. Motivation of managers, professionals, and employees appears to be quite high. Most seem very interested in the work they do.

The company is interested in further diversification in order to reduce their dependence on federal government contracts. Historically the company has focused on exploiting basic research knowledge from the field of optics.

1. What type of organization is this company?
2. Does it appear to be organized correctly for its situation? Why or why not?
3. What are the management and organization implications if Crozier Scientific Instruments seeks to grow in a more stable product line such as radios, stereo, etc.?

DISCUSSION QUESTIONS

1. In your opinion, what are advantages and disadvantages of the classical hierarchical (mechanistic) type of organization?
2. Compare the production subsystems of the mechanistic and organic organizations.
3. Why would the manager in a production subsystem of a mechanistic organization face different problems than a manager in a production subsystem in an organic organization?
4. Which boundary-spanning activities do you feel are most important in a mechanistic organization?
5. Would control systems differ much between mechanistic and organic organizations? How?
6. Why is the organic organization called a "flexible type"?
7. Would an organic organization ever want to "borrow ideas" from the mechanistic type? When and why?
8. What is organizational climate and why must the manager understand this concept?
9. Describe the TD-mixed organization and compare it to a mechanistic design.
10. Describe the MD-mixed organization and explain in which industries it would tend to exist.
11. What are differentiation and integration? Why are these concepts so important to the manager?

REFERENCES

1. Burns, T. and G. Stalker. The management of innovation. London, Tavistock, 1961.
2. Blauner, R. Alienation and freedom. Chicago, University of Chicago Press, 1964.
3. Kilbridge, M. D. "Do workers prefer larger jobs?" Personnel Journal, 1 (1960); 45–48.
4. Comstock, Donald E., and W. Richard Scott. "Technology and the structure of subunits: Distinguishing individual and work group effects," Administrative Science Quarterly, 22 (June 1977): 177–202.
5. Thompson, J. Organizations in action. New York, McGraw-Hill, 1967
6. Tushman, Michael L. "Work characteristics and subunit communication structure: A contingency analysis," Administrative Science Quarterly, 24 (March 1979): 82–98.

7. Lorsch, J., and J. Morse. Organizations and their members: A contingency approach. New York, Harper & Row, 1974.

8. Hall, R. H. Organizations: Structure and Process. Englewood Cliffs, N.J., Prentice Hall, 1972. "The concept of bureaucracy: An empirical assessment," American Journal of Sociology, 69 (1973): 32–40.

9. Schneider, B., and R. Snyder. "Some relationships between job satisfaction and organization climate," Journal of Applied Psychology, 60 (1975): 318–328.

10. Seiler, I. A. "Diagnosing interdepartmental conflict," Harvard Business Review, 41 (1963): 121–32.

11. Lawrence, P. R., and J. W. Lorsch. Organization and environment: Managing differentiation and integration. Graduate School of Business Administration, Harvard University, 1967.

Individuals and Groups
in Organizations

Organization systems are brought to life and continue to live because human beings effect changes using scientific, technical, and economic resources. Humans harness the energy, invent, and create both the organization itself and what it produces. The environment in which these organizations exist affects people, but it, in turn, is affected by them.

People in organizations are different—and the differences create a major problem for managers. Human beings bring very different attitudes, abilities, knowledge, and motivations to work. Because of such differences, performance varies among individuals.

If people acted predictably, like the solar system or machines, the life of a manager would be much easier. But they don't act predictably. Chapter 5 discusses differences in individuals, with a particular emphasis on how they are affected by the broader society and how these characteristics are related to the way people view their work.

Humans are social animals. They work with others—in groups—and groups affect the person. Organizations are sets of complex groups. In all but the rarest case, individuals are assigned to groups in organizations. Chapter 6 examines groups, what happens in them, and how groups affect organizations.

CHAPTER FIVE

People in Organizational Settings

Item 5.1 The Steelworkers

At 3:00 every working day the same act begins to unfold at Rose's Cafe. Dale and Art arrive about that time and order two beers. At 3:10 Smitty appears. He always has a low-calorie soft drink. Gerry and Nick are never later than 3:20. They all work the evening shift at the Valley Steel Company, a steel fabricator that is the major employer in this small town nestled in the Ohio River Valley. Everyone in the town works for Valley Steel, or a service business that supports it.

The men gathering at Rose's all work in the tub and bucket department. The department produces a whole range of steel buckets and small tubs, from mop pails to wash tubs. Dale and Smitty have worked thirty years for Valley Steel. Art, Gerry, and Nick each have over fifteen years service.

Rose's is a convenient place for them to meet before they report for the four o'clock shift. It is just up the street from the plant gate, a three minute walk from the Rose's front door to the time clock they all punch. Meeting together gives them some time to prepare for the day's work. It is a relaxing time and it has been a habit to stop by Rose's since they were all assigned to the tub and bucket line six years ago. There are only a few things they talk about during this period: family, sports, politics, and work. Today, Gerry talks about work.

"I'm tired," he says in a quiet voice. "I spent all morning putting a new roof on Mom's house. I'm going to find a place to sleep today."

Everyone knew what Gerry meant. There were large rolls of steel that were stored in the department to be made into tubs and buckets. When these rolls were brought in, the crew always stacked them so there were some nooks and crannies to hide, to catch a rest or maybe even a nap.

This was easy when work was slow, and it was always slower in the afternoon than on the day shift. Emmett, the department foreman, did not particularly care if one of the workers was away from his work station unless there was a heavy production schedule. There was this week—and the crew knew it. If Gerry left his position, the rest of the crew would have to cover for him.

"C'mon, Gerry," Dale was disgusted. "Not today. We have a lot to do and I'm not covering for you, not today or any day. I really don't understand you. We have a good job compared to what other people have. The work is pretty interesting. Besides you get paid for a full day's work. When you sign on with Valley, you've got to do your job. When there's work to do, you've got to do it."

Nick wasn't quite so adamant. "Look, Gerry, there are a lot of things I'd rather do, fish and hunt for two. But a job's a job and one's as good as another. Valley's an OK place to work, better than a lot. What'll you do if Emmett fires you?"

"Fires him! You've got to be kidding." Art was laughing. "We have a union contract and we're protected, buddy. They can't do that. Besides they didn't give us enough in the last contract. They owe us, and Gerry—and the rest of us—should take it. I say if he needs a nap, he should take it. We'll cover."

By now it was 3:55. They got up, walked past Bennie, the bartender, and hurried down to the plant gate to clock in.

What these men say about their work reflects very different views. Their attitudes toward work range from quite positive to very negative. Why do they feel differently about their work? The most obvious answer, of course, is that they are different people so they bring different characteristics to the job.

Why should there by any difference at all since they work for the same firm, are on a similar wage scale, have very similar jobs, and come from very similar socioeconomic backgrounds? Even though these workers share very similar experiences, each has different skills, values, and attitudes. Therefore, the same work situation may trigger very different reactions for one person than for another. Like others, these steel workers differ because of different events that occurred in the formative years of the human development of each of them. This process of development is called "socialization," by which a culture, or society, or other institution conditions the behavior of individuals.

From the time a person is born until his death, he or she is subjected to group norms and values, cues, and consequences that over a period of time develop and shape his or her behavior and attitudes. People develop, or learn certain modes of adapting to situations they encounter. This pattern of adaptation is called "personality." In general, personality is the unique pattern of psychological and behavioral characteristics of a single individual. The characteristics that make up personality are (1) skills, ability, and knowledge, (2) attitudes, (3) values, and (4) needs or motives.

Many who have studied personality believe that it is fairly well formed in early years and that once it is formed it is difficult to change. Childhood experiences are important in personality formation. The individual psychological and behavioral patterns that persist in adults reflect the experiences they had as children. The adult as a young person, learned then—or did not learn—how to solve some basic problems. Erik Erikson[1] points out that the orderly development of a healthy personality requires the successive resolution of certain conflicts at each stage of personality development. These life stages and the particular problems of each are shown in Figure 5.1. How these problems are resolved determine the personality.

FIGURE 5.1 Erickson's Stages of Personality Development

Approximate Chronological Phase	Specific Problem	Resolution
Infancy	Trust vs. mistrust	From and through his parents, the child hopefully concludes that the world is not a hostile or random place, and some people can be trusted.
Young childhood	Autonomy vs. shame Initiative vs. guilt	Again from and through parents (mainly in the conflict over toilet training and freedom to explore his house), the child should learn that he is an autonomous person who can and should exercise his independence without guilt.
Childhood and adolescence	Industry vs. inferiority	Success in exercising initiative tends to reinforce itself; the young person should become energetic and confident in seeking productive activity and challenge.
Adolescence	Identity vs. confusion	From examples of his elders and personal exploration, the young person should come to know who he is and what he can do.
Young adulthood	Intimacy vs. isolation	Clarity about self should facilitate the ability of the person to enter into close relationships with others.
Adulthood and middle age	Generativity vs. stagnation	With success and maturity, the individual faces the problem of maintaining effort and interest.
Old age	Ego integrity vs. despair	With declining physical and mental states, the individual struggles to maintain a sense of self-worth and optimism.

Source: Reprinted from ''Identity and the Life Cycle'' by Erik H. Erikson. From *Psychological Issues,* vol. 1, no., 1. By permission of W. W. Norton & Company, Inc. Copyright © 1959 by International Universities Press, Inc.

Certain aspects of the personality are of special importance in the world of work. For example, people differ in their reaction to authority. This is so because of differences in their early conditioning. Reaction to authority plays a significant role in organization performance. All organizations have authority systems, and authority issues pervade their day-to-day functioning. Reactions to authority learned by a child in coping with demands of parents, teachers, and other authority figures determine, to a great degree, responses as a superior or subordinate later in life.

SKILLS, ABILITY, AND KNOWLEDGE

Human beings differ widely in the knowledge, abilities, and aptitudes they bring to a job. Some people have high levels of competence in certain areas, say mathematics, while others have great difficulty understanding the subject. Others have the ability to perform physical activities well while others do not. Some people have extremely high finger dexterity, others fumble putting on gloves. **Knowledge** is an acquaintance with facts or principles. **Ability** is the capacity to do something. **Aptitude** is the potential to develop future skills or knowledge.

Managers (and others as well, of course) often underestimate the magnitude of individual differences in skill, ability, and aptitude. Even within a group of people who are apparently very similar there may be wide differences among individuals on some characteristics. In a group of highly trained scientists, for example, there can be substantial differences in the degree and the type of knowledge. The widest differences, however, are typically found in lower occupational groups, since in higher-level occupations a prerequisite level of ability may be a requirement for admittance. In one study, for example, intelligence test scores varied between 100 and 170—a spread of 70 points—for engineers, but between 45 and 160—a 115 point spread—for coal miners.[2]

Some aptitudes and skills are inherited. A person's finger dexterity, for example, cannot be changed significantly by special training. And while there is a great deal of controversy about the relative effects of heredity and environment on intelligence, it is clear that certain levels of intelligence make it easier to acquire certain levels of specialized knowledge.

Research shows that levels of different aptitudes of the typical individual vary.[2] A person may be very high on finger dexterity, medium on color discrimination, and low on intelligence. What is important to management is that characteristics relevant to a job be determined and that they be measured specifically and accurately.

NEEDS AND MOTIVES

Most people who study human behavior believe that a large part of it is goal-directed, that we behave as we do to satisfy some individual human need. Needs, or motives, are goal states that an individual strives to achieve. A need exists when an individual determines that the present state of being is not what he or she desires to be. When the difference between *what is* and *what is desired* is great enough, the person acts to reduce the disparity. This is goal-directed behavior.

An early and influential approach to the human need structure is that of Maslow,[3] who describes five categories of needs (see Figure 5.2).

1. ***Physiological Needs.*** Physiological needs are the basic requirements for survival. Man must have food in order to live. He must find some shelter to protect him from the elements. Physical well-being must be provided for before anything else can assume importance.

2. ***Security Needs.*** Once a person has food and found shelter, he can worry whether or not he will have them in the future. He desires protection against loss of shelter, food, and other basic requirements for survival. The security needs also involve the desire to live in a stable and predictable environment. It may involve a preference for order and for structure.

3. ***Social Needs.*** The need to interact with others and have some social acceptance and approval is generally shared by most people. For some, this need may be satisfied by joining groups. Others may find sufficient affection from their family members or other individuals, without joining groups.

4. ***Ego Needs.*** The ego needs have to do with the human desire to be respected by others, the need for a positive self-image. Individuals strive to increase their status in the eyes of others, to attain prestige or a certain reputation or a high ranking in a group. Self-confidence is increased when the self-esteem needs are satisfied. The thwarting of these needs produces feelings of inferiority or weakness.

5. ***Self-actualization.*** Maslow describes the need for self-actualization as the individual's desire to do what he is fitted for. Individuals want to achieve their potential. This is called the "highest-order need."

Maslow believed that the higher-level needs are not important to an individual until the lower-level needs are at least partially satisfied. In other words, an individual will not be concerned with social needs if there is not adequate food or shelter, or if security needs have not been met. Another important idea in this approach is that a person is not motivated by a need that is satisfied. Once a need is satisfied, the person is concerned with the need at the next level of the hierarchy.

A simpler approach to needs is to differentiate between primary and higher-order needs. Primary needs refer to physiological and security needs. Primary needs are satisfied in fairly standard ways among people, especially people from the same culture. They are easiest to satisfy in a reasonably active economy, so long as adequate income is provided. An individual with income can obtain the particular kind of food and shelter that is desired, within wage limitations, and security needs may be partially satisfied through union contracts or work agreements, as well as

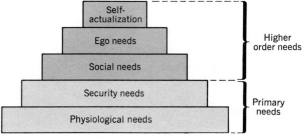

FIGURE 5.2 Maslow's need hierarchy.

social program such as unemployment compensation and welfare benefits. Letting an employee know what is expected at work also helps satisfy primary needs.

The higher-order needs are psychological. Different people want different things, and this is precisely the reason why the need hierarchy is difficult to translate into a motivational strategy for the manager. There is no way that managerial strategy or policy can be tailored to meet the very different nature of higher-order needs, which include social, ego, and self-actualization needs.

There are many differences among individuals with respect to the needs that are important to them. More important, there are many ways in which a particular kind of need may be satisfied. For instance, one person's ego needs may be satisfied by being recognized as the best worker in a department. Another may find this need satisfied by others' recognition of his or her dress style—being acknowledged as the sharpest dresser in the group. An individual's need structure is determined by socialization, or early learning experiences.

How an individual satisfies a particular need is learned by experiences that some situations are more desirable (rewarding) than others, and we seek these out. Other situations are ones we seek to avoid. With respect to social needs, for example, it may be particularly comfortable to interact with others of a certain ethnic or religious background, and very uncomfortable to interact with those from other backgrounds. Research has led to a number of conclusions about how primary and higher-order needs are related.

1. *It appears that as the primary or existence need becomes satisfied, it becomes less important.* When higher order needs are satisfied, they may become more important. For example when self-actualization or growth needs are met for a person, that individual may seek more, rather than be content. Wanous and Zwany[4] found that relatedness and growth needs of employees in a utility company were more important for those who reported those needs to be satisfied already.

2. *If lower-level needs are highly deficient, there is diminished concern for the higher-order needs.* The individual is preoccupied with lower-level need problems.[5] This has been shown for individuals who are known to be very hungry, for example, or who have found their jobs threatened, as when a firm faces bankruptcy. Thus, extreme fear or anxiety about lower-level needs precludes thoughts and concerns about higher-order ones.

3. *Social needs may be especially critical for satisfaction of other needs.*[6] If they are not satisfied, the individual may become concerned almost entirely with lower-level needs. If the social needs are satisfied, however, the person becomes primarily involved with the higher-level needs.

4. *Needs differ among occupational groups.* Rank-and-file workers generally consider the lower-level needs to be more important in work situations than do managers.[7] Managers, especially those at the highest echelons, consider the higher-level needs more important than the lower-level needs. Workers from urban backgrounds seem to be more concerned with satisfying lower-level needs than do workers from rural backgrounds.

5. *Psychological needs are reflected in what a person wants from work.* For example, it has been shown that employees with higher needs for security place a higher value on having clear work assignments.[8] There is also evidence that among managers there is more concern for security in the early years on the job, when the manager is unsure of organizational expectations and perhaps of his own abilities.[9]

Security needs then decrease as individuals grow older. For rank-and-file workers, however, concern for security increases with age. Lower occupational groups place higher value on security and money than do higher occupational groups.[10]

Another approach to needs is that of David McClelland.[11] McClelland emphasizes three human needs; achievement, power, and affiliation. Individuals high in **need for achievement** spend much of their time in thinking about doing their jobs better, advancing their careers, or accomplishing important things. They like situations in which they can take individual responsibility for accomplishment, where specific feedback exists on how well they are doing, and where their work goals are of moderate difficulty rather than being too easy or too difficult. Individuals high in **need for power** are concerned primarily with influencing and controlling others. Those high in need for power prefer positions that allow them to exercise power over others. They are often interested in reaching the highest levels of management or government because of the power in the position. Individuals high in **need for affiliation** are most concerned about their relationships with others. They seek out jobs and other activities in which there is an opportunity for friendly interaction and for helping behavior. Certain professional fields such as teaching, nursing, and counseling would have special appeal to those high in this need.

ATTITUDES

An attitude is an individual's feelings and beliefs about other persons, objects, events, and activities. These feelings and beliefs about persons, objects, events, and activities can be positive or negative. Attitudes reflect some preference—like or dislike toward an object.

Attitudes are formed over time. They are learned in a variety of ways. In the many groups to which an individual belongs, certain attitudes are developed. In a work group, for example, fellow workers will show approval and disapproval after a person expresses attitudes about management, unions, work procedures, performance standards, and other matters. Since most of us seek social acceptance, it is not surprising that the group has an influence over attitudes.

Attitudes are, of course, also formed and strengthened in our neighborhoods and homes both as children and as adults. Certain attitudes develop out of personal experiences with an event in question. If something, for instance a low grade in a particular subject in school, has contributed to a person's failure to get into college, it is likely that he or she will have negative attitudes toward that subject.

Most managers believe that a person's attitudes affect the way he or she behaves at work. They believe attitudes to be predictive of behavior. The way a person feels about something—and what he or she believes about it—determines their behavior toward it. Indeed, some research has shown that the changing of attitudes toward a person can change behavior toward the same person.[12]

Attitudes also might follow, instead of precede, experiences and behavior. In one study a group of workers' attitudes toward their job and company were measured. Later, some of these workers were promoted to foremen. They then were acting as managers, not as workers, and when their attitudes were measured again, they were found to have changed to be more like those of management. Other workers who were studied became union officials. Their attitudes became different from those of the workers, more like those of union officials.[13] Another important research study shows the significant effect of organizational position on an employee's attitudes and behaviors. Rousseau[14] found that job characteristics (such as autonomy, task identity, feedback) and position characteristics (such as time of work, status) accounted for a very significant effect on job satisfaction and propensity to leave an organization. She concluded that these characteristics of the work itself were more influential on attitudes and behavior than were the psychological characteristics of the person who was in the job. These two studies show that when an individual is in a particular situation, attitudes may change so that they are consistent with what he or she does. For example, if an employee works alongside a member of a group toward which he or she has a negative attitude, but treats the other person in a way consistent with a favorable feeling about the person as a person, it is more likely than not that favorable attitudes will develop toward the entire group. This is because individuals attempt to maintain some consistency between their behavior and their attitudes. In general, a person must be able to justify his or her behavior with an appropriate attitude, and that behavior influences the attitude— which in turn influences future behavior. There is, then, a reciprocal relationship between attitudes and behavior.

Human beings have many attitudes toward different things. We have attitudes toward work, politics, education, sex, leisure, and so on. These different attitudes tend to be consistent with each other as well as with behavior. This consistency helps us make sense of the world and to behave consistently. The attitude system is therefore one guide to reality.

Attitudes are important factors in a person's identification with a particular group. Holding attitudes in common with others contributes to a strong sense of unity with them. Because attitudes perform so many valuable functions for us, it is hardly surprising that we strongly resist attempts to change them.

VALUES

Values are more deeply ingrained and more general than attitudes (which are aimed at quite specific individuals or objects). Values are what an individual considers good or bad, important or unimportant. They serve as a means or a standard for evaluating things and events and therefore they help a person to deal with his or her environment. They are especially useful in comparing decision alternatives, since the alternatives can be scaled against values.

Values are the base from which attitudes emerge, perceptions develop, and behavior occurs. England[15] says that values and value systems are important because they:
1. Influence perceptions of the situation
2. Influence decisions and solutions to problems
3. Influence interpersonal relationships
4. Influence perceptions of organizational and individual success
5. Set the limits of ethical behavior
6. Influence the amount of organization pressures a person can tolerate

Values develop primarily from the background of individuals, for example, their religious and ethical upbringing. Some come from the culture itself. For example, in the United States a high value is placed on competition, while in Japan, the opposite is true.[16] Need for esteem is more important to Italian managers than to U.S. managers, while concern for security is much higher among managers in underdeveloped countries than those in the United States.[17] Some research shows much more respect for authority among Japanese workers than among U.S. workers.[16]

Work values are also a result of what actually happens to a person on the job. If, for example, we have worked hard on a task for little money, then we will perhaps convince ourselves that the task has much more intrinsic satisfaction built into it than it actually has. Finally, individuals who have been very successful on a job often come to place a high value on performance itself.[9]

Gerald Cavanaugh,[18] an observer of values in the business sector in the United States, concludes that the following values seem to be pervasive in the society:

1. Achievement and success
2. Activity and work
3. Practicality and pragmatism
4. Humanitarianism
5. Freedom
6. Quality
7. Patriotism
8. Material comfort
9. External conformity
10. Rationality and measurement

As you might expect, different individuals or groups rank these differently. For instance, material comfort may take precedence over practicality for one person, while for another achievement may be the predominant value.

A study of the values of over 1,000 managers shows how these values take on different importance to managers in their work.[15] **Operative values** are those that have the most influence on the work behavior of managers. They are most important to managers and fit their "pragmatic" orientation. Operative managerial values are:

1. Achievement and success
2. Activity and work
3. Practicality and pragmatism

Intended values are those that are important to a manager but that do not seem to fit the work situation. For instance, rationality is an important criterion for the behavior of managers, but experience often leads them to conclude that when they are rational they have not always been organizationally rewarded. Intended values of managers are:

1. Rationality
2. Patriotism
3. Freedom

Finally, some values have **low behavioral relevance** to managers. These are values that are unlikely to affect a manager's work behavior directly and are not consistent with the pragmatic view of managers. The "low behavior relevance values" are:

1. Equality
2. Material comfort
3. External conformity

Reactions to work have their roots in early life. In the young childhood stage, as shown in Figure 5.1, the child learns about autonomy and freedom. The child could develop high autonomy or could become very dependent in the young childhood stage.

Parents are the first "authority figures" the child deals with. Authority figures have power. They can give rewards or withhold them. They can administer punishment or refrain from its use. As authority figures, parents can provide a wide range of need gratification to a child by virtue of the way in which they reward or sanction the child.

In their very early years, children begin learning how to respond to authority and authority figures. As they grow, they continue to learn how to adapt to and cope with the world. The responses to authority figures first learned at home become further developed and strengthened by later experiences in churches, schools, and other organizations such as the Boy Scouts or Girl Scouts. Teachers, scoutmasters, and group leaders, as well as parents, represent authority figures.

Much of what is learned in these early experiences carries on into later life. Children who have learned that they can obtain affection from their parents by compliance are very likely to do what they are told by teachers in school. If they follow directions, they will win recognition. They will try to please their teachers. Doing this will result in positive reinforcement, probably praise. This increases the likelihood that they will do as they are told later. As they continue to comply with teachers, they continue to be rewarded. A cycle develops. Children who are "good" students are rewarded and reinforced—and they become "better" students. Teachers look for "good student" behaviors to reward. Often they ignore the "bad" behavior of good students. They may selectively perceive only "good student" cues.

There is a reverse side to this coin, and it is the one in which a child is unable to get attention by compliance. Suppose a young boy has a smaller sister. When he is told to be "good," he does so, but sees his parents spending time with his smaller sister, even so. The older child perceives the consequence for being good as having his mom and dad ignore him—no affection. In time he learns that to get attention it is better not to be "good." He learns that he must compete for his parents' time and that this can be done most effectively by being a problem, by adopting an alternative mode of behavior from that of complying. He becomes aggressive, a problem child.

When he goes to school, he carries this pattern of problem behavior to the classroom. The teacher expects a certain behavior (complying with teacher's requests), and this child acts in the opposite way. There may be negative sanctions of this behavior from the teacher, but the child's fellow students may give him a lot of social support. Thus, when the teacher publicly calls attention to his misbehavior this may, in a sense, be the very recognition he is seeking before his fellow students. Such a situation increases the likelihood that his "undesirable" behavior will continue. In time, teachers come to expect him to be "bad," and they will look for that particular behavior and reinforce it accordingly. So will his peers.

Thus, from early life, people develop different ways of coping with and adjusting to the world around themselves, and to authority figures. By adolescence "the young person should come to know who he or she is and what he or she can do.''[1] And reflecting on our own experiences and those of others, we know how differently people learn to accommodate to the world of work. These accommodations to work begin, as we have said, to take shape very early; family characteristics and values are related to work values. Our choice of work or career is also affected by early experiences.

FAMILY CHARACTERISTIC AND WORK VIEWS

Family background is associated with later work values. The socioeconomic level of the family, for example, is a consistent predictor of how one sees work. So is the nature of family relationships. One study, for instance, found that being a member of a close family, having many close friends, being subjected to parental discipline, and having social activities such as dating and taking part in community projects were all related to placing a high value on job security, a desire for good working conditions, and a desire for having good relations with fellow workers. A stress on independence and cultural activities in the home, however, was related to more concern with status, responsibility, and independence on the job.[19] Another study found that individuals raised in a home environment in which independence, achievement, and self-control were emphasized tend to be more active and have a task orientation as an adult. On the other hand, they found that individuals raised where family ties are emphasized tend to be passive and socially dependent, and to place a higher value on social acceptance.[20]

Career Choice

The occupation we choose is also affected by our early socialization. Although there are many chance factors that affect one's career choice, it has been shown that the parent's occupation is related to the occupation a person chooses. The children of individuals in higher-status occupations, for example, tend to end up in similar high-status occupations themselves. Which jobs are high-status jobs? Professional (scientist, engineer, lawyer, physician) and managerial (bank manager, production manager) jobs are consistently ranked at the top of the status hierarchy by the general population.[21] The offspring of those in lower-level occupations tend to take jobs similar to those of their parents. This tendency, of course, is to some extent determined by the educational opportunities available, which are most often dependent on the income of the family.

Chance or luck, as well as parental pressures and individual characteristics, also plays a role in occupational choice. Chance seems especially important in choosing jobs among the lower occupational levels.[22] Parental pressures are especially important for individuals who have low self-esteem, or a low self-image.[23]

Individual factors, however, do play a role in occupational choice, especially in choosing from among occupations with similar educational and experience requirements. One study of those entering the field of management showed that managerial success (given a high level of initial ability) was determined by the capacity to understand one's work environment and demands, competence in handling a wide variety of tasks, willingness to take risks, and ability to learn about oneself and then adapt to change as needed.[24] Individuals gravitate toward occupations congruent with their personal orientations. For example, individuals who tend to be rule oriented and conforming tend to prefer certain jobs such as accounting and finance. The applicant for a manager's position may, on the other hand, be an "enterprising" type who has verbal skill that he or she uses to dominate rather than help others.[25]

"CAREER" SOCIALIZATION

For individuals who choose occupations for which specialized training is required, work socialization continues during their educational experiences. For some, occupational socialization begins in professional school (e.g., engineering, medical, nursing, law schools) where the would-be professional is first exposed to the perspectives, values, and ways of thinking characteristic to the chosen field. A professional set of beliefs is acquired by participation in formal student groups, from taking courses, and through interaction with teachers. These beliefs are internalized; that is, they become part of the needs, attitudes, values, and self-concept of the individual. The person acts as a "professional" without thinking about it. Teachers are especially influential in shaping the new professional since in many professions the professor has much to do with the placement of students. The process of developing a professional self-image is a slow one, however, and students probably do not begin to think of themselves as professionals until they are treated as one by those who have already achieved that recognition.

CAREER ADJUSTMENT

These socialization experiences result in a "life structure" for a person.[26] The life structure is the way the following aspects of life are interwoven.

1. Work
2. Family
3. Peers
4. Other loved ones

These facets of life take on various degrees of importance for different people. The term "adjustment" refers to the balance that exists between these different aspects of life. When the balance between work, family, peers, and love relationship leads to high self-esteem and good relationships with others, we characterize that as successful adjustment.

Individuals sometimes find this balance disturbed. This change may then trigger an occupational adjustment problem in the later stages of a work career. Such changes are partly responsible for the so-called mid-career blues that seem to strike some individuals after age forty and the dissatisfaction of many women with the role of housewife. Successful career or occupational adjustment and involvement depend on the level of psychological success achieved, congruence of personal values with work demands, and how competitive work roles are with other life roles such as the role of parent, community member, or church leader.

Occupational and Job Expectations

If the status of an occupation is below the aspiration level of the individual in that occupational role, he or she is likely to be dissatisfied and experience a sense of personal failure. A major determinant of aspiration level is occupational level of parents. Young people expect to do at least as well as most of the relatives and neighbors they have contact with. People expect to attain at least the status of individuals similar to themselves. There is evidence that individuals from a managerial or professional background who become workers will not identify with the rest of the work group.

There is often a period of intense dissatisfaction shortly after a person moves into a new organization, begins a new career, or takes a different job. This has been found for younger rank and file workers[27] and for college graduates.[28] This dissatisfaction may be true of most new relationships that one enters and can likely be attributed to unrealistic expectations about how satisfying the new relationship will be.[6] Often people move into new work situations expecting them to be much more challenging and exciting. Over time, the person learns the more realistic set of work demands and morale improves as the individual changes early incorrect expectations about what is required.

Psychological Success

Psychological success is equivalent to high self-esteem. When individuals are successful in an occupational field, they will feel more positive toward it and develop high self-esteem. Motivation and occupational involvement will increase.[25] On the other hand, a sense of failure is likely to have the opposite effects.

Value Congruence

Occupational adjustment is influenced by the degree to which the individual's values are similar to the occupational role requirements. Many cases of career failures are due to this lack of value congruence. Policemen must be willing, at times, to engage in interpersonal conflict. Managers must be willing to direct subordinates to carry out unpleasant tasks.[29]

Compatibility Among Roles

Individuals in our society are in multiple roles. If the requirements of one of these roles, such as a manager's job, interferes with the performance of other valued roles, such as mother, father, or community leader, there will be an adjustment problem with the role of manager. When one important aspect of the life structure, such as work, conflicts with another one, some reconciliation of these imbalances must take place.

ORIENTATION TOWARD WORK

What we are is determined by where we have been and the experiences we have had. Parents, school, college, friends all shape our personalities. We have certain skills, some greater than others. We expect certain things from life and we react according to whether or not we get them. Where we work and what we do at work is a major part of life. How we react to work and the work organization is reflective of our personalities. As shown in item 5.1, the three steelworkers had different orientations to work.

These orientations are initially shaped early in life, though they may shift as people have different work experiences. Some people are highly committed to their work organizations. Others seem to be extremely interested in what they do but have little commitment to the organization.

Those who are highly committed to the organization, whether a business firm, a government agency, or an educational institution, we call **organizationalists.**[30]* The **professional** orientation is one that is characterized by a strong commitment toward the career or work itself, not the organization. The third type is called the **indifferent.** The indifferent orientation is dominated by the person's wish to be away from work, doing something better.

These categories are a type of organizational personality stereotype, suffering the limitations of any classification scheme or stereotyping. Each orientation is described as a kind of "pure type," an ideal description of sorts. And while there is probably no such thing as a pure type, having such a classification allows us to use the types as benchmarks. We can observe people and see how closely they approximate these pure types.

These categories are useful in our later analysis, since these different personality types appear in different proportions in different types of organizations. We expect to find more professionals in some organizations. In others, we expect to find more organizationally oriented types.

THE ORGANIZATIONALIST

Large and small companies, universities, and government agencies all have some highly loyal members who function very well within the system. A person highly committed to the place where he works is called an "organizationalist." John DeLorean, who left a successful career at General Motors, described his perceptions of senior executives in that company

> . . . As he saw it, the senior officers spent most of their day confined to meetings on the fourteenth floor of the corporation's headquarters in Detroit. Most executives worked ten-hour days, leaving for home around 7:00 P.M., lugging bulging briefcases. On Saturdays many reappeared in the office, this time in shirtsleeves, to put in a few more hours.

> Most G.M. executives lived in Bloomfield Hills or neighboring Birmingham, where they socialized together. When they weren't playing golf with suppliers or dealers, they frequently formed foursomes with one another at the Bloomfield Hills Country Club, because few made close friendships outside General Motors. While debate was allowed within the company, it was never to be aired in public, and since G.M. dominated the field, this meant there was little open self-criticism in the industry. Dinner conversations with G.M. executives, DeLorean felt, tended to concentrate on narrow interests—automobiles or finance and engineering—and to exclude such subjects as films or music.[31]

The organizationalist does well in the unit in which he works, seeking organizational rewards and advancement and identifying with the system. His or her

---

*The classification system we use here is drawn heavily from the work of Robert Presthus.[30] He uses the term *upward-mobile* as we use *organizationalist*, *ambivalent* as we use *professional*, but we have used the term *indifferent* as does Presthus.

"I yessed him to death."

FIGURE 5.3   An organizationalist's treatment of his boss.

self-concept is inextricably tied to the organization. The organizationalist has relatively high morale and job satisfaction. He or she is likely to be concerned about his position in the organization. He wants to know what his job is, for what he is responsible, and to whom he is accountable. The organizationalist is concerned with the effectiveness and efficiency of the organization. Organizational success is important to him because it is reflective of his own success. He is highly committed to the organization's goals. Identifying with a superior, he finds it easy to rationalize organizational pressures for conformity and performance, since he is seeking promotion and other rewards from the system. Status in the organization is very important to the organizationalist. His life values may be defined, or reflected by, the level achieved in the organization; belonging to the "right" clubs, having the "right" friends, and looking "right" reflect status. Because status is so important to him, he probably experiences a great deal of status anxiety, or fears that his position in the organization is threatened in reality or potentially. The organizationalist avoids controversy. He is a stickler for maintaining himself within the "channels" of the system, not readily going outside them to handle problems. Figure 5.4 outlines some characteristics of the organizationalist.

1. Loyalty to work
2. Identifies with the organization
3. Seeks organization recognition
4. Low tolerance for ambiguity
5. Concern with effectiveness
6. Deference to superior
7. High status anxiety

The Socialization of the Organizationalist

How does the organizationalist get to be what he or she is? The organizationalist develops an early respect for authority figures. Early experiences lead him or her to recognize the importance of authority, realizing that authority figures have power to dispense rewards and/or sanctions. Presthus[30] has suggested that the organizationalist comes from a family in which rewards and sanctions are applied primarily by the father. Organizationalists are success oriented. They acquire this early, learning to avoid failure experiences.

THE INDIFFERENT

Some people seem to work just for their pay. Their jobs are not a critical part of their lives. Tony, the lawyer described in item 5.2, is an indifferent though he is highly trained, technically proficient, and working in a "gray flannel" career. Work and the firm are not the center of life for Tony. Indifferents may perform well but are not highly committed to the organization. In effect, they act right but feel wrong. They may be managers, lower-level employees, or highly trained professionals. For many reasons they do not actively seek the rewards of the organization nor strive for higher position. They accept what they have. Given a choice, they would rather be doing other things. They also experience a great deal of role ambiguity.[32] They seek satisfaction of higher-order psychological needs outside the organization by doing things that are not related to where they work or what their work is. This is in marked contrast to the organizationalist, who seeks need satisfaction from a connection with the firm. This is supported by research that shows that persons who do not have strong values toward work are not highly committed to the organization.[33]

The Indifferent

**Item
5.2**

Tony made it five years ago. He was designated a partner in the largest law firm in the city. He was a good lawyer. As an associate in the firm, he was successful in handling several disputes between a large regional utility and the Environmental Protection Agency. Over the last five years, his work and his demeanor was above reproach. Since becoming a partner, Tony's success has continued. There were several partners who produced more business, but there were several who did not do as well as he.

Tony's work habits were fairly precise. He arrived at work every day by 8:00 A.M., but left the office by 5:00 P.M. He was never there on weekends and left instructions with the associate lawyers not to disturb him at home unless it was an emergency. If necessary he would see clients after business hours, but he preferred to keep his working time during the regular working hours.

He had only a few friends in the firm, not mingling with the other partners or associates socially except for the annual office events. He and his family were more involved with several local church and theater groups. His social life did not center around Snyder, Finch and O'Donnel.

"My life is mine," Tony would say. "I give them what they pay me for. I generate my share of the business. Why should I have to give them my soul, too?"

Some of the founding partners do not like Tony's particular view of S, F and O. They think it would be more appropriate if he were, as they said, "more involved and committed to the firm."

Interestingly, also, several of the younger associates who have been recently hired by S, F and O were concerned about Tony's work habits. There seemed to be the feeling that Tony did not have quite the correct manner and bearing of the partner of a major law firm in this city.

Recently one of the young associates had just become a partner and expressed this view in a comment to Tony. Tony did not reply but smiled and turned away. He thought, "Go to hell," as he walked away.

The indifferent generally prefers to withdraw from work. Greene[32] found that indifferents are more alienated from work than either organizationalists or professionals. He may be alienated by the tedium of the work itself. He does not get extensively involved with the work organization and participates in only a minimal way beyond work requirements. There are other, more important things in life than the job and the company. Rather then emphasizing the work ethic values as does the organizationalist, the indifferent seems more concerned with leisure.

The indifferent rejects the status and prestige associated with the job. He separates work from what he regards as the more meaningful aspects of life. He is essentially adapting to his work environment by withdrawing from it as much as possible, seeking his psychological satisfaction from neither the work itself nor the organization. Some of these characteristics are shown in Figure 5.5.

The Socialization of the Indifferent

Presthus[30] believes that the indifferent person generally comes from the lower middle class. Opportunities for advancement in an organization are restricted. If he is in the lower levels of the organization, he is likely to stay there.

We must not assume, however, that only lower-level personnel are indifferents. Many managers have a similar view. Often a person, whether a manager, a specialist, or an operative worker, turns the direction of his life to other things. Employees who were once fiercely loyal to the point of following orders without ques-

1. Seeks need satisfaction outside work
2. Withdraws from the organization
3. Less emphasis on "work ethic"
4. Rejects organization's status symbols

tion may change. For example, early in a manager's career he or she may be extremely committed to the organization. He or she may seek its rewards and want to advance. However, in middle age and in later career life, this individual may find that he or she has been passed over several times for promotion. Often a person finds that someone else gets the job that he or she expected to get. When this happens, the person turns elsewhere for support. So it is possible that with their promotion practices, organizations may turn managers from highly committed organizationalists to externally oriented types. Certainly we would expect to find fewer indifferents at higher levels, but it is not uncommon to find them in the higher-management ranks.

We must be careful, however, not to jump to the conclusion that the indifferent is necessarily a less effective employee than an organizationalist. The indifferent orientation, as are the others, is a state of mind. It may be only indirectly related to competence or quality of performance. The indifferent may not care as much about the organization as the highly committed person, but if he has high skill levels he may be able to perform extremely well. Ability, as well as state of mind, is an important component in determining level of performance.

THE PROFESSIONAL

Not all those who look outward from an organization are alienated from their work. The professional view is illustrated by the description of John, the counseling psychologist described in item 5.3. He cares about *what* he does and shows much less concern for the workplace (his university or the hospital). He wants them to support his activities.

THE PROFESSIONAL

**Item
5.3**

John is a thirty-seven-year-old counseling psychologist. He is a Professor of Psychology at an important West Coast University and also conducts a private counseling practice. His annual income is well over $100,000. He has investments and book royalties in addition to client fees and his university salary. He has recently been appointed as an adjunct instructor of psychiatry at a local teaching hospital.

His work schedule is grueling. He teaches a full load of courses at the university, advises several doctoral dissertations each year, has written two books and over fifty research articles in addition to seeing thirty clients each week.

He is highly regarded by everyone he works with. Students, clients, and other faculty members all want to be involved on projects with John. His research and his success in his counseling practice draw their attention.

John was not always so successful. As a young boy he did reasonably well in grade school and high school, and later in college. He was always in trouble, though, with teachers and superiors. In grade school he did everything to get the teachers' attention. He was such an active, rowdy youngster that one teacher thought he needed treatment for hyperactivity.

He had some modest athletic skills, but excelled as a jazz musician. He stumbled on this quite by accident. The high school band director goaded him into taking saxophone lessons. John surprisingly turned out to be quite good.

As a youngster he was never marked by his peers, his teachers, or his family as a high achiever. They did not pay much attention to him. But he found himself the center of attention when he played his music at the local jazz hangout.

He continued his music throughout high school and college. Music contributed to his feelings of self-esteem as well as financially to his college education. When he graduated with a degree in education, he took a teaching position at a local high school. John liked teaching; it was a lot like performing his music. However, he never felt that he had the same freedom teaching that he experienced while playing; there were too many restrictions—the other teachers, the administration and the teachers' union.

He decided to go back to graduate school, mostly to escape the job but also because the master's degree in teaching would mean a higher salary. Money was becoming more critical to him since he had recently married and his wife was pregnant.

John planned to get a M.A. in history. In his first term in school, however, he enrolled in a course in counseling psychology. Part of the course requirement was to serve as a psychological assistant in the psychology laboratory. As a psychological assistant, John worked with an undergraduate student who was experiencing test anxiety. As John continued to work with the student, the student's test anxiety was reduced. She became less threatened by tests and publicly gave John a good deal of credit for her more relaxed state of mind while taking tests.

The professor who taught the course used John's case study as an illustration in a class session. She singled out John's excellent work with the student. John began to feel as he did when he played his music—the individual performer in him came out. He decided to change his major to psychology.

He was admitted to the doctoral program, and while in it he published several articles in highly respected psychology journals. His professors thought him to be very good; some thought him to be outstanding. He had a good deal of freedom in designing his program. He could do almost anything he wanted during his graduate work. John developed some strong research skill and advised other students in graduate school about their research projects.

John graduated with a Ph.D. and was appointed to an assistant professor's position. His research was well executed and highly regarded by his peers. He felt extremely excited and rewarded when he would receive a letter from someone at another university who had read one of his articles. Now John had developed very high quality and quantity standards. He was not very tolerant of other faculty members who did little writing and research or little publication.

His success in publication began to attract graduate students and other colleagues. Students sought him out, though the course he taught was generally regarded to be the most difficult in the department. He had a reputation though for grading the students' work, not the personality. He was seen as "tough but fair." After his appointment as assistant professor, he began to engage in some private counseling work. He started by doing some volunteer work for the local juvenile court. Within five years he had developed a much more extensive and successful practice.

His waking hours were consumed with work. He spent very little of his time doing anything but writing and counseling. He took additional clients, often at no charge because they presented a challenge when they had a psychological problem he found interesting or novel.

His wife and children had little opportunity to spend time with him. Although his office was in his home, he spent more time with clients than family.

John poses problems for the administration of the university and the teaching hospital where he works. He rarely attends meetings. He never has work to the typing pool far enough in advance to have it done neatly. He makes heavy demands on the staff and chairman. "You are here to help me," he argues, "not the other way around. Don't bother me with administration trivia. Tell me when I teach, what I teach, and get the facilities for me. I'll do the rest."

Over the years, John's musical tastes progressed from jazz to opera. The dean said of John, "He's like one of those temperamental prima donnas. They raise all kinds of problems in rehearsal, but you get a great performance from them."

Professionals have external orientations but are preoccupied with their jobs or, more specifically, their careers. While the organizationalist has his or her self-concept linked to where he or she works, the professional has his or her self-concept tied to what he or she does. The professional has probably been heavily exposed to occupational socialization. In many cases the occupational socialization experiences conditioned him to believe that he must perform his work extremely well. However, in an organization, there must be compromises with the needs of the system. When the professional is subjected to managerial pressure to conform to organization demands that are inconsistent with his professional values, the professionally oriented person may believe that such directives are not rational. For instance, a researcher working for a pharmaceutical firm may believe that a particular drug needs more extensive testing before it is released in the market. But there are economic considerations in the decision that must be made. The decision to release a drug might be made by a manager who is less technically qualified than the researcher, and the professional may then believe that a bad decision has been made.

Professionals are likely to be particularly disturbed when they believe they are in a situation where they are unable to utilize all their skills most effectively. In such a situation, the professional feels underutilized. Most important, his self-esteem may be threatened because he does not have the opportunity to do the things he has been trained to do best. Professionals tend to feel more alienated toward work organizations than do organizationalists.[24]

FIGURE 5.6   Some Characteristics of the Professional

1. Oriented toward work, not the organization
2. Highly ideological about work values
3. Finds organization authority bothersome
4. Seeks to utilize skills to personal satisfaction

Often professionals refuse to play the organizational status game, looking outward to professional colleagues for approval. They would rather not be in the organization. They would rather be operating independently. Yet an organization is necessary to them, since it is imperative that they have a place to work, a base of operations and an economic base for their work. The professor who does not declare loyalty to his or her university must still be in *some* university to teach and conduct research. Without the university, teaching or other scholarly activities are not possible. The professional must adapt in some way to these needs for organization support, and often these accommodations are highly conflicting. Greene[32] found this to be the case for a group of scientists. He found that professionals reported more role conflict than organizationalists. The characteristics of the professional are outlined in Figure 5.6.

The Socialization of the Professional

The professionally oriented person often comes from the middle class and has become successful through higher-level education or by his or her own efforts to increase his skill.[30] He or she is likely to have a strong "ideological" orientation and to be extremely concerned that he or she does well in the chosen field. Success, for the professional, is usually defined in terms of personal achievement. In the illustration (item 5.3) John likes the recognition that comes from being able to work or perform solo. He measures success by the recognition he receives from external colleagues at other universities, in the profession, and in music more than by the rewards received internally in the organization. Organizational rewards are not valueless, however, since they do represent a way that the professionalist may estimate the importance of his contribution relative to others in the system.

ORGANIZATIONAL ORIENTATIONS
AND TYPES OF ORGANIZATIONS

In Chapter 3, we described three types of organizations: the mechanistic, the organic, and the mixed organization. The mixed organization contains both mechanistic and organic units. The three different personality types described in this chapter appear in different proportions in different types of organizations.

PERSONNEL COMPOSITION
OF THE MECHANISTIC ORGANIZATION

In a mechanistic organization the largest proportion of employees will be rank-and-file workers, for instance, blue collar in manufacturing and white collar in insurance companies or government agencies. Most of this rank-and-file group can best be characterized as having an indifferent orientation (see Figure 5.7). They tend, in general, not to be highly ego-involved or committed to their work and/or the organization. They tend to seek psychological satisfactions outside the workplace. This is due partly to their narrow job definition, that is, the tasks are not extremely challenging, and there is relatively little opportunity for advancement to positions where rewards are greater. One reason why promotion opportunities are limited is that there are fewer positions at the higher levels. Another is that often the requisites for promotions include advanced education, which the lower-level group is less likely to have. An indifferent orientation should not be construed to mean an unwillingness to work, however. Rank-and-file workers will probably do what is expected of them, but they do not obtain their primary satisfaction from their work.[34,35]

The middle management and specialist groups in the mechanistic organization will also contain a large number of indifferents—in this case managers who have reached career plateaus and have little opportunity for advancement. They become increasingly committed to their life away from work rather than to the work of organization.

We can also expect, at the mid-levels, to find a group of "organization-oriented" managers and specialists, people on the way up who seek the values and rewards of the system itself, high in achievement orientation and loyal to the organization.

PERSONNEL COMPOSITION OF THE ORGANIC ORGANIZATION

The organic organization will, of course, employ much larger proportions of professionals than the mechanistic organization. The greater volatility in the outside environment requires the employment of highly skilled specialists, and the lack of internal formalization will make it necessary to employ skilled rather than unskilled workers. Most of these employees are likely to have a professional orientation rather than an organizational or indifferent orientation. The mixture of organizational types in the organic organization is shown in Figure 5.8.

At the lowest level of the organization there will be a professionally oriented group of specialists, highly trained and skilled. The indifferents will probably be a smaller group of operating personnel charged with carrying out routine tasks. They will be longer-term employees.

At the mid-levels, the mixture of types changes. Two groups of roughly the same size will be found, one of organizationally oriented managers and one of

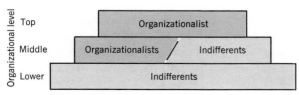

FIGURE 5.7 Personal orientations in mechanistic organizations.

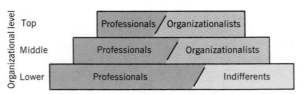

FIGURE 5.8 Personal orientations in organic organizations.

professionally oriented managers. The organizationalists will be administrators who are making a managerial career with success defined by their organization's achievement of primary work goals. The professionally oriented group will be specialists who have been promoted to managerial positions because of their high competence, but who have retained their original professional value system.

The distribution of types changes again at the top level, which will have a proponderance of organizationalists. This occurs because selection decisions for higher managerial ranks are made by those already in high positions, and they are likely to place value on the organization as such rather than on professional commitment. Technical skills are still important at this level, however, and some of the top management group will have a professional orientation.

PERSONNEL COMPOSITION OF THE MIXED ORGANIZATION

The mixed organization contains subunits that have mechanistic characteristics and subunits with organic characteristics. This is because the mixed organization's subunits face different environments, some of which are volatile and some of which are stable. In this type of organization the organic units are likely to have larger proportions of professionals relative to the mechanistic units. The mechanistic units will have a smaller proportion of professionals and a higher proportion of indifferents and organizationalists. This mixture of organizational personalities in the mixed organization will create difficulties in interrelating the work of the subunits in this type of organization.

THE PSYCHOLOGICAL CONTRACT: ORGANIZATION SOCIALIZATION

Each of the different types of individuals want different things from organizations. Early socialization experiences have caused the person to develop some ideas about how to interact with an organizational system. Early socialization experiences are the basis for values, expectations, and beliefs about what to do at work.

By the same token, there are expectations by the organization about what employees should do. The psychological contract refers to the mutual expectation between an organization and its members about what is expected of each.[36] An industrial organization and its employees, whether managers, specialists, or operative workers, have expectations about how much work is to be performed for the pay received. Students and professors have a set of expectations about what is appropriate performance for the other in a course when a grade is to be given. The expectations of the psychological contract, however, are not limited to compensation only. They may focus on demands such as loyalty to the firm or the special rights of long-term workers. Organizationalists, professionals, and indifferents all seek to strike a different bargain with the organization.

The psychological contract between an organization and an individual informally emerges through organization socialization. New members learn what superiors expect as well as the organizationally preferred values and ways of doing things. Like early socialization experiences, this learning occurs in a variety of ways. The teaching may be direct, as when a new employee is told about performance standards and rules during an induction program. Learning may occur through "behavioral modeling," in which the employee imitates others in the organization. Most behaviors, however, are probably learned through exposure and influence from the dominant reference group. A new production employee, for example, may be far more concerned with approval from worker peers than from a supervisor. A student's fraternity brothers or sorority sisters are likely to have more influence on the development of his or her values than will the college dean.

The new organizational member comes to the job with a set of work expectations. He or she expects certain things about working conditions, the mode of supervision, type of work assignments, and organizational life. Very often there is a divergence between what the employee expected and what the organization expects. In a study of college graduates hired by one of the large automotive companies, typical graduates found most of the job characteristics were worse than they expected.[28] In this study, it was also found that there was a wider divergence between what the graduate expected and what was present in the job situation for those who quit the firm as compared to those who stayed.

Thus, more often than not the typical new organizational member has a set of expectations about work that are somewhat unrealistic in terms of the organization's expectations. This has been demonstrated in a study that examined the relationship of early work experiences and expectations about work prior to taking the job. Over one thousand college graduates who were recently hired in a large manufacturing firm were studied. About five hundred of these had stayed with the company and an equal number had quit. Those managers who reported that their early job experiences were unsatisfactory, not challenging, and generally poor were likely to feel less successful at the job, more dissatisfied with it, and also were likely to leave. On the other hand, when a person had high achievement and security needs that were met on the job, had very positive expectations about what the job would be, and also had positive job experiences, he or she was more satisfied, felt more successful and was less likely to leave.[37]

The stereotyped idea of an individual as simply a pawn molded by an organization is not an accurate way to view reality. It is certainly true that individuals are shaped by their experience at work. However, organizations must adapt to the needs and values of various individuals or their very existence is threatened. An organization must continue to secure the services of new members or it will atrophy and die.

When a person changes organizations, he or she must be "resocialized." Schein[38] has followed business school graduates through various stages of their careers. He has found, as expected, that the values learned by students in the university setting change once they take jobs. When they are in school, the values of the students reflect those of their professors. After a time in an organization, the

FIGURE 5.9   The process of individual adaptation to the organization.

students' values become significantly less like those of faculty members and more like those of top management personnel in the organizations where they work.

SUMMARY

Not all people react to work in the same way. Some like work, others do not. Figure 5.9 illustrates the sequence of how these reactions to work begin to develop very early in one's life. As a child one begins to interact with authority figures. This continues through adolescence. Schools, churches, and community organizations all contribute to the early experiences that shape one's view of work.

Three types of work orientation develop from these early experiences. The organizationalist view is one in which the person is very committed to the company or place of work. The professional is more interested in a career, in the job done. Others work because they have to; they are called indifferents and are committed neither to their work nor to the organization.

These three different types of persons seek to strike different bargains with the work organization. The psychological contract refers to the overall exchange relationship between an individual and the work organization. This exchange agreement covers more than work for pay. It involves such things as loyalty and commitment from individuals in return for often long-term security for the individual. The psychological contract develops over a long period of time, starting when the person joins the organization. It changes over time, as conditions change. As long as there is an acceptable balance of benefits for the individual's contribution, the person is generally willing to remain. When the balance is too far in the advantage of the firm, the person tends to be dissatisfied and will seek to leave. This, of course, can work to the advantage of the organization as well as to the individual concerned.

Case
5.1   A Conversation with Two Factory Workers

WORKER #1

Q. "How long have you been here?"
   A.   "Two years."
Q.   "How do you like the work?"
   A.   "I don't. It's boring."
Q.   "What do you mean boring?"
   A.   "It doesn't interest me. It's not interesting, so it's boring."

Q. "Tell me, what do you think about during the day?"
A. "My check, what I'm going to do tonight or next weekend. I don't think about my job."
Q. "What do you think about those workers who have been here all their lives?"
A. "They're crazy."
Q. "The fellow next to you has been here for forty years."
A. "He's crazy."
Q. "Will you be here all your life?"
A. "Naw, I don't think so. This job is just temporary."
Q. "Would you advise a young man to go into factory work?"
A. "No."
Q. "What would you advise him to do?"
A. "Nothing. That's his business."

WORKER #2

Q. "How long have you been here?"
A. "Twenty-eight years."
Q. "What would you do with these kids today who are always protesting against the government?"
A. "Draft 'em."
Q. "Why do they do it?"
A. "I think the communists started this."
Q. "Why do you say that?"
A. "It must be run by somebody and I think it's the communists. These kids are dopey enough to be led by them."
Q. "What about capitalism? Some of these kids say that the workers like you are being exploited by their bosses. Do you think so?"
A. "No."
Q. "How about capitalism?"
A. "It's all right with me."
Q. "How much do you make?"
A. "$257 a week."
Q. "Do you regret taking this job?"
A. "It's all over and done with. What am I going to do about it now?"

1. What do these conversations with an older and a younger worker, assumed to be typical, tell us about problems of worker adjustment in this factory?
2. Contrast the different perspectives of the younger and the older worker.

Jack Graves

Case 5.2

Jack Graves was corporate director of industrial relations for Smith and Lamone Industries, a large worldwide manufacturer of industrial machinery with plants in many different countries. Jack had originally been a marketing manager for another firm, but was hired by Smith and Lamone in industrial relations on the strength of his energy and personality. Jack was an extremely personable, dynamic and socially aggressive person.

Over the first few years with Smith and Lamone, Jack developed and successfully implemented many innovative and effective personnel programs. Many of these programs were developed after Jack had a serious bypass heart operation in 1972.

In July 1980 Jack went back into the hospital for another bypass operation. Although he was supposed to spend three weeks in the hospital recuperating and another two months at home, Jack voluntarily left the hospital after two weeks and went back to work. He immediately launched a new personnel program and scheduled an exhausting set of meetings in the various company plants around the world to sell the program to the key managers in these plants. Jack's superior, Ed Geagen, upon hearing of the new program and planned trip from Jack, tried unsuccessfully to persuade Jack to take it easy. He then called up Frank Watson, the company's president, and explained Jack's plan and recent illness. "Shouldn't I forbid Jack from doing all of this, considering his health?" Ed asked.

Frank did not agree. "I think Jack's health is his own business," Frank replied. "If he wants to work that hard it's up to him."

1. Do you agree with the company president's answer? Why or why not?
2. Evaluate Jack's behavior. Why does he act the way he does?

DISCUSSION QUESTIONS

1. How is Maslow's need hierarchy (five categories) related to motivation within the organization?
2. How would McClelland's needs relate to Maslow's hierarchy?
3. Attitudes are formed in various ways. Discuss two important attitudes you have and how you feel they were formed.
4. How are attitudes and values different? The same?
5. Why should the manager be very aware of values and their priorities among his employees?
6. What influences do your family and childhood experiences have on your future work values and career choice?
7. Robert Presthus coined terms to classify people according to orientation toward work. Explain these three categories.
8. Could you change from one category of job orientation to another? Why or why not?
9. Name each type of organization in Chapter 4 and describe the types of employees that would be attracted to each.

REFERENCES

1. Erikson, E. "Identity and the life cycle," Psychological Issues, 1 (1959).
2. Tyler, L. The psychology of human differences. New York, Appleton-Century-Crofts, 1956.
3. Maslow, A. H. "A theory of human motivation," Psychological Review, 50 (1943): 370–96.
4. Wanous, John P., and Abram Zwany. A cross-sectional test of need hierarchy theory. Organizational behavior and human performance. New York, Academic Press, Inc., 1977.

5. Lawler, E. E., and J. L. Suttle. "A causal correlational test of the need hierarchy concept," Organizational Behavior and Human Performance, 7 (1972): 265–87.

6. Alderfer, C. P. Existence, relatedness, and growth: Human needs in organizational settings. New York, Free Press, 1972.

7. Porter, L. W., E. E. Lawler III, and J. R. Hackman. Behavior in organizations. New York, McGraw-Hill, 1975.

8. Carroll, S. J., and H. Tosi. Management by objectives: Applications and research. New York, Macmillan, 1973.

9. Hall, D. T., and K. E. Nougaim. "An examination of Maslow's need hierarchy in an organizational setting," Organizational Behavior and Human Performance, 3 (1968): 12–35.

10. Nash, A. N., and S. J. Carroll. The management of compensation. Monterey, Calif., Wadsworth, 1975.

11. McClelland, D., et al. The achievement motive. New York, Appleton-Century-Crofts, 1953.

12. Zimbardo, P., and E. B. Ebbesen. Influencing attitudes and changing behavior. Reading, Mass., Addison-Wesley, 1970.

13. Leiberman, S. "The effects of changes in roles on the attitudes of role occupants," Human Relations, 9 (1956): 385–402.

14. Rousseau, Denise M. "Characteristics of departments, positions, and individuals: Contexts for attitudes and behavior," Administrative Science Quarterly, 23 (December 1978): 521–540.

15. England, G. W. "Organizational goals and expected behavior of American managers," Academy of Management Journal, 10 (June 1967): 107–117.

16. Whitehill, A. M., Jr., and S. Takezawa. The other worker. Honolulu, East-West Center Press, 1968.

17. Haire, M., E. Ghiselli, and L. Porter. Managerial thinking: An international study. New York, Wiley, 1966.

18. Cavanaugh, Gerald. American business values in transition. Englewood Cliffs, N.J., Prentice-Hall, 1976.

19. Paine, F., D. Deutsch, and R. Smith. "Relationship between family background and work values," Journal of Applied Psychology, 51 (1967): 320–323.

20. Witkin, H. A., R. B. Dyk, H. F. Faterson, D. R. Goodenough, and S. A. Karp. Psychological differentiation. New York, Wiley, 1962.

21. Inkeles, A., and P. H. Rossi, "National comparisons of occupational prestige," American Journal of Sociology, 61 (1956): 329–39.

22. Myers, C. A., and G. P. Schultz. The dynamics of a labor market. Englewood Cliffs, N.J., Prentice-Hall, 1951.

23. Korman, A. K. "Self esteem as a variable in vocational choice," Journal of Applied Psychology, 50 (1966): 479–86.

24. Dill, W. R., T. L. Hilton, and Walter Reitman. The New Managers. Englewood Cliffs, N.J., Prentice-Hall, 1972.

25. Hall, Douglas T. Careers in organizations, Pacific Palisades, Calif., Goodyear Publishing Co., 1976.

26. Levinson, Daniel J. The season of a man's life. New York, Knopf, 1978.

27. Herzberg, F., B. Mausner, R. Peterson, and D. F. Capwell. Job attitudes: Review of research and opinion. Pittsburgh, Psychological Service of Pittsburgh, 1957.

28. Dunnette, M. D., R. D. Arvey, and P. A. Banas. "Why do they leave?" Personnel, 50 (1973): 25–39.

29. Miner, J. B. Studies in management education. New York, Springer Publishing Company, 1965.

30. Presthus, Robert. The organizational society. New York, St. Martin's Press, 1978.

31. Loving, R. "The automobile industry has lost its masculinity: Reflections on the abbreviated career of John DeLorean. A nonconforming executive at General Motors." *Fortune,* September 1973, pp. 186–191.

32. Greene, Charles N. "Identification modes of professionals: Relationship with formalization, role strain, and alienation," Academy of Management Journal, 21 (1978): 486–492.

33. Aryeh, Kiddron. "Work values and organizational commitment," Academy of Management Journal, 21 (1978): 239–247.

34. Dubin, R. "Industrial workers' worlds: A study of the central life interests of industrial workers," Social Problems, 3 (1956): 131–42.

35. Kornhauser, A. Mental health of the industrial worker. New York, Wiley, 1965.

36. Schein, E. Organizational psychology. Englewood Cliffs, N.J., Prentice-Hall, 1970.

37. Briscoe, D. Early Career Attitudes and Behaviors of Recently Hired College Graduates. Ph.D. Dissertation: Michigan State University, 1977.

38. Schein, E. "Organizational socialization and the profession of managements," Industrial Management Review, 9 (1968): 1–16.

CHAPTER SIX

Groups in Organizations

The Bank Wiring Room[1]

One important description of group behavior at work comes from the report of the Hawthorne study. Before this particular part of the Hawthorne study began, output records for the previous eighteen weeks were obtained from the department from which the men were chosen. In addition, all thirty-two workers in the department from which the men were chosen were interviewed prior to the study period. During these interviews, the men expressed their attitudes toward their jobs, supervisors, and working conditions. The fourteen men chosen were told by their foremen that they were to be part of a study and were asked to cooperate.

The experimental subjects were then introduced to the man who would observe them in the observation room. They were assured that no information obtained by the observer would be used to their disadvantage. All but one of the men studied were between twenty and twenty-six years of age, and only one had any college education.

The Bank Wiring Observation Room was separated from the main department by high partitions. In it, in addition to the fourteen subjects, there was the observer and, for a good part of the time, a trucker who brought in materials and removed completed work, and a group chief, the lowest grade of supervisor. As in the main department, the wiremen who wired "connectors" were placed in the front of the room and the wiremen who wired "selectors" were placed in the back of the room.

Group piecework was the system of wage payment for the department. Each piece of equipment completed by the department as a whole was credited to the department as a fixed sum. Each worker was paid an hourly rate of pay, depending upon his efficiency rating, plus a bonus.

Observation of the group at work showed that the actual behavior of the workers was different from, and more elaborate than, the work behavior described in the official descriptions of the jobs. For example, the men helped each other when someone fell behind in his work, though not all workers were helped and not all workers helped. In addition, the wiremen and the soldermen traded jobs (with the offer to trade being made by the wiremen).

The men also formed two friendship cliques within the Bank Wiring Observation Room. Each clique participated in its own games and other social activities. In addition to conversations, there was kidding and horseplay within the groups. The men gambled in a number of different ways. They organized pools and together would choose and place bets on horse races. They also matched coins, shot craps, and played cards. The men bought candy together and shared it, and they ate lunch with each other.

The researchers soon realized that the men in the Bank Wiring Observation Room, as a group, were controlling the rate of production. They had a definite idea of what constituted "too much" and "too little" work. At times, slower workers were bawled out for not working fast enough.

In addition to setting norms, the group felt that no worker should "squeal" to higher management about another group member, and no group member should attempt to put himself in a superior position in relation to the other workers in the room. One of the inspectors, the oldest man in the room and the only worker with some college education, was teased by the men. They adjusted his test set so that it did not work and reported to the supervisor that he delayed them. He retaliated by reporting the men to a higher level, an act that created so much hostility toward him that he had to be transferred out of the room.

The Bank Wiring Observation Room study ended in May, 1932, after 6½ months. During this time, the researchers observed that the men had created an informal social organization that developed an unwritten, but clearly understood, set of rules governing the behavior of the men in the group and specifying the nature of the relationships among them.

The Bank Wiring Observation Room group illustrates many important characteristics of all groups, characteristics that will be discussed later in this chapter. Groups of all kinds and sizes exist in work organizations. Departments, committees, integrated task teams, and the like are all formally designated groups. Within these units, members may go on to act in ways not specified in their job descriptions. No job description, for example, defines the individuals with whom an employee has lunch or travels to and from work. Yet from these activities may develop lasting relationships that can affect job performance.

Many problems in organizations can be understood only when the group is the unit of reference. Conflict between labor and management, for example, or between production and sales units, or between line and staff may be considered as special cases of group conflict. For these reasons it is important for managers to know something about group characteristics, phenomena, and processes.

All groups are collections of individuals who come together for some purpose. The purpose may be to accomplish some common personal objective of the individuals or to accomplish either a temporary or more enduring objective of the organization or of a manager with authority over the individuals that make up the group. For example, a group of workers or managers may voluntarily get together to form a car pool or to discuss possible approaches for obtaining a change in a policy. Or a department head may form a committee of six subordinates to produce a set of recommendations for reducing customer complaints. Or several general lathe operators may be put together in a particular section of a new plant to perform various assigned tasks.

These permanent or temporary collections of individuals then develop norms, roles, a status hierarchy, and other group characteristics. Then, depending on the degree of attraction the members develop for the group and the group's success in achieving its objectives and the objectives of its members, the group becomes more or less cohesive over time. This chapter introduces concepts that help us understand why and how groups are important in work organizations.

GROUP—A DEFINITION

A group is a collection of individuals who regularly interact with one another, who are psychologically aware of one another, and who perceive themselves to be a group. Two key concepts embedded in this definition are (1) identification and (2) interaction.

Identification means that persons consider themselves, along with others, as part of a group. Members of a group share something in common. It may be working for the same employer, having similar ethnic backgrounds, or being graduates of the same school. Identifying with a group simply means that a person recognizes a commonality with others. A manager of a quality control department may see herself as an employee of General Motors. Another group with which she might identify is the quality control department (of which she is the designated head) of the Oldsmobile assembly plant. Still a third focus of group identification for her might be the Society of Automotive Engineers.

These are all different groups with which the quality control manager may identify, but it is rarely the case that her role in all of these groups will be activated at any one time. Generally, the person interacts with individuals from one group at a time.

Interaction is another key group concept. Interaction is a process that occurs when one person's behavior affects a second person's behavior, and the second person responds in some way to the first. Say, for example, that our quality control manager meets with an inspector and gives him an instruction, ''Check the scrap rate in Department X.''

''I will, I'll go right now,'' says the inspector. An interaction sequence between the manager and the inspector has occurred.

In groups, certain interaction sequences are repeated over time. The pattern of interaction between group members can be analyzed and used as a way to identify individuals as group members. Thus, when we see an interaction sequence, as above, occur repeatedly we know that individuals are "in the same group."

REQUIRED AND EMERGENT BEHAVIOR IN GROUPS[2]

The interaction between the quality control manager and the inspector is part of their work assignment; it is activity to achieve the goals of the organization. Organizational units such as departments and committees are established on the basis of task requirements, or the job to be done. They are set up as a result of a rational decision-making process or they may, in part, simply evolve as a response to some organization need. *Required behavior refers to those behavioral requirements established for, and expected of, the members.* It is an organizational requirement. *Emergent behavior is that behavior that actually occurs in the group.* It is a result, not only of job requirements, but of a wide range of individual and group characteristics. Emergent behavior is likely to be different from, and more complex than, required behavior. Required behavior considers only the needs of the organization, not the needs of individuals and of the group itself, while emergent behavior—the behavior you actually see in a group—is the result of an accommodation between organizational demands and the interests of group members.

Most emergent behavior is probably functional for the group. It helps the group to cope with the stresses arising from the nature of the work and the interaction between individuals in the group. Where workers have monotonous jobs, as in the case of the Bank Wiring Room, the monotony may lead the workers to trade jobs, gamble, or engage in horseplay and other social activities—all diversions that enable them as a group to cope with the demands placed upon them by boring and repetitive work. It can also improve productivity.

Some emergent behavior, of course, may be highly undesirable from the organizational point of view. Restriction of production, for example, is undesirable from a company's perspective, but it may also be a way by which workers adjust to managerial pressures that conflict with individual or group needs, a way to avoid threatening comparisons between group members, for instance. Or, since the restriction of production is a group activity, it may provide the excuse for social interaction that gives the group a sense of purpose and a reason for existence. Production may also obviously be restricted in order to protect the jobs and income of group members.

TYPES OF GROUPS IN ORGANIZATIONS

Persons may be part of several groups that affect them at work. In some of these groups, the membership and much of the interaction between members is determined by others, usually higher-level managers, in the organization. For instance, the quality control manager we just discussed was probably selected for her job by the plant manager. The inspector to whom she gave an instruction was selected by her, or perhaps the previous quality control manager. That she gave him an instruction and expected him to comply probably stems from the job descriptions for the quality control manager and the inspector. These spell out what each is to do in the respective jobs and to whom each is responsible for work. When several people interact predictably and the interaction is specified in written documents, this is an example of a *formal* group.

A ***formal*** group, according to our definition, has two predominant characteristics:

1. Membership is usually determined by an official (such as a manager) in the organization. It is by appointment or selection, as is the case when someone is hired, given a specific job assignment, or appointed to a position.
2. The major interaction patterns are determined, defined, and specified by managers, officials, and/or technical specialists. This is just another way to say that there are some limits on how work is done.

Informal groups in organizations are not so completely influenced by the organization in which they exist. There is less "required," more emergent behavior. Individuals become identified with nonformal groups because in these groups individuals may find kindred souls with similar values, attitudes, and beliefs. Nonformal groups can make life pleasant by providing comfortable friends and companions to pass the work day with or make it miserable, as when a person becomes the focal point of jokes, personal attack, or similar hostile behavior of others.

FORMAL GROUPS

Formal groups in organizations have their membership and "required" behavior defined, for the most part, by officials, managers, or technical specialists. The basic purpose of formal groups is to enhance the goal-directed activities of the members, that is, to design work and select those who can do it effectively to achieve organizational goals. There are several different types of formal groups in any organization; departments, systems groups, committees, and temporary work groups.

Departments

One type of formal group is the department. A department is comprised of several individuals who have similar work roles or interdependent work roles. An example of people in a department with similar roles would be the case of several lathe operators all assigned to the lathe operations. An example of a department formed where work roles are interdependent is the personnel unit shown in Figure 6.1. This department is composed of several people who perform very different personnel tasks. There are interviewers and recruiters, compensation specialists, safety specialists, and labor relations staff in this unit. As we shall see in the section on organizing, there are several different ways to group work assignments to form departments. Briefly, however, work can be grouped on the basis of similarity of tasks (i.e., the lathe operators), similarity of purpose (i.e., personnel department) or geographic area (i.e., Eastern region and Midwest region), or in other ways. Some characteristics of departments that distinguish them from other types of formal groups are:

1. *Departments are supervisory units.* Departments are formed so that work roles can be grouped together in them, and also because the responsibility for supervising that work and authority to make decisions about it can be assigned to

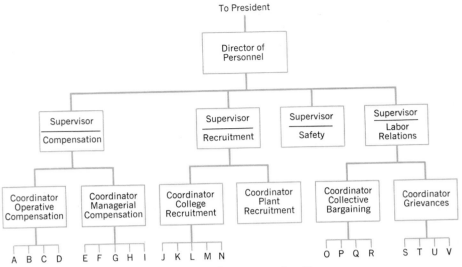

FIGURE 6.1   Departments as groups (in the personnel unit).

one person. Therefore, not only is a department a group of people that work together, but they are also responsible to the same person.

It is probably easiest and most appropriate to think of a department as a supervisory unit. As work is differentiated and jobs created, new work units (departments) are created within other work units (departments). In Figure 6.1, for instance,
those staff (A,B,C,D) who work for the Coordinator of Worker Compensation comprise a departmental unit, as do those (E,F,G,H,I) who work for the Managerial
Compensation Coordinator. Both of these formal groups can be thought of, also, as
being a department called "Compensation" headed by the Compensation Supervisor.

When the frame of reference is the Compensation Department, Worker Compensation and Managerial Compensation are called subunits.

2. *Departments are administrative conveniences.* In any work organization,
there are many things that need to be done for the staff. Personnel must be paid,
for example, as well as other actions taken that affect the individual's involvement
with the organization. A department is a conduit through which these personnel
actions can be processed.

3. *Departments are relatively permanent.* Departments are relatively permanent units that are created in organizations. They usually come into existence to
perform activities that are repetitive and ongoing. They are intended to, and usually
do, last for a very long time. For example, when a pipe coupling manufacturer
found that it was necessary to increase efforts to comply with affirmative-action
programs, it established an Affirmative Action Program office. This department was
staffed by several employees with major responsibilities of insuring compliance with
federal and state regulations.

The permanence of departments is illustrated by the fact that often even though
there may be major changes in the mission and purpose, the department is restructured and reorganized rather than simply disbanded. An example of this is the way

in which many firms that had already existing safety programs reacted to the new Occupational Safety and Health law. In the past it was rather common practice to have the safety function located in the personnel department of a firm. The new safety laws require a good deal more technical compliance with, concurrently, more extensively trained personnel. In most instances, the new safety staff were simply added to the already existing unit in the personnel office.

System Groups

Another type of formal group is a "system" group. In Chapter 3 we pointed out that the various subsystems in an organization often cut across **departmental** or **subunit** lines. People may interact regularly, as part of their assignments, with others from different departments to do their jobs. When this cross-unit interaction is frequent, it will usually be outlined in a **procedure,** a set of written steps that indicates who is to do what, when, and which person has decision-making authority. The procedure may also specify the executive with whom the system group must clear a recommendation for action they might make. The shaded area [A] in Figure 6.2 shows a systems group, that is, individuals from various departments who coordinate their work to carry out the interdepartmental function of college recruiting for a company. A staff interviewer (person N) visits a college and interviews prospective candidates for marketing research positions. A recommendation will be made to a manager of market research about which candidate is most promising. The recommendation will be approved by the Coordinator—College Recruitment. But, be-

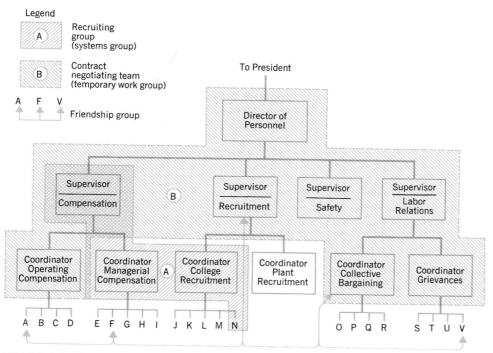

FIGURE 6.2   Groups in the work setting.

fore an offer is made to the applicant, the interviewer (N) and the College Recruitment Coordinator must obtain approval about the appropriate salary level for such a position from the Coordinator—Managerial Compensation.

A person may be a member of several system groups at the same time. Of course, as the number of involvements with others outside the formal departmental assignment increases, the person may experience many conflicting pressures from the different sources. Like a department, a system group may be relatively permanent. Unlike a department, it is usually not a self-contained supervisory unit, nor does it have an administrative support function.

Temporary Work Groups

A special group might be formed to solve a particular problem or work on a project. The group designated [B] in Figure 6.2 might be the temporary group designated to negotiate the union contract for the company. This negotiating group is made up of the personnel director, the compensation supervisor, the recruitment supervisor, the safety and health supervisor, the labor relations supervisor, and the coordinators of operative compensation, collective bargaining, and the grievance systems.

Temporary work groups have a life that coincides with the length of time the problem it is created to solve exists. When the contract is settled, for example, the negotiating group will disband until the next negotiation period. Temporary work groups are particularly common in organic organizations, which use project management structures. Project management structures will be more extensively considered in Chapter 11.

Committees are a special case of the temporary work groups. Committees are contrived groups that generally work in problem-solving, investigating, reporting, idea-development, and perhaps decision-making activities. For example, suppose the company shown in Figure 6.1 must change its current hiring policies to meet affirmative-action requirements. A committee may be formed of the Director of Personnel, the Director of Manufacturing, and the Director of Marketing to determine a new hiring policy. Such a group, with representation from the various functions of the firm, could consider the availability of potential personnel with the different skills required and the future vacancies in each department. Finally, the committee might recommend what general and specific action should be taken to comply with the legal requirements.

NONFORMAL GROUPS

Nonformal groups are those fairly persistent relationships among individuals that are not defined or specified by officials and managers in a work organization but still affect members in their work roles. Nonformal group goals may be economic, such as benefits arising from union membership, they may be professional benefits, such as those arising from membership in professional associations, or they may be psychological, such as the social-emotional benefits that a person obtains by the satisfaction of human social needs. The goals of nonformal groups are generally the well-being of individuals, as opposed to the organizational purpose (or task goals of formal groups). Two general categories of nonformal groups are (1) extra-organization groups and (2) friendship groups within the organization.

Extra-organization Groups

Groups of which persons are members that are outside the boundaries of their work organization are ***extra-organizational.*** All employees and managers of an organization share some involvement with extra-organization groups. Family, social clubs, as well as religious and political groups to which one belongs are examples of extra-organization groups. When employees and/or managers in a work organization are members of the same, or similar, extra-organizational groups it is likely that they share common bonds that will have some effect at work. Figure 6.3 illustrates the extra-organizational involvement of several of the staff of a firm. The president belongs to an association of young company presidents, is active in the local Chamber of Commerce, and collects stamps seriously. A member of the legal staff belongs to the American Bar Association, The Kiwanis, and church groups. The worker belongs to a labor union and Jaycees and is a member of city council. All have families.

There are two facets of extra-organization groups that are key to understanding how they affect individuals and the work organization. First, the structure of the external group is determined by its members, independent of the work organization. Incidentally, we call these groups nonformal because their structure is not defined by the work organization but by the external group itself. Nonformal groups, within themselves, may have their own formal structure but this formal structure is not designed or sanctioned by the work organization. Second, some extra-organization groups seek to exert pressures on the work organization, particularly with respect to the external group members. The amount of pressure and success in exerting it varies. Unions, for example, often have a very significant impact on work practices, as well as the pay of members, when they represent a work group. Professional

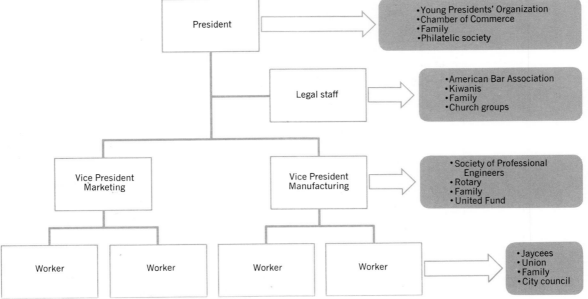

FIGURE 6.3   Extra-organizational group affiliations of organization members.

associations, like the American Bar Association, have codes of ethics and standards that presumably govern members' work practices in the firm that employs the members. Some professional associations determine "accreditation standards" that must be met by schools that train people who join the profession. Some external organizations have screening and approval mechanisms, like the medical practice exams for physicians or the bar examinations for lawyers.

The effects of other extra-organization groups on the work organization may be less extreme. For instance, family problems interfere with one's work but, by and large, there are no concerted efforts made by such groups to affect the policies and practices of the work organization.

Internal Friendship Groups.

Oftentimes individuals form friendship groups with others who work in the same firm. Members of friendship groups interact with each other because they find it relatively pleasant and satisfying. Friendship groups cut easily across formal subunit boundaries. For example, in Figure 6.1, the Supervisor of Recruitment, the Coordinator of Collective Bargaining, A, F, and V may constitute a friendship group.

Later in this chapter we will show how friendship groups form an informal communication network, the grapevine. Information that may not be available in the department where one works may be obtained from friends in other departments.

A GROUP EFFECTS MODEL

One of the more interesting and informative accounts of how groups affect members is a research study by Donald Roy called "Banana Time—Job Satisfaction and Informal Interaction.[3] Roy became a participant observer in a group of factory machine operators for a two-month period. His report is an analysis of how "one group of machine operators kept from 'going nuts' in a situation of monotonous work activity." What he uncovered is that the workers had developed a very systematic, predictive pattern of relationships which affected their satisfaction, individual performance and productivity.

The work was repetitive and dull,

> standing all day in one spot . . . looking through barred windows at the bare walls of a brick warehouse, leg movements largely restricted . . . hand and arm movements confined, for the most part, to a simple repetitive sequence of place the die— punch the clicker—place the die—punch the clicker, and intellectual activity reduced to computing the hours to quitting time.

Roy soon became aware of all sorts of other things going on. Workers did not simply stand at their machine all day and "place the die—punch the clicker—place the die—punch the clicker." He found that the work day was broken up into "times" and each "time" had a fairly regular theme. "Times" were often, but not always, announced by one of the group. Peach time was the first of the day when peaches brought to work were shared among the group after a call of "peach time!" by one of the workers. Then came banana time. Window time was next, followed by lunch time, pick-up time, cake time, and fish time.

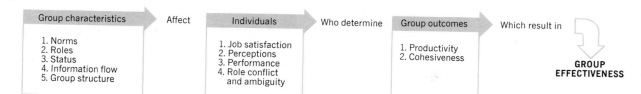

FIGURE 6.4 A model of group characteristics, individual effects, and group outcomes.

During these "times" the workers talked about various themes, and particular individuals had particular roles. For example, "kidding themes" were usually started by one of two specific workers. There were "serious themes" and "play themes" and the "professor theme." In the "professor theme" one worker, whose daughter had married a professor's son, described how he and the professor got along together, what they talked about, or the children of the professor's son and the worker's daughter.

This work group study, rich in detail, illustrates the relationships between the various aspects of our **group effects model. Roles, norms, status,** and **structure** within the group are clearly apparent. The relationship between these different aspects of the group effects model and how the individual feels about the job is shown when one worker was absent and the "times" got confused. For example, the "professor theme" was always started by a worker named George. On one day it was initiated by another worker, Ike, and the discussion drastically changed. George's discussion of the "professor" always turned on the professor's high-status profession. Ike started the "professor theme" by exclaiming that he had seen the professor teaching at a barber college. George, a key person in the group, became outraged, sore. George's bad feeling spread to others and there was a good deal of dissatisfaction within the group.

In the remainder of this chapter we discuss the group effects model in detail to provide a set of analytical concepts that can be used to understand "Banana Time," and "The Bank-Wiring Room." The group effects model is shown in Figure 6.4.

CHARACTERISTICS OF GROUPS

Groups, like individuals, can be described along certain dimensions that are characteristic of the group, not of any single member. These group characteristics are (1) norms, (2) roles, (3) status systems, (4) information networks and (5) group structure.

Norms

A norm is an expectation that one person has about what another person "should do." Norms are rules, of a sort, and standards that govern the conduct of group members. They are ideas that others have about how another "should" behave. In this sense, they are behavioral expectations. A norm is a guide to what behavior is acceptable. For instance, it may be perfectly appropriate—consistent with the norm—for a quality control supervisor to give instructions to one of her inspection

Groups in Organizations

133

staff in her office. However, there may be another norm against giving these instructions in the presence of lower-level workers. When both the supervisor and the inspector are aware of and comply with the norms, the interaction will be rather smooth and easy. If the norm is "violated" there will be problems as was the case in the Bank Wiring Room when workers violated the "production" norm set by the group.

Norms will be congruent with the values that permeate a group. They are a means of social control, as well as of evaluating the behavior of others. Norms guide an individual as to what to do and what not to do with others in the group and outside it.

LEARNING OF NORMS. Norms are learned in a variety of ways. They may be learned by simple observation of other group members, by being directly taught, or by conditioning. Conditioning occurs as a result of reinforcement from other group members. When, for instance, a new member works at too fast a pace the first day on the job, he may be subjected to derogatory comments such as, "Look at old speed king there," "Look who's trying to make us look bad," "Look who's trying to impress the foreman," "Look who's trying to make us lose our jobs," and so on. A little of this goes a long way in obtaining compliance with group norms.

Norms of a group are enforced by sanctioning violators. Sanctions may range from communications of disapproval, such as those cited above, to social ostracism, threats, and actual physical attacks, pranks, and the direct sabotage of another's equipment, raw materials, or finished goods. For example, in a steel mill a work team found that the previous shift filled the furnace with grit each morning until they reduced their level of production to the norm of the other furnace teams. A worker in a sweater factory found that other workers cut his yarn and damaged his machine when he worked at a pace which they considered too fast.

Some norms are more important than others. Schein calls the most important norms—those that must be accepted by all organizational members—pivotal norms.[4] The peripheral norms are less important. Compliance with them may be desired, but is not essential.

FACTORS AFFECTING THE LEVEL OF COMPLIANCE. There are usually varying degrees of compliance to group norms. Some individual members are quite conforming, while others are not. A number of personal characteristics seem to be related to susceptibility to group influence. One such personal characteristic is the degree of identification with the group. Some individuals identify strongly with a group, while others do not. A higher level of education or being of higher social class than most other workers may generate less conformity. In the Bank Wiring Observation Room study, the individual who violated the group norms had a higher level of education and was older than the other group members.

Since most organizational members are the members of several groups, when the norms and values of the other groups conflict with those of organizational groups, a problem is created. This problem often becomes a matter of which group the organizational member primarily identifies with. The group with which an individual identifies most strongly is a primary reference group—the one to which he or she looks for guidance in behavior and attitudes. Some research has indicated that the professionals in an organization, such as scientists, engineers, and economists, are more likely to identify strongly with their professional colleagues outside the firm. They may, of course, be less loyal to the firm than are managers.

Certain personality characteristics seem to be associated with the degree with which people comply with norms. Individuals with low levels of security or with a fear of being different are likely to be more responsive to group influence than are individuals who do not mind being regarded as different.

One's status in the group also influences norm conformity. The lower a person's status in the group, the less the other group members expect of him. In general, individuals in high-status positions are expected to be models of conformity to group norms.

Role and Position

Norms define the kind of behavior another person should exhibit. The behavior sequences of an individual's interaction with others is called a "role." ("Role prescription" is another way to define norm.) In a group, formal or nonformal, an individual may interact with several others. For instance, at work a quality control manager may interact with subordinates, other managers, her secretary, and other secretaries. The manager's relationship with subordinates is one role. The relationship of a manager with fellow managers is another role. Each of these different role partners have expectations (or norms) about how the manager should act. These several roles are shown in Figure 6.5.

All of an individual's group roles, as a cluster, define that individual's position. The related roles performed by an individual in a group locate her in relation to others "with respect to the job to be done, and the giving and taking of orders."[5]

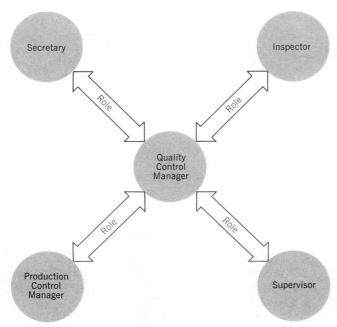

FIGURE 6.5   **Roles and positions—the role set.**

Thus, the position of quality control manager is defined, at the minimum, by the role relationships shown in Figure 6.5.

Since different individuals may occupy the same position at different times, it is expected that there would be some differences in role behavior between individuals in the same position, but also much similarity. Role behavior would depend upon the role incumbent's own personal characteristics and his or her perceptions of what others expect in the behavior of a person in his or her position, as well as the demands of others. Behavior of different individuals in the same position would be similar in many ways because of the expectations of others, and would be different in many ways because of differences in abilities and personality. In the Bank Wiring Observation Room, there were two inspectors, and they perceived their roles quite differently, one ingratiating himself with the group and not carrying out his officially assigned duties, the other acting quite officiously and informing on the men.

An individual may have many roles simultaneously, but in any particular instant of time it may be that only one role is activated. Which one it is depends upon with which group an individual is acting at the time and with which individuals he is interacting.

The roles that an individual may have vary from one group to another and from one group member to another. At times an individual is the superior and at other times, a subordinate. At times one is expected to provide information, and at times to receive information. At times a person must make a decision, and at times must carry out another person's decision. And at yet other times, of course, an individual may be a parent, a Little League umpire, or the secretary of the local bridge club.

Status

Role relationships are defined in terms of interaction between incumbents of positions. Roles may also be different in terms of status within the group. Status refers to the hierarchical ranking of roles in a group so that some roles may be said to be "higher" than or "superior" to others. Such distinctions may be functions of "skill, wealth, power, popularity."[6]

Individuals may have high or low status because they belong to particular professions (such as the medical), have particular formal positions (such as the vice president), have particularly important skills for the group (such as a computer programmer), or have achieved recognition in other areas (such as a person retired from baseball). Having high status gives one a set of rights and obligations. For example, individuals in high-status positions have the right to make suggestions to individuals occupying lower positions. At the same time they may have an obligation to provide certain types of advice and help incumbents of lower-status positions. In the Bank Wiring Observation Room, the higher-status wiremen always initiated the request to change jobs with the lower-status soldermen. For a solderman to initiate such a request would be considered inappropriate behavior for a person in the low-status position. In addition, the soldermen obtained lunches for the higher-ranked group members and otherwise behaved in a way appropriate for their social ranking.

The deference to those of higher status is clearly seen in the practice of bowing common in the prescribed interactions with royalty in some European countries. One is expected to bow when introduced to various members of royal family.

Similarly, in the Orient, Japanese businessmen typically bow when being introduced to each other. The depth of the bow is determined by the relative status differences among the individuals introducing themselves. When two or more Japanese businessmen meet each other they first exchange business cards, which contain information as to the bearer's job title or rank. Then the lower ranked person tends to give the deepest bow to the other as a sign of respect and deference.

Deference to higher status or authority seems to come about through socialization. Probably deference to higher authority is conditioned through the emotion of fear since individuals learn that authority figures can harm them in a variety of ways.

The status of an individual is often unclear without some obvious symbols of status and authority. Organizations confer authority or status on certain individuals through job titles, special clothes or uniforms, privileges, salary levels, sizes of offices, richness of office furnishings, and by other means. Given the influence of such status indicators on patterns of relationships among individuals, it is not surprising to observe the concern of organizational members with such status symbols. Tremendous amounts of effort and energy are often expended on obtaining larger desks or offices or more expensive office furnishings. In informal groups, an individual's status is not as obvious and must be determined through behaviors themselves; certain individuals attempt to dominate others and other individuals appear to accept or not to accept these domination efforts.

Information Networks

The pattern of information flow among members of a group is the communication network. The basic process that links one group member to others is interaction, an action–reaction sequence. In interaction, information (or a message) is transmitted from one person to another. Communication occurs when the information is understood by the recipient.

Because a key element of interaction is communication, it is quite logical to consider groups in terms of the information flows between members. The information flow will be affected not only by what the content of the information is, that is, who is supposed to know what, but also by the way the group has developed—who sees whom and how frequently. Information flows take on different patterns in the different types of groups. For example, the flow of task-oriented (work) information is more predictable in a department with its formal structure than in a loosely knit friendship group.

NETWORKS IN FORMAL GROUPS. The majority of information that flows through the formal channels is intended to trigger the task-oriented work in the different organization subsystems. Messages travel through this formal structure generally to

1. Provide information about how one job is related to another job.
2. Give instructions about how to perform a task
3. Provide evaluative feedback about how well individuals have done their jobs
4. Motivate individuals to perform better
5. Justify decisions made by managers at higher organization levels.

Figure 6.6 shows this flow, which corresponds to the form of the designed structure.

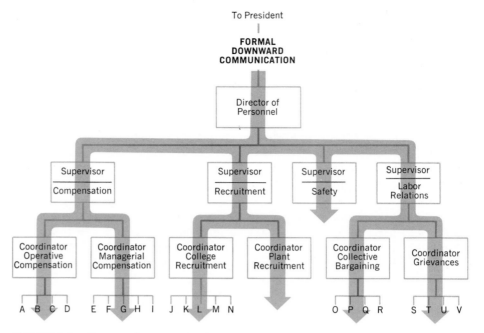

FIGURE 6.6   Ownward communication.

The formal organization system is a very effective information conduit. A good deal of information will flow along according to the lines of authority identified in the formal structure. For example, in Figure 6.6 information about changes in managerial pay policies may be transmitted from the Personnel Director to the Supervisor—Compensation to the Coordinator of Managerial Compensation. However, the same information is unlikely to be found in other channels, say to Coordinator of Collective Bargaining, unless an effort is made to get it to that person in staff meetings, or perhaps through a nonformal channel. If the whole department were formally structured differently, quite a different information flow would occur.

Some information flows laterally between units. For example, coordination between the supervisors of Compensation, Recruitment, Safety and Health, and Labor Relations is necessary for managing certain personnel problems, as may be the case where these managers are part of a team formed to negotiate a labor contract with a union.

Some formal communications flow upward, but upward formal communication differs sharply from the downward type. Most upward communication is for control purposes. It is intended to provide managers at middle and higher levels of the organization with data to compare the performance of those at lower levels to plans. Reports of production levels, quality, and compliance with policies and regulation make up a large proportion of upward communication. Mechanisms such as management and accounting information systems are designed to channel this information flow upward.

Few communication channels exist to transmit information on the attitudes of lower-level personnel upward. Many human problems at lower levels never find their way to higher organization levels because no way exists to get this information there. There are some conduits such as grievance procedures, employee surveys, and open door policies, but they are not as effective transmitting up the organization as are those channels that transmit downward.

COMMUNICATION AND NONFORMAL GROUPS. The communication networks of each nonformal group is different from that of others. Extra-organizational groups that represent employees of the organization seek to establish a formal upward communication channel with it. A union, for example, that represents the work force has union stewards who are always in the work place to protect the interests of employees. The union contract specifies who is to represent the union in negotiation and generally how these negotiations are to be conducted.

Other extra-organizational groups have less formal, but often influential, links with an organization. The American Medical Association sets standards for its members, but rarely is directly involved with the operation of, say, a hospital or clinic. Other extra-organizational groups may have very little relationship with the work organization. Social organizations, such as the Kiwanis, Rotary, and Jaycees (see Figure 6.3) rarely get involved in work organizations. Neither do families or other social groups outside the work organization.

Friendship groups within the work organization have communication systems that are extremely effective information transmission mechanisms. For example, the Coordinator of Collective Bargaining may obtain information about the impending pay change mentioned above because he is in the same friendship group as the Supervisor of Compensation, even though he is not in the formal communication network.

Information moves very quickly through friendship groups, and because friendship groups in an organization overlap, the information may spread very widely and rapidly through the organization. Figure 6.7 shows how friendship groups might

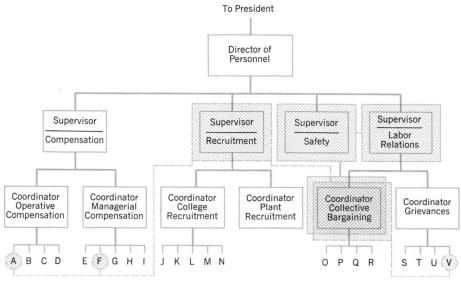

FIGURE 6.7   Overlapping friendship groups—communication links.

overlap. The Coordinator of Collective Bargaining is in two friendship groups. One group contains the Supervisor of Safety and Health and the Supervisor of Labor Relations. The second friendship group includes the Supervisor of Recruiting and persons A, F, and V.

Information usually flows very rapidly through friendship groups because of the inability of the formal structure to satisfy the information needs of personnel. This would be especially true of compensation issues since nearly all employees are concerned about their wages and salary. Potential changes in the pay structure may be threatening, especially when people are not sure how these changes will affect them. To satisfy this information gap, rumors will develop. The rumors will not only explain the change in pay policy, but also reduce the anxiety associated with the change.

Rumors explain uncertainty and relieve individual tension. The speed of rumors "concerning a given subject matter will circulate in proportion to the importance and the ambiguity of this subject matter in the lives of the individual members of the group."[7] You can expect rumors to spread when members of an organization feel unclear about work roles, pay, promotion, and the like. Rumors will fly with wild abandon whenever there is insecurity about an important facet of work; rumors are rampant during impending layoffs, strikes, cutbacks in the work force, and similar threatening events.

Even though rumors do not flow through "formal channels," they are very accurate. The *grapevine* is a term for the channel through which rumor flows. Studies of the grapevine show that rumors about work-related information may be as high as 75 percent correct. There may be an 80 to 90 percent accuracy rate for noncontroversial information. People *think* the grapevine is less accurate because "errors are more dramatic and consequently more impressed on memory than its day-by-day routine accuracy."[8]

The most predominant grapevine pattern is the cluster chain shown in Figure 6.8. In a cluster chain, information is passed from one person, say the supervisor of recruitment, to several others (Persons A, F, V and the Coordinator of Collective Bargaining). The Coordinator of Collective Bargaining then tells the Supervisor of Safety and Health and the Supervisor of Labor Relations. From this research, it seems that only a few persons in the network pass on information, others do not. Those who pass on information are called "liaison" individuals.[8]

Group Structure

The work and non-work activities of the machine operators in "Banana Time" were very predictable. The "times" occurred regularly and were generally initiated in the same way by the same person. Information networks, norms roles, and the status of each worker were known by the others. When there was a deviation from regular practice, the group members became suspicious. *Group structure* is the term we use to describe how predictably these different elements (norms, roles, networks, and status) are related to each other.

When the interaction patterns among members are predictable with a great degree of accuracy, as in "Banana Time," there is said to be a **high group structure.**

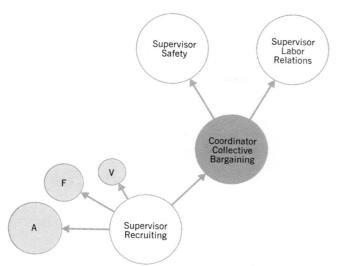

FIGURE 6.8   The cluster chain grapevine model.

When interaction patterns are less predictable and are not quite so clear to members, there is *low group structure.*

In a highly structured group, there will be little tolerance by the members when a person deviates from the norms. This is so because the members learn to depend on one another to do as expected. It is obvious that in highly structured groups an individual does not have much freedom or latitude to act in ways different than expected by others. When Ike, of the "Banana Time" group, violated the group norm that George should introduce the "professor theme," it led to hard feelings in the group for thirteen days. Such is the control of member behavior in highly structured groups. Everyone knows what should be done and who should do it. There should be little deviation.

When group structure is very low, it is correspondingly difficult to predict what others will do. This ambiguity may be unsettling, particularly to new members. When there is low group structure, members will seek to develop some degree of certainty so they can be relatively comfortable in carrying out the group roles.

The predictability of interaction patterns in groups can arise from different sources, such as *job descriptions, organization charts,* and *procedures* of the formal organization. These specify who is to do what and to whom they must report. *Charges of responsibilities* to committees and the *assignment of a special project* to a temporary work group also defines work group relationships.

The source of structure in nonformal groups is the social interaction of the members. As a person finds it reinforcing to engage in continued interaction with others, behavior patterns develop that may become very stable. Of course, when stable nonformal patterns develop along with very specific and detailed formal group specifications, the group structure can be very high, such as in the "Banana Time" group.

The second facet of the group effects model highlights *individual* reactions to group involvement. In this section we will describe the effects of groups on job satisfaction, perceptions, performance, and role conflict and ambiguity.

Job Satisfaction

The evidence seems clear that workers who are accepted as members of industrial work groups have higher job satisfaction.[9,10] Other studies show that as opportunities to interact with other workers are diminished, job satisfaction decreases.[11] Satisfaction seems to be higher in smaller groups. This is logical, since in large groups it is difficult to interact frequently with most members. A study of 228 industrial work groups in a machinery company found less anxiety among workers in highly cohesive groups.[12] There is other evidence that shows that individuals feel less tension and anxiety when they associate with others more frequently.[13]

Perception

Perception is the way we organize the things that we observe. Groups can affect perception or the way that reality is organized in significant ways. There are several classic studies that demonstrate these group effects very clearly. In one study a group of people were asked to each make and record an individual judgment about the length of several lines that all of them were shown. A large majority of the group had been coached to say that, for example, line A was the shortest when in fact line B was shorter. Initially the subjects reported that line B was shorter, but after being exposed to the group for a period of time eventually changed their report to conform to the majority.

Another study demonstrated how managers' perceptions of the "most important problem" are related to the departmental affiliation. This study illustrates how formal departmental assignment affects perceptions. In a management development program, a group of mid-level executives from sales, production, accounting, and staff departments were presented a complex written case to solve. They were asked to indicate which was the "most important problem" to be solved in the case. Their responses were closely related to their departmental affiliation. Generally, from the same set of facts, sales people identified a "marketing" problem, production executives identified an "organization" problem, the staff executives thought "human problems" were the most critical. The study's conclusion is that "each executive will perceive those aspects of a situation that relate specifically to the activities and goals of his department."[14]

Performance

The group can also affect a person's level of performance success. Seashore, in the study of industrial work groups,[12] found that attitude toward management was an important determinant of whether performance norms for a group were set at high or low levels. The Bank Wiring Room Study shows production norms, set by a work group and possibly different from standards set by management, having an effect on production.

Being with other people instead of being alone may improve or have a negative effect on performance. Everyone is familiar with assertions from the entertainment world that a receptive audience makes an actor better or that playing on the "home field" is an advantage in sports. Shaw[15] says that the "mere presence of others increases the motivational level of a performing individual when the person expects to be evaluated."

Social facilitation occurs when the person's level of performance increases in the presence of others. This is most likely to happen when persons are performing tasks that they have previously learned. So, in cases where people are doing things in which they have already developed competence, being in a group will likely have positive results, assuming such individuals are concerned about how others will evaluate them.

Social inhibition[16] occurs when the presence of others inhibits, or diminishes, performance. Such inhibition may occur when group members are learning new tasks or trying things that they do not do well. Anxieties brought about by the presence of others may have the effect of lowering performance.

Whether or not a person even shows up at work seems related to one aspect of the group; its size. Turnover and absenteeism are greater in larger groups than in smaller ones. This is not surprising since there is also higher individual dissatisfaction in larger grops and the level of satisfaction is negatively related to turnover/absenteeism. It is likely that individuals in smaller groups will feel that the presence will be more likely to affect the well-being of others than would be the case in a larger group.

Role Conflict and Ambiguity

Role conflict and ambiguity are stresses to which an individual is exposed in groups and which can affect the way group members perform and feel.[5]

Role conflict occurs when a person is subjected to inconsistent demands with respect to his behavior. There are several types of role conflict. *Intersender role conflict* occurs when the inconsistent demands come from different individuals in the role set. The quality control manager whose role is illustrated in Figure 6.5 may experience intersender role conflict if her supervisor asks her to present a forecast of monthly production levels for a meeting the next morning at the same time that she is supposed to hold a staff planning meeting called by her own work staff. She will, obviously, be unable to be in both places at the same time.

Intrasender role conflict occurs when the inconsistent demands come from the same source, as when the quality control manager expects a subordinate to complete an inspection project that requires more personnel to do it, but at the same time refuses to assign added staff to the subordinate's unit. The subordinate is in a position of intrasender role conflict generated by the manager.

Interrole conflict exists when a person outside the role set imposes demands that cause problems within it. The family of a manager may expect the manager to spend time with them, rather than at the office, thus inducing role conflict.

Person-role conflict occurs when the demands in the role are inconsistent with the individual's own value system. This problem could occur, for example, in cases when a work assignment calls for a legal but perhaps unethical activity that the person feels is wrong. Role conflicts exist in all organizations, and people learn to adapt to some moderate levels. Organization structures that define jobs and accountability are efforts to minimize this condition.

The condition in which individuals may not be clear as to what the role requirements are—that is, they may not know precisely what to do—is called **role ambiguity.** Two types of role ambiguity may exist. Ambiguity with regard to what behavior, or task, is expected is called **task ambiguity.** Or a person may be unclear about what others think of him. This may be related to how his supervisor rates him or what his status in a group is. This type of role ambiguity is sometimes called **social-emotional ambiguity.**

SOURCES OF ROLE CONFLICT AND AMBIGUITY. There are several causes of role conflict and ambiguity. Perhaps an individual is a new group member. It will take some time to "learn the ropes." Or role relationships may be unclear due to rapidly changing membership in a group. There may be high role ambiguity when there is rapid growth or change in an organization. Role conflict may be high, for example, when the organization structure must be constantly changed to accommodate developing markets or changing technology. Role conflict and role ambiguity tend to be higher in the organic organization than in the mechanistic organization. In the organic organization, organizational members may work for several supervisors rather than one, as in the mechanistic organization, and this may increase the problem of social-emotional ambiguity. Also, in the organic organization individuals may be assigned to several different projects and work teams at the same time. This makes it more difficult for a person to be aware of his or her roles or responsibilities since they might be expected to be different from one group or another.

Person-role, interrole, and intersender conflict may also be higher in the organic than in the mechanistic organization. The person-role conflict may come about through a professional being made a supervisor. Professionals may experience inconsistencies between their responsibilities to the organization and their professional values. Some research shows that professionals feel that managers often act in ways that are unethical.[17] Research also shows that organic organizations may require much more involvement from their members than mechanistic organizations, especially when individuals are in a managerial role.[18] These organizational requirements may interfere with home and community roles. We might also expect more intersender role conflict in the organic organization than in the mechanistic since the individual may be required to work on several project teams, each with its own supervisor.

GROUP OUTCOMES

In our group effects model the various dimensions of groups (roles, communication networks, status relationships, and group structure) are related to productivity and cohesiveness. The "Banana Time" workers developed, for example, social relationships with each other that were more complex and intensive than the work relationships that were prescribed by the design of the formal work system. Over time, these intragroup relationships (1) were supportive of the level of productivity of the group (they were hardly supervised at all—there was little need for it since their production met standards); (2) helped the group work through a crisis when the "times" did not take place as the members had come to expect; and (3) gave the group a sense of identity that was different from both managerial groups and other work groups.

"Cohesiveness"

Cohesiveness refers to the hold a group has on its members. How important the group is for its members is related to the ability of the group to maintain itself, or continue to exist, when it is subjected to pressures and stress.[19] Some groups are closely knit, while others are much less so. A number of factors have been found to be associated with group cohesiveness. Size is an obvious factor; other factors being equal, smaller groups are generally more cohesive than larger. Interaction opportunities contribute to cohesiveness. In many organizations it may be quite difficult for members to talk to each other or be in close contact. Noise, physical separation by machinery, and other similar factors may limit interaction.

Cohesiveness generally increases as a group experiences success in its collective activities. Repeated failure often leads to internal dissension and bickering within a group, but if a group is successful in meeting its objectives, pride in being a member may increase, and members may increase their commitment to the group. External attacks and pressure may also greatly increase group cohesiveness. To meet a common threat, the members will pull together.

Personal characteristics of members may also influence group cohesiveness. Individuals with similar backgrounds are likely to have common values and are therefore less likely to disagree. A common background may contribute to patterns of similar interests, making communication easier. Similar backgrounds may make individuals more comfortable in one another's presence.

Status factors are also important. If one believes his professional, ethnic, or racial group is superior to those of others, he may not want to associate with those believed to be of lower status. Also, persons may not want to associate with others whose status is ambiguous, because the uncertainty makes them uncomfortable. Status congruence means the degree to which the factors associated with group status line up with respect to each other for a particular individual.[20] A person has high status congruence if his personal characteristics are consistent in placing him at a high-, a middle-, or a low-status position in the status hierarchy. Low-status congruence means there are inconsistencies with respect to such factors. The important factor is consistency.

Productivity

All groups produce something. We call this outcome of group effort ***productivity.*** Productivity results from the task performance (required behavior) by the members on the resources used by them. Since the group comes together to create values (or results) that a single person alone cannot create, productivity is a result that can be greater than the sum of the individual contributions. For example, to provide social and welfare services for a community, government agencies (formal groups) are created that bring together all sorts of specialists in social work, counselors, career advisors, and health support specialists. The underlying premise, of course, is that one hundred organized people can provide social services more efficiently to clients than the hundred people working singly.

Productivity refers to the task-oriented output of a group. It is often the measure used to judge a group's effectiveness. The productivity of a formal work group such as a department, a systems group, or a temporary work group means the product, service, report, or other work-required outcome created. The outcome of a product-planning group might be demand forecasts and raw materials forecasts, which later become the basis for planning and control decisions by other departments.

Nonformal groups also "produce" something. There is "required behavior" in nonformal groups but of a different kind than in formal groups. In formal groups required behavior is related to organizational purpose—product, profit, service, etc. In nonformal groups the required behavior is for the members' purposes. Another way of saying this is that the "required behavior" in a nonformal group in an organization is the "emergent behavior" in the formal group. So a friendship group creates social satisfactions for its members, which is why the group exists. For example, for a friendship group at work that meets at noon to play poker, the "productivity" is the game itself and the enjoyment rising from it.

Differences in productivity can be associated with differences in group factors; one that seems especially important is ***group structure.*** Group structure is thought to have a curvilinear relationship to productivity. Figure 6.9 shows that productivity is highest when there is a moderate level of group structure. When group structure is very low (high unpredictability), productivity is low because group members spend too much time trying to figure out what to do and less time doing it. At the other extreme, high group structure, there is also lower productivity because the work relationships and requirements are so well defined that they are too restrictive. When there is high group structure the group may have trouble adapting to even very minor changes. When the very high structure of the "Banana Time" group was disturbed by a change in the "professor theme," the disruption lasted thirteen days.

We must point out, though, that individual characteristics such as skills, abilities, and motivations of individual members are important determinants of how

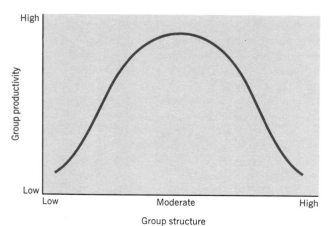

FIGURE 6.9   Relationship between group structure and productivity.

much a group can produce. A well-organized group of outstanding salespersons will almost always produce more than an equally well-organized group of average performers. On the other hand, a poorly organized group of highly skilled performers may perform at a significantly lower level than a better organized group of low-ability performers.

Groups in
Organizations

Interrelationships Between Cohesiveness and Productivity

One of the most important factors determining group productivity is cohesiveness. That is because when the work within a group is interdependent, helping behavior among the members may greatly contribute to productivity. Helping behavior is especially important when the tasks are complex and variable and individuals need the assistance of others to solve them. This assistance may be in the form of physical help or mental assistance in the form of ideas or suggestions. A study in a steel company showed that a more cohesive furnace room was more productive than another room low in cohesiveness because its members were more willing to help one another when something went wrong with one of the blast furnaces.[21] Similarly, the combat effectiveness of military units has been related to the cohesiveness of those units and the resulting helping behavior.[22] Cohesiveness is critical to miners because of the work problems and the hazards they face in their work locations. The work problems in underground mines are quite variable and dangerous, depending on factors such as soil composition, types of rock formations, the presence of water, and so on. There are many dangers in underground mining such as fire, gas, smoke, explosion, and roof collapse. When problems emerge in the mine, workers must get help from their fellow miners. Helping behavior is very functional for the miner, and work group cohesiveness tends to be very high among underground miners. Groups of surface workers in mining companies, on the other hand, are less cohesive. Surface miners do not put the emphasis on good work group interrelationships that the underground miners do.[23]

Group cohesiveness also influences productivity when the work is independent. This occurs through control of individual output as a result of norm adherence, as shown in the Bank Wiring Room experiment.

When there is high group cohesiveness there is less variability in individual performance than when it is low. The group, however, may exert a positive or negative effect on productivity depending on whether they attempt to raise the productivity of the lower-producing individuals or attempt to decrease the performance of the members with greater ability or motivation.

When the task of a group is planning and innovation and not physical output, high cohesiveness may prove detrimental. Research shows that high cohesiveness in a group contributes to lower rates of innovation and creativity.[24] Highly cohesive groups often emphasize solidarity over creativity and negatively reinforce new ways of behaving and thinking.[25] They become "frozen" groups and may overemphasize "group think." In group think, emphasis is on going along with the rest of the group and protecting the group from new ideas or criticisms of its operations.

Thus, cohesiveness and productivity, two outcomes of groups, are interrelated. Sometimes a manager must make a judgment as to whether cohesiveness or productivity is the more important outcome, particularly when increasing one will decrease the other.

GROUP EFFECTIVENESS

Productivity is a measure of a group's success or its effectiveness. However, effectiveness is a broader concept than productivity. Group effectiveness is the ability of a group to achieve its goals, whatever they may be. Sometimes an effective group is one that produces large numbers of units of output on schedule. Sometimes the group's effectiveness is determined by the quality of the ideas or suggestions it produces. In nonformal groups, effectiveness may be best measured by the satisfaction or degree of individual growth experienced by their members.

The effectiveness of a group can be judged only by its purposes or goals. A group's goal may be to achieve high productivity in a quantity or quality sense. A group's goal may be nothing but cohesiveness itself. In fact, groups have multiple objectives or goals and the group's effectiveness must be assessed by determining the degree to which several goals are simultaneously achieved.

SUMMARY

Organizations are composed of several different types of groups. Some of these are formal groups, such as departments and committees. Other groups are nonformal, such as friendship groups formed simply because certain individuals like each other.

Dimensions that can be used to describe groups are norms, roles, status systems, information networks, and group structure. These factors all affect individuals in groups. Individuals' job satisfaction, perceptions, performance, and stress all have been found to have some important roots in the pressure groups exert on individuals.

The effect of the group can be thought of as being twofold. First, groups produce something, called productivity. Second, groups also create some intensity among the members to "stick together." This result of groups is called cohesiveness.

Case
6.1 Hal Forkins*

Four years ago, Tasty Food Value Co., a regional retail food store, established an Internal Auditing Department to measure the losses it sustained in its stores and warehouses because the company estimated that losses on waste and mishandling of goods were $3 to $5 million annually. The purpose of the Internal Auditing Department was to determine where and why these losses are occurring. To do this, the auditing department established an inventory crew whose objective was to determine the total retail value of goods in each store every six months. Due to a limited budget, the inventory crew employed only part-time workers, with one full-time supervisor. I was one of the first members of this crew.

---

*We express appreciation to Richard Parry, who wrote the original version of this case, for permission to use it.

The Internal Auditing Department set up some guidelines for the operation and control of the inventory crew. The crew consisted of one supervisor and a group of workers. The number of workers on the crew varied, depending upon the size of the store in which the crew was working. The inventories were scheduled to begin at 5:30 P.M. and would continue until the entire store was covered. All crew members were expected to be present from the beginning of the inventory to the end of it. Each individual worker was expected to arrive at the designated store. If they drove, there was no compensation for mileage. The workers were paid an hourly rate. Each punched a time clock at the beginning and at the end of the work period. The workers were given a ten minute rest break. On this break, coffee and assorted pastries were supplied by the supervisor, who was allotted a weekly budget to pay for these items.

Before beginning the inventory, each crew member was given a calculator and a clipboard. Each crew member was assigned a certain aisle within a store. That crew member would then go to the specified aisle with the clipboard and worksheet. Then the crew member sectioned the aisle off into ten to fifteen foot segments. The worker would then start counting the goods on the top shelf of the specified aisle segment, and then work down to the bottom shelf. The worker would count the entire number of each item on the shelves. By punching the item price times the quantity of each item, the worker recorded the total retail value of each item in the memory of a specially designed calculator. Upon the completion of a shelf, the worker could easily determine the total retail value of the shelf. This figure was then recorded. The worker followed this procedure for every shelf in the aisle.

The only requirements for the position of inventory clerk were the ability to count accurately and quickly. Applicants for the position were given a test in the store to determine their ability before they were hired. The crew was usually made up of college students and others who wanted part-time work or a second job. The inventory actually began at 6:30 P.M. and the crew members arrived from their daytime jobs or colleges at that time. All the crew members considered this work to be a secondary job.

There were fifteen members in my inventory group. We were supervised quite loosely. Our supervisor generally allowed the four most senior workers to decide just how each store was to be inventoried. The group really tried hard to finish the inventory as quickly as possible so everyone could go home. The group really put a lot of pressure on anybody who tried to goof off. In spite of the very high productivity of our group, the inventory error rate never exceeded 0.5 percent of the total inventory.

The internal auditing department considers the part-time inventory crew so successful that they plan to organize another group as soon as the company has enough new stores to justify the group's existence.

1. Why does this group perform at such a satisfactory level?
2. What specific factors do you think cause this group to be so productive? What do you think would happen if the group were composed of permanent, regular employees?
3. What are the implications of this case for the management of other groups in this organization?

Case
6.2 National Regulatory Service

The National Regulatory Service, a government regulatory agency, received and evaluated reports sent to them yearly by several hundred thousand U.S. business firms. Like all government agencies, the NRS was charged with the responsibility of upgrading the job status of women and minorities. Many of these individuals had graduated from very poor high schools and their English and quantitative skills were deficient for the higher-level auditor jobs that the agency wanted to open up to minorities.

Two proposals have been made to meet these affirmative action goals. Lisa Berger, director of training, proposed that the agency decided to launch a massive voluntary training program in remedial English and mathematics to its clerical force. However, this proposal was criticized by the organization's human relations officer, Duncan Dickinson. Dickinson proposed that the agency should instead redesign the work that the auditors did. It is possible, he argued, to make the auditor's job easier by simplifying the forms that businesses sent to the government agency.

Lisa Berger protested this decision in a staff meeting. She argued that the training approach would result in more benefits both to the agency and to the individuals than the job redesign approach.

1. Why would the training department and the human relations group take such different views? How can this difference be resolved?
2. How might the views of Lisa Berger and Duncan Dickinson be affected by their work assignments?

DISCUSSION QUESTIONS

1. How did the Hawthorne study contribute to the study of management?
2. What is the Hawthorne effect?
3. What are the basic types of groups in organizations? Which type do you think is most important and why?
4. Why do informal groups emerge in organizations? How do they meet the needs of the organizations and of the individuals in them?
5. How do required and emergent behaviors interact and depend on one another?
6. In which type of formal group do you think you would be most effective? Why?
7. Departments are one of the most important units of organizations. Discuss the types and uses of departments.
8. Discuss how temporary work groups can be the moving forces in an organization.
9. Discuss the influence of organizations to which people belong outside of the work organization.
10. Why should the manager be very aware of norms? Roles? Group pressures? Values?
11. What are communication/information networks and why are they so important to the manager?

12. Discuss the various types of role conflict and the effects they have on the organization.
13. How important is group cohesiveness? How is this related to productivity? Defend your answer.

REFERENCES

1. Roethlisberger, F. J., and W. J. Dickson. Management and the Worker. Cambridge, Harvard University Press, 1939.
2. Seiler, J. A. Systems analysis in organizational behavior. Homewood, Ill., Richard D. Irwin, 1967.
3. Roy, D. "Banana time—job satisfaction and informal interaction." Human Organization 18 (1960): 158–68.
4. Schein, E. Organizational psychology. Englewood Cliffs, N.J., Prentice-Hall, 1970.
5. Katz, D., and R. L. Kahn. The social psychology of organizations, 2 ed. New York, John Wiley, 1978.
6. Newcomb, T. M., R. H. Turner, and P. E. Converse. Social psychology: The study of human interaction. New York, Holt, Rinehart & Winston, 1965.
7. Allport, G. W., and L. J. Postman. "The basic psychology of rumor," in L. Maccoby et al. (eds.), Readings in social psychology, 3rd ed. New York, Holt, Rinehart & Winston, 1958.
8. Davis, K. Human relations at work. New York, McGraw-Hill, 1962.
9. Vroom, V. H. Work and motivation. New York, Wiley, 1964.
10. Helmreich, R., R. Bakerman, and L. Scherwitz. "The study of small groups," Annual Review of Psychology, 24 (1973): 337–354.
11. Jasinski, Frank J. "Technological delimitation of reciprocal relationships: A study of interaction patterns in industry," Human Organization, 15(2) (1956): 24–28.
12. Seashore, S. E. Group cohesiveness in the industrial work group. Survey Research Center, University of Michigan, 1954.
13. Schachter, S. The psychology of affiliation. Stanford, Calif., Stanford University Press, 1959.
14. Dearborn, D. C., and H. A. Simon. "Selective perception: A note on the departmental identification of executives," Sociometry, 21 (1958): 140–144.
15. Shaw, Marvin. The psychology of small groups. New York, McGraw-Hill, 1976.
16. McGinnies, Elliott. Behavior in small groups. Social behavior: A functional analysis. Boston, Houghton Mifflin Company, 1970.
17. Moore, D. G., and R. Renck. "The professional employee in industry," Journal of Business, 28 (1955): 58–66.
18. Burns, T., and G. M. Stalker. The management of innovation. London, Tavistock, 1961.
19. Stogdill, R. M. Individual behavior and group achievement. New York, Oxford University Press, 1959.
20. Zaleznik, A., C. R. Christensen, and F. J. Roethlisberger. The motivation, productivity, and satisfaction of workers: A prediction study. Division of Research, Harvard Business School, 1958.
21. Lawrence, P. R., et al. "Century company," in Organizational behavior and administration. Homewood, Ill., Dorsey Press, 1961.
22. Ginzberg, E. The ineffective soldier. New York, Columbia University Press, 1959.
23. Gouldner, A. Patterns of industrial bureaucracy. New York, Free Press, 1954.
24. Filley, Alan. Interpersonal conflict resolution. Glenview, Ill., Scott Foresman, 1975.
25. Janis, Irving L. Victims of groupthink: A psychological study of foreign policy decisions and fiascos. Boston, Houghton-Mifflin, 1972.

The Managerial Process

The groundwork is now in place so that we can turn to the topic of what managers do and how they should do it. Management process contingency theory is based on the premises that the management process must vary to fit organizational and human considerations, these having been explained in Parts II and III, respectively.

Now we turn to the management process. *Decision Making*, an activity common to everything a manager does, is discussed in Chapter 7. *Planning* and the implementation of plans is the subject of Chapters 8, 9, and 10. *Organizing*, the process of insuring the proper relationships between people and resources, is treated in Chapters 11, 12, and 13. *Leading* and the related topic of motivation are presented in Chapters 14, 15, and 16. *Controlling*, coordinating, and control approaches are discussed in Chapters 17, 18, and 19.

In each of these chapters, we begin with a discussion of key elements of each process. Then we outline what we believe to be the most effective way to apply that process in either organic or mechanistic organizations. For instance, Chapter 14, "Leadership," begins with a discussion of the most popular theories or approaches to leadership. After that discussion, however, we point out the things that we think a manager can do to increase leadership effectiveness in organic and in mechanistic organizations. We hope, with this approach, to make useful prescriptions about what one can do to manage better.

CHAPTER SEVEN

Decision Making

Item
7.1 Penn Electronics

Penn Electronics has successfully produced and marketed electronic components, transistors, and quartz crystals for the last six years. They began in the late 1960s, as did many firms in this growth industry, but unlike many of their competitors that branched into minicomputers, microprocessors, and specialty memory products, Penn continued to produce standard memory chips. Also unlike their competitors, Penn's growth was not spectacular. Penn's sales last year were $150 million and next year were predicted to be $225 million. But Fon-tel, a firm that began the same year as Penn, had achieved sales in excess of $650 million last year. Fon-tel had been more aggressive in the expansion of their product line, and with this came success.

Six months ago, Hayes Woodward was appointed president of Penn Electronics. He replaced the founder, Jim Shaw, who was an electrical engineering genius. Shaw remained as chairman of the board, but Woodward was to assume a very important role in seeking to increase the sales of Penn.

"Woody, I want you to make this company another IBM," Shaw said to Woodward when he was appointed president. Since then, Woody has spent most of his time working on several alternative plans for Penn.

Two major projects, Woody thought, had to be undertaken. First, it was necessary to expand the product line. Penn had to get new products into new markets. Failure to take advantage of past opportunities was the reason that Penn had never been one of the glamour electronic growth stocks that was the "recommendation of Wall Street brokers."

Second, Woody knew that the plant had to be expanded. Their current production facilities could handle customer requirements and normal growth for another two years, but if he had any degree of success with new products, Penn would need another plant and it would have to be started soon.

Woody had two very important decisions to make. What new products should Penn Electronics seek to develop? Where should the new plant be located?

Every aspect of a manager's job involves making choices. "What resources are necessary to accomplish an objective?" "How much can be allocated to a project?" "Who should perform a job?"

Decision making is the act of choosing from among alternatives—coming to a conclusion about what should be done in a particular situation. In itself, the act of choice is not particularly difficult, like deciding to call "heads" or "tails" when a coin is flipped. What is difficult is to make a good decision. Making a good decision means that the choice that we make maximizes the likelihood that our choice will result in the most desirable outcome for the decision maker.

To make good decisions regularly we believe that persons should follow a sequential set of steps, each one of which will make the following step more likely to be successful. These steps are:
1. Recognizing a problem
2. Diagnosing causes of problems
3. Generating alternatives
4. Selecting alternatives and
5. Implementing decisions

These steps have long been thought to comprise the decision process by decision theorists[1,2] and by researchers studying decision making.[3] Over a period of five years, a research team studied twenty-five strategic decisions made in different types of organizations.[3] Among the decisions studied were whether or not to employ a new form of treatment by a hospital; acquire jet aircraft for a regional airline; purchase new equipment for a hospital; develop a new TV program; produce a new beer in a brewery; introduce a new container terminal in a port; develop a new market for a deodorant; implement an urban renewal program; construct a new building for a college; and build a new plant for a firm.

After studying these strategic decisions and the process by which they were made, Mintzberg and his fellow researchers identified stages in decision making which are similar to those listed above. The act of choosing, that is, selecting an alternative, is embedded in the several other necessary important steps of decision making. If managers do not go through this sequence, they are likely to make a decision that will solve the wrong problem.

RECOGNIZING A PROBLEM

This first step in the decision process is recognizing situations in which a decision is required because an opportunity, a problem, or a crisis exists.[3] A crisis or a severe problem is likely to be quite noticeable, generally will engage a fairly large number of people in seeking a solution, and demands immediate attention. The coal strike of 1977–78 became a crisis when stockpiles were running low and there was no apparent agreement in sight. A crisis occurred for one large automobile manufacturer when there was not sufficient cash on hand to meet current debts and payroll. The crisis was alleviated by a large loan to obtain the necessary cash. Then the firm had another problem to solve. It had to restructure its financial situation to repay the large debt incurred. Crises occur in firms in the defense industry when government spending is cut back without notice. On the individual level, a crisis may be exemplified when a person has a very serious, obviously unforeseen, auto accident.

Opportunities and problems, on the other hand, are often not so obvious; yet the firm that is most successful in the long run will be the one that can deal with problems and opportunities most effectively. Thus, a major responsibility of a manager is to seek out opportunities in the mass of information that confronts him or her every day. One major manufacturer in the United States, for example, has a reputation among its competitors for being very deep in management talent. The company achieves this by careful manpower planning. When an industry experiences a recession, it allows personnel attrition to cut back the work force, but during such periods, the company will remain overstaffed in managers in order to maintain the quality of its management for periods of resurgence. Competitors, on the other hand, reduce their work force by firings and layoffs. When business picks up again, the competitors are scurrying to build their managerial and technical staffs, while the first firm has its team well in place.

WHAT IS A PROBLEM?

A problem exists, and therefore a decision is necessary, when there is a difference between **what is** (or **will be**) happening in a particular situation and **what should be** happening, defined by a goal, a standard, or an expectation. When this difference between "should be" and "is" is large enough, something must be done to reduce it. We make a decision so that things will be different than they presently are, or are likely to be in the future.

Some situations (a current crisis or a current problem) demand immediate improvement in the situation. Other situations involve anticipated problems or opportunities that may call for a present action. Sometimes the achievement of a future desired state (what should be) requires a long sequence of interrelated and well-planned steps, as when a business organization wishes to develop and market a new product. The development, design, and marketing of the Polaroid SX-70 Instant Camera took several years and very large investment of capital.

In identifying **what should be,** both explicit and implicit performance standards may be used. An explicit standard is objective, obvious, and often expressed in quantitative terms. Rates of return, scrap rates, and cost standards are explicit standards. A subjective, or implicit standard, is in the brain of the observer and may not even be formally stated. A subjective standard is a "feeling" of what would be. Good morale, better leadership, or better customer relationships are examples of implicit standards. Standards are typically based on the past experience of the organization or manager, what is being accomplished in comparable organizations, or expectations of the manager or his superior, which may stem from the individual's personality, motives, or degree of self-confidence.

Objective standards make it easier to identify problems. With subjective standards different individuals will disagree about the existence and severity of problems.

Which Problems to Solve?

Just because a situation is identified as a problem does not mean something must be done in order to solve it. Problems abound in an ongoing organization, and managers, with limited time, must continually make choices about which problems to try to solve now and which problems can be worked on later.

Several guidelines have been proposed to rate problems in terms of the priority for solution.[2] One consideration is the problem's **potential** for becoming more serious. Some problems, if left unattended, will grow worse while others will not. In other words, we must look at the trend suggested by the problem. Because a machine turns out a particularly high rate of low-quality products in a period does not mean, necessarily, that maintenance is needed. We would want to see if this trend is increasing. If it is, then we should do something; otherwise it may be better to wait to take further action.

Another consideration is how a problem is **related to other potential problems** in the organization. Those are problems that, if not solved, will create other difficulties in different parts of the organization. A quality defect that occurs in an operation at the beginning of an assembly line may be reflected in slower production times and more rejects at later stages in the assembly process.

Still another consideration in determining problem priority is the **time constraint.** An order that is due to be delivered tomorrow must have a higher priority than an order for next week.

Problems can also be viewed in terms of **cost–benefit analysis.** For a manager the cost of working on one problem is to forego the opportunity to work on other problems. Managers must determine which allocation of their time will result in the greatest possible benefits for the organization or the unit involved.

DIAGNOSING CAUSES OF PROBLEMS

The real, or most probable, **cause** of the problem must be identified. Suppose, for example, a student desires an A in a course. In her first exam she receives a C. She knows that if she continues as is, she will receive a C in the course. If the C grade is unacceptable, some action must be taken. The student must change what she is doing.

When the student generates alternative courses of action, they reflect her perception of the cause of the problem. Consider some possible alternative actions and how they are associated with possible causes of the problems.

1. *Spend more time studying.* This assumes that the cause of the C grade is simply not knowing enough and that the student is capable of learning the material at the desired level.

2. *Do additional reading.* This solution assumes that the student does not understand the concepts, and that by additional studying she can become capable of learning the material by providing a more appropriate foundation of knowledge.

3. *Change course selections.* This solution assumes that the cause of the problem is the instructor, his standards, the time of the class, or perhaps the size of the class.

Which is the best alternative? It depends upon the cause of the problem. If the student has a night job and the class meets at 8:30 A.M., the best alternative may be to change classes to one that meets later in the day. If the student is in an advanced course and does not have the necessary background, the best alternative may be to do additional reading. If the student has not read the assignments, the best alternative is to spend more time studying.

What happens if the student is in an advanced course without the necessary background and changes sections? The discrepancy between the desired and actual grade is likely to remain. Or suppose the standards of the instructor are so high that the student's potential in the course with her present instructor is only a C grade. Or assume that the student may not have the time to devote to more school work. In either of these cases, the discrepancy may be reduced by changing from the present course section to one with an instructor with lower standards.

In the study of twenty-five top management decisions by Mintzberg and his colleagues,[3] diagnosis of causes was of special importance in dealing with the problems (as compared to **crises**). In dealing with crises, at least the immediate "causes" are likely to be obvious and will cry out to be resolved without delay. With the less critical situation, however, unless the real causes of the deviation of **what is** from **what should be** are identified, the problem will remain in spite of taking corrective actions. We may prescribe aspirin when surgery is needed.

We stress the stage of diagnosing causes because there is evidence that individuals tend to be too "solution minded" when dealing with problems.[4,5] The pressure of events may lead us to jump to very premature conclusions about the causes of a problem, and then rush into the next stage of the decision-making process, searching for alternatives.[2] For most problems there are several possible causes, as we have seen in the example of the student above. The difficulty is in determining the one most likely to lead to the deviation.

The way to determine the most likely cause involves two major steps. First is to list all the possible causes. The second step is to "test" each cause, trying to decide whether one is more likely than another to have created the deviation.

One very well developed approach is the Kepner and Tregoe[2] problem-solving method. This method requires the decision maker to describe each problem precisely by answering the questions: What is it? What is it not? Where is it occurring? Where is it not occurring? When is it occurring? When is it not occurring? And when the deviation does occur its extent is _____? and is not _____? The real cause of the deviation or problem will become apparent when there are distinctions between the *is* and *is not* answers.

For example, suppose a manufacturing firm experiences a decline in profits.

(The characteristics of the problem and how they are related are shown in Figure 7.1). A group of managers get together to discuss the cause; several possibilities are suggested:

1. Poor marketing
2. Employee concern with a new promotion policy
3. Excessive administrative staff
4. A recent labor dispute on shift[1]
5. New raw material supplier

By answering the questions listed above, as is shown in Figure 7.1, these several possible causes can be evaluated and all but the most likely one of them eliminated. It is unlikely that a poor marketing effort is the cause since the sales revenue continues to be high. Indirect administrative costs are similar to those in the past, eliminating that possibility. It is clear that the increase in direct costs is an area for more fruitful search.

When the different shifts are examined, it is found that the cost increase has been on the first shift only, pinpointing the possible cause a little more sharply. What remains as possible causes now are

1. Employee concern with the new promotion policy
2. Recent labor dispute on Shift 1
3. New raw materials

The new supplier and the employee concern about the new promotion policy can be ruled out. Why? Because these two factors affect all shifts. It is possible that the staff on the first shift might have reacted, coincidentally, with the introduction of the new promotion policy, but the best choice for "most likely cause" of the problem is the recent labor dispute.[2]

FIGURE 7.1   Problem Cause Analysis

		Is	Is Not	Distinctive Features	Any Change From Past
What?	Profits	Low	High	Drop	5% decrease
	Sales revenue	High	Low	None	
	Indirect costs	Low	High	None	
	Direct costs	High	Low	Over standard	Usually in line
Where?	Shift 1	Over standard	Within standard	Excessive	Usually in line
	Shift 2	Within standard	Within standard	None	
	Shift 3	Within standard	Within standard	None	
When?	Shift 1	Last 3 months	Not before	Recent	Labor dispute
	Shift 2	—	—	—	
	Shift 3	—	—	—	
How much?		200% increase	Within tolerance limits	Very high	

Most likely cause—to be further tested:
Recent labor dispute

What such a diagnostic strategy does is to uncover the most likely cause of the problem, not tell the manager how to solve it. Now the manager must look for alternative courses of action to take that will bring costs back into line. The managers in this plant can now try to find solutions to labor problems, not quality control problems or production system design problems.

To aid in identifying problems, organizations often provide managers with rather frequent performance data. In one dental supplier, managers receive projected data for each type of product, based on prior sales. Managers also receive information about what other companies in the industry sell in each of these product categories. These industry data are provided by the dental supply trade association to which the firm belongs. Projected cost figures for each product are determined in advance as well. Then monthly revenues and costs are compared with those that should be obtained according to projections. These data not only point out problems, but help identify where they are.

GENERATING ALTERNATIVES

After the most likely cause (or causes) of the unsatisfactory state of affairs is identified, we must find what different ways there are to eliminate the cause. There is disagreement among decision theorists about how people generate and evaluate alternatives. A rational decision is the selection of the *best* alternative, the implication being that all possible alternatives are evaluated. In most decision-making situations, however, all of the possible alternatives are not known, and even if they were, a human being would generally find it impossible to consider all alternatives. Herbert Simon therefore argues that a person cannot "maximize" in decision making because of this human limitation.[6] Simon draws a distinction between "economic" man and "administrative" man. Economic theory assumes that in a particular decision-making situation, a manager knows all of the alternatives and their outcomes. It is further assumed that the choice among alternatives will be according to a system of values that involves the maximization of an economic referent, such as profits. This "economic man" is contrasted by Simon with "administrative man." He points out that in real life "administrative man" is *not* aware of all of the alternatives available and cannot possibly know all the consequences of choosing one alternative over another. So "administrative man" reduces the complexity of a problem to the point at which his knowledge and judgment limitations can make the decision. The typical decision maker, then, is subject to "bounded rationality," since his capacity for solving complex problems is limited to the alternatives of which he is aware. In addition, the manager makes decisions on the basis of his perception of the situation, and this may or may not be what the situation actually is. Subjective, idiosyncratic, and individualistic elements play highly significant roles in the making of decisions.

"Economic man," then, is assumed to have full knowledge of all alternatives, of the consequences of each alternative, and of the probability of occurrence of various conditions affecting the decision. "Administrative man," on the other hand, has limited knowledge of alternatives and consequences, and he makes guesses about the likelihood of certain events occurring in the future.

Simon argues that administrative man has the goal of "satisficing" instead of optimizing or maximizing, as does economic man. *Satisficing* is a decision strategy in which one searches for an alternative that achieves some minimum level of satisfaction for the desired objectives. This is the alternative usually selected. In other words, the decision maker will not identify *all* possible alternatives in order to choose the best from among them, but rather will stop his search for alternatives when he finds one or two that seem to be adequate, given his objectives or expectations. Of course, standards may change from one situation to another, depending upon personal experience. If the decision maker has great difficulty in finding an alternative that meets his standards, he may lower those standards in the future. On the other hand, if he easily achieves his objectives, he may raise his level of expectations the next time he is making a similar decision. Doing this would clearly suggest that better alternatives were available in the past.

Most people first search for ready-made solutions, a solution designed by others, or, perhaps, by oneself in the past. The search for ready-made solutions may begin with the individuals inside the organization or in the organization's records. External consultants, suppliers, or even governmental agencies may provide possible ready-made alternative solutions to problems. According to the research of the Mintzberg group, organizations first look for ready-made solutions in close and familiar locations. If they are unsuccessful, they then proceed to possible sources of alternatives that are less familiar.[3]

PROGRAMMED DECISIONS

In programmed decisions the alternatives are presented to the decision makers. They simply choose from a preestablished set of alternatives the one that is most appropriate given the specific dimensions of the problem. The possibilities and their consequences are worked out in advance. Programmed decision making is widely used where the tasks and/or problems are routine and stable as, for example, in a factory assembly-line operation. In such an operation if the equipment stops working, for instance, the manager immediately chooses a preestablished strategy based on the nature of the stoppage. Similarly, a dentist or physician often applies a standard procedure whenever he encounters a dental or medical problem of a particular type. (The available procedure may be memorized by the decision maker in advance or may be available to him in the form of written instructions.)

All of us make many programmed types of decisions every day: for example, with respect to eating, the time to eat, the sequencing of food to be eaten, and the choice of eating utensils may all be highly programmed. For a wide variety of situations, our culture has provided specific alternatives that are available, along with the criteria necessary to guide us in our choice among them. Programmed decisions are most applicable to situations where the decision-making problem is quite common or frequent so that solutions can be specified in advance. They are also most useful when a decision must be made very rapidly or when the qualifications of the decision maker are low.

The manager in a mechanistic organization (see Chapter 4) will have a very high proportion of programmed decisions. In fact, one of the problems often cited by people who work in mechanistic organizations is that creativity is stifled, that they are not permitted to make decisions. This is certainly true, but the nature of these organizations lends itself to such programmed guidelines.

Policies, Procedures, and Programmed Decisions

Policies and procedures are organizational guides for making programmed decisions. **Procedures** specify the steps required for a given situation; for example, how to handle customer complaints. They tend to focus on specific, narrow problems. **Policies** are general guides to action and often give only a broad context within which a manager should make a decision. A company policy may be "to operate within the legal constraints applicable to the firm and industry." The manager must use his judgment in selecting alternatives that fall within these guides.

The formulation of procedures and policies for programmed decisions is an important organizational task, since they have a significant effect on how efficiently an organization operates. All too often, however, procedures and policies are designed without fully considering their implications for the overall effectiveness of a unit. In one major company, for example, it was concluded that absenteeism was high enough to be a problem that required the attention of top management. It was then discovered that one of the major reasons for the large number of absent days was that when a worker's wages were garnished by outside creditors, the employee automatically received a three-day suspension. This suspension policy made the application of discipline uniform, but because of a large number of garnishments, it generated a large number of three-day absences. It also added to the initial problem, since it created further financial difficulty for workers.

In any case, managers must live with programmed decision rules. They generally have to implement alternatives required by such rules, and if they want to change the rules, they must seek higher-level approval. In effect, managers do not make decisions in programmed situations. It is in the unprogrammed area where managers need a decision-making strategy.

NONPROGRAMMED DECISIONS

In only five of the twenty-five top management decisions did Mintzberg and his group find that ready-made solutions were used. This is no problem since some research shows that custom-made solutions produce superior results than do ready-made solutions.[4] The design of new solutions is necessary when there are no readily available solutions of acceptable quality, and this is often the case in the practice of management. Cases of this type are called "nonprogrammed decision" problems.

In the organic organization the decision maker faces a high proportion of nonprogrammed decisions and must exercise a high level of judgment (or creativity). Research indicates that the ratio of nonprogrammed decisions to programmed decisions is higher in organizations in which there are many product changes and where the tasks tend to be nonroutine and complex—as, for example, in an organization involved in research and development work.[7] In such organizations nonprogrammed decisions have to be made for unfamiliar types of problems.

Obviously, nonprogrammed decisions require more competence and experience on the part of the decision maker than do programmed decisions. Thus, in organizations characterized by rapid product changes or complex tasks and employing highly trained and experienced personnel, there will be found a greater frequency of nonprogrammed decisions than in organizations with the opposite characteristics. Often nonprogrammed decisions require the help of experts, or the use of group decision-making methods, to improve the quantity and quality of alternatives to be evaluated, as well as the evaluation itself. Some approaches that may be used to generate alternatives to solve problems without ready-made solutions are the use of models, research, and creativity.

The Use of Models

A model is an abstraction of reality. It is an attempt to portray, in some miniature fashion, a particular state. Models can be useful in generating alternatives. For example, suppose you want to build a bookcase for a room. You take some measurements of the space where it is to fit, draw a rough diagram, evaluate its appearance, change the design, check the measurements, and build it.

There are different kinds of models, ranging from very simple to complex, and from real to abstract. A physical model often is a miniature version of the real thing. Aircraft designers test alternative "scale models" of planes in a wind tunnel and make changes that improve the final product. Qualitative models explain a phenomenon with everyday language or sometimes symbols. For example, you explain to a friend why costs increase as the size of the firm grows.

In management today there is an increasing use of mathematical models. Relationships between the characteristics of the subjects of interest are represented by numbers. For example, the relationship between the amount of investments and the interest rate may be represented by an equation. Mathematical models are more precise and less ambiguous than qualitative models and are therefore of greater value in obtaining specific answers to certain managerial questions. Since the mathematical model describes how various critical factors in a situation relate to each other, it is possible to use the model to generate alternatives.

In a mathematical model the objective is referred to as a ***dependent variable.*** The factors in the situation that affect the attainment of the objective are referred to as ***independent variables.*** For example, a model might describe the relationship between the objective—profit—and an independent variable—amount of output. The model might show that profits steadily rise up to a certain point as quantity of output rises, but that after that point, profits decrease because costs rise when any given facility is used to excess capacity. Such a model would show what the profits will be at alternative levels of output and the decision maker can select the optimum output for the profit objective. A mathematical model might also be developed that describes the relationship between machine speed, material strength, and the number of rejected pieces. In this model, the number of rejected pieces is the dependent variable and machine speed and strength of raw material are the independent variables. The varying combinations of machine speed and material strength are alternatives that a decision maker will consider.

Research

Preferably, the form of the mathematical model should be determined through research. Research involves the use of systematic observation in order to find the answers to problems. Frederick Taylor emphasized research as a means of managerial problem solving. In his famous metal-cutting experiments conducted over a period of twenty-six years, locomotive wheels were cut up in order to identify the factors affecting the cutting of metal. Taylor found that eighteen factors were important. The interrelationships between these were specified in a series of equations and converted to notations on a slide rule, which could then identify the various alternatives for a situation in which metal was to be cut. For example, the decision maker could choose between increasing machine speed and changing the composition of the metal to be cut. Thus, through careful research, a mathematical model was developed that identified the various feasible alternatives.

Creativity

In many situations it is not possible to use previous experience, standard responses, research, or models in order to generate alternatives. New or novel alternatives must be generated. In some organizations the creation of new or novel alternatives is considered so important that much effort and energy are expended in an attempt to increase creativity. (See Figure 7.2 for a humorous but not unrealistic view of creativity.)

Identifying creative individuals is not easy. Many research studies have attempted to identify the personal characteristics related to creativity. Intelligence and certain personality factors such as dominance, resourcefulness, and self-sufficiency have been associated with creative persons.[8,9] While this would seem to indicate the feasibility of the selection approach, other research shows that creativity is specific to the situation.[10] Other research shows that creativity is high in environments in which individuals have the freedom to express novel ideas and where these ideas are recognized and valued by supervision or by the organization.[10]

Several approaches have been suggested for generating creative solutions, especially from groups. One of the earlier methods, brainstorming,[11] requires individuals to gather in a group setting and to generate as many ideas as possible without criticizing anybody else's ideas. Some studies of this process, however, have shown that the individuals working alone may generate more and better ideas than groups.[12] The synectics approach requires the decision maker to form analogies from nature to the problem at hand (e.g., ability of some species to change color), to use fantasy, or to place himself in the role of some element in the problem ("Assume you are the machine").[13]

SELECTING ALTERNATIVES

Most of the writing and thinking about decision making focuses on selecting alternatives, but it is apparent that a wise selection of alternatives depends upon success in the recognition, diagnosis, and generation stages of the decision-making process. Those who have looked carefully at the research on decision making conclude that most individuals are poor decision makers,[14] but there is some research

*"Don't laugh—he was doing that the day he figured out
how to scoop up Trans-American Ramex, Inc."*

FIGURE 7.2

showing that managers trained to move through the steps of the decision process,
rather than their natural inclinations, make better decisions.[14]

The choice process can be improved using ideas from **decision theory,** a set
of concepts that seek to guide one to the best choice. In a decision theory approach,
the decision maker is required to determine which objectives are important so that
each alternative may be compared against these objectives. It is also necessary for
a decision maker to take into account, somehow, the nature and amount of uncertainty that is always present.

All organizations face some uncertainty in their environments. Even the most
logical, best alternative at the time a decision is made continues to be the best
choice only if the particular set of environmental circumstances prevail that were
predicted to prevail when the decision was made. Suppose we make a decision to
expand plant capacity when economic conditions are good and demand is growing.
If economic growth continues, and we have made a decision based in growth
premises, we have made a good choice. Suppose, however, that the economy turns

downward unexpectedly after we have made the decision and the plant is completed and operating. Now, the once "good" decision is a "bad" one. Such a situation occurred recently in a furniture manufacturing firm. Consumer demand was increasing, so the firm borrowed heavily to make its plant one-third larger. Just as the expansion was finished, the general economy took a downturn and consumers reduced furniture expenditures. Though revenue fell drastically, bank payments still had to be met. The firm was near bankruptcy but was saved by a sudden turnaround in the economy.

BASIC CONCEPTS IN DECISION THEORY

In order to use a decision theory approach in selecting alternatives, a manager must make some determination of three factors: the state of nature, probabilities, and expected values. These are basic concepts in decision theory.

State of Nature

When choosing from several alternatives, a decision maker must make some assumptions about the different environments, or situations, in which the choice made will be implemented. The environment **outside the control** of the decision maker is called the "state of nature" and will determine the success or failure of a decision. For example, the "states of nature" for the furniture manufacturer might be diffeent levels of economic activity, say (1) economic growth or (2) economic downturn. The manufacturer can do little to determine growth or recession, but whichever occurs will affect profits. State of nature that would affect the decision of a processor of tomato juice might be defined in terms of weather and growth conditions, such as (1) ideal growing conditions, (2) average growing conditions, (3) poor growing conditions. For both the furniture manufacturer and the tomato juice processor the "bestness" of any decision depends on which state of nature occurs *after* a choice is made and implemented, and since this is not known in advance, there is uncertainty in the environment.

Probability

One way the decision maker can translate the environmental uncertainty into useful inputs is to make a probability estimate of the likelihood of each state of nature. Probability simply refers to the frequency of occurrence of a particular outcome—the percentage of times that an outcome occurs if an event occurs a large number of times. We can be certain, for example, that if we flip a coin 1,000 times, very nearly 500 heads and 500 tails will occur. If an event is certain to happen, it has a probability of 1. If it occurs 1 time in 5, the probability is .2 or $\frac{1}{5}$.

There are three types of probability: **a priori, empirical,** and **subjective.** An a priori probability is determined on the basis of something known about the possible outcomes of the situation itself. For example, if a coin is evenly balanced, then a priori it can be said that the odds of a head when it falls are 1 in 2. The same is true of a tail, while the probability of a head *or* a tail is 1.

An empirical probability is one that has been derived from experience with an event. For example, it may be the experience of a university that only 75 of 100 incoming freshmen continue to graduation. The empirical probability of graduating then is ¾ or .75. Another example is the probability associated with the different weather conditions and the states of nature for the food processor. The probabilities for those different weather conditions would be determined from a study of past weather records. Both a priori and empirical probabilities are called *objective probabilities*.

Subjective probabilities can be defined as one's best estimate of the probability. Subjective probabilities are educated guesses based on one's experience, intuition, and feelings.

Expected Value

Evaluating probabilities of states of nature allows the decision maker to compute expected values for strategies or alternatives. An expected value is calculated by multiplying the payoff (what we would win or lose) if an event occurs by the probability.

$$EV = \text{probability} \times \text{payoff}$$

Expected values may be thought of as the average value (or loss) one would receive by making a particular decision a large number of times. If you, for instance, can win $5.00 if you flip a coin and heads comes up, the expected value is $2.50

$$\$2.50 = p(.5) \times (\$5.00) \text{ payoff}$$

If you have to pay $3.00 to get into the game (i.e., to flip the coin), then getting into the game is a bad decision, since the cost is greater than the expected value. If the game costs $2.00, getting into the game is a good decision.

TYPES OF DECISIONS

In the decision theory approach, the decision maker must make some determination about the probabilities of the different states of nature. When decision makers are very sure that a particular state of nature will be in existence, they are operating under **conditions of certainty.** When they are not sure that a particular state exists, they make decisions under **conditions of uncertainty.** Often it is possible to estimate the likelihood of the different states of nature, in which case decisions are **made under risk.** In this section we discuss these three types of decisions, particularly decisions under risk and decisions under uncertainty.

Decisions Under Conditions of Certainty

In situations of certainty, the decision maker knows the state of nature, or what the environment of the decision will be, before the decision is made. Therefore, he or she can calculate, in terms of the objective, the consequences (or payoff) for each alternative. A situation such as this sometimes exists for problems involving internal operations of an organization. For example, in making a decision about alternative work assignments among various machines in a shop, the capacity and availability of each machine is known. Or the manager may have to decide which of several engineers should be given a problem to solve. If only one engineer possesses the skill to solve the problem, the decision is easy to make.

In decisions under certainty, the decision maker chooses the alternative that has the largest payoff in terms of his objective. The primary problem may be calculating the payoff for all possible alternatives. For example, if you have twenty productions jobs to perform and twenty machines that can perform them, several million alternatives would not cover all possibilities. Various techniques such as linear programming have been developed to solve these kinds of problems.

Decisions Under Conditions of Risk

The decision environment is one of risk whenever the decision maker does not know for certain what state of nature will occur but is willing to assign a probability to each of the states of nature that may occur. We may know from past experience, for example, that a worker obtaining a certain score on a finger dexterity test has a 25 percent chance of failure at a certain task. Thus, if we hire a worker for that task who obtains this score on the test, he would have a .25 probability of failure and a .75 probability of reaching an acceptable level of performance by the end of the probationary period of employment. Of course, probability derived from past experience will not be accurate in the present unless present conditions are quite similar to those in the past. For example, if the production worker's job was changed so that finger dexterity is no longer as important as it was, employees obtaining that certain score on the test would not fail at the same rate as in the past.

Here is an example of decision making under conditions of risk (refer to Figure 7.3). Let us suppose that you are the owner of a chain of small gift shops. You have two alternative sites for your shop, one in the center of town and another in a new shopping center being constructed just outside of town. You are not certain what the future holds for the downtown business district or for the shopping center. In any case, you feel that you should seize a good opportunity if it arises.

You know that there are risks involved. Several things could happen that might make either alternative good or bad, and you must assess the risks and evaluate the alternatives.

States of nature are a way of conceptualizing the world, especially the relevant environment for persons making decisions. For your problem, your experience has led you to conclude that the best way to define the state of nature is the movement of local population. You believe that where people move will affect your profits and income. You determine that three general population trends are possible:

1. People will move away from town
2. People will stay where they are
3. People will move into town

These are the states of nature for your decision problem.

In order to make the best decision, you must make some estimate of the probabilities of each of these states of nature occurring, so you turn to the local population experts (the Chamber of Commerce, the state department of commerce, consultants, etc.) and they tell you, "We can't be certain what the movement of the population will be in this town, but we have made some estimates of the probability of each of your three states of nature occurring." These estimates are subjective probabilities, but you regard them as acceptable and reasonably accurate. The probability estimates for the states of nature are as follows:

State of Nature	Probability
1. Away from town	.4
2. No change	.3
3. Movement toward town	.3

THE PAYOFF MATRIX. You are now able to prepare a payoff matrix. A payoff matrix is a way to represent a decision problem. Such matrixes are constructed with the states of nature in the columns, the available strategies in the rows. The payoff for a particular strategy and a given state of nature is the point where the row and column intersect. Figure 7.3 shows the payoff matrix for your problem. In the matrix are entered the various estimated payoffs that would be obtained for each state of nature and each alternative, or each row and column in the payoff matrix.

These payoffs are called conditional values (CV), or what you can expect if a particular strategy is chosen and a particular state of nature occurs. To arrive at the conditional values for our problem, you make, say, sales forecasts for each of the six cells in this matrix. For example, as shown in Figure 7.3, the conditional value of the strategy "to locate in the center," if population moves away from town, is $60,000, or what the company would make if the strategy were selected and this state of nature occurred. Another forecast indicates the company would make $50,000 with the strategy of locating in town if population moves toward town.

Naturally it is important to specify conditional values as accurately as possible, since they are forecasts of what you will get if something happens. How can conditional values for this particular case be developed? Basically, for your problem you would forecast your profits, or income, for each cell in the payoff matrix. This means that you must:
1. Determine sales levels for each state of nature
2. Determine costs for each state of nature
3. Compute the profit for each state of nature

COMPUTE EXPECTED VALUES. Once you have done this you can calculate the expected value for each alternative. The rational decision maker will select the strategy that has the greatest expected value. Selecting this strategy will be the best decision.

FIGURE 7.3   Payoff Matrix to Locate Gift Shop in Town or in Suburban Shopping Center

State of Nature / Strategy	Movement Away From Town $p = .4$	No Change $p = .3$	Movement Toward Town $p = .3$
Locate in town	$25,000	$40,000	$50,000
Locate in center	$60,000	$40,000	$20,000

The total expected value for each strategy is calculated by multiplying the probability of the state of nature times the payoff for that state and adding these values for all states of nature for that strategy. This is shown in the formula

$$\Sigma EV = p_1(CV_1) + p_2(CV_2) + p_3(CV_3) + \ldots p_n(CV_n)$$

where

$$\Sigma EV = \text{the total expected value}$$
$$CV_1 \ldots CV_n = \text{conditional values of each state of nature}$$
$$p = \text{the probability}$$

You are now in a position to compare the two strategies by computing the expected values of each. To compute the total expected value for each strategy, you multiply the conditional value by the probability for each state of nature and add them together. This is done for each alternative strategy. For the "locate in town" strategy the expected value is $37,000:

$$\Sigma EV = .4(\$25,000) + .3(\$40,000) + .3(\$50,000)$$
$$= 10,000 + 12,000 + 15,000$$
$$= \$37,000$$

For the "shopping center" strategy, the expected value is $42,000:

$$\Sigma EV = .4(\$60,000) + .3(\$40,000) + .3(\$20,000)$$
$$= \$42,000$$

Applying the rule of rational decision making, the best alternative is to move to the shopping center. The reason for this is that the decision maker will, on the average, be advantaged in the amount of $5,000 ($42,000 − $37,000 = $5,000) when selecting the shopping center over the in-town location.

PROBABILITIES MEAN MAYBE. Is the decision maker absolutely better off by using such a stragety as just described? In the long run, yes. But it is possible to select an alternative that has a lower expected value than another and yet fare much better with it than one with a higher expected value. Suppose, for example, that an electronics manufacturer must decide between using his available resources to build a new computer or a new electric typewriter. If the states of nature are defined as two different conditions of demand, then the following payoff matrix represents the profits from each strategy.

	Demand I	Demand II	ΣEV
	$p = .5$	$p = .5$	
Computer	$1,000,000	−$300,000	$350,000
Typewriter	$400,000	$400,000	$400,000

Clearly the rational decision would be to manufacture the new typewriter. But if the manufacturer decides to build the computer and the state of nature proves to be Demand I, he wins big. Do you feel lucky? Then build the computer. Rational? Manufacture typewriters.

UTILITY AND EXPECTED VALUE.   To return to the gift shop problem, suppose that in order to locate in the shopping center, you must take a long-term lease, immediately paying $15,000 to the owners—but in town you need only take a monthly lease. In both cases you will still realize the returns in the payoff matrix of Figure 7.3.

If the decision maker is not willing to risk (or spend) $15,000, then it is preferable to locate in the city. Another example may make the point more clearly. Suppose you are involved in a gambling game, flipping coins. You have been told that if you flip a head, you win $100 and if you flip a tail, you lose $50. Clearly the expected value is high; where 0.5 is the probability of a head appearing or of a tail appearing, the expected value of the situation can be computed as follows:

$$.5(\$100) + .5(-\$50) = EV$$
$$\$50 - 25 = \$25$$

This means that on the average you are $25 ahead each time you flip a coin. But suppose that you must bet only in $25 amounts, you have only $25, and you have to pay that much for a bus ticket home. You cannot afford to lose; therefore, you cannot afford to bet. You cannot make the "rational" decision, because the utility of having a sure way home is greater than the potential payoff.

Decision Making Under Conditions of Uncertainty

When the decision maker, for one reason or another, is unable or unwilling to make a probability estimate of the different states of nature, there are still ways to use decision theory. Decision making under uncertainty is possible. When decisions fall into this category, the personality of the decision maker plays a much more influential role.

Let us go back to the problems of Penn Electronics, the firm described in item 7.1. Their primary market has been to produce electronic components for other firms, acting as a main supplier for companies that manufacture and market digital watches, electronic calculators, and minicomputers. After evaluating the success of these firms, Penn's president Hayes Woodward and the executive committee decide that it may be profitable for them to enter one or more of these fields. The executive committee meets and proposes four product strategies for Penn, which seem equally acceptable. The product strategies are:

S1.   To manufacture and market medical technology
S2.   To manufacture and market electronic calculators
S3.   To manufacture and market digital watches
S4.   To remain in the current business

Today the planning group is meeting with the executive committee to present the results of their study of each of these alternatives. The planning group was asked to forecast the returns to Penn Electronics for each of these different strategies so that the executive committee could select the "best" alternative. Due to the innovative character of each of these strategies (except S4), no one in the planning group is really willing to make any guesses about the probabilities of market changes that might affect the profits. No one, then, feels able to make a good estimate of the different states of nature that might occur. Yet the planning group has made some projections based on certain possible market conditions (but not whether or not these will occur, or their probabilities). These states of nature are:

N1. Increased demand in the medical field
N2. Increased demand for electronic calculators
N3. Increased demand for digital watches
N4. No change in the current demand state

The resulting forecast for each strategy and the return (conditional value) for each state of nature is shown in Figure 7.4 as a payoff matrix with the conditional values (the entries) representing changes in projected profits for Penn Electronics. Note that these decision makers are faced with a substantially different problem from the one faced by the gift shop, discussed earlier, since they cannot, or will not, make probability estimates about the states of nature. The expected value (EV) for each strategy cannot be computed since EV = (p) (CV). So how can a "rational" decision be made?

Problems of this type are called decisions under uncertainty. Miller and Starr say that

> One of the most interesting results of decision theory has been the discovery that there is no one best criterion for selecting strategy. Instead, there are a number of different criteria, each of which has a perfectly good rationale to justify it. The choice among these criteria is determined by company policy and/or the attitude of the decision maker.[15]

When these different criteria are applied to a decision under conditions of uncertainty, it is possible that any of a number of different strategies may be selected. Here are how these decision criteria apply to the problem of Penn.

THE PESSIMISTIC CRITERION. The decision maker may adopt an attitude that is pessimistic, that the worst is likely to happen. Given this set of assumptions, the decision maker should select the strategy that yields the greatest amount under the worst conditions. Consider the problem of Penn Electronics. For each strategy, we find the lowest or minimum payoff. These are shown for Penn in the payoff matrix in Figure 7.5.

FIGURE 7.4   Payoff Matrix for Penn Electronics' Strategy Decisions

	States of Nature—Market Conditions			
Strategy	N1 Increased Medical	N2 Increased Calculator	N3 Increased Watches	N4 No Change
S1. Enter medical field	300	250	100	−100
S2. Enter calculator field	100	400	200	−150
S3. Enter digital watch field	50	300	600	−300
S4. Stay the same	−50	−75	−100	150

FIGURE 7.5 Applying the *Pessimistic* Criterion to Penn Electronics' Strategy Decision

	States of Nature—Market Conditions				
	N1	N2	N3	N4	
	Increased	Increased	Increased	No	Worst
Strategy	Medical	Calculator	Watches	Change	Payoff
S1. Enter medical field	300	250	100	−100	−100
S2. Enter calculator field	100	400	200	−150	−150
S3. Enter digital watch field	50	300	600	−300	−300
S4. Stay the same	−50	−75	−100	150	−100

Decision: Stay in same area or enter medical field.

Now assuming that the worst will happen, if we select the strategy "no change in product structure" (S4), then we will obtain the maximum minimum payoff. This same outcome will occur if we enter the medical field (S1). This criterion for making decisions is called **maximin.** If our conditional values are correctly forecast, then the worst that can happen to Penn Electronics is that it will not lose more than $100 million if they stay in the same business (S4) or enter the medical field (S1).

THE OPTIMISTIC CRITERION.   Just as one could assume the worst might happen, it could also be assumed that the best might occur. The decision maker may feel fortunate, rather than unfortunate. The **maximax** criterion selects the strategy that has the greatest payoff. This approach, of course, is just the opposite of the pessimistic criterion. To determine the best decision using the maximax or optimistic criterion, the decision maker determines the largest payoff for each strategy. For Penn Electronics Company these are shown in the payoff matrix in Figure 7.6.

In this case, Penn Electronics would select the alternative of entering the digital watch market (S3). If the assumption about good fortune holds, then the company will make $600 million.

FIGURE 7.6 Applying the *Optimistic* Criterion to Penn Electronics' Strategy Decision

	States of Nature—Market Conditions				
	N1	N2	N3	N4	
	Increased	Increased	Increased	No	Best
Strategy	Medical	Calculator	Watches	Change	Payoff
S1. Enter medical field	300	250	100	−100	300
S2. Enter calculator field	100	400	200	−150	400
S3. Enter digital watch field	50	300	600	−300	600
S4. Stay the same	−50	−75	−100	150	150

Decision: Enter digital watch field.

THE REGRET CRITERION. There is another way to look at the choice problem. Once we make a decision and know the results, it may be that we would have been better off had we done something else. The regret criterion is based on the idea that

the decision maker should attempt to minimize the regret which he may experience. Exactly what is his regret? It appears to be the fact that he may not have selected the best strategy in terms of the particular state of nature that did, in fact, occur. Savage suggests that the amount of his regret might be measured by the difference between the payoff he actually received and the payoff he could have received if he had known the state of nature that was going to occur[15]

Making these assumptions, it is possible to construct a regret matrix for Penn Electronics. The entries are the "amount of regret" for each strategy and each state of nature (Figures 7.7 and 7.8). First consider what the best strategy would be in the event of the occurrence of the state of nature N1, increased medical product demand. Examining that row in the payoff matrix, it is clear that the medical field strategy (S1) would be best. If we select that alternative, we would be most satisfied and have no regrets ($300 − $300 = 0). This was computed by taking the highest payoff for that state of nature ($300) from the payoff for the medical field entry alternative.

We can continue in the same fashion to obtain a regret measure for the "calculator" alternative for the same state of nature (increased medical demand—N1). Penn Electronics would have made $100 million if they had decided this way, but they could have made $300 million if they had done something else (entered the medical field, S1). They would have lost the opportunity to make $200 million: $100 million (the calculator payoff), which they received, less $300 million (the medical field alternative), which they did not get. The regrets for the other two strategies (S3 and S4) if the market increases in medical technology are given at $250 million and $350 million (see Figure 7.8).

Now consider the regret computations for another state of nature, for example, if the market shift is to "increased demand for digital watches" (column N3 in the payoff matrix, Figure 7.8). If this state of nature occurs, then Penn would experience no regret (0) if they "enter the digital watch market" (S3). But if N3 does occur and they have selected S1, then they would experience $500 million worth of regret. This means they made $100 million but lost the opportunity to make $600 million. The $500 million is obtained by subtracting $600 million (payoff for S3, N3 in

FIGURE 7.7   Regret Computations for the Penn Electronics' Strategy Decision

	States of Nature—Market Conditions			
Strategy	N1 Increased Medical	N2 Increased Calculator	N3 Increased Watches	N4 No Change
S1. Enter medical field	300(−300)	250(−400)	100(−600)	−100(−150)
S2. Enter calculator field	100(−300)	400(−400)	200(−600)	−150(−150)
S3. Enter digital watch field	50(−300)	300(−400)	600(−600)	−300(−150)
S4. Stay the same	−50(−300)	−75(−400)	−100(−600)	150(−150)

FIGURE 7.8 Applying the Regret Criterion to Penn Electronic's Strategy Decision

| Strategy | States of Nature—Market Conditions | | | | |
	N1 Increased Medical	N2 Increased Calculator	N3 Increased Watches	N4 No Change	Maximum Regret
S1. Enter medical field	0	−150	−500	−250	−500
S2. Enter calculator field	−200	0	−400	−300	−400
S3. Enter digital watch field	−250	−100	0	−450	−450
S4. Stay the same	−350	−475	−700	0	−700

Decision: Enter calculator field.

Figure 7.7) from the $100 million (payoff for S1, N3). By continuing with computations such as these, the regret matrix in Figure 7.8 is constructed.

We are not yet finished, however, for Penn wants to select the strategy that leaves them with the least regret. Penn Electronics can now examine each strategy and find the greatest regret score for it. The strategy selected using this criterion is to enter the calculator market (S2), since the company would experience the least amount of regret ($400 million) if they did this.

THE RATIONAL CRITERION. This approach is based on the idea that for decisions under conditions of uncertainty, it is impossible to make a reasonably adequate estimate of the probability of a particular state of nature occurring, but that if there is no cause to believe that one state of nature is more likely to occur than another, it can be reasonably assumed that they are equally likely to occur.

Making this assumption means that for a decision problem under uncertainty (where we apply no probability estimates), we assign equal probabilities to all states of nature. In the case of Penn Electronics, this means that we assign probabilities of .25 ($\frac{1}{4}$) to each state of nature. When this is done, then it is possible to compute the total expected value for each strategy, and this leads to the decision to enter the digital watch market (S3). This computation is shown in Figure 7.9.

FIGURE 7.9 Applying the Rational Criterion to Penn Electronics' Strategy Decision

| Strategy | States of Nature—Market Conditions | | | | |
	($p = \frac{1}{4}$) Increased Medical	($p = \frac{1}{4}$) Increased Calculator	($p = \frac{1}{4}$) Increased Watches	($p = \frac{1}{4}$) No Change	ΣEV
S1. Enter medical field	300	250	100	−100	137.5
S2. Enter calculator field	100	400	200	−150	137.5
S3. Enter digital watch field	50	300	600	−300	162.5
S4. Stay the same	−50	−75	−100	150	−18.75

Decision: Enter digital watch field.

THE KEPNER–TREGOE APPROACH

Another approach to making decisions has been developed by Kepner and Tregoe.[2] This is a method widely taught to practicing managers and has the advantage of being somewhat more straightforward. It forces managers to be more specific about what they expect to achieve through a decision as each alternative is evaluated. This approach involves the following steps:

1. Determine objectives against which to evaluate alternatives
2. Classify objectives according to importance
3. Evaluate alternatives against objectives
4. Choose the best alternative as a tentative decision
5. Assess the adverse consequences of the tentative decision

Suppose the management of Penn Electronics decides to move ahead and buy another plant that must have at least 200,000 square feet of operating space. Four locations are available that meet this requirement: Atlanta, Annapolis, Chicago, and Boston. Before selecting a location the management must know more precisely what the objectives of the decision are, as follows:

1. Determine objectives against which to choose. Basically, setting problem-solving objectives means that the decision maker should list what he or she expects to obtain when the alternative is selected. This may include several desired outcomes. For example, a decision maker might want an alternative to have (1) 200,000 square feet of space, (2) $2.50 unit cost, (3) $1.00 unit shipping cost; and to be (4) near a major port, (5) close to the home office, (6) in a locale with warm winters, and (7) in a rural area.

2. Classify objectives according to importance. Problem-solving objectives are classified into two categories: musts and wants. "Musts" objectives specify the outcomes that have to be achieved. Unless these "must" objectives are met by an alternative, the problem will not be considered solved. For example, given the list of objectives stated above, the decision maker might determine that (1) the space requirement, (2) unit costs, and (3) shipping costs are "must" objectives. Figure 7.10 shows how this management distinguished between those requirements.

FIGURE 7.10 Evaluating Location Alternatives for Penn Electronics

		Atlanta	Annapolis	Boston	Chicago
	Must Objectives				
	200,000 sq ft	Yes	Yes	Yes	Yes
	$2.50 unit cost	Yes	Yes	Yes	No
	$1.00 unit shipping costs	No	Yes	Yes	Yes
Rank	**Want Objectives**		Annapolis (Score × Rank)		Boston (Score × Rank)
4	Near major port		5 × 4 = 20		5 × 4 = 20
3	Near home office		3 × 3 = 9		4 × 3 = 12
2	Warm winter		3 × 2 = 6		2 × 2 = 4
1	Rural—not urban		4 × 1 = 4		1 × 1 = 1
	Total score		39		37

"Must objectives also frequently contain resource limits. Problems are solved with resources that are usually in limited supply in any situation. Any alternative that does not meet all the "must" objectives is eliminated from further consideration. Those that do are then assessed against the "wants."

"Want" objectives are outcomes that are not necessarily critical, but are desirable. They are, in a sense, extras that may be obtained when an alternative is selected. Naturally the decision maker will select the alternative that, after meeting the "must" objectives, satisfies the most "wants."

These "want" objectives should be weighted or ranked in order of importance to the decision maker. In our example he may rank the remaining decision objectives as follows:

1. Near a major port
2. Near home office
3. Warm winters
4. Rural—not urban

Numerical weights can be assigned to these "wants." Here we have concluded that locating near a major port is more important than being near the home office and given it a weight of 4.

3. *Evaluate alternatives against objectives.* Each alternative is compared against each "must" objective first, since the "must" objectives set maximum and minimum limits. Any alternative that stays in contention must meet all the "musts." Since Atlanta's shipping costs are too high, as are the unit costs in Chicago, both of these cities are eliminated from further consideration (see Figure 7.10). The remaining alternatives are then evaluated against the "wants." A 1–to–5 scale can be used, with 5 representing meeting a "want" to the highest degree and 1 the lowest degree. The scores assigned to how well both the remaining alternatives satisfy each "want" are shown in Figure 7.10. These scores are the best judgment the decision maker can apply based on his knowledge of the facts.

4. *Choose the best alternative as a tentative decision.* The best tentative alternative will be one that meets all the "must" objectives and satisfies the most "want" objectives to a significant degree. This can be determined by simply multiplying the weight assigned to a particular "want" times the score that each alternative gets for meeting that "want." For instance, the weight for the objective of being near the home office is 3. If the home office is in Hartford, Connecticut, then since Boston is closer to Hartford than Annopolis, it would be given a value of 4. Since Annapolis is not too distant, it is given a score, still high, of 3—but not as high as Boston. The weighted score on this dimension is Boston 12, Annapolis 9. The alternative with the highest total score is probably the best alternative. From Figure 7.10 it can be determined that the best alternative is to locate in Annapolis.

5. *Assess the adverse consequences of the tentative decision.* It is not enough that an alternative meet the "must" and "want" objectives, however, since its implementation may generate other problems, and an alternative that creates a problem worse than the one it solves is not a feasible alternative. Decisions often involve change, and change itself can create problems. Therefore, it is important to identify possible future problems that may be created if the alternative is chosen and implemented, together with the possible seriousness of those problems and the probability of their occurrence. Such an evaluation may lead to the rejection of what initially apears to be a highly desirable alternative. If it does, the manager goes back and evaluates the next most desirable alternative.

Why Not Annapolis?

Figure 7.11 reflects a managerial judgment that there may be two possible future serious problems with the Annapolis alternative, but only one problem with the Boston alternative. Annapolis is a relatively small city. Penn Electronics might experience a labor shortage with limited labor supply, because when new companies move in they attract the existing labor supply from other jobs leaving all other employers with an insufficient supply of workers. We might further conclude that it will be difficult to attract workers from other geographical locations. This potential labor shortage problem for Annapolis is given a seriousness rating of 9 on a 10-point scale. The probability of a labor shortage happening is judged to be 7. The seriousness of the problem times its probability equals 63 (see Figure 7.11).

Another potentially serious problem for the Annapolis location is the threat of large tax increases in the future. The management might rate the probability of future excessive taxes as 6. Excessive taxes might be given a seriousness score of 8. In Boston, however, the probability of large tax increases is even higher, as Figure 7.11 indicates. However, our analysis shows the Boston alternative to be more favorable than Annapolis because the Penn Electronics managerial group does not foresee other serious future difficulties in Boston.

The degree to which alternatives meet the "must" and "want" objectives must now be weighed against the seriousness and the probability of future problems. This must be a subjective evaluation since there is no generally acceptable, or correct, approach for determining how likely each alternative is to lead to serious future problems. In the example of Penn, we are likely to choose the Boston location, since it scores only slightly less than Annapolis on the "must" and "want" objectives, but much better on the possibility of future problems.

SOME OTHER CONSIDERATIONS
IN COMPARING ALTERNATIVES

There is no easy way to select what criterion should be used in evaluating alternatives. Not every alternative considered by a manager is weighed against profits or costs. Often there are many criteria against which alternatives are evaluated. It is possible that the alternative must meet all the required standards, as would be

FIGURE 7.11   Future Problem Evaluation of Penn's Locations

Future Problem	Annapolis			Boston		
	Seriousness	Probability	Weight	Seriousness	Probability	Weight
Labor shortage	9	7	63			
Excessive taxes	8	6	48	8	9	72
Total			111			72

the case when a decision maker lists the "must" criteria. However, often when an alternative is available, it may also be assessed against various other criteria, or "wants."

Compensatory and Noncompensatory Criteria

In establishing criteria it is important to decide whether they are compensatory or not. If the criteria used are compensatory, then high scores on one criterion can offset low scores on another. Compensatory criteria are often applied to decisions to admit students to graduate programs; here, high test scores can often compensate for low undergraduate grades. The criteria for promotion to associate professor, on the other hand, are often teaching ability, scholarly accomplishment, and service to organization and community, but these are typically noncompensatory today. That is, insufficient publication, for example, will not be compensated for by high scores on teaching or service. An early illustration of a compensatory system for evaluation of alternatives is described in this passage from a letter from Benjamin Franklin to Joseph Priestley in 1772:

> When I have thus got them all together in one view, I endeavor to estimate their respective weights; and where I find two, one on each side, that seem equal, I strike them both out. If I find a reason pro equal to some two reasons con, I strike out the three. If I judge some two reasons con, equal to some three reasons pro, I strike out the five; and thus proceeding I find at length where the balance lies; and if, after a day or two of further consideration, nothing new that is of importance occurs on either side, I come to a determination accordingly.

DECISION MAKING
AND TYPES OF ORGANIZATIONS

There will be dominant decision-making patterns in different types of organizations. These dominant patterns are illustrated in Figure 7.12 for the organic and mechanistic organizations.

Decisions under certainty will constitute a larger proportion of decisions in mechanistic organizations. To make decisions under certainty (deterministic approaches) the environment must be well defined, known, and relatively constant—as it is for mechanistic organizations. The decision maker can specify costs, conditions, and circumstances with some accuracy.

Decision making under risk will also be employed in mechanistic organizations. Often, even though managers cannot be certain about things, they may be able to make probability estimates about them. This may be because of past experience, or perhaps because data have been collected and analyzed. These two approaches are the most prevalent in hierarchical organizations.

In the organic organization there will also be a large proportion of decisions under risk. However, we believe the most dominant decision type will be *decisions under uncertainty.* The difficulties with which organic organizations must cope stem from the fact that not only must the changes in the external environment be perceived and assessed, but also that these changes may well alter the way goals are sought.

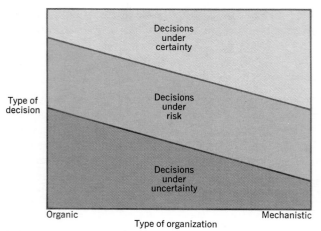

FIGURE 7.12   Type of organization and predominant types of decisions.

The emphatic thrust, then, in organic organizations will be colored by the volatile environment, for which there are few good data. This leads to much more subjectivity and personal evaluation of different states of nature the firm might face.

SUMMARY

Decision making is a skill that cuts across everything managers do. Managers decide what to produce, how to produce it, who to hire, how to lead, and so on. Decision making can be improved by following these steps in sequence:

1.   Be aware of a problem
2.   Diagnose causes of problems
3.   Generate alternatives
4.   Select alternatives
5.   Implement decisions

In this chapter we have emphasized the first four steps. The last will be more fully explored in later chapters. There are some useful guides that are helpful to managers for each of these steps. Recognizing a problem requires that a manager be sensitive to the surrounding situation. Problems exist when something is not as it should be. It is when this deviation is important that some action is called for.

Recognizing a problem and knowing its cause are two very different things. Problems can be solved only when the real cause is removed. A good deal of careful analysis is necessary to insure that we make a decision that has a high probability of removing the cause of the problem.

Once the cause of the problem is settled upon, the next step is to figure out what the alternatives are. There is more than one way to skin a cat, and there are often many ways to solve a problem.

There are many different ways to evaluate which alternative is best. All of them involve making some determination of objectives that we are trying to reach. The approach to selecting alternatives can depend very much on the degree of certainty that exists in the environment. When there is great stability, the manager can use approaches for "decisions under certainty." When the environment is volatile, a manager may choose to use either a "decision under risk" or "decision under uncertainty" approach.

Sinclair Publishing Company

Bob Sinclair has just resigned from Foreman Publishing Company because he decided to start his own firm. He is an experienced editor and publisher and knows the technical and the marketing side of publishing very well, especially business and economics. His new firm, Sinclair Publishing, will specialize, particularly, in publishing management books because his experience is in that field.

Sinclair Publishing is a small company. Bob does all the manuscript acquisition, some of the editing, and all of the marketing. His marketing strategy is to use mail advertising to sell the books he publishes. He has a secretary, a part-time editor, and a part-time inventory clerk. Such a small organization is not uncommon in publishing, since almost everything that has to be done to produce a book can be free-lanced, that is, editing, printing, graphics, and so on.

There is currently adequate capital to produce Sinclair's first two books, but not much more than that. If these two books can be even modestly successful, Sinclair can get off the ground. If they fail, he will go back to work for another large publisher.

He has received three manuscripts from authors who he believes are capable of writing successful texts. One is a textbook for a basic management course, the second is for a book designed for the introductory MBA course, and the third is a book for an advanced consumer behavior course.

Sinclair has decided that he will publish one of three books now, and then another book (not any of those remaining) at a later time. He sizes up the problem this way. He is not very familiar with the consumer behavior market, though he has reason to believe he might sell 5,000 copies of the book each year. This would be used primarily at the graduate level.

If he publishes the undergraduate management text, and it is very successful, he could do very well. The market for this book is estimated to be over 300,000 units each year. However, there are over 100 texts that compete in this market, and many of them are published by major publishers with large sales forces who call on professors who will use the book. Bob has no sales personnel. In addition, Bob estimates that he would sell only a few copies of this book at the graduate level.

The third book, the introductory graduate level text, would probably sell no more than 5,000 copies each year. However, the number of potential users is much smaller and easier to reach by mail than those who use the undergraduate text. Bob knows that this book would not sell for any undergraduate courses.

1. Can you construct a payoff matrix for Sinclair Publishing?
2. What should Bob Sinclair do? Why?

Case
7.2 The Automobile Industry

The U.S. automobile industry has been facing one difficult circumstance after another—oil shortages, oil embargoes, effective competition from foreign manufacturers, and some outright bad decisions. A group of managers from different auto firms were discussing the situation and what could be done to alleviate it. Here are some of their comments.

TOM McCAIN: Everyone thought we should worry in the '50s and '60s about the Volkswagen and the U.S. auto market. Japanese manufacturers have been more of a problem. What we should do is to impose a high import tax on foreign cars. That way, they'll be too expensive, and consumers will buy U.S. cars.

JACK FELTON: The real problem is oil. If we can increase the supply of gasoline, people will buy bigger cars. They want them anyway.

We could do two things. First, we might get control of oil suppliers. This could be done by finding our own, or helping our friends get control of the oil cartel.

The second thing we could do would be to develop alternative sources of energy for other uses. That would free up a lot of oil that could be manufactured into gasoline.

P. HOROWITZ: The government needs to get out of the business of regulation. If they would let oil prices loose in the free market system and remove most of crazy controls on the auto industry, we would be able to solve the problem.

JOE RIGHT: We were asleep at the wheel. We should have seen it all coming and started to downsize ten years ago. Instead, we closed our eyes. Now we know what we have to do and it is going to take some time. We can do it, if the clock does not run out on us.

1. What do these different statements suggest about the cause of the problem?
2. How would you suggest that these managers begin to analyze the problem to determine its most likely cause?
3. What solutions are dictated by the problem definition of each of these managers? How likely is it that the solution would solve the problem? What are other effects of each of the solutions?

DISCUSSION QUESTIONS

1. Name the recommended sequential steps to be followed for good decision making. Do you think this sequence includes all the necessary steps?
2. What do you think the priorities should be when deciding which problems to deal with?
3. How would you go about identifying problems and causes of those problems that a firm must deal with?

4. What is a programmed decision? What is the difference between a programmed and a nonprogrammed decision?
5. Why would a manager want to have his subordinates make "programmed decisions"? Under what conditions would he not want to constrain them in such a fashion?
6. What is a model and what is the importance of using models?
7. How do the three factors of decision making (state of nature, probability, and expected values) affect the process?
8. Discuss the Kepner–Tregoe approach to decision making.
9. What is the "rational" decision if you have the following payoff matrix:

	States of Nature		
	(1) $p = .5$	(2) $p = .3$	(3) $p = .2$
Strategy 1	$2,000	$10,000	$12,000
Strategy 2	4,000	11,000	8,000

10. Suppose you have the following payoff matrix:

	States of Nature		
	(1)	(2)	(3)
Strategy 1	$2,000	$10,000	$12,000
Strategy 2	4,000	11,000	8,000
Strategy 3	9,000	8,000	6,000

   a. What is the decision that the "optimist" would make?
   b. The "pessimist"?
   c. To minimize "regret"?
   d. The "rational" manager?
11. What are the dangers in using "experience" as a basis for solving problems?
12. Is betting on the flip of a coin a decision under risk or a decision under uncertainty?
13. What is the difference between "maximin" and "maximax" approaches to making decisions?

REFERENCES

1. Simon, H. A. The new science of management decision. New York, New York University Press, 1960.
2. Kepner, C. H., and B. B. Tregoe. The rational manager: A systematic approach to problem solving and decision making. New York, McGraw-Hill, 1965.
3. Mintzberg, H., R. Raisinghani, and A. D. Theoret. "The structure of unstructured decision processes." Administrative Science Quarterly, 21 (1976):246–275.
4. Maier, N. R. F. Problem-solving discussions and conferences: Leadership methods and skills. New York, McGraw-Hill, 1963.

5. Maier, N. R. F. Problem solving and creativity in individuals and groups. Monterey, Calif., Brooks-Cole, 1970.

6. Simon, H. A. *Models of Man*. New York, Wiley, 1957.

7. Friedlander, F. "The relationship of task and human conditions to effective organizational structure," in Bass, B. M., R. Cooper, and J. A. Haas (eds.), Managing for accomplishment. Lexington, Mass., D. C. Heath, 1970.

8. Taylor, C. W. Creativity: Progress and potential. New York, McGraw-Hill, 1964.

9. Torrance, E. P. "The Minnesota studies of creative behavior: National and international extensions," Journal of Creative Behavior, 1 (1967): 137–54.

10. Miner, J. B. The management process: Theory, research and practice. New York, Macmillan, 1973.

11. Osborn, A. F. Applied imagination: Principles and procedures of creative thinking. New York, Scribner's, 1957.

12. Dunnette, M. D., J. P. Campbell, and K. Jaastad. "The effect of group participation in brainstorming effectiveness for two industrial samples," Journal of Applied Psychology, 47 (1963): 30–37.

13. Gordon, W. J. J. Synectics. New York, Harper and Row, 1961.

14. Slovic, P., B. Fischoff, and S. Lichtenstein. "Behavioral decision theory," in M. Rosenzweig and L. Porter (eds.), Annual Review of Psychology, (28) 1977: 1–39.

15. Miller, D., and M. Starr. Executive decisions and operations research. Englewood Cliffs, N.J., Prentice-Hall, 1960.

CHAPTER EIGHT

Strategic Planning

Henry Ford II leaves a strategy for the '80s

Item 8.1

In an interview with Business Week on Apr. 10, Henry Ford II laid out his company's plans for the 1980s. The company must have separate strategies for domestic and foreign markets because the problems and challenges in the U.S. differ from those abroad. At home Ford Motor Co. must regain the market share lost to General Motors Corp. in the last two years, gains GM made by taking an early lead in downsizing its autos to meet tough federal fuel economy laws. Ford Motor also must regain a reputation for quality in the U.S. That image has been badly tarnished by well-publicized defects in the Pinto and mechanical malfunctions in other models.

Such demands are forcing Ford Motor to spend heavily in the U.S. But the expenditures come just as GM is challenging Ford Motor's traditional hegemony over U.S. carmakers in Europe and other foreign markets. Fully 48 percent of last year's earnings came from outside North America. In Europe, where growth in the next decade is expected to outpace that in the U.S., safety and emission laws are less stringent. Still, Ford Motor faces large investments overseas, too, if it is to maintain leadership in the face of increased competition. In the following excerpts from Ford's interview, he describes the strategy for meeting the different challenges:

IN THE U.S.: COMPLIANCE

"Our strategy in the U.S. is plain and simple. It's dictated by government regulation. Those are fuel economy numbers—19 mi. [per gal., fleet average] this year, 20 next year, and 27.5 in 1985. We have decided to remain a full-range company. We want to offer the consumer a subcompact car, a compact car, an intermediate car, a standard car, and a luxury car—with different nameplates.

"We've got to figure out what engine sizes go with what combination of transmissions and rear axles to meet the fuel economy laws. We've chosen to go the PROCO—or programmed combustion—route. [PROCO involves modifying an engine's cylinder head to produce a high-compression engine that runs on gasoline but delivers the better fuel economy of a diesel. GM is leaning toward the diesel.] You don't have the odors, the hard start, and the NOX [emissions] at low revs that you have with diesels. On the other hand, it's a very complicated manufacturing process, which we've been working on with Bosch in West Germany [the manufacturer of spark plugs and other engine components]. Dr. [Hans L.] Merkle, the chairman of Bosch, told me this was the most complicated manufacturing job they've ever undertaken.

RESIZING THE MARKET. Meanwhile, we're resizing and reclassifying the [U.S.] market as we go along. One [car size] slips into another so easily, it's hard to classify them. We're hitting it from both ends, with new models and downsized cars.''

A SHORTAGE OF MONEY. "One of our problems is a shortage of money. Meeting fuel economy, safety, and emission laws in the U.S. will require tremendous capital investments: Our estimate now is $20 billion between 1978 and 1985. We have to be very careful about expenditures outside the U.S. during this period, so that we can do what we have to to meet the laws of the U.S. and still keep a competitive range of products and not just have a four-seater car with a diesel engine.''

GROWING PROFIT MARGINS. "We're certainly not going to make the kind of money on our smaller cars that we make on our larger cars. We have to make sure that our total [domestic] profit margins grow. We have to be smart enough to make derivative vehicles—specialty kinds of cars—on which our margins can be very substantial.''

IN EUROPE: COMPETITION

"First, we rationalized our operations in Europe. Instead of having, as we used to, companies in France, Britain, and, West Germany that all did their own thing, we rationalized the whole thing under one corporate umbrella that we call Ford of Europe. It's a management company, not a holding company. GM is working toward this.''

MECHANICAL EMPHASIS. "Three years from now, the competition from GM [Europe] is going to be much more difficult. They're strong, but not anywhere near as strong as we are. We've got to be sure we stay as far ahead of them as we are today. We've got to put our emphasis, in Europe particularly, on new engines, new drivelines, new mechanicals. Europeans are very, very interested in the mechanicals, the innovative things that are under the sheet metal. Over here, people look at the sheet metal and the interior, and they don't give a damn [about mechanicals]. Over there, we've got to make sure that our engines and everything to do with the mechanical side of the vehicles are strong.''

CAPACITY SHORTAGES. "We figure we'll have capacity shortages [in Europe] by 1982. The question is whether we should build a new plant or enlarge a present facility." [Ford Motor is weighing a major expansion in Spain or West Germany against a new plant in France or Austria.]

A SPECIALTY MARKET. "It's unbelievable to me, particularly abroad, how people spend almost any amount of money on a car of a specialty kind. I saw a Porsche 928 in Australia for $51,000. You've got Rolls Royces and Jensens. Even our own larger [European] Granadas cost $10,000 or $11,000. . . . Maybe we don't have [to construct] new assembly capacity [in Europe]. Maybe we run along with what we have and get better products with the money. That possibility hasn't been crossed off."

NEW TRUCK LINES. "We're also expending in Europe a considerable amount of money to modernize our truck line. In Europe, there are many, many truck manufacturers doing a very good job. We've got to modernize ours to make them wholly competitive, from the small Fiesta or Escort vans right up to the Transcontinental, which is a big heavy-duty truck."

"We're particularly well-qualified [to meet these challenges] on the international side. The real problems are in North America—to get our profit margins up, to meet all the laws, to build top-quality cars. The most important things we've got going in this company right now are quality, reliability, and durability. We've got to make them better, and we've got to continue to make them better, so the consumer is satisfied and doesn't write to his congressman or some consumer agency and bitch all the time. It starts right down in the engineering department, and it goes right through the company until the damn car goes out the door. Our big effort has got to be North America."

Source: Business Week, April 30, 1979. Reprinted from the April 30, 1975, *Business Week* by special permission. Copyright © 1975 by McGraw-Hill, Inc.

Planning is the managerial process of determining what human and technological resources are required to reach a goal, when these resources will be needed, and at what rate they should be used. Planning is future oriented; it may concentrate on the long run or may be short range, considering the immediate future. In this chapter we will focus on long range or strategic planning. In the next chapter we will examine short-range planning and budgeting problems.

In planning, managers constantly make decisions about resource allocation—which to use and how to use them. These decisions are communicated to lower levels of an organization through budgets, rules, policies, and procedures so that the probability of achieving goals is increased because of the increased likelihood of concerted action at all levels of the organization.

In today's turbulent economic and social environment, planning is becoming, if anything, increasingly difficult and complex. As resource shortages such as energy and raw materials continue to be often unpredictable, better planning is a vital necessity.

Planning is also an integral part of other aspects of the process of managing. *Control,* for instance, is defined as seeing that events conform to plans. In planning, performance standards are set that become the criteria against which the execution of an activity is measured. For example, suppose we plan to achieve a 20 percent return on investment for a given period. To do this, let us say that we determine that we cannot exceed a manufacturing cost of $2.00 per unit. This cost becomes a control standard for the production department. When costs exceed it, some corrective action must be taken.

The *organizing* process is also linked to planning. In organizing we seek to develop a structure of departmental relationships to facilitate the coordination of activities. The goals determined in the planning process govern recruitment, selection, individual performance evaluation, and pay systems.

It is for reasons such as these that managers need to pay attention to the planning process. It is at the very heart of successful performance.

THE STRATEGIC PLANNING HORIZON

Strategic planning is a term that is often used interchangeably with *long-range planning.* How far into the future does a manager have to be thinking before it is long-range or strategic planning? The length of the strategic planning period varies directly with the confidence managers have in predicting the environment. Where there is a stable environment, the long-range planning period may be in the range of five to ten years or more.

Long-range planning, five to ten years into the future, is quite common in stable industries such as steel, public utilities, and automobiles. Take the case of automobile manufacturers. Product styling is a process that has about a four-year lead time, so designers and product engineers are working now on cars that will not be on the road for four years. But the strategic planning problems are certainly more complex than those of design. The Federal government has imposed fleet mileage requirements that manufacturers must achieve in the 1980s. To do this means cars must be smaller and lighter, and engines must be more efficient. Planning to meet these requirements was begun in the 1970s.

Top management in the auto companies must make a number of key decisions today if they are to be profitable ten years from now. Item 8.1 describes how Henry Ford II sees the strategic approach of Ford Motor Company for the 1980s. The mix of car sizes in the product lines must change. In general there will be "downsizing," which means that there will not be as many big cars in the future. The rate at which these smaller cars are to be introduced into the market must be determined. Should General Motors lead Ford? Or should Ford test the waters first? These decisions have to be made before the designers and engineers can be turned loose to translate the strategy decision into a specific product. New materials, lighter but as strong as such traditional materials as steel, must be developed for use in the product. Much testing is required to know where these new materials will work and where they will not. For example, a fiberglass-plastic material is being evaluated for use in wheel rims. One strategic decision is how much money to spend on R & D for a project that will not go on line for, maybe, five years.

And not all strategic decisions result in successful outcomes. The auto industry spent much money and time testing the Wankel engine. The Wankel is a rotary engine that operates on a very different set of principles than the reciprocating piston engine. After several years of testing and evaluation, it was scrapped. Other key long-range decisions have to do with plant location, marketing and distribution policies, and financing strategies.

Contrast this long-range period with the long-range planning in an electrical engineering consulting firm. One such company bids and works on as many as a hundred different projects each year. These projects are for several different clients, they are often one of a kind, and the projects all have different time requirements. Some projects take six weeks, others six months, and some six years. When the president was asked about long-range planning, three to five years into the future, he said

> "We can't do it. Long-range planning for us is, maybe, one to two years ahead. We just don't know where—or who—our business is."

Does this mean that the auto executives who plan five to seven years ahead are better managers than the president of the engineering firm? No, because the planning cycle is different for the two different firms. If a company tries to plan beyond the natural industry or firm cycle, that is really "blue sky" planning and probably of not much use for anything except as a good mental exercise.

THE EFFECTIVENESS OF PLANNING

There is good evidence that planning pays off. Several studies show that the economic performance of companies that have formal planning activities is far better on most traditional performance criteria than companies that do not plan.

There are two related studies in which this evidence is impressively clear. Thune and House[1] studied thirty-six companies in six industries. They compared "formal planning" companies to "nonformal planning" companies on sales, stock prices, earnings per share, return on equity, and return on capital employed.

> Formal planners . . . significantly outperformed informal planners with respect to earnings per share, earnings on common equity and earnings on total capital employed.

Planning benefits may be especially critical for firms that have highly uncertain markets or technological environments. Thune and House[1] found that the gains from long-range planning were greater in more rapidly changing industries, and Khandwalla[2] also concluded that it is probably more important to emphasize strategic planning when the environment is volatile.

Following up on the Thune and House study, Herold[3] found that during a seven-year study period drug and chemical companies that engaged in long-range planning outperformed those that did not. For example, over the study period (1962–1969) formal planning companies increased profits by 139 percent, while the profits of informal planners increased *only* 59 percent. Other studies show equally strong results. Ninety-three companies that had engaged in mergers and acquisitions were studied. The "strategic planning" companies outperformed the "nonplanners."[4] Stagner[5] studied 109 firms and found that those companies that used their top managers in long-range planning consistently obtained better results than those that did not have a strong planning activity. This evidence, we believe, is very strong. These studies are systematic and serious efforts to examine how useful long-range planning really is, and they support the countless individual cases of companies that swear to the importance of long-range planning. There is good reason for confidence in long-range planning.

TYPES OF GOALS

Goals, or objectives, are inherent in the planning process. An objective is simply a *desired end state*—someplace you want to be in the future, something you want to have, or a condition you wish to exist. We make plans to get there.

In planning, managers must be concerned with what these goals are, how to measure the success of achieving them, and how resources should be used to get there. This is no easy task. First, different individuals and groups in organizations will be strong advocates of different goals, often goals that conflict with each other. For example, one coalition of top executives may advocate that a firm should expand through acquisition and merger; another group in the same firm may believe the firm should seek to grow by increasing its sales and, hopefully, profits in its current product line. Second, there are problems with determining how success should be measured, even when there is agreement on what the goal should be. Take the case of an advertising agency. Its stated objective may be to provide high-quality service to clients. What does that mean, operationally, in terms of what the agency does? Is this objective best measured by the number of campaigns the agency conducts, its billings, or its profits? Each of these different measures of goal achievement could lead to a different plan. For instance, if the number of campaigns is the measure for what management selects as the primary indicator of success for that agency, the agency might actively seek new clients. With a profit measure as the primary objective, the firm might focus on cost-reduction strategies in current programs without vigorously seeking new clients. All this is to say that the way the goals become specific for its members can markedly affect what they do.

There are three types of goals that must be considered in the management process, especially planning. ***Strategic goals*** are those that are related to meeting the survival needs of the organization as imposed by the external environment. ***System goals*** are requirements of the internal operating units of an organization. ***Individual goals*** are those demands that individuals place on the organization.

STRATEGIC GOALS

Strategic goals are those that are derived to meet the requirements or demands placed on the organization from the existing environment. We have already described how the external environment (markets, technologies, or other sectors) affect the structure of the different subsystems of the organization. The basis of the different strategic goals are related to the environmental sectors. A fundamental strategic goal for any business firm is the market it will seek to serve. Customers and clients have very different needs and preferences, which must be determined by the firm. Publishers, for example, may seek to target the market for college textbooks or to target the trade markets (fiction, nonfiction, etc.). Computer manufacturers may direct their efforts at customers who use small terminals or those who need gigantic computers, like research facilities. The definition of the market the organization will serve depends upon current and potential capability of the organization. The analysis of capabilities is basic to the strategic planning process.

Thus, the market strategy is related to the second strategic goal area—the technological strategy. This strategic area is a limiting factor on the firm's capacity to satisfy marketing goals. The computer manufacturer mentioned above must have technical staff (computer scientists, engineers, and programmers) capable of designing and implementing the market strategy decision. Suppose a computer manufacturer should decide to compete against IBM. Can the members of the staff design the hardware and the software program packages that will do what IBM does? If they cannot, even though a share of the market may be available, it is probably unattainable because the firm cannot produce a "good product" for that market.

If other segments of the environment have a significant effect on the organization, then strategic goals must be considered in these areas also. How, for instance, should a pharmaceutical manufacturer that has significant relations with governmental agencies such as FDA, FTC, and the Justice Department act in matters of quality control or potential antitrust violations?

In order not to go out of business and, as important, to operate profitably, the firm must focus on strategic goals and put the organization processes and systems in place to achieve these strategic goals. This is what we mean by strategic planning. Strategic planning is spelling out the strategic objectives and making resource (both human and physical) acquisition decisions to achieve them.

An Example of a Strategic Goal

Power tools such as saws, drills, routers, and sanders have been the product line of Black and Decker for many years. In the early years of the company, the major market for these tools was the construction trade. These tools had a long life and were favored by skilled tradesmen. The tools were high priced, but the durability and quality were more than worth it.

This market became increasingly competitive, especially with the entry of large retail department stores, such as Sears, which sell their own "private brand" tool. At about the same time, the "do-it-yourself" movement began to grow. Hobbyists and others who did not need such quality and durability in their tools created a large new market.

Black and Decker management was faced with the following decision: should it continue to produce tools for the skilled tradesmen or should it seek to produce tools for the larger but less technically demanding market? It chose the latter. The firm is now a leader in electric power tools, lawn care products, and other related consumer products. The decision led to a substantial change in the product image among skilled tradesmen, who now prefer other tools. But the profitability and growth of the company over the last fifteen years has been extremely strong, justifying the change of course.

Internal system goals are those of the subunits of the system. If the whole system is to achieve the strategic objectives, every unit must have inputs from other units, and each unit must provide an output to be used by others. These outputs are internal system goals.

When a strategic goal is made operational, it is broken down into specific subgoals, and these are assigned to specific units of an organization as an internal system goal. Production output goals for a manufacturing unit, cost goals, market share goals, and efficiency objectives are all "end states" that are typically associated with a particular organizational unit (auditing, manufacturing, sales, and so forth).

When a manager speaks about goals for his or her unit, the manager is talking about internal system goals. Because of the divergent interests of the various units of an organization, it is often difficult to successfully integrate the different points of view into a harmonious set of system goals.

A strategic goal is translated, through the strategy decision, into more refined and specific objectives (internal systems goals) for the various units of the organization. These may be ***product*** goals, ***market share*** goals, ***productivity*** goals, and ***profitability*** goals.

Product Goals

Product goals state the character of the output. How long should the product last? How should it look? What components are to be used in its manufacture?

The answers to these questions represent how the strategy decision is translated in the firm; that is, what kind of product to make to achieve the strategic goal. Design standards, quality-control levels, and manufacturing methods may all be thought of as forms of the product goal.

Market Share Goals

For Black and Decker market share goals specify at what particular group of tool users the product is aimed and what proportion both of the total market for power tools and of the particular market segment the firm believes it can obtain. Some tool users, of course, will continue to demand high quality and durability, even though the price may be higher. Another group will want lower price and less durability. In opting for the high-volume, low-price segment of the market, the firm will consider the probable size of that market segment relative to the total market for power tools, as well as the total share of that market segment it is possible for the firm to obtain. Typically, the firm will then measure at least one aspect of market success by determining how much of the market it has relative to competitors, and its current share relative to the share of previous years.

Market share goals set the tone for the development of specific sales strategy and planning. What kind of advertising program is most likely to be effective in reaching the desired group of customers? Geographically, where are the majority of potential customers located? How can the sales staff sell most effectively? What channel of distribution is most efficient?

Productivity Goals

Productivity goals measure the efficiency with which resources are used. Productivity is the output obtained relative to inputs. Productivity goals typically are expressed as ratios, such as sales per employee, or units produced per worker. Productivity goals may be set for manufacturing activities, marketing functions, and other areas of operation. Setting productivity goals is an attempt to give managers some idea of what they must achieve to contribute to the effectiveness of the whole system.

Productivity goals may be derived from a number of different sources—past ratios of outputs to inputs, for example. If previously ten employees produced 1,000 units per day, then we would want to add two more employees if projected levels increased to 1,200. On the other hand, by adding only one more employee and improving the operation, perhaps we could still attain an output of 1,200 units; thereby we have improved productivity and very likely reduced costs.

Profitability Goals

Profitability goals are a form of productivity measure that refer to how well the organization has performed, overall. Typically, profitability goals are assessed by considering returns obtained on sales or investments. Profit as a percentage of sales or as a proportion of assets are common measures of profitability.

Profitability goals focus less on how well a specific component of the organization is doing and more on the whole firm, although it is possible to devise such indexes for specific units. Profitability is generally used as a measure of managerial effectiveness and may have significant effects on the acquisition of capital. For example, investors will be more willing to risk their funds in a firm that has higher profitability than another, presuming that both offer similar prospective returns in the form of dividends to the investor.

INDIVIDUAL GOALS

These are goals that individuals, or specifically identified subgroups, expect the organization to provide to them. Each person or group wants something slightly different from another in an organization. Workers want wages, managers want salaries, owners want profits. These are inducements that an organization must provide to obtain the contribution of these various groups. Individual goals are reflected in the planning documents of an organization. Wage levels, for example, will be shown as estimates of part of the product cost. Profit levels will be set as goals. The individuals and groups who expect payoffs from the system will, of course, press to increase their return. Owners will want higher profits and dividends, workers will want higher wages.

The final overall plan adopted by an organization will reflect all of these individual and subgroup goals. The final plan derives from the pressures that each brings to bear on the others. In this sense, then, plans to achieve objectives represent compromises among the subgroups.△

THE PLANNING PROCESS AND OBJECTIVES

One way to look at planning is as a factoring, or breaking down, of the strategic objective into system goals for both the long and short range. Basically, strategic decisions are made about the nature of products and markets. These are then translated into profit and cost objectives for the total firm and the specific operating units.

Figure 8.1 illustrates the planning and control cycle for an organization. For the coming year it is necessary to develop specific goals and strategies, operational plans and controls, for marketing, production, and support functions. From these projections, control standards are developed that become the basis for evaluating how effectively the firm operates.

At the same time that planning is being done for the short run, long-range considerations such as capital acquisition and new products must be considered and evaluated. This strategic planning requires an intimate knowledge of products and costs, as well as of strengths and weaknesses of the firm. It requires a long-range estimate of changes in the economy, society, and the political environment that will affect the capacity of the organization to survive.

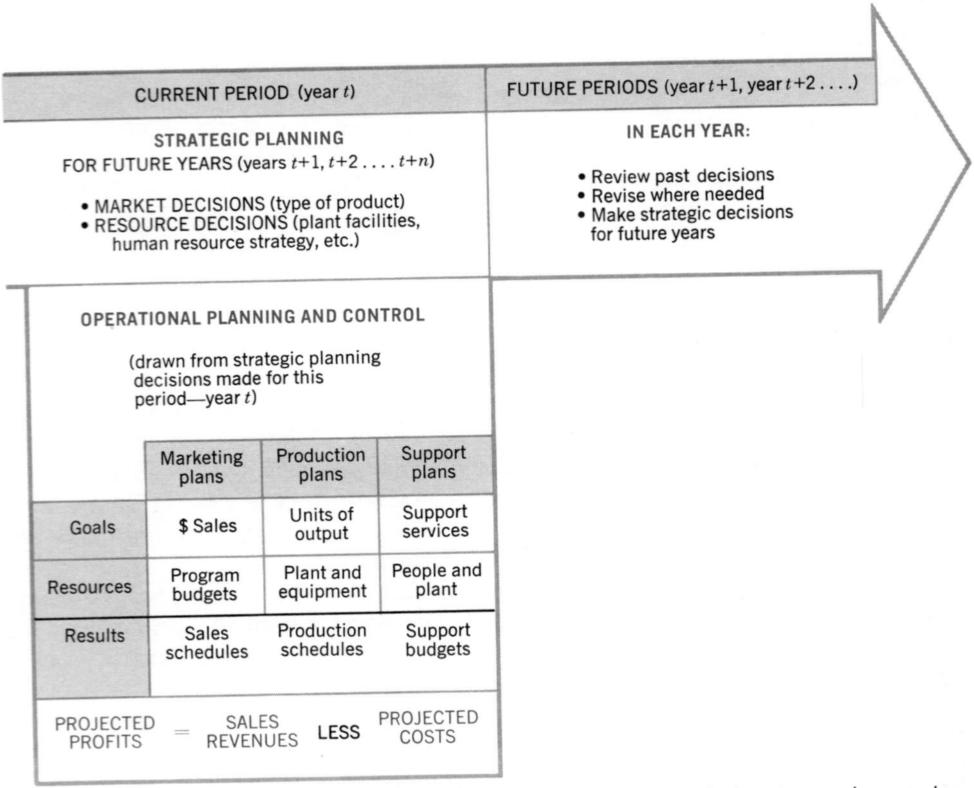

CURRENT PERIOD (year t)	FUTURE PERIODS (year $t+1$, year $t+2$ ....)
STRATEGIC PLANNING FOR FUTURE YEARS (years $t+1, t+2 \ldots t+n$) • MARKET DECISIONS (type of product) • RESOURCE DECISIONS (plant facilities, human resource strategy, etc.)	**IN EACH YEAR:** • Review past decisions • Revise where needed • Make strategic decisions for future years

OPERATIONAL PLANNING AND CONTROL

(drawn from strategic planning decisions made for this period—year t)

	Marketing plans	Production plans	Support plans
Goals	$ Sales	Units of output	Support services
Resources	Program budgets	Plant and equipment	People and plant
Results	Sales schedules	Production schedules	Support budgets

PROJECTED PROFITS	=	SALES REVENUES	**LESS**	PROJECTED COSTS

FIGURE 8.1   The link between strategic planning and operational planning and control.

Figure 8.1 shows a "comprehensive managerial planning system."[6] Comprehensive managerial planning involves the development of a whole family of formal plans including long-range and short-range plans. Strategic planning is at the heart of the comprehensive planning process. The medium-and short-range plans are the operational component of the comprehensive planning system. These shorter-range goals and plans are the means by which longer-range organizational strategy is implemented. The medium- and short-range operational plans involve the specification of resource use in the organization.

THE STRATEGIC PLANNING PROCESS

The steps that an organization takes to define its mission and domain, the strategic goals for that mission and domain, and the policies to guide managers toward the strategic goal are called the **strategic planning process.** This process is illustrated in Figure 8.2. The steps in the process are:

1. Analyze the environment (characteristics of the industry, product demand, technological environment, government)
2. Analyze the organization (product and market situations, capital structure, technical skills, organization structure, and human resources)
3. Analyze key skills required (critical skills necessary for success)
4. Assess the problems and opportunities that may be the basis for organization action.
5. Generate, evaluate, and select alternative strategies to take advantage of opportunities.

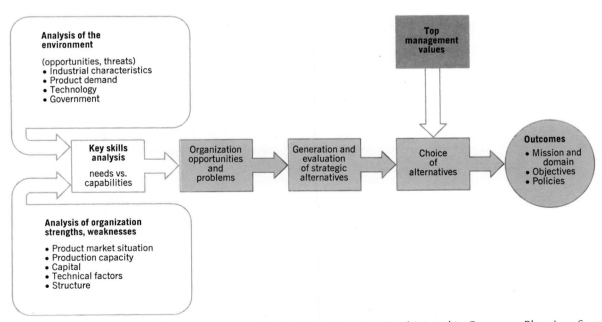

FIGURE 8.2   The strategic planning process. (Adapted from Denning, Basil W. (ed.). *Corporate Planning: Selected Concepts.* McGraw-Hill, London, 1971, Figure 1.2, p. 8.)

The outcome of these steps is the determination of mission and domain, strategic goals, and policies.

The **mission and domain** marks out the general technological and market sectors within which the organization will operate, or to say it another way, those environmental sectors to which the company must adapt. For example, some companies have redefined their mission and domain as "entertainment," rather than "movies." There would be no Disneyland unless the Disney Company broadened its mission beyond cartoons and feature length films. Companies once in the oil business are now in "energy," with broader interests in electricity, coal, nuclear, and solar power.

But not all firms that broaden their mission and domain are successful. Some bite off more than they can chew. The Rucker Company was a small engineering company in the early 1960s. By the mid 1970s, Rucker had acquired twenty-six different types of firms. Sales had increased dramatically, yet eventually the profitability began to decline. Rucker reevaluated its domain—and retrenched, getting rid of many of those firms it had acquired.

The mission and domain statement is of value to investors and lenders, as well as those in the firm. For investors it gives a basis for judging whether or not the firm has an adequate resource base to operate profitably. For those in the firm it provides a basis for understanding the strategic goals.

The **strategic goals** are embodied in the mission and domain statements. Strategic goals will target markets and define growth objectives. One manufacturer, Parker-Hannifin, redefined its mission and domain as the capital goods and the automotive aftermarket and set strategic growth goals that took seven years to implement. Parker-Hannifin set about to increase its automotive supply sales from $8 million to $100 million over this period.[7]

The Parker-Hannifin strategy of growth through merger flowed from this objective. *Business Week* reported that for Parker-Hannifin

> it made no sense . . . to try building new product lines internally to compete with large and established aftermarket supplies like Delco. . . . The biggest hurdle was to bring off the first major merger.[7]

The strategy for Parker-Hannifin was merger, but for other companies increasing current product or service sales may be equally viable approaches.

Strategy is the overall master plan of how to provide goods and services within the bounds of the mission and domain, given the company's resources. Strategies are conceptual ideas about how to achieve the strategic objective. Strategies are the long-term plans that relate the organization's characteristics to competitors, regulators, and customers and the technological base that defines the production system.

Internal system goals are derived from the strategy. Operational planning and control must be fully integrated with the strategic plan. **Policies** are developed to achieve this integration. Policies are decision rules, to be followed by managers at lower organization levels, designed to guide behavior and decisions made at lower levels within the boundaries of the mission and domain statement. Policies reflect the direction that top management believes decisions should take. They may be derived from management's values, they may be a means to implement a strategy, or they may be imposed by external groups such as the government. In any event, policies are means that top management uses to control activities in the organization, minimizing the need for personal supervision to insure that events conform to plans.

ANALYSIS OF THE ENVIRONMENT

One of the first steps in strategic planning is to understand, as clearly as possible, the environment of the organization. General concepts like markets and technology must be translated into specific products, estimates of product demand, and governmental impact. Some, but surely not all, environmental factors are considered below.

Demand for Products.

The long-term demand for current products and for potential products must be assessed. In strategic planning the primary concern is the trend of demand, rather than short-term fluctuations. Short-term fluctuations, generally due to seasonal variations or the stage of the business cycle, are of more concern in short-range planning.

Long-term trends may be predicted using different sources of data, depending on the industry. For example, capital goods manufacturers of machinery and equipment may look very hard at projected rates of economic growth. Consumer goods manufacturers may develop their long-term forecasts from projections of societal and family characteristics, such as changes in the birth rate, in the length of the work week, in age at which people marry, or in leisure interests.

The "product life cycle" must also be considered in long-term projections. (The product life cycle is shown in Figure 8.3.) Products go through periods of growth

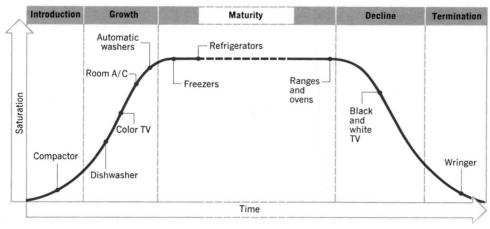

FIGURE 8.3 Life cycle stages of various products. (*Source:* Smallwood, John W., "The product life cycles: A key to strategic marketing planning." *MSU Business Topics,* vol. 21, 1973, pp. 29–35.)

and profits for new products may be higher at first, when the products may be sold in specialty outlets to high-income market segments. As the product becomes more widely accepted, distribution may move from specialty stores to department stores and finally to discount stores. As it moves through the cycle, unit profits may drop but total product profits may be high because of large volume.

There are several different ways of making long-term demand forecasts. According to Wheelwright and Makridakas,[8] the choice of which approach to use depends on the characteristics of the decision situation and the characteristics of the forecasting techniques. Some important characteristics of the planning situation are:

1. Time horizon: This is the period of time into the future for which the forecast is made. We have already said that time horizons vary for different types of firms.
2. Number of items that make up the product or service line: This refers to the aggregation of units in the forecast. Will the forecast be by product line or for the total number of units? For example, General Motors may forecast sales by division (e.g., Oldsmobile, Chevrolet, Buick), or it could simply forecast the total number of cars to be sold.
3. Stability: The degree of uncertainty and change in the environment will affect the planning approach. Of course, this suggests that there will be a different planning strategy for organic and mechanistic organizations.

The characteristics of the forecasting methods will also affect the approach used. These characteristics to be considered are:

1. Time horizon: Generally, for very long forecasts qualitative methods are more useful for short-run plans.
2. Pattern of data: Some techniques vary in their ability to identify different patterns.
3. Accuracy: In some instances, it is necessary to be generally in the ball park. For other cases, a variation of no more than 5 percent may be necessary.
4. Ease of application: The user of the forecast must understand the method, or be reasonably confident about the outcome.

In general, the manager should evaluate different planning methods against these guidelines and the benefits of each method compared against the cost.

AN EXAMPLE OF DEMAND FORECASTING. California Calculator, Inc. (CALCAL) manufactures electronic calculators. In the past they have found that their own level of sales bears a fairly constant relationship to the level of sales for the entire industry, about one percent. In order to plan, long-term and short-term, the company bases a forecast on projected industry activity. In our example, total demand is predicted to be as shown in Table 8.1, along with the expected level of sales for CALCAL (one percent of industry volume).

Figure 8.4 is a hypothetical projection of total industry sales derived from the data shown in Table 8.1. Industry forecasts such as this are often prepared by organizations themselves, but are also available from trade associations, industry groups, and very often from governmental sources.

TABLE 8.1   Projected Industry and CALCAL Sales (in units)

Year	Total Industry Volume	CALCAL Volume (1%)
19__1	1,500,000	15,000
19__2	1,800,000	18,000
19__3	2,000,000	20,000
19__4	2,500,000	25,000
19__5	3,000,000	30,000

Industry Structure

This refers to the number of firms, their size and output, and how sales are distributed in the industry. Some industries are highly competitive. Entrance into some product areas is relatively simple because capital requirements are low. Others, such as pharmaceuticals, are oligopolistic, where a few firms dominate the industry.

THE CALCAL EXAMPLE.   CALCAL is in a highly competitive industry. In California, south of San Francisco, are many firms that manufacture the same type of product, semiconductors. The industry seems to spawn new companies. A bright engineer who wants to be in the business need only find a few investors and a small plant, and a new company is born.

The Technological Environment

We have already shown in Chapter 3 how the technological environment may affect a firm. In a rapidly changing technological environment, successful firms this year may be out of business next year because of technological breakthroughs. Some estimate must be made of the rapidity of changes that will cause the current product line to become obsolete. For instance, in recent years the watch industry has undergone very significant technological changes. With the advent of quartz crystals and

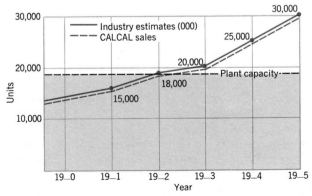

FIGURE 8.4   Projections of industry sales of electronic calculators and CALCAL sales.

digital devices, manufacturers of spring-driven watches were seriously threatened. Some adapted, others did not.

Manufacturing technology may also change drastically. At one time the assembly of television sets required a great deal of skilled hand labor. Presently television production is so automated that assembly is carried out by only a few workers.

Government

Governmental action can be a key element in the environment. Governments often take actions to support and protect an industry from foreign competition. A government may set quotas or import duties on foreign products. These quotas or import duties may apply to raw materials, components, and finished products. Such government actions are often designed to stimulate domestic production of certain products or services.

Government regulation may have significant effects on various industries. Air pollution regulations have resulted in the closing of some chemical plants, paper mills, and steel mills. Changes in the tax laws can stimulate or discourage investment. Other governmental action can support some industries, such as aerospace. The role of the government is so pervasive that its effects, present and potential, must be assessed.

ANALYSIS OF THE ORGANIZATION

The objective of organization analysis is to discover or clarify the strengths and weaknesses of the organization. The strategic plan should be based on the strengths of the firm and these should be judged as realistically as possible. Some areas to be evaluated in organization analysis are (1) product, (2) production capability and capacity, (3) technical knowledge, (4) capital structure, and (5) organization structure.

Product

What the company sells and how this product is seen by the market is of significant importance. A product/market analysis may reveal such factors as the quality image, the availability of dealers and dealer service organizations, or other strengths on which the firm can capitalize. A market/product analysis may show that the way management conceives of the product could lead to a less effective marketing strategy. One marketing expert, for example, thinks that a manufacturer of power drills, such as Black and Decker, should view its product as $\frac{1}{4}$-inch holes that the consumer wants, not $\frac{1}{4}$-inch power drills. IBM's product is viewed as "solutions to problems," rather than computers.

Analysis may show that different products are in different stages of the product life cycle. For example, an appliance manufacturer may find that its microwave ovens are in the growth stage, while blenders are in a stable period. This information can be used to decide which markets are most profitable and those in which resources should be utilized.

Production

Two important facets of the production system are capability and capacity. ***Capability*** is simply whether or not the firm can produce the current or planned products. In the computer industry, for instance, there are, and have been, many firms that are able to manufacture equipment that is equivalent to that of competitors. Major electronics companies (RCA and GE) with the capability to compete technologically with IBM have been relatively unsuccessful in the market. It is not enough to be able to produce something.

Capacity means whether or not production resources are available that can be used for manufacturing the product or delivering the service. If there is unused capacity or slack resources, the company may be able to make lower bids to customers, since the incremental cost of producing additional orders may be relatively low. If demand exceeds capacity, and if the company wishes to increase its sales, then it must evaluate the alternatives of adding new facilities or not.

> **CALCAL.** One fact is evident from Figure 8.4. With plant capacity of 18,000 units, CALCAL will be unable to increase 19_2 sales to the potential level of 20,000 components. So this year the president must also make a capital investment decision. Should he expand current facilities, add new ones, or simply stay the same size? Unless there is an increase in the production capacity, CALCAL will be able to produce only 18,000 units annually.

Technical Knowledge

Closely linked to production is a set of technical considerations. Technical knowledge and research and development facilities are often important prerequisites in exploiting strategic opportunities. In one major firm that had a costly and important component, which it purchased from a supplier, it was decided that the firm itself should manufacture the component. They abandoned this project when they found that their staff did not have the engineering skill, and they were unable to recruit adequate technical staff to design and manufacture the part.

Having adequate technical skill is not always enough to insure success, either. Certainly manufacturers like RCA, GE, and Sperry Rand UNIVAC have in-house capability to design competitive computer equipment, but for the most part, when these companies have ventured into this market, they have had only minimal success.

Capital Structure

Financial strengths and weaknesses are important considerations in strategy. New markets and available technology are opportunities only if they can be financed. The capital strength of the firm is an important determinant of future growth and, subsequently, profitability.

Organization Structure

The organization structure may be a barrier to growth. In one firm it was found that the older, more established departments hindered the new-product development unit. This can happen when the evaluation of new projects is performed in one unit and a report must be cleared by other units before the report is accepted. Often a manager who feels threatened by the proposed strategy might use delaying tactics, such as requiring that the project be reported to an evaluation committee. If the committee is slow, or the threatened manager can delay the project in the committee, the time may pass for the proposal to be a viable option.

KEY SKILL ANALYSIS

Key skill analysis is important in strategic planning. The assumption of key skill analysis is that there are a small number of critical organizational skills necessary to succeed in a particular environment. Figure 8.5 shows that these key skills vary from industry to industry. International marketing skills and contract negotiating skills are key skills in an oil company. For an auto firm, cost control and mass production skills are musts. Capital acquisition skills are critical in mining, and in advertising creativity is of great importance.[9]

Once these required key skills are identified, they can then be compared to those that are present. If the skills required for a particular industry are greater than or different from those identified as existing in the firm, the firm should be very cautious in moving ahead with strategic plans. Management must decide whether the skill gap can be overcome by hiring or training. If not, it should be very reluctant to risk a move.

OPPORTUNITIES AND THREATS

The assessment of the environment, the evaluation of the organization, and the key skills analysis will allow management to compare these three factors. It then can

FIGURE 8.5 Capability profile and key skills. (*Source:* Denning, Basil W. (ed.). *Corporate Planning: Selected Concepts.* McGraw-Hill, London, 1971, p. 15.)

seek to identify opportunities for the organization that might exist and/or threats to which the company must respond.

Threats may be in the form of current or anticipated government action, increased foreign or domestic competition, technical obsolescence, declining markets, or changing product image. A threat to the firm might therefore result from changes in the environment or from internal weaknesses of the organization itself. For example, one of the major computer manufacturers felt threatened and *reduced* the price of its major computer when IBM announced it was introducing a new machine that, as it turned out, was not delivered for three years.

When a threat is discovered in planning, it is important, at all costs, to avoid reacting without careful thinking. For a company to make a major change just because something *could* happen is, obviously, unwise.

An **opportunity** exists when there is a real or predicted market or technological gap and the firm has the capacity to fill it. For instance, McDonalds, the restaurant chain, found and exploited an opportunity by uncovering and developing the market for home parties. Now, they provide food for all sorts of parties in homes.

Opportunities may be identified in a number of ways. One expert believes that growth and success are most likely when the firm chooses propitious niches.[9] The propitious niche is meeting or exploiting a particular need in the environment, choosing where to concentrate or what factors to emphasize.

Success depends on organizational strengths. Organizations that match their strengths with the factors needed for success in a particular situation are likely to perform better than their competition. One foreign firm built a successful dealer organization in the United States very early in its history, on the advice of consultants. This dealer organization now enables the firm to distribute noncompeting products of other international companies, with a considerable profit for itself.

Success is a matter of exploiting strengths and avoiding weaknesses, whether we are speaking about a business organization, a military unit, or an athletic team. Tactical mobility may win a military victory over an enemy of superior numbers and resources, or a basketball team can sometimes exploit its superior ball-handling skills to overcome the superior height or shooting prowess of another team.

THE AUTO INDUSTRY THREAT. A threat was faced by the auto industry, magnified by the oil crisis of 1973. Even though imports and small cars had been in the U.S. auto market for years, there had been little effective response by domestic manufacturers. There was little effort to build and market a U.S.-manufactured automobile that delivered high gas mileage.

The threat for the auto industry was created by the growing fuel shortage—and highlighted by the 1973 oil embargo. For General Motors, in particular, the problem was severe. *Fortune* reports that:

> When the Arab oil embargo hit at the end of 1973, GM had the worst average gas mileage among U.S. automakers—a dismal twelve miles per gallon. As buyers turned away from gas guzzlers in panic during the following year, GM's share of the U.S. new car market slipped to 42 percent, the lowest point since 1952.[10]

It was clear that the U.S. auto industry was in trouble. Public confidence was falling, along with sales and stock prices.

Of course, GM and the other auto manufacturers had been planning before 1973, and there was some discussion about trying to increase mileage and "downsizing," that is, producing smaller cars. But the oil embargo disrupted—very severely—the smooth planning that had traditionally gone on in this industry. Up to then, design and introduction of new models had proceeded at a rather orderly pace. Suddenly, in 1973, it was apparent that the planning would have to be sped up.

The Opportunity/Threat Gap

An opportunity, or a threat, should be viewed as a current (or predicted) gap between where the firm is (or will be) and where it should be. As in the case of the auto industry—and GM in particular—it was clear that the market would not continue to accept the types of cars that were being manufactured in 1972. When this gap is large, or if it is growing, the firm must find a way to reduce it. That is the purpose of the next stage in the strategic planning process.

GENERATION, EVALUATION, AND
SELECTION OF STRATEGIC ALTERNATIVES

There are "many ways to skin a cat." There are also many ways to reduce the opportunities/threat gap. The generation and evaluation of strategic alternatives is of prime importance because the choice sets the organization on a path that may take several years to travel. So the process of finding alternatives and evaluating them should be as open and rational as possible. Yet there is a grave danger that political considerations in the firm will take over in the evaluation of strategic alternatives. Why? Because it is likely, since different directions will be advocated by different groups, that the strategy chosen will place one person or group in a stronger power position than others.

Where do these strategic alternatives come from? The previous chapter discussed several ways to generate alternatives, and these approaches would be useful here. However, in strategic planning there is a great deal more subjectivity and intuition in the process of generating alternatives.

There is also more subjectivity and qualitative factors when managers evaluate the strategic alternatives. Because the selected "strategy" will have such a long-run effect, and because of the uncertainty of the future, human judgment enters in and plays as important a role as forecasts and more quantitative or systematic predictions. Some considerations are:

1. *Resource availability.* Human and physical resources limit what the firm can do. The basic question here is whether or not the company has the resource base to be able to carry out the plan. If it does, then it can proceed. Otherwise it should postpone implementation or seek resources from other sources.

2. *Capacity to obtain resources.* If the firm does not have the resource base, can it be acquired? Does the firm have a strong enough financial reputation to borrow or to raise equity capital? Often strategic alternatives require very large amounts of capital. Lender and investor confidence are useful assets for any business.

3. Risk. Generally speaking, the longer the time horizon for the strategy, the greater the risk. Ten-year plans are more uncertain and risky than three-year programs. Not only might environmental conditions change over time, but the firm's skill and resource base may change as well. Plans may become obsolete, valuable technical personnel hired away.

The risk of a strategic decision will also increase as a larger proportion of total resources of the firm is committed to it. Very large losses, while important, can be absorbed more easily by larger companies. A loss of $500,000 may be easily taken by a very large multinational firm, while such a loss could destroy a small firm.

4. Strategy congruence. Strategy congruence is the fit between current activities and planned activities. Past objectives, policies, and plans that are currently being implemented will have an effect on the future. To the degree that there is a good deal of congruence between long-term and short-term plans, the long-term strategy will be easier to implement.

5. Economic/cost considerations. When a company makes a long-range plan, it is making a commitment of resources. But costs must be thought of as more than just the cash outlay. Several aspects of costs must be taken into account.

The **sunk cost principle** means that a resource is worth, not what it cost in the past, but what it will bring in the future. Old or specialized equipment, though very expensive to purchase, is worth only its scrap value unless it produces some economic benefits. Past investments are history and must be forgotten, written off, and discarded if they have no earning capacity, no matter what their value is "on the books."

The difference between **implicit** and **explicit** costs is that explicit costs can be assessed or verified because they are formalized in the accounting or information system. Because of this, resources to which it is difficult to attach explicit costs are often used poorly. The best example of implicit costs is human resources. Human talent is of great value to an organization, but it is not treated as an asset. A firm seeking to reduce costs may reduce explicit costs but incur tremendous implicit costs by taking actions that increase personnel turnover, reduce productivity, or increase resistance to new programs.

An instance of how different companies treat the explicit and implicit cost of human resources is illustrated in the example of the manpower strategy of two firms in the same industry. Over the years the more successful firm has reduced its work force during recessions by attrition (resignations, retirements, and deaths). Such an approach increases managerial and technical costs above what they might be during the business lull, but when demand increases and sales pick up, the people are in place to take advantage of new opportunities. The practice of the other firm is very different. During recessionary periods, managers and engineers are "laid off" or terminated. The short-run costs are reduced, but when demand increases, the second firm goes on a hiring spree. It takes the new personnel quite a period of adjustment and learning the system before the slack is picked up. Product design is slower because of the less experienced staff. This difference in handling human resources is thought by many to be a key factor in the success of the industry leader.

Marginal costs are added costs incurred when a decision is made. Marginal costs must be compared to the marginal gains, and so long as the marginal gains are greater, then the decision maker is gaining.

Opportunity costs are those costs that are incurred because when we commit resources to one strategy, we cannot use them for another. Therefore, we have given up an "opportunity." Often resources such as equipment, human factors, capital, and facilities are used for a product for which demand has slipped considerably when those same resources could have been used for products with increasing demand.

THE GENERAL MOTORS STRATEGIC DECISION. In 1973 the auto industry faced a threat from the impending fuel shortage. To the most naive observer, it was clear that cars were going to have to be lighter and smaller and get more miles per gallon. GM, like other automakers, adopted a "downsizing" strategy—make the big cars smaller. But which ones? When? When one considers the size of these giant corporations in the auto industry, it is easy to understand that it is impossible to downsize all auto lines in the same year. The investment in new capital equipment is just enormous.

According to *Fortune*, General Motors decided to "downsize" its line starting from the top—with the Cadillacs, Buicks, and Oldsmobiles.

> By downsizing the top of its line first, while competitors started from the bottom, GM has ended up with the standard car market almost to itself for the next year or so.[10]

Of course, there was more involved in the whole process of making and implementing this strategy. According to *Fortune*, three years after the "crisis" began, GM had increased its mileage from the lowest average among the carmakers (12 mpg) to the highest average mileage (17.8 mpg) in 1978.

PIMS APPROACH TO STRATEGIC PLANNING

A wide range of factors, forces, and effects must be evaluated in the strategic planning process. Product design, plant location, marketing strategies, corporate image, and the like are important considerations. Perhaps the most important set of considerations revolves around how, and whether, an organization is going to make expenditures for projects that have the promise of generating future returns.

One approach to evaluating these considerations is the PIMS approach (Profit Impact of Marketing Strategies). PIMS originated from some extensive planning work at General Electric. The approach is based on the profit experiences of over six hundred businesses in several different industries. The profit experiences of these firms were analyzed to find answers to the following questions:

1. What is the "normal" profit rate for a particular type of business, considering factors such as technology, competitive position, and cost structure?
2. If such business continues its present course, what is its future economic performance likely to be?
3. What strategic changes might improve its performance?

4. What are the consequences of specific strategies for profitability and/or cash flow in the short run and in the long run?

With answers to such questions, a firm can estimate what its returns should have been over a particular period of time. If these returns are exceeded, the company can seek to determine why, and then assess whether or not it should continue doing whatever it was doing. If the actual returns are less than the "normal" rates, then there is the need for a different strategy.

One use of PIMS was in an international firm manufacturing and selling abrasives and other industrial products. The company had eighty-five plants located in twenty-one different nations. Traditionally, abrasive goods were sold in mature markets where the company had significant market shares. The abrasives business depended on careful cost control, keeping products up-to-date, and maintaining the current market share of the company. The abrasive product line provided the company with much cash but little growth. The newer nonabrasive product lines had higher cash needs, but they also had high growth potential.

The company's operations were divided into sixty different "businesses," which in turn were grouped into thirty strategic business units. Each of these thirty strategic business units (SBUs) prepared a strategy book in which its proposals were outlined for review by a top level strategy guidance committee every two years. In the strategy book each SBU had to identify its mission, strengths and weaknesses, likely competitive developments, trends, and strategy. These were then compared to the overall corporate strategy and to the strategies developed for other product groupings. Of course, this almost constant review of the various strategy books prepared by the different units enabled the top corporate management team to know, not only what was currently going on, but also what was supposed to happen in the future for all of their products on a worldwide basis. This gave top management much more control and flexibility than many other top management groups in multiproduct companies who are often forced to react to problems after they have occurred when it is too late to do anything about them.

ORGANIZATIONAL TYPES AND PLANNING

When the environment is well-defined, known, and relatively constant—as it is for mechanistic organizations—deterministic techniques can be applied to planning problems. The decision maker assumes that certain costs, conditions, and circumstances can be specified with accuracy. With such an assumption various alternatives can be evaluated, and the one that best achieves the goal can be selected. This is decision making under certainty.

Decision making under risk is also likely to be employed in mechanistic organizations. Often, even though a manager cannot be certain about things, he may be in a position to make a probability estimate about them. As we noted in Chapter 7, this may be because of his past experience, or perhaps because of data that have been collected and analyzed. These two approaches to decision making and resource allocation are the most prevalent in mechanistic organizations.

The difficulties with which organizations operating in a volatile environment must cope arise from the fact not only that changes in the external environment must be perceived and assessed, but also that the changes themselves often alter the organization's methods of goal achievement. This means that organizations operating in a volatile environment must have a flexible structure, one in which both human and technical resources are adaptable to changing tasks. Since the opportunities to develop fixed production systems that are present in the mechanistic organization are not present in the organic organization, resources in the latter must be kept mobile.

What the manager in the organic organization must do is adopt planning strategies for short time periods, recognizing that subsequent periods may require vastly different organizational activities. Starr[11] addresses this problem by noting that one

> approach is to speed up management's response rates and to plan for periods that are short enough to be relatively stable. Short planning periods have all the dangers of suboptimization . . . , but, if consecutive periods are relatively independent, then a good deal can be gained from faster decision making, more rapid action, and so on. Speed is accomplished largely through increased experience. . . .

The emphatic thrust, then, in organic organizations will be to make decisions about what environmental goals should look like, based on the changes that managers feel will occur, and to focus on the development, design, and effective managing of project-like task activities.

The manager in the organic organization therefore needs to know how to make decisions when there is high uncertainty in the environment. He must deal with two problems: (1) selecting a strategy likely to be successful in an unpredictable environment, (2) implementing the strategy. Item 8.2 describes GE's approach to evaluating various strategies. It shows the "subjectivity" involved in strategy decisions in a volatile environment.

Item 8.2   GENERAL ELECTRIC'S "STOPLIGHT STRATEGY" FOR PLANNING

General Electric Co. thinks it has found at least a partial solution to an age-old corporate planning problem: how to put a value on those critical elements in planning it is impossible to attach a number to. In a decision on whether a product will live or die, for example, the value of a patent or the impact of social change cannot be quantified. By using its Strategic Business Planning Grid, or "stoplight strategy," GE can at least evaluate such factors with something more than just a gut reaction.

"It's the best way we've found to sort disparate businesses," says GE planner Reuben Gutoff. "You eventually have to make a subjective decision, but you put into it all the hard information you can. It's one way to compare apples and oranges."

GE, with 43 distinct businesses, has a lot of apples and oranges. In every annual planning review, each individual business is rated, not only on numerical projections of sales, profit, and return on investment, but also on such hard-to-quantify factors as volatility of market share, technology needs, employee loyalty in the industry, competitive stance, and social need. The result is a high, medium, or low rating on both attractiveness of an industry and GE's strengths in the field.

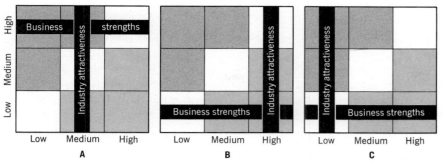

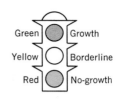

General Electric's Spotlight Strategy for Planning

HOW IT WORKS. If industry attractiveness is seen as medium and GE's strengths as high (chart A), an "invest and grow"—or green light—decision would result, because the evaluation bars cross in a green square. Both industry attractiveness and business strength are low in chart B, indicating a red light strategy, or a business that will continue to generate earnings but no longer warrants much additional investment by GE. Chart C represents a business with high industry attractiveness but low GE strength—a "yellow" business that might go either way.

A green business is expected to grow. A red operation's strategy, on the other hand, may involve consolidation of plants, limited technology infusion, reduced investment, and strong cash flow. A yellow business could be borderline or the business—say, electronic components—could be diverse enough to have both red and green units.

"We don't give definitive weights to the non-numerical factors," says Gutoff, "but they do have weights. At the end of our discussion there is a good consensus on what's green, red, or yellow." The result, he says, is "semiquantitative." After three or four critiques at various levels, the final grids—and decisions—are made by the corporate policy committee—the chairman, three vice chairman, five senior vice presidents, and the vice president for finance.

The process is not just window dressing. It may prevent costly mistakes. "Interestingly," says one GE planner, "the financial projections are often best on businesses that turn up worst (in the red) on the grid."

Source: Business Week, April 28, 1975. Reprinted from the April 28, 1975, *Business Week* by special permission. Copyright © 1975 by McGraw-Hill, Inc.

SUMMARY

This chapter examined strategic decision making and planning, activities generally carried out by top management in organizations. Strategic decisions are converted to plans when the organization commits itself to various courses of action in exploiting and coping with its environment in the future, whether the period is for the next year or over the next ten years. These strategic plans must then be converted to operational plans carried out at lower levels, since top management does not execute the plans it develops. However, top management must review such operational plans to insure that they are in conformity with strategic plans, that they are executed as intended, and that they achieve the results anticipated.

Strategic Planning

Case
8.1 Applied Chemistry Research Corporation

Applied Chemistry Research Corporation has produced batteries since the 1930s. In the late 1960s research began on a new type of battery that had a long life but which could be made much smaller than batteries in the past. The company was successful and gained worldwide patents for these new batteries. One of the first applications of these new batteries was in a pacemaker, which many heart patients need to stay alive.

The emphasis in ACRC has been on quality, rather than quantity, to such a degree that fast workers are transferred out of the pacemaker battery production room. The company has not had to stress quality; the workers seem to take great care with their product on their own initiative. By the mid 1970s, the product improvement measures ACRC had introduced had given the batteries such a long life that one of the marketing managers complained to the president, "We are taking ourselves out of a replacement market entirely." The president looked at him and answered, "Yes, that's true, but we have to do it. It's the right thing for ACRC."

1. Why does there appear to be such an emphasis on quality among the workers in this company?
2. Evaluate the comments made by the marketing manager and the president.
3. What strategic decisions has Applied Chemistry Research made?
4. What must they do to continue their success? How risky is this strategy? What kinds of risks are there for ACRC?
5. Compare ACRC's strategy with that of a more traditional battery producer.

Case
8.2 Universal Electric

Universal Electric is one of the largest multinational firms in the world. Although UE initially produced only electrical products, the firm now manufactures more than 30,000 different products and services, many quite unrelated to each other. The firm has centralized financial and personnel activities, but all other functions are delegated to the various product divisions of the company. Some of these divisions are highly centralized, though others are decentralized.

Bob Muzik, manager of the Nuclear Power Systems Division, is very worried. His division develops, manufactures, and sells nuclear reactors—very large, complex, and costly products. Over the years this division has hired and retained some of the finest nuclear reactor specialists in the world. In 1971 Universal Electric sold four nuclear reactors to foreign nations. Their chief U.S. competitor sold another four reactors. Foreign reactor producers sold only one nuclear reactor. A few years later, the U.S. government, fearful of the spread of atomic weapons, placed many restrictions on the sale of nuclear plants to other countries. This had a devastating effect on the sales of nuclear reactors. In 1976 Universal Electric sold no nuclear reactors. U.S. manufacturers, in fact, sold only one nuclear reactor to an overseas buyer. In 1976 European companies sold nine nuclear reactors. In 1977 U.S. firms sold no nuclear reactors, but its European competitors (to whom Universal Electric had sold their patent rights) sold four.

Bob Muzik wondered whether the division could stay afloat if it could depend only on domestic sales. "It's so unjust," he thought. "If we don't sell them a reactor somebody else will, so what's accomplished by this policy?"

1. What might the company do at this point?
2. Evaluate Bob Muzik's last statement.
3. What does this case illustrate about factors that might affect strategic planning activities?

Strategic
Planning

DISCUSSION QUESTIONS

1. Long-range planning has been proven to be effective within an organization. Discuss how and why this is true.
2. Strategic goals are related to the survival needs of the organization. These relate to the market and technology. What would happen if there were other relevant sectors of the environment? Discuss these two areas.
3. Internal system goals involve the subunits of the organization. Discuss this important aspect of planning.
4. Market share goals reflect the specific group of customers the organization aims at. Discuss the importance of these goals.
5. What do productivity goals measure and why are they so important?
6. How are profitability goals related to productivity goals?
7. Why are individual goals of greater importance than other goals used in planning?
8. Why is it necessary for a manager to take the position that in the final analysis a plan is detailed as though no worthwhile opportunities for deviating from the plan will occur?

REFERENCES

1. Thune, S., and R. House. "Where long-range planning pays off," Business Horizon, 13 (1970).
2. Khandwalla, Pradip. The design of organizations. New York, Harcourt Brace Jovanovich, 1977.
3. Herold, D. "Long range planning and organizational performance: A cross validation study," Academy of Management Journal 15 (1972): 91–102.
4. Ansoff, H. I. "Does planning pay?" Long Range Review, 3 (1970): 2–7.
5. Stagner, R. "Corporate decision making," Journal of Applied Psychology, 53 (1969): 1–13.
6. Steiner, G. "Comprehensive managerial planning," in J. McGuire (ed.), Contemporary management. Englewood Cliffs, N.J., Prentice-Hall, 1974.
7. "Parker-Hannifin: The acquisition route into the auto aftermarket," Business Week, March 20, 1978, pp. 129–130.
8. Wheelwright, S. C., and S. G. Makridakas. Forecasting methods for management. New York, Wiley–Interscience, 1979.
9. Newman, W. H. "Shaping the master strategy of your firm," California Management Review, 9 (1967): 77–78.
10. "How GM turned itself around," Fortune, January 16, 1978, pp. 87–100.
11. Starr, M. Management: A modern approach. New York, Harcourt Brace Jovanovich, 1971.

CHAPTER NINE

Operational Planning and Budgeting

Item 9.1 Green Springs Bedding Company

The Green Springs Bedding Company produces mattresses in a plant located in an industrial park in Maryland. The company employs about forty workers and individuals in managerial level positions. The company makes a well-known brand of mattress, which is sold in department stores, in furniture stores, and to hotels and motels.

The production of mattresses involves the use of standard procedures that have been widely used in the industry for many years. The Association of Bedding Manufacturers has published these procedures along with performance standards involved in the manufacture of a mattress. Most mattress factories use individual incentive wage plans for their employees since the availability of performance standards makes their use quite feasible.

Purchasing is quite an important function in the manufacture of mattresses since the components of a mattress amount to about 60 percent of the total cost of manufacture. Labor costs amount to only 7 or 8 percent of total costs. Changes in the prices of the steel springs or foam used in the mattress or in the fabric used to cover the mattress can significantly affect the costs and thus profits of the mattresses.

Sales of mattresses tend to follow furniture sales quite closely. These, in turn, are related to economic conditions and especially disposable income. Households tend to postpone furniture purchases when family income decreases, as many furniture purchases are to replace existing furniture. A 10 percent decrease in disposable income can contribute to a 50 percent drop in the sale of mattresses and other furniture items. In estimating mattress sales, heavy reliance is placed upon various economic forecasts, especially those that relate to a local area or region, since mattresses are not typically shipped long distances.

Sales to department stores or hotel chains involve a bidding procedure. Various mattress manufacturers may offer a given number of mattresses at a certain price. In these situations it is important to estimate as closely as possible the probable bids of competitors. Since costs will determine the nature of the bids as well as the company's anticipated amount of unused capacity, the costs of the competitors are usually predicted before making a bid. The costs of the competitors is determined by Green Springs Bedding by buying one of their mattresses and then stripping it down to reveal all its components. The costs of these components can then readily be determined through the use of catalogues published by the component manufacturers. The labor costs of manufacturing a mattress are also well known. This produces quite similar bids for various potential orders. When this is the case, reliability of delivery may become an important factor.

Recently new government legislation has been passed that requires mattresses to be resistant to fires caused by cigarettes. The mattresses are covered with a substance to prevent a lighted cigarette from setting a mattress on fire. This will protect individuals from death caused by falling asleep while smoking in bed. To test for the flammability of the mattresses, periodically mattresses must be selected at random from the production line and taken to a special room where several burning cigarettes are laid on each side of the mattress. The mattresses subjected to these tests are then destroyed.

The president of Green Springs calculates that these new standards will add $10 to the price of each mattress to compensate for the costs of the tests. Since retailers then typically double the wholesale price, the new standards may cost the consumer about $20 a mattress. The president wonders what effect this will have on the sale of mattresses in the future. He is concerned about this issue because his profit margin is narrowing. Green Springs will have to plan for the coming years' operations a good deal more carefully.

Generally only a few managers at the highest levels will be extensively involved in the development of strategy and strategic plans. Most managers, like the president of Green Springs Bedding, will be involved with short-range planning of activities in the firm. Still, understanding the concept and practice of strategic planning is useful because the strategy is the umbrella under which the short-range planning and budgeting of operations occur.

The overall planning process is a factoring, or breaking down, of the strategic objectives into internal systems goals, i.e., product, market share, productivity, and profitability goals. Basically, strategic decisions are made about the nature of products and markets. These are then translated into profit and cost objectives for the total firm and specific operating units. For operational plans for the coming year, for example, it is necessary to translate the strategic decision into specific plans, targets, and programs for marketing, production, and support activities. From these plans, targets and program standards are developed that become the basis for evaluating how effectively the firm operates.

To show how planning and budgeting are done, we will continue with the illustration of the CALCAL company from Chapter 8. We have already seen that CALCAL has prepared a long-term demand forecast that leads the president, Pat Redwick, to believe that sales will increase over the next several years. He places some confidence in the analyses and now wants to decide whether or not CALCAL should invest in new fixed resources to take advantage of this growth.

CAPITAL BUDGETING

Capital budgeting is the process of assessing the value of future expenditures to implement these decisions. If we build a new plant, the costs may be incurred over a short time, but the benefits may accrue for longer periods. Programs for research are similar investments that must be made currently but that have long-run payoffs.

The problem faced by CALCAL can be used to illustrate capital budgeting. We have already seen (from Figure 8.4) that CALCAL cannot produce enough calculators unless they expand their plant capacity. The president must make a long-range planning decision: should CALCAL expand its production facilities to seek the additional sales possible?

The president, Redwick, can see that the present plant capacity of 18,000 units is adequate for the next two years. However, if the current sales projection is correct, in year 19__3 CALCAL could sell 20,000 units, 25,000 the following year, and 30,000 the following.

Let us assume that the president has $50,000 available for investment. He must decide how to expend this amount to obtain the greatest return. For the sake of simplification, we will consider only two alternative investments.

The first is leasing production facilities near the existing location. Production space is available near the existing plant. Due to space limitations, however, the maximum production capacity of the total facilities if the lease is taken will only be 28,000 units. In the first year after the lease begins, CALCAL capacity will increase to 25,000 units; the next year it will go to the 28,000 maximum. The cost will be $40,000.

The second alternative is to lease a new plant on the West Coast. But there will be no output from this facility until the second year, at which time total CALCAL capacity will be 30,000 units. The cost for this alternative is also $40,000. Table 9.1 gives some of the relevant data the president will consider. (We have made a number of simplifying assumptions here to show conceptually how such decisions can be made.)

For CALCAL the selection of either of the alternatives will have significant consequences. First, there will be loss of flexibility. Committing $40,000 to either alternative means that the money cannot be spent elsewhere, in product development or advertising, say. It also means that for the life of the lease (five years), CALCAL has a fixed commitment that could seriously affect the profitability of the

TABLE 9.1 Comparative Returns from Two Investment Alternatives for CALCAL

Year	Sales Potential[a]	Increase Local Lease			Increase West Coast Lease[c]		
		Sales	Units	Profits	Sales	Units	Profit
19__3	20,000	20,000	2,000	$ 4,000	0	0	$ 0
19__4	25,000	25,000	7,000	14,000	25,000	7,000	14,000
19__5	30,000	28,000	10,000	20,000	30,000	12,000	24,000
19__6	30,000[b]	28,000	10,000	20,000	30,000	12,000	24,000

[a.] From Table 8.1
[b.] Estimated; not shown on Table 8.1
[c.] Estimated at $2.00 per additional unit.

firm. Suppose, for instance, that the basic premise on which this decision is made is incorrect and that sales do not increase as predicted to 30,000 units by year 19__5. Then CALCAL is stuck with capacity to produce something no one is buying.

Second, as the firm increases in size, it must begin to plan for other situations. Personnel must be added, distribution channels developed, additional related product lines considered. The future commitments that one makes can have important ramifications beyond the immediate problem. Even so, capital budgeting is of benefit to a firm. For example, by preparing market forecasts and comparing them with future and current production capacities, the construction of new facilities can be timed. Acquisition of land and financing can be obtained so that resources will be ready when needed, not too early and not too late. Some capital equipment, such as buildings and machines, takes long lead times for acquisition.

Lenders and investors are more receptive to well-planned projects. Capital budgeting will also be useful to the financial manager, making it easier to decide when to enter capital acquisition markets to secure necessary funds.

SELECTING FROM ALTERNATIVE PROPOSALS

The basic aim in capital budgeting is to choose those proposals that provide a return to the organization in excess of the cost of the capital of the firm. Funds that are used to obtain assets have a cost. Interest must be paid on loans, and dividends to equity shareholders, and even funds generated internally (for example, through retained earnings) have alternative uses that can be viewed as a cost. These costs can be estimated and weighted to obtain a cost of capital for a firm.

Basically, the returns from any investment decision should exceed the costs of capital. In some instances this may not be so, especially when external factors cause a firm to make an expenditure. For example, pollution controls may be expensive and generate few, if any, added returns, yet the firm may be required to provide them. In such a case the firm must raise prices or perhaps be willing to accept a lower total return than in the past.

At any rate, the firm should select those investment proposals that exceed the costs of capital. A number of different methods of evaluating return on investment

*Operational
Planning
and Budgeting*

215

provide a basis for making capital budgeting decisions. All take the costs of capital into consideration. Rather than illustrating each of them by example, we will show how one of these methods would be used by CALCAL company to determine whether it should select the local lease or the West Coast lease.

Net Present Value Method

To use the net present value method, the costs of capital to the firm are used to discount the future stream of cash flows. The present value of these cash flows is obtained and then compared to the cost of the project. If the net present value is greater than the outlay, then the investment should be made. If there are two alternatives, then the alternative with the greatest net present value should be selected, if only one investment can be made.

This method assumes that the cost of capital is determined. At CALCAL, for example, we assume it to be 12 percent. Then the value today (present value) of a future inflow of $1,000 in one year is less than $1,000, or $893. This amount ($893) invested at 12 percent will yield $1,000 in a year. One thousand dollars received two years from now has an even lower current value, $797, which is how much would have to be invested at 12 percent, compounded annually, to yield $1,000 in 2 years. (Tables giving present values of $1.00 for different rates are given in most financial management texts.)

Since the (assumed) cost of capital to CALCAL is 12 percent, we can now compute the net present value for each alternative investment. Table 9.2 shows the incremental profit for each year of the investment. The return for each year for each investment is multiplied by a discount factor from present value tables, and a total net present value is obtained. Table 9.2 shows this computation for the alternatives facing CALCAL. If the available funds are $40,000, then the most desirable alternative for CALCAL is the West Coast lease, since the net present value is $3,510 for this alternative compared to $1,690 for the local lease.

Alternative Methods

There are other ways to evaluate capital investment decisions. Basically, any one of three methods that take into account future cash flows and discount them will give results similar to those of the net present value method just discussed. The internal rate of return method and developing a profitability index would have yielded the same results; that is, the West Coast lease is the preferred alternative. Under some conditions, however, different results might be obtained with the different methods. Weston and Brigham[1] note that the following project characteristics will yield different results using different methods:

1. If the projects have different lives
2. If the costs of one project are higher than those of another
3. If cash flows increase over time for one project, while they decrease for the other

Another method for assessment of these projects—not recommended by finance experts, but widely used—is payback. The payback method simply determines which of the several alternatives return the total invested amount to the firm first.

TABLE 9.2   Comparative Present Value of Two Investments

Local Lease		Discount Factor	Present Value	
19__3	$ 4,000	.893	$ 3,572	
19__4	$14,000	.797	11,158	
19__5	$20,000	.712	14,240	
19__6	$20,000	.636	12,720	
			$41,690	Present value of returns
			40,000	Cost of lease
			$1,690	Net present value
West Coast Lease		Discount Factor	Present Value	
19__3	$0	.893	$ 0	
19__4	$14,000	.797	11,158	
19__5	$24,000	.712	17,088	
19__6	$24,000	.636	15,264	
			$43,510	Present value of returns
			40,000	Cost of lease
			$3,510	Net present value

PLANNING FOR CURRENT OPERATIONS

The president is ready to plan for the coming year. He is about to determine what will be manufactured and sold, when, how, and at what rate. His ultimate plan will also tell something about whether he will have extra cash for particular periods during the year or need short-term financing. He will learn something about raw materials requirements and how many employees he may have to add. From his final, comprehensive plan, he should be able to determine what the profit level is likely to be and, more important, whether or not it is satisfactory.

What does this executive know to begin with? First, he has a reasonably good estimate of what sales levels will be in 19__1, the coming year (15,000 units) and in the future if:

1. The industry forecast is fairly accurate
2. The firm continues to operate (i.e., manufacture and sell) in the same industry
3. There are no major changes, such as a strong new competitor or a major technological shift

He also knows a great deal about his costs of operations from previous years. Collecting historical cost information allows him to estimate the costs necessary in producing a unit of product and to make a judgment about what level of sales is required to break even.

The plant has a capacity of producing 18,000 units per year, or 1,500 per month. It employs ten persons, whose positions are given in the organization chart shown in Figure 9.1.

First, the president must know how profitable CALCAL will be next year at the predicted sales level. This evaluation can be done using break-even analysis. Then, assuming that CALCAL can make a profit, specific information about production schedules, inventories, and costs are prepared in the form of budgets.

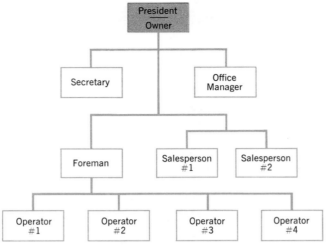

FIGURE 9.1   CALCAL's organization chart.

BREAK-EVEN ANALYSIS

Forecasts are estimates, and estimates may be inaccurate. It would be useful to know what the profit might be for various levels of sales. It would also be useful to know how much must be produced and sold in order to cover costs, or to break even. Break-even analysis shows the relationship between fixed costs, variable costs, and sales volume. The break-even point is that point where sales and costs are equal.

Fixed costs are those costs that are fairly constant and remain the same regardless of the level of production. Of course, all costs change over time and in this sense are not fixed, but for purposes of break-even analysis, it is safe to assume that at least for the planning period there will be such minor variations in these costs that they are, for all practical purposes, fixed. Rental or lease payments, interest charges, and executive salaries are examples of fixed costs.

Variable costs, on the other hand, are those that change as the production level changes. They are costs incurred each time an additional unit is produced and/or sold. Materials, direct labor, portions of changes for utilities, and sales commissions are examples of variable costs.

The total costs (TC) for a firm, at a given level of production are equal to the fixed costs (FC) plus the total variable costs (VC), or

$$TC = FC + (VC \text{ per unit} \times \text{number of units})$$

The total costs for a firm vary, based on the level of production. Assume that CALCAL has determined that fixed costs and variable costs can be estimated with reasonable accuracy as follows:

Fixed costs (monthly)

Administration costs	$2,500
Fixed manufacturing cost	1,000
Miscellaneous costs	250
Monthly fixed costs	$3,750
Yearly costs—$3,750 × 12 =	$45,000

Variable costs per unit

Direct labor	$2.00
Direct materials	2.00
Variable manufacturing	1.00
Marketing costs	.50
Total variable cost per unit	$5.50

To estimate the total costs to CALCAL for a particular level of production, we use the formula given above, TC = FC + (VC per unit × number of units), so that at 18,000 units of production the total cost is:

$$TC = \$45,000 + (\$5.50 \times 18,000)$$
$$TC = \$45,000 + \$99,000$$
$$TC = \$144,000$$

At 8,000 units it is $89,000

$$TC = \$45,000 + (5.50 \times 8,000)$$
$$TC = \$45,000 + 44,000$$
$$TC = \$89,000$$

and if the forecast of 15,000 units is correct, total costs will be

$$TC = \$45,000 + (\$5.50 \times 15,000)$$
$$TC = \$45,000 + \$82,500$$
$$TC = \$127,500$$

By examining the total costs line on the break-even chart in Figure 9.2, we can see how costs vary as a function of production level. The costs at the different production levels are marked (x) on the Total Costs line. At each point, it is clear on the break-even analysis chart of Figure 9.2 what part of the total costs is the variable and what the fixed component.

But these costs are important only in relation to the sales revenue of CALCAL. The sales revenue for particular sales levels is shown by the Revenue line, if we assume CALCAL sells each unit for $10.00. If CALCAL were to produce and sell its total production capacity (18,000), then it would have sales revenue of $180,000. Projected sales revenues for 18,000, 8,000, and 15,000 units are:

18,000 units	=	$180,000
8,000 units	=	$80,000
15,000 units	=	$150,000

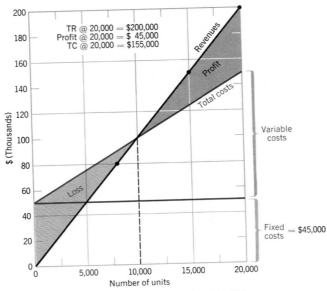

FIGURE 9.2   Break-even analysis for CALCAL.

Profit levels can now be computed simply by deducting total costs from revenues. These are shown in Table 9.3. Determining the specific level of sales at which the CALCAL company will break even can now be determined. The break-even point is the point where revenues equal costs. Since

sales volume = price (P) × number of units (N)
   total costs = fixed costs (FC) + (variable costs (VC) × number of units [N])

The break-even point is where **sales volume = total costs**, or

$$P \times N = FC + (VC \times N)$$
$$(P \times N) - (VC \times N) = FC$$
$$N (P - VC) = FC$$
$$N = \frac{FC}{P - VC}$$
$$\text{break-even } N = \frac{\$45{,}000}{\$10 - \$5.50}$$

The firm breaks even when the difference between the price and unit variable costs ($P - VC$) is enough to cover the total fixed costs. These relationships can be

TABLE 9.3   Profits (Loss) for CALCAL Company at Different Sales Levels

Production Level	Revenues	Less	Total Costs	Equals	Profit or Loss
18,000	$180,000		$144,000		$36,000
8,000	80,000		89,000		(9,000)
15,000	150,000		127,500		23,000

seen in Figure 9.2. It shows that at a sales and production level less than 10,000 units, CALCAL experiences a loss; for example, at 8,000 units, a $9,000 loss is incurred. But profit begins to occur above 10,000 units.

THE DEVELOPMENT OF OPERATIONAL PLANS AND BUDGETS

Knowing that the predicted sales level of 15,000 units will result in a profit, the president of CALCAL can now translate this into more specific plans. For example, the 15,000 units will not be produced and sold in a single day or week. The demand and production will flow over the year to produce total sales, and there will be a steady stream of payments (for materials, labor, leases, etc.) throughout the year.

It becomes useful now for the manager to think about at what rate sales will occur, revenues will be received, and payments will have to be made and to plan for these eventualities. Budgets are such plans. They are projected levels of revenues and expenditures that are targets or goals that will, if achieved, result in the desired level of performance.

If the president feels reasonably sure that CALCAL will sell 15,000 units in the coming year, this information can be translated for use in other specific plans or budgets. A complete budget system includes (1) a production budget, (2) a materials purchases budget, (3) a cash budget, (4) a budgeted income statement and balance sheet, and (5) a capital expenditure budget. These plans can be used to estimate whether or not the firm can achieve its objectives and what spending limits must be maintained if it is to do so.

When the various budgets have been developed, they become the basis for other planning. For instance, the production budget can be an important source of information for a personnel manager because from it he can predict when to enter the labor market to add new staff. The cash budget will show when shortages of funds will probably occur, so that the firm may be able to anticipate and secure short-term loan commitments substantially in advance of need.

Based on previous sales patterns, the planners in CALCAL estimate that the 15,000 units are to be sold in the following quarterly pattern for the year:

Quarter	Volume
1	3,400
2	3,600
3	3,900
4	4,100

A set of the different budgets can be derived for each quarter (or, for that matter, for any time period). Suppose first-quarter sales of 3,400 units are broken down on a monthly basis as follows:

Month	Units	Unit Price	Sales Volume
January	1,000	$10.00	$10,000
February	1,200	$10.00	$12,000
March	1,200	$10.00	$12,000

Production Budget

If the standard cost for each unit of product is now, say, $6.00 and the monthly sales forecast is as noted above, a production budget for each of the months can be prepared. The production budget shows the number of units that are to be produced and how much of the production will have to be held in inventory.

This budget has many uses. For instance, a weekly production schedule can be prepared for February and March. For the purposes of production planning, CALCAL company management can estimate future labor requirements. If, for example, some worker is planning for vacation in January, arrangements can be made to fill the position. In this way production schedules will not slip.

Materials Purchases Budget

The materials purchases budget shows the level of raw material requirements that must be maintained to meet the plans. CALCAL must buy raw materials in each month of the quarter. If these quantities are bought and delivered on schedule, the production budget and production schedule can be met. The materials purchases budget is derived from the production budget. We can develop it only after we know how much we are going to produce.

Of course, inventories are a form of investment for the CALCAL company. As such they must be managed carefully, as must any asset. Materials purchases budgets provide information that can help in inventory management. Inventories of raw materials will depend on a number of factors, such as anticipated changes in price, reorder times, the storage space available, and the costs of money required to purchase inventories.

Cash Budget

When production schedules, material requirements, and the manner in which sales dollars flow into the firm are known, the cash budget can be prepared. These budgets show the projected flows of cash into and out of the organization. Preparing a cash budget allows the manager to estimate whether or not there will be excess cash (or a shortage) at the end of the period. This will facilitate improved cash management since borrowings or investments may be more rationally undertaken.

Cash budgeting can be helpful to the management of CALCAL. If this analysis shows, for instance, that cash excesses exist in certain periods, the cash may be invested in some way to earn a return. These cash surpluses can be invested because they are not immediately needed for payments to suppliers, for labor, or for services. Short-term government securities are frequently used for this purpose.

Cash budgeting can also show when cash deficiencies are predicted. It often happens that cyclical swings in payments produce excesses in one period but a shortage in another. Short-term borrowing might be necessary, and lenders are more likely to be receptive to requests when the borrower appears to have planned and knows how much is needed.

With the materials purchases and cash budgets, a forecasted income statement and balance sheet can be prepared. The budgeted income statement shows projected gross income from sales, minus the cost of goods sold, labor charges, depreciation, and other expenses. With this budget the president can see what the estimated income will be for each period. This statement can also be used to assess whether or not the company can meet its profit objective.

The budgeted balance sheet shows the future financial position of the firm; that is, the impact of the projected operations on CALCAL's assets and liabilities. This information is especially useful when a firm seeks to secure added funds from external investors.

PLANNING FOR HUMAN RESOURCES

From these data, other plans may be developed. For example, manpower needs may be forecast. CALCAL's organization chart (Figure 9.1) shows that four operators are employed. These four workers produce 1,000 units, or 250 units per worker monthly. If we assume this represents a normal output, then it is clear that in the second and third months of the quarter, CALCAL is in trouble, because the average production per worker must increase from 250 to 300 units.

$$1,200 \text{ units} \div 4 \text{ workers} = 300 \text{ units per month}$$

To add another employee would not be economical. With an average output of 250 units, productive capacity would then be 1,250 units, and this level of production is not required during the first quarter. This is a problem for the production foreman. Certainly it can be seen that adding the fifth employee is inefficient since CALCAL's output capacity would be 1,250, 50 units more than needed. Thus, the production foreman must make a decision. He must decide whether to hire the additional worker, make some arrangement for overtime with other employees, or develop some more efficient method of production.

Knowing that the average monthly production in the second quarter will be 1,200 units (3,600 ÷ 3), the fifth employee could be sought at the beginning of, say, March, so that in April he can be fully productive. Knowing production schedules and predicted demand is valuable to a personnel manager, since from it he can estimate how many production employees will be needed.

In similar fashion a judgment about increasing the marketing staff can be made. With two salespersons the average monthly sales per employee is 500 units (1,000 ÷ 2). As the level of sales increases, the marketing staff will undoubtedly be working harder. Since an additional salesperson will not be needed until the average monthly volume is 1,500 units, it may be unnecessary to hire a new salesperson next year. However, if the 18,000 units forecast for the following year become the sales objective, clearly an additional salesperson will be required, since average monthly sales are 1,500 units, enough to support three salespersons. For personnel planning, however, the search must begin in the last quarter of next year, probably in early

November so that by January 1 the marketing group is fully staffed. By the end of the current year, the organization of CALCAL will change.

THE HUMAN EFFECTS OF PLANNING AND BUDGETING

There are human problems that result from planning and budgeting processes. People are affected by plans. Plans mean more than just numbers—or standards—that are used for guiding the actions of organizations. Plans, and actually all decisions made in an organization by others, which have to be carried out by a person are constraints. They limit the actions available. When constraints such as plans are imposed, they cause people to react. In this section we will examine some possible human consequences of being involved in and affected by planning. The sequence of activities that produce the plans and budgets themselves and then their actual use by organizational members is shown in Figure 9.3.

The first stage (Stage 1) includes those activities that produce the final documents. Managers meet with subordinates, and projections of expenditures are formulated, evaluated, consolidated, and coordinated. Competition occurs between units for available resources. Out of Stage 1, budgets and plans emerge. The budget (Stage 2 in the model) is a set of quantified goals. It is used to provide guidance to individuals and to subordinate units. The goals may be very specific or more general. The latitude a particular manager has over resource allocations may be narrow or broad. Plans may be more extensive than budgets, defining and clarifying how certain things should be done. Finally, the budget can be used (as in Stage 3) as a standard of comparison to evaluate performance as a basis for rewarding managers.

BUDGET PROCESS (STAGE 1)

A budget is a document that allocates resources among different units in an organization. When resources are scarce there is likely to be competition among units for increased amounts, relative both to their past funding levels and to other units. In one study[2] the budgeting process at the University of Illinois was examined in an attempt to determine how resources were distributed among the university's departments. The study considered budget allocations and examined their relationship to the power of the various departments, their work load, and their national reputation. The study found that to the extent that a department had power, measured by presence in university committees, it had an advantage in the budgetary process regardless of its work load and concluded that "subunit power affects the allocation of resources within the organization."

FIGURE 9.3   Sequence of planning activities.

Anxiety from Budgeting and Planning[3]

A characteristic of the budgeting process that may cause problems is that budget negotiations are likely to be carried out in secrecy. This secrecy and the fact that budgetary allocations are likely to be based on power, as well as the amount of work to be done, will generate a high level of anxiety for those managers involved. If the planning and budgeting process leads to fear that there will be inequitable or inadequate distribution of resources, this can lead to one or more of the following reactions by managers:

1. *Political Behavior.* Managers may attempt to increase their power in an organization by political behavior. They may, for instance, withhold important information until the last minute to magnify its significance. Or they may be excessively ingratiating toward superiors or those in positions of influence. Providing favors beyond the normal courtesies and requirements of the work assignment are also political forms of behavior.

2. *Negative reactions toward planning and budget units.* Perceived inequity of resource allocation may trigger negative reactions toward those units responsible for the collection and preparation of budget data. Personnel in the controller's office (probably a group of staff specialists) are likely to have the major responsibility for putting together a budget's final figures. They may end up bearing the brunt of criticism since they are more convenient targets than line managers. After all, an individual's superior will be responsible for promotion decisions, making it unwise to alienate him by directing aggression toward him.

If this mode of adaptation becomes at all widespread, it will hinder the planning group's effectiveness because it will become increasingly difficult to interact with other units to obtain accurate and timely information.

3. *Overstatement of needs.* To protect a perceived equitable share of future resources, managers will sometimes pad estimated budgetary needs. They learn quickly that cuts are usually made in requested amounts and, in order to be equitable, all units have to experience relatively similar budget cuts. Therefore, the honest manager, estimating his needs with some degree of accuracy, is penalized. He quickly learns that an overstatement of requirements helps him secure his "fair" share.

4. *Covert information systems.* If there is a high degree of secrecy regarding budget allocations to other units, managers will seek to make some estimate of how they fare relative to others. They will probably overestimate the amounts obtained by other units. Nevertheless, because the allocations may represent something other than need—for example, the power one has—information will be sought about the amount received by others. Secretaries, staff members from the budget offices, and those with access to data will be prodded for information. A communication network may develop that provides some information, although it may quite possibly be inaccurate.

The Use of Participation for Anxiety Reduction

Acceptance of plans and budget requirements may be substantially increased through "participatory management" strategies. March and Simon have concluded that participation may minimize problems when there is a "felt need for joint decision-making."[4] Certainly if power is a major factor in determining budget allocations, then a participatory strategy is warranted.

PLANS AND BUDGETS (STAGE 2)

The outcomes of the preparation stage are plans and budgets. Basically, a budget is simply a listing of physical and human resources with authorized expenditure levels which a manager uses in performing his job. It is a formal document which constrains or regulates an individual manager's behavior in such a way as to increase the predictability that subordinates will act in a particular way. There is a fundamental assumption that if resources are expended as allocated and plans carried out as developed, satisfactory performance will result.

Plans and Budgets as a Set of Goals

Plans and budgets are goals for a manager. There is much empirical literature on the subject of goals that yields some useful insights into how they affect performance.

Some of the most extensive work on the relationship between goals and performance has been reported by Locke.[5] He reasoned that if "goals regulate performance, then hard goals should produce high performance." The results of several studies he conducted, as well as other reasearch he cites, leads him to conclude that "the results are unequivocal: The harder the goal, the higher the level of performance." However, and perhaps more relevant to the problem of plans and budgets, he found that when subjects had specific goals, they were more likely to do better than when they had general or nonspecific goals. Carroll and Tosi,[6] in their research on goals and objectives, concluded that

> . . . for all types of subordinates, the superior should make sure the goals established focus on significant and important areas of departmental need, are clearly stated, and the relative importance of goals pointed out. The difficulty of goals, however [had different effects]. For example difficult goals were related to decreased effort in managers with low self-assurance and among less mature and experienced managers. However, difficult goals were associated with increased effort among managers with high self-assurance, managers who associated their performance with the reward system, and mature managers.

In a study of two state agencies that had different types of control systems, one having more specific goals than the other, Turcotte found that

> Demanding objectives, quantitatively expressed and understood . . . , were essential foundations of the effectiveness of the high performing agency.[7]

From these studies it seems that the "motivating" effect of the budget derives primarily from the fact that it is a statement of explicit goals.

BUDGET IMPLEMENTATION (STAGE 3)

Finally, the important question is, "How are plans and budgets used by the manager?" The manager brings plans to life, but the effects previously noted—anxiety in the preparation, the effects of goals—have taken place and are likely to form the perceptual base from which individual reactions will develop.

Both plans and budgets may be viewed as instruments that specify, at least partially, certain actions that a manager must take to achieve goals. So the manager must use these instruments—make them work. Otherwise they will be useless.

The Budget and Performance Evaluation

The seductive nature of plans and budgets is that they are "objective." Goals are quantified in a way that makes sense to the pragmatic manager—dollars and cents—and are likely to have a significant weight in the evaluation of managerial performance. How budgets are used in performance evaluation is crucial, since a manager may, using them wrongly, reinforce behavior that can have negative effects on performance.

When a behavior is reinforced (i.e., rewards or punishments are seen as its consequences), the probability that an individual will act similarly in later periods changes. Therefore, when a person is rewarded for, say, meeting a budget requirement, it can be predicted that he will later work to meet other budget requirements. It is important to ask the question, "What are we reinforcing when we use the budget as a basis for evaluation?" The answer is, of course, "It all depends."

Suppose the superior rewards or sanctions a subordinate based solely upon whether or not a budget requirement is met; for example, a subordinate who exceeds expenditure levels is not given a salary increase, while one who stays below budget is given a substantial one. *In this case, the reinforced behavior is achievement of a particular level of a measure.*

It is possible that the methods used to achieve this goal may be organizationally suboptimal. For example, a manager may meet a budgeted maintenance expenditure by not having maintenance performed, or by having it done but arranging for billing in the next fiscal period. In either instance, what is intended may not be accomplished.

When the superior's concern is with the budgeted level and it is used as described above, then those who have to live with the budget learn the ropes of manipulating outcomes with little regard for what is really intended as the purpose of the activity. This is because budgets, and most managerial controls, give little guidance on *how* to do something. Rather, they simply specify the approved level of resources to be used. Effectiveness depends *both on the quantity of resources and how they are used.*

To use plans and budgets effectively, then, a manager must go beyond them. He or she should, of course, communicate to subordinates the intended level of achievement. But a manager must also monitor the way subordinates go about achieving that level. The manager may have to coach subordinates extensively about *how* to achieve goals. This means that performance evaluation must focus on both budget requirements *and* behavior so that, from a reinforcement point of view, the subordinate not only learns how much is expected, but how to do it.

Other Factors in Evaluation.

The utility of the budget as an evaluation device may be diluted by a number of other factors. First, the rewards for achievement of performance goals may not be seen to be as valuable by the subordinate as by the superior. Second, the budget contains only one type of performance criterion, while overall performance may include more subjective facets. Third, the frequency of performance reviews is not great, generally once or twice a year. Such a schedule usually does not allow sufficient opportunities to link rewards strongly to performance measured against the budget. And, finally, some superiors simply may not regard the budget as a useful enough evaluative device to give it prominence in assessment.

SUMMARY

This chapter has shown how budgeting planning may be done and how it links into the strategic planning process. Plans are vital to successful performance. Developing them takes time, but it is certainly time well spent. The operational plans become an important ingredient in the other steps in the management process. They become the basis for determining job specifications in the organizing process. They become objectives for individual manager's to meet which are formulated during the implementation phase of the management process. Finally, the plans form the basis for standards that are used for central purposes.

Case 9.1 The Citizen's Bank

The Citizen's Bank is a relatively small bank located in eastern Ohio. It was founded in 1962 and now consists of the headquarters bank in Lafferty, Ohio, and six branches in several nearby towns. In 1975 a new president, Janet Darley, was hired by The Citizen's Bank from another bank in West Virginia. The new president asked her staff to prepare proposals relating to several new bank services.

One staff member was assigned the responsibility of developing a plan for a new bank overdraft system. Under this system customers would be allowed to write checks in excess of their bank balances. These checks would be considered a charge against the customer's line of credit and, as such, prevailing interest rates for the use of this money would apply.

Customers would have to apply for a line of credit, and these applications would be evaluated on the basis of the perceived ability of the customer to repay the loans. The perceived ability of the customer to repay the loan is determined by income, job security, community stability, and past credit performance.

The program devised by the staff involved an extensive advertising compaign in local newspapers and brochures describing the new program inserted with the monthly statements sent to present customers. In addition, a special training program to explain the new service to present employees was to be carried out at each branch after regular working hours.

Darley decided to change the proposed program. Instead of advertising being carried out from the bank's headquarters, each branch was to market the new service itself, although flyers announcing the service were to be inserted in the customers' monthly statements. A cash bonus system was set to award cash prizes to the branch that signed up the most customers for this new service. Each branch was to conduct its own training of its staff using the flyers sent to the customers. Customer applications to enroll in the program were to be evaluated by a special three person committee at the Bank's headquarters at 5 P.M. every day. Customers with applications that were disallowed were to be sent letters explaining the reasons for the denial by the special committee.

1. Predict the success of this new program.
2. Evaluate the modifications made by the president in the staff members' plan to introduce the new service.

Craig Kive

Craig Kive is the training and education director for the National Association of Building Contractors. This association is located in Washington, D.C., and conducts research, communication, educational, and lobbying activities on behalf of its thousands of members located all over the United States. Most of its members are small businesspeople who joined the association in order to support efforts to improve the condition of building contractors.

The association sponsors research on more efficient construction methods. It serves as a clearinghouse for research done by others on this subject. NABC also attempts to influence Congress on legislation having relevance to the construction industry.

One of Kive's responsibilities in the association is to conduct training programs for its members on subjects of relevance to the industry such as bidding, subcontracting, safety, and contract law.

In the spring of 1979, George Slocum, a professor at a nearby university, was asked by Kive to conduct a training program on planning and control methods in the construction industry the next autumn. George, a nationally recognized authority on management, said he would if the association would meet his fee schedule. Slocum told Kive that he charged an hourly fee for consultations and preparation of materials in addition to a fee for conducting the training.

Kive said there would be no problem with the fees, but that he must have an opportunity to watch Slocum conducting a seminar. He also asked for the names of other groups that Slocum had trained since he wished to check with them. Kive went on to say that, in the previous year, he had hired a college professor to conduct a training program for him and the participants had very strong negative reactions to the training. Kive did not want this to happen to him again.

Kive had to settle for watching Slocum conduct a seminar for executives at the university, since Slocum was not involved in any outside training activities at the time. Appearing satisfied, Kive told Slocum that he would like Slocum to carry out the training but wanted him to share his training time in the program. Kive wanted also to use a training consultant who had worked with NABC before and who made a favorable impression on association members.

Over the next several months, Kive and Slocum met several times to go over—in great detail—the extensive training session outlines, cases, and other materials that Slocum had prepared. The other consultant came down from New York City to participate in some of these meetings. Every minute of the planned training session was to be accounted for in the training plan, according to Kive's wishes for a tight seminar. The training program preparation costs skyrocketed.

The training program was scheduled for early November 1980 in Washington, D.C. Unfortunately, only thirteen association members attended the course and paid the $1,000 fee. The total loss to NABC for this management training program was $6,000. Kive attributed the low attendance to the unseasonably good weather across country. Potential training program participants wanted to stay home to take advantage of the weather to complete the projects they had in process. The training program was rated very high by the participants because of the very high preparation costs. Kive was warned by the association's executive manager never to run a program with such losses again.

1. Evaluate the reasons for Kive's behavior in this situation
2. How is Kive likely to behave in the future given what has happened?
3. What aspects of planning did Kive overlook?

DISCUSSION QUESTIONS

1. Explain why capital budgeting is one of the most important aspects of planning in an organization.
2. The net present value approach is probably the most widely used system for determining whether or not to invest in a new project. Discuss how a business would use this method.
3. Explain what a break-even analysis is and define each component used to determine the break-even point.
4. Total costs, fixed costs, variable costs, sales volume, and number of units are terms necessary to understand to be able to compute a break-even analysis. Define each term in detail.
5. A complete budget system includes five plans. Name these and discuss each one.
6. How would a weekly production budget prove to be advantageous in an organizaton?
7. Inventories, being a form of investment, are of ultimate importance to the organization. Discuss how inventories are related to the materials purchases budget.
8. Cash budgeting reflects shortages and excesses of cash. How can an organization deal with these?
9. Discuss the effects on people from planning and budgeting. Include negative and positive reactions evoked in individuals and groups.
10. Why is it so important for a manager to understand strategic planning?
11. Explain how a capital budget is formed.
12. Capital budgeting is an excellent example of the use of the decision-making process. Explain.
13. Briefly describe the three basic methods of capital budgeting.
14. Estimate the break-even point for Product Y. It sells for $15.00 per unit. Total costs for different sales levels are as follows:

Units	Total Costs
2,000	$40,000
4,000	$50,000
6,000	$60,000

REFERENCES

1. Weston, J., and E. Brigham. Managerial finance. New York, Holt, Rinehart and Winston, 1972.

2. Pfeffer, J., and G. Salancik. "Organizational decision making as a political process: The case of the university budget," Administrative Science Quarterly, 19 (1974): 135–151.

3. Tosi, H. "The human effects of budgeting systems on management," Business Topics, 22 (Autumn 1974): 53–63.

4. March, J., and H. Simon. Organizations. New York, Wiley, 1958.

5. Locke, E. "Toward a theory of task motivation and incentives," Organizational Behavior and Human Performance, 3 (1968): 162.

6. Carroll, S. J., and H. Tosi. Management by objectives: Applications and research. New York, Macmillan, 1973.

7. Turcotte, W. "Control systems, performance and satisfaction in two state agencies," Administrative Science Quarterly, 19 (March 1974): 60–73.

CHAPTER TEN

Implementing Plans

Item 10.1 Implementing Plans at CALCAL

CALCAL's president, Pat Redwick, has worked out the strategic plan for the next several years. He has also determined that the sales of CALCAL will exceed the break-even point, so he is relatively optimistic.* Budgets have been prepared (as outlined in Chapter 9) and have been presented to the board of directors. They have approved these plans, so the president is ready to begin implementing them.

Last week he had a staff meeting. The following staff were in attendance:

Peter Gabriel—Production Foreman
Bill Oliver—Office Manager—Personnel
Victoria Holt—Secretary
Nicole DeBlasis—Sales
Frank Doneson—Sales

At this meeting Redwick told the staff about the plans that were developed. "The board has approved the plan leasing a site on the West Coast," he said. "The local site just did not prove to be the best. With any luck, it is going to turn out well for us."

---

*See Chapter 9 for information about CALCAL's sales forecast

FIGURE 10.1   CALCAL Production Budget, 1st Quarter

	Month 1	Month 2	Month 3
Unit sales	1,000	1,200	1,200
Beginning inventory	500	600	600
	500	600	600
Ending inventory	600	600	600
Production required	1,100	1,200	1,200

Then Pat began to be a little more specific about next year. "The sales forecasts for next year is that CALCAL will sell 15,000 units. If we do, our profits will look fairly good. I think we can be happy about the next year, at 18,000 units."

"Frank, you and Nicole should expect sales to increase a little each quarter. The first quarter, we should move 3,400 units, it will increase to 3,600 for the second quarter. From July thru September, 3,900 units are predicted. We'll close out the year with 4,100 units."

"How does that affect me?" Peter Gabriel, the production manager, wanted to know. He had been caught in a squeeze before when he did not know that sales were increasing until it was too late for him to develop a production schedule to get the product out.

"Here is the production budget for the first quarter, Pete." Pat replied as he handed everyone a sheet of paper (see Figure 10.1). He looked at Gabriel and said, "The unit sales for the first quarter are broken down monthly. I estimated your monthly beginning inventory to be one-half of the current month's sales and year ending inventory should be one-half of next month's sales. I want to meet with you next week, after you've had a chance to go over this production budget. Let me know whether or not you think it is a budget you can live with."

"I know right now I'm going to need more help," Peter told Pat.

"That's where I come in." Bill Oliver, the office manager–personnel director could see that he was going to have to look for at least one new worker and probably a new salesperson.

"Right, Ollie. You and I can talk about this next week. We'll meet and see how these plans will affect the office and personnel. But now I want you all to see the cash budget." Pat spoke as he shuffled through a pile of papers. He pulled out a folder, opened it and passed copies of the cash budget to everyone [Figure 10.2].

Victoria Holt was the administrative secretary. She spent most of her time handling the books and making sure that costs did not get out of line. She was also responsible for suggesting ways to handle short-term cash excesses. Pat was glad to have her at CALCAL. She had been a financial analyst at a large bank in Capital City, but wanted to get more involved in managing. When Pat hired her she told him, "I'm bored with my job. I want to have some responsibility and excitement in the next one." Pat had given her responsibility, at least. Victoria knew the short-term financial position of CALCAL better than anyone.

"I'll look at this budget, Pat. Let's meet on Monday, and I'll have a plan for you," Victoria said as she placed the cash budget in her folio.

"Meeting's over, folks," concluded Pat. "Go away and work on this stuff. I

FIGURE 10.2   CALCAL Cash Budget, 1st Quarter

	Month 1	Month 2	Month 3
Receipts (previous months sales)	$10,000	$10,000	$12,000
Disbursements (accounts payable) direct labor, administrative expenses, etc.	9,300	9,900	9,900
Cash available from operations	700	100	2,100
Initial cash (from previous month)	6,200	6,900	7,000
Cumulative cash	6,900	7,000	9,100
Desired cash level	5,000	6,000	6,000
Cash available (needed)	$ 1,900	$ 1,000	$ 3,100

want to meet with each of you next week individually and go over these plans. Call me and we'll arrange to get together."

One week later, the president meets with Peter Gabriel. Pete has worked out a weekly production schedule and is somewhat concerned because according to his estimate he thinks he will need to hire an additional worker.

"I'm going to meet with Bill Oliver next week and see what he can do for me," Pete told Pat.

"Pete, if it's at all possible we should try to get increased production for the workers we have. I know you can average 250 units per worker pretty easily. Can you raise it to 300?" Pat asked.

Pete knew the cost of labor, and he was more than a little worried because he did not think he could do much to raise output.

"I'll get some work layout consultants," Pat continued. "There's a company that was recommended to me by Larry Blair at UBM."

"Pat, we can't do it. We've squeezed everything out of the plant operation possible. If you help me by making sure that I have raw materials inventory when I need it, I can meet your production budget," Pete said. "How about that?"

"OK," Pat was convinced that Pete and he had thought through the question of improved productivity and that another worker was needed. "I'll talk with Bill Oliver for you. I'll see that he gives you all the support you need, Pete."

Two days later Pat met with Victoria Holt. Victoria had examined the cash budget in detail. "Pat, I don't think that we have enough of a cash surplus to worry about the first two months. Toward the end of the quarter, the situation will be different. I am going to hold the first and second months surplus in our bank account. Then later I'll probably try some short-term treasury notes."

"Good, but can't we do something with that excess cash?" Pat asked.

"We could, if you want. I am more concerned with the cash flow for the second quarter, though." Victoria answered. "We seem always to have a slump in the payments of receivables. I know you didn't give us second-quarter budgets. I did one on my own and if my figures are right, we're going to be going to the bank to borrow."

Pat thought for a minute. "Do something with the cash for those two months.

I think I want it that way. Now, tell me more about the cash shortage in the second quarter."

"The best laid plans of mice and men often go astray" or "The road to hell is paved with good intentions." Both of these proverbs have the same meaning—that planning and organizing may be important but that it is carrying out the plans that leads to the intended result.

The plans developed in the planning process need to be disseminated throughout the organization and carried out by other personnel, managers, and operatives. This requires that they be understood and accepted. By acceptance of plans we mean, at least, that those at lower levels are willing to carry out the actions necessary, not that these persons are psychologically committed or endorse them heartily. Generally, acceptance should not be too much of a problem because most plans will likely fall within the boundaries of the person's "psychological contract." The major problem in implementing most plans is to insure that they are understood throughout the organization and that the necessary resources are available to carry them out.

One way to insure that an organization's strategic and major operating plans are carried out is to convert them into goals and action plans that are executed by individuals at the operating levels. Much research shows that directing individual work efforts with specific objectives contributes to very good performance.[1] Goals direct work activities in specific and desired directions. People can always find things to keep them busy, but these energies can be better used if they are aimed at organizational goals. Employees, if left entirely on their own, will choose what is most interesting to them. Such choices may or may not be in the organization's interests.

Thus, the general strategic goals of the organization become internal systems goals (market shares, profitability, productivity, etc.) and eventually become converted to work plans and performance requirements for individuals. The goals and plans of top management must be communicated to lower management levels to insure accomplishment. This is what Pat Redwick, CALCAL's president, did in the meetings he held with his staff. He wanted to insure that the company's goals were achieved.

WORK PLANNING SYSTEMS*

In any modern work planning system, a superior and a subordinate attempt to reach consensus about (1) what goals the subordinate will attempt to achieve in a given time period, (2) the plan or means by which the subordinate will attempt to accomplish the goals, and (3) the means by which goals progress will be measured and the dates for such measurements. After there is such agreement, the superior will periodically review performance; this may involve quarterly performance re-

---

*Work planning systems are also called management by objectives (MBO), management by results, work planning and review, and goals and control systems.

*"Mr. Mott, may I remind you that the success of this company
has been largely due to our attention to detail."*

FIGURE 10.3.

views as well as a final performance review at the end of the year. Such work planning systems help insure that strategic goals are attained.

ENDS AND MEANS

The heart of this process is the ***objective and the action plan.*** Success depends on how well both the objective and the plan are defined, communicated, and accepted. Objectives are goals (or ends); action plans are the maps (which spell out the ***means***) for reaching those objectives. The organizational work planning process works best when the individual members of an organization work with one another to identify common goals and coordinate their efforts in reaching them.

Objectives can be thought of as statements of purpose and direction. They may be long range or short range. They may be general, to provide direction for an entire organization, or they may be highly specific, to provide detailed direction for an individual.

Objectives may be general, for a larger organization, or specific, for an individual, because two purposes of work planning systems are to make it possible to

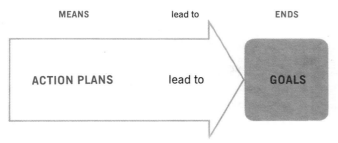

FIGURE 10.4   Relationship between goals and action plans.

derive specific from general objectives and to insure that objectives at all levels in the organization are meaningfully located structurally and are linked to each other. A set of individual objectives is a form of job description and can be thought of as a different way to provide that job description. Once objectives (ends) are determined and assumed by organizational units and by individuals, it is possible to work out the means (performance) required for accomplishing the objectives.

The "end result" (or objective) represents a desired condition or situation, a purpose to be achieved. Objectives may be specific achievement levels, such as product costs, sales volume, and so on, or they may be completed projects. For instance, the market research department may seek to complete a sales forecast by a particular date so that the production facilities can be properly coordinated with market demands. Objectives, or end states, are attained through the performance of some activity. These activities are the means to achieve the end. Figure 10.4 shows the relationship between goals and action plans. The goal (the end state) is attained when certain activities are completed.

To use work planning effectively, managers must be concerned with both the goals *and* the action plans of those who are accountable to them. The reasons are that:

1. Some objectives can be attained with ineffective action plans.
2. Some projects will not be completed until the relatively distant future.
3. Some objectives cannot be easily quantified.

1. *Ineffective action plans.* Often there are several ways to achieve an objective. Some are more appropriate than others. For instance, suppose Pat Redwick of CALCAL decided that the marketing goal of the next year would be a sales increase to 16,000 units, 1,000 more than the market prediction. One way to increase sales

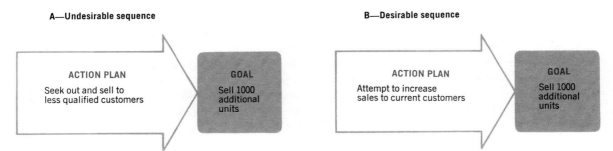

FIGURE 10.5   Desirable and undesirable ways to achieve a goal.

FIGURE 10.6   Goal and action plan sequence in which the goal is nonquantifiable.

would be to simply find more customers who will pay current prices—expanding the market. Another way would be to sell products to customers who are poor credit risks. If they fail to pay, the profitability of CALCAL is reduced. Another way to increase sales might be to offer very high discounts to motivate retailers to buy in larger quantities, but this has the effect of reducing profits. It is in the president's best interest to know which of these action plans the sales force intends to implement. This problem is illustrated in Figure 10.5.

2. Long-term objectives. Some goals may not be completed until a long time in the future. A new product development manager will never know how successful he or she has been until the products on which the staff is working hit the market. This may be several years in the future, yet that new product development manager must be evaluated in some way. In these situations it is possible only to judge whether or not the action plan is being carried out as it "should be."

3. Nonquantifiable objectives. Some goals cannot easily be quantified (see Figure 10.6). How, for example, can one judge whether not a manager with a goal of developing subordinates has performed well? Clearly the end result cannot be easily measured. It is possible only to assess how the action plan is carried out.

TYPES OF OBJECTIVES AND ACTION PLANS

There are two types of objectives that must be managed: performance objectives and developmental objectives. In this chapter we will discuss performance objectives, and in Chapter 13 we will examine developmental objectives in more detail.

It is impossible to develop objectives for a manager that would cover each and every area of responsibility, because the structure of most jobs is too complex. Yet once objectives are set for a position, they comprise the major description of the job, and their achievement in light of what is known about total job requirements should be assessed. Once objectives are set for a person, a basis exists for insuring that there is a "balance" of activities in the job; for example, that a worker is performing the normal duties, while at the same time working on activities thought to be important to higher management.

The **relative importance** of objectives should be kept in mind when these goals are used for evaluation. For example, a person who fails on a difficult, but creative, objective should not be evaluated in the same way as one who fails to maintain a critical recurring operation. The former may have undertaken a high-risk project, say a new product design that would have had high payoffs, at the suggestion of the boss. The latter may simply be failing at meeting normal job requirements.

PERFORMANCE OBJECTIVES

A performance objective is derived directly from the job assignment, from the major areas of an individual's responsibility and activity. Included in these areas would be the maintenance of recurring or routine activities, the solving of problems, or the creation of innovative ideas, products, services.

Routine objectives represent the normal requirements of the job, the kind of thing commonly found in a job description. Quantity requirements, the time one is supposed to come to work, and normal deadlines for reports are all routine objectives.

Special-project objectives are those objectives that take on special importance for a number of reasons: emergencies, change in priorities, or management decisions. A special project goal for one position may be routine for another. A special-project goal for a lower-level manager might be a routine goal for his superior. Developing a computer-based information system for personnel records might be a highly creative objective for the personnel department, yet would be a routine goal for a systems analysis group.

What a Performance Objective Should Look Like

The first critical phase in setting objectives is the statement that describes the end sought. This statement should be:

1. Clear, concise, and unambiguous
2. Accurate in terms of the true end-state or condition sought
3. Consistent with policies, procedures, and plans as they apply to the unit for which the objective is being set
4. Within the competence of the unit, or representing a reasonable developmental goal for it
5. Interesting, motivating, and/or challenging whenever possible

Some examples of goal statements might be: "Increase sales 10 percent." "Reduce manufacturing costs by 5 percent," "Reduce customer complaints." "Increase sales by 5 percent by December 1," "Increase quality with a 5 percent increase in production control costs." "Develop understanding and implementation of computer techniques among subordinates." The production budget of CALCAL, for example, states the monthly objectives for the production foreman.

Notice that most of these goal statements have at least two key components. First, each clearly suggests an area of activity in which accomplishments occur. Second, four of the six clearly specify a level of achievement, the quantity or deadlines to be met. The desired level of achievement is the performance level.

THE ACTION PLAN

The "action plan" is the means by which an objective is attained. The action plan should summarize what is to be done. The action plan for a complex activity should be broken down into major subprograms and should represent the "best" alternative, of possibly many, that would achieve the goal level. Action plans might be stated in the following manner:

1. For a sales increase, develop more penetration in a particular market area by increasing the number of calls to dealers there.
2. For a reduction in manufacturing costs, analyze the overtime activities and costs and schedule more work during regular hours.

Subordinates may base their own action plans on those developed by their manager, using those plans to guide their own roles in their unit's effort. We can see how action plans for the CALCAL production foreman are beginning to develop. Victoria Holt, the secretary, is beginning to shape an action plan for the investment of short-term cash surpluses.

It is important to recognize the distinction between measuring an objective and determining whether an event has occurred. If we are unable to measure or specify the goal level adequately, then we simply assume that the desired goal level has been achieved *if* a particular event or set of activities takes place. For example, while it is very difficult to measure whether or not a manager is developing the talents of subordinates, we can determine whether he or she has provided them with development opportunities. If they have participated in seminars, attended meetings, or gone off to school, it can be assumed that the development activity is being properly conducted (see Figure 10.6).

Some benefits of and opportunities for developing good action plans are these:

1. It aids in the search for better, more efficient methods of accomplishing the objective.
2. It provides an opportunity to test the feasibility of accomplishing the objective as stated.
3. It develops a basis to estimate time or cost required and deadline for accomplishment.
4. It examines the nature and degree of reliance on other people in the organization toward coordination and support needed.
5. It uncovers anticipated snags or barriers to accomplishment.
6. It determines resources (manpower, equipment, supplies, facilities) required to accomplish the objective.
7. It facilitates control if the performance is well-specified and agreed upon; reporting need only occur when problems arise in implementing. This is a form of planning ahead; when plans are sufficiently complete, only deviations from it need be communicated.
8. It identifies areas in which the superior can provide support and assistance.

Coordination of Action Plans

Success or failure in reaching an objective may depend upon the contribution and performance of other individuals or departments. They must therefore be considered. Some contingencies apply to all objectives, of course. For example, delays in the availability of resources, change in support or priorities from higher management, equipment failures, delayed information or approval, and the like, which are unplanned, should be taken into account when the assessment of objective accomplishment is made. For CALCAL there is a need to coordinate the production plans of the foreman and the recruiting plans for the personnel manager. If the new staff member is not hired in time, production levels cannot meet the levels required to meet demand. Other contingencies specific to the objective might be inadequate authority of the surbordinate, lack of policy covering aspects of the objective, possible failure to gain cooperation from others, and known delays in the system. Once these are uncovered, several actions are possible:

1. Reexamination of the objective (e.g., alteration of a deadline) when and if the contingency occurs
2. Commitment of the superior to aid by overcoming or preventing the contingency
3. Revision of the performance required to accomplish the objective
4. Establishment of a new objective. If a contingency is serious enough, an objective aimed at overcoming the problem may be justified

Constraints on Action Plans

Any action plan must take deadlines and constraints into account. Deadlines and budget constraints can and should be strictly specified in some cases, and not in others. A great deal depends on:

1. The importance of the objective
2. The ability to determine the time or costs required in performance
3. Whether or not written plans or objectives of other people require coordinated completion dates
4. The amount of time and money the subordinate will spend on the particular objective under discussion
5. The predictability of problems or barriers to accomplishment

Discussing these constraints furthers understanding between superiors and subordinates and establishes the constraint's use in evaluation. Expectations become known; realities can be tested. Deadlines and costs should be viewed as "negotiable." Deadlines especially should not be set simply to insure that action is initiated.

THE CASCADING OF OBJECTIVES

In Chapter 8 we discussed goals. Strategic goals are synonymous with the basic purpose of an organization; they seek to meet the demands placed upon the organization for its product or service, delivered in a way that will satisfy the desires of the organization's clients. Internal system goals are the objectives that organizational subsystems must meet to accomplish strategic goals.

The responsibility for developing strategic goals is typically top management's—usually the chief executive's, in conjunction with the board of directors or a group of vice presidents. Once these goals are developed, then internal subsystem goals (marketing, production, etc.) are stated, usually in the form of general plans. When these have been developed, they are communicated to the next-lower levels. This can be done by a series of cascading meetings between superiors and their subordinates and work groups, continuing from the top management level to the lowest point of supervision. This is what is described in the CALCAL example at the opening in item 10.1.

In the cascading process the corporate executive officer determines strategic objectives and the general program to achieve them. Then he meets with his immediate subordinates, including staff and operating executives in charge of major divisions. At this meeting, objectives and plans for the group are defined—a statement of the major activities and goal areas for the following year. The purpose of this meeting, for the subordinates, is informational. They are given the opportunity to increase their understanding of how the chief executive sees the direction, goals, and plans of the company.

Negotiable and nonnegotiable areas and plans should also be discussed, because these will become operating constraints for lower-level managers. A nonnegotiable area is one in which the chief executive requires that a specific approach be taken. In these areas lower-level personnel have no discretion. For instance, the chief executive may insist that certain products not be produced, because he has been so directed by the board of directors. In the CALCAL example, the president had decided what production levels for each month will be. These were nonnegotiable. Negotiable areas represent activities and goals where the chief executive is willing to modify his positions. Whether or not a new employee should be added to the CALCAL production staff was a negotiable goal area.

At the first meeting between the chief executive and the immediate staff, there is little emphasis on specific goals and objectives of the subordinates. From the information received, each subordinate manager should be able to develop a plan of action, goals, and appropriate performance measures for each relevant organizational objective in his or her own unit or division. Then in a private meeting with the chief executive officer, he or she undertakes an assessment of goals and what can be done to achieve them. When these goals and specific plans of action are agreed upon, specific goals and ways of achieving them exist for two levels of management.

Once a second-level executive knows what his or her objectives are, a meeting is scheduled with the operating and staff personnel. At this meeting, he makes known to that group the goals and action plans that he has agreed to with his superior. Again, this group meeting is essentially an informational one, and subordinates are encouraged to ask questions and engage in discussion that will help them understand the kinds of commitments that have been made. The subordinate can then make a more accurate assessment of his or her discretionary area as well as those areas that are nonnegotiable or nondecision making.

After this group meeting, each third-level executive individually prepares a set of action plans and objectives for himself and his unit and then meets individually with his superior. At this time the superior and the subordinate agree upon the goals, activities, and criteria for assessment of success.

When some consensus has been reached and the executive has his set of goals, he then schedules a meeting with his subordinates and the process continues as described. This cascading process proceeds to the lowest level of the organization at which it is still feasible. At each succeeding lower level, the amount of individual discretion becomes less and less, of course. This may seem that for the lowest operating managerial level, the meetings are essentially communication, with activities being specified and the subordinate being given a fairly well-developed set of operating measures and action plans that must be implemented. The nature of the organizational beast is such that the lowest-level managers operate within tighter constraints than managers at higher levels; the latter formulate the goals of the organization, and the former translate them into work.

Problems in Cascading Objectives

Some difficult problems must be resolved in this cascading process. The first is timing, especially in large organizations. For the cascading process to occur, meetings between superiors and subordinates must be fairly tightly scheduled; otherwise, the goal-setting process may extend over too long period of time. A specific, relatively limited period should be devoted to goal setting—perhaps the two-week period immediately following the final budget determination for the following fiscal year. If managers know that a particular time is scheduled for goal setting, they can schedule their own commitments appropriately.

A second problem occurs if there is a break in the goal-setting chain. If at any level a manager fails to set goals, those at lower levels will not receive the guidance they need. This is perhaps the primary reason that goal setting should be done during a specific time period. Managers can then be held accountable for setting goals. One goal, in fact, that should be set for all managers by their superiors is the setting of goals for their subordinate groups. Their success in this area can be verified later in the evaluation of performance.

PARTICIPATION IN GOAL SETTING

To implement plans effectively requires a good deal of subordinate involvement—or participation—in decision making about objectives and action plans. Participation can have two very important effects. First, when people participate in making decisions that affect them, they are more likely to accept and implement them. They not only feel that they have had something to say about what they are going to be doing, they also are more likely to understand more clearly what is to be done.

Second, participation is often necessary because subordinates have information that would be more useful in making decisions than does the superior. In this case the decision maker needs their ideas or information that they possess. Under these conditions, participation is a wise and necessary strategy.

Participation means that a person can influence—have something to say about—a decision that is normally beyond the formal authority in their job. Participation means sharing of power. But the implicit nature of power and authority must be recognized. Unless they have the approval of their superior, lower-level managers cannot legitimately influence goal levels and action plans in areas in which they have no formal authority or discretion. Therefore, it is necessary to spell out areas in which subordinates have some freedom, so that they know what their decision limits are. Otherwise they may mistakenly believe that they can participate in decisions, while in fact their superiors will not allow them more extensive influence. When a person expects to participate and then cannot, negative consequences can occur. Below are some considerations that influence whether or not a person should influence goals or action plans.

1. *Boundary-spanning functions.* Persons in a boundary-spanning activity affected by conditions outside the organization, for example, may be in the best possible position to determine both the goals (or ends) and the most appropriate means to achieve them because external conditions may not be clearly known to internal managers. For instance, marketing executives are in constant touch with the external environment. They should be in a better position to determine possible sales penetration and programs than anyone else in the organization. However, not having authority over goal levels should not preclude involvement of a lower-level manager in goal setting. Here, work planning should focus on developing the best action plans for goal attainment.

2. *Technical considerations.* High levels of skill and technology required in a particular function may make the specialist better able than a nontechnical person to assess what can be done in a technical field. Thus, the specialist should be involved in determining goal levels, as well as in carrying out activities.

3. *Organization level.* An important limitation on discretion is organizational level. The lower the organizational level, the narrower the zone of a manager's discretion. That is, managers at the lower levels are responsible for fewer, more specific, and more measurable activities and can commit smaller quantities of resources than those at higher levels.

4. *Changing competency.* Another factor that should affect influence is the changing competency levels of the incumbent. A person learning a job may need a great deal of guidance from his superior. As his or her skills increase, however, the superior may spend less time with the subordinate since he or she can capably handle more activities and make more decisions.

What about those decisions that fall outside the discretion limits? For these, the role of subordinates may be to contribute information and assistance, inputs to the decision-making process of superiors, which the superiors may elect to accept or reject. But contributing information and assistance must be differentiated from goal setting.

EFFECTIVE OBJECTIVES

A "good" objective for any aspect of a managerial job has two characteristics.
1. If achieved, it will increase the probability that the organization's level of effectiveness will increase. We call this the ***"quality"*** dimension.
2. The person who is expected to carry out the action plan to achieve the goal will be willing to put forth the necessary effort to do so. This is the ***"acceptance"*** dimensions of an objective.

A good objective is one that is technically adequate (has "quality") and is implemented (i.e., accepted). This idea can be summarized by the formulation.

$$\textit{effective objectives} = \textit{quality} \times \textit{acceptance}$$

Objectives can be classified into one of three categories based on acceptance and quality requirements.[2]

Q/A Objectives

The first type is a Q/A objective. This is dominated by the quality aspect. Acceptance is of little consequence. This type of objective would occur when one of two conditions exists. First, an objective may be of such critical importance to higher organizational levels that it is set there and the lower levels must carry it out. Such an objective might be the desired rate of return and subsequent general strategy to achieve it. Second, subordinates, for any number of reasons, may be willing to carry out the objective set at higher levels. The most effective approach to Q/A objectives is to have them set by higher organizational levels and then simply transmitted to those in lower levels.

A/Q Objectives

The second type of objective is an A/Q objective. For this type acceptance requirements are more important than quality requirements. Such objectives could exist because either (1) top management knows that those at lower levels will make good decisions and have high trust in them or (2) top management may be unable to make a good decision about an objective because they lack necessary information. For example, in one electronics firm, project leaders are allowed to form their own project work teams. After they have selected those whom they would like to have on a specific task, they report to the appropriate senior official about the team composition. In all but a few cases, the membership on the team is approved. The best way to implement A/Q objectives is to have them set by those who are to implement them. This requires a participative approach to goal setting.

A = Q Objectives

The third type of objective is a A = Q objective. For these objectives both acceptance and quality are of equal—and probably high—importance. Organizational success depends on a high quality decision to which the members are highly committed. Major research and development projects often fall into this category. Another problem of this type is selecting which capital investment projects should be undertaken, provided that the firm has several from which to choose and a limited amount of investment capital. For A = Q objectives, the superior must play a very active but not a dominating role in setting objectives. Objectives are set through a process of mutual influence by the superior and subordinate.

WHEN TO USE PARTICIPATION

The most effective approach for setting two of the three types of objectives requires a participative management approach. Managers must know two things about it: **when** to use it and **how** to use it. Various degrees of participation are possible. Subordinates may have complete autonomy in setting some objectives and developing action plans, or the decision maker may consult with them and then make the decision unilaterally. The degree of participation that is appropriate depends upon the situation and the type of problem to be solved. The important things a manager must decide are:

1. In what performance components of a subordinate's job is participation appropriate?
2. What is "participative" management behavior?

Performance Components

Any job has several parts to it. We call these different parts performance components. (We discuss this idea in more detail in Chapter 15.) Participation in setting goals may be very critical for some parts of a subordinate's job, but not for others. Consider the position of supervisor of a men's wear department in a large retailing operation. The performance components of this job might include at least the following:

1. Maintaining adequate inventory levels
2. Selecting and purchasing the different clothing lines and styles for the department
3. Determining prices for goods
4. Planning various sales, determining when they will be held and the markdowns on sale goods
5. Supervising sales personnel
6. Maintaining records of the department

The sales manager, to whom the supervisor reports, must decide how to manage each of these performance components, i.e., what measures of performance (criteria) will be used to judge each of them and how much influence the department supervisor should have in deciding goals and action plans for each of them. Company policies may specify the nature of records and the frequency of reports. Over that performance component (number 6), the men's wear department supervisor has little influence. But selecting and purchasing the lines to be sold (number 2) may be decentralized to the department level. The sales supervisor has influence in this performance component and therefore the sales manager should use some form of participative strategy.

It must be clear which performance components a subordinate will be able to influence. Developing this clarity is primarily the responsibility of the higher-level manager. When a subordinate knows what is expected (the goals) and the amount of influence he or she has over decisions, it is more likely that there will be better performance.

HOW TO BE PARTICIPATIVE

Knowing in which areas of a subordinate's job participation is appropriate is only part of the solution to implementing decisions. Knowing how to act in a participative fashion is of equal importance. Many managers think their subordinates participate in decision making or setting objectives when they meet with the subordinate and talk about future goals. There are several different degrees of subordinate influence that might be used in setting goals.[3]

1. The manager allows the subordinate to set goals. The manager accepts whatever goals the subordinate sets.
2. The manager and subordinate both have thought very carefully about the subordinate's future goals. A problem solving discussion takes place, from which the objectives are developed.
3. The subordinate prepares a set of goals, but the manager has thought little about them. During the goal-setting meeting, the manager decides which goals are to be assigned to the subordinate.
4. The manager calls the subordinate in and hands him or her a set of goals that are unilaterally determined by the manager.

All these approaches may be used and can work. However, here we focus on how to behave in a participative goal-setting mode since that behavior is most difficult to enact.

To Improve Quality of Objectives

Once managers have decided to encourage subordinates to influence goal setting, here is how the quality of the goals can be improved.[2] Quality of goals, as used here, means that the final goal set makes a significant contribution to organization success.

1. *The superior must participate in the discussion.* The boss must be willing to engage in meaningful discussion about the goal. He or she must be well-prepared, which means doing background work on the subordinate's job. The higher-level manager must be a good listener but also a good contributor to help the subordinate.

2. *Discussions should be developmental, not follow a "free" mode.* The superior and subordinate should not discuss anything that happens to be of interest at the moment. Digressions about nonrelevant issues should be avoided. While it is important to be pleasant and conversational, setting goals should be seen by all involved as the major reason for the meeting.

3. *Identify causes of problems.* Rather than spending most of the time talking about what is going to happen, more time should be devoted to identifying obstacles that may stand in the way of achieving the goal. For instance, instead of a district sales manager and a sales person arguing over whether or not a sales quota is too high, the sales manager should perhaps ask, "Why can't this goal be achieved? What stands in the way?" By answering these questions, both can work toward a solution of the problem by removing the obstacles.

4. *Do not discuss alternatives until the problem cause is clearly identified.* People too often suggest objectives and plans that they prefer to carry out or that they are most competent to perform. These are frequently not the most effective ways to achieve a goal. For instance, when sales drop, the market research director might propose an analysis of changes in demands because, let us say, the market research staff has most competence in this area. If the loss of sales has come about because of changing patterns of salesperson's calls, the proposed demand analysis will be of little value. Only after it is reasonably certain that obstacles (causes of problems) have been clearly identified should alternatives be evaluated.

5. *Do not hurry in setting goals.* Too often there is quick acceptance by either party in goal setting of a suggested objective just because it seems appropriate. A plant superintendent might tell the plant manager that next year's labor cost reduction goal is 3 percent. If that seems appropriate on the surface, the plant manager might immediately agree and want to move quickly to the next performance component to set goals. Setting goals is too important an activity to hurry through. There should be adequate time given to allow for discussion and evaluation.

6. *The superior should refrain from making suggestions.* If at all possible, the superior should not tell the subordinate what he or she thinks should be done. Subordinates, often anxious to please or worried about doing what their boss wants, often accept these suggestions even though they are not particularly good. The superior should make every effort to see that any suggestions he or she might make carry relatively equal weight, certainly no more weight than the subordinate's. Remember that this is a participative decision area, one in which the superior has decided with good reason that the subordinate should have some influence.

7. *Once an objective has been set, think about it and talk about it again.* Research on group decision making has demonstrated that if people who have solved a problem start again and try to reach a second solution, the second solution is better than the first.

To Increase Acceptance of Objectives

To increase the degree of subordinate acceptance of, or commitment to, the goals and action plans in participative goal setting, there are some things managers should do.

1. *Insure that subordinate input is reflected in the final decision.* There is nothing more disheartening to a person than to make a suggestion to a superior or to solve a problem only to have it presented to others as formulated by the superior. When possible, it should be made known when an idea comes from another person. One way would be to say in group meetings, "It was Frank's idea." Unless subordinates who are asked to participate in goal setting retain ownership of their good ideas, the climate will not be developed to get sound input.

2. *Subordinates must feel free to make suggestions.* Subordinates must not be afraid to make inputs. This requires a climate of trust in the superior–subordinate relationship. A higher-level manager should reinforce, as much as possible, suggestions and ideas from others. When an idea is rejected, there should be some explanation of why.

3. *Superiors should not dominate discussions.* Almost everything about setting goals supports the dominant position of the boss. The meeting is usually held in his or her office. The subordinate rarely sets the agenda or schedules the time for the meeting. The physical arrangement of the office is usually such that it clearly marks the different status between a lower- and higher-level manager. Therefore, extra care must be taken to encourage subordinate contributions.

4. *Conflict of ideas must be tolerated.* When two or more different goals have strong advocacy, it is best if the relative merits and disadvantages of each can be aired. This requires a tolerance for other views that may conflict with pre-established ideas. This tolerance of conflict is as important for the lower-level manager as it is for the higher-level person. Both must be willing to evaluate other positions so that the best outcome is selected.

5. *"High quality" objectives should be set.* There is nothing that will insure the demise of participative goal setting more quickly then having low-quality goals. When this happens everyone loses confidence in each other and in the system. There will be a very quick shift toward more unilateral goal setting.

DANGERS IN THE PARTICIPATION APPROACH

There are several reasons why some managers resist using participation to increase acceptance of goals.[2] First, managers may fear that subordinates will make a low-quality decision. Second, managers may feel that subordinates may expect to participate in future goal setting. Third, supervisors may feel that respect for them will diminish, since as a supervisor the role is to lead, not follow. Fourth, many managers feel that it is their responsibility to make the decisions and that subordinates do not wish to participate in setting goals and developing action plans. Many managers probably feel they do not have the ability to handle a participative situation in a group and are uncomfortable in such a situation.

Perhaps the most significant obstacle to the effective use of participation is "pseudo participation." Many managers openly acknowledge that goals are more readily accepted when subordinates are "involved," so they bring together a group ostensibly to discuss a problem, set objectives, and develop plans. After an airing of facts, there sometimes emerges a consensus among the group for an alternative unacceptable to the manager. He will then say , in effect, "Those are great ideas, but we have to do it another way." In reality he expected the group to select his alternative. Since they did not, he overruled them. This tactic can only lead to problems. The manager will find it difficult to obtain much involvement later, since trust will be destroyed.

PARTICIPATION IN GOAL SETTING AND TYPES OF ORGANIZATIONS

Participative approaches to setting objectives are more likely to be used in some organizations than in others and especially at certain levels in those organizations that use them. Decision making about objectives becomes more participative at the higher levels of management.[4] This can be expected, since higher-level managers are often perceived to be more closely identified with the organization's goals, to be more worthy of trust because of higher competence, and to have the appropriate work values. They are more organizationalist in outlook. In addition, their jobs are more important and less structured and they possess or have access to the necessary information for a decision.

Environmental uncertainty has an important effect on the extent to which clear-cut goals can be set and communicated to the rest of the organization. The strategic goals of the mechanistic organization are likely to be relatively stable over time. This will make it easier to break them down into goals for lower units. In organic organizations, where the environment is more turbulent, goals are less well fixed. So many factors will determine how to get effective implementation of decisions that a manager must not only have the technical expertise to make sound judgments, but he or she must also be skilled at analyzing the kind of problems faced, in order to have a decision implemented at the point where it will be carried out. This may make it impossible to centralize goal setting.

Organizations in different types of environments will differ with respect to the frequency with which participative decision-making approaches are used. Professionals and specialists often feel that they have a right to participate in the making of decisions and will be less accepting of autocratic decisions.

Also, in organic organizations problems are less structured and the information relevant to solving the problem is dispersed among different specialists. On the other hand, organizations faced with environmental certainty will have more structured problems and more narrowly defined jobs with limited discretion than those faced with environmental uncertainty; this is likely to decrease the frequency with which participative and group decision-making approaches are used.

Work planning can be used for implementing decisions with managers and professionals in the mechanistic organization since this approach works well under conditions of organization stability. However, there are ways that implementation of plans can be improved.

Set Objective Goals and Action Plans

Managers may incorrectly emphasize results, to the exclusion of the means by which goals are achieved, because there are likely to be output measures that are presented as "acceptable" standards. Excessive emphasis on objective performance standards in the stable organization can lead to dysfunctional behavior. For example, Blau,[5] in a study of a state employment agency, found that interviewers evaluated on the basis of the number of applicants processed paid little attention to placing the applicants and in fact avoided those applicants who required more of their time and effort. There are many other examples of how the establishment of "objective" performance standards against which individuals or groups were to be evaluated resulted in deliberate distortion of performance records, omission of information that would reflect adversely on performance, and the generation of false statistics.

Used correctly, however, goal setting can be an effective device. If the manager both sets goals with subordinates *and* develops acceptable means of achieving those goals, it can be determined both whether or not a goal was achieved and whether or not an action plan was carried out. The supervisor can focus on problems resulting from performance, rather than on personality deficiencies, and there should be less defensiveness than with the more traditional type of rating system.

The Use of Participation

In some cases participation is necessary. In others it may not be, since both task requirements and technology are known in the mechanistic organization to both the superior and his or her specialized staff. However, participation in setting work goals and objectives may still be desirable for purposes of achieving higher motivation and worker commitment. Some studies show that when a person participated, he or she was more committed to the decision.[2] If participation clarifies goals, that is good, since goal clarity is related to better performance.[6,7]

Evaluation by the Superior

In the mechanistic organization the superior is in a position to make judgments about performance. He or she typically knows the task objectives and the best approach for achieving them. The manager is usually in frequent contact with the person being evaluated. The existence of objective performance data makes rating easier than in an organic organization, and there is probably less need for the service of a staff rating expert. However, with a single rater the possibility of bias and favoritism is higher; a staff rating expert might prove useful in the mechanistic organization to keep the superior's ratings "honest." On balance, however, it seems that the most desirable method is to have the supervisor conduct the rating and provide feedback so that an opportunity is provided to improve supervisor–subordinate relationships and to bring job-related problems to the attention of both the rater and rated.

GOAL SETTING IN ORGANIC ORGANIZATIONS

Because relatively objective output measures are difficult to obtain in the organic organization, goal setting must be undertaken on a different basis than it is in the mechanistic organization. End results (objectives) may be specifiable only in general terms; for example, "increased quality" or "production of a low-cost unit." But since neither quality nor cost level can be precisely defined, management must concentrate on the definition of means for goal achievement, or the action plan.

Emphasize Action Plans

To set objectives in an organic organization, the ***general objective*** is stated and an action plan is given in detail. When an individual is evaluated, the focus is on whether or not the action plan has been carried out. It is assumed that if activities are proceeding according to the plan, the objective will eventually be reached. In effect, this strategy attempts to get employees to go through the steps that are assumed to lead toward the goal. For example, suppose a project group has the following goal: "To develop a new product that performs better than Competitor A, and at a lower price." (See Figure 10.7). Such a project may take two or three years to complete. But in the interim period, the individuals assigned to it expect pro-

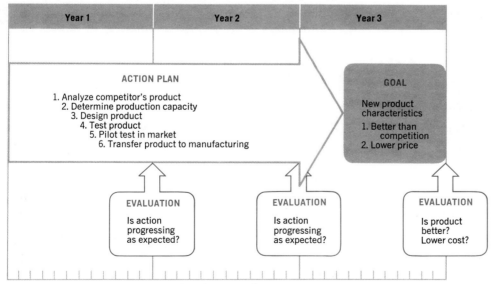

FIGURE 10.7   Project group goal and action plan.

motions, wage increases, and other rewards. About all that a manager can do in such a case is to make sure that the project group members are engaging in the activities that, based on experience, are most likely to achieve the desired result. The action plan for such an objective might be given in the following steps.

1. Analyze the competitor's product's characteristics. (To be completed in six months.)
2. Determine this company's capacity to produce a similar product. (To be completed in eight months.)
3. Design the product with less expensive components. (To be completed in fourteen months.)
4. Test the product for performance. (To be completed in sixteen months.)
5. Prepare plans for a pilot test of the product in the marketplace. (To be completed in twenty months.)
6. Transfer the design to the manufacturing division for production. (To be completed in twenty-four months.)

If such an action takes two years to carry out, then a manager evaluating the performance of the project group must determine whether or not the group is carrying out the elements in the plan. This evaluation must be done at regular intervals long before the achievement of the objective can be measured in the marketplace. So, periodically, at specified dates, the manager assesses whether or not the competitor's product was analyzed, a study of capacity was conducted, and so forth, step by step through the action plan.

Use Extensive Participation

Participation in setting objectives of this type requires extensive involvement of those who will carry out the action plan. The supervisor may not have the technical competence needed to develop an action plan for activities that are not so routine and will vary from project to project. He often does not know what subordinates do nor how they do it, and therefore he must solicit their ideas in establishing work objectives for both individuals and project groups. Thus, because subordinates often know more about what is possible, they should have more to say about goals and action plans than would be the case in a mechanistic organization.

Use Others for Help in Evaluation

The superior in the organic organization will be directing individuals who are using skills and knowledge unfamiliar to her, and therefore it is difficult for her to judge their performance. In addition, if she is directing higher-level personnel who are individually working on different projects with different task teams, she will not have the knowledge—or the time—to evaluate their performances. Thus, in the organic organization, inputs for evaluations are more likely to come from a group of professional peers and/or the various supervisors or project team members with whom the organizational members work. While the supervisor may herself provide feedback directly to subordinates, she must rely on these other sources of information for much of that feedback.

Change Objectives When Tasks Change

Goals should change often in the work planning system because the environment will be rapidly changing. Organization members may lose confidence in work planning unless these changes are reflected in work assignments. Thus, when goals change, any documents that have the obsolete goals written in them should also be changed.

SUMMARY

Plans must be executed if they are to be effective. Implementing them requires a good deal of communication between all levels of an organization. Work planning, as we have described it, is one way to approach the implementation of plans. Plans and objectives are communicated to subordinates. In many instances it is necessary that subordinates be very extensively involved in the planning and setting of objectives. Participation, when used wisely may, increase the extent to which subordinates understand and accept the plans set.

The approach to implementing plans will be different in mechanistic and organic organizations. In mechanistic organizations, we can expect to see less participation and more centralized planning. In organic organizations these will have to be a good deal more participatory because of the uncertainty in the environment.

Foster Glass

Case 10.1

The purchasing department of Foster Glass has the responsibility of insuring that the quantities of raw materials used in making the company's glass bottles are sufficient for meeting anticipated production schedules. Doug Wortman is the purchasing agent in charge of buying soda ash, a key ingredient in the manufacture of glass bottles. In March of 1979, he was told by his primary supplier, PGS corporation, that deliveries of previously ordered soda ash could be as much as two months late. The severe winter in the Midwest tied up the railroad cars needed to transport soda ash, and now the railroad cars were being used to fulfill earlier commitments.

When Doug Wortman reported this news to the manufacturing manager Cliff Hall, Cliff became enraged:

> I'll have to reduce my planned production by one half to stretch out the soda ash we have until we can get some more. You idiot—how could you do this to me? How am I going to meet my objectives this year? I'll never make my bonus now. I'm going to complain to Ed Scott (company purchasing director) about this. You should have anticipated this kind of a problem and built up inventories of soda ash.

Doug thought to himself, "It's my butt if we have excess carrying costs for these supplies. I can't win this case."

1. Evaluate Hall's statement about Wortman's competence. Is he justified in what he says?
2. What does this case illustrate about managerial control?
3. What should be done, if anything, about this type of problem?

Case 10.2 Urban Trust Company

The Urban Trust Company located outside Austin, Texas, has forty-five branch locations. Recently the bank installed a management by objectives program in the branch operations. Under this program, each branch manager established a set of specific objectives with his or her regional branch supervisor.

As part of the corporate objective of increasing the number of customers, one of the objectives established for each branch manager was to obtain a certain number of new customers for the branch. At the end of the year, almost every branch manager had achieved the objectives for obtaining new customers. However, the total number of customers served by the branch did not change very significantly, some thought, because the branches lost almost as many old customers as they had gained during the year. The personnel manager of the bank wondered if she should do something about the situation, especially since the MBO program seemed to be one of the causes of the problem.

1. What does this case illustrate about use of the management by objectives to help implement an overall company program?
2. What might a personnel manager of the bank do about this particular problem?

DISCUSSION QUESTIONS

1. Work planning is a *very* prominent and important approach to having plans implemented. Carefully explain work planning.
2. Explain how forming objectives and determining action plans interrelate and lead to successful work planning and goal setting.
3. There are long-term, short-term, and nonquantifiable objectives. When is each of these important to formulate and use?
4. What are the advantages of goal setting?
5. Write three performance objectives and be prepared to defend them.
6. Briefly explain what is meant by cascading objectives and problems associated with this process.
7. Why is subordinate participation so important in work planning?
8. Discuss Q/A, A/Q and A=Q objectives.
9. List and briefly discuss the suggestions given in the chapter to improve quality of objectives.
10. List and briefly discuss the suggestions given in the chapter to increase acceptance of objectives.

11. In which organization type do you feel that work planning would be most effective? Why? What would the problems be?
12. In which type of organization do you feel work planning would be most difficult to use? Why?

REFERENCES

1. Latham, G. P., and G. A. Yukl. "A review of the research on the application of goal setting in organizations," Academy of Management Journal, 18 (1975): 824–835.
2. Maier, N. R. F. Problem-solving discussions and conferences: Leadership methods and skills. New York, McGraw-Hill, 1963.
3. Tosi, H., and S. Carroll. "Some structural factors related to goal influence in the management by objectives process," MSU Business Topics 17 (Spring 1969): 45–51.
4. Heller, F. A., and G. Yukl. "Participation, managerial decision making and structural variables," Organizational Behavior and Human Performance, 4 (1969): 227–41.
5. Blau, P. The dynamics of bureaucracy. Chicago, University of Chicago Press, 1955.
6. Carroll, S., and H. Tosi. Management by Objectives. New York, Macmillan, 1973.
7. Locke, E. "Toward a theory of task motivation and incentives," Organizational Behavior and Human Performance, 3 (1968): 162.

CHAPTER ELEVEN

Departmentation

Item 11.1 Westinghouse Opts for a GE Pattern

Westinghouse Electric Corp. has never admitted that it is excelled by its larger rival, General Electric Corp., in anything but size and profits. But when Robert E. Kirby assumes command of Westinghouse next week as chief executive officer, he will preside over a trimmed-down corporate structure that is modeled in part on a GE management concept.

Fighting a severe profits slump, Westinghouse has recently lopped off losing businesses that account for about $700-million in annual sales. It has been preparing for the time when Donald C. Burnham, chief executive since 1963, steps down under a preretirement program for top officers that he himself devised. When he reaches 60 next week, Burnham will become an "officer-director" at two-thirds of his former pay. Last week, the 56-year-old Kirby, former head of Westinghouse's profitable industry and defense group, told 200 line and staff managers at a Lancaster (Pa.) meeting how the corporation will reshape itself when he takes over as chairman on Feb. 1.

SHRINKAGE   Instead of doing business through five operating companies, West-inghouse is shrinking back to three, each headed by a president who serves on a top, five-man management committee. The change eliminates the Consumer Products Co., already decimated by the pending sale of Westinghouse's $600-million-a-year major appliances business to White Consolidated Industries. Other consumer lines are being absorbed by two of the remaining companies—Industry Products under Douglas D. Danforth, fifty-two, and Public Systems, headed by Thomas J. Murrin, forty-five. Public Systems also gets five business chunks from the old Broadcasting, Learning & Leisure Time Co., which is reduced to subsidiary status under Chairman Donald H. McGannon and contains only the money-making Group W television and radio stations. The third company, Power Systems, headed by Gordon C. Hurlbert, fifty, continues as at present.

Replacing an old, seven-man policy committee, the five-man management committee will meet more often and make "more coordinated" corporate decisions. The fifth member, along with Kirby, Hurlbert, Danforth, and Murrin, is Marshall K. Evans, fifty-seven, vice chairman and chief of staff. Faster decision-making at the top supposedly will be aided by the most interesting facet of the reorganization: the grouping of Westinghouse's 120 divisions into thirty-seven "basic business units," each headed by a general manager. The divisions will remain profit centers, but "strategic planning" decisions on market growth and capital expansion will be coordinated at the business unit level instead of in the divisions. "We had gone too far in the decentralization to divisional profit centers and had fragmented several businesses that weren't fragmentable," says Evans.

The model for this approach is the "strategic business unit" plan adopted in 1970 by GE, which is divided into forty-two SBUs. Westinghouse had been grouping its divisions by markets for some years, but now it has taken the final step to the unit concept. "We learned a helluva lot from GE," says Evans. "We struggled like mad to find something better than GE has, but theirs is as good as there is. Ours is not a copy of GE's, but we're coming out at the same place."

OTHER CHANGES   In a further effort to make the new units cost-accountable, Westinghouse is reassigning corporate technical staff to the unit level. This will result in a "significant reduction" in corporate staff, Evans says.

Whether these and other changes will reverse the erosion of profits that had taken place over the last two years remains to be seen. The decline occurred in large part because the company moved too fast into service businesses unrelated to electrical equipment manufacturing and nuclear power. In recent months, in addition to the huge appliance business sale—which awaits Justice Dept. approval—Westinghouse has disposed of $100-million worth of business that had lost a total of $59-million in 1973. Included are a mail order company, water pollution control equipment operations, military and low-income housing, and a French elevator company. The divestiture program, now completed, will require write-offs of $66-million on 1974 income. But, says Evans, "we've managed to shoot all the dogs."

Source: Business Week, Feb. 3, 1975. Reprinted from the Feb. 3, 1975, *Business Week* by special permission. Copyright © 1975 by McGraw-Hill, Inc.

Organizing is the managerial process that includes (1) the design of organization structure, (2) attracting people to the organization, and (3) creating conditions and systems that insure that they work to achieve the strategic and internal system goals.

In this chapter we discuss designing the organization structure. This activity results in the formation of departments and the chain of command. The specific issues are what kind of departmentation should be used, how many departments or subunits there should be at each organization level, and how these units should be integrated with each other by the authority and responsibility relationships. These are the problems that Westinghouse had to solve, as pointed out in item 11.1. Westinghouse concluded that they had far too many separate units and made the decision to reduce the complexity of the organization structure.

ORGANIZING AS A DECISION PROCESS

The process of organizing goes on constantly. As the external environment changes even slightly, there is continuous rearrangement and reassignment of activities within the firm to adapt to changes. Sometimes the changes are modest, requiring only a small change in activities of one person. For instance, as federal and state environmental protection activity increased, a lawyer with the legal department of a large public utility was assigned complete responsibility for handling the firm's Environmental Protection Agency relationships. Some of his previous duties were assigned to other staff lawyers, and other duties were simply eliminated because they were now unnecessary.

Sometimes these organizing changes are drastic, as in the case of a large mid-western university, which created an Office of Affirmative Action to move into compliance with federal and state equal opportunity requirements. A new department was created with a director, several assistants, and other support staff. Some general outlines of the activities of the new department were developed. It may take several years for such a new unit really to find its niche and settle in with the rest of the organization subunits. The Westinghouse example is another case of a major organizational change.

Figure 11.1 shows how organizing is related to other aspects of the management process. Organizing follows planning and the analysis of objectives. In planning, objectives are determined, and activities are selected that are likely to achieve the goals. In organizing, these activities are assigned to different departments.

Assigning tasks ineffectively could lead to poor performance. It is no easy matter to decide who should perform which tasks and when these tasks should be performed. Also, there are different ways to group activities, some better than others.

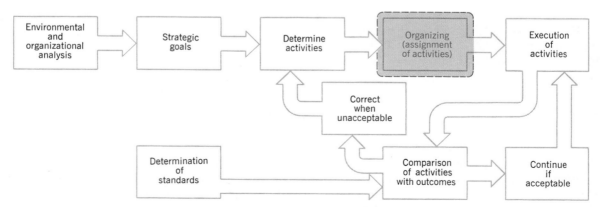

FIGURE 11.1   Organizing and the other management processes.

The choice and design of an organization structure for integrating these differentiated tasks and specialists must be made. Therefore, organizing can be viewed as a **de-cision-making** process, deciding "what is the best way to differentiate and integrate the subsystem activities?"

Figure 11.2 illustrates the decision aspect of organizing. First, the manager is dissatisfied with the current state of affairs, aware of a difference between **what the manager thinks should be** and **what is.** Some problems that might be caused by poor organization, hence leading to a need to reorganize are:

1. Higher-level managers spending too much time handling current problems and not enough time planning.
2. Delays in meeting delivery or production schedules, especially when there are adequate physical resources.
3. When product (or service) quality is lower than desired, and there are no recent changes in raw material or production technique.
4. When a new task is necessary, as would be the case when a new product is developed or a new market is found.
5. Managers spending large amounts of time coordinating activities of their subordinates or of their own unit with other units.
6. Managers unable to get information needed for decision making in time.
7. When individuals are uncertain about what their major responsibilities are.
8. When there are poor relationships between different organizational levels.
9. When there are disagreements over which manager has authority and responsibility for which activities and for which people.
10. When the organization seems swamped with excess reporting and information requirements.

When problems such as these exist, the next step is to determine the probable cause. In Figure 11.2 three possible causes are suggested. The problem could be a result of **people, physical facilities, resources,** or the **organization structure.** If after evaluating the different possible causes of the problem, the manager determines that the most likely cause is the current organization, then a set of "organizing decisions" must be made.

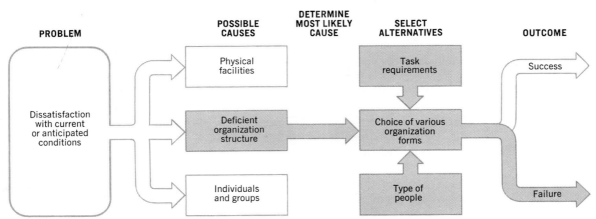

FIGURE 11.2 Organizing as a decision process.

Organizing Decisions

There are two types of organizing decisions, "differentiating" and "integrating" decisions. "Differentiating" decisions are choices made about which ways the organization subsystems are to be separated or unbundled. There are alternative ways to unbundle these subsystems. This is illustrated in the Westinghouse example. Their business activities can be organized in different ways. Before the change, Westinghouse was a loosely structured group of 120 divisions. After the reorganization these became thirty-seven strategic business units. The two major differentiation decisions are

1. What types of departments should be formed?
2. How large should the "span" of control be?

The departmentation decision results in the formation of different types of organizational subunits. The span of control decision determines how many organizational units there will be at each organizational level.

The "integrating" decisions are the choices about how the departments that have been formed are to be linked together. The primary integrating decision is

How should authority relationships and responsibility be designed?

The Westinghouse case shows how the authority relationships will be different. First there will be fewer major units. Second, decisions will be centralized in the top management of each business unit, instead of in the 120 divisions. Differentiation and integration decisions result in the system of formal authority and responsibility relationships, or who is responsible to whom and for what.

TYPES OF DEPARTMENTATION

When the activities of different subsystems are separated, they are regrouped into departments. Departments are the skeleton of the organization on which the different subsystems hang. They are the most visible components of organizations, though they may show very little about how the organization really operates since the subsystems (i.e., production, boundary-spanning, etc.) cut across departmental boundaries.

Departments should be formed only after an analysis of the work necessary to achieve the strategic objectives of the firm. For example, consider CALCAL, the firm that manufactures electronic calculators. Here is the way we would proceed with such an analysis to organize the manufacturing department.

1. *Determine the strategic goal.* In this instance, the goal would be to produce a low cost calculator to meet the computational needs of students, engineers, and home users.

2. *Define the product or products.* Several different calculators might be designed, ranging from one that could handle highly sophisticated analytical problems to one that is a simple four or five function calculator.

3. *Determine the components, or parts, of each product.* The basic elements of the calculator would be the case, the display elements, the integrated circuitry, and the registering mechanisms or keys.

4. *Develop a procedure for making each part.* For those subassemblies that the firm will manufacture, we must design the production process. Each subassembly will require a different manufacturing process.

5. *Determine each step in the manufacturing procedure.* In other words, we must determine what different steps must be done and in what sequence these steps must be carried out.

6. *Determine how each step is related to other steps.* What are the similarities and differences between steps? Do several steps require similar machinery, like a lathe, for instance? Do some steps require similar worker skill?

7. *Decide which steps should be grouped together and which should be separate.* This is the last part of the analysis and determines the type of departmentation.

Of course, such an analysis would also lead down many other different paths. For instance, after we have answered the question "what product?", a series of marketing questions must be considered about how to get the product to the different users.

The types of organizations that might emerge from such an analysis are (1) functional organization, (2) product organization, (3) matrix organization, and (4) project organization. Of these, the functional and product form are the most frequently used forms in industrial organizations.

FUNCTIONAL ORGANIZATION

The ***functional*** form of organization is one in departments (or subunits) that most closely parallel the organization subsystems (see Chapter 3). The primary subsystems (production, boundary-spanning, and monitoring), are largely self-contained in departments. In an organization with functional departmentation, we might find the production, boundary-spanning, and external-monitoring subsystems located in departments as shown in Figure 11.3. The maintenance subsystems would be staff departments (which we will discuss later in this chapter) such as personnel, quality control, and auditing.

Figure 11.4 is an abbreviated organization chart of a firm departmentalized along functional lines. Managers, specialists, and other personnel are assigned to groups that perform similar kinds of work, e.g., marketing, production, and finance. Most of the staff in the different departments probably have similar backgrounds and

FIGURE 11.3 Departments and Subsystems in Functional Organization

Department	Subsystem
Manufacturing	Production
Marketing	Boundary spanning
Finance	Boundary spanning
R & D	External monitoring

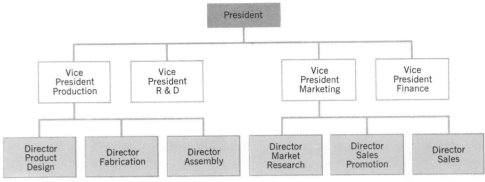

FIGURE 11.4   A functional organization.

training. This, along with their work experience, means they are likely to be very knowledgeable specialists, able to direct their attention to a limited area of activity.

Communication will be simpler within functional departments because of these common backgrounds, interests, and experiences. The jargon in each functional area will be more easily understood by the department members. On the other hand, there may be communication difficulties among departments because of the differences between, say, production and marketing personnel in the respective departments. Coordination among the different departments may be very difficult and often require higher levels of management to become involved in solving co-ordination problems. For instance, the Marketing Division might actively press for a policy to produce a wide range of products, which would make them better able to meet varied customer needs. The Manufacturing Division in the same company might wish to pursue a policy of product line simplification, which would ease substantially production scheduling problems and reduce manufacturing costs. These two different policies sought by marketing and production are incompatible with each other, and some balance must be struck. A higher-level managerial decision must be made to resolve this disagreement. This problem exemplifies one of the main difficulties with the functional organization, that is, relating goals of each functional division to overall corporate objectives.

PRODUCT ORGANIZATION

A second widely used form of departmentation is the **product** form. Organizational subunits are built around different products or service. These are also called "goal oriented organizations."[1] The different organizational subsystems may be present in each of the different product divisions. Figure 11.5 shows such a product organization structure. The manager of a product unit is responsible for the operation of what may be an almost complete business.

In the product organization, people are grouped with others from diverse backgrounds like marketing, engineering, and manufacturing into a unit that produces and markets a product different from that of other major organization units.

Accountability and control are somewhat simplified in the product organization since manufacturing and marketing costs may be allocated to each of the different products. The product group, as a whole, can be held accountable for virtually the complete task of producing and distributing the product.

Product divisions may produce different, **noncompetitive** products. An electronic data processing equipment manufacturer has a product division for typewriters, another for computers, and another that develops computer programs and other software.

Divisions of product organizations may be **competitive.** In General Motors, which has always had a strong product-oriented organization, there is strong competition between Oldsmobile, Buick, and Pontiac. The different divisions compete with each other for sales.

At the present time, a majority of the largest companies in the U.S. are organized on a product division basis. In all of these companies, the major organization units are product divisions that tend to have a great deal of autonomy over such matters as marketing, manufacturing, and engineering. However, control of certain activities, such as finance and industrial relations, is often retained by the company's top management at the corporate headquarters level because of the need for uniformity and consistency of decisions in these areas.

MATRIX ORGANIZATION

The **matrix** organization is useful when it is necessary to integrate the activities of many different specialists while at the same time maintaining specialized organizational units.

In the matrix organization, technicians from specialized organizational units are assigned to one or more project teams to work together with other personnel. For example, chemical, mechanical, industrial, and electronic engineers, and other specialists may be assigned to functional units to develop a new product. The specialists should be able to integrate their efforts better when they are members of a group than when they are merely the representatives of their own specialized departments.

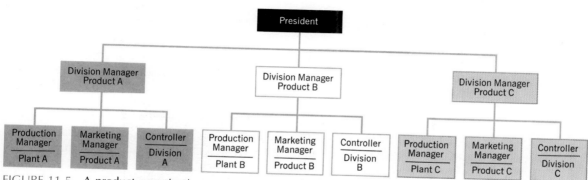

FIGURE 11.5   A product organization.

Each member of the team is subject to dual authority. The team member takes orders from the project manager and from the manager of the department to which he or she is assigned. The goals of each of these different managers may be incongruent. In the aerospace industry, for example, project managers tend to be concerned about meeting schedules within budgetary limitations and in producing output within previously planned specification. Specialized unit managers, on the other hand, are more concerned with full utilization and the long-term development of resources as well as high technical performance.[2]

Retaining the specialized organizational units as a relatively permanent subunit enables the individual specialist to obtain help from professional colleagues on technical problems. It also provides the opportunity to identify with a professional group as well as continue professional development, perhaps with the help of others. Specialized organizational units also make for more efficient utilization of human resources for the organization and less duplication of resources, since these highly trained and probably well paid technicians would have to be assigned to other units.

This form of organization can help achieve high technical performance and integration of diverse specialities at the same time.[3] It does this, however, at the cost of higher role ambiguity and stress for the individuals involved as compared to the other forms since many in the matrix organization work for two superiors at the same time.

Figure 11.6 shows the matrix organization of the Aerospace Division of Universal Products Company. There are several functional (or specialist) units: production, engineering, materials, personnel, and accounting. There are three projects in the division (if this firm produced consumer goods, these might be three different products, say, automobile brake system, water pumps, and hydraulic lifts). Managers and technicians from each of these functional units are assigned to each different project. Thus, those production specialists assigned to the Venus project (until its completion) report to both the production facilities manager and to the Venus project manager.

The matrix organization is also used outside industrial settings. For example, one college of business administration uses a matrix structure. Faculty members are assigned to their specialized departments such as marketing, finance, management, accounting, and so on. There are program managers (associate deans) for the undergraduate program, the graduate program, the management development program, and so on.

While effective, the matrix form presents some organization problems. Disagreements occur between different project managers and between project managers and managers of specialized departments. In addition, project team members themselves often receive incompatible requests from their two superiors and, therefore, experience considerable role conflict and stress. They also often experience insecurity because they are working on temporary projects.

Matrix organization requires member emphasis on cooperation, rather than competition. Matrix organization often creates the potential for harmful conflict since often diverse and contradictory objectives and values come together in it. Some organizations using the matrix system feel that training in the management of conflict is essential to making this approach a success.

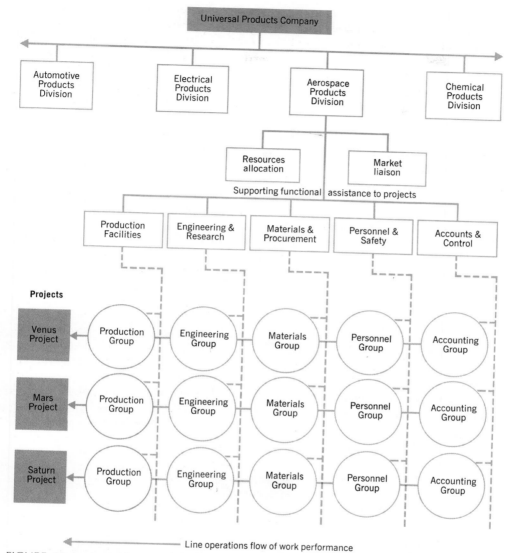

FIGURE 11.6   A matrix organization. (*Source:* Mee, John, "Matrix organization," *Business Horizons,* Vol. 10, Summer 1964, p. 71.)

PROJECT ORGANIZATION

When the nature of the work changes very rapidly, due to changes in the environment, an organization must have a structural form that changes with it. When this situation exists, a **project** form of organization may be appropriate. A "project" is a series of related activities required to achieve a work outcome, say a product or a design and plan for constructing a new building. One characteristic is that projects are generally unique; no two are the same as are different brands of refrigerators or different makes of automobiles that may be produced by the same manufacturer. For example, the lunar landing and return of U.S. astronauts was a unique space project. Once the astronauts came back and the data were analyzed, workers were shifted to other projects.

Project organization recognizes this need to change and allows the shift of both physical and human resources as needed. Individuals are assigned to temporary work teams that exist for different project time periods, since each project will have a different life. Each project has a planned termination date to which planning and control activities are tied. The main factor that determines the composition of the work team is the project needs. When different skills are needed for different projects, the composition of the team will change.

Figures 11.7 and 11.8 show two typical project organizations (A and B) for the electrical engineering consulting firm, D. Clements. Suppose the company is working on six different projects (Table 11.1) in January 19__1. Teams are assigned to a project leader (Tom, Janina, etc.) and each group has the responsibility of finishing the project assigned to it. Each project has a different date, as shown in Table 11.1, and by the time January 1, 19__2 (as seen in Figure 11.8 and Table 11.2) rolls around, Tom's project (1), Floyd's project (3) and Debby's project (5) have been completed and new ones have been added.

Floyd switches from a medical to an industrial project and he now reports to a different vice president. Tom switches from an industrial to a medical project, and he too changes bosses. Debby's new project is still in the commercial section, so her boss stays the same. Gene, a new project manager, has been hired during the first year and is assigned to the Shift's Department Store Project (10).

There has also been a reassignment of the technical staff. In the previous year, Phil, Harold, and Larry worked for Debby. Now she supervises Kathy, Phil, and Pete, a new employee. Thus, when the nature of the business changes, there is a major job change for technical and supervisory staff of D. Clement Engineering.

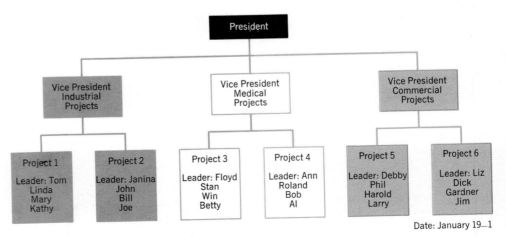

Date: January 19__1

FIGURE 11.7   Project organization A for D. Clement Engineering.

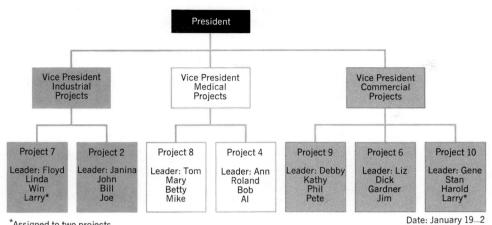

*Assigned to two projects

Date: January 19__2

FIGURE 11.8   Project organization B for D. Clement Engineering.

TABLE 11.1   D. Clement Project Schedule A, January 1, 19__1

Project	Team leader	Project responsibility	Team members	Completion date
1. Auto plant lighting	Tom	Vice president Industrial	Linda Mary Kathy	6/1/__1
2. Utility cooling tower	Janina	Vice president Industrial	John Bill Joe	12/30/__2
3. W. C. Field Hospital addition	Floyd	Vice president Medical	Stan Win Betty	8/1/__1
4. Generating System-Medical Center	Ann	Vice president Medical	Roland Bob Al	7/1/__2
5. Westgate Shopping Center	Debby	Vice president Commercial	Phil Harold Larry	10/30/__1
6. Pine Mission Development	Liz	Vice president Commercial	Dick Gardner Jim	11/30/__2

TABLE 11.2   D. Clement Project Schedule B, January 19__2

Project	Team leader	Project responsibility	Team members	Completion date
2. Utility cooling tower	Janina	Vice president Industrial	John Bill Joe	12/30/__2
4. Generating System-Medical Center	Ann	Vice president Medical	Roland Bill Al	7/1/__2
6. Pine Mission Development	Liz	Vice president Commercial	Dick Gardner Jim	11/30/__2
7. Power transmission system	Floyd	Vice president Industrial	Linda Win Larry[a]	1/1/__3
8. East Medical Clinic	Tom	Vice president Medical	Mary Betty Mike	11/11__4
9. Shower Office Project	Debby	Vice president Commercial	Kathy Phil Pete	9/21/__2
10. Shift's Department Store	Gene	Vice president Commercial	Stan Harold Larry[a]	6/7/__3

[a]Assigned to two projects.

OTHER FORMS OF DEPARTMENTATION

Activities can be organized in other ways as well. For example, departments may be formed as geographic units (see Figure 11.9) or type of customer served (see Figure 11.10). This is especially likely when detailed knowledge of specific geographic locations or customers is required, as is often the case in marketing. For example, in selling industrial goods, technical knowledge of the salespersons tend to be much more important than in selling consumer goods. In the marketing of goods in Japan, special knowledge is needed of the very complex sales and distribution systems used in that country, which are quite different than those found anywhere else in the world.

These other forms of departmentation are often used in conjunction with the product and functional forms since the typical organization is often a hybrid of several forms of departmentation.

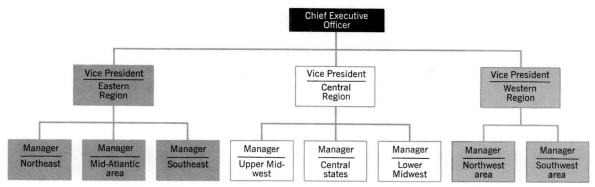

FIGURE 11.9   A geographically organized firm.

STAFF DEPARTMENTS

Staff departments are support units. Their primary objective is to **support,** to help, the line or primary activities. This support occurs in the nature of their relationship with the primary activities. The role of staff units should, in general, be advisory or supportive in their relationship with these line units. Except in rare instances they should **advise, not control or make decisions.** This is what is meant by the support role of staff.

Staff support can take several forms:

1. Staff departments may perform routine activities. For example, typing pools and maintenance departments may be created when the volume of this type of work is large enough.
2. Staff departments often perform planning and control activities. Auditing groups, information processing groups, and quality control units all collect information that is used to evaluate performance of the line units of the organization. Product planning and production scheduling staffs generally engage in operational planning activities that make the production systems more efficient.
3. Staff units may be groups of highly trained technicians and professionals whose

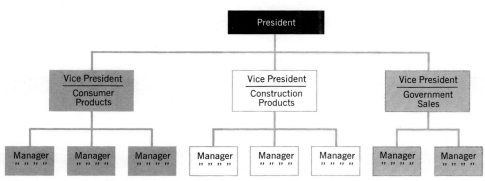

Departmentation

FIGURE 11.10   Organization by type of customer served.

269

assistance is needed throughout the firm, but there is not enough demand in any one subunit to justify the position. Take a legal staff, for example, which might work on marketing problems, antitrust problems, and environmental problems. It is probably uneconomical to assign a lawyer full time to, say, the marketing department, so a legal staff is created that serves the whole firm.

Figure 11.11 shows some different types of staff units in the functional organization (see Figure 11.4). The staff departments are

1. Corporate legal staff
2. Vice president of personnel
3. Personnel (production)
4. Personnel (marketing)
5. Production control

The corporate legal staff reports directly to the president. The role of this staff is to advise the chief executive officer about compliance with regulations and laws that govern the business. The final decision to what action to take in any matters, however, is the president's.

The personnel staff is an example of one that has several units at different points throughout the firm. If the personnel problems of the production units are different from the personnel problems of the marketing unit, separate personnel departments might exist in each functional unit. This would certainly be so if the production facilities and the marketing operations were separated geographically; say, the plants were located in Michigan and the sales office in New York. Because there are some personnel problems that cut across all units, the office of vice president of personnel

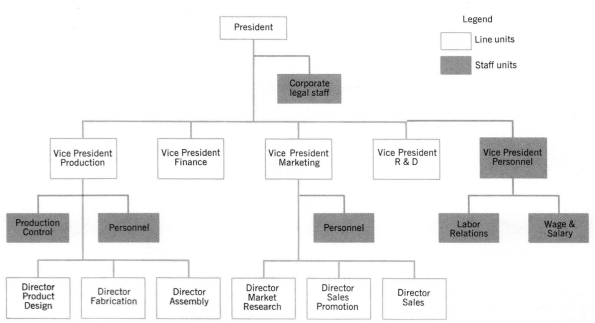

FIGURE 11.11   Staff units in a functional organization (see Figure 11.4).

is at the corporate level. Personnel activities assigned to this corporate level office might be for instance, reporting on an Affirmative Action Program or Occupational Safety Program and conducting labor negotiations for all units. This central office would coordinate the personnel activities of those units that have been decentralized in the marketing and production divisions.

The production control staff has the assignment of assisting the production department. The production system can operate more efficiently when work is scheduled properly and materials are available as needed. The production control department does this for the manufacturing department. The vice president of production and the other production managers receive the scheduling advice and operational information they need to help do the production job better.

WHICH FORM OF DEPARTMENTATION?

A few years back, it was viewed as avant-garde to propose that highly bureaucratic organizations were like dinosaurs, becoming extinct. This premise was based on the following faulty assumptions:

1. Technology was increasing so rapidly that the traditional bureaucratic organization would have to change to survive.
2. Human beings would rebel against bureaucratic forms because these forms restricted human growth; these organizations did not provide an opportunity to satisfy higher-order human needs.
3. A manager had a *wide* range of choice about which form of organization and the degree of formalization would be used.

The view we think makes more sense is that the environment drives the general form of structure and the general level of formalization required. A manager may have some choices to make but must select a type of departmental organization that falls within the boundaries defined by the environment.

Of course we know, and it is now widely agreed, that the rates of technological changes vary. In some cases there is rapid change, as in electronics. In others, like the transportation industry, change is slower. And human beings also have varied needs that are satisfied elsewhere than in work organizations. Also, some people prefer a more structured work environment while others prefer a less well-defined work setting.

These different environmental pressures and individual preferences will always require diverse types of formal organization structures. The person who designs an organization must keep these givens in mind and realize that the starting point for prescribing the way an organization should be designed is constrained by them.

DEPARTMENTATION IN STABLE ENVIRONMENTS

When the several major external environmental sectors are for the most part stable, then the organization will be mechanistic. The subsystems will be differentiated into formal organizations that will have either a functional departmentation or product departmentation form. These two forms seem to be predominant structures, and it is less frequent that we find major departmentation along customer or geographic lines.

Choosing Between Product and Functional Organizations

Often a firm has the choice: it can organize along either product or functional lines. In fact, most organizations are a mix of product and functional types. A good example is General Motors, which is, as we noted, primarily a product organization, but the General Motors Acceptance Corporation (the consumer finance unit) and the General Motors Assembly Division are functional units.

But, still, a firm will choose one or the other of these two forms as the predominant structure. One major consideration that affects the choice is risk. In a functional organization a poorly managed functional activity can affect the whole firm. For instance, if the marketing division of a company making three product lines is poorly managed, sales of all of the three products will be affected and overall profits will be low. On the other hand, when marketing and production functions are placed within a product group, a poorly managed functional unit will affect only that product or product line. If the marketing function is placed in each product division, as in Figure 11.5, and the marketing manager of Product B does a poor job, the rest of the organization may still benefit from profits from the other two product lines.

There is some research on American and European industrial organizations that outlines the consequences of using either the functional or the product form of departmentation.[1,3,4,5]

1. The functional form results in higher levels of technical knowledge applied to problems than in the product form.
2. The functional form results in more conflict among organizational subunits than in the product form.
3. Communication within organizational subunits is easier, but communication between organizational subunits is more difficult in the functional than in the product form.
4. Functional organizational units generally produce higher-quality products than product organized groups.
5. Organizations with functionally organized subunits generally have more consistency of action throughout the organization than product organized organizations.
6. Functional organizations have less duplication of staff and facilities than the product organizations.
7. There is more efficient use of highly trained technical manpower in the functional form as compared to the product form.
8. Specialists for the functional form of organizations are easier to find and recruit than the more general managers required by the product organizational form.
9. Greater group and professional identification occurs in the functional organized units as compared to the product groups.
10. The product form of organization results in better customer service and delivery than the functional form.
11. The product form results in easier control and accountability than the functional form.
12. The product form results in better training of top managers than the functional form.
13. The product form of organizations results in better performance than the func-

tional form when very tight production schedules and interdependence among specialized personnel are required by the situation.

14. The product form of an organization requires less elaborate coordinating mechanisms than the functional form.

15. A greater concern with long-term organizational issues develops in the product organized units as compared to those organized on a functional basis.

In the last analysis, the choice may be dictated by the firm's philosophy about what leads to maximizing its goals. When it seems that the strategic goals can be best achieved by emphasizing customer or client services, the firm will probably choose a product organization. If it believes the strategic goal is most likely to be attained by emphasizing internal efficiencies, it should choose a functional form.

DEPARTMENTATION IN VOLATILE ENVIRONMENTS

For those organizations that have one or more environmental sectors that are volatile, the form of departmentation must provide flexibility to match. The two environmental settings that an organization planner might face are:

1. Generally volatile environments
2. Mixed environments

Generally Volatile Environments

When several of the key environmental sectors are highly volatile, the organization should take the "project" form. The governing factors that determine a specific project group (which can be seen as a sort of temporary department) are the project time horizon and the skills required.

A project team will be formed for the life of the project, from planning through execution and perhaps evaluation. The work group, however, is unlikely to be constant in size and/or makeup. As skills are needed, members can be added. When the project is completed the members will be reassigned.

Mixed Environment

When the organization's environmental sectors have very different degrees of volatility (i.e., some stable and some volatile), the matrix form is most likely the appropriate way to organize. Technical specialists can be assigned to more permanent departments to provide them with the type of assistance necessary for effective performance.

In a technology-dominated organization, the technical specialist will have engineering or scientific competence that can be brought to the organization. For example, Figure 11.6 shows a firm in the aerospace industry. Functional departments of production, engineering, and so forth have a "project coordinator" who assists them.

In a market-dominated organization, the technical specialist will bring marketing competence to the operation of a functional unit. For example, in the recording industry, companies that produce music ranging from country to classical have A & R personnel for each of the different types of music. It is the A & R representatives' responsibility to select the artists and the repertoire of music for each area. For example, the A & R representative for country music would help determine which of several performers under contract should record certain music. The A & R representative for classical music would perform a similar function, but selecting from classical artists and music. The production and distribution facilities (the functional departments) would be used for both types of recording.

THE SPAN OF CONTROL

The second differentiation decision is "How large should the span of control be?" The span of control is the number of subordinates that report to a particular manager. The span of control may be wide, as when a manager has fifteen to twenty subordinates reporting directly to him, or it may be narrow, as when a manager has three or four subordinates reporting directly. The span of control is related to departmentation in that the size of the span determines the number of different subunits at a particular level of organization. For instance, the president in Figure 11.4 has a span of control of four vice presidents, while the president in Figure 11.11 has a span of control of five.

How Large a Span of Control?

The size of the span of control can affect how well a manager does his job. When the span is too large, then too much time may be spent coordinating and interacting with subordinates. The manager will have less time to devote to planning and executing his or her own work assignments. On the other hand, if the span is too narrow, the manager may have time that could be devoted to developing subordinates, to help them do their jobs better. A narrow span may often mean the manager's job is not big enough, that there is "unused" managerial capacity.

The "right" span of control has been the subject of much controversy among management writers. Filley, House, and Kerr, after examining several studies that examined how large a span of control should be, conclude that:
1. The optimal span is in the range of five through ten.
2. The larger spans, say eight through ten, are particularly appropriate at the highest policy-making levels of the organization.[6]

This was also found in an extensive study of British manufacturing, which showed in the most effective large-batch manufacturing firms, the "chief executive . . . controlled no more than the recommended five or six subordinates."[7]

At the operative level, technology may be a very important factor leading to different spans of control. For example, when there are real-time information reporting systems, the operative work is controlled by the speed of an assembly line or work is defined by standard procedures, and the span of management may be larger since there are fewer things that the supervisor must personally check. However, if the supervisor must spend a lot of time working with employees, helping them solve work problems, then the span should be smaller.

Some factors that affect the span of control are:

1. *Degree of interdependent work.* When the work of subordinates is highly interrelated, or interlocking, the span of control should be smaller because the supervisor must spend more time coordinating the work of the subordinates. Consider, for example, the D. Clement Electrical firm (Figures 11.7 and 11.8). The project leaders have a small span of control, three engineers. The reason is that these engineers and designers must work very closely together to accomplish the project goal. The Project 2 (Utility Cooling Tower) team of John, Bill, and Joe will have to coordinate the electrical plans and construction plans of each other. Supervisor Janina must work closely with all the team members individually and with the group.

2. *Similarity of jobs supervised.* When a manager supervises subordinates whose jobs are very similar, the span of control may be larger than when the jobs of subordinates are very different. This is the case for the president in a product organization (Figure 11.5); each immediate subordinate has a similar job, and the responsibilities of the different division managers are very much alike. However, the work of the vice presidents in the functional organization (Figure 11.4) is very different. When there is a great difference in what is done in the supervised groups, the span of control should be smaller. There is research support for this conclusion. Udell studied the relationship between the span of control and functional similarity and found that spans were greater where the work of subordinates was similar.[8]

3. *Personal characteristics of subordinates.* Personal characteristics, especially the competence and values, of those supervised affect the span of control. Highly skilled subordinates need less supervision than those who are less skilled.

Subordinate values also come into play. When subordinates' and manager's values are similar, it takes much less time to gain acceptance of directives. For instance, subordinates who have an "organizationalist" orientation toward work will act in ways they believe to be in the best interest of the firm.

Selection, development, and training programs will affect the level of skills and types of values. When selection efforts are successful in finding highly competent employees, the organization designer can plan for larger spans of control. This is also true when the firm's training and development efforts improve the skills of both managers and employees.

4. *Dispersion of activity.* Where people work affects the span of control. The dispersion of activity has a curvilinear relationship to the span of control. When activities of those managed are not widely dispersed, the span can be large. As subordinates work farther and farther apart, it will be necessary to reduce the span. But if there are such great distances between those supervised that it is impossible to see each subordinate frequently, the span may be larger.

For example, if the work group is located within one plant and the supervisor does not have to travel too far to see most of the members, the span of control may be larger. When a foreman must supervise a group whose members have jobs spread widely throughout the plant, the span should be smaller. However, when there is great geographical distance between subordinates, as when there are district supervisors in different geographic regions, the span may be larger. In one nationwide consumer-loan company, each regional manager supervised as many as twenty-five branch offices. The distance between offices was so great that the regional manager called there regularly, but infrequently. In the place of direct personal supervision, written reports were substituted.

5. *Routineness of work.* When the work of those supervised is relatively routine and repetitive and there are standard procedures that spell out how to do a job, the span of control can be larger. Work of this type requires less close personal supervision and can be ***managed by exception.*** In managing by exception, only major deviations from the standards are brought to the attention of a manager.

There will be, of course, more routine jobs at lower organization levels. Standard procedures will be used more often to define the duties and activities of lower organization positions. This means that the span of control can be greater at these levels of the firm than at higher managerial levels.

6. *Specialized staff.* When specialized staff units exist, the span of control may be larger. Suppose we would want to increase the number of product divisions for the firm shown in Figure 11.5 from three to seven. A corporate staff unit (shown in Figure 11.11) would make it easier for the president to deal directly with the larger number of product division managers. The president's corporate staff might include personnel specialists, legal specialists, and auditing and control personnel. The role of these different staff employees would be to draw together relevant information from all the different divisions and prepare summary reports for the president. Having these data condensed and organized by the staff group will save time and will allow the president to devote more time to working with the larger number of managers in his span of control.

AUTHORITY AND RESPONSIBILITY

Departments are linked together, in large part, by the authority structure. The authority structure is the system of authority/responsibility relationships between different individuals and subunits—the "chain of command" that links the top levels of the organization with its bottom levels.

There are three concepts that help one understand the authority structure: authority, responsibility, and accountability. ***Accountability*** is reporting to another person, usually a superior, about how well the first person has met his or her responsibility. ***Responsibility*** is the obligation a person has to perform the organizational tasks assigned in a satisfactory way. One accepts responsibility when he or she takes a job. Responsibility is usually defined in a job description stating the activities that a person is to perform in the job. However, responsibility of an individual may be broader or narrower than the job description. The "psychological contract" (see Chapter 5), which eventually governs the person's relationship with the organization, is the real obligation for performance and involvement with the work organization.

A person may have responsibility for performing tasks, for example, doing work necessary for the achievement of organization objectives. A person may also be responsible for the work of other people. This latter type is managerial responsibility, an obligation to see that the work done by others meets standards of performance.

To meet work obligations, the person must have authority. ***Authority*** is the right of decision and command over others and resources. This right always includes the physical facilities such as plant equipment and tools; when a person has managerial responsibility it is necessary that the right cover decisions about others, the exercise of some command over subordinates, and the way subordinates use resources.

Authority associated with a particular position and specified in organizational documents is called ***formal authority.*** Formal authority gives a person discretion over others or over resources. It is made legitimate, or appropriate, because it is sanctioned by those at the highest level, who have responsibility of running the organization.

Formal authority associated with an organization position is usually spelled out in the job description. Job descriptions define two things in addition to specifying what tasks a person must perform:

1. The areas in which a person can make decisions
2. How much discretion the person has in these areas

Decision-making areas differ, as can be seen by examining the figures in this chapter illustrating the different organizations. Figure 11.4 shows the Production Vice President responsible for the production. This vice president makes or approves decisions about product design, fabrication, and assembly. The Marketing Vice President has responsibility for and makes decisions about market research, sales, and sales promotions. Comparing Figure 11.4 with Figure 11.5 shows that the decision-making areas are different in product organizations from those in the functional firm. Here, all vice presidents are responsible for production, marketing, and finance decisions and each makes these decisions about **different** products, for instance product A, product B, and product C.

The **amount** of discretion or authority a manager has in each decision area is not shown on any of these charts, but is usually defined in job descriptions. **Decision discretion** is the amount of authority a manager has. The manager with much discretion has correspondingly more authority. Take the case of the product division managers shown in Figure 11.5. These managers may have the right to decide on production levels of their own product, or the level of production may be determined by the president. In this second case each product division manager only implements the decision. In the first instance the vice presidents have much discretion. In the second instance discretion is much lower and authority limited.

CENTRALIZATION–DECENTRALIZATION

The way that the authority is distributed among positions in an organization is called "decentralization." The more decisions are made at the higher levels of the organization, the greater the centralization of decision making. In a highly centralized organization, authority, power, and discretion are concentrated at the top levels. Individuals at lower organizational levels have little discretion. Control is in the hands of the higher management levels.

When the right to make decisions (authority) is dispersed throughout the lower organizational levels, decision making is said to be decentralized. Of course, some decisions will always be made near the top of an organization (e.g., major policy decisions) and others will almost always be made near the bottom (e.g., work schedules). But there are some differences between organizations with respect to the level at which relatively important decisions are made.

Advantages of Decentralization

There are some clear advantages to a more decentralized approach to decision making. These are:

1. More rapid decision making. When a problem develops, it can be dealt with more rapidly because the problem solver is closer to the point of difficulty. There is no need to "clear" with management for approval of what action to take. The person at the point of the problem makes the decision.

2. *Better information.* Those closer to the problem may have better information about the problem, its possible causes, and the most effective way to solve it. The further away a person is from the point of a problem, the less accurate will be the information used to make the decision.

3. *Development of personnel.* The best way to learn how to make decisions is to make them. Decentralization gives managers at lower levels the opportunity to make decisions and learn how to manage. It also gives higher-level executives an opportunity to see how well subordinates can manage, which is of great assistance when making promotion decisions.

4. *Effective use of top management.* There is little reason for top-level managers to get involved with much of the day-to-day activities of running the organization. A decentralized approach will give top management more time to engage in strategic planning and policy formulation.

Advantages of Centralization

A centralized decision approach is not without its advantages. Obviously, Westinghouse felt that it would be much more profitable if it centralized some of the important, previously decentralized decisions. When power, authority, and decision making are concentrated at the top levels instead of being dispersed, the possible gains are:

1. *Consistency of decisions.* There is going to be less variability of decisions in lower-level units when decision making is centralized. Suppose, for instance, that the product organization shown in Figure 11.5 manufactured automobiles and that each division produced a different car, intended for a different market. If each division manager decided what the price of the division's product was to be, there might be undesirable competition between divisions. So the pricing decision for all products are made by the president or some group at the very top management level.

2. *An overall organization perspective.* Managers at higher levels should have a wider perspective than those at lower levels. They may be able to see the internal system objectives of the different departments in terms of the strategic objectives of the whole firm. This may lead to better decisions in terms of long-range interests of the firm.

3. *Lower managerial costs.* More centralized decisions could reduce total management costs to the firm. Making more important decisions is equivalent to more responsibility and authority, and managers who make them will generally be paid more highly than those who manage more routine work and make less important decisions. If there are several levels of managers, then the total managerial bill may be less because each manager at lower levels might be paid less than if he or she had more responsibility. And if managerial talent happens to be in short supply, centralization may result in fewer costly errors than if there were decentralization with less competent managers.

The degree of centralization may have important consequences for organizational change. As a general rule, there are two reasons why we would expect change to be initiated more rapidly in centralized than in decentralized firms. First, decentralization is likely to result in managers who have more concern with subunit goals rather than organization goals. Second, if these managers are successful they will be more self-confident than managers in highly centralized firms. Operating together, these two factors are likely to result in less resistance to changes initiated by top management in decentralized organizations.

RESPONSIBILITY CENTERS

One approach to assigning authority and responsibility to a manager is to designate departments as "responsibility centers." A responsibility center is an organization subunit evaluated by the degree to which it is able to achieve cost and/or revenue goals assigned to it **because the unit is fairly self-contained and integrated.** Yet the subunit must be differentiated (separated) clearly enough from the rest of the firm so that costs it incurs or revenues it generates can be reasonably accounted for and associated with it.

Two types of responsibility centers are profit centers and cost centers. **Profit centers** are organization units to which large portions of both revenues and costs can be allocated. This permits the determination of the profitability of each responsibility center. The management of the profit center is then held accountable for the profits or losses the subunit sustains.

To establish a profit center, a set of transfer prices and policies must be developed. These transfer prices are to determine prices to be charged to each unit for goods and services produced elsewhere in the firm. Administrative rules and policies are established to guide subunit managers in making decisions within their unit, yet managers typically have much latitude to make decisions within these policy limits. The value of the subunits output is computed and the charges for services levied, then evaluation is based on "profit" performance of the unit, the "profit center."

Establishing profit centers is not easy. It is difficult to find organizational subunits independent enough from each other so that they may be viewed, almost, as separate businesses. To use "profit centers," authorities recommend that each one have:

1. Operational independence in the sense of having control over most operational decisions that affect profits (e.g., volume, production methods, and product mix)
2. Complete freedom to buy and sell in alternative markets both inside and outside the company
3. Separable costs and revenues to facilitate "profit measurement"

The several product divisions of General Motors are profit centers. Costs and revenues can be determined for the Chevrolet, Pontiac, Buick, Oldsmobile, and Cadillac divisions. Commercial Credit Corporation uses this approach in evaluating the performance of its branch loan offices. The cost of money used by each branch office and the profits on branch office loans can be determined. Because each branch office is independent of each other branch, especially with regard to costs and revenues, the profit center approach is quite useful.

Cost centers may be established when it is not possible to associate revenue with a unit, but costs that it incurs in its operation can be reasonably well determined. We could not determine how much revenue is generated, for instance, by the corporate legal staff (Figure 11.11), but it can be a cost center since we can determine the costs necessary to run it. A manager of a cost center will be evaluated by how well those costs under his or her control stay below some goal level, and whether or not the unit still provides the required support to the rest of the organization.

The use of responsibility centers often occurs as organizations grow and become diversified (i.e., the production and sales of many, quite different products or services). Responsibility centers may ease some management problems by, in effect, creating many separate businesses. Those managers in charge of the responsibility centers can then be evaluated on the return on the investment for the use of resources or, in case of a cost center, on the basis of how they contributed to the profits and losses of a unit. In a highly diversified company where there are many different profit centers, the annual performance of each responsibility center may be compared and the executives in charge of them rewarded accordingly.

The responsibility center approach develops a profit (or cost) consciousness in managers. Since these are the criteria used for evaluating performance, managers will emphasize those factors related to the objectives of profits and efficiency. Responsibility centers may also support motivation through competition since the rewards given to managers of different profit centers often depend on their relative standing at the end of the accounting period. Some case studies show performance improvements with the use of responsibility centers. At Squibb and Sons direct hourly labor costs were reduced by 30 percent over a five-year period with introduction of the cost center system.[9]

TYPES OF AUTHORITY

Authority and responsibility relationships could take different forms in organizations. This is so because organizations are not simple, and different conditions develop that lead to various types of authority relationships. These different types of authority relationships can be classified as *line authority, staff authority,* and *functional authority* relationships.

Line Authority

The chain of command that results from the differentiation of production, boundary-spanning, and external-monitoring subsystems is the *line organization.* Personnel performing these activities are in the line organization. Thus, the product organization shown in Figure 11.5 is a line organization, and so is the project organization shown in Figure 11.8. *Line authority* is the right that a manager has to allocate resources and assign tasks to personnel in the unit for which he is responsible. It is the right of a manager in the line chain of command to make decisions about subordinates in *their* work assignments.

Staff Authority

The relationship between the individuals in the line organization and those in staff units (see Figure 11.11) is generally not a direct command relationship. *Staff authority* is advisory, which means that the staff, a support unit, recommends action or alternative actions to the appropriate line manager. The line manager then makes the decision about whether or not to implement the staff recommendation. For example, the production control staff in Figure 11.11 might recommend several different production plans to the production manager. Even though those in the staff are specialists and are very well qualified to suggest which plan is the best, the production vice president usually has the line authority to make the final decision because he has the responsibility for results and is accountable to higher levels for them.

Functional Authority

Another type of authority relationship is called *functional authority.* This is the right of decision and command that a person outside a chain of command has over very specific activities (or functions) of someone in it. Figure 11.12 shows the functional authority relationship of a quality control staff in a production department. The production manager decides on schedules, plans, and runs the department. However, when product quality drops below a particular level, say the scrap rate exceeds 10 percent, the quality control inspector can close down the production line *without* the approval of the production manager.

There are several situations that give rise to the need for functional authority. When there is a problem area very crucial to organization success and the skill required to make decisions is very specialized, as in the quality control problem just discussed, it is common to use functional authority. A second instance when functional authority is widely used is in the matrix organization. Figure 11.12 shows that product managers have influence in operating departments across department lines.

UNITY OF COMMAND

Whenever authority relationships are more complicated than simple line authority, there is great potential for problems. Multiple authority relationships occur in a situation when a person has more than one direct supervisor. The **unity of command** principle, which states that a person should have only one superior to whom

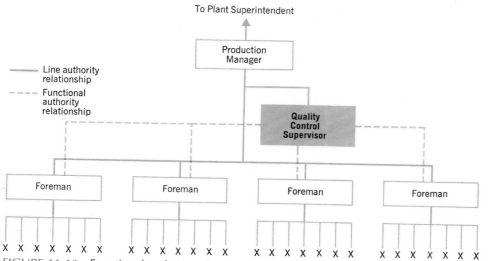

FIGURE 11.12 Functional authority of a quality control supervisor in a production department.

he or she is accountable in an organization, seeks to minimize problems that might arise from multiple authority relationships.

When a person receives orders from two or more bosses, role conflict exists. There is much strong research evidence showing that high role conflict is associated with much job anxiety and low job satisfaction. Paine and Gannon also found that having more than one boss was associated with lower performance.[10] Personnel who were judged to be "low performers" reported receiving orders from more than one boss.

Of course, it is impossible for unity of command to be absolutely maintained in a very large organization. It is somewhat easier to do so in product and functional forms of organization, though there will always be staff and functional authority relationships that lead to multiple supervision. These, however, will probably be few in number, and role conflict can be minimized by clearly specifying the cases when staffs or other units may exert functional authority.

But in the matrix organization (Figure 11.6) and the project firm (Figures 11.7 and 11.8) it is impossible to maintain unity of command. The product managers and the unit managers of the matrix organization will have to spend a good deal of time determining, as clearly as possible, who is responsible for what. In the D. Clement Engineering firm (Figure 11.7), in which staff members are reassigned from supervisor to supervisor depending on the project, unity of command breaks down. In project and matrix organization structures, managers must be aware of the high conflict potential. They will probably have to devote a good deal of their time resolving problems between individuals and departments.

AUTHORITY–RESPONSIBILITY— THE LINKING ELEMENT

When authority–responsibility relationships (i.e., who is responsible to whom and for what) are defined, this pulls the differentiated organizational units back together, linking them in the organization form. This linking process pulls the highest and lowest levels together, as well as those units horizontally differentiated. This linking function is shown in Figure 11.13. Manager A is responsible for the whole organization, but since it is impossible to supervise all personnel and activities directly, we separate the activities horizontally and vertically. Managers B and C report directly to A. They are part of his immediate work group (designated as 1). In work group 1, B and C are subordinates who transmit information upward to A from those units below them. They also transmit information from A to their units. This is the linking role of supervisors B and C, to join the level above them with the level below.

Work group 2 is headed by manager B, and D, E, and F are part of it. In this group, manager B is the superior and D, E, and F are subordinate managers. Manager B is responsible for the performance of this organizational unit, which includes the lower level units 4 and 5. Managers D and F link the lower units (4 and 5) to the higher-level units. Manager C is the head subunit 3, with a group of subordinate managers G, H, and I. Manager H is shown as the linking manager who ties unit 6 to unit 3 and, ultimately, to unit 1.

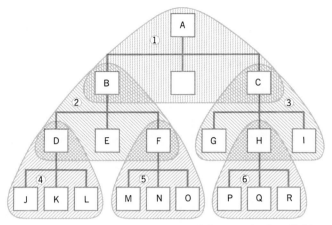

FIGURE 11.13 Authority–responsibility and the linking process.

ORGANIZATION STRUCTURE AND FORMALIZATION

In any organization that attains modest size (say as few as four or five), there will generally be some documentation of different facets of work relationships. Some written rules or policies will govern what a person does. Relationships prescribed in rules, policies, job description, and other documents are called "formal" and the organization is said to be "formalized" when these exist.

Rules, policies, and procedures that specify job behavior will vary greatly from one organization to another. For instance, there may be differences among organizations in such matters as which executive must approve pay increases of a certain amount. In one large company the stated policy was that merit increases in excess of $1,000 per year had to be approved by the vice president of personnel. In another company in the same industry, plant managers could make the decision.

High formalization exists when an organization makes considerable use of standing policies, procedures, methods, and rules. At this high end of the formalization continuum are mechanistic organizations. Low formalization, the other end to the continuum, exists when there are fewer rules, policies, and so on. This would be characteristic of organic organizations.

Formalization increases the accuracy with which behavior can be predicted. It has some positive and some negative effects. It leads to more consistent behavior among organizational members, quicker performance, and fewer mistakes. This is so because when a task is carried out in the same manner each and every time, people become quite competent in performing it. If a task or procedure has been previously analyzed and the most efficient method of performing it identified, developing a formal procedure can contribute significantly to higher performance.

On the other hand, high formalization limits new ideas and changes in organizations.[11] It may also lead to higher degrees of alienation of those who must follow the rules,[12] more rigidity in behavior, difficulties in dealing with individuals outside the inside organization, timidity, conservatism, and insecurity.[13-15]

Formalization is especially a problem when there are highly trained professional specialists in an organization, because formalization and the training of professionals are both designed to do the same thing—obtain more consistency and predictability in behavior. Formal procedures may be seen as unnecessary and, perhaps, insulting by highly trained professionals since presumably they already know how to handle the types of problems for which they were hired.

A narrow view of organization structure is that it is comprised of formal factors such as procedures, job descriptions, policy manuals, and organization charts. These only partially prescribe and explain the behavior of workers and managers.

Not all the patterning of behavior comes from the formal definitions prescribed in manuals, job descriptions, and procedures. Much of it, even in bureaucratic organizations, stems from the individual characteristics of the members and pressures from groups. This is especially true in new or small organizations. Organizations accommodate to members as well as to environmental demands, especially to key members.

The organization structure should be viewed as the pattern of predictable interaction among organization members. When the behavior pattern is not so stable and clear, or when it changes in short intervals of time, the organization structure can be called "loose," or flexible. When the behavioral patterns are very stable, enduring, and clear, we can say that the organization structure is rigid, or "tight." Such a tight structure is easy to observe and probably simple for new members to comprehend. They can come into the organization, read the appropriate job and procedural description, and begin to contribute very rapidly.

In new organizations predictable patterns of behavior develop as members interact with each other over time. They find that certain behaviors are accepted by others, make their own work easier, or simplify problems of dealing with others. Consider what happens when two strangers are brought together, for whatever reason, to work on an activity. Without guidance from a third party, they will work out who should do what and when. Over time, if they continue to work together they will begin to interact in a predictable way. As new people are added to work on the activity, they will initially have to fit into the existing pattern. But that pattern will change over time to accommodate the new members. Regular interaction patterns will appear. Behavior can become as predictable and stable as if there were written specifications such as job descriptions and procedures. Think about a time when you were in a large class and you were not assigned a seat by the instructor. After a short period of time, you find that you come to class regularly with certain people. As the term progresses, seating patterns become fairly stable. You sit in, or close to, the same seat most of the term, and you may find that you regularly interact with certain people in certain ways. Predictable behavior patterns have emerged even though there have been no efforts to impose any structure on the group.

SUMMARY

Departmentation, span of control, and authority are related. The product form of organization, for example, is typically associated with a higher degree of decentralization than the functional form. The heads of product units are usually delegated authority and are held responsible by headquarters for results. But, within itself, a decentralized product division may be highly centralized. Formalization—clear rules and policies—is a prerequisite of effective decentralization. Decentralization is less likely to lead to errors when unambiguous policies and rules exist for the guidance of lower-level managers. Formalization also allows a large span of control, because the guides, procedures, and rules act as "substitute" leaders in the sense that they give direction to subordinates and also serve as control standards.

Departmentation, centralization, span of control, and formalization should be compatible with each other. It is possible to use the product mode of department with either centralization or decentralization. One of the largest companies in the United States uses a product division system in which there is considerable decentralization down to the level of the product division manager. Within the company's various product divisions, however, the degree of decentralization varies considerably, probably depending on the nature of the environmental demands on the unit, the values of the divisional top management group, and the characteristics of the individuals employed.

This chapter has focused on the departmentation, span of control, and the authority structure as important elements of the organizing process. Once the need for organization is recognized, many alternatives exist as to mode of departmentation, degree of centralization, type of authority to be delegated, and the size of span of control. All of the alternatives have their offsetting considerations, and choices among them must be made.

The Harrisburg Group Practice

Two faculty members of The University School of Dentistry visited a large dental practice in Harrisburg, Pennsylvania, which is reputed to bring in more revenue than any other dental practice in the state. The faculty members of the dental school were interested in the practice because of its use of modern management methods.

The practice was located on the entire top floor of a six-story office building near downtown Harrisburg. There was a large parking area, reserved for dental patients and visitors. The two professors parked their car and entered the building. They took the elevator to the sixth floor. As they stepped out of the elevator on the sixth floor, they found themselves in a beautiful reception room with thick plants and a curved reception desk staffed by three auxiliary receptionists. Dr. Brown, the principal founder of the four-man partnership, was called and came out to meet them. Dr. Brown then took them on a tour of the facilities.

Immediately to the right of the reception area was located the waiting room, which also included a small playroom for children. The waiting room was well furnished and provided seats for over twenty-five patients. Near the waiting room was a preventive dentistry unit. This unit consisted of separate small offices in which patients could be taught how to properly handle tooth care. This wing of the facility also included a staff conference room, magazines, several bathrooms, X-ray facilities, private small offices for each dentist, and a staff room with a kitchen.

To the left of the reception area were the fifteen operatories. In each were a dental chair and equipment. Each dentist was assigned two operatories, separated by a small two-counter laboratory and storage area. Each of the three hygienists (auxiliaries who only cleaned teeth) had one operatory. The other operatories were used for taking dental histories and for other purposes.

There were several restrooms and telephone rooms for patients' use. In the telephone rooms patients could sit at a desk and transact business by telephone while waiting for their appointment. The operatories and rooms were separated by movable partitions and large movable plants.

The visiting professors found out the following during their visit.

1. Each of the four dentists was middle-aged and had been in solo practice for several years before coming together in the group practice.

2. One dentist, a recent dental school graduate, was a salaried associate.

3. Each dentist had brought his or her own practice to the group. The group practice had records for about ten thousand patients. The records were stored in five large circular files in a room near the reception area and were color coded for easy access.

4. All of this equipment was very modern and was leased by the corporation from the manufacturer.

5. The building in which the practice was located was a condominium. The partners had purchased the facilities for the practice.

6. A very rigorous schedule was kept. Only a certain amount of time was allowed for each procedure.

7. All dentists drew the same salary from the practice. In addition, each participated in a generous retirement system and received dividends from stock in the parent corporation.

8. The partners had established a gross amount of revenue to be earned in one year. This was then broken down into monthly, weekly, and daily figures. Each day in the middle of the afternoon, an auxiliary determined whether the daily revenue was sufficient to cover the quota for that day. The yearly figure was established on the basis of anticipated expenses for salary, equipment payments, taxes, and so on, for the year, annuity payments for retirement benefits, and an adequate return on invested capital.

9. Patients paid by cash, check, or could use a major credit card. The credit card company then assumed all losses for unpaid accounts. The charge to the practice by the credit card company varied by the amount billed, but generally ran about 2.5 percent. A daily credit to the account of the practice was made by the credit card company.

10. The dentists passed their patients from one to another when necessary to perform certain specialized tasks. All practiced general dentistry, but some were more specialized in certain types of dental problems.

11. The practice employed twenty-one people, either as dentists' assistants or to carry out some of the specialized services provided by the practice.

12. The biggest personnel problems occurred when auxiliaries from the various solo practices were assigned work in the reception and record keeping areas.

13. It was difficult for staff members to identify with the staff as a whole. In addition, the new scheduling and record-keeping procedures still had bugs in them.

Being especially interested in how such a large and efficient practice had come into being, Professors Middleton and Davis interviewed Dr. Brown, who was the founder of the practice.

DR. MIDDLETON: Dr. Smith, Dean of University Dental School, mentioned that all of you had discussed your philosophy of management for the practice together while the facility was being planned. How were your meetings carried out when you did this? We are interested in the process of planning.

DR. BROWN: We discussed together our philosophy of treatment since it is important that we all agree on this when we join together in a group practice. In going about it, each of us wrote out our personal philosophy on patient care. Then we met together to discuss these. We also wrote down our long-term goals and our short-term goals and then discussed these as well. At this point, we found we had to get very specific about the meaning of various terms. For example, we had to define what constitutes quality care of patients. We wanted to make sure that we all had the same ideas for these terms. We did not, of course, at first, but after our discussions we more or less came to an agreement.

With respect to patient care, we decided to take a preventive dentistry approach, which obviously does influence the design of our facilities. We decided to refuse to do extractions unless absolutely necessary. We also decided we wanted to take a total and comprehensive approach to the treatment of our patients. This, of course, requires sufficient time on diagnosis, treatment planning, and so on. It also requires that the practice as a whole can cover most problems that come up.

In our planning meetings, we concluded that the five of us had to cover fifteen areas in all. Thus, each of us had to cover three areas. We each wrote down the areas we agreed to specialize in, based on our interests and our competence, and then we got together and worked out an agreement. We agreed to study and to keep abreast of developments in these areas. There were a few uncovered areas because of lack of interest by any of us. Here, instead of pressuring somebody to do something that he had no interest at all in, we decided to hire some salaried associates in the future who had an interest and skill in these areas.

DR. DAVIS: How about planning for facilities? How did you go about that?

DR. BROWN: I had long thought about starting a group practice. To prepare for this, I attended several group practice seminars sponsored by the American Dental Association and collected a lot of literature on the topic. I passed out my literature to the other prospective partners so that we would have a common background of knowledge in this area. In addition, we all had observed several group practices in operation. We then set goals for our facilities to use in evaluating different facility arrangements.

We evaluated two systems in detail. One manufacturer, hearing of our plans to put in fifteen or sixteen operatories, invited us down to Atlanta to discuss what they might provide for us. We discussed our plans with them but they did not come up with a specific plan for us. We then went to another manufacturer, and they worked up a plan for us after we had given them our physical limits and some idea of what we wanted.

DR. MIDDLETON: Did they charge you for service?

DR. BROWN: They charged us $300 per person for a group practice, but this is credited against any future sales of their equipment. There is no charge for individuals.

Let me continue on with our experience in planning the facilities. The manufacturer gave us a plan that we considered unsatisfactory. We rejected it. We then met with their representatives to tell them where they fell down and they then reworked the plan. In the meantime, the first manufacturer submitted a plan to us, also. At this point we had a disagreement about which plan was best, and we had some meetings in which we went over the goals or criteria that we had established earlier. We then decided to accept the plan of the second manufacturer. One of the factors in our decision was that the system we chose seemed to be more flexible and we wanted a flexible system. In addition, much of the equipment from the first manufacturer was very new and they would be experimenting on us. We wanted equipment with a proven reliability.

Our next step was to hire an interior designer. We found one who had previously designed some dental offices, but he did not specialize in this kind of work. He modified the plan we had from the manufacturer and came up with a plan we really liked. We are finally realizing it now.

DR. MIDDLETON: Let me say that I'm very impressed with your facilities. Unlike some other large group practices that I've seen it does not have a sterile, hospital-like appearance to it. It appears much smaller than it really is. In addition, you get the impression of an unhurried and comforting type of atmosphere.

DR. BROWN: Yes, we it like very well. It's so much better to work here than in my old building. After all, it's important that we work in an atmosphere that pleases us. I just feel good when I look around me every day. It's a pleasure to work here. In fact, each day I notice things I was not aware of before. In other words, I receive little daily surprises and this is stimulating.

DR. DAVIS: How about your planning for auxiliaries or staff? Did all of you get together on this?

DR. BROWN: I could talk for an hour on that, but unfortunately I have a patient who is waiting for me. Why don't we get together later on that.

1. This case describes a very successful practice. How much do organizational structure and systems contribute to this success?
2. What happened in the organizational planning process that contributed to the later success of this practice? Why?
3. How well does this form of organization meet the needs of the patients? The dentists? The work staff? Why?

Benton Public Schools*

BACKGROUND

In December, Dr. Joan Howard, Deputy Superintendent of Public Instruction for the Benton City Public Schools (BCPS), was quite concerned. She was receiving a growing number of complaints from new teachers hired in September who had yet to receive their first paycheck. More than a hundred teachers had not been paid, and frustrations were increasing as Christmas rapidly approached. The newspapers, radio, and television news commentators, learning of the problem, publicly criticized the administration at BCPS. Pressures on the administration from the teachers' union mounted.

Dr. Howard approached Mr. Bill Grant, Assistant Deputy Superintendent for Fiscal and Business Management, whose responsibilities included overseeing the staffing and payroll operations. Mr. Grant told her his ideas about the location and the cause of possible bottlenecks in the system. However, when Dr. Howard approached these "bottleneck offices," they blamed the problem on Mr. Grant and other personnel and staffing offices.

Dr. Howard, who had left her previous position in Philadelphia for this one, began to realize that no one had a thorough understanding of internal operations of BCPS. Furthermore, she learned that this "late pay" situation had occurred for the past three years, and that each year was worse than the year before. She felt the school system was facing a potential crisis.

Immediately, Dr. Howard arranged for emergency loans from local banks for those teachers who had not been paid. Then, with the approval of Superintendent Dr. John Hoffman, she hired two data systems consultants to head a task force. This group was scheduled to convene on the first of February to identify, document, and "detangle" the vastly complex personnel and payroll processes.

The team was composed of the two consultants, three representatives from BCPS' Personnel Division, two from the Data Processing Division, one from Fiscal Management, and one from Position Control. They met as scheduled and began work. In the initial phase of the study, the team interviewed key employees about their jobs to develop work descriptions and process flow charts. The second phase of the study was to be an analysis of the findings of the first phase, to make recommendations to improve the current system, and to offer specific implementation plans for revised procedures.

*We express our appreciation to Fran Silber, who wrote the original version of this case, for her permission to use it.

The interview phase took longer than anticipated—three months—to complete. In May the team presented a progress report to Dr. Hoffman, Dr. Howard, and Mr. Grant. This report spelled out the major findings from the interviews and process analysis. However, though there was enthusiastic support of the three administrators, they decided that the task force should be temporarily dissolved because another priority, that of beginning the staffing process for the next school year, required the efforts of the BCPS task force team members.

The task force never reconvened. The following description of the personnel environment and workflow of BCPS is based in part on the task force report.

THE PERSONNEL ENVIRONMENT

The goal of the Personnel Division, as stated in its most recent policy manual, is to "provide support services in the staffing of schools so as to afford maximum opportunity for educational excellence to all pupils." Specifically, this involves the recruitment, selection, assignment, and promotion of the best-qualified, state certified teachers. Additionally, the Personnel Division provides policy and procedure information to all employees and furnishes data to top management for improving human resource planning. In carrying out these objectives, the Personnel Division is divided into two units to serve the needs of educational and noneducational (Supportive Services) staff separately; both offices are subdivided by function (see Figure C.1).

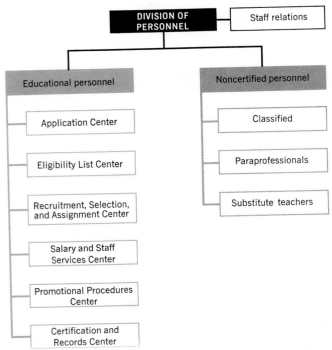

FIGURE C.1   The division of personnel—organization chart.

Within the organization, the Personnel Division interfaces with the following four departments involved in the staffing process for all municipal employees.

Regional Offices of the BCPS
Position Control
Educational Data Processing Center (EDPC)
Payroll

In addition, because the BCPS is municipally controlled, Personnel must also work closely with the city's central payroll office (see Figure C.2). The following work flow description will illustrate the vital role played by each of these internal as well as external offices in the staffing and payroll functions for the BCPS.

This discussion will focus exclusively on the personnel environment affecting educational staff members only since this is the group experiencing pay problems. The functional subgroups or centers within the Educational Section of the Personnel Division include:

Application Center
Eligibility Center
Recruitment, Selection, and Assessment Center
Promotional Procedures Center
Salary and Staff Services Center
Certification and Records Center

(See Figure C.3). These offices operate interdependently with each other within the educational section as well as other departments inside and outside of the school system.

FIGURE C.2 Responsibilities of other (nonpersonnel) offices in the staffing process

Regional Office
1. Alerted by the school principal of an existing teacher vacancy (via the telephone)
2. Contacts Personnel for referral of eligible teacher applicants
3. Refers candidates for interview with the Principal
4. Initiates the paperwork flow in order to hire new teacher and, later, assists in its processing
5. In general, acts as a liaison between schools and BCPS headquarters

Position Control
1. Maintains manually a job file of all funded positions
2. Assists in paperwork processing by transferring information on BCPS in-house form ("ticket") to those required by the city's payroll office

Educational Data Processing Center (EDPC)
1. Keypunches the information from the in-house form
2. Enters applicant information from the in-house form onto computer records

City Payroll Office
1. Officially places the teacher on the school's payroll
2. Enters applicant information for their required form ("ticket") onto computer records

FIGURE C.3   Responsibilities of centers within personnel in the staff process

Application Center

1. Keeps files on all teacher applicants
2. Houses credential papers and applications for all candidates

Eligibility Center

1. Manually compiles and maintains eligibility lists of certified teachers
2. Provides list to Recruitment, Selection, and Assignment Center (RSAC) for candidate referred to fill vacancies

Recruitment, Selection, and Assignment Center (RSAC)

1. Receives vacancy reports from regions on a weekly basis
2. Reviews files of candidates on the eligibility list and makes referrals to regions for placement in reported vacancies
3. Assists in manually processing paperwork in the hiring process

Salary and Staff Services Center (SSSC)

1. Makes salary determinations for all newly hired teachers
2. Assists in manually processing paperwork in the hiring process

Certification and Records Center

1. Maintains manual personnel records for over ten thousand educational employees
2. Maintains microfilm records for all educational employees inactive for more than five years

THE WORK FLOW

The complexity of the staffing and payroll operations can be shown by the procedure for filling only one teaching vacancy (refer to Figure C.4). The process begins when the school principal reports the vacancy to a regional office. The regional office, responsible for all administrative functions for approximately twenty-five schools, includes the vacancy on a weekly report sent to the Recruitment, Selection, and Assignment Center (RSAC) in the Division of Personnel. RSAC, equipped with a list of eligible teacher applicants (from the Eligibility List Center) plus the regional vacancy reports, arranges a possible match between openings and applicants. RSAC then refers three candidates per vacancy to the region, and the region informs the appropriate school. The principal of the school with the vacancy, having interviewed the candidates, makes a selection. This choice is communicated to the regional office, where the paperwork flow is subsequently initiated.

A "request for employment" form is sent, by the region, to Position Control. Position Control's primary responsibility is to maintain a file of all funded positions to make sure that the city's budgetary allocation for teachers is not exceeded. Upon receiving the "request for employment" form, Position Control checks the job file to verify that a vacant funded position does, in fact, exist. The funded position is only considered vacant if the leaving teacher's paperwork had been completely processed. If a position is available, Position Control approves and returns the request form to the regional office, thus granting the region permission to hire the candidate selected by the principal.

Upon receiving Position Control's approval, the regional office completes an "entry authorization," which summarizes the applicant's personal data, and for-

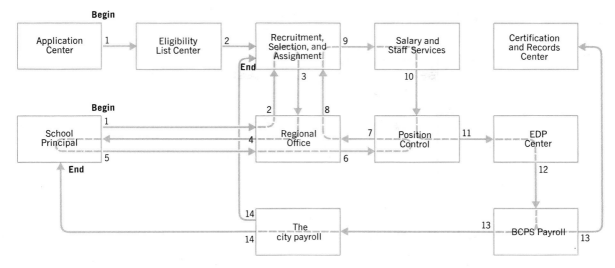

Begin

| Application Center | 1 → | Eligibility List Center | 2 → | Recruitment, Selection, and Assignment | 9 → | Salary and Staff Services | | Certification and Records Center |

End

3

Begin

2   8

| School Principal | 1 → ... 4 ... 5 | Regional Office | 7 → | Position Control | 11 → | EDP Center |

10

End

6   12

14 | The city payroll | ← 13 | BCPS Payroll | 13
14

Note: The same number on more than one portion of the work flow indicates that the processes occur simultaneously.
The following offices are located outside of headquarters: 1. payroll, 2. EDP Center, 3. the city payroll.

FIGURE C.4   The paperwork flow in the staffing process.

wards this document along with the approved "request for employment" form to the Personnel Division. The forms first arrive in Personnel's RSAC where they are manually logged in. Then they are forwarded to the Salary and Staff Services Center (SSSC) for salary determination—and duplicate back-up logging. Both offices edit the forms to correct readily detectable errors.

The forms are then sent to Position Control, which performs two functions. First, Position Control now finds out that the position they approved earlier is going to be filled, so they manually update their "open position" file accordingly. Second, Position Control retypes all the information from the "entry authorization" onto a "ticket" form. The "ticket" is the form required by the city's payroll division, while the "entry authorization" is for BCPS' internal use only.

Then, the entire paperwork package (original "request for employment," "entry authorization," and new "ticket") is sent to the Educational Data Processing Center. Here the applicant's information is entered onto the computerized master personnel record file.

From EDPC, the forms are mailed to the BCPS Payroll office, which is located several miles from BCPS headquarters. The Payroll office manually records the applicant's salary information (as stated on the "entry authorization") in its own files and disburses the carbon copies of the "ticket" to the Records Center, a unit within Personnel, and to one external agency, Central Payroll. This transaction is the key link connecting the personnel and payroll records with those of the municipal government.

Once the ticket information is posted to their records, the city payroll office completes the paperwork flow in two important ways: (1) the employee is placed on the payroll of the school to which he or she has been assigned and then (2) a final copy of the "ticket" is returned to Personnel, which signals the completion of the entire process for one person. Finally, payment with pay can be made.

1. What are some of the reasons for this organization's problems?
2. What can be done to alleviate the problems?

DISCUSSION QUESTIONS

1. Discuss the differences between low formalization and high formalization. What effects might high formalization have in an organization?
2. Discuss the ten problems listed in the chapter that might be caused by poor organization. Can you add any others?
3. What is a differentiating decision? Give an example.
4. What is an integrating decision? Give an example.
5. How is a functional organization departmentalized and what is its primary problem?
6. Why do you think that a majority of the largest corporations in the U.S. have product organizations?
7. What are the advantages in having a matrix organization? How is this different from the other forms?
8. Would working in a project organization appeal to you? Why or why not? Would you prefer a functional organization?
9. Describe the two environmental settings that can affect an organization.
10. There are advantages and centralizing approaches to decision making. Explain these and how they affect organizational change.

REFERENCES

1. Filley, Alan. The compleat manager—what works when. Champaign, Ill., Research Press Company, 1978.
2. Galbraith, J. Designing complex organizations. Reading, Mass., Addison-Wesley, 1973.
3. Galbraith, J. Organization design. Reading, Mass., Addison-Wesley, 1977.
4. Child, John. "Organization structure and strategies of control: A replication of the Aston study," Administrative Science Quarterly, 17 (June 1972): 163–176.
5. Khandwalla, Pradip. The design of organizations. New York, Harcourt Brace Jovanovich, 1977.
6. Filley, Alan C., R. House, and S. Kerr. Managerial process and organizational behavior. Glenview, Ill., Scott, Foresman, 1976.
7. Woodward, J. Industrial organization. London, Oxford University Press, 1965.
8. Udell, J. G. "An empirical test of hypotheses relating to span of control," Administrative Science Quarterly, 2 (December 1967): 420–439.
9. Carroll, S. J. "The use of objective performance indicators in performance appraisal, Proceedings: American Institute for Decision Sciences, Chicago, 1977.
10. Paine, F., and M. Gannon. "Unity of command and job attitudes in a bureaucratic organization," Journal of Applied Psychology, 59 (1974): 392–394.
11. Hage, Jerald, and M. Aiken. "Relationship of centralization to other structural properties," Administrative Science Quarterly 12 (June 1967): 72–92.
12. Aiken, M., J. Hage, and C. B. Marrett. "Organization structure and communications," American Sociological Review, 36 (1971): L, 860–871.
13. Crozier, Michael. The bureaucratic phenomenon. Chicago, University of Chicago Press, 1964.
14. Merton, R. K. Social theory and social structure. New York, Free Press, 1957.
15. Thompson, V. Modern organization. New York, Knopf, 1961.

CHAPTER TWELVE

Changing Organization Structure

The Turnaround at Mohawk Data

In recent years entrepreneurs have found a lot of scope in the computer industry. Attracted by the high profits common to the field, countless young men have left the security of jobs with the mainframe manufacturers to strike out on their own. But as the industry has become more competitive, the high growth that attracted them in the first place has often proved to be their downfall. Now, more and more professional managers are moving in.

Mohawk Data Sciences Corp. (MDS) is one company where this has occurred, and as a result, a classic turnaround is shaping up. Founded by a general manager from the Univac division of Sperry Rand Corp. fifteen years ago, MDS in the 1960s was a high-flying manufacturer of data-entry equipment. But it had lost $41 million over three years when the board brought in the current president in 1975. Since then, Ralph H. O'Brien, with twenty years in business systems at Litton Industries Inc., has pulled MDS back into the black. The Parsippany (N.J.) company posted a $2.9 million profit on sales of $178 million for the year ended April 30. More important, MDS has developed a new line of products that puts it squarely in the flourishing market for distributed data processing.

SPRINTING, THEN SPUTTERING O'Brien attributes much of the company's recent progress to what he terms, simply, professional management. The old MDS started with a good idea and was well stocked with technical talent, he says, but lacked the management sophistication needed to perform in the competitive environment of the computer industry. "It was going in too many directions at once for a company of its size and capital structure," he adds.

MDS got off to a brilliant start in 1964 when it introduced a key-to-tape data-entry device called the Key Data-Recorder, a faster, more economical replacement for the traditional keypunch. With a headstart in the field, the company prospered; by 1968 the stock had soared over 100.

Flush with success, Mohawk took off on the acquisition path, picking up such diverse businesses as printers, plug-for-plug replacements for IBM disk and tape drives, and factory data-collection systems. But then, in the early '70s, things started to go wrong. Preoccupied with expansion, MDS let its competitors get the jump on key-to-disk products—the next generation of equipment in data entry. "They took their eye off the ball in their basic business," says Robert L. Christensen, an analyst with A. G. Becker Inc. in New York. "They overextended with a lot of acquisitions that didn't fit that well."

Since the company had financed these acquisitions on the basis of its high stock multiple, rather than earnings, it was hit hard when stock prices for secondary high-technology companies collapsed in 1970. MDS stock dropped to $1, demand softened for MDS products, and in 1971 the company slipped into the red. The lack of any new products, plus the fact that MDS then rented a much higher proportion of its products than it does today, compounded the company's problems, and by 1975 MDS was staggering under a debt load of $164 million.

At this point, O'Brien stepped in, bringing with him his own team of managers. Of the seventeen executives at MDS today, fifteen have arrived since 1975. Among the key members of O'Brien's team are R. Watson Bell, a former chief financial officer at Lenox Inc., the china company; Douglas A. Davidson, former vice president for North American operations at Honeywell Information Systems Inc.; and William J. Mann, a former senior vice president at General Automation Inc. "The key element was to be able to attract a highly motivated professional group of managers," says O'Brien, who used his reputation as a manager, financial rewards, and the lure of a challenge to draw them.

RESTRUCTURING   This handpicked group set about restructuring the company. They terminated a number of the product lines picked up through acquisitions and closed six domestic and two foreign plants, leaving the company with four manufacturing plants in the U.S. and a refurbishing facility in Germany. In the meantime they converted rental equipment to sales. By the end of the first year, they had paid off $45 million of Mohawk's debt.

They they set about working with what was left. "Our tactics in the short term," says O'Brien, "were taking systems in manufacture—the 1200 and 2400 data-entry systems—and upgrading hardware and software capabilities. But we obviously needed a new product line." Building on its data-entry background, the company spent two years and more than $25 million on the development of the Series 21, a family of systems designed for the distributed-processing market.

With this, MDS entered one of the hottest growth markets in the computer industry—one likely to expand at 60 percent a year, according to International Data Corp., a Boston market research firm. Distributed processing entails the use of small systems at customer sites that are linked to more powerful central computers only for complex tasks.

'LOTS OF ROOM'   MDS is in the low end of this market. Aimed at sophisticated computer users who want to develop a distributed-processing capability, a typical "starter" configuration of the Series 21 costs between $12,000 and $14,000. That is a small fraction of the cost of IBM's highly sophisticated network-oriented offering, the 8100, which is priced from $90,000 to $180,000.

Nor is the MDS product as advanced as those of Datapoint Corp., of San Antonio, Tex., or Four-Phase Systems, Inc., of Cupertino, Calif., the two leaders in the market. "[Mohawk's] strength is more in their customer base and marketing service than in their hardware technology," says Otis T. Bradley, an analyst with Alex. Brown & Sons in New York.

According to IDC, $1.1 billion worth of terminals aimed at the distributed-processing market had been installed by the end of 1978; MDS has almost 3 percent of those terminals, and market leader Four Phase has almost 33 percent. But, says IDC's Ellen S. Rogers, "there is lots of room in this market. A crumb will do." She expects MDS to be a legitimate competitor in the future. "They are spending money where it counts," she says.

The money is being spent mainly on software. Some 55 percent of the research and development money the company spends goes into software, and the company plans to up that to 75 percent or 80 percent by 1984. "Five years from now we'll be spending more on hardware than we are now, but it will still be only about 20 percent of our R&D," says O'Brien.

O'Brien thinks that his emphasis, plus the marketing strength that is a legacy from the old MDS, will be a winning combination. The company has 300 branches worldwide, as well as a distributor network that handles sales, support, and service in fifty smaller countries. "Only fourteen other companies can say as much," boasts O'Brien.

A SMALL NET   Now, as part of the effort to keep the company moving in a new direction, MDS is once again looking for acquisitions. But this time the company is seeking only companies with products that complement its product line and that can use its distribution system advantageously. A recent acquisition Trivex, a small Costa Mesa (Calif.) supplier of controllers and displays compatible with the IBM 3270 line, fits these requirements well. "Theirs is very close to the product line we have," says O'Brien, "and at present it is doing almost nothing outside the U.S."

In this manner, says O'Brien, the company is seeking to offer a "continuum" of products for sophisticated users. MDS recently added a word-processing capability to its Series 21, and analysts anticipate further extensions of the line at both the lower and the upper end. "The world out there is our marketplace," says O'Brien. "And it is a world created not by IBM but by MDS and Datapoint, so we have a lot of credibility."

Source: Business Week, July 9, 1979.

In Chapter 3 we showed how the organization's structure is related to its technological and market environment. Those organization structures, of course, must change as the environment changes. The relationship between groups and departments changes, even in mechanistic organizations. In the mechanistic organization the change is less rapid and more predictable and takes place in smaller degrees than it does in the organic organization, but there is change. The basic idea is this: if an organization's structure is a function of the environment, then when the environment changes, the structure must also change if the organization is to survive.

What causes the structure of an organization to change? First, a major cause of change is organization growth. Everyone has seen what happens when a church group or a civic association that started as a small informal group of interested people becomes popular and attracts membership. Growing pains follow. Rules develop, formal procedures for the election of officers must be designed, and so forth. Business firms are no exception to this rule of change.

Second, major changes in the structure of an organization result from changes in the environment. If the environment of an organic organization becomes more stable, the firm must begin to take on more mechanistic characteristics. Conversely, when the stable environment of the mechanistic firm becomes more uncertain, there is no choice but to loosen up the fixed rules, policies, and guides that govern the system.

In this chapter we examine how an organization can adapt to changes in the external environment. We will discuss two aspects of structural development and change: first, the problems associated with change in organization structure in growth periods; and second, problems that an organization must face when it finds environmental circumstances changing.

GROWTH AND STRUCTURE CHANGE

What happens to the structure of an organization when it grows? As an organization grows, it goes through three stages.[1] The first stage is the "small firm stage." The second stage is the "growth phase." The third stage is the "administrative organization." Figure 12.1 illustrates the growth cycle of a firm and Figure 12.2 summarizes characteristics of organizations at these different stages.

STAGE 1: THE SMALL FIRM

Initially, when the firm is small the owner-manager does nearly everything: producing the product, marketing it, and arranging for financing. He plans, organizes, and controls the operation alone, performing all the managerial functions himself. As the market for the product grows, with a corresponding increase in production, new personnel are hired and assigned work. This brings about the initial differentiation of activities—a split between the managerial functions (planning, organizing, etc.) and the operating activities. The new personnel brought in will be responsible for doing the work, but not much of the managing. For example, a small book publisher manages the business and is also actively engaged in the operational

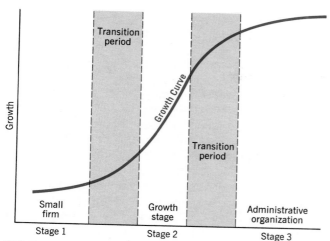

FIGURE 12.1 Growth stages of an organization. (*Source*: Filley, A. C., and R. J. House. *Managerial Process and Organizational Behavior*. Glenview, Ill.: Scott, Foresman and Company, 1969.)

functions of manuscript acquisition, editing, producing, and marketing. When he adds his first permanent staff, their assignments may be copy editing or proofreading and carry no managerial responsibilities.

The second stage of differentiation in the small firm will be a separation of the functional activities. Marketing will be separated from production, and the begin-

FIGURE 12.2 Critical Factors in Stages of Growth

Continua of Growth	Small Firm	Growth Stage	Administrative Organization
Objectives	Comfort-survival	Personal achievement	Market adaptation
Policy	Traditional	Personal	Rational
Leadership	Craftsman	Entrepreneur	Professional
Work-group bonds	Fixed roles	Interaction-expectation	Homogeneity
Functional development	Single	Successive emphasis	Full development
Structure	Power levels	Field of force	Rational hierarchy
Staff	Housekeeping	Technical-personal	Technical-coordinative
Innovation	No creativity	Innovation	Development
Uncertainty-risk	Nonrisk	Uncertainty	Risk
Growth-size economies	Size benefits	Growth-size benefits	Size benefits

Source: Filley, A. C., and R. J. House, *Managerial Process and Organizational Behavior*. Glenview, Ill.: Scott, Foresman and Company, 1969.

ning of formal departmentalization will occur. Probably the owner-manager will still continue to perform the control process and the acquisition of both physical and human resources. The financial control activity will be the last to be completely differentiated in the small firm. The owner-manager will keep a hand on the helm of the ship.

In a small organization, relationships between employees and the manager are likely to be very personal. In this stage there are few of the written, formal aspects of organizaton structure that are commonly found in larger organizations. Assignment of work responsibilities is usually done verbally, thus providing flexibility to shift employees from one job to another as necessary. This allows the owner to maintain a high level of operating efficiency. What formal structure there is will probably be imposed by governmental record-keeping requirements such as the maintenance of wage records for social security purposes, reports that may have to be submitted to comply with health and safety laws, and financial reporting for tax purposes.

The objectives of the small firm will be a reflection of those of the owner-manager. The owner-manager expects a reasonable income and living standard, and at the same time an opportunity to be independent, working for himself in a job he likes.

A firm may remain small (in stage one) if the owner-manager does not want to become involved with, or feels unable to manage, the problems associated with managing a complex organization. For example, the owner-manager of a small electronics component firm that supplies highly specialized circuitry for the space program could have tripled the firm's sales and profits, but only by adding more technical and managerial staff, moving to a different part of the country, and reducing the personal control he has over the business. Even though there is a high potential for growth, the owner elects to stay small. Many owners of small firms have made such conscious choices, even though the conditions for growth were present.

The Transition to Growth

To enter the **growth phase,** a number of conditions must exist. Unless they are present the firm cannot begin rapid growth. The following circumstancess facilitate rapid expansion.

1. Innovation. Something must occur that makes larger markets available. A new product may be introduced, or an old product may acquire a new potential. A firm may discover a new production method that substantially reduces cost. An invention may provide the innovation necessary. Item 12.1., which opened this chapter, describes such an innovation, the Key Data-Recorder, which made the initial rapid growth of Mohawk Data possible.

2. Significant returns for risk. With innovation there is usually high risk. There are many innovations that are useful to a small number of people but do not seem to have the potential of large-scale returns. Thus, the risk of undertaking the production and marketing of them may not seem worthwhile. The owner-manager of a small firm must see the potential payoff of an innovation as far exceeding the risk involved before he will consider expansion and growth.

3. *Entrepreneurial orientation.* The entrepreneur is an innovator willing to assume risks for expected returns. The owner-manager of the small firm must have an entrepreneurial orientation—that is, be willing to take risks—in order to obtain the returns associated with growth. The comfort-survival objective of the owner of a small firm must change; if the opportunities are present but the owner-manager is not entrepreneurially oriented, he or she will not make the decisions required to move into the second stage.

4. *Additional resources.* In the growth stage substantially more resources will be necessary both to produce and to distribute the product. Often the firm, at this stage, does not have the capacity to generate enough resources to take advantage of the innovation and its potential. An outside source of capital must be found. If this capital comes from borrowing (which will heavily commit the owner to financial institutions), the lending institutions themselves must see an opportunity for aggregate return.

These are the conditions that must be present if an organization is to grow. If it does, then its relatively informal atmosphere will change.

STAGE 2: GROWTH PHASE

The organization grows because it exploits an innovation in an increasingly larger marketplace. Sales rise, new employees are added, production increases. Initially growth may be very rapid, occurring at an increasing rate. Later in the growth stage, the rate of growth may begin to slow down (see Figure 12.1).

Leadership in the growth phase must be different from that in the small firm. It will still be highly personal, but more entrepreneurial and charismatic. This highly emotional atmosphere will pervade the firm, especially those members close to the chief executive. It is possible that in the growth stage the leader must be someone other than the owner-manager of the small firm. While the owner-manager of the small firm may be willing to grow, he or she may find difficulties in managing a growing organization. The owner-manager may step aside to become the chairman of the board and hire an entrepreneurially oriented president. The founder can set the tone, make policy, and handle the more ceremonial and ritualistic activities. The actual operation of the firm will be in the hands of the entrepreneur-president.

The objectives in this stage are a reflection of those of the key executive. These are usually goals that reflect "personal achievement." Growth, success, and its attendant status and prestige are reflections of the personal needs of the entrepreneur. *Playboy,* the magazine phenomenon of the 1950s and 1960s, was successfully launched by Hugh Hefner on a relative shoestring. As its appeal grew, the organizational and entrepreneurial talents of a small group of loyal Hefner staff members provided the advertising program and nationwide distribution that allowed the magazine to convert that appeal to a spectacular success.

When the organization grows in size, it has to add new staff. New personnel will be strongly influenced by the charismatic personality of the leader. Like the entrepreneur, they will be concerned with growth and will be willing to take risks for the possibility of large long-term payoffs. In the early part of the growth phase, while the organization is still relatively small, new members may seem to be an extension of the personality of the leader. Through them the leader will manage the growing organization. It is likely that they will make decisions in a fashion consistent with the entrepreneur's beliefs, attitudes, and general policies.

During the early phase of growth, managers will devote their energies toward exploiting external opportunities rather than to internal problems of efficiency and effectiveness. This lack of attention to internal control problems may impose a cost later, but at this time it can be ignored. For instance, both human and capital resources may lag substantially behind the level that is necessary adequately to support sales. Mohawk Data, the company described in item 12.1, had personnel with the necessary technical talent but they neglected to add staff with managerial skills to see them through growth.

During the growth phase the production system may be extended beyond its capacity in order to meet market needs, possibly resulting in earlier equipment replacement. There is a cost when a firm must replace a capital asset before it would have been necessary had proper precautions been taken.

Often in this growth stage decisions are made to acquire capital resources to support a projected level of activity that in the end proves unrealistic. When this happens, the organization will find itself with excess resources that become a critical managerial problem in the administrative organization stage. For instance, during the late 1950s and early 1960s, university enrollments were expanding rapidly. During that time many classrooms and dormitories were built on the assumption that ever-increasing enrollments would require these facilities. The buildings took three to four years from planning to completion, and during that period of growth classrooms and housing facilities were crowded. The resource base lagged behind the level required. In more recent years, however, enrollments have tapered off, and now many universities have excess classroom and dormitory space.

During rapid growth, large revenues from increasing sales provide a cushion for internal inefficiencies. High sales and income can cover up many managerial mistakes. If, for example, costs increase more than they might were there more planning and control, these increases can easily be passed on to the consumer. This is especially true of a growing firm that has control of a particular innovation through patent or simply because there are few other firms in the industry or market. In early years Mohawk Data was so successful with their Key Data-Recorder that they allowed competitors to take advantage of other innovations, which course of action later proved to be harmful to Mohawk's competitive position.

Changes in Structure

As the organization grows it will be necessary to add more personnel, and as more and more people are brought in it is less likely that those selected will reflect the character of the leader and his or her initial associates. To insure consistency in decision-making, policies and procedures will be formalized to provide guidelines for the growing number of new people. It will not be possible to permeate completely the growing organization with the strong personality of the entrepreneur. Thus, the structure of the organization will begin to emerge more formally and clearly. The informality of earlier periods will give way to job descriptions, organization charts, and policy manuals.

The control and managerial subsystems (the authority relationships) will become more pronounced and clearly separate from the production and boundary-spanning units. Greater predictability of relationships between organizational members will be sought by the development of guidelines that specify authority and work relationships between individuals. Employees will then know what kind of decisions to make under what circumstances, to whom they must report, and the general scope of things for which they are accountable to their superior.

In the growth phase the status system in an organization will become more clearly defined. Those close to the leader will have access to a larger proportion of organization benefits and prerogatives, both formally and informally, than those not close to the leader. At the same time, as the organization develops it may be difficult to determine exactly who is close to the leader and who is not. Some lower-level managers may misrepresent their relationship to the leader in order to enhance their own status.

More policy and procedures will be added to insure predictability and control. But their proliferation may be the beginning of such a reduction in the organization's members' freedom that it could become difficult for the organization to take full advantage of the growth situation. Individuals will be constrained by job descriptions, procedural rules, and control systems. They will be reluctant to go beyond them. One reason for this is that the staff added later in the growth phase will not have an opportunity to get to know the entrepreneur personally. If they are not as risk-oriented as the entrepreneur is to begin with, they will tend to stay within their position guidelines in order to avoid the risk of failure and subsequent job loss.

The Transition to an Administrative Organization

As the organization moves up the growth curve, it may begin to experience competition from other firms. The market that was once its own is now invaded by others who see the opportunities for growth and profitability. The firm begins to lose its market advantage. As the market is shared with others, profits begin to diminish. Because of competition, it is more difficult to pass on increased costs to the consumer. Growth begins to slow not only because of competition, but also because the presence of the more formal structure begins to set the organization in its ways. It becomes less able to capitalize on outside opportunities because it has built up an investment in human and physical resources with particular skills. This was one of Mohawk Data's problems. Competitors in a very dynamic industry were more alert to new product opportunities, which Mohawk did not see.

The transition to an "administrative organization" begins as market growth starts to slow. The assets begin to catch up with the output, and pressures emerge for more efficient use of resources. To operate at an acceptable level of profit, the organization is forced to look inward for effectiveness. That means better, more efficient management of its resources. *Playboy's* successes of the 1960s brought competition from other publications directed at a similar market. *Playboy*, once the daring innovator, suddenly found that a shift in tastes had occurred. Other magazines were successful in their appeal to the market, reducing *Playboy's* market share. Playboy clubs were in financial trouble, the price of Playboy stock dropped rapidly, and profits suffered. The management of *Playboy* responded by moving toward a more stringently controlled operation. It "tightened up."

During the transition from the growth stage to an administrative organization, the formal structure of the organization finally becomes very clear and well-defined. Policies, rules, job descriptions, and the authority structure become fairly firmly set. Managerial and control subsystems to support the production and distribution functions that developed earlier in the life of the organization become more important. This is because many of these subsystem activities will have—and will control—the necessary information and technical competence required to increase the effectiveness of internal resource utilization.

There is an important change in the nature of the managerial style. In the growth period, the firm is dominated by the entrepreneur-promotor. As the organization moves to the stage of the administrative organization, the managerial style becomes more professional, shifting toward a more impersonal form evidenced by the use of more bureaucratic structure. "Successfully achieved, this provides the firm with a defensive posture against decline, allowing it a solid and stable base upon which to expand further."[2] For instance, Edwin Land, the key figure at Polaroid, was an entrepreneur-innovator who almost singlehandedly developed instant photography. He had been chief executive officer from the beginning. He stepped down shortly after the introduction of the SX70 camera. His replacement began to introduce more planning and financial control into the firm at that time.

STAGE 3: ADMINISTRATIVE ORGANIZATION

When the organization enters the administrative organization stage, it has many of the characteristics of the mechanistic organization described in Chapter 4. It will be structured by a well-defined set of tasks with explicit job definitions, authority-responsibility relationships, and a clear hierarchy of authority and responsibility. The managerial emphasis will be to plan, organize, and control activities in such a way to insure long-term survival. Under its new president, Polaroid is moving toward a greater emphasis on long-range planning. As Mohawk Data moves into this stage, professional managers are thought to be essential for long-term survival and profitability.

For the administrative organization, the rate of increase in organization size will be relatively modest compared to the growth phase. By now the opportunities for rapid growth created by the existence of innovation in the early stage will be gone. Growth will slow down and markets will become more stable. Because of the stability of the external market and technological sectors, along with the internal tendencies toward a mechanistic formal structure, it is unlikely that the firm can easily experience a rapid, dynamic growth period again. It may be too large with too much investment in resources that cannot be shifted easily to new and different markets where there may be greater opportunities. If a large administrative organization is to experience the rapid growth phase again, it may have to do so through acquisition and merger with other organizations in the growth stage and integrate them into the existing structure of the firm. This will often pose difficult problems of integration for the two different organizations, but it may well be the only way that rapid growth can again occur.

If the structure of an organization and the most effective approach to managing it are related to the environment, then when the environment changes, so too must the structure and the managerial approach. Sometimes the environment changes because of events over which the organization has little or no control. In other cases, the organization may be able to influence the environment to change in a way that is most optimal for the organization.

EXTERNALLY INDUCED ENVIRONMENTAL CHANGE

Those in an organization may have little or no control over how and when the environment changes. Environments may change for several different reasons, for example, innovation, or market saturation, or changing consumer preferences, or changes in legal requirements, or actions of other organizations, or effects of pressure groups.

1. *Innovation.* We have seen that innovation is necessary for growth to occur. Innovation may change the competitive character of the environment to which an established organization must adapt. For instance, the development of high-speed transportation along with refrigeration capabilities in trucks and rail cars made it possible to provide off-season fresh vegetables and fruit nationwide. This changed the marketing patterns of both food producers and food processors. The development of microcircuitry made possible both cost reduction and size reduction of computers. They are now more readily available to smaller firms and are now being sold for use in homes. The development of scanners to read product and cost data from food packages makes it possible to use computers at supermarket checkout counters. The implications of this innovation for the supermarket industry are enormous. The nature of the checker's job is changed. Inventory managers must revise their systems to use the new technology; inventory levels may be determined almost instantaneously. Ordering can be more responsive to sudden shifts in demand. Such an innovation not only has implications for the supermarket and the customer, but also for the manufacturers of the scanning equipment, who must develop different sales strategies and programs to support the use of this equipment in supermarkets.

2. *Market saturation.* A firm in a volatile market with a volatile technology and control of innovation may find, over time, that the market becomes more stable as demand begins to peak. Or the technological advantage it possesses because of patent control may diminish as other competitors develop similar processes or products.

As products become widely distributed, eventually the demand may diminish to a point where the market is primarily a replacement market. Then growth in sales will come from replacement and increase due to changes in population levels. As this happens, the managerial strategy of the firm will become more inward-looking, seeking to increase profitability through internal efficiencies. This will result in tighter procedures and controls.

3. *Changing consumer preferences.* The market may change because of shifts in consumer tastes. The women's fashion industry has long been cited as an example of changing consumer tastes with attendant impacts on the profitability of clothing manufacturers. This same kind of phenomenon may be emerging in men's fashions.

Clothing styles are much more varied for men than they were in the past. Such uncertainty makes it difficult for manufacturers of men's suits to predict sales levels as accurately as in the past. Production methods, procurement, and purchasing have to be more responsive to shifts in taste.

4. *Changes in legal requirements.* Often the environment is changed by action of the government. These actions sometimes cause a firm to change its method of production. For example, legislation now requires automobile engines to produce lower emissions of certain chemical compounds. These requirements mean a change in the design of automobile engines, which necessitates changes in production methods. As another example, the Food and Drug Administration often requires pharmaceutical manufacturers to take certain drugs off the market or imposes stricter controls on the distribution of these drugs. The drug company must respond—adapt—to these changes in their environment.

There have been instances where certain products have simply been made illegal. Perhaps the classic example is the prohibition of alcohol sales during the late 1920s and 1930s. The ban on cigarette advertising on television forced advertisers to look for new media.

5. *Other firms' action.* Changes for a particular organization may be induced by what other firms in that environment do. High profitability and growing markets may bring about the entry of other firms into an area and as competition begins to develop, prices, as we have seen, may begin to drop. The market may become saturated, bringing about a degree of market stability. New manufacturing processes may be developed by other firms, more efficient ways of production may be developed by a competitor, or a competitor may locate its production facilities closer to the market. Organizations must adjust to all these environmental disequilibria.

6. *Pressure groups.* In some cases, the internal structure of an organization changes because of interest groups outside the organization. These pressure groups may be able to affect the decision making within a particular firm. The ecology movement in the United States is an example of such pressure. Another example is change caused by local governments' and citizens' groups' pressure on the Tennessee Valley Authority. These pressures caused not only in a change in the TVA's policies of operation, but also in its structure. This method of adapting to pressure groups is "co-optation."[3] Co-optation is the process of absorbing the external group into policy- and decision-making structure of the organization.

ORGANIZATION ATTEMPTS TO INFLUENCE THE ENVIRONMENT

One should not have the impression that an organization reacts to its environment like a cork, passively bobbing on the ocean waves. Organizations need not simply react to changes in the environment; they can undertake to influence the external circumstances that directly affect them. There are different ways to influence the environment, but the objective is essentially the same. Firms may try to induce changes in the broader segment of the environment to make it more compatible with their own method of operation. Some of the approaches a firm may use to influence the environment are to:

1. Influence demand

2. Lobby
3. Control inputs
4. Induce market volatility
5. Induce technological volatility
6. Control the introduction of innovation

1. *Influence demand.* Most organizations, either individually or collectively as an industry or interest group, try to influence markets, smoothing out fluctuations in demand. They may do this by increasing marketing efforts during slack periods. Pricing policies often have the same objective. By offering discounts during periods of low demand, consumers may be induced to purchase the product or service at a time when the firm's sales level might otherwise be low.

2. *Lobby.* An obvious example of environmental control tactics are government lobbying efforts designed to yield legislation making external conditions more favorable. Agricultural groups, for example, press for government programs to insure stable prices and stable farm income in the face of foreign competition and the vagaries of nature. The meat industry seeks protective tariffs, one purpose of which is to minimize competition from imports.

3. *Control inputs.* In some cases, a firm may reduce external uncertainty by securing control of inputs and/or raw materials. One way that this is done is to enter into long-term contracts with suppliers, as did a large aluminum plant that contracted with a public utility that agreed to provide electricity for a very extended period at a guaranteed price. Another way to control inputs is to acquire a firm that produces raw materials. It is also possible to enter the business of producing raw materials. This latter approach is called ***vertical integration*** and a classic example is Ford Motor Company, which has its own steel mill that produces a substantial amount of metal used in the manufacture of Ford products.

4. *Induce market volatility.* A firm may find itself selling its product or services to a rather stable market. The volatility of a market may be increased by generating demand for the product in other segments of the population where the product is not used extensively. For example, Black and Decker, a manufacturer of power tools, has consistently reduced the price of power drills. Several years ago these tools were bought primarily by professional tradesmen in the construction industry and by hobbyists who used them frequently. Through the development of more efficient production systems and product redesign using less expensive components, Black and Decker reduced the price of power drills to a point where they became inexpensive enough to be bought by those who make only intermittent use of them. Thus, the company made its product attractive to a larger number of consumers and substantially increased the market. Applying this same strategy to other products such as circular saws, Black and Decker experienced very rapid growth in sales and profits since the mid 1960s. Its products have essentially the same functions as they did when they were first introduced. The market shift was caused by their strategy of cost and price reduction.

5. *Induce technological volatility.* In some cases it is possible to develop a product that performs the same function as another, but uses a different technology. Electronic calculators are an example. Another is the development of microwave ovens by manufacturers of kitchen equipment. Item 12.2 describes the recent development of a new, very expensive, but energy efficient light bulb by GE. Such an innovation, if successful, has consequences for other firms in the industry.

Item
12.2 Technological Breakthrough

FROM GE, A $10 BULB THAT SAVES MONEY

General Electric Co. apparently took the light bulb industry by surprise with a scheduled June 14 announcement that it has developed a "revolutionary" new household bulb that will last five times longer than the typical 1,000-hour life of ordinary incandescent bulbs and use only one-third as much electricity to generate the same amount of light. GE says that the new bulb will be launched commercially in early 1981, following extensive market tests starting late this year to gauge consumer response to a bulb that will cost $10 but save $20 over its rated life in lower electric bills.

All light bulb makers have been working on similar energy-saving products, spurred by Energy Dept. pronouncements and some token funding but until now only two small companies, Duro-Test Corp. and Lighting Technology Corp. (Litek), have touted the promise of new-technology bulbs for home use. The other major manufacturers, Westinghouse Electric Corp. and GTE Products Corp., have been concentrating on the commercial and industrial market, where the idea of a high-cost but energy-saving bulb is easier to sell.

GE officials admit that persuading consumers to spend $10 for a light bulb is a marketing challenge, but they feel that the steadily rising cost of electricity and the support of consumer education programs from Energy will help sell the bulbs. "We know we're going to make it happen," declares K. Gary Mason, manager of market planning for GE's Lamp Products Div.

REDUCING DEMAND. "We honestly believe that this is going to revolutionize lighting in a manner very similar to what was done by the introduction of the fluorescent lamp in 1938," says Ralph D. Ketchum, general manager of the division. By the end of the next decade, GE hopes to have the new bulbs in 10 percent of the 840 million screw-in sockets that are now burning 100 watt and bigger bulbs. Attaining that level of penetration—which is only about one bulb in each 1985 household—would reduce electrical demand by some 8 billion kilowatt hours annually, GE claims, or the equivalent of 14 million barrels of oil.

The first bulb that GE will offer will be a two-way model for three-way sockets. Inside the glass envelope is a mercury-vapor, or metal-halide, arc lamp—the same sort of lamp used in the latest street lights—plus two conventional tungsten filaments. One filament is a 50-watt incandescent light source for a fairly dim level of illumination. The other filament emits light as soon as the arc lamp is turned on, to provide light during the 30 seconds that it takes the arc lamp to warm up. Then the current to the filament is automatically reduced by an electronics package in a plastic housing at the base of the bulb—hence the new bulb's name, Electronic Halarc. GE says that the bulb never burns more than 50 watts of electricity even though the arc lamp produces as much light as a 150-watt incandescent bulb.

Until now, it had looked as though Duro-Test would be the first to market an energy-saving bulb. The North Bergen (N.J.) producer of long-life bulbs puts a special coating on the inside of bulbs that reflects back much of the heat now lost from conventional bulbs. Reflecting the heat back at the filament, which produces light by glowing with heat, means that the filament can continue to glow brightly while consuming up to 60 percent less electricity. "We have not yet made a 60 percent-conserving bulb," admits Luke Thorington, Duro-Test vice president of engineering, but he hopes to do so this year. If all goes smoothly after that, Thorington says that Duro-Test could also be on the market in 1981 with a $4, 2,500-hour bulb.

The lamp that Litek wants to make is a screw-in bulb that works like a fluorescent tube—emitting light from a phosphor coating that fluoresces when it is activated by high-frequency radio waves. The Millbrae (Calif.) company is now lining up private capital and hopes to make a bulb that would last more than 10,000 hours and sell for about $10.

GE'S INVESTMENT.   GE is also working on both these concepts, and Ketchum says that the radio-frequency fluorescent technology is especially promising. So far, GE has spent more than $20 million and five years on the new electronic bulb— and will spend $24 million more on production facilities. It has several patents issued and scores of applications. Yet Ketchum says that GE intends to make the technology available "as quickly as possible" to any company that wants to license it. "The energy-saving idea is something the country needs," he asserts.

Source: Business Week, June 25, 1979.

Unless someone is quite lucky, such technical innovations are possible only if a firm is willing to expend vast amounts for research and development at a corresponding risk. Because of the cost and risk involved, it is likely that most organizations will seek to adopt new technology after it has been developed, rather than attempt to find a significant breakthrough itself. This is especially likely to be the case where the current technological formation of a firm, or industry, represents a large investment in capital resources. Firms in the automobile or the basic steel industry, for example, will not introduce technological changes that alter the basic nature of their production processes in a short time period. Their strategy is more likely to be one of gradual introduction of the new technology, to be discussed next.

6. *Control the introduction of technology.* A firm may control breakthroughs either in products or production technology and will introduce these innovations gradually. To do otherwise may require dismantling of the capital assets and an enormous reinvestment. By controlling the rate of introduction of new products, the organization is not only able to experiment but is also able to make the change slowly enough to avoid major reshuffling of the production side of the firm. For example, the automobile industry gradually changed from the standard transmission to the automatic transmission. At General Motors, it first became available in one line, the Oldsmobile, and then in another product line as retooling took place. It would have required a substantial investment if the changeover had been made across the whole product line. The rate of introduction of new products is controlled—or at least control is attempted—because even though changing over to a new product may be technologically feasible, economically it is not. The auto industry again moved in a similarly cautious fashion in introducing small cars to meet the competition of European and Japanese imports. The market for small cars was obviously there, but the industry felt it had to make the changeover at a rate that was economically feasible. This, of course, created problems in the United States auto industry when fuel supplies suddenly became more scarce. In fact, one of the major causes of the Chrysler crisis in 1979 was the very sudden decline in oil supply, which caused a tremendous increase in demand for small cars. Chrysler was not able to increase production of small cars fast enough, and it ran out of money to finance the changeover of production facilities from large cars to smaller ones.

HOW ORGANIZATIONS ADAPT TO ENVIRONMENTAL CHANGES

The environment can change in two directions. It can increase in uncertainty—that is, move from stable to volatile—or it can increase in certainty—move from a volatile to a stable condition.

Increasingly Stable Environments

There will be a "natural" tendency for all organizations to seek stable environments and move toward mechanistic structure. This will lead to changes in structure similar to those that occur with growth, which we discussed in the first part of this chapter. The control subsystem will seek greater predictability of members' behavior. Those in the environmental monitoring sector will seek ways to reduce variance in the volatile environment. The control and the managerial subsystems will develop ways to keep track of both people and resources for internal control purposes. Procedures such as governmental reporting requirements on tax withholding and social security will be implemented and they require regular reports. As the number of systems and procedures increase and become permanent, the organization structure becomes less flexible.

There are two ways that a firm may cope with an environment that is becoming more stable. It can (1) become more mechanistic or (2) withdraw from the stable sector.

1. Become more mechanistic. If the environment is becoming progressively more stable, then the organization should increase the degree of structure. Jobs should be defined more exactly, more permanent authority-responsibility relationships should be established, and the freedom of organization members to make decisions should be lessened. There will be a need for greater coordination with other units as work becomes more interdependent, and this creates a situation in which it is especially important to be able to rely on another person to do his job. Thus, it becomes less efficient to allow people to decide how and what to do. They must have operating definitions of their work.

The major concern in this changing situation is the congruency between the rate of the development of structure with the changing environment. The development of a more rigid structure must keep pace with the changing, reduced, degree of volatility of the environment. But if it becomes too inflexible too soon, creativity may be stifled.

A high volatility environment will not turn into a stable one overnight. The change will be gradual and thus the increasingly rigid organizational structure should also emerge gradually. For example, as the rate of technological change begins to slow, the production subsystem may become more mechanistic as methods become more routine. But if the market is still volatile, the structure of the marketing department should remain flexible. It should move toward more rigidity only in concert with the external environment.

If the organization proceeds too swiftly in imposing structural rigidity, it may find itself unable to cope effectively in an environment that is still fairly volatile. For example, suppose a firm manufactures several lines of specialized furniture. It may decide to standardize production for a mass market. If the market is not there, losses will occur. On the other hand, if organization structure lags substantially behind the rate of environmental change, then the organization may find itself at a competitive disadvantage. If more efficient, standardized operations can produce similar products at lower costs, then the firm that moves most quickly to standardize operations will have the competitive cost advantage.

2. *Withdraw from the stable sector.* A firm often has the capacity to operate in a stable environment, but may choose to function in a more volatile one. For example, the women's fashion industry is characterized by a wide range of market volatility. Some firms manufacture more "traditional" clothes for women. Chanel and Villager are companies noted for their classic designs, which do not change markedly from year to year. Others in this industry, by design, choose to stay on the frenetic world of high fashion. Manufacturers like Yves St. Laurent or Rudy Gernriech attempt to remain in the forefront of the industry by introducing radical or even shocking change in each new fashion season. One reason why this segment of the market is so volatile is that this condition is fostered by these designers themselves. Figure 12.3 shows how these two types of women's wear firms are situated differently in the environment grid.

Increasingly Volatile Environments

If the environment shifts from stability toward volatility, there may be great difficulty in adjusting. The stable mechanistic organization generally has a substantial investment in both people and physical resources and will find a great deal of internal resistance to change. Thus, the large organization in a stable environment will attempt to minimize the possibility of such a shift.

The degree of volatility does not have to increase dramatically to cause problems for a firm. It only needs to move a little beyond the capacity of the firm to adapt to change. The Chrysler crisis of 1979, for example, occurred because Chrysler could not change its facilities over from manufacturing large cars to producing small cars in time. Chrysler was apparently planning to make exactly such a change, but one more year was needed to shift capacity successfully to smaller cars. The environment changed just a little ahead of the firm's capacity to adapt.

An increasingly volatile environment may be a serious problem in industries composed of a large number of small organizations. For example, the restaurant

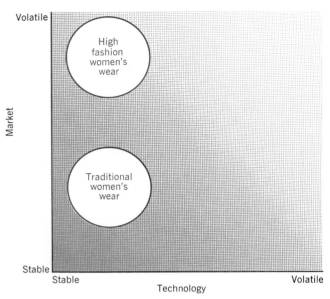

FIGURE 12.3   Similar firms in different environments.

industry was once composed of a large number of small independents who operated in a traditional small-business fashion. Then the rapid development of quick-food service franchises such as McDonald's and Kentucky Fried Chicken caused a major change in the nature of the industry. Small traditional restaurants were not able to take advantage of the new opportunities and found themselves losing the competitive battle with the quick-food franchises. The calculating-equipment industry is another example. Prior to the development of integrated circuitry, adding machines and calculators were largely mechanical, relying on electrically driven gear mechanisms. Suddenly the development of integrated circuitry made possible extremely rapid calculation with smaller and more reliable equipment. Manufacturers of adding machines and calculators were faced with the problem of surviving in a market substantially changed by innovation.

There are three things that a firm can do when its environment becomes more volatile. First, it can change its strategy to take advantage of the new opportunities. Second, it can seek merger with or acquisition of an organization currently capable of functioning in that enviornment. Third, it can elect to withdraw from the volatile segment of the environment.

1. *Change strategy.* Changing strategy requires a shift in the way a firm is managed as well as in the technological processes of production and distribution. The product may be redesigned to parallel more closely that of competitors. This new design may change the way the product works, or it may simply be a change in appearance. If there has been a shift in the way the product is built (as in the case of electronic calculators), the organization may not have either the production methods or the staff to operate under the new system, and so it must acquire the services of a new group of product engineers capable of dealing with the change. If the change is a style change (as might be the case in men's fashions), new designers must be obtained. When the change in strategy requires a change in production methods, the organization will have to invest heavily in the new technology, scrapping the old production system and replacing it with a new one. The substantial investment with the attendant risk requires a decision that should be very seriously evaluated before the change is undertaken. This is the type of adaptation that Disney World (See item 12.3) is making to what is believed to be a shift in their market. They are adding attractions that will appeal to adults who, as children, were the previous clientele of Disneyland.

Less Mickey Mouse

DISNEY TO SHIFT TARGET ON SOME PARKS, MOVIES TO TEENAGERS, ADULTS

PLANNED FACILITY AT ORLANDO TO DISPLAY TECHNOLOGY; A "SNOW WHITE" PARODY
"BABY BUST" SPURS THE SWITCH

Orlando, Fla.—If you visit the Experimental Prototype Community of Tomorrow when it opens in 1982 at Walt Disney World here, leave your mouse ears at home.

Dubbed Epcot, it will be designed for adults instead of children. So forget about going through the haunted mansion or riding the merry-go-round. Instead, for an all-inclusive ticket price of about $10, you'll be able to learn about many new forms of technology in "Future World" and about the history of arts and crafts of thirteen countries in "World Showcase."

Disney sees Epcot as a rich opportunity to tap a new market. Some 30 million tourists come to Florida each year, and Disney now attracts only about 25 percent of them to its resort and theme park near Orlando. "Our visitors now come in family units, and with Epcot we hope to draw adults without children, too," says Disney's research director, Frank Stanek.

Epcot is the centerpiece for a changing corporate strategy at Walt Disney Productions. Long dependent upon young children and families for its theme parks and movies, Disney is broadening its appeal to teenagers and adults.

OTHER CHANGES. Besides Epcot, the company is making more sophisticated movies with bigger name stars, writers, and directors. It is planning a new type of animated film to attract older audiences. And it is hoping to build and operate a ski resort when the right property becomes available.

The reason is clear: The number of American children aged five through nine years is expected to decline 5 percent in the next eight years, and the number of ten-to-fourteen-year-olds is projected to drop 14 percent. "In the U.S., the prime market for Disney products is the five-to-eight-year-old," says Lee Isgur, a securities analyst with Paine Webber, Mitchell Hutchins, Inc. "Disney can't get much more of that shrinking market. So to grow, it must penetrate the teenage-to-adult market." . . .

Source: The Wall Street Journal, January 26, 1979.

2. *Acquire a firm in the volatile environment.* Merging with a firm that is already successfully in the volatile environment, or merging with one that has the technical capability but perhaps has not been profitable due to limited resources, is another way to deal with environmental change toward volatility. The joining of the two organizations is likely to produce a synergistic effect that will substantially increase the resource base and, if the fit is a good one, potentially increase the returns of both organizations.

3. *Withdraw from the volatile sector.* To withdraw from the volatile segment of the environment and continue to produce and market existing goods and services is a third possibility. The organization may elect to stay as it is, but it will face problems of managing in a retrenched position, since a segment of the market is gone. If the new environment is stable and the market is large enough, in absolute terms, however, effective managers may continue to operate a firm profitably. The remaining customer segment in the industry may be large enough for a few, but not many firms. As the less profitable and more inefficient competitors who remain in the stable sector begin to drop out, the remaining firms may increase internal efficiencies to be acceptably profitable, still operating as they did in the past. Olivetti, an Italian office equipment manufacturer, found that it was not able to support the research and development necessary to compete in the United States market with United States firms. Olivetti chose a strategy of withdrawing from the U.S. market, but adopting U.S. technology for the European Market.

SUMMARY

In this chapter we have described several ways in which the external environment may change, bringing about corresponding internal changes of the organization. There are many current trends that will influence organization structure in the future. Some will act to increase formalization and predictability and contribute to more of a bureaucratic design for organizations, while others will contribute to less formalization and to more of a dynamic design for organizations.

As organization structure changes, the management processes must also change. When the environment shifts from volatile to stable, the firm must move to the managerial techniques appropriate for a mechanistic organization. Decision making will shift from decisions under uncertainty to decisions under certainty or decisions under risk. As an organization's structure becomes more rigid, with more specific job descriptions, different personnel with different attitudes, needs, and motivation should be recruited. Of course in the event the change is in the other direction (from stable to volatile), the managerial strategies should shift accordingly from those appropriate for a mechanistic organization to those effective in organic ones.

A change in the structure of an organization will create different role pressures on incumbents, and they must adapt to these if the organization is to survive and survive efficiently. Some of these structural changes can be anticipated, though not easily influenced, by the firm. Other structural changes may be planned and implemented in order to increase the effectiveness of the organization within its current operating environment. Organizations interact with the environment; they do not simply react.

Personnel Communication Inc.

Gary Mugnolo founded Personnel Communication Inc. (PCI) in 1967 in New York City. The basis for PCI was Gary's belief that employee alienation in U.S. industry was high primarily because organizations did not effectively communicate to their rank and file employees. Companies failed to tell their employees about their stake in the company's future and what the company was doing for them. Gary, very creative in communications, developed a personalized communication yearly report that was sent to each employee in the company. It recognized the rank and file employees as individuals and did not refer to a person in an impersonal way.

A company furnished PCI with data on each employee and PCI prepared a personalized report. Gary sold his communication reports to companies on a trial basis. Initially he produced them in an old garage with five employees, who had a great deal of experience in advertising. The first employees of PCI were very devoted to Gary. They worked very hard and for long hours.

The product proved quite successful, and the number of PCI's clients expanded rapidly. PCI moved to larger quarters, which proved to be both more attractive and more efficient. However, Gary still retained his old warm and informal ties with all employees. The work was done, still, with hustle and effective teamwork.

In the early 1970s, Gary sold PCI to a large national advertising firm, but he remained in control as president of the subsidiary company, still named Personnel Communication Inc. Shortly after becoming a subsidiary of the advertising firm, Gary hired Bill Pownall. Bill, an accountant by training, became PCI's executive vice president. Bill was an excellent person to carry out details of the business. He was effective in following through each customer's orders and insuring that delivery schedules were met.

Gary was able to spend more of his time developing other unique and creative products for the firm. Sales of PCI's products and service increased and employment rose. This caused some problems. The company, for example, began to experience some space and working capital shortages.

Gary died rather suddenly of cancer in 1977. Bill was appointed as temporary president, though he said he did not want the job. Bill remained as president for the next three years.

This was a period of rapid growth during which the company added many more employees. For the first time employees were grouped into several specialized departments. Before this, those employees concerned with a particular type of communication program were all located together. Now there was a writing group, a printing group, and a sales group.

Integrating the work among the specialized departments began to be a problem. The old informal coordinating approaches did not seem to work. The communication reports to clients' employees were delivered late. Bill attempted to insure that schedules were met by frequent personal intervention, but this did not work. Coordination problems continued to increase.

The managers and supervisors began to express a lot of dissatisfaction because they did not know what was happening in the company or where the company was going. Some complained about the salary system, which required them to take the initiative in negotiating a salary increase each year with Bill. PCI was experiencing precisely the problems that Gary Mugnolo solved so well for others.

The parent firm, upset at the chaotic conditions in the company, told Bill that it was necessary to get things under control. He decided to install a management by objectives system in PCI by the end of the year. One of the organization development specialists of the parent firm was quite knowledgeable about this topic. The specialist, Page Meade, visited PCI and helped a committee of the department heads to develop a MBO system that was suitable for them. Page pointed out that for the program to succeed, organizational goals must be established by the president and there must be improved coordinating mechanisms. Page also warned the committee that they should have a flexible MBO system, given the diversity in the firm's services and products.

A year later, Page called Bill's company to find out how the program was working. She found out that Bill had not established organizational goals and, although he did not resist his subordinates' use of the MBO system in their units, Bill did little to help or support them in their efforts.

The parent company was upset. They felt they needed a more systematic approach in PCI, so they hired an insurance executive to become Bill's boss, as chairman of the board of PCI. The new chairman of PCI's board quickly introduced a highly quantitative and formalized management by objectives system, which he had used in his previous work in the insurance company. New budget systems and performance standards were also introduced.

Shortly after, Bill quit PCI and took a position with a national accounting firm. Most of the department heads were not sorry to see Bill go. However, they are having some problems in adjusting to the management systems introduced in PCI. Many feel that "It's not the same old place."

1. How does the growth of PCI compare to that of other business organizations?
2. Evaluate the parent company's action in relating to their acquired firm.
3. Predict the consequences of the latest managerial changes in this company.
4. Why would old-timers in PCI have troubles adjusting to these new approaches?

Case 12.2 D.O.C.E.

D.O.C.E. is a state regulatory agency with offices in all the major cities of the state. The agency is subdivided into various specialized departments involved in various aspects of regulation and enforcement. These different units have the responsibilities of (1) collecting reports from businesses, (2) auditing or evaluating these reports, (3) investigating violations of the regulatory laws, and (4) developing and publishing various statistical reports from the data collected. In the agency is also an internal systems analysis group that seeks to develop more efficient procedures for D.O.C.E.

Two years ago, the internal systems analysis group discovered a practice they judged to be very inefficient. Each of the specialized units maintained its own set of files of the reports from the regulated businesses. The systems analysis group calculated the costs of maintaining these separate files to be in excess of $500,000 a year. Given this, the systems group recommended that a new unit—central files—be established. This would be the only department in the agency with the authority to maintain the files of reports from businesses. Each of the deparments could then request the central files group to provide it with the files required for its operations. The head of D.O.C.E., seeing an opportunity to save several million dollars over a period of several years, endorsed the plan and the new department was created.

Things did not, however, go as planned. The other departments still kept their files long after they were supposed to give them up. After a year, the director became very concerned about the slow implementation of the plan to centralize files. He wondered how to obtain compliance with the plan to reorganize the files of D.O.C.E.

1. What are some of the reasons why the new change has not taken place as effectively as hoped?
2. What can be done to make a change in this situation more quickly and effectively?

DISCUSSION QUESTIONS

1. What are the major causes of structural change in an organization?
2. Trace the stages of growth in an organization.
3. Give several reasons why a firm's owner may not want his firm to grow.
4. How does the role of the owner-manager change when an organization's structure changes through growth?
5. What conditions were stated as necessary for growth to occur? What others might be effective or influential?
6. How would decision making change when the environment changes?
7. What external factors might influence a change in structure in an organization? Explain these. Can you think of others?
8. How do organizations attempt to influence the environment? Can you think of any other ways?
9. How would organizations adapt to changes in the environment? Explain.
10. What happens, when rapid growth occurs, to managers of small organizations?
11. It seems implicit that a person who starts a business that becomes exceptionally successful and large will have to step aside if the success is to be continued—or does it?

REFERENCES

1. Filley, A. C. The compleat manager—what works when. Champaign, Ill., Research Press Company, 1978.
2. Filley, A. C., and R. J. House. Managerial process and organizational behavior. Glenview, Ill., Scott, Foresman, 1969.
3. Selznick, P. TVA and the grass roots. Berkeley, University of California Press, 1949.

CHAPTER THIRTEEN

Human Resource Management

Fred Blair was appointed president of National City Bank fifteen months ago. National City is located in the suburbs of a large metropolitan area in the southwestern United States. In the five years before Fred was appointed, National City had expanded rapidly, increasing the number of branch offices from six to fifteen.

Fred was appointed to the position of chief executive officer because the board of directors was unhappy with the profitability of the bank. Though deposits had increased sharply, profits had not kept pace. The board was particularly disturbed at a seeming lack of control of the branch operations.

Two moves were made within Fred's first three months as president. First, he initiated a very aggressive marketing effort to increase customers and deposits. Second, he replaced nine of the fifteen branch office managers.

The replacement of the managers, Fred thought, would have the greatest effect on bank performance. Fred believed that "good management" could solve most problems at National City, so he made every effort to select branch office managers who had not only excellent technical qualifications in banking but also a strong commitment to the developing human resources.

One year ago, when all the new branch managers were in place, Fred held a staff meeting with them. At that time he reaffirmed his commitment to training and development and urged them all to begin working on programs for each of their branches.

As the year passed, Fred met periodically with each branch manager to review progress. Several branch managers had instituted on-site training programs for the branch staff. Other branches were working closely with the local community colleges in cooperative classes (computer programming). All the branches had sent managers to training programs at universities (managerial skills and human development) all over the United States.

When Fred examined the performance records of the several branches, he was pleased with the progress that had been made. On all measures of performance, every branch was doing better. Deposits were up, complaints were down, and branch costs seemed to be coming under control.

The performance of one branch was quite notable, though. The Shadyside office had shown a remarkable 35 percent increase in output and work accuracy was up 10 percent. This was, by far, the most significant improvement in any office. When Fred became president, the performance of the Shadyside branch was about average for National City's branches. At that time he had appointed Ann Smith to replace John Jensen, the previous branch manager.

Ann, like the other branch managers, had met with Fred to talk about her plans for training. Like the others she had a manager or two in a university program and had most of the clerical employees at the Shadyside branch participate in some training to update their technical skills. It seemed, at least on the surface, that she was operating like the other branch managers.

Fred wanted to find out what Ann was doing differently from the rest of the branch managers. Perhaps Ann's approach might help them. Fred asked Ann to meet with him one morning. Fred listened while Ann told him how she had been managing in Shadyside, about the training, and about the marketing efforts.

Then, she said, "Fred, you might think this is crazy, but I think that this increase in productivity is due to my donuts and pizza plan."

"What in the devil is that, Ann?" Fred queried.

"Well," Ann said, "you know that we keep daily records on transactions, error rates, and quality for most of the people in the bank. Usually I would go over these reports on a weekly basis with the group supervisors and ask them to go out and get their staff to do better.

"I decided to try an experiment. I began summarizing the reports daily for each department and for each individual. These reports show how everyone compares against our standards for quality and accuracy. Any time one of the bank staff meets or exceeds a standard, I buy him or her coffee and donuts that day on their break. If the department meets or exceeds their goals every day for a week, I buy pizza and beer for the department on Friday afternoon.

"Here's what I do. For example, Jerry Foster works in our branch. Every day he knows whether he has processed enough customer information such as account numbers, payments, and so forth into the computer to reach a daily standard. Jerry knows, every day, exactly where he stands. Every day Jerry meets his goal, he gets treated to coffee and donuts. If he doesn't, no one says anything."

"What I'm trying to do, Fred," Ann continued, "is make sure that people get some kind of reward for doing their job well. It's not much, it's not money, and it's not a big deal. But still it's something. I also have worked hard with the supervisory staff. I want them to give some reinforcement to their group every day, even if its just to say 'Good job, Charlie.' "

Fred listened attentively. Ann seemed convinced that her "donut and pizza" plan worked. She went on, giving him other examples. An hour later she left Fred's office, the meeting over.

"Get Lew Richards on the phone!" Fred commanded his secretary. Lew managed the Bellaire branch. The Bellaire branch was the worst of all the branches. Even since Lew had been appointed by Fred, the branch's performance had been consistently low. Fred knew he had to do something. He was starting to think about replacing Lew Richards but believed that Lew might improve with some time and, especially, some coaching from Fred.

"Hi, Fred," Lew's voice boomed in Fred's ear. "What's going on?"

"Lew, Ann Smith was here today. I had a long talk with her about what she's doing in Shadyside," Fred told him. "I think you might drive over and talk with her, Lew. Her approach might work in Bellaire."

"The old 'donuts and pizza' plan, huh, Fred," replied Lew." I think it's crazy. This is a bank, not a schoolroom. Ann treats her people like school kids. I won't do it. It will never work in Bellaire."

Lew Richards talked to Fred for the next twenty minutes about why Ann's approach wasn't sound. When he finished, Fred hung up.

"You're right, Richards," Fred mused out loud, "nothing ever works in Bellaire."

Human beings give life to the structure and systems of an organization. Women and men execute the plans and insure that objectives are achieved. People make decisions about and carry out the activities of each subsystem.

One of many outcomes of planning is that it provides valuable information for managing human resources of the organization. Staffing activities can be initiated to bring in the required human talent. Human resource development activities, such as training, can be undertaken to improve the skills of those already in the organization. In this chapter we will discuss the managerial aspects of these two activities.

Staffing and human resource development complement each other since developmental activities can be used to provide new organization members with the necessary levels of knowledge, activities, skills, and attitudes to operate effectively in the organization. It is sometimes impossible to hire people who have necessary skills. Often they must be developed.

Staffing and human resource development are continuous activities because human resources, unlike physical resources, may voluntarily quit or retire. In addition, as we have indicated in Chapter 12, organizational tasks and structure may need to change in order to adapt to the environment. Such changes may require different human skills. This change in skills may be brought about by selecting individuals who possess the required skills or it may be sought through development. Fred Blair, president of National City Bank (see item 13.1), changed the skills in that organization primarily by selection. He was also using a developmental strategy to fine tune performance.

Human resource planning provides the overall framework for specific developmental or training experiences. In most organizations training and development programs emerge from specific short-range situations. For example, when the government environment changed civil rights employment legislation, making it necessary that more women and minority group members be moved into managerial positions, many firms attempted to reduce the resistance of the incumbent work group with training. It is important, though, that long-range organization planning be undertaken, because then it is possible to consider every training effort as it fits into an overall theme.

Without the foundation of human resource planning, organizational development and training efforts cannot be related to the long-range performance requirements of the organization. This argument is strongly supported by the illustration in item 13.2. Many firms have formalized the idea that a particular type of manager is needed for the particular problem a unit faces. Human resource planning requires two steps. First, it is necessary to forecast needs. A second phase of human resource planning is auditing the personnel currently in the organization.

Wanted: A manager to fit each strategy

**Item
13.2**

Manpower planning and strategic planning have become two of the most popular catchphrases in management parlance. Of chief executives responding to a recent survey, 85 percent listed manpower planning as one of the most critical management undertakings for the 1980s. The popularity of strategic planning—and particularly the phase known as product portfolio analysis—is pointed up by the growing practice of diversified companies to identify products by market share and growth potential, and to base long-range capital allocations and operational goals on individual product life cycles. Under this concept, products with a high market share but a low growth potential, for example, are used as cash cows to fund star performers that may not yet be self-sufficient in cash flow.

A JOINT CONCEPT All too often, however, chief executives speak of manpower and strategic planning as though they were separate functions. Management experts warn that corporations failing to link the two concepts may be sounding a death knell for both. The problem, as these experts perceive it, is that corporate manpower officers still tend to weigh specialized, product-line knowledge more heavily than general management skills in making executive assignments. They ignore the fact that the entrepreneurial type of manager who brought a product line from only, say, a 2 percent share of market to 20 percent in three years may not be the right person to continue managing that line with equal effectiveness once it becomes a mature product with little growth potential. Very likely the entrepreneurial type's forte is risk-taking and innovating, while cost-cutting and pushing productivity—the essence of operating a mature, cash-generating business—may well be anathema to him.

"Too often it's like trying to put your best guard into the quarterback's slot—it just can't work," says consulting psychologist Harry Levinson, of Belmont, Mass. Adds Richard J. Hermon-Taylor, vice president of Boston Consulting Group: "I just don't think companies give a lot of explicit attention to the personality attributes of management when they are considering significant changes in strategy."

But some companies do recognize the link between manpower and strategic planning and are striving to match a manager's orientation or style with operating strategy.

CHASE MANHATTAN BANK   When the trust manager retired, corporate management decided that the department, whose operations had been essentially stable, should focus on a more aggressive growth strategy. Instead of seeking a veteran banker, Chase hired a man whose main experience had been with International Business Machines Corp. "We felt he had that strong IBM customer marketing orientation," explains Alan F. Lafley, Chase's executive vice president for human resources. Similarly, when Chase reoriented its retail banking business from a low-margin operation, in which the stress was on keeping down costs, to a more expansionary enterprise offering broader consumer financial services, it hired—because of his entrepreneurial skills—an executive who had been a division chief for a small industrial firm overseas. The former head of retail banking, who was viewed as a strong cost-cutter, is now successfully whipping some of Chase's European operations into better financial shape.

HEUBLEIN'S UNITED VINTNERS INC.   The subsidiary split its wine operations in two in 1977, forming a premium wine division to stress quality over volume and a standard division to emphasize aggressive pricing and efficient volume production. The company chose a wine professional, Robert M. Furek, its previous marketing vice president for all wines, to run the premium wine business. But it tapped Harold G. Spielberg, formerly personal products manager for Gillette Co., to be general manager of United's new Standard Wines Div. The sales staff was drastically reshuffled along similar quality-vs.-volume lines. "People in our premium wine company tend to have more wine background, while those in our standard wine company come out of consumer products and food companies," an official concedes.

CORNING GLASS CO.   It has projected fast growth for its fledgling optical fibers business over the next decade, and it shifted the head of the company's television tube business to direct the new venture. The growth of the tube business had leveled, and its manager had shown himself to have entrepreneurial flair, says Richard A. Shafer, Corning's director of management and professional personnel. "Optical fibers is clearly an entrepreneurial thing," Shafer explains. "We don't know what the i's and t's are, so we can't get someone who dots i's and crosses t's." A manager from Corning's more mature electronics business replaced the television tube head.

In December, ironically, Corning reshaped its electronics strategy, deciding that the market was starting to expand again, and that it needed a growth-oriented manager. It placed a manufacturing specialist who had "shown a great deal of flair in working with customers" in the top marketing slot for electronics, and, says Shafer, "it looks like he's turning it around."

Although such moves sound simple to arrange, many companies are reluctant to choose managers primarily on the basis of managerial orientation or personality traits. Appointing outsiders as managers can be demoralizing for executives who assumed they were next in line. Finding a challenging spot for a competent manager whose only fault is that his department's strategy has changed can also be a problem, particularly for companies that do not have the luxury of numerous divisions and products. Moreover, appraising an individual's managerial orientation or style and determining the type needed for a specific job are imprecise tasks at best. "Too few people are keeping adequate records of their employees' behavior patterns, and too few companies are writing job descriptions focusing on needed behaviors," Levinson says.

THE TI STORY It can be a hit-or-miss proposition. For example, Texas Instruments Inc. has adopted a manpower planning policy that sounds as if it comes out of a behavioral science textbook. "As a product moves through different phases of its life cycle, different kinds of management skills become dominant," says Charles H. Phipps, manager of strategic planning. "It may be in the nature of an entrepreneurial manager to continue to take risks, but if the business gets too large, then top management can no longer tolerate wide swings in performance."

But although TI takes great pains to assess its managers in terms of personal orientation, it failed to capitalize on its early lead in integrated circuits largely because it misjudged the style needed to manage the product line. The story goes back two decades. Jack Kilby, one of TI's foremost researchers and a pioneer in integrated circuit technology, had been pegged as a brilliant scientist but not a strong manager. In 1959, when TI formally launched its IC development program, it placed an executive skilled in administrative chores in charge, with Kilby subordinate to him. The company ignored Kilby's "strong desire to lead his brainchild into the marketplace," Phipps recalls.

To placate Kilby, TI moved the new manager elsewhere in 1961 and let Kilby manage the fledgling IC department. Not surprisingly, Kilby stressed innovation and research at the expense of financial controls, and a few years later he was gently eased out of the department and back to research. Top management brought in managers from TI's technically mature germanium transistor department to provide tighter cost controls.

The tighter controls were introduced, but TI failed to recognize that Kilby's research orientation was really what the IC department needed at that stage. The new management team did not provide the technical push needed to get the IC operation, still in the development phase, off to a fast commercial start. When J. Fred Bucy became head of TI's semiconductor operations in 1967, he swept out most of the IC management and again put in technically oriented people. The result: TI went on to pioneer brilliantly in bipolar integrated circuits and became a competent follower, though not a leader, in the newer metal oxide semiconductor technology.

A chastened TI has since redoubled its efforts to match management orientation with job needs. Bucy, now president, personally reviews the records of the top 20 percent of TI's managers. But Phipps admits that the company still has no all-encompassing answer as to how to fit the manager to the strategy.

Several companies are trying hard to formalize programs that will at least keep them heading in the direction of making perfect managerial meshes. Chase's Lafley, a twenty-seven year veteran of General Electric Co. who was recruited in 1975 to set up a strategic manpower planning program, says his group has "started at the top of the bank and addressed every one of the positions, checked the strategy of the division, and checked whether the people leading the divisions had the proper [behavioral] criteria." It has not been painless. Lafley says that 200 to 300 people have left the bank, "at least half of whom were encouraged to leave because their skills didn't fit our strategies."

"GROWERS" VS. "UNDERTAKERS"   At GE, an adherent of product portfolio analysis, strategic objectives for the company's wide-ranging products are defined as "grow," "defend," and "harvest," depending on the product life cycle. Now its general managers are being classified by personal style or orientation as "growers," "caretakers," and—tongue-in-cheek—"undertakers" to match managerial type with the product's status. Notes one consultant and GE-watcher: "I hear they have a shortage of growers, but they are making great efforts to remove the undertaker types who are heading up growth businesses."

A look at the game of musical chairs recently played in GE's Lighting Business Group in Cleveland tends to support that observation. "The lighting business is mainly mature, but we just designated international operations as a growth area in our five-year forecast," explains Harry T. Rein, the group's manager for strategic planning. John D. Hamilton, the manager responsible for its manpower planning, says he and the executive manpower staff at corporate headquarters "looked at the whole pool of corporate talent." They decided to move in a manager from GE's motor division who had an industrial rather than lighting background, but who seemed to show an entrepreneurial flair.

CORNING'S MATCH-UPS   Perhaps the most formal integration of personal managerial styles and strategic objectives is being done by Corning Glass. A personnel director has been assigned specifically to assess the company's top 100 managers for such qualities as entrepreneurial flair. Each of eleven other personnel development managers is responsible for gathering skills data for about 300 lower-echelon managers. "We're asking incumbents and their bosses what you need to have on the job, because we want to know what goes into success," Richard Shafer says.

The process is easier for small companies, which can assess the types of managers employed by larger competitors and emulate their approach to staffing. In 1974, Prime Computer Inc., a Wellesley Hills (Mass.) minicomputer maker, had sales of only $6.5 million and was operating in the red. The next year, Kenneth G. Fisher left Honeywell Inc. after twenty years to become Prime's president, and he immediately started to hire new managers from companies like his former employer.

"We wanted people from big companies that had already been through what we were going through," Fisher explains. "We assumed that we were going to succeed extraordinarily, and we needed men who had been through all the plateaus before." Fisher has since increased the managerial staff from fifteen to 260 people. Last year, Prime's sales were up to $153 million and net income to $17 million, but Fisher is still looking for managers from much larger companies. "We're building a management substructure that can manage a $500 million company," he says.

DOUBTS ABOUT IT ALL   Fisher notes that recruitment of executives with the sophistication gained at giant companies induced Prime to automate its process for laying out printed circuit boards much earlier than competitors of its own size. Similarly, Prime computerized factory scheduling, material control, and other functions long before sales volume justified such an investment. This has let the company operate with an administrative staff at least one-third smaller than would otherwise have been required. Fisher boasts that Prime gets revenues of about $70,000 per employee, compared with an average in the minicomputer industry of about $35,000.

Despite such successful results from strategic manpower planning, many companies remain uninterested in the concept. Says Chairman James L. Ketelsen of Tenneco Inc., who prefers versatile, jack-of-all-trades managers: "It doesn't make that much difference to us whether it's a growth business or a stable business per se. Most good managers can run any kind of business." Many behavioral scientists shudder at such views, but they hope that ten years from now fewer chief executives will hold them.

Source: Business Week, February 25, 1980.

FORECASTING NEEDS

To forecast the need for the use of human resources it is necessary to make predictions and plans about the future structure of the organization.

Organization Planning

Organization planning consists of making projections of what the organization will look like in the future—three, five, or even ten years hence. These projections can be constructed from data available from strategic planning, such as long-range building or capital expansion projects. Thus, we can arrive at an "ideal" organization structure for some time in the future.

"Phase plans" can be used to bridge the gap between the ideal and the present organization structure. Phase plans are intermediate plans or steps to achieve the desired structure on a sound and practical basis. The use of phase plans forces planners to consider changes in economic conditions, product line, span of control, or loss of key personnel. The projected structure is broken down into phases with respect to time and organizational units. For example, at stated future times, certain subunits may be split off and reorganized in an orderly manner. The phases may be timed to coincide with major additions, planned operational changes in plant and equipment, introduction of new products, and the planned retirement of executives. The final form of organization at a given time will no doubt differ from the ideal structure originally conceived for that time.

Future Performance Requirements

Requirements for future performance can be inferred generally from the long-run organization plan. For example, if we assume that future decision making will require increased use of operations research and information technology—tools based on mathematical skills—the fundamental mathematics can be taught immediately. Then managers will be prepared for advanced training in specific applications in a relatively short time. Training in specific applications of these tools may then be included in development programs concurrently with the fundamental concepts of managing and organizing human behavior.

At best, we can make only qualified guesses about what specific types of training and development will be most useful for the future. As a general guide, however, we can analyze future requirements for managers in terms of the different skills that they must bring to bear on their work. These are technical skills, human relations skills, and administrative skills.[1]

Technical skill is the specialized knowledge needed to perform the major functions and tasks associated with a position. Human relations skill is the capacity to work with people and motivate them in such a way that they want to perform well. Administrative skill is the ability to make decisions and conceptualize relationships directed toward organizational goal achievement, rather than toward maximizing return to some specific subunit of the firm. These skills, of course, necessarily include the ability to plan, organize, and control the organizational system and structure.

There are different skill requirements for different organizational levels. At the lower supervisory levels, technical and human relations skills are primarily important. At the higher levels, administrative skill assumes major importance. The skills mix differs, also, for different stages of organization growth and development. Therefore, as a person progresses through a career in an organization, the nature of development experiences should change. Moreover, as an organization progresses through various stages of growth, skill requirements can be anticipated. For example, before the firm moves into the stage of "administrative organization," managers can be given training in systematic management processes.

THE HUMAN RESOURCE AUDIT

The human resource audit is a systematic analysis of the strengths and weaknesses of the human assets in an organization. The results of this analysis can be compared to the organization plan to provide the following benefits:

1. *Better development efforts.* Knowing something about the strengths and weaknesses of individuals and the projected needs of the organization will make it easier to determine developmental objectives (see Figure 13.1).

2. *Improved promotion decisions.* Individuals can be directed into positions for which they are most qualified or for which they have the capability of being trained.

3. *Better selection.* Selection decisions can be based on future requirements. In addition, the audit will point to areas in which there are no capable people currently in the organization. Staffing efforts can be aimed in these deficient areas.

In order to conduct a human resource audit, it is necessary to obtain information about the current performance and the potential, or promotability, of each individual. Usually, the evaluation of current performance is carried out by a manager's superior. These judgments about how well a person has accomplished his or her job should reflect the responsibilities of the current position assignment.

Making an estimate of a person's promotability (potential) is very complicated. In most organizations that carry out performance audits, the "potential" estimate is

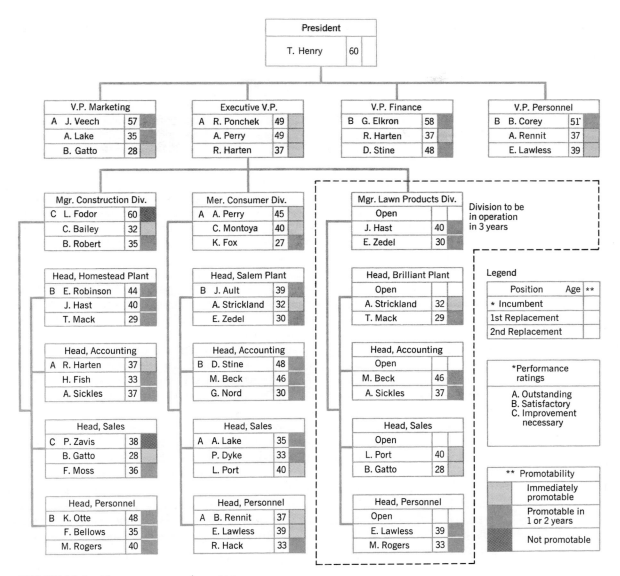

FIGURE 13.1 Human resource inventory.

made by several persons who have had an opportunity to supervise the person. This is because this promotability judgment can be vitally important to a person's career and care should be taken when making it. For example, in one firm that made promotability evaluations, one branch manager was graded as "highly promotable" even though her branch had shown losses for the last three years. Her supervisor's first inclination, when required to rate her promotability, was to give her low scores. However, two other managers involved in the judgment pointed out particular competitive circumstances the branch manager could not control. When these three managers took these into account, their assessment was that the branch manager was, indeed, promotable in spite of the current problem.

Many firms that systematically use human resource planning seek to uncover exceptionally promising personnel in the audit. These firms designate these outstanding people as "hi-pots" (high potential) or "fast track." These are usually the budding stars of the firm, and their progress is carefully marked. In one large U.S. manufacturer, a study completed by their personnel research group showed clearly that "hi-pots" moved more frequently, advanced more quickly, and received higher salary increases than did a group of comparably aged managers.

When the human resource audit is completed, it is usually summarized in a form shown in Figure 13.1. This is a Human Resource Inventory Chart containing much information of the type we have just been describing. It shows the current structure of positions in the firm as well as a future addition to structure, that is, the Lawn Products Division, which is to be in operation within three years.

Figure 13.1 contains much information that is useful in human resource planning. It shows who is a potential replacement for every major position and the current state of readiness of that candidate. For example, there are two very strong prospects for the job of Executive Vice President, currently held by R. Ponchek. If Ponchek leaves the company or is promoted to the presidency, few problems are anticipated. The same cannot be said for the top job in Marketing. The incumbent, J. Veech is performing well. The two replacements are A. Lake and B. Gatto. Should Veech leave, Lake is the first replacement, but she still needs some development. Gatto is the second replacement for the vice presidency of marketing, and while he is currently readily promotable, he is young and inexperienced, working for P. Zavis in the Sales group of the Construction Division. This audit shows that the marketing staff needs some development.

Charts like that shown in Figure 13.1 can be helpful at assessing strengths and weaknesses of different units. A simple visual inspection of the Consumer Division shows it has more immediately promotable people (five) than the Construction Division (three). This might signal a need to develop a plan to distribute high-potential people throughout the firm, rather than allowing them to concentrate in one unit. Recently, for example, a consultant to a large manufacturer conducted a human resource audit of the management in its U.S., European, Asian, and South American divisions. The U.S. division had the preponderance of highly promotable staff. The consultant showed the president charts such as Figure 13.1 for each of the major divisions. The president saw all the high potential personnel on the U.S. chart and few on the charts of foreign operations. This led him to institute extensive development plans for those overseas units.

STAFFING

Staffing is the process of providing needed human resources to the organization. It includes the activities of recruitment, selection, and placement. Recruitment attracts applicants to the organization; the selection process chooses those to whom employment offers will be made; and placement determines the appropriate position, or role, or field for the individuals selected. The objective of staffing is, of course, to increase organizational effectiveness. This objective is achieved when individuals with the necessary skills, attitudes, needs, and self-concepts are matched with organizational requirements. This matching contributes in a number of different paths to effectiveness. Outputs are achieved—products, services, and ideas—that contribute to profits or returns, and turnover and absenteeism are minimized. A review of research on turnover and absenteeism by Porter and Steers[2] concludes that level of job satisfaction is directly related to levels of turnover and absenteeism, and one study found a significant relationship between the level of unsatisfied needs of employees and absenteeism.[3]

While individual needs are important considerations in staffing strategies, however, abilities may today be the easiest factor to measure, since more research has been directed at this problem than at the others. In some individuals, abilities improve over time; in others they do not. Determining which individuals have the capacity to grow, develop, and learn becomes especially important when selecting individuals for a career (e.g., managers and professionals) as opposed to selecting for just one position.

RECRUITMENT

Usually, recruitment precedes selection—the process of choosing from among applicants—but sometimes the selection comes first. For example, an organization first chooses a person it wants to become an organization member. Then it does all it can to recruit or entice him or her to come to work for it. Supply and demand obviously influence organizational recruitment. When there is a shortage of workers in a particular occupational group, recruitment receives great emphasis. When the demand for candidates exceeds the supply, there is no selection: You hire whoever is available. On the other hand, when the supply is plentiful, recruitment is quite easy and selection becomes a problem.

Candidates for any position may be found both inside and outside the organization. For instance, transfers and promotions fill vacancies, but often the organization must go outside itself to find viable personnel alternatives.

SELECTION AND PLACEMENT

In the selection approach one particular position or role is kept in mind when evaluating applicants, and applicants are compared against the requirements for it. With the placement approach the individual's strengths and weaknesses are determined with a view toward finding the organization role or situation in which that individual's talents can best be utilized. In selection the emphasis is on rejection. The purpose is to select from a large group of applicants the person best suited for a particular role. In placement, however, the emphasis is on how a particular individual can best be used.

In periods of labor shortage, most organizations emphasize the placement approach. Contrarily, the selection approach is most favored when many applicants exist for a vacancy. Also, the selection approach has probably been traditionally used for lower-level personnel, the placement approach most frequently for college graduates, such as those entering the first level of management.

To use the placement approach, a number of different positions must be available, which is most likely to be the case in large organizations. The task in such a case is to maximize both role performance and role satisfaction with a given, fixed group of applicants, who differ in individual characteristics, and a finite group of vacancies to which they can be assigned. Perhaps the most striking example of an organization that must deal with this problem is the military, into which there flows a continuous stream of untrained recruits who must be assigned to a wide variety of specialized roles.[4]

In using the placement approach, Dunnette recommends the identification of task clusters.[4] In each cluster are jobs with some similarity in task content, although there are some differences. For example, an engineering cluster may have research jobs, applied production jobs, and technical services to customers. Prospective engineers are assigned differentially to these various jobs, based on abilities, preferences, and task demands.

HUMAN RESOURCE DEVELOPMENT

Figure 13.2 is the Development Model on which the remainder of this chapter is based. This model rests on the simple premise that in order for any change attempt to be successful, it is necessary that basic relationships between the following factors must be taken into account.

1. The targets of change
2. The change process
3. The objectives of change

A great deal of theory and research supports the idea that change efforts must be more broadly based and consist of more than mere classroom exercises. It is not hard to predict what would happen if Lew Richards, manager of the Bellaire branch of National City Bank, were forced by Fred Blair to institute the "donuts and pizza" plan that worked so well for Ann Smith in Shadyside. Without Lew's support the program would fail miserably. Change efforts not only must be compatible with the type of change desired but also must be supported by the organizational climate.[5,6,7] This means that the management group must be willing to support change efforts with organizational reinforcements. Only when this is done can management expect change efforts to result in the kinds of behavior intended. This support can be provided only in the form of specific top management decisions and practices. It is not enough for management to support development "verbally." They must do so with their practices and policy making. The change model in Figure 13.2 outlines those factors that must be considered when different change objectives are desired.

PREREQUISITES OF CHANGE

Unfortunately, people do not change just because someone wants them to change. Even if a manager determines that there are some serious weaknesses in a work group and decides that these differences can be overcome through training, the training may or may not take, because before individuals or groups can be changed, certain conditions must be present.

FIGURE 13.2 The Developmental Model

Targets of Development	Individual		Group	Organizational
Objectives of Development	Ability and Knowledge	Attitudes	Intergroup Cooperation	Organization Effectiveness
Development Process — Diagnosis	• Motivation to change • Mental capacity • Physical capacity	• Low to moderate levels of authoritarionism • Individual values and group norms that are not inconsistent with change goals	• Task interdependence between groups • Resource interdependence	• Congruence of basic structure with environmental uncertainty • Skill and competence of personnel
Development Process — Change	• Instructor-centered methods • Lectures, cases • Programmed instruction • Skills practice • Job rotation • Special assignments • Delegation/ coaching	• Individual- and group-centered discussions • Role playing • Discussion methods • Sensitivity training	• Confrontation • Action research interventions • Gather data, feedback, and action planning	• Management by objectives and performance based appraisal • Coaching, counseling, and frequent review based on objectives
Development Process — Process maintenance	• Opportunity to use skills on the job • Informal group norms consistent with new skills and ability	• Organization climate consistent with change goals • Organization practice consistent with change goals	• Climate of trust • Organization structure that promotes cooperation, not conflict	• Compensation and reward system based on desired practices • Attitudes and values supportive of organizational goals

1. *The cause of the present unsatisfactory state of knowledge, behavior, or attitudes must be understood.* If change in an individual or group is desired, it is because behavior or attitudes are not what they should be. Change attempts have the best chance of success when the causes of present behavior and attitudes can be determined.

2. *The obstacles standing in the way of change must not be insurmountable.* If there is to be a change in knowledge, for example, certain minimum levels of learning ability must be present, since limits in individual learning abilities place limits on the amount and type of material that can be learned. Certain behavior

patterns or attitudes may be so deeply ingrained and so important to the functioning of the individual that they can be changed only with great expenditures of time and energy, if at all.

3. *There must be some motivation to change.* An individual or group must be motivated to change an existing level of knowledge, behavior patterns, or attitudes, or the influence programs will fail.

4. *Defensiveness must be minimized.* Most individuals are not inclined to accept negative information about themselves. A person performing at an unsatisfactory level, for example, is likely to shift the blame for low performance to other people or to the situation, such as a lack of resources. In general, the person refuses to acknowledge that performance is unsatisfactory or that errors are serious. All of this hampers change.

Research has identified some critical situational factors related to a positive reaction to training by the participant.[7,8] In these studies it was found that trainees reacted more positively to the program if

1. They believed that good performance would result in pay increases or promotions.
2. They desired a promotion.
3. They were relatively satisfied with their jobs and the organization.
4. They felt the company was supporting the program.
5. They felt their superior was supporting the program.
6. They perceived they had the power to make changes in their jobs.
7. They perceived the content of the program to be related to the solution of their current problems.

In other words, participants are more favorable toward change efforts when they see them as a means of accomplishing personal objectives. Those who react most favorably to a program expect that it will help them attain outcomes they think are important (promotions, pay increases, solution of current problems). Those employees with favorable attitudes toward the company are more favorable toward training programs that the company endorses than those with less favorable attitudes toward the company. In addition, it was found that those who feel they can utilize the training on their jobs are also more positive about the programs.

Behavioral scientists believe that if an individual participates in the making of a change, he is predisposed to accept the change. Why? First, because he has a greater understanding of it, and thus less uncertainty, which is a source of resistance to change. Second, with participation the individual (or group) becomes ego-involved with the change. If a person makes a suggestion, and if she believes it is a good suggestion, she will be motivated to try to make it work. If she does not try to make it work, and if the suggestion ultimately proves to be no good, that will be a negative reflection on her as a person, and she will have to reevaluate her opinion of herself. Third, if a person commits himself to successful accomplishment of a change, he will be motivated to make it succeed, because people see themselves as individuals who keep their word, and they try to live up to this aspect of their self-concept. Finally, in a group setting, the individual perceives that the change is being accepted by her peers, whose opinion she values.

Participation does not always overcome resistance to change, however. It is generally not effective when the individuals involved do not have the competence or information needed to contribute to the development of the change, or when they lack motivation or interest in the subject of concern, or when they do not consider their participation in the change decision appropriate.

TARGETS OF DEVELOPMENT

Development and training are usually thought of as very important activities that must be carried out to insure an adequate supply of competent managers. Yet there is very widespread disappointment with many change efforts because when they are systematically evaluated, it appears that they have little impact. For example, one large bank in the Southeast has spent a great deal of money to send their executives and bank officers to an executive development program designed especially for managers in financial institutions. The analysis showed the bank had not changed its competitive position relative to other banks in its region. The evaluation showed that the managers were very well versed in financial management, human resource management, and other topic areas that are commonly a part of an executive development program. However, there was extensive intergroup conflict between various divisions, which was associated with an unwillingness to cooperate effectively. When the researcher told the bank president of this conclusion. The president said

> "I can't understand it. All these people have been to 'banker's school.' I am certain they know what needs to be done because I have spent the money to insure it. These training and development programs must not work."

The president, who planned the bank's development effort, really did get what he paid for, that is, an increase in knowledge and ability of individual managers who worked in the bank. He did not have any training and development effort directed at improving group functioning and cooperation.

To have development work—or take effect, as it were—it is necessary to understand that development may be aimed at different targets and that it may be very effective for one target and not another. The targets for development can be

1. The individual
2. The group
3. The organization

The Individual

The managers in the Southeastern bank were involved in a type of change effort that was aimed at the individual. The individual may be the focus of efforts to improve ability, increase knowledge, or change attitudes.

When the individual is the primary target of development, it is not likely that overall organizational effectiveness or teamwork will result from development efforts. Individual development efforts can change people, but whether or not that change is carried into the work place depends upon many other factors. For example, individuals can learn how to use certain techniques like systems analysis and computer programming. Or the person may learn much about human behavior, motivation, and personnel practices. Still, this may not have any significant effect in how well the person performs on the job or works with other people.

The Group

There are many problems that occur between groups that can be solved with development approaches. We have already discussed many of these in Chapters 4 and 6, particularly. Attitudes of group members and intergroup cooperation may be of concern to management, and, therefore, the group may be the target of a development effort.

The Organization

Overall improvement in organizational effectiveness can be the target of development. Certainly, this is the most complex and difficult target and requires not only a good deal of developmental work but also may take much time for the developmental effort to work. The reason that the president of the Southeastern bank was disappointed with the results of the bank's development efforts and expenditures is that he expected an increase in organization effectiveness (an *organization* target), but made use of developmental approaches that were more effective in improving skills (an *individual* target).

THE DEVELOPMENT PROCESS

An analysis of what effective development programs have in common has led to the identification of steps in the establishment of successful change efforts.[9] The successful development process involves three basic stages: (1) diagnosis, (2) change, and (3) maintenance.

Diagnosis

Diagnosis is the process of trying to determine whether or not the conditions are present that will allow the change to be successful. The type of information sought in diagnosis depends upon the objectives sought and the targets of change.

There are many techniques for diagnosis. Some diagnosis may be performed using questionnaires completed by organization members. Another diagnostic approach is observation. Interviews are frequently used.

Change

Changing individuals, groups, or organizations requires two steps: unfreezing and changing.[5] **Unfreezing** is the first step in the change process. At this stage attempts are made to motivate the target person, group, or organization before the actual change is introduced. Common to the unfreezing stage is the removal of social support to the individual for the old behavior or attitudes by insulating him from his habitual social system. For example, when trying to change attitudes, it may be useful, at least initially, to take the person away from his normal work setting, where he may be finding strong reinforcement of his present attitudes, to a location where he may obtain a new perspective. Next, rewards for willingness to change may be introduced, along with punishments for lack of willingness to change.

Changing is accomplished through the use of some process directed at a development target and intended to achieve a different state in one of the objectives of development. This could be anything from lectures intended to increase knowledge to the use of very extensive interventions in the organization, such as action research. These techniques, and how effective they are, will be discussed later in this chapter.

Change programs seem especially effective when identification and internalization occur. Identification occurs when the target person identifies with one or more role models in the environment and thus tries to behave as they do. When there are appropriate role models present, it facilitates change since the role models exemplify the new behavior in their actions. The other effective change process is that of internalization, by which the target person discovers for himself that the new behavior or attitude can become part of his personality system.[5]

Process maintenance

In the process maintenance phase of development, the conditions that support the desired behavior or attitudes must be put in place if they are not already there. This is done so that the organization structure, the groups that make up the organization, and especially the managers of those who are exposed to developmental efforts reinforce the change efforts made.

OBJECTIVES OF DEVELOPMENT

The objectives of development are the kinds of changes that are sought. Sometimes the intent of development may be simply to increase knowledge. Often the goals are more ambitious, such as improved organization results. The developmental model (Figure 13.2) describes the factors that must be diagnosed, the type of change approach, and the conditions that must exist to achieve the following change objectives:

1. Ability and knowledge
2. Attitudes
3. Intergroup cooperation
4. Organizational effectiveness

The objectives of development are not the same as the targets of development. Targets define the level at which the change effort is aimed (e.g., individual, group, or organization), while the development objective refers to the type of change. For example, Figure 13.2 shows that an attitude change objective could be directed at the individual or the group level, as could an intergroup cooperation objective be aimed at subgroups within a department or at the whole organization itself.

Knowledge and Ability Goals

In our developmental model (Figure 13.2) knowledge and ability goals are targeted at individuals. Knowledge-change goals refer to efforts to increase the level of information a person has. A developmental objective, for example, may be to make employees more aware of certain technical or management techniques, such as linear programming or capital budgeting. Another possible knowledge-change objective could be to increase an employee's understanding of current theory about managerial practice and behavior. In the National City Bank case in item 13.1, many of the managers who are attending university training programs are involved in knowledge-change efforts.

Ability is one's capacity to act in a particular way or solve problems. Ability-change efforts are aimed at improving how well a person can do certain things or how the person might solve problems. Many developmental efforts are aimed at improving abilities needed in organizations. Managers are trained to make better decisions. Specialists may be trained to use computers. A person in a training program may learn how to program a computer or run a group meeting more effectively, but whether or not these skills are used at work is determined by the job.

According to Figure 13.2, to increase knowledge, the participant must be willing to learn (be motivated) and be exposed to instructor-centered methods such as lectures, tapes, textbooks, and so on. So long as the instruction is competent (contains the necessary information), it is likely that one will learn.

One problem with such development is that even when these conditions (learner motivation and competent instruction) are present and people do learn, managers on the job expect other outcomes (e.g., improved job performance). It is like expecting all those who understand and appreciate Bach to be able to play his fugues.

To increase abilities the change effort must be experiential; that is, the person must be able to practice the activity. For example he or she must formulate a plan, solve a problem, run a meeting. Such techniques as role-playing and group discussion often provide interpersonal skill development. Business games, simulations, special assignments, and job rotation fall into this category.

Behavioral modeling is an important factor here. The superior must do the things she is seeking to develop in the subordinate. Or if she does not have the capacity to do so, then she should give the subordinate the opportunity to use the skill. For example, the goal of development might be to improve computer-programming skills. The superior may not need such capacity in her own work and may have no ability to program, but she can make available to the subordinate every opportunity to use these abilities in problem solving.

Attitude-Change Goals

Attitude-change objectives may be targeted at individuals or groups. Many firms try to change attitudes of both workers and managers not only toward the company, but also toward women and minorities. They have done the former to increase loyalty, job satisfaction, and commitment. They have done the latter to facilitate affirmative action programs, as well as to minimize problems in the work place when women or minorities are hired.

For attitude change to occur, methods such as role-playing, sensitivity training, or group discussion methods are effective. In these, participants have an opportunity to consider how their current attitudes affect their work, and whether and how changing them may improve the job situation.

In attitude change efforts, however, rigid attitudes—or those that are very important to the individual's psychological adjustment—will be difficult to change. Norms and values must also be diagnosed to insure that the direction of attitude change is consistent with them.

After the training, the environment to which the person returns is important. He should find a sympathetic leader, groups norms that are not conflicting, and organization policies that do not make it difficult to change. For example, if the goal is to change attitudes of male managers toward women executives, then it would be necessary to have nondiscriminatory selection and promotion policies.

Intergroup-Cooperation Goals

The goal of intergroup cooperation can be directed for both group and organization targets. Intergroup cooperation goals focus on developing smooth and effective working relationships between different groups. To diagnose whether or not conditions for group cooperation exist, we must look at the degree of interdependence between groups. When two or more groups must work together or are otherwise dependent upon the same resource base, then some degree of cooperation is necessary. The change efforts to achieve cooperation can be confrontation approaches (such as we discuss in Chapter 18) or an ***action research intervention.***

In an action research intervention we try to identify the causes of the problem by gathering information from those involved with the problem. These data are then fed back to the participants and a solution is worked out, usually with the aid of a consultant.

When action research or confrontation does bring about the desired change, a climate of trust and an organization structure that promotes cooperation, not conflict, must exist for the change to hold. In the hospital group problem, cited in Chapter 18, the confrontation approach did change the working relationship immediately after the groups had gone through it. However, six months later problems resurfaced because there had been no major change in the organization structure. The work setting and formal structure to which people returned still fostered low cooperation.

Organizational Effectiveness

This is the most difficult of change objectives to achieve because so many factors must be taken into account in order to improve results. First, the general structure of the organization and the environment must be congruent. Second, those in the organization must have an adequate level of skill to perform, as well as the motivation or willingness to do so.

The developmental method for improving effectiveness is to give personnel an opportunity to use these capacities on the job. A person must be permitted to make mistakes. The leader must offer coaching and guidance, providing help, support, and feedback about how well the subordinate is doing. The different facets of organization structure must support the desired performance. For example, in promotions, we must recognize the need to fail. A manager may have had some very important and useful learning experiences early in a career.

Improved organizational results will not occur unless the system (the structure) is designed so that it supports such results. For example, the compensation system must pay for, not penalize, good performance. Managers must be able to use both objective and subjective rewards to reinforce subordinates. These reinforcers must be consistent with, not contradictory to, the predominant climate in the organization. This is what Ann Smith, of National City's Shadyside branch, did with her "pizza and donuts" plan. Whenever employees achieved goals, they were rewarded for it.

AN INTEGRATED DEVELOPMENT EFFORT

The Developmental Model (Figure 13.2) suggests that the achievement of organization effectiveness is sequential, that is, change objectives begin with the individual and then move through to organizational development. This can be done several ways, and the approach taken by Blake and Mouton[10] illustrates one frequently used. Their approach emphasizes changing the whole organization in a series of six sequential steps. Each step represents a particular phase of the total change program.

Phase 1

Phase one involves approximately five days of training, during which managers participate in various exercises that illustrate group and intergroup problems. These exercises emphasize the advantages of certain problem-solving techniques, stressing primarily involvement and participation. These exercises focus on how other groups solve problems and illustrate the difference between high- and low-effectiveness groups.

Group members also receive feedback from the other participants as to their leadership style. Each participant compares this evaluation with his or her own self-evaluation. Then the gap between this style and the desired style (a combination of people orientation and work orientation) is considered. In phase one individuals are encouraged to commit themselves to closing the gap between their present style and the desired style. During this phase each participant also evaluates the general leadership behavior patterns that exist in his company.

Phase 2

In this stage, teamwork development is emphasized. Here each team member evaluates her or his group at work and then meets with the other members of the group to discuss perceptions of the culture of the work group. Each member's leadership style is assessed, primarily how he or she relates to the group. Also, the group meets to study, and attempt to resolve, the problems of operating together. A project derived from some specific difficulty in the work place is investigated by the group. Phase 2 begins with the top group in the organization and slowly works down to the lower-level work groups.

Phase 3

In this step, all groups review their external relationships and identify other groups with which they have problems of coordination, cooperation, or conflict. The emphasis is on improving intergroup relations. Key members of the different groups with unsatisfactory intergroup relationships then meet to understand the type of relationship they actually have. They attempt to define what kind of relationship they want to exist between their groups and then to develop a plan for overcoming the difficulties.

Phase 4

In this phase, a top management team designs an ideal strategic corporate model. This defines what the organization would be like if it were truly excellent. This ideal model takes into account the type of structure, the type of personnel, problems that will be encountered in implementing it, and so on. After a careful analysis, the model is developed and is then evaluated by other organization members and units.

Phase 5

Now comes the implementation of the ideal model. In this stage, the organization is broken down into components and a planning team is created to help implement the model in each part, with the assistance of a general consultant. Each team must, of course, implement the model with consideration for the unique character of its own organizational component.

Phase 6

Phase 6 is a critique of the whole program. Instruments are used to assess how the organization has changed since the complete developmental program was initiated. Problems uncovered in phases 1 through 5 that hamper effectiveness are raised, and these problems become the issues for future development plans.

DEVELOPMENT TECHNIQUES

There are many ways that organizations can change individuals and groups. These methods are the technology of the trainer. They are techniques for learning and change, activities intended to bring about a change of skills and attitudes in another. Here we discuss various off-the-job and on-the-job training methods and then review what is known about their effectiveness in accomplishing various kinds of change.

OFF-THE-JOB METHODS

Off-the-job methods are learning environments away from the work setting. Usually in a classroom situation, the training content is presented. The content can range from skills training, for example, how to type, to lectures and discussion of subjects such as human relations, quantitative decision-making techniques, finance, accounting, and economics.

Lecture

Perhaps the most common form of training is the standard lecture, in which a person competent in a topic area presents a set of concepts and ideas to a group. Often questions and answers are used to determine understanding, but the lecture is generally considered an "instructor-centered" method.

Lectures are effective for knowledge acquisition. Study after study shows that college students learn as much through lecture methods as they do through discussion methods.[11-14] The same would probably be true for managers. Managers, in fact, seem to prefer lectures, at least over discussion methods. Studies on managerial acceptance of the lecture compared to the discussion approach indicate that managers prefer the lecture or more leader-centered approach.[15-18]

Films and Videotape

Another instructor-centered method is the use of film or TV. Sometimes the instructor appears on the screen and presents material in much the same fashion as in a lecture, and sometimes the instructor is interviewed. Usually, questions and answers are not used unless someone, such as a trainer, is present and using the films as a vehicle to stimulate discussion with the group of trainees. Sometimes the film presents dramatizations of certain incidents in order to provide examples of the concepts being taught.

These methods seem to be about as effective as the conventional lecture in increasing knowledge. A review of nearly 400 studies that compared television courses with conventionally taught courses found that in 65 percent of the comparisons there were no differences in learning, in 21 percent of the comparisons the television approach was more effective, and in 14 percent of the studies the participants in the television courses learned less than in conventional classes.[19] There is a tendency, though, for individuals to be more satisfied with lectures than with videotapes and films.

Programmed Instruction

Programmed instruction is another instructor-centered approach. However, it is also interactive in that the learners move at their own pace, not moving on to a more advanced set of concepts until preliminaries have been mastered.

With conventional programmed instruction, concepts are presented to the learners and then a series of diagnostic questions are asked. Only when all questions are answered correctly does the learner move on to the next concept. If questions are answered incorrectly, the learner is directed to additional material on the subject. Programmed instruction is theoretically based on principles of reinforcement, the reinforcement ostensibly coming from the satisfaction of answering the diagnostic questions correctly.

Programmed instruction is effective for knowledge acquisition. In several individual studies that compared programmed instruction to both conventional lectures and discussions, learning was at least 10 percent higher under programmed instruction in one-third of the studies, and there was no practical difference between the conventional and programmed instruction in the remaining two-thirds.[20] Some studies show that programmed instruction is preferred by managers to the lecture method,[21,22] but several studies show that participant acceptance of a training approach is a function of their experience with it.[23-25]

Simulations—Business Games

The simulation is an attempt to create a learning situation that approximates the real world. In most simulations the learner is faced with a series of decisions to be made—for example, decisions about how many units should be produced. These decisions are then fed into computer models and their effects are shown. Simulations may be extremely complex, or very simple, and they may deal with a wide variety of problems—manufacturing, retailing, or even governmental management.

There is little research on the effectiveness of business games as a method for teaching problem-solving skills. The students who were in a class where a game was used reported they did not seem to learn much about specific problem-solving solutions or strategies that could be used in other situations.[26] When simulations plus lectures were used however, students understood the interrelationship between organizational factors better than students in sections with cases and lectures.[27]

Raia[28] found that a business game was not favored over other methods of instruction by students. Business students in sections of a course that used a business game had similar attitudes toward the course as those students in sections without the business game. Only a few of the students participating in business games believed that the game was a valuable learning experience.

Case Studies

The case is a narrative, written presentation of a set of problem facts that the student analyzes and then solves. Cases are used to stimulate discussion of topics and of all types. Like simulations, they can be simple or complex.

The case study is a widely used training method. Unfortunately, there is little research on the effectiveness of the case study as a training device to improve problem solving. It appears, however, that case studies can be effective ways to increase knowledge. In a well-controlled study where a class taught by the case method was compared to a class taught by a lecture-discussion approach, the case-study section scored significantly higher on achievement tests.[29] Fox found that about one-third of the students exposed to case-study analysis improved significantly in their ability to handle cases, about one-third made moderate improvement, and one-third made no improvement.[30]

The case study method is high on participant acceptance. Fox found that attitudes in the form of testimonials toward the case study method were very favorable.[30] However, interest in cases seems to dwindle after a period of exposure to them.[31]

Conference (Discussion) Methods

The conference method is a group-centered method of instruction in which the participants, with a conference leader, engage in discussions to develop ideas that can lead to greater understanding of what is being taught. It may be used with or without cases and simulations. Students may be assigned material for reading and the instructor will then use a series of questions to stimulate discussion. The conference method involves the participant more extensively in the learning process than do lectures or films.

Discussion methods are superior to lecture methods and the other directive methods of instruction for changing attitudes and behavior. In two fairly well-controlled studies where the lecture and discussion approaches were compared in situations involving attitude change among adults, the discussion approach was more effective than the lecture method in changing behavior.[32–34]

Role Playing

Role playing is an experiential, student-centered method of instruction. In role playing, the student (learner) is asked to act as another person. For example, in a management training program one participant assumes the role of a company negotiator while another acts as a union representative. Each person receives a set of facts and is instructed to represent his or her side in determining the final form of a labor contract. Role playing is especially useful in developing interpersonal skills because the consequences of behaving in different ways are actually seen. By taking another person's role it is also possible to develop a greater awareness of his or her perspective.

Managers generally like role playing as a training method.[35] There is a good deal of research showing that role playing can be quite effective in changing attitudes, especially if the subjects participating in the role-playing situation are asked to take the point of view opposite to their own and to verbalize this opposite point of view to others.[36–39]

More evidence is available on the effectiveness of role playing in developing problem-solving skills. These studies indicate that problem-solving skills can be improved for both students and managers with the use of role playing.[40–45]

Role playing can also improve interpersonal skills. A study by Bolda and Lawshe showed that role playing can increase sensitivity to employee motivations if the participants become involved in the role play.[35] Role playing can also be effective in improving interviewing skills[46] and group-leadership skills, which are a form of interpersonal skills.[41–43]

Sensitivity Training

Sensitivity training explores the nature of interpersonal relationships. Individuals are brought together in groups with little or no structure. Under the guidance of a leader, group members in an ambiguous situation must work out their own group structure and relationships.

Sensitivity training is an attempt to increase the interpersonal skills of the participants. It is generally felt that such objectives are achieved when individuals become more accepting of feedback about themselves from others, more candid about expressing their own feelings, more trusting, more spontaneous, more flexible, more sincere, and more willing to face up to conflict and personal problems.

In sensitivity training sessions an effort is made to establish a learning atmosphere in which self-examination and criticism are rewarded, where constructive feedback is given to others, and where social support is given for change efforts. Various experiential exercises, tests, and role models are also frequently used to facilitate such learning.

The evidence is quite clear that sensitivity training is fairly effective in changing attitudes and behavior. Several studies have attempted to see whether behavior was changed as a result of sensitivity training, and these studies did find behavioral changes.[47–51]

With respect to attitude change, other research on groups using a before-and-after design with student and adult participants found attitude changes as a result of sensitivity training.[52,53]

Much sensitivity training research has examined its effects on developing interpersonal skills. Several studies of sensitivity training show that participants describe others in more interpersonal terms than people without such training.[53]

ON-THE-JOB METHODS

Some feel that experience is the best teacher—that putting a manager into a sink-or-swim situation is the best approach to development. This approach, taken in a systematic way, is the "on-the-job" developmental method. Not only can a person learn the job content, but there is also the opportunity to observe others at higher-level managerial positions and pattern behavior after them.

Members of any organization can learn from watching others and modeling their behavior. Human beings can learn from observation and/or direct experience. As Bandura concludes:

> Research conducted within the framework of social-learning theory demonstrates that virtually all learning phenomena resulting from direct experiences can occur on a vicarious basis through the observation of other persons' behavior and its consequences for them.[54]

There are at least four types of experiences that can be classified as on-the-job development: (1) job rotation, (2) special assignments, (3) delegation and coaching, and (4) management by objectives.

Job Rotation

With job rotation—a fairly common method—an individual is systematically moved from one position to another in an organization. The purpose of these moves is to allow the person to learn something about each of the positions and what the purpose and function of various organizational units are, relative to each other.

The sequence of different positions is planned in advance, with both the individual's and the organization's needs in mind, so that two people do not always get exactly the same experience. In one major aircraft company, for example, a new trainee worked for six months in production at Los Angeles, four months in the finance division in Seattle, and another six months in the marketing division in Washington, D.C. Then the employee selected the division in which she wanted to work and, after consultation with supervisors in each division where she had trained, the personnel department assigned her a position.

Another type of job rotation system is **career progression planning.** Rather than a horizontal series of jobs, a vertical sequence is planned as the individual moves up the hierarchy of the organization. For instance, the first position may be as an assistant foreman in manufacturing, then foreman. From there the employee may move to a higher-level position in the personnel department, after which he may be promoted to assistant plant superintendent. This type of job rotation system is usually used with employees who are considered to have high potential; that is, those destined for high managerial positions.

Special Assignments

An individual may also undergo development through special assignment. For example, a manager may be assigned the responsibility of evaluating the organization's compensation program. In completing this assignment, the manager learns a great deal about compensation. Or a marketing manager may be assigned to a production committee to obtain a better appreciation of the problems in the production area. Such assignments are often tailored to the needs of the individual.

Delegation and Coaching

Delegation and coaching are also traditional developmental methods that can be quite effective. The subordinate is assigned—delegated—responsibility for a particular task, which he then carries out. He learns how to carry it out both by doing and by consulting with his superior when problems arise. Such a method works most effectively when the assignments made are challenging and when the superior spends sufficient time on coaching and provides useful feedback about the subordinate's performance. Research has shown that, as would be expected, a climate of helpfulness and supportiveness contributes to the effectiveness of coaching sessions,[55] and that supervisors will do a better job of coaching when they receive credits or rewards for their efforts and when they have received training in conducting performance appraisal and appraisals interviews.[56]

Management by Objectives as Development*

It would be more desirable not to have to resort to programs or strategies, as outlined above, but rather to build development into everyone's job. With management by objectives (MBO) this is done, because emphasis is placed on establishing goals, developing ways to achieve these goals, and providing feedback about how well someone has done. We discussed goal setting, an important facet of MBO, in detail in Chapter 10. There, however, we examined only performance objectives, which have to do with the work itself. Of course, this is developmental to the extent that a manager develops goals with subordinates that represent learning experiences for them. In addition to setting performance goals, however, MBO should take a more pointed orientation toward development. Managers should work out personal development goals with subordinates.

A personal development goal is an objective with increased human potential as an end. It should focus on improvement of skills and abilities, attitude change, or better interpersonal relationships. Every manager can, when needed, work out personal development goals for those who work for him or her.

These personal development goals must be based on problems or deficiencies, current or anticipated, technical skill, or interpersonal problem areas. They may also be aimed at developing a subordinate for transfer and promotion within the organization. The importance of personal development objectives lies in their potential for; combating obsolescence, given our rapid expansion of knowledge; for preparing people for increased responsibility; and for overcoming problems in organizational interactions.

---

*Management by objectives (MBO) was discussed in Chapter 10. We used the tern **working planning systems** there.

Setting development goals is probably more difficult than setting performance goals since they are personal in nature and, as such, must be handled with care and tact. This difficulty, of course, may be avoided by simply not setting them, and it could be argued that they should be avoided, since they are an intrusion into an individual's privacy by the superior or the organization. However, when perceived personal limitations hinder effective performance, the problem must be treated.

So, if at any time the superior believes an individual's limitations stand clearly in the way of the unit's goal achievement, that should be made known to the individual. He may not be aware that he is creating problems and would gladly change—if he were aware. Many technically competent people have been relieved from positions because of human problems they create. Many might have been retained had they only known that problems existed or were arising.

When there is a need for them, personal development objectives should be a basic part of the MBO program. If there is no real need, then an effort to set them probably will produce general and ambiguous objectives, tenable only if the organization wishes to invest in "education for education's sake." Personal objectives should attack deficiencies related to performance, containing specific action proposals for solving the problems.

Effectiveness of On-the-job Methods

There has been no research evaluating the use of various on-the-job methods. Organizations must, therefore, assess whether or not the costs of learning on the job are excessive. If so, then some sort of training away from work must be devised.

There are some important considerations to training. Perhaps much of the value of on-the-job development comes from the "modeling" effects noted earlier. This means that there must be careful selection of the model, and the situation in which it is hoped modeling behavior will occur can contribute to improved outcomes.

The primary problem with an on-the-job development strategy is the variability of supervisors under whom an individual will work. One supervisor may be strong developmentally, another weak, so that the progress of the trainee is impeded. Moreover, if supervisors are given the responsibility for such "temporary" employees, they may not spend adequate developmental time with the trainees, since the supervisor knows that the employee's ultimate assignment will be elsewhere than his or her own unit.

There is some evidence that changes do occur when MBO is used as a strategy for development. In an extensive study of MBO in two firms over a three-year period, managers reported changes in how they set goals, dealt with their bosses, and provided feedback to subordinates.[57]

SUMMARY

Ensuring that human resources are compatible with task and system requirements is one of the most important keys to an effective organization. Human resource planning is the first step in this process. A forecast of the future organization is prepared and skill requirements for it are determined. Then an audit of current human assets is conducted. This audit assesses the present performance and the promotability of those in the firm.

Comparing the results of the audit with the forecasted needs will give some indication of the specific staffing and development objectives that must be achieved. Development programs tend to be much more successful when they have specific rather than general change objectives. Change or development objectives can be aimed at an individual, group, or organization. The specific goals might be (1) increased skill and ability, (2) changing attitudes, (3) promoting intergroup cooperation, and/or (4) increased organization effectiveness.

These goals can be sought through off-the-job as well as on-the-job development efforts. What is of most importance in determining the success of any change effect is that it be reinforced by and congruent with the social system and the organizational structure within which it is sought.

Case
13.1   MISCO Industries

Gary High was appointed Training Director of MISCO Industries last week. His first assignment is to prepare a training strategy to increase the work effectiveness of first-line supervisory personnel.

These supervisory personnel all work in the shop, which is a continuous-process assembly line. There are ten shop supervisors, and each one has a crew of eighteen to twenty-five hourly workers assigned to his or her department. The work in the shop is machine paced, the speed of the operation determined by the production scheduling department.

Lately there have been quality problems. Scrap rates have shot up from 2 percent to 13 percent. A very careful investigation has concluded that these problems *cannot* be attributed to the equipment or to the materials.

Mary Vine, Gary's boss, thinks that the quality of supervision is not high. "The supervisors are capable," she told Gary, "but they need some training." Mary continued, "I don't know what to do, Gary. We have sent these supervisors all to the 'first-line supervisors' workshop. There are good trainers there and the content is fine. The supervisors go and seem to learn something, but when they return, the training doesn't last."

1. Why do you think the past training has failed?
2. If you were Gary High, how would you analyze this problem? What factors are important? Why?

Case
13.2   Vickery Limited

Ray Vickery is the crusty old manager and owner of Vickery Limited, a company that manufactures lawn furniture and garden implements. Vickery is growing rapidly because of the high-quality products that are attracting more customers. Ray now has twenty-five managerial personnel and a hundred hourly employees working for him.

Recently, Ray was asked by Joan Renato, a professor of management at the local university, to be a guest lecturer in her personnel management class. She wanted Ray to discuss his philosophy and practice of personnel management, particularly developing new managers.

Ray came to the class at the appointed time. After a few opening remarks, he said, "I believe that it is impossible to really develop managers. You can't train or teach someone how to be a good manager. You've got to be born with it."

Professor Renato was surprised. She thought that because Vickery was so successful that the firm would have quite an advanced personnel program. She was, apparently, quite mistaken.

She asked Ray, "Don't you think our university's Management Education Program for Executives is useful? Many firms send a lot of managers here for training."

"I believe they are wasting their time," Ray replied. "I think they are wasting money."

1. What are the differences between the philosophies of Ray Vickery and Joan Renato?
2. If you were Joan Renato, how would you rebut Ray's position?

DISCUSSION QUESTIONS

1. Explain the steps necessary for human resource planning.
2. What are the different skills that managers must be aware of if they are to forecast the future with any confidence?
3. Why would you think a human resource audit might prove important and/or useful? How easy or difficult do you think it is to assess human beings for this type of audit? Why?
4. The authors note that certain conditions must exist for change to take place. List these and explain them. Are there other factors that you feel should be included?
5. How can we relate change as presented in this chapter to work planning discussed previously?
6. Why is it so important that the managers be able to distinguish targets for development, that is, separate efforts directed at the individual, the group, or the organization?
7. Discuss the three basic stages of the development process.
8. Using Figure 13.2 as a base, discuss the developmental methods directed at the individual as compared to those directed at groups.
9. How does the diagnosis stage differ in the three categories that are the targets of development?
10. How would you deal with Ann Smith (item 13.1) in terms of explaining intrinsic versus extrinsic motivation? (See Chapter 15 for a discussion of intrinsic and extrinsic motivation.)
11. The integrated development model developed by Blake and Mouton[10] outlines steps for total change within an organization. Does this model seem feasible to work with? Why or why not?
12. Do you think "on-the-job" or "off-the-job" methods of development techniques are more effective? Why? When?

REFERENCES

1. Mann, F. "Toward an understanding of the leadership role in formal organization," in R. Dubin et al. (eds.), Leadership and productivity. San Francisco, Chandler Publishing, 1965.

2. Porter, L. W., and R. M. Steers. "Organizational work and personal factors in employee turnover and absenteeism," Psychological Bulletin 80 (1973): 151–176.

3. Hrebiniak, L. G., and M. R. Roteman. "A study of the relationship between need satisfaction and absenteeism among managerial personnel," Journal of Applied Psychology, 58 (1973): 381–383.

4. Dunnette, M. D. Personnel selection and placement. Belmont, Calif., Wadsworth, 1965.

5. Schein, E. "Management development as a process of influence," Industrial Management Review, 3 May (1961): 59–76.

6. Sykes, A. J. N. "The effects of a supervisory training course in changing supervisors' perceptions and expectations of the role of management," Human Relations, 15 (1962): 227–243.

7. House, R. J., and H. L. Tosi. "An experimental evaluation of a management training program," Academy of Management Journal, 6 (1963): 303–315.

8. Carroll, S. J., and A. N. Nash. "Some personal and situational correlates of reactions to management development programs," Academy of Management Journal, 13 (1970): 187–196.

9. French, W. L., and C. H. Bell. Organizational development. Englewood Cliffs, N.J., Prentice-Hall, 1978.

10. Blake, R., and J. Mouton. Building a dynamic corporation through GRID organizational development. Reading, Mass., Addison-Wesley, 1969.

11. Buxton, C. E. College teaching: A psychologist's view. New York, Harcourt-Brace, 1956.

12. Dietrick, D. C. "Review of research," in R. J. Hill (ed.), A comparative study of lecture and discussion methods. Pasadena, Calif., The Fund for Adult Education, 1960.

13. Stovall, T. F. "Lecture vs. discussion," Phi Delta Kappan, 39 (1958): 225–258.

14. Verner, C., and G. Dickinson. "The lecture, an analysis and review of research," Adult Education, 17 (1967): 85–100.

15. Anderson, R. C. "Learning in discussions: A resume of the authoritarian-democratic study," Harvard Educational Review, 29 (1959): 201–205.

16. Filley, A. C., and F. H. Reighard. "A preliminary survey of training attitudes and needs among actual and potential attendees at management institute programs," Madison, University of Wisconsin, 1962; cited in R. J. House, "Managerial reactions to two methods of management training," Personnel Psychology, 18 (1965): 311–319.

17. House, R. J. "An experiment in the use of management training standards," Journal of the Academy of Management, 5 (1962): 76–81.

18. Mann, J. H., and C. H. Mann. "The importance of group tasks in producing group-member personality and behavior change," Human Relations, 221 (1959): 75–80.

19. Schramm, W. "What we know about learning from instructional television," in Educational television—the next ten years. Stanford, Stanford University Press, 1962.

20. Nash, A. N., J. P. Muczyk, and F. L. Vettori. "The relative practical effectiveness of programmed instruction," Personnel Psychology, 24 (1971): 397–418.

21. Hughes, J. L., and W. J. McNamara. "A comparative study of programmed and conventional instruction in industry," Journal of Applied Psychology, 45 (1961): 225–231.

22. Neidt, C. O., and T. Meredith. "Changes in attitudes of learners when programmed

instruction is interpolated between two conventional instruction experiences," Journal of Applied Psychology, 50 (1966): 130–137.

23. Guetzkow, H., E. L. Kelly, and W. J. McKeachie. "An experimental comparison of recitation, discussion, and tutorial methods in college teaching," Journal of Educational Psychology, 45 (1954): 193–207.

24. Harris, C. W. (ed.). Encyclopedia of educational research. New York, Macmillan, 1960.

25. Hughes, J. L. "Effects of changes in programmed text format and reduction in classroom time on achievement and attitudes of industrial trainees," Journal of Programmed Instruction, 1 (1963): 143–155.

26. Dill, W. R., and N. Doppelt. "The acquisition of experience in a complex management game," Management Science, 10 (1963): 30–46.

27. McKenney, J. L. "An evaluation of a business game in an MBA curriculum," The Journal of Business, 35 (1962): 278–286.

28. Raia, A. P. "A study of the educational value of management games," The Journal of Business, 39 (1966): 339–352.

29. Butler, E. D. "An experimental study of the case method in teaching the social foundations of education," Dissertation Abstracts, 27 (1967): 2912.

30. Fox, W. M. "A measure of the effectiveness of the case method in teaching human relations," Personnel Administration, 26 (1962): 53–57.

31. Castore, G. F. "Attitudes of students toward the case method of instruction in a human relations course," Journal of Educational Research, 45 (1951): 201–213.

32. Bond, B. W. "The group discussion-decision approach: An appraisal of its use in health education," Dissertation Abstracts, 16 (1956): 903.

33. Levine, J., and J. Butler, "Lecture vs. group decision in changing behavior," Journal of Applied Psychology, 36 (1952): 29–33.

34. Lewin, K. "Group decision and social change," in E. E. Maccoby, T. Newcomb, E. L. Hartley (eds.), Readings in social psychology. New York, Holt, 1958.

35. Bolda, R. A., and C. H. Lawshe. "Evaluation of role playing," Personnel Administration, 25 (1962): 40–42.

36. Culbertson, F. "Modification of an emotionally held attitude through role playing," Journal of Abnormal and Social Psychology, 54 (1957): 230–233.

37. Janis, I., and B. King. "The influence of role playing on opinion change," Journal of Abnormal and Social Psychology, 49 (1954): 211–218.

38. King, B., and I. Janis. "Comparison of the effectiveness of improvised vs. non-improvised role playing in producing opinion changes," Human Relations, 9 (1956): 177–186.

39. Janis, I., and L. Mann. "Effectiveness of emotional role-playing in modifying smoking habits and attitudes," Journal of Experimental Research in Personality, 1 (1965): 84–90.

40. Solem, A. R. "Human relations training: Comparisons of case study and role playing," Personnel Administration, 23 (1960): 29–37.

41. Maier, N. R. F. "An experimental test of the effect of training on discussion leadership," Human Relations, 6 (1953): 161–173.

42. Maier, N. R. F., and R. A. Maier. "An experimental test of the effects of 'developmental' vs. 'free' discussions on the quality of group decisions," Journal of Applied Psychology, 41 (1957): 320–322.

43. Maier, N. R. F., and L. R. Hoffman. "Quality of first and second solutions in group problem solving," Journal of Applied Psychology, 44 (1960): 278–283.

44. Maier, N. R. F. "Using trained 'developmental' discussion leaders to improve further the quality of group decisions." Journal of Applied Psychology, 44 (1960): 247–251.

45. Maier, N. R. F., and A. R. Solem. "The contribution of the discussion leader to the quality of group thinking," Human Relations, 3 (1952): 155–174.

46. Van Schacck, H., Jr. "Naturalistic role playing: A method of interview training for student personnel administrators," Dissertation Abstracts, 17 (1957): 801.

47. Boyd, J. B., and J. D. Ellis. Findings of Research into Senior Management Seminars. Toronto: The Hydro-Electric Power Commission of Toronto, 1962. Cited by J. P. Campbell and M. D. Dunnette, "Effectiveness of T-group experiences in managerial training and development," Psychological Bulletin, 70 (1968): 73–104.

48. Bunker, D. R. "Individual applications of laboratory training," Journal of Applied Behavioral Science, 1 (1965): 131–148.

49. Miles, M. B. "Changes during and following laboratory training: A clinical-experimental study," Journal of Applied Behavioral Science, 1 (1965): 215–242.

50. Underwood, W. J. "Evaluation of laboratory method training," Training Directors Journal, 19 (1965): 34–40.

51. Valiquet, I. M. "Contribution to the evaluation of a management development program," unpublished master's thesis. Massachusetts Institute of Technology, 1964. Cited by J. P. Campbell and M. D. Dunnette, "Effectiveness of T-group experiences in managerial training and development," Psychological Bulletin, 70 (1968): 73–104.

52. Smith, P. N. "Attitude changes associated with training in human relations," British Journal of Social and Clinical Psychology, 3 (1964): 104–113.

53. Campbell, J. P., and M. D. Dunnette. "Effectiveness of T-group experiences in managerial training and development," Psychological Bulletin, 70 (1968): 73–104.

54. Bandura, A. Principles of behavior modification. New York, Holt, Rinehart and Winston, 1969.

55. Carroll, S. J., and H. Tosi. Management by objectives: Applications and research. New York, Macmillan, 1973.

56. Douglas, J., and C. Crain. "Activity reaction forms: Measurement of dyadic perceptions of managers using a management by objectives program." Working paper presented at Midwest Academy of Management. University of Michigan, Ann Arbor, Michigan, April, 1975.

57. Tosi, H. L., J. Hunter, R. J. Chesser, J. Tarter, and S. J. Carroll. "How real are charges induced by management by objectives?" Administrative Science Quarterly, 21 (1976): 278–305.

CHAPTER FOURTEEN

Leadership

Harry Louis

Harry Louis has been with Stone Mountain Insurance Company for twenty years. He began with SMIC shortly after he graduated from high school. He had no chance to go on to college to study law, his dream from childhood, because he had to contribute to the support of his parents, brothers, and sisters.

As an agent he enjoyed enormous success. Year after year he led his office in sales production. After sixteen years with Stone Mountain, Harry was promoted to staff manager. A staff manager supervises six to nine agents and is responsible for their performance.

His first staff was a challenge. Mike Hesley, the District Manager who appointed Harry told him, "Harry, in this district the staff you have was 250th out of 250. Go to it. Let's see how you can do with this bunch of losers." Hesley couldn't find another prospective staff manager, so he picked Harry Louis as a last resort. Louis didn't fit Hesley's concept of a staff manager. Harry dressed in a conservative style, not quite as fashionable as Hesley thought a manager should. Harry spoke in a quiet voice, not an overpowering, firm voice that Hesley preferred. Harry also had a different approach to selling than Hesley. Harry refused to sell any insurance policy that he didn't think was right for the client. Hesley thought that Harry was too conservative in his sales efforts. Still, Harry got results. He was consistently the office sales leader, and the rate at which his clients canceled insurance was among the lowest in the whole region. Hesley concluded that he didn't have much to lose by promoting Louis. The staff couldn't be any worse, and he would demonstrate that he rewarded good sales performance with more than pay.

"A manager's job has to be easier than this," mused Harry as he wondered how to approach this first supervising job. So, he began. Two agents resigned because the work was too hard. Harry began spending many hours with the remaining staff members. "Hell," he realized, "these men don't know how to sell insurance." He trained them carefully. The staff learned the importance of developing prospects, being well prepared, being quite persistent, and simply working long hard hours.

Harry set goals for each one of the staff members. These were different for each person, set depending on the sales potential of each territory. The goals were challenging but realistic. When one of his agents had problems and wanted help from Harry, he was there.

Harry did not hurry to fill the two vacancies on his staff. He looked around among his acquaintances and carefully recruited Frank and Joe, salesmen in a local department store whom Harry had known since high school.

Eighteen months after he had been appointed staff manager, Harry's staff had improved, almost miraculously. The staff had risen in the rankings from last (250th place) to 110th place. Harry had taken them into the "upper division."

At just about the time that Harry was beginning to think he could relax, Mike Hesley invited Harry to lunch. Mike said, "Harry, you're going to get another chance to prove you are a good manager. I am giving you Charlie's staff. Charlie wants to sell again and his health isn't good. Let's see how you can do. Go get it, boy!"

Harry felt a lump in his throat. He knew that Charlie Collins' staff was terrible. They ranked 193rd in the district and had never been above 160th since Charlie took over.

So he began again; training, coaching, setting goals, recruiting, hiring, and firing.

Gradually the staff began to improve, though not as rapidly as his first one. At the end of the first twelve months, the staff ranked 145th, but at the end of the second year, the Collins' staff was 50th in the district.

Mike Hesley couldn't figure out how Harry did it. He never thought Harry would do so well. Harry didn't look like a manager, he didn't even act like one. Some way or other, though, Harry got the staff to produce extremely well.

Managers know from their experience that leadership matters. We have all read of failing companies that were turned around because of leadership. Similar things occur in sports. In 1978, early in the professional basketball season, the Seattle Supersonics had one of the worst records of all teams. The coach was replaced, and the team reached the championship finals. Was it the coach? Or was it the players?

Leadership is a rather interesting phenomenon. We can see it when it is present, as during the era of Martin Luther King, Jr., and the civil rights movement. It is also obvious when it is absent, as when a football team gets confused because no one takes charge.

But it is rather difficult—perhaps impossible—to create or select leaders. By that we mean that so little is known about what makes a good leader that it is very difficult to predict who will be effective as a leader. For example, Mike Hesley, the district manager of Stone Mountain Insurance, never thought that Harry Louis would be such an effective leader (item 14.1).

WHY DO PEOPLE COMPLY?

Leadership is the process of influencing others to do what you want them to do. Such a concept may seem simple enough on the surface, but in reality it is quite complex. Suppose Harry Louis asks an agent to work some evening to meet a prospect. The agent agrees. Has Harry exercised "leadership"? Perhaps, and perhaps not. Maybe the agent needs the extra pay, or perhaps he works because he knows he is needed, or because he is afraid he will lose his job if he does not.

Many things that people do at work—following orders, doing what is required of them, working harder than is necessary—cannot be explained in terms of leadership alone. This is why we should start our discussion of leadership not by asking, "How does one person influence others?" but by asking, "Why do people comply?"

THE PSYCHOLOGICAL CONTRACT

A powerful, but relatively simple, concept that can account for a great deal of compliance in organizations is the psychological contract. Schein states the concept of the psychological contract in this way:

> The individual has a variety of expectations of the organization and the organization a variety of expectations of him. These expectations not only cover how much work is to be performed for how much pay, but also involve the whole pattern of rights, privileges, and obligation between the worker and organization.[1]

Basically this implies that people in any situation—including at work—will do many things because they believe they should. And for what they do, they expect reciprocation in the form of pay, benefits, and favors.

The content of the psychological contract is affected by what one has learned and experienced before he or she arrives in an organization and by what the organization needs. The professional, the organizationalist, and the indifferent all, because of their different values, strike different "bargains" with their work organization. Socialization experiences contribute to the development of personal values, which usually cause the individual to feel that it is "right," under certain circumstances, for those in higher authority to tell him and others what to do. When the individual feels this direction to be right, the authority is said to have "legitimate" power.

Legitimate power refers to whether or not a person subjected to an attempt to influence by another believes it is proper for the other person to influence him or her. Legitimacy stems from the internalized values of a person. The organizationalist, for example, believes that many directives from a superior are legitimate. The professional may feel more legitimacy in influence from colleagues. The indifferent responds primarily to organization demands so long as they are made during job hours.

The legitimate power of a person over others is not unlimited. As Barnard has pointed out, organizational members believe that some directives from a leader are legitimate and some are not.[2] The psychological contract defines that set of directives that will be followed without question, since they are clearly legitimate for a superior to make. Directives that fall outside the psychological contract are considered nonlegitimate by those to whom they are given.

The Boundaries of the Psychological Contract

The psychological contract is not static. It often changes by mutual consent, as when a person is promoted and expected to put forth more effort for the increased pay, status, and privileges that come with the new position. Sometimes it is changed by pressures from one or the other of the parties, as when a union is able to obtain increased hourly wage rates from management or when a manager makes a new work assignment that a subordinate accepts, even grudgingly.

As long as the request, commands, directives, and suggestions fall within the boundaries of the psychological contract, there will be compliance with them. Figure 14.1 shows the psychological contract of a salesperson on Harry Louis' staff. In general, he will do without question anything that falls within the public boundaries of his contract. The *public boundaries* encompass those things he wants others, especially his superior, to believe he will do as part of his job. They are generally-agreed-upon work activities. But they do not represent the effective outer limits of his bargain with the organization. The real boundaries for the salesman are broader. He will do more than is represented by the "public" zone. The real boundaries do, however, define the limits beyond which he will not go.

For tactical reasons, the salesman may want his superior to believe that the public boundaries of his psychological contract represent his actual limits. Then

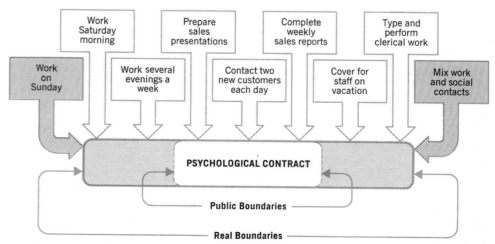

FIGURE 14.1   Public and real boundaries or the psychological contract of a salesperson.

when he complies with requests that fall between his public and real boundaries, he will appear to be giving up something. He may do this to extract a "favor" at some future date. He has made it appear that he has gone beyond the normal call of duty and thus expects a quid pro quo—a favor—in return for exceeding the normal requirements of his job. Suppose, for example, that in the past he has created the impression that he believes he should not have to cover when another staff member is ill. When Harry Louis asks him to do so and the salesman complies, he may feel that Harry now owes him a concession of some kind in return. He may well be able to have his superior feel that way, too.

It is when an individual receives orders that fall outside the real boundaries that problems begin to occur. Any request beyond these real limits is excluded from the range of things the salesman will normally do. For example, if asked to work on Sundays or to perform clerical tasks he may resign.

However, as we have said earlier, the boundaries of the psychological contract can be moved. When faced with a request to act outside the real boundaries, the person may decide to comply, especially if no other job alternatives are available. Thus, a person who is pressured by his superiors to act in a way he does not want to, may do so, but at great personal and psychological cost. This would be true if he cannot find a job elsewhere or must stay in the organization for some other reason.

LEADERSHIP, ADMINISTRATION, AND THE PSYCHOLOGICAL CONTRACT

Accomplishing goals through others is done by means of administration as well as leadership. There is, however, a significant difference between these two concepts. By **administration** we mean the use of the prerogatives, techniques, and rights associated with one's position in an organization, such as making decisions and giving directions. Managerial tools such as budgets, standard operating procedures, compensation systems, plans, and other control mechanisms are the devices used in the administrative process. When these are used to obtain compliance from subordinates, within the real boundaries of the psychological contract, it is administration, not leadership.

Administration is an important concept, for it means that a very significant part of what a manager does can be taught. The way to design these administrative tools, as well as their effective use, can be taught to others by commonly used teaching methods. For instance, a person can learn how to prepare a budget, design a procedure, or develop a compensation program.

Understanding the boundaries of the psychological contract and requiring subordinates to perform within the real boundaries rather than the more narrow public boundaries is part of the administrative process. Generally, reasonable requests from a superior, although they may be outside the public boundaries of the psychological contract, are within the real boundaries, and typically subordinates will do more things if they are asked. For example, much of Harry Louis' success after he took charge of the staff was due to the fact that he asked staff members to perform in the zone between the public and real boundaries of the psychological contract.

Often, however, there is a need to go beyond even the real boundaries. Obtaining compliance to requests beyond the real boundaries of the psychological contract is leadership. Katz and Kahn "consider the essence of organizational leadership to be the influential increment over and above mechanical compliance with a routine directive of the organization."[3] When a person is able to broaden or expand the real boundaries of another's zone of indifference, either permanently or temporarily, it is an act of leadership. Some of the ways in which one might shift the boundaries of the psychological contract are: (1) fear or threat, (2) reciprocity, (3) reinforcement, (4) job design, (5) team building, (6) competition, and (7) ego involvement. These managerial strategies are discussed in Chapter 16.

It is possible to learn and to improve administrative skills in schools and by experience, but the elusive dimension of the manager's job is the leadership process. While it is easy to conceptualize why people comply (the psychological contract) and the bases of power (organizational, skill, and personal), it is extremely difficult to characterize the qualities, or behavior, of individuals who exert influence and are capable of managing in a way to achieve organizational goals.

POWER—THE BASIS OF COMPLIANCE

Influence is a process, a series of actions that one initiates intended to get another person to do something. When one is successful at influencing another—either because the influence attempt falls within the boundaries of the psychological contract or because the boundaries are moved—power has been exercised.

Power is a force one can use to obtain compliance. Power, the force, is activated in the influence process. The use of power is leadership. People act and decisions get made. Things happen when power is exercised.

Power comes from several different bases: (1) organizational factors, (2) skill and/or expertise, and (3) the personal qualities of the leader. These relationships are shown in Figure 14.2.

ORGANIZATIONAL FACTORS

Organizationally based power resides in the position, not the person in it. The person may only use it. When he leaves the position, he loses this power base. For instance, the production control manager in one plant determines when different products are scheduled for assembly. When John Smith is production control manager, he makes scheduling decisions. When he is transferred, and his assistant Ruth Jones becomes production control manager, she makes scheduling decisions. Two organizational factors—formal authority and organizational location—are determinants of power inherent in a position.

Formal Authority

Formal authority is the right of decision and command a person derives from the position held. These decision-making rights are delegated from higher organizational levels. In a managerial position, one has the right to allocate resources, make decisions, and distribute rewards in certain amounts and under certain conditions,

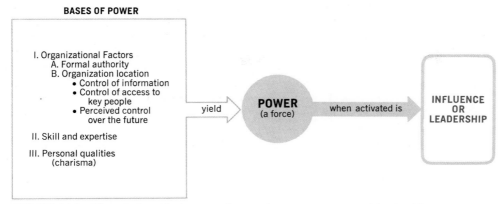

BASES OF POWER

I. Organizational Factors
   A. Formal authority
   B. Organization location
      • Control of information
      • Control of access to
        key people
      • Perceived control
        over the future

II. Skill and expertise

III. Personal qualities
    (charisma)

yield

POWER
(a force)

when activated is

**INFLUENCE
OR
LEADERSHIP**

FIGURE 14.2   The relationship between bases of power, power, and leadership.

typically specified in the job description. The responsibility corresponding to the rights of a person in a position is the obligation to perform well.

Formal authority is the amount of designated discretion that an individual has in determining who gets what. In most instances, the higher the position, the greater the discretion. Consider the case of a manufacturing vice president. His position may give him discretionary power over how to expend funds for capital investments, who at lower levels in the manufacturing division should be promoted, and so forth. These will be the rights of anyone in the position of manufacturing vice president.

Influence can be exercised in other ways than through decision making. A person in a high-status position in an organization, whether the status derives from the position's importance or level, can exercise a great deal of control over who interacts with him, and when. For example, a subordinate generally sees his superior at the superior's convenience, not his own. And, typically, the superior will determine how long the meeting lasts.

Those at higher levels make another significant decision that gives them much power. The higher the position, the more likely it is that the incumbent will be able to determine either who gets promoted or what criteria are used to determine promotions. Thus, those in higher positions usually have significant effects on the career patterns of those in lower positions. This leads people, generally, to respond to influence from those at higher levels.

Organization Location

The location of a position within an organization setting may be a base of power, sometimes without regard to the level of the position. In some positions, for example, a great amount of important information is collected for dissemination to other organization points. ***Desired information, when controlled, gives power to the person who has it.*** The finance group may have information about future spending plans and plant site locations, for instance. If there is internal competition among managers for, say, the positions of plant manager at these new plants, having advance information that others do not have can give those who have it an advantage in making the strongest possible personal case for a plant managership. The finance group, with the information, has power.

Control over access to key people is another source of organizational power. In order to see the president, we may have to clear an appointment with his or her administrative assistant. In such a case lower-level personnel have a great deal of influence over others in the organization at higher levels.

Perceived control over the future is another source of lower-level influence. The personnel unit is a classic example of this case. Often managers, rightly or wrongly, feel that those on the personnel staff have a great deal of influence over whether or not they get future assignments. So in their efforts to insure favorable consideration, they often comply with requests from personnel staff in order to stay on their "good side."

SKILL AND EXPERTISE

Sometimes a person may be successful with attempts to influence because he or she presumably has more skill or knowledge in a particular area than most people do. It is common practice to rely on expert opinion in our personal lives, accepting the advice of accountants, lawyers, and doctors because we believe their training and knowledge can solve problems. At work, the same thing happens. In designing and implementing a computer-based management information system, we rely on computer experts to define the capacity of the equipment and what it can provide. When a customer threatens legal action, we go to the company's attorney for advice. When the director of engineering wants to know company policy on travel expenses, she will call the administrative assistant in personnel.

Expert power is very specific to the type of problem and to the person with the skill. We are unlikely to ask the company attorney for marketing advice, or the computer programmer for legal advice. Expert power is task-specific, but—more important for this discussion—it is generally associated with a particular person. It is not easily transferred to another person, as is organizationally based power. When a person becomes a plant manager, he generally has the same formal authority as the previous manager, but a person gets expert power only through demonstrating competence or by having it "given" because he or she has the appropriate education, experience, and appearance. When an individual with expert power leaves the organization, his or her replacement will probably not have the same amount of influence, even though he or she may have the same organizational title.

PERSONAL CHARACTERISTICS OF THE LEADER

In some cases individuals are susceptible to influence because they identify with another person. French and Raven call this "referent power."[4] Referent power is based largely on the attraction exerted by an individual on another person, or on a group. The stronger the attraction, the stronger the power.

Identification with another may come about because he or she possesses personal characteristics and qualities highly valued by the group, such as family background, appearance, or athletic ability. Or the identification may come about because of the leader's ability to articulate the values and concerns of the followers.

Persons who exert this kind of influence are called "charismatic" leaders. They have the loyalty and commitment of their followers, not because they have a particular skill or are in a particular position, but because their followers respond to them as individuals. Like the skill and expertise power base, this power base is unique to the individual and the situation. Charismatic influence cannot be transferred to another person.

LEADERSHIP, POWER, AND DEPENDENCE

Leadership can be viewed in terms of dependence. If a leader can influence others, it is because they are dependent upon him. This dependence can arise because of psychological identification or because someone has the power to allocate rewards—pay increases, promotions, or prestige and status symbols. Dependence can also occur because a person can impose objective sanctions—disciplinary actions, demotions, or removal of rights.

Subjective rewards and sanctions are less tangible; they exist in the mind of the individual. Recognition or disapproval from a supervisor may or may not be viewed as a reward or a sanction by subordinates; it depends upon their esteem for him. A way to increase leadership effectiveness is to increase the dependency of the subordinate on either the manager or the organization.

POWER AND TYPE OF ORGANIZATION

Since mechanistic and organic organizations have different patterns of structural relationships and different organization personality types among their members, it follows that the bases or sources of power will also be different in the two.

Power in Mechanistic Organizations

In mechanistic organizations power will be distributed as a function of
1. The formal authority system
2. The possession of important information
3. The making of recommendations that are likely to be accepted
4. The importance of the unit's function

   1. The formal authority system. Status differences between management levels are maintained because of the nature of resource-allocation decisions in a stable organization. Resources are allocated from the top of the hierarchy down, and at each level how much is passed on to lower levels is usually a relatively unilateral decision. Managers are likely to hoard resources, maintaining discretionary funds where possible, which means that lower levels of management must constantly go to the higher levels to obtain additional resources. Since the organization is relatively stable, there are few external pressures to change this resource-allocation process, and this leads to concentrations of power and to conflict.

   2. The power of information. A person must understand a job before he or she can do it. He must know how decisions are made before he can influence them. He must know what criteria are used in making decisions before he can work to achieve them.

In some organizations, for instance, budgeting units are extremely influential because information flows to them from several different units. This information is reshaped into budget proposals. It would be useful for a manager to have information about the budgetary allocations of other units in order to present her own case in the most favorable way. Because they hope to obtain such information, some managers will respond to demands from the budgeting unit that go far beyond its scope of formally defined authority.

3. *The power of recommendation.* Over time certain individuals and departments develop the capacity to influence others' decisions. For example, the president of a major magazine publisher relied heavily on advice from a trusted colleague who started the business with him but who, for personal reasons, never achieved high position. This confidant was at least four organization levels below the president, but when major decisions were under consideration, his advice was sought and usually heeded. This led many managers at all levels to seek the confidant's assistance in gaining the president's ear.

Personnel departments often have similar influence, especially in large, dispersed organizations. When the manager of the branch plant away from headquarters needs a production supervisor, the personnel department may supply the list of potential candidates. Those who aspire to success in the firm know that the personnel department can be of great help to them. In many firms personnel files are closely guarded to prevent individuals from learning how their performance is evaluated and what they can expect in the way of promotions. This is a common form of secrecy. When questioned about the reason for not telling an employee about what has been planned for him, a personnel executive said,

> "It can cause more headaches than it's worth. Suppose we think someone is capable of taking over the Birmingham plant in a year and it looks like the plant manager will be moved to make room. If the economy changes, or any number of things happen to freeze the present plant manager in his position, we can't promote the person. He'll be disappointed, frustrated, and may leave because he feels we haven't kept our promise, even though we never really made one."

4. *The importance of the unit's function.* The balance of power between the production and boundary-spanning systems is an important relationship. Most organizations will find that one function is more critical than another, and the unit performing the critical function will generally have the most power. How can this happen in a mechanistic organization? Suppose that a firm has a captive market; suppose it is the primary producer of product A and can sell all it can produce. As long as such demand exists, the production function will be the most powerful in the firm, especially if there are manufacturing problems that might restrict output if not effectively overcome. The production function is the controlling factor, and thus the most powerful. In another firm, production problems may be minimal, while the chief problem will be to keep sales constant or growing. In such a firm, marketing will be the dominant unit.

The dominant unit, being more influential, will receive larger budget allocations. It may also have access to important information. This advantaged position may cause those in other units to be more aggressive in their dealings with it, breeding discontent and coordination problems that hinder effective cooperation.

Because of the need to adapt to constantly changing environmental demands, the location of power in the organic organization is more likely to change than in the mechanistic. In the organic organization, power will be a function of

1. Expertise and skill
2. Boundary positions
3. Financial interest in the organization
4. Project priority

   1. *Expertise and skill.* An organic organization succeeds or fails depending on whether or not the technical competence is present. The organization may be more dependent on the expert than vice-versa. It is unlikely that managers possess the technical skill required to evaluate alternatives and design projects well, because, even though they may have had technical skill early in a career, moving into an administrative job makes it difficult to maintain competence in rapidly developing and changing fields. In organic organizations, this leads to hierarchical (formal position) power being less important.

   2. *Boundary positions.* Those positions in an organization that interface with the external environment are called *boundary positions*. Individuals in boundary positions must have the ability to interpret changing environmental conditions and translate them into meaningful actions for the organization. Such individuals will have a great deal of power because their ability to do this is important, indeed critical, to the survival of the organization.

   3. *Financial interest.* In a smaller organization where the ownership is not broadly dispersed among a large number of small shareholders, financial interest can be especially powerful. That is, an owner can exert a great deal of influence on the setting of organizational objectives—and he may do this completely arbitrarily, with only minimal competence.

   4. *The priority of a project.* The priority assigned a project can be another base of power. Managers in charge of a project assigned a high priority will have a great deal of power in the organization. For example, a firm may have three projects under way simultaneously. One may involve several million dollars; the other two, only several hundreds of thousands of dollars each. Obviously, the economic success of the firm is more contingent on the first than on the last two, and the manager of the first will have much more organizational power than the managers of the other two.

LEADERSHIP: THEORIES AND RESEARCH

Leadership has been the subject of much study, research, and theory. The ultimate purpose of this study and research, of course, is to be able to select those individuals most likely to be able to influence others to achieve organizational goals, then to place them in a position that enhances this capacity.

Early research studied leadership as a collection of personal traits and characteristics. Subsequently, research emphasized a behavioral approach that looked upon leadership as a series of acts, or a behavioral repertoire, designed to help a group achieve its objectives. Viewed from this perspective, leadership was seen as acting out a set of behaviors that would vary, depending upon the group's need for greater task effectiveness, member satisfaction, and cohesiveness. More recently, attention has been directed toward developing "contingency" theories of leadership. This view recognizes the fact that effective leadership is a function of the situation in which leader and followers interact.

THE TRAIT APPROACH TO LEADERSHIP

The underlying premise of the trait approach to leadership is that leadership is an attribute of personality, that a certain identifiable trait or collection of traits makes a person effective as a leader, and that better organizational results can be obtained by selecting as leaders those who have these identifiable qualities.

There are literally hundreds of suggested lists of the traits of a good leader. Trustworthiness, initiative, good judgment, and honesty, are examples of these proposed leadership traits. Hundreds of studies sought this "magic list" of traits with little success. By 1948 Stogdill reviewed many of these studies and concluded that the long lists of leadership traits simply were not useful or theoretically sound.[5] There seem to be no readily identifiable traits related to possession of leadership status, or to effectiveness as a leader, in all situations.[5]

This may, however, be principally because the research has been done with leaders in a wide variety of situations and jobs. When studies are more situation-specific—for example, relating various personal characteristics to managerial (a special kind of leadership, as we noted earlier) success—consistencies are found. Dunnette,[6] for instance, reviewing research on traits associated with executive success, found that successful executives tend to be dominant, self-confident, and assertive and to have a high aspiration level as well as a general success pattern throughout life. Ghiselli[7] found self-perceived intelligence, initiative, supervisory ability, self-assurance, and occupational level to be positively related to general management success in terms of upward mobility and rated job success.

One reason for some of the difficulty in finding leadership traits is that mere possession of a characteristic is not in itself a sufficient condition for assuming a leadership (or management) position and then being successful. Many people have high enough levels of intelligence, but not all wish to be in leadership or managerial positions. In addition, the characteristics related to leadership do not operate singly, but in combination. Thus, individuals who seek the responsibilities of leadership and who possess the combination of traits commonly associated with success as a leader—such as initiative, self-confidence, and persistence—have an advantage over those individuals without these characteristics or those who have them but lack the interest.[8] (Many of the references in this chapter can be found in the extensive review of research and theory on leadership by Stogdill.[8])

Some early leadership scholars concluded that situational factors determined who would emerge as the leader.[9] Today it is recognized that individual characteristics and situational factors are important. As Stogdill[8] points out: "Most recent theorists maintain that leader characteristics and situational demands interact to determine the extent to which a given leader will prove successful in a group."

Disappointment and failure with the trait approach led a change in the direction of research and theory. Instead of looking at what a leader is (a trait), the research on leadership behavior aimed at finding out what a leader does. Many studies sought to relate specific behaviors of individuals in managerial, supervisory, or leadership positions to group effectiveness—that is, the productivity and satisfaction of group members.

Some of the earliest studies focused on very specific behavior. The different supervisors of groups with high and low performance, or with high or low satisfaction levels, were compared with respect to the amount of time they spent planning, how they disciplined employees, communication patterns, the amount of recognition given to subordinates, the amount of pressure exerted for higher production, and other supervisory behaviors.

Many studies have been conducted on how much influence the leader allowed subordinates in the decision-making process.[8] From these studies, a particular classification system for describing leader and managerial behavior became popular. In these studies, following the early work by Lewin, Lippitt, and White,[10] leaders were described in one or more of the following terms:

1. *Autocratic* or dictatorial. The leader makes all decisions and allows the subordinates no influence in the decision-making process. These supervisors are often indifferent to the personal needs of subordinates.

2. *Participative* or democratic. These supervisors consult with their subordinates on appropriate matters. They allow their subordinates some influence in the decision-making process. In addition, this type of supervisor is not punitive and treats his subordinates with dignity and kindness.

3. *Laissez-faire* or free reign. Supervisors in this group allow their group to have complete autonomy. They rarely supervise directly, so the group makes many on-the-job decisions itself.

Thus, the amount of influence of either the superior or the subordinate can be viewed on a continuum, as in Figure 14.3.

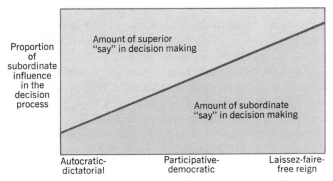

FIGURE 14.3   Subordinate influence in decision making.

Many research studies have directly compared the autocratic and democratic styles of leadership. Such studies usually show that the democratic, or participative, leadership style is associated with higher subordinate satisfaction. High performance is also often present under democratic leadership, but there are no consistent performance differences between democratic and autocratic styles—in some studies there were no performance differences between groups even though different leaders used different approaches. However, the participative style is more often associated with greater acceptance of change and more organization identification than is the autocratic.[8]

The relationship of the laissez-faire supervisory style to satisfaction and performance has not been studied as extensively as the autocratic and democratic leadership styles. What little research has been done seems to indicate that subordinate satisfaction and performance under laissez-faire is less than under the democratic approach but higher than under the autocratic approach.[11]

The Ohio State Studies

Beginning in the late 1940s and continuing through the 1950s, a group of researchers at Ohio State University conducted extensive studies of leadership effectiveness in industrial, military, and educational institutions. These studies were supported by large grants from the government. After World War II there was much interest in seeking ways to improve leadership and selection, for obvious reasons. If it was possible to select and train leaders more effectively, this would minimize costs incurred if we picked a poor manager and had to wait for improvement. For the military it meant they could select and train officers more easily, thereby allowing more rapid expansion of the services, important particularly in the event of war.

The Ohio State research ranged from the development of instruments to measure leadership to the evaluation of factors that might determine group effectiveness. From these studies emerged two leader behavior characteristics often associated with group effectiveness:

1. *Consideration.* The extent to which the individual is likely to have job relationships characterized by mutual trust; respect for subordinates' ideas, and consideration of their feelings. High scorers tend to have good rapport and two-way communication with subordinates.

2. *Initiating structure.* The extent to which an individual is likely to define and structure his role and those of his subordinates toward goal attainment. High scorers are those who play an active role in directing group activities and communicating information, scheduling, and trying out new ideas.

According to the Ohio State studies, effective leaders were high on both these measures. That is, the leader had to show both a concern for those who worked in the group (high consideration) and an ability to plan, organize, and control its activities (high initiating structure). The two factors are measured with a scale called the "Leader Behavior Description Questionnaire" (LBDQ), the widespread use of which facilitates comparison of results from different efforts. Here are some examples of the kinds of descriptions of leader behavior on the scale. Subordinates were asked to indicate how frequently their supervisor behaved in the way stated in the question.

"Initiating Structure" items

1. He lets members know what is expected of them.
2. He encourages the use of uniform procedures.
3. He decides what shall be done and how it shall be done.

"Consideration" items

1. He is friendly and approachable.
2. He treats all members of the group as his equals.
3. He gives advance notice of changes.

Most studies show that consideration is generally related to high employee satisfaction; it is related much less often to high performance, although occasionally it is so related.[8] In a number of studies, initiating structure has been found to be related to high job satisfaction, less often to high productivity, low absenteeism, and low turnover.[8] However, in other studies no relationship of any kind was found between initiating structure and subordinate behavior.

The relationship of consideration and initiating structure to performance and satisfaction varies from one study to another. Some of the inconsistencies are due to the fact that there are very different organization settings where these studies have been done. Other discrepancies may arise because researchers use slightly different versions of the LBDQ, and thus arrive at different conclusions.[12] Some researchers might try to adapt it to a particular site in which data are being collected by changing the wording of the questions. For instance, an item above might be changed to read "He encourages the use of uniform procedures *in the CALCAL company.*" Making several changes like this could produce different results.

The Michigan Studies

The Institute for Social Research at the University of Michigan was formed after World War II. This group has made significant empirical, theoretical, and practical contributions to the study of leadership and organizational effectiveness. They conducted a number of leadership studies in offices, railroad settings, and service industries. From their studies they concluded that leadership behavior could be described in terms of two dimensions, *"production centered"* or *"employee centered."* These are similar to those used by the Ohio State group, but there is an important difference. In the early stages of the Michigan studies, leaders were described as engaging in behavior that was either production-centered or employee-centered.[8] This was different from the Ohio studies, since the Ohio studies attempted to characterize an individual on both the dimensions.

The production-centered supervisor was defined as one primarily concerned with achieving high levels of production and viewing subordinates merely as instruments for doing this. The employee-centered supervisor, on the other hand, was one concerned about subordinates' feelings and attempting to create an atmosphere of mutual trust and respect.

Some early interpretations of the Michigan research concluded that the most effective style was employee-centered, that employee-centered supervisors were more likely to have highly productive work groups than were production-centered supervisors. Other studies, however, showed that effective supervisors engaged in both employee-centered and production-centered behavior at the same time.[8]

A later study at Michigan expanded the number of important leader behaviors. They found four supervisory behaviors associated with satisfaction and performance in a study of forty agencies of an insurance company. These four basic supervisory behavior dimensions are:

1. Support: Behavior that enhances someone else's feelings of personal worth and importance.
2. Interaction facilitation: Behavior that encourages members of the group to develop close, mutually satisfying relationships.
3. Goal emphasis: Behavior that stimulates an enthusiasm for meeting the group's goals or achieving excellent performance.
4. Work facilitation: Behavior that helps achieve goal attainment by such activities as scheduling, coordinating, planning, and providing resources such as tools, materials, and technical knowledge.

The Michigan research strengthened the case for conceiving of leadership as a complex activity. It has been instrumental in shaping much of the work on situational theories of leadership.

THE CONTINGENCY APPROACH TO LEADERSHIP

It has long been known that the situational context within which a human being operates makes a difference, but until recently this idea was not part of the leadership research literature. Situational factors were not prominent facets of either the Ohio State studies or the Michigan studies, though the researchers were aware of their importance. In all contingency approaches an attempt is made to specify how a leader's or a manager's behavior is related to effectiveness in different situational circumstances. This, of course is quite consistent with managerial process contingency theory. Such work on leadership provides us with more specific prescriptions about how a manager should function in different types of organizations. Some of the situational factors that seem to be especially important to the effectiveness of a leadership style are (1) the characteristics of subordinates, (2) the organizational situation, and (3) the style of one's superior in an organization.

1. *Subordinate characteristics.* The characteristics of the subordinate are related to leadership effectiveness. Leadership style that varies from what a subordinate expects may meet with a negative reaction.[13] For example, the participative management style was found to be ineffective when subordinates were not used to influencing decisions of their superior. Subordinates seem to have a better response to the participative approach when they feel it is the way a manager *should* behave.[14,15] The autocratic approach may be preferred by individuals who do not feel competent to participate in the decision-making process.

2. *The situation.* The organizational situation also influences the supervisory approach. The degree of crisis and the type of work are but two possible situational factors that could be important. For example, in an emergency where a decision is quickly needed, it may be unwise to use a participative approach, since this would take undue time.

If a person's job is well-defined, narrow, and highly routine (often the case with lower-level employees in a bureaucratic organization), then directive leadership styles might have negative effects. The employee will feel pressure from both his job and his boss. While he may perform better, dissatisfaction will be higher. When the task is less well-structured, however, directive behavior may provide the employee with needed guidance, improving effectiveness.[16,17]

3. *The leader's boss.* The style of one's superior can also affect one's own supervisory approach. Fleishman[18] found that a manager's style was more related to the way his superior managed than whether or not he had been in a training program. Carroll and Tosi[13] found that a subordinate models his behavior after that of his superior, especially when the subordinate finds himself in situations where he is unsure of what to do. For example, an assistant manager of a department store may be given the assignment of presenting an advertising program to the board of directors. If he has never done this before, he may pattern his approach after what he has seen his boss do. Likewise, in dealing with subordinates, a manager may handle a troublesome employee as he has seen his boss do it. The way many people learn to manage is by modeling their behavior after those who are already in management jobs.

Fiedler's Model of Leadership

Fiedler[17] has developed a formulation about how leadership style, the group, and the situation interact to affect group performance and satisfaction. The style of a leader is, in part, a function of his or her own needs and personality. Therefore Fiedler suggests, leadership style, like personality, is relatively well-fixed and established.

Leadership style is measured by the "Least Preferred Co-worker" scale (LPC). On the LPC, a manager is asked to describe the co-worker with whom he least likes to work. From this description, two classifications of leadership style are developed:

1. *People-centered* (high LPC). This style is one in which the leader is oriented toward the feelings and relationships in the work group, with a tendency to be permissive.

2. *Task-centered* (low LPC). This style focuses on the task, with a tendency to be directive and controlling.

These two dimensions are much like those found in the Ohio State and Michigan studies. Fiedler, however, extends both those approaches by defining what characteristics of the situation are important in determining which style is more effective. The important situational characteristics are:

1. *Leader–member relations* refer to the amount of trust and how well-liked the leader is.

2. *Task-structure* refers to the extent to which the job is defined. High task structure refers to well-defined jobs in which each aspect is spelled out. Low task structure is present where job requirements are unclear and ambiguous.

3. *Position power* is a function of the formal authority structure; that is, whether or not an individual has the right to reward, sanction, evaluate, or promote those who work for him.

Figure 14.4 shows the eight possible combinations of these three factors and which supervisory style is predicted to be more effective in each. Task orientation

FIGURE 14.4   Classification of group task situations and the predicted relationship of group performance and leadership style

Task Structure	Leader–Member Relations	Position Power	Suggested Leader Orientation
High	Good	Strong	Task (low LPC)
	Good	Weak	Task (low LPC)
	Poor	Weak	People (high LPC)
	Poor	Strong	People (high LPC)
Low	Good	Strong	Task (low LPC)
	Good	Weak	People (high LPC)
	Poor	Weak	Task (low LPC)
	Poor	Strong	People (high LPC)

Source: F. Fiedler. *A Theory of Leadership Effectiveness.* New York: McGraw-Hill, 1967, p. 37.

is generally best in situations where leader–member relations are either very good or very bad. When relations are good, the group may be quite willing to accept a *task orientation* **(low LPC).** Where all situational factors are bad for the supervisor, the group will fall apart unless the leader takes charge and controls their behavior.

Under some of the moderately unfavorable conditions the leader must use a people-orientation approach, either to motivate group members to deal with an ambiguous task or to win their support. **High LPC** leaders are most likely to be effective when there are not extreme negative conditions.

Fiedler's work has some important implications. One is that if leadership style is not flexible, then when an organization is not performing well, the situation should be restructured to make it more favorable to the style of the person leading—or the leader should be replaced.

The research evidence supports some, but not all, of Fiedler's predictions as to the most effective supervisory approach for each of his eight conditions.[19] Obviously, there could be other situational factors not considered by Fiedler, which could also have an effect on performance.

Path–Goal Theory

Path–goal leadership theory asserts that the leader obtains good performance from his work unit by making sure that subordinates know what they have to do (the path) to be rewarded for good performance (the goal) and also by reducing barriers to effective performance.[16,20]

In addition, the supervisor must behave in such a way as to help subordinates satisfy their needs through their high performance. Since different groups of employees have different needs and different types of work problems, the most appropriate leadership approach depends on the types of individuals involved and the characteristics of their work situation. Research indicates that when the task requirements are ambiguous, a leader's attempts to clarify what subordinates are supposed to do contributes to high satisfaction. These same efforts to clarify work requirements may reduce satisfaction when the task requirements are quite clear.

In the latter case, the supervisor's efforts to explain already clear task requirements are viewed by subordinates as unnecessary and, perhaps, insulting. Path–goal theory suggests that a manager's emphasis on either consideration or on initiating structure can be effective, depending upon the needs of the individuals in the situation at the time.

The importance of path–goal theory is that it not only specifies what leaders should do in different situations but it also explains why or how this effect occurs. This explanation is found in four general propositions that link performance and leader behavior through motivation (see Chapter 16). These propositions are:

1. The leader's role in motivation is to increase to the subordinate the utility (positive value) both of achieving work goals and of the work itself. Where there is uncertainty, he should also clarify the path (the things that have to be done) to achieve work goals.

2. With clear paths to work goals, the subordinate will be motivated because he can be more certain of how to achieve goals (or his role ambiguity will be reduced). When, for example, an employee is given a new assignment, if he does not know how to do it, then he should receive some help or coaching from his superior.

   Clarification of the task assignment also permits the manager to reinforce desired behavior because it may then be easier for the individual to perceive the link between performance and rewards (or sanctions), since they are now specified.

3. If the path to the work goal is already clear because of the nature of the work or the rigidity of the structure, then the leader who is directive (exercises high initiating structure) may increase performance through added pressure, but will decrease satisfaction. Close supervision of a skilled worker may upset him greatly, though he may produce more because of it.

4. If the leader acts to satisfy subordinate needs, better results will occur only when increased satisfaction results in the individual placing greater value on the work, or goal-directed effort. This means that if a manager provides, say, favors to a group and they are happier but do not like their work assignment, performance will not increase.

Perhaps one of the most important contributions of path–goal theory is that it gives some insight into how a particular behavior affects performance. A manager can affect individual and group motivation in these ways:

1. *A manager can define the link between performance and rewards.* This can be done by spelling out relationships between efforts and performance levels and between performance levels and various outcomes such as rewards or punishments (salary increases, promotions or demotions). When he does, he may be able to reward high performance. Even if he has few rewards to allocate, he still has the capacity to use social rewards, such as recognition or approval, but for these rewards to be effective the subordinates must see this social recognition as important. Kahn and Katz found that productivity of work groups was related to beliefs by group members that high performance would lead to the receiving of the reward of supervisory approval.[21] Such supervisory recognition must be given only for high performance. If it is also given for average performance, then subordinates assume that average performance is perfectly satisfactory.

2. *A manager can set goals.* Motivation may also be affected by the difficulty of work goals the supervisor establishes for individuals or groups. In one study it was found that when work goals set for foremen were viewed as impossible, very poor performance resulted.[22] On the other hand, when goals were perceived to be difficult but challenging, performance increased. In another study it was found that there was more enjoyment with goals of intermediate difficulty than there was with quite easy or quite difficult goals.[23] It should be kept in mind, however, that personal characteristics affect the perception of the relative difficulty of goals and of the response to this perception. In one study, for example, managers low in self-esteem reported diminished effort expenditures when given goals they believed to be difficult, while managers high in self-esteem reported they worked harder when they had difficult goals.[13]

3. *A manager can clarify how to achieve work goals.* The clarification of work goals is another way that performance can be affected. As pointed out in path–goal theory, a leader's high initiating structure can reduce role ambiguity, which can increase motivation by making it more probable that effort will result in goal attainment. On the other hand, confusion among subordinates as to why, when, and how something should be done wastes time and energy and contributes to personal frustrations, which in turn leads to diminished motivation.

The Vroom–Yetton Model

Vroom and Yetton,[15] extending the pioneering work of Norman Maier (see Chapter 10), described different methods of decision making and devised an aid for deciding when different leadership patterns should be used. Leader behavior can range from making the unilateral decision to the other extreme of allowing a group to make the decision. The different leadership approach strategies are described below. As the decision approach moves from AI toward GII (*A* stands for autocratic, *C* for consultative, and *G* for group), the amount of subordinate influence over the final decision increases.

AI   The manager makes the decision alone with currently available data.

AII Necessary information is obtained from subordinates, but the manager still decides alone. The role of the subordinates is input of data only. They have nothing to do with generating or evaluating alternatives.

CI   The manager discusses the problems with relevant subordinates individually. Then, without bringing them together, he makes a decision that may or may not reflect their input.

CII The manager shares the problem with subordinates in a group meeting, gathering ideas and suggestions. He then, alone, makes the decision that may or may not take the input of the group meeting into account.

GII Problems are shared with the group. The manager functions in the participative style described by Maier. (See Chapter 10.) His role is to provide information and help, facilitating the group's determination of their own solution, rather than his.

The Vroom–Yetton (V–Y) model takes a number of factors into consideration which influence the degree of success in using a participative approach. It is called a normative, or prescriptive, model because it's how a manager *should* act or behave. The appropriate leadership style is contingent upon the following characteristics of the situation in which the problem arises:

1. *Importance of the quality of the decision.* How important is it to achieve a high-quality solution? If there is no quality requirement, then any acceptable alternative will be satisfactory to management and the decision becomes a relatively easy one to make and the group can make the decision itself.

2. *Extent to which the decision maker has the information necessary to make decisions.* Vroom and Yetton point out that there are two kinds of information that may be necessary to make an effective decision. One type of information pertains to the preferences of subordinates about alternatives. The second type of information is whether or not there are rational grounds on which to judge the relative quality of alternatives.

When the leader is not aware of subordinates' preferences, he must obtain this information somehow, and participative approaches are one such means. If the leader has this information, however, and the problem is such that an individual decision is more likely to produce a better solution than that of a group, then clearly the situation calls for the manager to make the decision alone.

In what kinds of situation is a group likely to make a better decision than an individual? Research indicates that an individual can do as well as a group when either (1) the problem has a highly verifiable solution, or when (2) the solution requires thinking through complicated interrelated stages, keeping in mind conclusions reached at earlier times. This same research shows that a group is superior when the problem is complex, has several parts, and the group members possess diverse but relevant talents and skills. Insight and originality can then be more likely obtained from a group than from an individual.[24]

3. *Extent to which problem is structured.* In structured problems, the alternatives or at least the means for generating them are known. In most organizations at least some use is made of standard procedures that give individuals all or most of the information necessary to take a previously planned action. In an ill-structured problem, on the other hand, the information may be widely dispersed through the organization, with a number of individuals each possessing a part. These individuals will probably have to be brought together to solve the problem or to make a joint decision.

4. *Extent to which subordinates' acceptance is important.* Acceptance by subordinates is not critical when a decision will be implemented by someone outside the specific unit in which the decision is made or when it falls in the boundaries of the psychological contract. In the latter instance carrying out the decision is a matter of simple compliance rather than a matter of exercise of initiative, judgment, or creativity. The more commitment required from subordinates in the carrying out of a strategy, of course, the more important subordinate acceptance becomes.

5. *Prior probability that a unilateral decision will be accepted.* If a decision is accepted by subordinates without participation, it falls within the boundaries of the "psychological contract."

6. *Extent to which subordinates are motivated to attain organizational goals.* Organization members may have objectives in a particular situation inconsistent with those of management. In such cases participation in decision making in order to increase acceptance of a needed change may be more risky than in those situations when the goals of the two groups are the same. Thus, participative decision making could be expected to work best when there is mutual interest in the problem.

7. *Extent to which subordinates are likely to disagree over solutions.* Subordinates may disagree among themselves over prospective alternatives because of different gains or losses from an alternative or because of differences in values or other critical factors. The method used to reach a decision must facilitate resolution of the disagreement, and thus group involvement is necessary.

These situational characteristics are presented in the form of questions in the Vroom–Yetton model in Figure 14.5. The questions are answered on a yes–no basis. The decision tree format establishes the sequence of the questions of concern to the decision maker in various situations. At the end of every path in the decision tree is a leader style that is suggested for that situation. According to Vroom and Yetton, the best method for making decisions can be determined by using such an approach.

To illustrate, say that a manager wishes to change the work schedule so as to have at least one maintenance engineer on duty at all times between 9 A.M. and 9 P.M., six days a week, and that this represents a departure from previous work schedules. He has a number of alternative ways to make his decision. He starts with question A in Figure 14.5, "Is there a quality requirement?" He decides that there is none since he will be satisfied with a wide variety of different work schedules so long as a maintenance engineer is on duty at all times between the hours of 9 A.M. and 9 P.M., six days a week. Because he answered "No" to question A, he must go to question D, "Is acceptance of decision by subordinates critical to effective implementation?" Suppose that in his opinion the answer to question D is "Yes," since acceptance of the schedule is critical to its effective implementation. (If he had answered question D "No," the decision tree shows a recommended leader style AI, making the decision himself.) But the manager could use, if he chose, any of the decision-making methods for dealing with a group listed earlier—AI, AII, CI, CII, GII.

Because he answers "Yes" to question D, he must next answer question E, "If I were to make the decision by myself, is it reasonably certain that it would be accepted by my subordinates?" A "No" answer to question E, according to the decision tree of Figure 14.5, shows the recommended approach for making this type of decision is GII, which requires the decision maker to share the problem with the group and to agree to accept any alternative that the group supports.

In all cases where a recommended style is other than GII, the person may still elect a participative strategy. As noted above, if the suggested style were AI, any more consultative approach would work. Then the manager must look at other aspects of the situation to determine what to do. The decision maker may want to use the alternative that requires the fewest number of worker hours to make and to implement the decision—but here it should be remembered that although a manager may be able to make a decision more quickly alone, it may take more time in the long run to communicate that decision to subordinates and to achieve an understanding of what is required than would a participative decision.

For the manager who finds the V–Y model too confusing, there is a simplifying way to approach it. One analysis of the V–Y model found that decision process CII

FIGURE 14.5 Decision-process flow chart for group problems

A. Is there a quality requirement such that one solution is likely to be more rational than another?
B. Do I have sufficient information to make a high-quality decision?
C. Is the problem structured?
D. Is acceptance of decision by subordinates critical to effective implementation?
E. If I were to make the decision by myself, is it reasonably certain that it would be accepted by my subordinates?
F. Do subordinates share the organizational goals to be attained in solving this problem?
G. Is conflict among subordinates likely in preferred solutions? (This question is irrelevant to individual problems.)

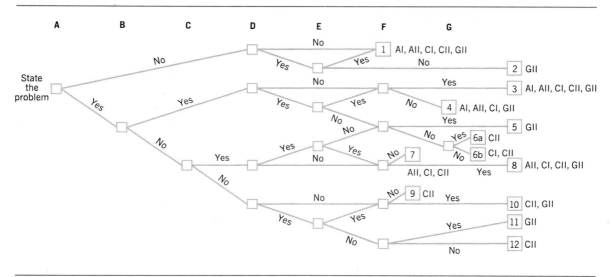

Source: Vroom, V. H., and P. W. Yetton. *Leadership and Decision-Making.* Pittsburgh: University of Pittsburgh Press, 1973. By permission of the authors and the publishers.

is an effective alternative for 80 percent of the problem situations. For the other situations, GII is a feasible alternative. The following simple rule is suggested: if acceptance of a decision by subordinates is critical to effective implementation and it is reasonably certain that subordinates would not accept autocratic decisions, but they share organizational goals (or decision quality is not important), use GII. Otherwise, use CII.[25]

A Summary of Leadership Concepts

Out of the leadership research, two basic and important dimensions of supervisory behavior emerge; one emphasizes task performance, one emphasizes satisfying individual employees' needs. Figure 14.6 shows the similarity between the different approaches to leadership behavior described in this chapter. The relationship of these factors to employee needs and performance is definitely associated with the situation. Especially important situational factors are (1) the structure and nature of tasks, (2) the needs and abilities of the group members, and (3) the superior.

FIGURE 14.6   Similarity between selected concepts of Leadership

Ohio State Studies	Early Michigan Studies	Bowers and Seashore	Fiedler's Contingency Theory	Path–Goal Theory	Vroom and Yetton
		Support	People-centered (high LPC)	Consideration	CI CII CIII
Consideration	Employee-centered	Interaction facilitation	**Situational Factors**		
			Position Power		
			Task Structure	Clarity of path–goal relationships	Acceptance Quality Information Conflict Goal congruence
		Goal emphasis	Leader–Member Relations		
Initiating structure	Production-centered	Work facilitation	Production-centered (low LPC)	Initiating structure	AI AII

LEADERSHIP AND TYPE OF ORGANIZATION

These ideas about situational leadership fit quite nicely with management process contingency theory. They are very helpful in prescribing what the predominant leadership style should be in the organic and the mechanistic organization. Our approach is based very much on path–goal theory. Five factors are taken into account: two leader behaviors (structuring behavior and consideration), one task characteristic (task structure), one situational factor (work climate), and the personal characteristics of subordinates.

1. Structuring behavior. Structuring behavior refers to behaviors of a leader directed at accomplishing tasks. It includes the assigning of tasks to individuals, letting group members know what is expected of them, and asking the group members to follow standard procedures. It involves planning and organizing the work.

2. Consideration. The establishment of socioemotional relationships between the leader and the group members is consideration. Supervisors high in consideration create a climate of psychological support, warmth, and helpfulness. Such supervisors show concern and trust for others.

3. Task structure. Task structure refers to the extent to which jobs are well-defined or ill-defined. Job requirements may be fairly well spelled out and relatively constant over time (as would be the case in mechanistic organizations) or they may not have clear requirements, as would be the case in an organic organization. In path–goal theory House refers to the ambiguity or uncertainty of tasks.[16]

4. Work climate. Fiedler[17] theorized that an important determinant of leader effectiveness is the relationship between the group members and the leader. House theorized that job satisfaction is an important determinant of leader effectiveness. The work climate is the ambience that exists within the work group. It is the degree of trust that subordinates have in the leader, the level of group cohesiveness, the general satisfactoriness of leader and group relationships, and the congruence between individual and organizational needs and values.

Satisfying work climates are those in which there is high satisfaction with work and with the superior. Individual values and attitudes of members do not conflict with those of the manager or the organization. In general, there is a great deal of mutual trust and respect, and good relations exist between the leader and the members of his organization.

In dissatisfying climates, organization members have little trust in the leader's competence and fairness. There may be disagreement between the leader and subordinates about the appropriate way to solve problems. The individual values of subordinates may be different from those of the superior.

5. Subordinate characteristics. There is much research on the effects of different subordinate characteristics on leader effectiveness. House and Mitchell[23] identify two subordinate characteristics—authoritarianism and ego-involvement—as especially important. First, the individual's authoritarianism has been found to be related to how one reacts to a boss. High-authoritarian people are dogmatic, rigid, and unwilling to change. Low-authoritarians are the opposite. A second personal factor is ego-involvement in work. People with high ego-involvement in work see their work with a professional orientation or the organizationalist orientation described in Chapter 5.

MANAGERIAL BEHAVIOR IN MECHANISTIC ORGANIZATIONS

The primary factor that differentiates the managerial position in the mechanistic organization from that in an organic one is that task structure is higher; that is, there is more certainty about job requirements. The production subsystem is likely to be repetitive, with jobs broken down into relatively narrow tasks, and organization structures will be fairly well fixed, with clear lines of authority, responsibility, and job definition. Since goals are relatively stable, the work assignments will be fairly constant over time. The work groups themselves will tend to be stable in membership. Often there is a fairly heavy investment in fixed, specialized resources capable of producing only a limited number of products.

If this is so, then the two factors that determine how a leader should act to produce effective results are (1) the level of subordinate authoritarianism, and (2) the work climate. When the work climate is satisfying and the group knows what the leader expects, the situation demands relatively low amounts of structuring behavior and greater emphasis on consideration, as shown in Figure 14.7. As House[16] points out, in such situations structuring behavior will be viewed as too much pressure and produce negative results. Structuring behavior is less necessary in the mechanistic organization since the work is already well-defined from the nature of the tasks.

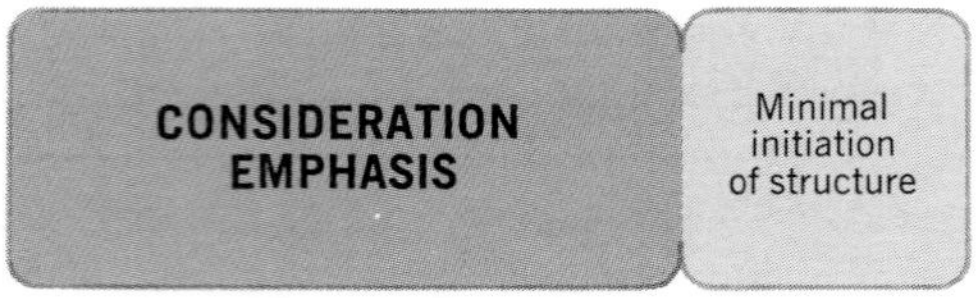

FIGURE 14.7 Leader behavior when the task is highly structured and subordinates are low in authoritarianism.

In a dissatisfying climate, consideration behavior should be emphasized, as shown in Figure 14.7. High levels of structuring behavior will make an already unpleasant situation more intolerable. So the leader must take action to improve the attitudes of the group toward him and the situation.

Due to the routine nature of work, especially at lower levels, most of the workers will be externally oriented and have low job involvement or identification with their work. The personality characteristic of authoritarianism plays an important role with regard to how a subordinate reacts. Subordinates who are low in authoritarianism will react favorably when they have an opportunity to participate in job decisions. High authoritarians seem to have less need to have much influence in work decisions. House and Mitchell[23] conclude that the high authoritarian, in fact, reacts negatively to such participative approaches. Of course the nature of participation in a mechanistic organization is restricted, since both ends and means (goals and plans of action) are already fairly well determined. Thus, participation in the stable organization will probably be seen as a form of "consideration" behavior. Under these conditions, the manager should emphasize structuring behavior, as shown in Figure 14.8.

How a Manager Can Improve Performance

The performance of a work unit will be high when there is some congruence between leader behavior, work climate, and the level of task structure. In a mechanistic organization the task structure is fixed and well-defined by the work system; therefore, top management has at least three possible strategies to consider in the event of poor performance.

1. *Change the technological system.* This strategy is one of job design or change. Suppose we find, in an assembly-line operation, that there are generally good relationships existing between the leader and his group. An analysis of the leader's behavior shows that his style is predominantly one of initiating structure. If poor performance occurs, it may be that the technological system needs to be redesigned. Improvements in efficiency may be made through methods study. Perhaps the jobs should be enriched and made more challenging, or perhaps they should be more narrowly defined, or it may be that old equipment should be replaced.

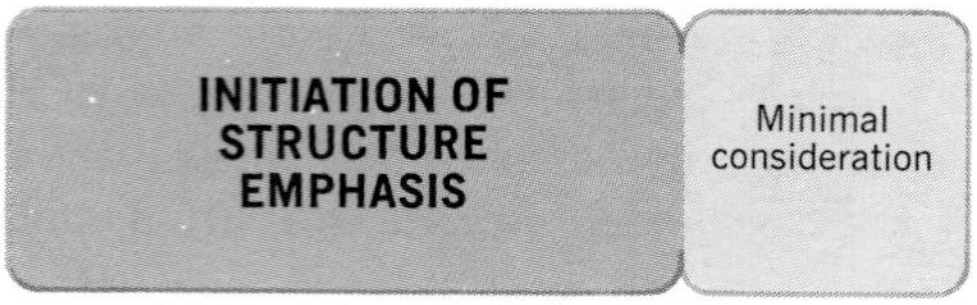

FIGURE 14.8 Leader behavior with highly structured tasks and high-authoritarian subordinates.

Clearly the suggested alternative to improve the results of the organizational unit calls for working in the technological system, not trying to change leader behavior from initiating structure to consideration. When technological limitations are the cause of poor performance, trying to change how a manager behaves may only serve to aggravate the problem.

2. ***Change emphasis of manager's behavior.*** Performance deficiencies could also be the result of the incongruency of the manager's style with situational demands. For example, say that the technological system is producing great stress in organization members. In this situation if the leader's behavior pattern is dominated by structuring behavior, then he or she should attempt to move toward a style dominated by consideration. A manager can show greater consideration by engaging in some of these activities:

a. Showing greater concern for personal problems and interests. This can be done, for example, by being willing to discuss the subordinate's personal objectives and interests.

b. Representing the interests of the employee to top management. Going to bat for members of the group or showing an interest in their advancement in the organization is a way to demonstrate concern for the individual.

c. Increasing the degree of subordinate participation in decision making. There are usually some opportunities for subordinate involvement that managers do not use. More frequent group meetings to solve problems not only may be a way to get better, more useful inputs, but could also be a demonstration of a considerate behavioral style.

d. Coaching or taking other constructive action in response to individual mistakes.

The emphasis on consideration presupposes that high task structure exists—that is, there is little ambiguity about the job. Often there is the need to provide some task structure through leader behavior (structuring behavior) even in a bureaucratic organization. When this judgment is made it can be done by employing a greater number of systemic factors available in an organization, such as budgets, procedures, and goals. The leader can increase structuring behavior by planning more extensively, by making more decisions, or by letting others know precisely where they stand on particular problems.

3. ***Change the leader.*** Suppose that an individual manager exemplifies either a predominant structure style or considerate style and is unable to change his behavioral emphasis. The most effective strategy may be to remove the leader and replace him with one whose style is congruent with the situation.

MANAGERIAL BEHAVIOR IN ORGANIC ORGANIZATIONS

In the organic organization, the leader contributes to performance and satisfaction to a greater extent than in the hierarchical organization because in the organic organization the work is not so preplanned and because more problems arise that require cooperation to solve. In addition, providing information to organizational members on the goals and activities of other employees and units facilitates task performance. With highly competent staff, as it often is in the organic organization, potential performance is high. The supervisor's responsibility is to insure that the potential is achieved—that human resources are used to capacity. The important factor that must be taken into account when considering leadership style for a dynamic organization is that the tasks are basically unstructured.

In organic organizations, professionals and managers are often shifted from one project to another as they are needed. Because of the volatile environment, projects will change periodically, and members will sometimes find themselves in ambiguous situations. They will, perhaps, not know how to do a particular job or solve a new problem. This can occur when they are not sure what skills are required or, if they do know, they do not possess those skills.

Another possibility is that an individual may not know how his or her particular competence fits with others in the organization. For example, suppose one employee is an expert on propulsion systems and another is an electronics communications specialist. Both of these persons may be extremely competent in their own fields of specialization, but if a project requires interdependent effort, then some way to integrate and coordinate their work must be devised. If they themselves are uncertain as to how to proceed, they will not function at maximum efficiency. Under the conditions of low task structure—when there is a high level of task ambiguity and a satisfying climate condition—the best leader approach is one that emphasizes initiating structure behavior, as in Figure 14.9.

Structuring behavior will have desirable effects on performance and satisfaction because, where "tasks are varied and interdependent and where teamwork norms have not developed within the group, initiating structure and close supervision will regulate and clarify path–goal relationships," or show the staff the way the job should be done.[16] In an organic organization, then, a manager must exhibit a behavioral style that is more directive and work-oriented than in the mechanistic organization. He or she should focus on defining subordinate tasks, fixing responsibilities, planning, budgeting, and controlling. This will impose performance pressures on the group, and so long as these pressures are not intense enough to induce dissatisfaction, good results may be obtained.

In the organic organization, structuring leader behavior will be seen as goal-oriented toward the accomplishment of organizational objectives. House and Mitchell[23] conclude that in an ambiguous work setting managers who are seen by their subordinates as achievement-oriented are likely to contribute positively to group satisfaction and performance. Part of the reason for this lies in the high task involvement of organization members. They desire high performance.

Of course when subordinates become very frustrated or come under great stress, then high consideration in addition to high structuring behavior may be necessary. In the organic organization, participation may be emphasized not only to obtain acceptance of a decision but because the leader lacks the information necessary to

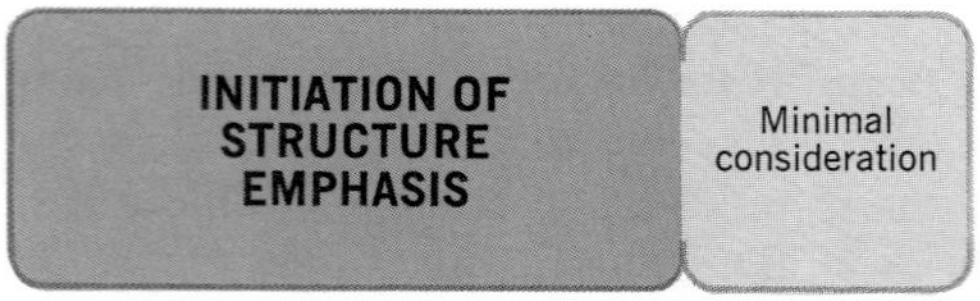

INITIATION OF STRUCTURE EMPHASIS	Minimal consideration

FIGURE 14.9 Leader behavior with low task structure and satisfying climate.

make the decision (see Figure 14.10). The low authoritarianism, high task involvement, and professional orientation characteristic of subordinates in the organic organization facilitates the use of participation.

How a Manager Can Improve Performance

There are a number of possibilities for dealing with poor performance in the organic organization, and here we will analyze some of the possibilities and suggest the circumstances under which they are most likely to be effective.

1. *Increase participation.* One way to improve performance is to increase participation in decision making. Tushman found that in research projects with complex tasks there was widespread reliance on participative decision making to deal with the complex information-processing requirements.[26] Management by objectives discussed in Chapter 10 is especially useful for this purpose in organic organizations.

2. *Replace members with others of greater ability.* Whereas in the mechanistic organization, technology, plant, and equipment are important, individual skill and ability are critical in the organic organization. When there is congruence between leader style and work requirements, but performance is still low, then it may be that employees, either managerial or professional, must be terminated (or transferred) and more competent ones hired. Of course, it may not be necessary to replace whole units. The least competent should be replaced.

3. *Change leader behavior style.* The leader may be able to shift his behavioral repertoire in order to obtain the required congruence. When a considerate leader wishes to engage in more structuring behavior, he may do so by emphasizing the following:

a. Facilitate the allocation of sufficient resources (time, supplies, equipment, etc.).

b. Increase emphasis on the importance of deadlines, budget constraints, and adherence to policy.

c. Schedule more meetings to develop plans for units at lower levels.

d. Take a more active part in the redefining of tasks and the design of projects, making subordinates more aware of the differentiation in organization levels that exist between superiors and subordinates.

e. Actively engaging in coaching functions, helping subordinates to understand their jobs better.

4. *Change leaders.* The acceptability of a leader to subordinates in the organic organization is, of course, as important as it is in the mechanistic. In the organic organization the legitimacy of the leader may be determined by professional credentials. If these are not sufficient to obtain "legitimacy," a change in leaders may be necessary.

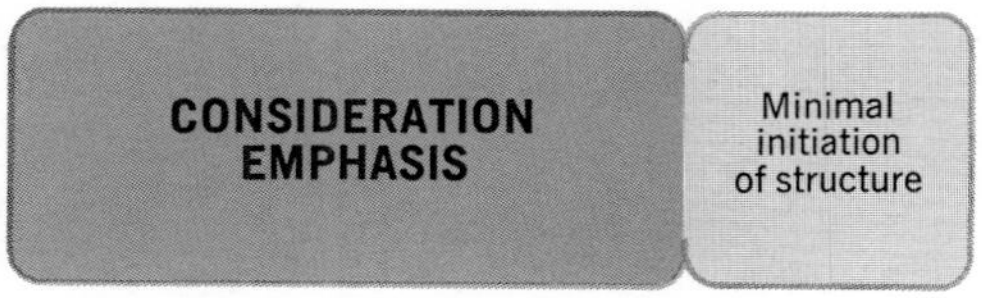

FIGURE 14.10 Leader behavior with low task structure and a dissatisfying climate.

CONSIDERATION EMPHASIS

Minimal initiation of structure

SUMMARY

We have already pointed out that organizations must first establish objectives and strategic plans and then convert these to operating plans and budgets. Organization structures and management systems must also be developed to facilitate the accomplishment of the tasks. Managers perform a leadership function when they take actions to get lower-level personnel to execute the plans. Leadership involves a variety of approaches to influence others to carry out assigned responsibilities.

Managers enact leadership by using power, some of which is granted by virtue of the position one holds. Power, a force one uses to extract compliance from another, is also derived from technical expertise and charisma.

Much of what is seen as leadership is the result of the psychological contract, the willingness of an individual to comply with organizational directives in return for some inducements. Actually, leadership is best thought of as the ability to get organizational members to go beyond those areas of the psychological contract, where compliance is virtually automatic.

A good deal of research has been aimed at discovering those behaviors and traits associated with effective leaders. Much of this research and theory was discussed in this chapter. At present, the state of research and theory seems to suggest that leaders are more effective when they behave in a way congruent with subordinate needs and with the structure of the task being performed.

Case
14.1 Southeastern Bay Telephone Company

In 1975 the repair unit of Southeastern Bay Telephone Company adopted a new performance evaluation system for their telephone repair clerks. These clerks received telephone calls from customers requesting various types of repair services. The clerks sent these requests to the supervisor of the repairpersons, who scheduled the actual repairs. Then the clerks called back the customer to insure that somebody would be home during the visit of the repairperson.

The new performance evaluation system required the company's internal audit group to listen in periodically on the phone conversations taking place between the customers and the repair clerks. The repair clerks were rated on the degree to which they opened the conversation with certain phrases (good morning, etc.), and the degree to which they exhibited a pleasant voice tone, proper grammar, and good manners. Objective performance standards were also used. For example, each incoming telephone call had to be answered within twenty seconds, no customer could be put on hold for more than sixty seconds, no customer could be put on hold more than twice in one conversation, and so on.

In 1981 after a severe windstorm had taken place, several repair clerks received negative ratings on their performance for failure to meet the above criteria. The operators complained to their union. They demanded the system of performance evaluation be abandoned on the basis of being a violation of their basic individual rights.

1. What leadership style is indicated by the method of performance evaluation described in the case?

2. How useful is this approach of evaluation given the task requirements?
3. What changes in the system would you recommend if any?
4. To what degree do you think there is an ethical problem with monitoring phone conversations?

Boone & Smith Asphalt Company

Boone & Smith Asphalt Company was founded in 1947. The company surfaced roads, tennis courts, playgrounds, parking lots, and other areas with asphalt. Boone & Smith was divided into three divisions, a paving division, an asphalt plant division, and an equipment leasing division in which trucks and other equipment were leased to the State and other clients when needed, especially in the winter months.

The asphalt plant division produces liquid asphalt. The plant is hot and dangerous. Asphalt is mixed under high temperatures and stored in a raised hopper, under which trucks drive to be loaded. When a truck pulls under the hopper, the hot asphalt is loaded by dropping it from the hopper into the truck. This material is quite hot and workers who handle the hot asphalt must be careful to avoid serious injury. Goggles and protective clothing must be worn by the asphalt plant workers at all times.

A new supervisor of the asphalt plant, Jack Tombari, has noticed that the workers often neglect to wear their goggles and helmets at the asphalt plant. Jack told his foremen that they should insist the workers wear the proper protective clothing at all times. In spite of his warnings, he notices the men still do not comply with the rules on this matter. He wonders whether he can do anything to get the men to protect themselves.

1. What are some of the possible reasons for the workers not complying with the safety regulations?
2. What actions might Tombari take to obtain more worker compliance?

DISCUSSION QUESTIONS

1. How would you define leadership in an organization?
2. Power has different bases in the mechanistic organization and the organic organization. Discuss these.
3. How has the direction of research about leadership changed from its beginnings to the present time?
4. Why do you think identifying traits for good leadership was a prominent approach? What are the results of those studies?
5. What did the Ohio State studies reveal about effective leadership? What are the two basic leadership styles that emerged from these studies?
6. What did the original Michigan studies reveal about effective leadership? How did the later study amend the original one?
7. The Ohio State and Michigan studies both made researchers aware that situ-

ational factors are relevant factors. Discuss some of these factors and their influence on effective leadership.

8. What assumption does Fiedler make in his model? How does he measure styles of leadership? What does he recommend for an organization that is not performing well?
9. The path–goal theory is based on the expectancy theory of motivation. Explain.
10. How does the Vroom–Yetton model approach effective leadership?
11. Which style of leadership do you feel would influence you in the future?
12. What are some strategies for a manager to use to improve performance in a mechanistic organization?
13. How can a manager in an organic organization improve performance?

REFERENCES

1. Schein, E. Organizational psychology. Englewood Cliffs, N.J., Prentice-Hall, 1970.
2. Barnard, C. The functions of the executive. Cambridge, Harvard University Press, 1938.
3. Katz, D., and R. Kahn. The social psychology of organizations. New York, Wiley, 1978.
4. French, J. R. P., and B. Raven. "The bases of social power," in D. Cartwright (ed.), Studies in social power. Research Center for Group Dynamics, Ann Arbor, Mich., University of Michigan, 1959.
5. Stogdill, R. M. Personal factors associated with leadership: A survey of the literature. Journal of Psychology, 25 (1948): 35–71.
6. Dunnette, M. D. "Predictions of executives' success," in F. Wickert and D. McFarland (eds.), Measuring executive effectiveness. New York, Appleton-Century-Crofts, 1967.
7. Ghiselli, E. E. Explorations in managerial talent. Santa Monica, Calif., Goodyear, 1971.
8. Stogdill, R. M. Handbook of leadership: A survey of theory and research. New York, The Free Press, 1974.
9. Gibb, C. "Leadership," in Handbook of social psychology, Vol. 2. Reading, Mass., Addison-Wesley, 1954.
10. Lewin, K., R. Lippitt, and R. K. White. Patterns of aggressive behavior in experimentally created social climates, Journal of Social Psychology, 10 (1939): 271–299.
11. Lippitt, R., and R. K. White. "An experimental study of leadership and group life," in E. E. Maccoby, T. H. Newcomb, E. L. Hartley (eds.), Readings in social psychology. New York, Holt, 1958.
12. Schreisheim, C., R. J. House, and S. Kerr. "The effects of different operationalizations of leader initiating structure: A reconciliation of discrepant results," Academy of Management Proceedings, 35 (1975): 167–169.
13. Carroll, S. J., and H. Tosi. Management by objectives: Applications and research. New York, Macmillan, 1973.
14. French, J. R. P., Jr., J. Israel, and D. Aas. "An experiment in participation in a Norwegian factory," Human Relations, 13 (1960): 3–19.
15. Vroom, V. H., and P. W. Yetton. Leadership and decision-making. Pittsburgh, University of Pittsburgh Press, 1973.
16. House, R. J. "A path goal theory of leader effectiveness," Administrative Science Quarterly, 16 (1971): 321–338.
17. Fiedler, F. A theory of leadership effectiveness. New York, McGraw-Hill, 1967.
18. Fleishman, E. A. "Leadership climate, human relations training and supervisory behavior," Personnel Psychology, 6 (1953): 205–222.
19. Graen, G., K. Alvares, J. B. Orris, and J. A. Martella. "Contingency model of leadership

effectiveness: Antecedent and evidential results," Psychological Bulletin, 74 (1970): 285–296.

20. Evans, M. G. The effects of supervisory behavior upon worker perception of their path-goal relationships. New Haven, Conn.: Yale University, Doctoral Dissertation, 1968.

21. Kahn, R., and D. Katz. "Leadership practices in relation to productivity and morale," in D. Cartwright and A. Zander (eds.), *Group dynamics: Research and theory.* New York, Harper and Row, 1953, pp. 612–628.

22. Stedry, A. C., and E. Kay. "The effect of goal difficulty on performance: A field experiment," Behavioral Science, 11 (1966): 459–470.

23. House, R. J., and T. Mitchell. "Path-goal theory of leadership," Journal of Contemporary Business, Autumn 3 (1974): 81–87.

24. Kelley, H., and J. Thibaut. "Group problem solving," in G. Lindzey and E. Aronson (eds.), Handbook of social psychology, Vol. 4. Reading, Mass., Addison-Wesley, 1969.

25. Field, R. H. George. "A critique of the Vroom-Yetton contingency model of leadership behavior," The Academy of Management Review, 4 (1979): 249–257.

26. Tushman, Michael. "Work characteristics and subunit communication structure: A contingency analysis," Administrative Science Quarterly, 24 (March 1979): 82–97.

CHAPTER FIFTEEN

The Motivation to Work

Item 15.1 A Warning That Worker Discontent Is Rising

The past has shown repeatedly that societal changes have a dramatic—sometimes a tumultuous—impact on the workplace. Yet companies and unions are lagging behind in adapting to major shifts in attitudes and values, and the rising level of education, since World War II.

This is borne out by the recently announced results of the third national survey on the quality of employment conducted by the University of Michigan's Survey Research Center under a Labor Department contract. It shows, among other things, that 36 percent of American workers feel that their skills are underutilized, 32 percent believe that they are "overeducated" for their jobs, and more than 50 percent complain about a lack of control over the days they work and their job assignment. These figures indicate a high degree of frustration on the job that seems unlikely to abate.

The 1977 household survey of 1,515 workers—a large sample, representative of all major demographic and occupational groups—asked the same series of questions about employment that the center had posed in 1969 and 1973. The latest results indicate a "slight but significant" drop in overall job satisfaction, particularly between 1973 and 1977. As measured by various polls over thirty years, job satisfaction had shown little change up or down. But the 1977 survey, says program director Stanley E. Seashore, "is significant because it's the first confirmed decline in the national level of job satisfaction. The degree of decline isn't going to shake the world, but it will if it continues."

The four-year decline in job satisfaction

	Percent responding "very true"	
	1973	1977
Good hours, pleasant surroundings, and job is free of conflicting demands	38.4%	30.2%
Interesting work with opportunity to develop abilities and freedom to decide how to do the job	51.3	41.5
Good pay, fringe benefits, and job security	45.7	33.8
Enough information and authority to get the job done	63.3	52.4

Data: 1973 and 1977 "Quality of Employment Survey," University of Michigan Survey Research Center; Work in America Institute Inc.

EXPECTATIONS   The decline was more marked in specific aspects of job satisfaction, such as the challenge posed by the job, comfort (hours and physical surroundings), financial rewards, and the adequacy of resources to perform the work. One likely explanation for the drop is that higher levels of education have produced rising expectations. "Jobs aren't getting worse, but people are getting better," Seashore says.

This trend is likely to mean continuing trouble in the workplace but not necessarily in overt forms of protest, such as strikes. Rather, the growing disdain with which Americans regard their jobs—although work itself is still highly valued—will probably mean increasing friction between supervisors steeped in authoritarian tradition and workers who want more challenge and more voice in decisions affecting their jobs.

Some companies have been trying various methods of making work more satisfying and reducing the reliance traditionally placed on hierarchical command. But such experiments are by no means sweeping corporate America. "The survey is a warning to companies that all is not as peaceful and productive as they might believe," says Jerome M. Rosow, president of Work in America Institute Inc., a nonprofit organization that promotes programs to improve the quality of working life. "When companies see their productivity drop, they should ask how they can improve jobs, and not merely by setting up new productivity targets but also by sharing gains with workers and responding to their needs."

Organized labor also appears to be responding slowly to societal changes. The 1977 survey asked for the first time comprehensive questions regarding workers' attitudes about unions and revealed some surprising results. Curiously, the unions do not seem to recognize their potential for organizing the unorganized. About 39 percent of all nonunion blue-collar workers, and 28 percent of white-collar workers, said they would vote for union representation in their workplace.

Furthermore, the survey shatters the stereotyped notion that Southern and women workers are hostile to unions. In an analysis of the findings on union attitudes, Thomas A. Kochan, an associate professor at Cornell University, reports in the April issue of *Monthly Labor Review* that 35 percent of workers in the South and 40 percent of women workers support unionization. Many union leaders have discovered in recent years that black and other minority workers are easier to organize than white workers, but the survey result is striking: 67 percent of blacks and other minorities would vote for a union.

THE REAL DIFFICULTY   Edmund Ayoub, research director of the United Steelworkers, points out that it would be wrong to apply these survey generalizations to any specific organizing situation, but he says that unions should learn something from the survey. "Perhaps the workers' attitudes in the South aren't the obstacles we once thought they were," Ayoub says. "The difficulty in the South may be more a function of employer resistance to unions."

"What the figures tell me," says Thomas R. Donahue, executive assistant to AFL-CIO President George Meany, "is that the American labor movement is not in the terrible shape its critics say it is." In many European countries, he notes, workers often join a union even if it is not their exclusive bargaining agent. "If we followed that practice and took into membership the 33 percent of nonunion workers who say they want to join unions, we'd be as large as the European labor movements," Donahue says. About 25 percent of nonfarm workers in the U.S. belong to unions.

But even if the pro-union workers are dispersed in the labor force and therefore hard to organize, the unions do not seem to be moving very fast to claim their natural constituency. This is indicated by National Labor Relations Board statistics. In fiscal 1978, there was a 10 percent drop in representation cases—mainly union requests for elections—filed with the NLRB. And the rate has not increased in fiscal 1979.

RATING   Aside from organizing, however, U.S. unions appear to be performing largely the way their members want them to. In the University of Michigan survey, a little more than one-quarter of union members were dissatisfied with their unions. But the unions received good marks in responding to the traditional desires of their members, in improving wages, benefits, and job security provisions. Their record on handling grievances, a matter of high priority, was not quite so good, and rank and filers generally want their unions to respond more quickly to workers' needs.

Organized labor also could do much better, according to rank and filers, on issues involving the quality of working life, such as providing more interesting work and giving workers more of a voice in their jobs. Even where companies want to install programs to make jobs more meaningful, unions often flatly refuse to cooperate, claiming that management's main goal is to increase productivity, not help the worker. In the future, unions may pay a price for this recalcitrance.

While improving the quality of working life does not rank among the top priorities of union members, 60 percent to 75 percent said they want "some" or "a lot of" effort exerted on these nontraditional issues. This creates a "dilemma" for unions, says Cornell's Kochan, because "in some places they will have to address quality-of-work issues as well as the bread-and-butter issues, and that means they can no longer apply a standard program to all workers."

DIVERSE DESIRES To some degree, as the AFL-CIO's Donahue points out, unions have always dealt with a diversity of rank-and-file desires in bargaining. And they have handled some work-quality issues in negotiating over working conditions. But workers now seem to be saying that they want more attention given to these problems, while unions must continue to produce on wages, benefits, job security, and health and safety protection. That will be difficult because it calls for a change in conventional bargaining. In addition, the USW's Ayoub notes, "We don't know what they really mean when workers say they want more 'say' in their jobs."

But the evidence indicates that union and management will have to be more innovative to meet shifting desires. For example, 54 percent of workers surveyed in 1977 complained about having no control over job assignments; 76 percent of nonunion and union workers believed that employees should have "complete say" or "a lot of say" on decisions affecting worker safety; and 77 percent mentioned the lack of control over the days that they work as a problem.

Indeed, says a Survey Research Center analysis, the growing concern about working days and hours points to "a sizable constituency of workers who would be receptive to flexitime and other experiments in which workers could help determine their own work schedules."

387
The
Motivation
to Work

Source: "A warning that worker discontent is rising," McGraw Hill, Inc., reprinted from the June 4, 1979 issue of Business Week by special permission. Copyright 1979 by McGraw Hill, Inc., New York, N.Y., 10020. All rights reserved.

Motivation is a prime concern of today's managers. Managers at all levels believe that if they can only "motivate" their subordinates, those subordinates will perform better. This concern with motivation is due, in large part, to the fact that measurable differences between companies, government agencies, departments, and other types of organizational units are very often attributed to human factors. If, for example, you were to enter an automobile plant in which all signs and symbols designating the company had been removed, you probably could not differentiate it from the plant of any other auto company. The assembly line at a Chevrolet plant looks very much like that at a Ford plant. Therefore, given this similarity between hardware and technology, it is easy to believe that differences in productivity and performance between a Ford plant and a Chevy plant are due to human factors—differences that can be rectified, it is commonly thought, by proper motivation of the workers.

Motivation is also a concern in contemporary culture because of the historic stress on the "work ethic" in the United States—the belief that to work is good and that everyone should want to work. The socialization experiences of large segments of our society have led them to believe that they should be involved and committed to their work.

Many managers subscribe to the work ethic, and they are upset when they discover that many who work for them do not—may, in fact, be alienated from their work. Many try to counter this alienation with "motivation," because it is widely believed, especially among those who subscribe to the work ethic, that if one is committed to and generally satisfied with work, he or she will perform better. If he thinks well of his job, he will do well at it. This is one concept of motivation frequently held by managers who wish to "motivate" their subordinates. The question is, is it a sound concept?

APPROACHES TO UNDERSTANDING MOTIVATION

The term ***motivation*** has two general meanings in the dictionary of management. One use of the term motivation is as an activity of managers. The second use of the term motivation refers to a person's psychological internal drive state, which causes the person to behave in certain ways particularly in the job setting.

The term ***motivate*** (used as a verb) means the act on the part of one person seeking to influence another person to behave in a particular way. Used in this way motivation describes a management activity, or something that a manager does to induce subordinates to act in a way to produce effective results, organizationally. In this context we might say, ''The role of the manager is to motivate the worker,'' or ''The teacher tries to motivate the student.'' There is a relationship between leadership and motivation, used in this sense. In the next chapter, we elaborate on this meaning, describing several ''managerial motivation strategies.''

Motivation also means the internal psychological state of tension that induces a person to behave.

A NEEDS APPROACH TO MOTIVATION

This approach to motivation assumes that people engage in particular behaviors to satisfy their needs. Goal-directed behavior, as we have shown in Chapter 5, occurs when a ''need'' is aroused and the person, feeling some tension, acts to reduce the need. Such a sequence is shown in Figure 15.1. Suppose a manager tells her work group about a vacancy at a higher organization level and says that the position will be filled by the most productive worker in her group. The information is a ''stimulus'' and the supervisor intends to arouse, perhaps, the ego needs of workers, specifically their desires to advance and earn more income, status, and prestige. If this need is aroused, those in the work group then search for ways to reduce the tension (or satisfy the need). They may work harder, which is the response desired by the manager. If the person is promoted, the need is then satisfied. If a person does work harder and there is no promotion *and* if the desire to be promoted (continued arousal) still exists, the person may suppress the desire for advancement or might try to find a better job elsewhere.

Such a model of motivation to work suggests that there is a relationship between job performance and need satisfaction. The person would have needs satisfied when he or she performs well and subsequently receives pay, advancement, or recogni-

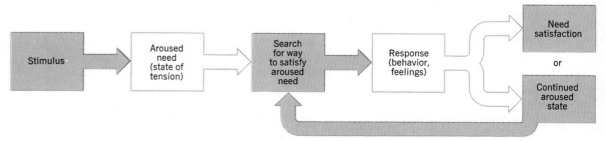

FIGURE 15.1 A needs model of motivation.

tion. If the "needs" model does indeed parallel real life, it can be used by managers to get better results from work groups. It would work this way: a manager arouses worker needs any number of ways, for example, opportunity to advance, threats to job security, improved working condition. When the worker produces more and the aroused need is satisfied, that is, the person actually is paid at a higher rate, the level of individual satisfaction should increase. This reinforces working harder and the individual should continue to work harder to obtain satisfaction.

Needs and Job Satisfaction

Job satisfaction is a generalized attitude toward work. This general attitude exists because of the specific facets of the job situation (like working conditions, pay) are linked together and associated with work. *Job facets* are identifiable aspects of work and the work situation. Pay, recognition from a supervisor, working conditions, relationships with peers and supervisors, and so on are job facets. The person assesses each of the separate job facets against a particular personal goal (desired end state). For example, in Figure 15.2, the person's judgement about "How the Boss *Is*" is compared to "How the Boss *Should Be*," and the results of these comparisons lead to the level of job satisfaction.

The general model that explains the level of job satisfaction is:

$$\begin{pmatrix} \text{what a job} \\ \text{facet} \\ \textbf{\textit{should be}} \end{pmatrix} \text{less} \begin{pmatrix} \text{what} \\ \text{job facet} \\ \textbf{\textit{is}} \end{pmatrix} = \text{discrepancy}$$

If there is a large discrepancy between "what is" and "what should be" for each job facet, and when several negative facets are compounded, a state of low job satisfaction exists. If there is only a little discrepancy between "what is" and "what should be" for all job facets or "what should be" exceeds "what is," there is high job satisfaction.

What an employee wants is determined by his or her values and is related to economic and psychological needs. What one feels one should receive is deter-

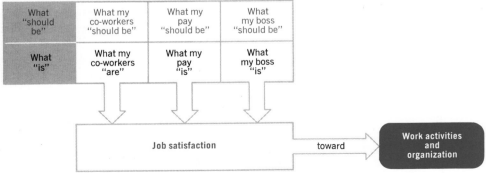

FIGURE 15.2   Some facets of work and their relationship to job satisfaction.

mined by a personal sense of equity—by one's perceptions of what other individuals are receiving for what they do compared to what one believes one does. Thus, if an employee finds out that another worker is earning more than he is, but is not exerting more effort or putting in more hours, or does not have more seniority or education, then he will feel a sense of inequity or injustice and will be dissatisfied. On the other hand, an employee may be satisfied with his pay even if he finds out that other workers doing similar work are getting more pay, if he perceives that they work harder than he does or have more seniority, education, or ability.

In certain circumstances pay satisfaction or dissatisfaction is not highly related to overall job satisfaction. If a worker places relatively little value on pay, as compared to the value he places on other job factors, pay dissatisfaction may not significantly reduce his total job satisfaction. And even when workers on similar jobs receive exactly the same benefits, we would still expect differences in job satisfaction among them because they will have different job values. Some employees place a high value on using their abilities; some do not. A variety of job satisfaction and dissatisfaction factors, then, and their relationship to one another, must be weighed and reckoned with when devising motivational programs.

All this is to say that if the manager expects to increase satisfaction, he must work on those facets that make a difference to employees. In one organization that was experiencing high dissatisfaction, the management believed a "communications" gap existed. They began bombarding the employees with "newsletters" and other informational devices. The general dissatisfaction remained. An evaluation by an outside consultant found that the problem came, not from lack of information, but from several policies the workers thought unfair. One cause of discontent was the "parking policy." Certain parking places were always restricted, even after 5:00 P.M. Some employees who worked a later shift thought this unfair, especially since the spaces were generally unused after 5:00 o'clock. A reconsideration of the policy led to a change, removing a cause of dissatisfaction.

Satisfaction with Work and Performance

Job satisfaction and its relationship to performance may well be the most studied factor in organizations, with much of the work resulting from the interest generated by the Hawthorne studies and the point of view known as "human relations." The logic underlying the human relations point of view is that if a worker is committed to a job, productivity will be higher. Such a commitment in work will be made because of, and reflected by, the level of job satisfaction. By increasing job satisfaction, goes the assumption, we will improve performance.

This belief that high job satisfaction should cause high performance is very strongly embedded in much of the writing and thinking about people and work. But why *should* satisfaction cause a worker to perform at a higher level when a basic postulate in Maslow's need theory would lead to just the opposite prediction? Maslow believed that a *satisfied need was not a motivator*. Therefore, people should be less likely to put forth more work when they were highly satisfied.

A worker may be perfectly happy in his job while at the same time be wholly uninterested in exerting much effort at it. Or a worker may perform at a very high level even though dissatisfied, because he fears losing his job. Or he may perform well because he believes it is his duty as a responsible person to do the best he can. (Professionals, especially, often feel this way.) He also may work hard because he needs the money to pay his bills.

That satisfaction causes high performance is an intriguing assumption and would be very useful if it were consistent with reality. Victor Vroom has examined research in which job satisfaction (or employee attitude toward work) was correlated with performance. He found that the average correlation in these studies between satisfaction and performance was very low, leading him to conclude that:

> There is no simple relationship between job satisfaction and job performance. . . . We do not know yet the conditions which affect the magnitude and direction of relationships between satisfaction and performance.
>
> . . . The absence of a marked or consistent correlation between job satisfaction and performance casts some doubt on the generality or intensity of either effects of satisfaction on performance or performance on satisfaction. It also suggests that the conditions which determine a person's level of job satisfaction and his level of job performance are not identical.[1]

Improving job satisfaction may not in itself necessarily improve job performance. On the other hand, there is some evidence that higher job satisfaction may follow better job performance.[2] This is most likely when the higher performance is followed by rewards important to the employee, such as a promotion when a job is done well.

At the same time, research has shown a definite and consistent relationship between job satisfaction and the turnover and absenteeism rate among workers.[1] Absenteeism and turnover can both, of course, affect costs and productivity. If a worker is absent from the job, for example, others may have difficulty performing their jobs because of that absence. If a worker quits, his equipment and machinery stand idle until he is replaced (perhaps by a less experienced worker). So while it is very difficult to associate job satisfaction with productivity levels, if we accept the idea that it is related to absenteeism and turnover, then it is clear that some substantial costs may be reduced if satisfaction can be increased.

High turnover and absenteeism can be very expensive. Consider, for example, a plant employing 1,000 workers at an average wage (salary and fringe benefits) of $20,000 per employee. If the absentee rate is 5 percent, this means that the plant must hire 50 additional employees at a yearly cost of $1,000,000 to offset the absenteeism. Cutting absenteeism by one-fifth (20 percent) would result in a savings of $200,000 a year. A recent *Wall Street Journal* article estimated that absenteeism cost U.S. industry $35 billion in 1978 (see item 16.1).

Some of the costs incurred by organizations due to turnover are fringe benefits, severance pay, overtime costs, underutilization of facilities, administrative expenses, training cost, and productivity losses. One very conservative estimate is that a rank-and-file worker who quits can cost a company at least $3,000.[3] If 10 percent of a work force of 1,000 workers quits each year, then turnover costs will amount to at least $300,000. Because of high cost associated with job dissatisfaction, leading as it does to turnover and absenteeism, managers must be concerned with job satis-faction.

TWO-FACTOR THEORY

There are two problems with a "needs" model of motivation to work. First, the categories of needs proposed by Maslow are simply too broad to be useful to a manager. How, for instance, can a manager arouse "social needs" of several various subordinates, especially when social needs are satisfied in different ways for different people? A manager must have more specific information about needs to know what to do to "motivate" employees. Second, the research on the different facets of job satisfaction produced divergent results. No job facet has demonstrated a consistent relationship over enough studies to justify a conclusion that it was related to pro-ductivity.

One approach, developed by Herzberg and called two-factor theory, seemed to resolve this dilemma. A study of two hundred engineers and accountants was conducted.[4] The accountants and engineers were asked to recall two types of work events:

1. Those events or circumstances that characterized a marked improvement in the work satisfaction, or when they felt exceptionally good about their jobs.
2. Those events or circumstances that characterized a significant reduction in their positive feelings about their jobs.

From an analysis of the interviews, the researchers concluded that the facets of the work situation that were associated with feelings of satisfaction were different from the facets associated with dissatisfaction. Those characteristics associated with posi-tive feelings about work were called satisfiers (or motivators). Factors associated with negative feelings about work were called dissatisfiers (or hygiene factors). Mo-tivators affected performance differently than did hygiene factors.

Hygiene Factors (Dissatisfiers)

Job characteristics associated with reports of dissatisfaction at work are:

1. Technical supervision
2. Interpersonal relations with peers, subordinates, and supervisors
3. Salary
4. Working conditions
5. Status
6. Company policy
7. Job security
8. Interpersonal relations with the supervisor

Notice that these factors describe the **context** in which work is done. They are not part of the job itself, but circumstances that surround it. The research concluded that when hygiene factors are present in a job, they are **not** related to better per-formance. For example, presence of good interpersonal relationships will not be associated with high productivity. But when good interpersonal relationships (a hygiene factor) are absent, the absence will cause dissatisfaction. This is why they were called dissatisfiers.

Motivating Factors (Satisfiers)

Satisfiers, on the other hand, are related to high job satisfaction and a willingness to work harder. When satisfiers are present, they may induce more effort. But if they are absent, the absence will not produce dissatisfaction in most people. According to Herzberg,[4] the following characteristics of the work situation are motivational in nature:

1. Responsibility
2. Achievement
3. Advancement
4. The work itself
5. Recognition
6. Possibility of growth

These are different from hygiene factors. Hygiene factors are part of the job context. Motivators are **job content** factors, a characteristic of the job itself. According to two-factor theory, when a person is in a challenging job, he or she is likely to be satisfied and motivated to perform better. The lack of responsibility, achievement, or advancement opportunities or any other "motivator" does not lead to dissatisfaction, but merely the absence of satisfaction.

A unique interpretation of job satisfaction came out of Herzberg's research. It was that a job facet worked in only one direction; it was unipolar. This means, for example, that a good pay level for a job would not cause satisfaction to exist. Rather pay (a hygiene factor) worked only on the "dissatisfier" side. Pay is a problem if not adequate, as shown in Figure 15.3, but not helpful when it is. But recognition (a motivator) worked in the other direction. It caused high "satisfaction" (or motivation), but when it was not given, there was no dissatisfaction.

The Appeal for Managers

The attraction of two-factor theory for a manager is quite obvious. The manager is no longer faced with the ambiguous direction to "provide a person with a job that satisfies ego needs." Two-factor theory helps a manager know **what to work on** to affect worker satisfaction and motivation. If a high level of dissatisfaction is present, then to improve the situation attention must be directed to the hygiene factors. For example, working conditions must be improved, company policy changed and made less a problem, or the technical competence of supervisors increased by training.

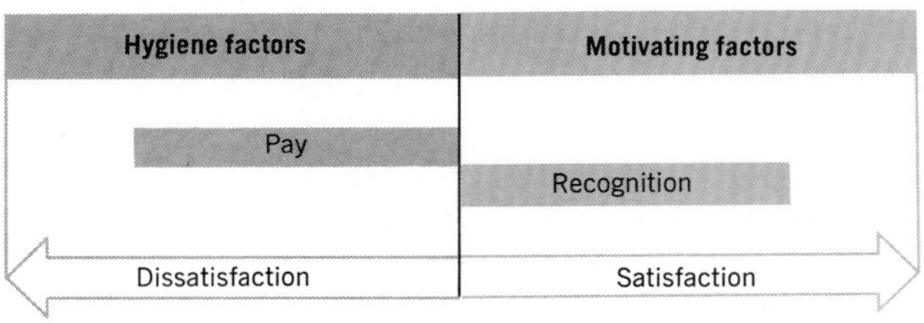

FIGURE 15.3   The unipolar character of job satisfaction factors, according to Herzberg.

But the manager knows this will not be adequate to improve performance. To get improved results, the manager must work on the motivators, and this means changing the content of the work to make it more challenging and intrinsically rewarding.

Criticisms of Two-Factor Theory

Two-factor theory has had an important influence on motivation theory, and it has accordingly been subject to a number of critical evaluations. Several of the criticisms are important enough to suggest a great deal of caution in using this approach. Some criticisms are:

1. A *method bias* led to the results Herzberg obtained.
2. The theory does not take *differences among* individuals into account.
3. The results are *inconsistent with other research.*

Method bias means that the findings from the research occurred because of the way the research was conducted, not the nature of the subject studied. The research technique Herzberg and his associates used was a semistructured "incident recall" method. A subject was asked to remember either a "good" or a "bad" experience at work. In other studies of job satisfaction that use such an "incident method" it has generally been found that job factors fall into similar "motivator–hygiene" classes as two-factor theory. However, this may be due to the kind of question that is asked.

The employee's answer when asked to think of a time when he or she felt unusually good or unusually bad about the job is influenced by the employee's memory, what has actually occurred, and the tendency toward selective perception. The criticism of such a research method is that a person attributes successful events to oneself and unsuccessful events to others.

Locke conducted several studies using such an "incident recall" method.[5] Locke's research shows that *individual differences* are not considered and that the factors listed by Herzberg as satisfiers and dissatisfiers are not as clear-cut and obvious as they may seem on the surface. For example, a person wants "challenging work he can cope with successfully." Self-confidence as well as skill will be a determinant here. One person may find it challenging to repair an automobile engine. The highly skilled mechanic who views an engine as a problem to be solved will be motivated to work on it. That same broken-down engine would be avoided by a person who has no knowledge of internal combustion engines, for he knows that if he works on it, the problem will probably become worse. Thus, individual characteristics and personality differences would also lead to different reactions to the factors classified as motivators and hygiene factors.

Inconsistency with other research is also a weakness attributed to the two-factor theory. After an extensive examination of other research that evaluated effects of the factors listed as satisfiers and dissatisfiers in two-factor theory, House and Wigdor concluded[6] that other studies found different results from Herzberg. Other studies that considered, say, recognition and the quality of working conditions as they related to effectiveness had a wide range of findings. In some studies these two factors were positively related to results, and in other studies they were negatively related.

The Contribution of Two-Factor Theory

With such limitations of two-factor theory, why does it deserve such attention? First, it has been a dominant model in the study and application of motivation theory for several years. It has been widely used by practicing managers as a basis for managing people, changing organizations, and designing jobs. Hackman and Suttle also claim that it directed attention to the motivating potential of the job itself.

> In sum, what the Herzberg theory does, and does well, is point attention directly to the enormous significance of the work itself as a factor in the ultimate motivation and satisfaction of employees. And because the message of the theory is simple, persuasive, and directly relevant to the design and evaluation of actual organizational changes, the theory continues to be widely known and generally used by managers of organizations in this country.[7]

EQUITY THEORY

Equity theory is a part of a broader theory called **exchange theory.** These theories focus on the motivational effects of perceived imbalances in exchanges between individuals and groups or among individuals themselves. Equity theory predicts the performance and attitudinal consequences of feelings of being underrewarded or overrewarded for work.

An individual exchanges with the organization such things as work behavior, education, skill, seniority, and the like (inputs) for factors such as pay, fringes, status, and other outcomes of work (outputs). The fairness of this exchange is judged not only by the ratio of a person's inputs to outputs, but by how that ratio compares to the inputs and outputs of others. So when the ratios of two individuals are equal, there is equity:

$$\frac{O_A}{I_A} = \frac{O_B}{I_B}$$

This means that person A believes that what she is getting relative to person B is in balance, or equitable.

Inequity occurs when the ratios are not equal. Thus, if A believes that she brings more to the job (inputs such as more education and skill) than B brings, then according to A, B is overpaid relative to A. B's ratio is more favorable, as

$$\frac{O_A}{I_A} < \frac{O_B}{I_B}$$

It is possible that B, finding out that this is true, will feel overpaid, while A feels underpaid. According to equity theory, the anger or the guilt resulting from such feelings of over- or underrewarding (i.e., inequity) will create tensions in proportion to the amount of perceived inequity.

The persons (A and B) will then be motivated to take actions to reduce the feelings of inequity.[8] A number of actions can be taken to reduce feelings of inequity.

1. A person can change inputs. One may put forth more or less effort, for example, to alter the equity balance.

2. Pressures may be exerted to increase outputs to bring equity into balance. For example, if there is a wage differential between two similar positions, which is believed to be unjustified, pressures may be applied to increase the output of the higher-paid group.

3. A person can withdraw. One may be able to leave the situation in which inequity exists. For example, a person may quit a job or ask for a transfer.

4. A person can change perceptions about the value of their, or others', inputs and outputs. It is often possible to do this by rationalizing in such a way as to either increase or minimize the importance and value of the factors that affect equity.

5. One can compare oneself to another person. For example, if person A feels that she is underpaid relative to person B, she might change her reference to person C. This could result in a better balance.

These actions to reduce feelings of inequity may affect performance and attitudes. Adams, a principal contributor to equity theory, makes some predictions about how equity will be sought.[9] He believes persons are more likely to reduce inequity by changing outputs. Individuals are unlikely to change inputs that are costly. People will resist changing their perceptions of value of inputs and outputs because this often affects their self-esteem. Adams also thinks individuals will not leave a situation unless the distress of the inequity is very high and there are no other easy ways to reduce inequity.

Research on equity theory also sheds some light on how inequity may be reduced. Several studies show that when people felt underrewarded it led to less effort put forth with subsequent lower quantity and quality of output. When an incentive payment plan is used, and there is underpayment, individuals produced an acceptable number of units per hour but with lower quality. Underreward also is related to higher absenteeism and turnover.

Feelings of overreward may be less common than those of underreward. Research in the overreward condition shows that when workers are paid on an hourly rate, higher quantity and quality result. When there is perceived overreward in incentive pay systems, the result appears to be lower quantity but higher quality. These behavioral reactions probably serve to reduce individual feelings of guilt in this situation.

There is a good deal of research support for the basic tenets of equity theory.[8] Yet to use such an approach in a work situation, managers must be able to know how employees compare themselves to others. Then management could take those actions to eliminate the undesirable behaviors associated with feelings of inequity.

EXPECTANCY THEORY AND PERFORMANCE

Understanding motivation to work will help us understand why one person might do better at work than another with similar skills. A person may be willing to exert more effort in a job for any number of reasons. He or she may "want to succeed" more than another. When we use the term motivation to work we mean the amount of drive or force a person has that is directed toward work requirements. One useful way to analyze motivation to work as a "force to perform" is with an **expectancy theory** of motivation. In expectancy theory

$$\text{motivation to work} = \Sigma \text{ (expectancies} \times \text{valence)}$$

An expectancy is a belief that the amount of effort put forth in work will lead to specific results. Valences are satisfaction that a person *anticipates* will occur when the result is obtained.

Expectancies

An expectancy is a probability estimate about how likely a particular amount of effort one exerts is to lead to some result. For instance, a student might have this expectancy about an examination, "Studying ten hours is likely (probability = .9) to lead to a grade of 85." Another expectancy about this exam is that "Studying eight hours will cause me to be very tired." These are two different types of expectancies that must be taken into account in determining how motivated the student is to study.

"Effort → Performance" (E → P) expectancy is the first type of expectancy. It refers to the person's expectations about the relationship of his effort expenditures to the attainment of certain performance levels. For example, a salesperson's expectancy about meeting a sales goal will depend on the salesperson's perception of the number of customer calls that will be required to achieve that goal and the effort this will involve.

Obviously the personal characteristics of an individual affect expectancies. Personality characteristics have been shown to be related to E → P expectancies. Managers high in self-esteem put forth more effort to achieve difficult work goals than did managers low in self-esteem.[8] Individuals with high skill in an area will have higher expectancies than those with less competence.

Technological factors may also affect E → P expectancies. When a person works in a technology-dominated job with poor equipment, neither high skills nor high self-esteem will be related to high E → P expectancies.

The *performance → outcome* (P → O) expectancy is the second type of expectancy. This refers to an individual's expectations about the relationship between achieving a particular performance level and the attaining of certain outcomes. For example, an employee may feel that if he consistently attains a particular high performance level there is a moderate probability he will become fatigued, a high probability that his co-workers will be angry with him, a high probability that he will get a pay increase, and a moderate probability that the foreman will give him a compliment.

The behavior of a superior can influence employee expectations. One study, for example, found that when supervisors increased the use of specific performance goals for subordinates and also reviewed their performance more frequently, employees increasingly felt high performance would result in pay increases and promotions for them.[10] When management switches to an incentive pay plan, employees perceive a stronger relationship between high performance and the receiving of economic rewards than they did before.[8]

Valence

Not all outcomes are equally desired by a person, of course. Different outcomes may have different valences. ***Valences are anticipated satisfactions that result from outcomes.*** They are the individual's estimates of the future pleasantness—or unpleasantness—of an outcome.

It is obvious that some of these outcomes are positive and some are negative. For the student above, ready to take the examination, some of the outcomes (Grade A) are very positive and desirable. The other expected outcome (getting tired from studying) has a negative valence. The degree to which a particular anticipated outcome has a positive or negative valence depends upon the person's anticipations and expectations of the outcomes. For example, an employee may expect that there is a high probability of receiving a pay increase if she achieves a particular performance level. How positive the pay increase will be to her will depend on her perception of the consequences of getting a pay increase. If she can use the extra pay to buy something she has long desired, then she will probably put a high positive valence on the pay increase. On the other hand, she may anticipate that the pay increase will be spent by others in her family or by somebody she owes money to and therefore put only a slight positive valence on the pay increase.

If we subscribe to expectancy theory, we would assume that individuals tend to choose performance levels that they are likely to be able to achieve and that are also anticipated to result in a set of outcomes with more positive than negative values to the individual, given his needs and situation.[11]

A Final Point

These expectancy theory factors are summarized in Figure 15.4, which shows how ability and motivation are linked to performance. This model shows that in order to get performance, both motivation and ability must be present. If one is absent,

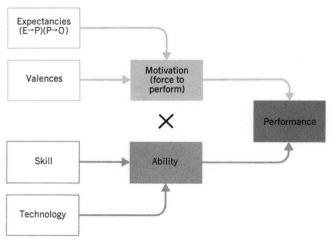

FIGURE 15.4 The expectancy theory approach to motivation.

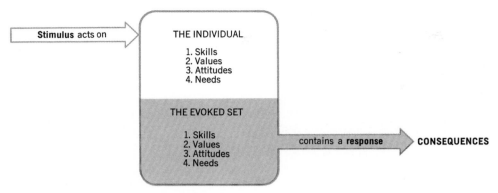

FIGURE 15.5   A model of human behavior.

there will be no performance. Motivation and ability are not equally important in all cases, either. Often motivation is the most critical factor to good results. Sometimes ability is more critical. We will expand on this point later in this chapter and in the next.

REINFORCEMENT THEORY

Figure 15.5 represents a reinforcement model of motivation.[12] The individual is a configuration of skills, attitudes, values, and needs and is affected this way: The person perceives a stimulus, or **cue,** in the environment. The cue triggers a certain part—a subset—of individual values, attitudes, and behaviors called the **evoked set.** A person acts, with behavior or emotions, and the action is called the **response.** When **consequences** (such as reinforcements or punishment) are associated with the response, then the likelihood of that cue triggering a similar response in the future is changed.

Stimuli

A stimulus is a factor or a condition that triggers a response. Stimuli, or cues, are those "aspects of the environment that have a significant impact on behavior in the next time interval."[13] A stimulus can be fairly simple—say, a whistle that signals a lunch break in a factory. Or it may be complex—a disciplinary interview in which a superior provides a great deal of information in the form of verbal criticism (what he says), as well as information convey by how it is said (e.g., with a frown and harsh tone of voice).

Evoked Set

Stimuli act on the individual, but not on all the values, attitudes, and behavioral alternatives. A cue evokes only the particular set of these elements that the individual associates with the cue. The set it acts upon is called the "evoked set," the set that contains the response of the person to the cue. For example, when the lunch whistle blows, it generally triggers a whole group of attitudes and behaviors associated with eating lunch—workers pick up their lunch buckets, head for the eating area, and so on.

Response

Part of the evoked set includes the response of the individual. The response may be behavior, or it may be an emotional reaction. It can be relatively simple (such as going to eat when the lunch whistle blows), or complex (such as changing the way an individual does a job after a disciplinary interview).

Consequences

A stimulus induces tension to act—the individual feels the need to do something or say something. When we respond to a cue with a behavior (verbal or physical) or the expression of an attitude and associate the behavior with reinforcement or punishments, the likelihood of the response occurring changes.

Some responses are associated with positive consequences while others result in negative consequences. In general a person will be more likely to repeat those actions (or respond to those stimuli) that produce positive consequences and avoid those that have negative consequences. In some instances the consequences of our behavior can be controlled by others. For example, suppose we perform our job particularly well and we receive a pay increase as a result of a recommendation by our boss. Or it may be that when we are late for work we receive a disciplinary notice. Figure 15.6 shows the effects of applying or withholding positive or negative consequences.

1. *Reinforcement.* This occurs when the probability of a response is increased. ***Positive*** reinforcement is the application of a positive or desirable consequence when a person acts. Positive reinforcement occurs, for example, when a person who has met a cost improvement objective receives desired recognition and a pay increase. For a consequence to be a positive reinforcer, the individual must have a need for more of whatever is used as the reinforcer. ***Negative*** reinforcement means that undesirable (or negative) consequences are withdrawn or withheld or do not occur. With a negative reinforcer, the probability of engaging in the behavior that avoids the undesirable consequence is increased. Hamner cites this example:

FIGURE 15.6   The relationship between the application and withdrawal of positive and negative consequences

Action Taken	Type of Consequence	
	Positive Consequence	Negative Consequence
Apply	***Positive reinforcement*** Effect: Increase the probability of the response	***Punishment*** Effect: Decrease the probability of the response
Withdraw	***Punishment*** Effect: Decrease the probability of the response	***Negative reinforcement*** Effect: Increase the probability of the response
Nonreinforcement	Extinction: Decrease the probability of the response	

Punctuality of employees is often maintained [in this way]. The noxious stimulus (undesirable consequence) is criticism by the shop steward or office manager for being late. In order to avoid criticisms . . . employees make an effort to be on time.[13]

2. *Punishment.* Punishment can occur, as shown in Figure 15.6, either by applying a negative consequence or by withholding a desirable one. When a subordinate who fails in one aspect of his or her job does not get an anticipated promotion, that is a form of punishment. When a salesperson fails to meet his or her quota for a sales period and as a result he or she is reassigned to a less desirable territory, that is punishment. Most of us can understand this notion when we visualize its application to children. When a child misbehaves and is spanked (an application of an undesirable consequence), it is clearly a case of punishment. Likewise, when the child misbehaves and is not allowed to have his friends in (withholding or withdrawing a desirable consequence), that too is punishment.

3. *Nonreinforcement.* Another way that behavior may be affected is by nonreinforcement. Extinction occurs when either positive or negative consequences that have been associated with a particular behavior by a person are withdrawn. As the reinforcement or punishment fails to occur for the action, the frequency of the action diminishes. For instance, a person may expect a supervisor to comment favorably on his or her work each time a project is completed. If over time the supervisor responds with recognition less frequently, the quality and quantity of work may fall off.

The individual must perceive the link between the consequence and the behavior (response). An employee, for instance, may engage in a wide variety of behaviors followed either by praise or censure from a superior. Often the employee does not know for such which of several behaviors resulted in the superior's approval or disapproval. Unfortunately, individuals often believe it was one kind of behavior that obtained approval when actually it was quite another. Therefore individuals often act in ways they believe to be pleasing to others, when actually those ways are not pleasing at all.

Reinforcement Schedules

The frequency and rate at which various contingencies (rewards or punishments) are associated with particular responses is called the ***reinforcement schedule.*** This schedule affects the speed with which responses are learned or behavior changes. Rewarding every correct response is a 100 percent reinforcement schedule. With 100 percent reinforcement, new responses are learned very quickly. However, if individuals become used to being rewarded every time they make a certain type of response, they stop behaving that way very quickly if the reinforcement stops. The nonreinforcement is very obvious to the individual, leading to a reduction in the frequency of the behavior, or extinction.

A variable schedule is one on which individual responses are reinforced or rewarded only intermittently. It takes longer for new behavior to develop with a variable schedule, but stopping the reinforcement will not stop the behavior immediately. The individual will continue to anticipate the reward, even though it is not forthcoming, since the nonreinforcement is not obvious. Research has shown that an intermittent and variable reinforcement schedule is slow to bring about new behaviors, but very effective for maintaining a particular type of behavioral response once it is learned.[14]

Behavioral Change

Individuals may learn to respond in a particular way in one situation, and then find themselves in another, similar situation in which the old response is not reinforced, or perhaps even sanctioned. If now a new behavior, even the opposite behavior, is positively reinforced, the individual will behave differently. This is, by definition, behavior change.

For example, let us say a person grows up in an anti-union household, where the family expresses negative attitudes toward labor unions. Negative comments about unions are reinforced with signs of approval. Later suppose the person goes to work in a unionized company. When he or she expresses negative views about unions, that view is met by disapproval from fellow workers. Since the individual may wish to have approval (rewards) instead of disapproval (punishments) from fellow workers, he or she may begin to express positive attitudes toward labor unions—and at work these may be positively rewarded. Ultimately, in order to justify the contradictory attitudes expressed in the two situations—home and work—the person may take a middle position, saying that unions have both good and bad features. The behavior, what a person saying about unions, has changed because of the contrasting reinforcements received.

THE MOTIVATION/RESULTS MODEL

Each of these approaches to understanding motivation is useful in some respects, but they fail to capture the complexity of managing performance. It is quite obvious that motivation is important, but so are other factors. We think that the proper way to examine the subject of motivation is to start by understanding performance, then considering the relationship between motivation and results. How is motivation linked to performance? What other factors intervene between motivation and performance? When is motivation important and when is it not? Our concept of the motivation/results relationship is shown in Figure 15.7.

This model shows that human factors and technological factors are the basic inputs to performance. The manager works to arrange these two factors in the appropriate relationship to each other. What the manager does will affect a person's expectancies about effort and performance. A useful motivation approach must take all of these factors into account.

PERFORMANCE COMPONENTS

What does it mean when we say someone is a good performer? A "star"? Think about any person's job. There are many parts to it. A quarterback of a football team must be able to pass, understand defenses, and run. A professor teaches and carries out research. The manager of an auditing unit must manage a staff, run meetings, and understand the financial structure of the organization. There are, it is obvious, several parts (or components) of any job, even the most simple.

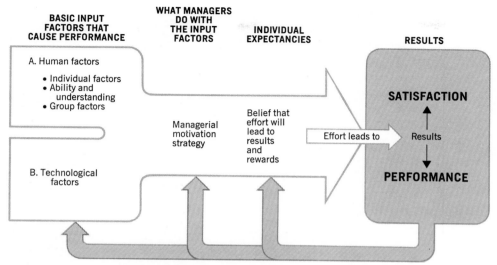

FIGURE 15.7   The motivation/results model.

A person may be highly competent in one work component, but not in another. He may be more motivated (interested) in one facet of performance than another. A quarterback may be most interested in throwing passes, either because he is most skilled at throwing or throwing gets the most public attention. We illustrate how performance components are related to the motivation/results model in the following example of a production foreman's job. Suppose that the foreman carries out these activities (see Figure 15.8):

1. Preparing work schedule
2. Ordering raw materials
3. Dealing with subordinates
4. Running departmental meetings

The foreman's superior may view some facets of performance as more important than others. Superiors may focus on, and reinforce, only one aspect of a job. It is possible that top management, being concerned with cost reduction, emphasizes raw materials' costs. Consequently, they create an incentive system that rewards cost reduction. This may cause the foreman to emphasize this aspect of his job, perhaps to the neglect of the other aspects.

Performance Components and Inputs

From Figure 15.8 we can see that the input factors of the motivation/results model are different for each of the various performance components of a job. Each performance component may have a different mix of technological and human input factors. For example, running departmental meetings will require more human skills than does ordering raw materials. However, ordering raw materials may require the use of computers and the ability to understand materials flow. There are clearly different skills required for the two job components, but the same person is expected to have them.

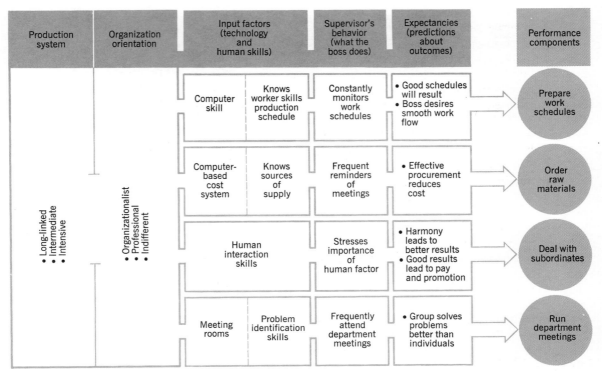

Production system	Organization orientation	Input factors (technology and human skills)		Supervisor's behavior (what the boss does)	Expectancies (predictions about outcomes)	Performance components
• Long-linked • Intermediate • Intensive	• Organizationalist • Professional • Indifferent	Computer skill	Knows worker skills production schedule	Constantly monitors work schedules	• Good schedules will result • Boss desires smooth work flow	Prepare work schedules
		Computer-based cost system	Knows sources of supply	Frequent reminders of meetings	• Effective procurement reduces cost	Order raw materials
		Human interaction skills		Stresses importance of human factor	• Harmony leads to better results • Good results lead to pay and promotion	Deal with subordinates
		Meeting rooms	Problem identification skills	Frequently attend department meetings	• Group solves problems better than individuals	Run department meetings

FIGURE 15.8 Performance components and the motivation/results model.

Expectancies and Performance Components

Similarly, the foreman will have different expectancies about each component of his job. He may feel that if he increases his effort at work scheduling, he will get a smoother flow of work. And if he does, then he may receive a pay increase, which he values. The foreman may thus spend more time on this activity than on the others.

He may not have the same expectancies about the other task components. He may have low expectations of the payoffs for ordering raw materials. He may know that this area is of great importance to top management, but he may have little control over the activity if he must clear his requests with, say, a purchasing department.

The Boss and Performance Components

Consider the different ways a manager of a group of finish carpenters working for a home construction firm and the manager of an assembly department in an automobile plant would try to solve the problem of poor performance. The construction foreman, faced with low quality and excessive costs, would most likely try to improve production by finding more highly skilled—or better—carpenters. How well a carpenter does the job is largely a function of personal skill. While tools and equipment are of some importance, getting better equipment is likely to have a marginal effect. For that type of work where human ability and skill are the most important contributors to results, we use the term **human-skill dominated.**

Supervisors on an assembly line have a very different managerial problem. The work they supervise is what we call **technology-dominated work.** Contrast the assembly line with the work of a carpenter (human-skill-dominated work). Only limited skills are usually required for assembly-line work. In fact, one advantage of assembly technology is that a lot of training and skill are not required. The most effective way to improve performance here would be to make improvements in the way the technology—the assembly line—is used. Investment in new machines and equipment may be most appropriate under these sorts of technological constraints, that is, the best way to improve productivity may be to emphasize improvements in technology itself.

The contrast between these two managers' problems illustrates an important point. To improve results, any manager must know how to determine the relationship between the human and technological factors in affecting output. The work a manager supervises must be analyzed along these lines. We cannot expect to improve performance simply because more competent personnel are hired when the work is technologically dominated. Similarly when the work is human-skill dominated, adding measurably to plant and equipment may have little effect.

In the next chapter we will show how problems of managers differ between technology-dominated and human-skill-dominated work. Now we examine the human input and the technological input factors briefly.

HUMAN FACTOR INPUTS

Human factors have already been extensively discussed in the preceding chapters. Here we highlight some particular facets of these discussions which we are very important to understanding the motivation/results model.

Needs and Values

Individual needs, attitudes, and values interact with other factors in the workplace to affect results. First, they affect the reaction to the strategies used by managers to motivate workers. In addition, work experiences contribute in many ways to the satisfaction of individual needs, often providing an opportunity to fulfill unsatisfied needs. (See the discussion of Maslow's hierarchy of needs in Chapter 5.) For example, doing well in a job may make an employee feel more secure, while performing below a certain level may be associated with a fear of job loss or negative reaction from the supervisor.

The relationship of individual needs to job characteristics has been shown in two studies. In one study of 200 employees in a telephone company, it was found that more complex jobs were associated with higher motivation, satisfaction, and quality of performance for those employees who were concerned with higher-order needs.[15] In another study it was found that dental assistants with high achievement needs had high job involvement, when many of the jobs were expanded to make the tasks more varied and complex.[16] In another, more structured unit, those who were primarily concerned with security needs were more involved with their work than were the dental assistants who were primarily concerned with achievement needs.

Achievement needs are of particular importance in managerial effectiveness in increasing performance.[17] Individuals high in achievement needs derive a deep feeling of satisfaction from competing against some standard of excellence.[18] They seek success for the sense of accomplishment that it gives them and they may perform at high levels even in the absence of material rewards for achievement. The standard of excellence may be an attempt to do better than others, or it may be simply an attempt to improve on earlier performance.

Some persons have a **need to avoid failure,** rather than a need for achievement.[19] Rather than obtaining need satisfaction by seeking to be successful in situations, they do so by attempting to avoid circumstances in which they might fail. Avoiding failure rather than attaining achievement is their main driving motive. These individuals, setting performance goals for themselves, tend to set them at either such a low level that they cannot fail, or at such an impossibly high level that no one expects them to succeed.

Group Factors

Groups often develop production norms—that is, what members consider appropriate performance levels—and they take actions to insure that members conform to these norms. We have seen that groups can affect perceptions and attitudes as well as behavior. Individuals, however, differ in their susceptibility to group pressures. Research indicates that compliance is greatest when a group member's previous values and attitudes are congruent with the compliance attempt and when the individual places a high value on group acceptance.[20] The individual then internalizes the group norm, and it governs his behavior.

Ability, Understanding, and Feedback

A person must have the ability to perform each of the performance components and must understand when those abilities are to be used. **Ability** is the capacity to carry out a set of interrelated behavioral or mental sequences to produce a result. One has the ability to play the piano when she can read music, understands chord structures, and has the manual dexterity to finger the keyboard appropriately. One has the manual dexterity to operate a computer when he is capable of preparing data, programming it, and processing it. Ability levels differ among and within individuals. It is important to be aware of this individual difference, since most jobs have several different characteristics that require different abilities. For example, the production foreman's job (Figure 5.8) includes scheduling of work, ordering raw materials, dealing with subordinates (handling grievances, supervising his crew), and running departmental meetings. Each of these separate activities requires different skills, and a person may be high in some and low in others. There may also be a wide range of performance among individuals who perform similar jobs. Some personnel managers are better than others. Some carpenters are more skillful than others. Some musicians perform better than others. As with needs, individual differences in ability must be taken into account when a manager makes a job assignment.

"Nonsense, Bentley! You can win 'em all!"

FIGURE 15.9

Understanding what to do, when something must be done, is also important. A person must know what is supposed to be done, when and how it is supposed to be done, and also how well it has been done. The problem of misunderstanding what is to be done is highlighted by research that shows that there is a good deal of disagreement between superiors and subordinates about performance expectations.[21] Many subordinates do not seem to know what their superiors expect of them, and this misunderstanding itself can contribute to poor performance. A number of studies have indicated that when individuals are given specific performance goals rather than being given the more generalized goal of "do your best," performance significantly increases.[22] Certainly part of this better performance can be attributed to the fact that the individual's efforts and energies are directed in specific directions rather than being diffused wastefully over a number of activities. Some of the performance increase can also be attributed to the individual's knowing specifically what will constitute good performance.

Feedback is necessary since it is sometimes difficult for a person to determine how well she is doing or has done without being told by a superior. Studies show that providing feedback on progress toward goals can improve performance.[10,23] One reason why feedback helps is that individuals selectively perceive their performance. They tend to rate their own performance higher than do their supervisors; they tend to assume their performance is adequate when it is not. In addition, if they are having difficulties, they tend to attribute them to outside forces rather than to themselves,[22] and thus they are not inclined to take actions themselves to correct such difficulties. In general, then, management can improve performance, first, by taking actions to communicate performance expectations clearly and, secondly, by providing appropriate feedback on such performance.

TECHNOLOGICAL FACTORS

''Technological factors'' are the tools, machines, facilities, and equipment a person uses in performing a task. Cooks use pots, stoves, and recipes to produce a meal. Auto workers use a complex assembly line with highly interdependent activities to manufacture a car. An artist uses a drawing board, paint, and a brush. Obviously the technological structure varies tremendously from one organization to another— as, say, between a steel mill and an advertising agency—as well as within organizations—as, say, where one group of employees must use computers and another group simply pencils and paper. The differences in the technological structure result from (1) degree of automation and (2) the arrangement of equipment and facilities.

Automation

Automation is the substitution of machine energy for human energy. A tool is automated when the force that drives it comes from some source other than a person. A pen, for instance, is a writing tool. It operates when it is guided and powered by a person. There is no automation. A kitchen blender is also a tool, but one that is more highly automated. Food is placed in a container, a switch is flipped, and the food is processed.

Arrangement of Facilities

How tools and facilities are arranged to complete a task also affects the technological inputs to performance (see Chapter 3). Work is sequentially arranged in ***long-linked technologies.*** In an ***intensive technology*** the arrangement and sequencing of work must wait to be done after the consumer requirements are known. The primary feature of the ***mediating technology*** is that several different users and several different customers are linked together through the production system, such as in a bank, which brings together those who wish to borrow and those who wish to save money.

Figure 15.10 shows different combinations of facilities arrangements and automation. The registration process at a university is a long-linked technology with low automation. There is a sequence of work activities to get students enrolled. They see advisors, sign up for classes, have fees calculated and so forth. This is very routine and much of the work is done manually. Food service at many fast-food restaurants is also long-linked, but more automated. Hamburgers are prepared in assembly-line fashion, though still with a good deal of manual labor. The epitome of the long-linked, highly automated process is automobile manufacturing.

A local farmers' market is an example of low automation in a mediating technology. Many farmers come to market and set up stands. Buyers come from all over

FIGURE 15.10   Levels of Automation of Different Types of Technology

Type of Technology	Level of Automation		
	Low and Simple	Moderate	High and Complex
Long-linked	University registrar	Fast-food restaurant	Automobile manufacturer
Mediating	Local farmers' market	Bank	Computer information system
Intensive	Home construction	Hospital emergency room	Heavy equipment manufacturing

to purchase fresh vegetables. At the other extreme is a complex computer information system, with several data sources used by a large number of people. For example, one large manufacturer has a system in which managers can access production information, cost data, budget position, and personnel information. All these different data from several different sources may be obtained at many different computer terminals.

Intensive technologies also have different levels of automation. Home construction is an example of an intensive technology with low automation. While these are power tools used by carpenters, most of the work is still manual. A hospital emergency room has complex equipment for analysis and treatment. Its use is governed by the technical personnel and the type of emergency being treated. An example of a highly automated and complex intensive technology is heavy equipment manufacturing. Large and complicated production machinery is used, but it is possible for each piece of equipment manufactured to be made to the specification of each customer.

SUMMARY

The motivation/results model shows the complex problems of managing. A manager must integrate the human factors and technological factors used in the work place. The manager must choose which of several motivational strategies is likely to produce the kind of results that are desired by the organization and the individual.

Basically, results at work (the output) are dependent upon the characteristics of the *inputs,* people, and the technology required to produce. The manager may do a number of different things to achieve the most effective blending of people and equipment. These are *managerial motivation strategies.* What a manager does, interacting with the input factors, affects individuals' beliefs about what their efforts will yield. These beliefs, called *expectancies,* are related to the amount of *effort* that a person is likely to put forth, and effort leads to *results.*

The results of effort can be broken down into two parts. One part is *performance.* By performance we mean either behavior or mental activity in which a person engages to produce the product, service, or idea necessary for the organization. A second component of results is individual *satisfaction.* When we accomplish any task, we may have positive or negative feelings about it. The important point in this chapter is that managers cannot rely on motivation as a way to improve performance. Quite often they must work to improve the technology to get better results.

Case
15.1 Toronto Safety Appliance Company

Toronto Safety Appliances Company was begun in 1934 in Toronto, Canada, by Chris Jacobs. Chris was formerly with the Canadian government as a supervisor of safety inspectors. He had developed a number of ideas for products that could help companies identify certain hazards associated with particular technological processes such as gas leakage from furnaces in steel mills.

The company was started in a small wooden building in Toronto. It grew unevenly over the next twenty years. As new products were developed, separate buildings and offices were added to the original building. Each building developed its own customs and norms of behavior.

In 1962 a fire destroyed the entire complex of wooden buildings. Fortunately, some of the equipment and supplies were saved and were moved into a very large abandoned factory building the company was able to rent. New supplies and equipment were purchased with insurance proceeds. The different manufacturing groups were placed together under one roof for the first time in the company's history.

The workers quickly saw that such matters as rest pauses, use of sick leave, discipline, and general supervisory style differed considerably from one group to another. Many of the workers soon became discontented. The number of complaints grew rapidly. Absenteeism increased.

1. Evaluate the causes.
2. Using the material presented in this chapter as guide, identify some of the most likely causes of this firm's current problems.
3. What would you recommend to alleviate the situation?

Case
15.2 National Retired Servicemen Agency

The National Retired Servicemen Agency (NRSA) employs a large number of lawyers to deal with the many claims of retired servicemen about their benefits and rights under a number of congressional statutes. Concerned with the level of performance of these lawyers and with the high cost of this activity, NRSA management initiated a new performance appraisal program suggested by an outside consultant.

With this new performance appraisal system, lawyers were evaluated in terms of the number of cases they processed in a given time period and the difficulty of these cases. These two factors were combined into an evaluation score. Each lawyer was supposed to obtain a particular number of case points in a particular time period. More points could be obtained for more difficult cases. The cases were rated as to difficulty by two of the supervisors of the lawyers. The performance standard was set at 100 points.

The range of points accumulated among the lawyers was from 50 to 190 for one time period. Lawyers with lower point scores were quite defensive. They defended themselves against criticism by their superiors by saying the case difficulty ratings were not accurate.

Recently, the Agency decided to change the required number of points for which lawyers are to be held accountable to reflect changes in the procedures for processing cases. More efficient methods for transcribing notes and quicker access to information through the use of modern computer systems have been installed. Many of the agency's lawyers have vigorously protested, not only about the proposed changes in the system, but about the original system itself. They claim the system is impairing, rather than helping, their performance. The lawyers have threatened to approach the largest veterans organizations, to which many of the Agency's clients belong, to enlist their support in this dispute with the Agency's top management.

1. Evaluate the likely effectiveness of this organization's performance appraisal system from the perspective of the motivational theories discussed in this chapter.
2. Would you recommend changes in this system? Why or why not? If so, what changes?

DISCUSSION QUESTIONS

1. What exactly is the work ethic that many managers subscribe to and feel that their subordinates should subscribe to?
2. What are some of the needs that an employee may see as necessary for job satisfaction? Why may they be seen as unnecessary?
3. How is job satisfaction related to performance? Defend your answer.
4. Is it true that job satisfaction is related to absenteeism and/or turnover? Defend your answer.
5. What problem did Herzberg try to deal with when he developed the two-factor theory?
6. Herzberg defined hygiene factors as factors associated with negative feelings about work. Name these dissatisfiers and discuss them.
7. Herzberg defined motivating factors as factors related to high job satisfaction. Name these satisfiers and discuss them.
8. What are the criticisms of two-factor theory? For an approach that has been criticized so strongly, why does it still persist?
9. What are expectancies and valences? How do they relate to performance levels?
10. Describe the reinforcement theory of motivation and how it explains behavioral change.
11. Which theory of motivation would you deem to be the most succcessful in a work situation? Defend your answer.

REFERENCES

1. Vroom, V. H. Work and motivation. New York, Wiley, 1964.
2. Greene, C. N. "Casual connections among managers' merit pay, job satisfaction and performance," Journal of Applied Psychology, 58 (1973): 95–100.
3. Nash, A. N., and S. J. Carroll. The management of compensation. Monterey, Calif., Wadsworth, 1975.

4. Herzberg, F., B. Mausner, and B. Snyderman. The motivation to work. New York, Wiley, 1959.

5. Locke, E. A. "Personnel attitudes and motivation," Annual Review of Psychology, 26 (1975): 457–480.

6. House, R. J., and L. Wigdor. "Herzberg's dual-factor theory of job satisfaction and motivation: A review of the evidence and a criticism. Personnel Psychology 20 (1967): 369–389.

7. Hackman, J. R., and J. L. Suttle. Improving life at work. Behavioral science approaches to organizational change. Santa Monica, Calif., Goodyear, 1977.

8. Miner, J. B. Theories of organizational behavior. New York, Dryden, 1980.

9. Adams, J. S. "Inequity in social exchange." In L. Berkowitz (ed.), Advances in experimental social psychology, Vol. 2, New York, Academic Press, 1965, pp. 267–299.

10. Carroll, S. J., and H. Tosi. Management by objectives: Applications and research. New York, Macmillan, 1973.

11. Mobley, W. H. "An interorganizational test of a task-goal expectancy model of work motivation and performance," Ph.D. thesis, University of Maryland, 1971.

12. March, J., and H. Simon. Organizations. New York, Wiley, 1958.

13. Hamner, W. C. "Reinforcement theory and contingency management in organizational settings." In H. L. Tosi and W. C. Hamner (eds.), Organizational behavior and management: A contingency approach. Chicago, St. Clair Press, 1978.

14. Nord, W. R. "Beyond the teaching machine: The neglected area of operant conditioning in the theory and practice of management," Organizational Behavior and Human Performance, 4 (1969): 375–401.

15. Hackman, R., and E. E. Lawler, III. "Employee reactions to job characteristics," Journal of Applied Psychology monograph, 55 (1971): 259–286.

16. Carroll, S. J. "Psychological needs as moderator of reactions to job enrichment in a field setting," *Proceedings, Academy of Management,* 23 (1977): 85–87.

17. McClelland, D. C. "Toward a theory of motive acquisition," American Psychology, 20 (1965): 321–323.

18. McClelland, D. C., J. Atkinson, J. Clark, and E. Lowell. The achievement motive. New York, Appleton-Century-Crofts, 1953.

19. Atkinson, J. W. "Motivational determinants of risk taking behavior," Psychological Review, 64 (1957): 359–372.

20. Helmreich, R., R. Bakeman, and L. Scherwitz. "The study of small groups," Annual Review of Psychology, 24 (1973): 337–354.

21. Maier, N. R. F., L. R. Hoffman, J. J. Hooven, and W. H. Read. "Superior-subordinate communication in management," American Management Association, 9 (1961).

22. Locke, E. A. "Personnel attitudes and motivation," Annual Review of Psychology, 26 (1975): 457–480.

23. Ilgen, D. R., Fisher, C. D., and Taylor, M. S. Consequences of individual feedback on behavior in organizations. Journal of Applied Psychology 64 (1979): 349–371.

CHAPTER SIXTEEN

Managing Motivation and Performance

Costly Problem

FIRMS TRY NEWER WAY TO SLASH ABSENTEEISM AS CARROT AND STICK FAIL

MORE TRY "JOB ENRICHMENT," SEEKING TO RAISE MORALE; A BOX PLANT GETS RESULTS

ALL "CURES" SEEM TEMPORARY

Northampton, Mass.—The midmorning sunshine darted through the windows as Jerry Hathaway, his wife, and his three-year-old daughter ("she's a great little camper") prepared for a weekend outing along the shimmering Quinebaug River.

With their gear assembled, one detail remained. Mr. Hathaway's wife, Donna, had to telephone a message to the local boxboard plant of Tenneco Inc.'s Packaging Co. of America. The message: "Jerry will be out sick today."

This popular lie plus legitimate absences adds up to a monumental headache for U.S. industry. Statistics suggest that absenteeism costs workers and the economy $20 billion a year in lost pay alone. In addition, industry spends $10 billion a year in sick pay and $5 billion on fringe benefits that continue whether or not the worker is there.

Absenteeism also can cripple production and profits. A computer analysis at the University of Nebraska for a major manufacturer showed that a 1 percent rise in absences could slash profits by 4 percent. Once when Mr. Hathaway and six co-workers failed to report for the forty-man night shift at the packaging company plant here, the evening's target of one million square feet of corrugated boxboard was sliced by 20 percent.

3.5 PERCENT OF HOURS LOST

In May 1976, according to the Federal Bureau of Labor Statistics, work-hours lost through absenteeism came to 3.5 percent. There is no later study, but Janice Hedges, who did the 1976 study, thinks the 3.5 percent figure still holds.

Some other labor economists wonder, however, whether the continuing business expansion hasn't produced a somewhat higher rate. Workers are more likely to take unnecessary days off in times of expansion because they are sure the job will still be there for them the next day.

Most researchers agree that absenteeism is an index of morale. "Workers who are turned off will stay out under any pretext," says Jerome Rosow, a former assistant secretary of labor. Mr. Rosow now heads the Work in America Institute in Scarsdale, New York, an organization that studies productivity and the quality of working life.

As hourly wages rise and leisure-time attractions proliferate, both the stick and the carrot—traditional discipline and newer attendance bonuses—are faring poorly in the campaign against absenteeism. Industry is increasingly turning to "job enrichment" programs aimed at giving the worker more pride in his job and more appreciation of its importance to the company. Such programs came along a decade ago, but about 75 percent of them involved white-collar jobs then; now, more of them are being tested on the factory floor, where absenteeism is more of a problem.

EVOLVING AT GE AND GM

Job enrichment programs are evolving at General Electric Co., General Motors Corp., and Ford Motor Co., among others, and they are already in full swing here at the boxboard plant.

Eli Kwartler, the plant manager, last year drafted a 100-item questionnaire on workers' attitudes. Among other things, the survey showed that night workers wanted a four-day week of ten-hour shifts, Monday through Thursday, instead of a five-day week of eight-hour shifts. So the company switched last June to a four-day night shift and reaped a double reward: Not only did absences fall, but the shift's production climbed 9 percent.

Even Mr. Hathaway, a fork-lift operator whose predilection for absences was common knowledge, took fewer days off after the changeover. He no longer had to skip Fridays to take long weekends.

The survey also showed that even conscientious workers were angered by a point-penalty system that management had imposed in an effort to cut absenteeism. Mr. Kwartler suggested that the workers come up with a better idea. A committee of four hourly workers and two supervisors did come up with a new system, and it took effect Dec. 1.

A POINT SYSTEM

415
*Managing
Motivation
and
Performance*

Under the old system, the penalty for absences without notice ranged from one point for an absence with a documented reason (this particularly infuriated the conscientious workers) to seven points for an outright no-excuse no-show. Forty points in twelve months meant dismissal; when June, say, of one year began, the points accumulated the previous June no longer counted against you. The new scale ranges from zero to three points. Thirty-one points bring dismissal, and the point total keeps accumulating; only by chalking up perfect-attendance periods can you reduce your point total.

Mr. Kwartler made other changes. Regular meetings were scheduled between employees and supervisors, and now full plant-wide meetings are held at least twice a year. "It's like an old town meeting," Mr. Kwartler says, "and the trust level has gotten to be such that these people have no compunction about letting me know where they stand. We don't necessarily do what they want, but the important thing is letting them know that their feelings are important enough to merit a response."

The company has begun posting weekly bulletins that include data on the company's backlog of orders. Mr. Kwartler says that this information formerly was kept secret lest workers use it to plan their absence. Workers are also told when they are doing well, and the entire work force can earn a bonus of up to 20 percent when it surpasses a week's production goal. Last October, the plant set a production record. Absenteeism is down to 3.5 percent from 4 percent.

More recent company bulletins entice employees to beat the production of an efficient sister plant in Syracuse, New York. "Everybody's got a little competitive spirit in them," says plant worker Stephen Burns, "and it's nice to set a record. It's also nice to be told when you're doing a good job." Mr. Burns is a machine operator who Mr. Kwartler says "used to be an absentee problem but lately has been producing better than ever."

A positive attitude also prevails in the front office, where secretary Mary Conti says, "Just look at the workers around here and you can see that it's worked out. We're not treated like peons here. That's a nice feeling, and we're pretty loyal."

A SWITCH AT THE LAMP PLANT

At a General Electric lamp plant in Memphis, manager Russell Colomb says casual absences fell to 2.2 percent in 1978, from 3.5 percent in 1977, after he instituted monthly plant-wide meetings where employees are told exactly what absenteeism costs the company.

"Most of our efforts now go into awareness programs and enrichment," Mr. Colomb says. "It's a matter of making workers feel they're important. There isn't anything that can beat that. We've tried to get our workers to realize just how important they are and how badly we need them here."

Worker teams meet with their supervisors weekly. They are congratulated when performance is good. When there is a poor production run on a certain type of light bulb, the supervisors don't point fingers: they ask for suggestions.

"We don't feel that wages are the primary motivator," Mr. Colomb says. "The real motivation is when the worker feels he's making a contribution. And a worker who feels he's contributing is the worker least likely to be an absentee problem."

Ford Motor Co. is trying similar programs, says Ernest Savoie, manager of labor relations planning, "and a lot of thought is being given now to expanding in the area."

"INTERCHANGE" AT GM

At some General Motors assembly plants, finished cars are pulled at random from the assembly line and put on display, their defects highlighted with big check marks. "Employees are asked, 'What can we do to see that this doesn't happen?'" says John Mollica, assistant director for labor relations. "We try for an interchange of ideas and principles—something more than a boss–employee relationship—in order to involve the worker."

Mr. Mollica says that a full-time staff is working on such methods. "We're growing in this area," he says, "but there's no handbook for this kind of thing."

On the other hand, there is enough experience with the old, punitive systems to indicate that they don't do the trick. One reason is that workers can learn to beat the system. Under the point-penalty method, for example, it isn't hard for a worker to keep his own record and simply make sure that he doesn't pass the dismissal level.

Despite the moves toward enrichment at Ford, a disciplinary system still exists there, but Mr. Savoie disparages it. "The group of chronic absentees just gets larger as more learn how to play the system," he says. Ford's short-term absence rate climbed to about 6 percent last year from 5.2 percent in 1972. "Obviously," Mr. Savoie says, "the old system isn't working very well."

CARROTS ALSO FAIL

More recent "well pay" and attendance bonus programs have also had disappointing results. Such programs reward perfect attendance with cash bonuses or paid time off.

Three of the nation's largest farm-equipment manufacturers have tried these programs. "The guys who were coming in kept coming in, and the guys we were trying to reach kept staying out on Fridays and sleeping in on Mondays," says a spokesman for International Harvester Co. A program providing paid time off for a week's perfect attendance was installed at Harvester, then was dropped from the current labor pact.

A spokesman for Caterpillar Tractor Co., which has a similar program, says that improvement, if any, has been slight. Deere & Co. says that latenesses and absences were somewhat reduced when its paid-time-off bonus for a perfect week of attendance was increased to 1½ hours from half an hour, but the company declines to give figures.

GM "tried a couple of reward programs, but they didn't work out," Mr. Mollica says. GM's absentee rate climbed to about 7.7 percent in 1977 from 5.8 percent in 1972. More recent figures aren't comparable because they have been inflated by inclusion of paid personal holidays.

While job-enrichment programs give some promise of alleviating the problem, no one views them as a cure-all. A particularly frustrating aspect of absenteeism is that any solution seems to be temporary at best. Ford's Mr. Savoie says, "There's nothing universal in this area, and you may have to change your techniques all the time."

Mr. Kwartler at the boxboard plant agrees. "We'll probably have to go right back into it in two years," he says, "and come up with something new."

Source: The Wall Street Journal, January 14, 1979, page 1.

Item 16.1, which opens this chapter, points out the different ways that firms use to deal with absenteeism. Several motivational strategies, most of them discussed in detail in this chapter, are being used to get people to come to work.

Managerial motivation strategies are manipulative in nature. This means simply that a manager is trying to get an individual to do what the manager wants that person to do. Motivational strategies, in and of themselves, should not be regarded as either good or bad. Goodness or badness depends upon whether or not an individual, so motivated by another, is ultimately placed in a position he or she might not have chosen freely, or is injured. To be "motivated" by a customer to take the afternoon off for a game of golf may be fully consistent with the desires of a salesperson. To be "motivated" by a superior to do something illegal is entirely another matter. Both the customer and the superior may use similar manipulative strategies. It is the outcome that causes motivation to be seen as good or bad.

MANAGEMENT MOTIVATION STRATEGIES

When a manager attempts to motivate others, he or she is acting primarily on the human input factor, within the technological constraints of the situation. Essentially, the manager attempts to increase the individual's drive to perform better. A number of different approaches can be used by managers. Each has its advantages and disadvantages and each varies in effectiveness from one situation to another. Some of the strategies have been evaluated by Carroll, who surveyed a number of different supervisory groups to assess which of these strategies they believed to be most useful in their work.[1] The effectiveness ratings given to some of these motivational strategies by several groups are shown in Table 16.1.

Fear or Threat

With the fear strategy, an individual is threatened with undesirable consequences unless he or she complies. "If you're late for work, you will be given a three-day layoff," or "You will be fired if you are insubordinate." The threat may be, then, something very specific, such as the loss of one's job. It may be unspecified, as when a person complies simply to avoid displeasing a higher level of authority. This approach seems to be fairly widely used, perhaps because it is easy. One study showed that this approach is effective in motivating organization members to perform at a high level if they have limited alternative employment opportunities.[2] The approach is not perceived to be effective by supervisors, however, in the typical situations they encounter, as Table 16.1 shows.

The use of threats or fear is limited. First, it only works in the short run. In the long run, most individuals can find alternative employment opportunities where there is less reliance upon fear as a managerial strategy. Second, it creates anxiety, which may disrupt rather than facilitate performance. Threats directed at some em-

TABLE 16.1   Supervisory Ratings of Various Managerial Strategies

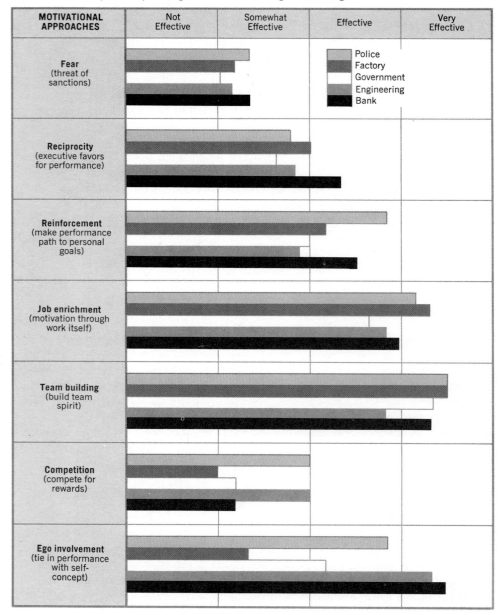

ployees may increase anxiety in others. Third, in order to work, the threats must have credibility. This is difficult to achieve when employees are protected by a strong union, tenure rights, or other safeguards. Fourth, threats induce hostile feelings toward the supervisors who make them, feelings that may be manifested in aggressive acts against either the supervisor or the organization. Finally, a problem with the fear strategy is that it creates a punitive climate in which individuals are afraid of being different from or of offending others. This diminishes creativity and can lead to intellectual stagnation.

Reciprocity

The expression "If you scratch my back, I'll scratch yours," describes reciprocity. The "norm of reciprocity" states that what one is given will be repaid in approximate equivalence.[3] Individuals who receive benefits from others feel guilty if they have a chance to reciprocate and do not do so. In fact, they feel a sense of relief at repaying an obligation when they can.

Using reciprocity, a supervisor may attempt to trade certain things of value to subordinates in exchange for satisfactory levels of performance. The commodities traded may include special privileges, special concern for the individual, and the acceptance of rule violations, in addition to more obvious favors. An office manager may permit members of the secretarial staff to take short periods away from work for their personal business so long as the quantity and quality of work is good.

Reciprocity is widely used and generally seen as effective (see Table 16.1). To some degree the popularity of this approach can be accounted for by its ease of use. But it presents problems. First, there can be disagreement about the value of the things exchanged as when a group of workers may feel their supervisor is asking them to do a "big" favor when he or she has done only "little" favors for them. Second, certain favors may become so common that the recipients no longer consider them to be favors. In a case where employees can leave early when their work is done, they may begin to plan on it and not see early departure as a "favor" anymore. The workers may become extremely upset when the supervisor seeks to have them remain on the job until quitting time. Finally, there may be resentment created when a recipient of a favor does not have the ability to repay; a person may feel he is getting more and more committed to do something for his boss.

The psychological contract is based on the concept of reciprocity. The employee agrees informally to meet some of the organization's performance expectations in return for the benefits the organization provides him. But, as they do with the individual supervisor, organization members often disagree with the organization as to the value of the benefits exchanged between them.

Reinforcement

Managers may use a reinforcement approach with those who work for them. With this strategy the manager attempts to reward workers who perform well and either not reward or impose sanctions on workers who perform poorly. Behaviors followed by desired rewards are repeated, while behaviors not followed by reward are extinguished (not repeated). Thus, if an individual sees a clear relationship between good work and the attainment of a desired reward, he or she has a tendency to perform at a high level. This is one of the approaches described in item 16.1. One plant manager points out that

> Workers are told when they are doing well and the entire work force can earn a production bonus of up to 20 percent when it surpasses a week's production goal.

People perform at a higher level when they perceive a relationship between high performance and the obtaining of desired rewards, such as pay increases and promotions. Experimental studies conducted in the laboratory situation, in the military, in educational organizations, and in industrial organizations demonstrate that using money, tokens, signs of social approval, or surrogate rewards can increase the frequency with which certain desired behaviors occur.[4] Studies on the effectiveness of incentive wage plans in industry lead to the conclusion that, on the average, there is an increase in production when workers are paid by the piece rather than on the basis of the amount of time they work.[5]

Recognition of the need to tie rewards to performance exists in the business world also. *Dun's Review* reported that

> Some companies that have long paid bonuses at the corporate level, like those in the oil, steel and food industries, are now seeking to devise comparable cash incentives for executives who head their best-performing divisions. Others are trying to fine-tune their compensation programs so that they can reward deserving individuals at any level in the corporate hierarchy. A compensation director of General Mills, notes: "There is hardly a compensation man today who is not aware of the need to develop rewards more closely related to individual performance."[6]

In general, managers view the reinforcement approach as effective (see Table 16.1), but it too has its problems. First, it is effective only if the rewards used are desired by those who are to receive them. Pay increases, promotions, social status symbols (such as office rugs), all may be regarded as different kinds of rewards, but there are substantial individual differences in preferences for payoffs. Some people prefer pay increases. Others seek promotion. Still others may desire new rugs on their office floors. Some may regard compensatory time off as a reward. Such individual differences in preferences for rewards make it very difficult for a manager to utilize organizational factors effectively as incentives. The value a person places on different incentives is internal.

Second, linking rewards with performance is especially difficult for those whose jobs are extremely interdependent with others. How do you determine the contribution of one worker on an assembly line to the final product? How do you assess the contribution of one research scientist in a team working on environmental pollution controls? It is also extremely difficult to measure individual performance for staff personnel, higher-level managers, and many professionals, since it is difficult to quantify results and isolate outcomes that can be associated with an individual.

Most pay systems are not consistent with the principles derived from the theory and research on reinforcement. In the typical organization, pay increases are given at regular, predictable times, say every six months. Often there is not much differentiation between good and bad performers. The research on reinforcement shows that awarding increases at unpredictable times is more effective than giving them at predictable intervals.[7] Organizations that reward members relatively equally, without regard to their performance, are in effect reinforcing the poor performers to maintain their present levels of performance while discouraging the better performers. When a group of employees receives an across-the-board pay increase of, say 10 percent, the poorer employees are treated in the same way as the good ones.

Job Enrichment

With job enrichment, emphasis is placed on motivating the worker through the task or job itself. The assumption is that if the work is challenging and more meaningful to a person, then the person will be self-motivated. This is especially true when the work is routine and/or broken down into such small components that the person cannot see how the work is related to that of others, or to the end product. Job enrichment involves assigning work to individuals so that they have the opportunity to complete an identifiable task from beginning to end. They are then held responsible for successful completion of the task. Basically, the motivational effect of job enrichment flows from the opportunity for personal achievement, challenge, and recognition.

Five characteristics of work are believed to be important in affecting individual motivation and performance. These job characteristics are:

1. *Skill variety.* The extent to which a job demands different skills of the person.

2. *Task identity.* The extent to which the job requires completing a whole, identifiable unit of work.

3. *Task significance.* The impact that the job has on others, whether inside or outside the organization.

4. *Autonomy.* The freedom of individual action.

5. *Feedback.* The degree of understanding that a person has about the level of job performance that comes from carrying out the job.

According to Hackman and Suttle,[8] the characteristics of variety, identity, and significance contribute to the **meaningfulness** of the job. Autonomy fosters feelings of **responsibility,** and feedback contributes to **knowledge of results.** When a job is high in all of these characteristics, it has a high "motivating potential." Low scores are associated with jobs that have a low "motivating potential."

A central idea of job enrichment is that "vertical loading" of a job enhances "motivation potential." This means that instead of merely assigning a person more different activities, the job should be expanded "vertically" in the organization hierarchy. Vertical loading means including some responsibility for deciding how to do a job and when to do it. It increases the amount of autonomy in a job.[8]

The experiment in job enrichment at the Saab–Volvo automobile manufacturers in Sweden (see item 16.2) illustrates how job enrichment works. Rather than the long-linked, potentially monotonous production system that characterizes auto manufacturing in the U.S., at Saab–Volvo they use a team-assembly concept in which workers rotate the tasks required for building an auto. Basically, the entire group, the team, is responsible for assembling the entire auto.

Item 16.2

VOLVO: Torslanda . . . Skövde . . . Kalmar
New Directions in Work Systems and Technology

Like other automotive companies, Volvo evolved from hand craftsmanship to moving line assembly and Methods Time Measurements system (MTM), with every phase of manufacturing and assembly worked out in infinite detail down to the last nut and bolt and kronor. However, labor unrest in the late sixties, expanding markets, rising demands for industrialization of the workplace, diversification of the company, a desire for a greater share of the export market, and societal problems dictated new approaches; since the sixties production layout has been based more and more on social/technical analysis.

As one of the first companies in Sweden to do so, Volvo, in consultation with Joint Works Councils, issued written standards for the physical makeup of the working environment.

If the working environment is to make up the basis for the comfort and work satisfaction of the employee, then psychological, social, financial, and technical factors must be coordinated in the planning stage. The psychological and social side, for example, consists of modified work organization, new working forms for supervisors and foremen, extended contract activities, etc. The technical side consists of the entire working environment: lighting, noise level, air, layout, human engineering, and medical factors.

Here are some guidelines that were used for the working environment:

1. In connection with all new projects started in the Volvo Group of companies, the employees are to be consulted.
2. Planning of new plants is to attain the best solution with respect to environmental and financial demands on the entire project.
3. The working environment is to be as risk-free as possible and give the employees a feeling of comfort and togetherness inside the company.
4. In connection with the purchase of machines, consultation must be carried out to ensure that environmental demands on the machine are satisfied.

THE TORSLANDA PLANT IN GOTHENBURG

At this, the largest assembly plant in the Volvo Group, intensive development in new forms of layout and work structures has been going on since the late sixties and much of the experience gained here has been used effectively at other plants, notably Kalmar. Job alternation, the expansion of working tasks, and the delegation of responsibility to working groups with common jobs, extended advisory and information activities, training and orientation, as well as management programs are some of the constituents of this development.

Several thousand people work in new forms of job layout; workplaces have gradually been adapted to suit these forms. Joint Work Council activities have become even more intensified by the appointment of cooperation groups which supplement subcommittees.

Job alternation, or job rotation, means that the job is changed once or several times daily. At different sections of the assembly line people within groups change jobs with each other and thus obtain physical and mental change, at the same time the individual learns a variety of jobs from assembly to repair and inspection. Procedures are determined within the groups in consultation with foremen.

A complete discussion of all the work changes at Torslanda would require a book; however, one example will give an idea of the system.

In the upholstery assembly department workers, mostly women, suffered from arm, back, shoulder, and wrist pains, which contributed to turnover and absenteeism. The first step was to develop mechanical aids to ameliorate the ailments by increasing the comfort of the workers.

Some relief was obtained by working with doctors, industrial engineers, and specialists, yet many uncomfortable tasks remained. Job rotation was introduced whereby workers switched jobs, two by two. It had its good and bad sides. Some employees found it difficult to maintain production by switching to new jobs requiring new work rhythms. Various forms of job rotation continued and a completely new system was developed. This required every worker to learn the jobs being done by all fifteen work stations included in the assembly process—each task carrying a time cycle of about two minutes. Rotation was done according to a one-day or half-day program.

This change added considerable variety to the assembly workers' jobs. The increased contact among workers resulted in new methods of quality feedback information and strengthened the workers' understanding of, and commitment to, group work. The workers were overwhelmingly in support of the new system.

In the third stage the group was given responsibility for all planning of work as well as doing it. The group constantly is aware that correct deliveries are made to the final assembly line. Information is constantly being supplied on auto models being assembled and which seats belong in each. Data on quantities, types of seats, seat covers is then translated into work assignments for the group. The planning of this work is now a regular part of the group's operation with various members doing the paperwork. Also, checking on incoming upholstery material has been delegated to the group, thus expanding the scope of the individual worker's job and giving him or her more responsibility. The jobs of four controllers who previously did this were abolished.

Physical ailments dropped drastically and along with them turnover and absenteeism. Versatility of workers has grown, their commitment and job satisfaction has risen substantially, and quality has improved.

Job alternation and group effort have consistently been implemented at the Torslanda plant. Currently about 60 percent of the 8,000 employees are part of groups in which this is practiced. Because some employees prefer the rhythm of one specific task, participation in job alternation is voluntary.

While Torslanda is still a traditional plant with a moving assembly line, work has started to change the system. Eighteen people, working in two groups of nine workers each, do final assembly in docks performing every operation including body work, chassis assembly, final trimming, mating chassis and body, and final checkout. An hour is required to assemble one car and production costs are competitive. Dock equipment and material handling costs are justified by improvement of job satisfaction and as aids in reducing turnover and absenteeism.

Incidentally, it is generally accepted that turnover and absenteeism have dropped well over 60 percent between the late sixties and the present.

VOLVO SKÖVDE PLANTS

The Skövde engine plants have been considered among the most advanced plants in the world in terms of industrial engineering. In the early 1970s an additional engine plant was started at Skövde which began producing engines in stages in 1973 with full production in 1974. It has a floor area of about 440,000 square feet and employs 600. Capacity is 250,000 gasoline engines per year.

Planning for the new plant coincided with the planning for the Kalmar plant. Managers, specialists from various areas, and employee representatives participated in the planning. Overall project committee included representatives from the local union. Project groups for the smaller areas included representatives from those employees who would be directly affected by the work areas.

The plant resembles an "E" but instead of three legs it has four, which are connected to the main body. The main body is the assembly area while the four legs house machining areas. Each of the legs, or machining departments, concentrates on one particular component or a group of similar components. The first makes the cylinder blocks; the second the crankshafts; the third the cylinder heads and connecting rods; the fourth produces the balance of engine parts, i.e., camshafts, manifold intake pipes, etc.

Machining operations are automated. Material handling is highly mechanized. None of the individual workers is tied to machines; jobs are primarily supervision and inspection. Employees work as teams and help one another as needed. As a result the work is more interesting, and there is a better social relationship among workers. Each worker feels a larger responsibility.

Each of the legs is separated from the other by walls and a green area. Exhaust devices on each machine eliminate smoke and dust; the walls and ceilings are soundproofed to a point where the sound level in each bay has been held to 80 dbA.

Located against the wall and facing the green are coffee rooms for breaks; during pleasant weather employees can take their break outdoors.

Components from the four machining bays come together in the assembly area, which features the most interesting innovation. Instead of a moving assembly line, "mini" assembly wagons are used. The wagons are battery powered and carry components between work stations. They follow a magnetic track in the floor and stop at preestablished points. The wagons are controlled manually by the workers; they are not computer controlled as at Kalmar. Fixtures on the wagons can be twisted into different positions in two different planes with a turn of the wrist; they can be lowered or raised for the most comfortable working positions.

Prior to assembly, the engine block is washed and painted. Crankshaft, flywheel and other heavy components are added. At this point the engine block and wagon come together and the block is mounted on the assembly fixture. The wagon begins its assembly journey on the magnetic track. Piston and connecting rods are assembled next. Workers switch jobs at will; each knows what's to be done. There are no fixed programs for these changes. The wagon now goes into a large buffer area prior to the next assembly. While in the buffer area it passes various preassembly groups where cylinder heads, valves, camshaft, push rods, etc., are assembled.

After the buffer zone the preassembled cylinder heads are affixed to the block. Then the wagon goes into two more assembly areas with two pairs of parallel "final" assembly flows. One engine goes through one pair of areas, the next through the other pair, before proceeding to final inspection and testing. Here, also, the workers control the wagon . . . there are always additional wagons in the buffer zone. In all areas natural freedom of work prevails, not job alternation tied to a rigid prearranged schedule.

A word about the buffer zones. These are storage areas used in the assembly operation. Each team is allotted a time cycle during which the team must finish its operations and push the wagon to the next team. If a team wants to work ahead to gain a longer break, or an additional break, it finishes its operations ahead of time and pushes the wagons into the buffer zone.

Currently, output is limited only by the market demand and the need for engines. The full capabilities of the plant have not yet been explored; however, on the basis of current volume and cost, the productivity of the new plant is equal to that realized from a conventional engine plant. In addition, there's better worker cooperation and job satisfaction from more interesting and varied work. The machining "factories" and assembly areas with their wagons function smoothly and efficiently.

KALMAR PLANT BREAKS NEW PATHS

The 430,000-square-foot factory is star-shaped. This permits extending the outer walls, ensuring plenty of daylight in the factory as well as maintaining a sense of contact with the natural environment. The architecture also retains the atmosphere of a small workshop in a large factory. By making use of the angular construction of the outer walls, the different work teams are able to work in clearly defined areas with their own entrances, rest rooms, changing rooms, etc. The plant has two stories in three of the bays; the fourth has one story. The office is a small wing directly in front of the plant.

Car assembly takes place along the outer walls, while the material stores are situated in the central part of the building.

Assembly is divided into three phases: body, chassis, and final. It begins on the top level of the plant where the body is placed on a carrier—or wagon, as it's referred to by Volvo—similar to those used at Skövde, only larger. It moves from one assembly team to another automatically and comes to a stop at prearranged stations. At the top level glass, interior roof, electrical system, etc., are installed. The doors are affixed and the body is moved to the lower level.

At the same time that the body is being assembled on the top level, the engine (assembled at Skövde and shipped from there), gear box, axles, and exhaust system are assembled at the lower level. At precise times the body comes from the top level and is joined with the chassis on the lower level for final assembly. Quality checkpoints, interspersed in the assembly process, permit immediate quality feedback to the teams. At the end of the assembly a final check is performed and the car is ready for delivery.

There is considerable flexibility within each group. Work stations and work organization can be freely arranged by its members. The work within the group is arranged according to two main models, the straight line assembly and the dock assembly.

In the straight line the team's work is divided among four or five stations and each station is manned by two or three workers who complete their tasks in about five minutes. In practice all workers learn the tasks of the other stations.

In the dock system, which is used in about one-quarter of the area, the wagon comes into a "dock" where it remains for the entire time required to complete the assembly. Two or three workers take over the particular assembly operations assigned to a group. Each worker has a time cycle of twenty to thirty minutes, but a problem is posed by the difficulty of providing enough space to accommodate the material required for thirty minutes of assembly work.

Amount of work done by the various assembly groups was calculated with the help of MTM systems. Methods and quantities of work are developed with the active support of union and employees. An agreement calls for maximizing the work load on different groups at a level corresponding to 111 percent MTM. This means that the quantity of work done will exceed by 11 percent the base standard indicated by the MTM system. This agreement is typical for Volvo's manufacturing units. Labor efficiency, as measured by the MTM system, is comparable with other Volvo assembly plants despite the lengthening of the task cycle to twenty to thirty minutes. A drastic reduction in specialization has not resulted in loss of efficiency.

The assembly wagons are electrically powered and computer controlled, as contrasted with Skövde, where control is manual; however, manual control is possible. Magnetic guide tracks are located in the floor. Assembly is performed when the wagons are in a stopped position. Furthermore, the fixture on the wagon is so designed that it can be tilted to facilitate assembling components on the underside of the auto; there are no assembly pits at Kalmar. Tilting was first successfully tried at Torslanda.

Two types of wagons are used, a high and a low. The low wagon is used on the upper level and is designed for maximum comfort and ease of assembling. The high wagon, used on the lower floor, can be raised or lowered to facilitate assembling the various components. Between the various teams are buffer zones for incoming and outgoing wagons.

All carriers are monitored by the computer, which keeps them moving on the electric track (carrier movement is agreed upon at union negotiations). The computer also registers all disturbances, holdups, number of cars in the various stages of production and keeps the teams informed via closed-circuit TV.

The entire factory is organized along team lines, there being thirty teams of fifteen to twenty workers each; one supervisor handles two or three teams. A consultive network exists based on "functional councils" of which there are six—two for production, one each for materials, quality, industrial engineering, personnel, and finance. At the functional council meetings problems are discussed and solved; they serve as communications links with work councils, management, and other employees. There are approximately 640 workers at Kalmar of which 540 are hourly and 100 salaried. Plant production capacity is 30,000 cars per year per shift.

What are the results of this method of assembling automobiles?

1. Turnover is down to about 12 percent and absenteeism down to around 14 percent—a tremendous reduction from highs of around 50 percent.
2. Direct assembly time, expressed in man-hours, is the same as for the conventional Torslanda plant. The assembly times at Kalmar are fixed to correspond to the times of a conventional plant.
3. Very little downtime. Utilization is at 96 percent efficiency.
4. It's easier to introduce new models and make changes in the line depending on new technical or work ideas.
5. Cost of the Kalmar plant was about 10 percent higher than for a conventional plant.
6. Advantages of Kalmar over conventional plants will become more marked as full production is attained. It is expected that all negatives will be wiped out.
7. Switching jobs within a team is considered to be a good way of working by eight out of nine workers.

A recent study of workers unearthed some interesting facts:

1. Workers are pleased with their work environment; 80 percent of the workers are satisfied with the low noise level; 83 percent are satisfied with the level of lighting.
2. Workers were not too happy with the design of body fixtures for the cars; access was considered sometimes too difficult and they suggest improvements be made.
3. Ventilation remains a problem; this is being worked on.
4. Workers believe they have more direct influence over their jobs than workers in a conventional plant.

We can do worse than conclude with Pehr G. Gyllenhammar's observation; "At Kalmar the objective is to organize automobile production in such a way that employees can find meaning and satisfaction in their work.

"This is a factory that, without any sacrifice of efficiency or financial results, will give employees the opportunity to work in groups, to communicate freely, to shift among work assignments, to vary their pace, to identify themselves with the product, to be conscious of responsibility for quality, and to influence their own work environment.

"When a product is manufactured by workers who find their work meaningful, it will inevitably be a product of high quality."

To appreciate Volvo's effort in work organization one should understand the Swedish business/labor/government relationships and Sweden's social policies. If Volvo (as well as Saab–Scania) activities are viewed as the result of these interacting forces one will begin to grasp the reasons for Volvo's direction and success.

For years the Swedish trade unions have pushed for democratization of the workplace. They believe the tightly controlled machine-paced processes, fragmented tasks, and virtually no opportunities for employees to take their own initiative generates big problems for the workers and for business. They believe the employees, or their elected representatives, should be brought in as equal partners toward shaping the means of production. Therefore, the objectives of work reform are generally expressed not only in terms of increased productivity and efficiency, but also in increased job satisfaction and more interesting and more stimulating tasks as worthwhile ends in themselves.

Sweden has had Work Councils since 1946, so the philosophy of employee involvement has a long history. In general, companies of fifty or more employees must have a Work Council. Each council consists of twenty members, half elected by the employees and half by the employer. It is directed toward improving productivity, job satisfaction, working conditions and it exerts an influence over job structures.

The Swedish government has enacted laws which strengthen the employees' position and their organizations in matters connected with personnel policy and the organization and direction of work. Laws govern dismissals, labor cutbacks, security of employment, industrial litigation, status of shop stewards, employee election to boards of directors, and employment of elderly.

In 1977 the government further implemented and sanctified a stronger democratization of industry through laws which call for full consultation of employees and their representatives ranging from the shop floor all the way up to the board room. Decision-making is no longer the sole prerogative of the employer.

Has this industrial democracy been all bad? Here's what Pehr G. Gyllenhammar, managing director of Volvo says; "The modern working man needs a sense of purpose and satisfaction in his daily work. He feels the need of belonging to a team, of being able to feel at home in his surroundings, or being able to identify himself with the good he produces and, not least, of feeling that he is appreciated for the work he performs.

"Factory work must be adapted to people, not people to machines. This calls for innovations in both the field of human relations and technology. At Volvo this has been done by interchange of work, by giving a greater insight into the job being done, and by entirely new technical conceptions in planning our production plants, both existing and those to be built in the future."

Sweden is not without its business problems.* Unemployment did not exist for many years and "guest workers" had to be attracted from other countries. (A similar situation existed in other European countries.) Turnover in automotive was horrendous. In addition, a better educated work force did not like working on a dull assembly line, when other, more interesting work at similar pay was available. Absenteeism was high. During our visit with Volvo we were told turnover reached as high as 50 percent in the sixties! (A published statistic states that personnel turnover in a Saab–Scania chassis line was 70 percent in 1969 and 29 percent in 1972.)

Volvo attacked the problem and found employee participation to be one of the answers. Incidentally, another crucial point to remember is the fact that the *potential* Swedish labor force mainly consists of women and well educated young men. Thus, Volvo, motivated heavily by social consciousness, a changing work ethic, and also by the desire to further increase profitability, developed the organizational work programs which culminated in the Kalmar assembly plant.

When viewed against this background a comparison of Volvo with Detroit is like comparing ice fishing in Wisconsin with ice fishing in Antarctica.

*Sweden has not remained unscathed by the current economic turbulence triggered by the oil price hike of 1973, part of the cause of the 1977 balance-of-trade deficit. Another has been the high labor costs, which affect Sweden's position in world markets. So far unemployment has been held to the "normal" 1.6 percent. The government has maintained employment levels through grants to firms which produce for inventory; when inventories overflowed the government introduced a system of grants amounting to 25 kronor ($5.57) an hour per employee to firms which trained their employees internally instead of laying them off. Companies have also used employees for repair, maintenance, and improvement work. When layoffs become absolutely necessary the unemployed are trained in public manpower programs or hired in the expanding public sector.

Source: William F. Schleicher, "Volvo: New Directions in Work Technology." From *Machine and Tool Blue Book,* William F. Schleicher. Copyright 1977 by Hitchcock Publications, Wheaton, Illinois, pp. 74–85. Reprinted by permission.

Such an approach is being widely experimented with in industry. Companies that have undertaken job enrichment programs are AT&T and Texas Instruments, among others. But these programs have not always met with success.[9] Research to date suggests that these efforts may improve morale and the quality of work more than the quantity,[10] as seen in item 16.1. Managers often feel like the GE plant manager in item 16.1. "Most of our efforts now go into awareness programs and enrichment. . . . the real motivation is when the worker feels he is making a contribution."

Job enrichment is generally seen as effective by managers, but is not without its problems. (see Table 16.1). When workers are given a more complex job, they realistically expect commensurate increases in compensation; otherwise they feel inequitably treated.

Some work—such as large-scale assembly operations—may not lend itself easily to job enrichment. Some production systems—such as long-linked technology—are very difficult to change without major redesign of a whole plant. This could be so very expensive as to be uneconomical.

Team Building

Team building is an effort to foster the formation of cohesive work groups that adopt a norm of high performance. The idea is that groups with a high standard of performance will pressure individual members to perform at a high level. This means that the individual is subjected to performance pressures from peers, as well as from superiors, and will perform at a high level in order to live up to the desires and expectations of fellow workers.

The supervisor can contribute to group cohesiveness and to high performance by isolating the group from others; by assigning tasks that require collective effort; by putting individuals together in a group who can work well with each other; by assigning tasks of an appropriate difficulty level so that the group can experience success; by rewarding the group collectively for their high performance; and by fostering the formation of positive attitudes toward the organization. In general, supervisors seem to rate this motivational strategy as quite effective (see Table 16.1). They believed that many workers could be pressured into high performance only by their peers, not by higher management.

Some problems in using the approach, however, must be taken into account. Some groups become cohesive, but adopt a low, rather than a high, standard of performance. In addition, in many work situations it may be difficult to get the workers together in group activities if their work is not interdependent or if they are physically separated from each other.

Competition

Using the competition strategy, individuals or groups compete against each other for a reward. This approach is especially common in sales work where there are sales contests for a variety of rewards, such as bonuses, vacation trips, automobiles, and so on. Competition has been used also, however, for motivating other types of employees. In one study it was found that a pay system that gave a bonus to only the five highest-achieving blue-collar workers was more effective than a traditional incentive wage system in which everybody received a bonus who surpassed a certain standard.[11]

Several case studies by Carroll[12] indicate that competition is effective only when the reward offered is desired by all the participants and when competing individuals or groups feel they have a good possibility of winning. When the reward is not considered desirable, or when the same individuals or groups seem to win most of the time, competition strategies do not have any good effect. Competition can also lead to blocking the performance of others.[13] Problems occur with this strategy when work is interdependent and competition would decrease cooperation. Competition can also lead to a great deal of hostility toward one group by another.[14]

Ego-involvement

One managerial motivation strategy is to try to increase the person's involvement with the work or the organization. Allowing organizational members to participate in the establishment of performance goals for themselves is one way to do this. It is felt that a person is likely to try to achieve a performance goal that he himself has established, since the person's self-concept or self-perception will be involved. Since most individuals think positively about themselves, they should feel positively about performance goals established by themselves. There is also evidence that individuals and groups are most likely to attain goals when they make a public commitment to do so.[15] This may be because such commitments are promises and most people view themselves as persons who keep their word.

Korman[16] and Vroom[17] have summarized research that indicates that individuals attempt to behave in accordance with their self-concepts. They try to make their behavior consistent with such self-perceptions. Thus, individuals who set a certain goal for themselves will be strongly motivated to be successful in achieving that goal. Individuals are more likely to apply high effort to tasks that are perceived to require abilities they take pride in.[17] Conversely, there is less effort expended on tasks with ability requirements that do not rate high in a person's self-perceptions. For example, people who think they are high on creativity will expend more effort on tasks they believe require creativity for success in order to validate their self-perceptions. The implications of this for motivation are obvious. An organization should be able to obtain higher performance if it can assign tasks to individuals that require the abilities the individuals take pride in. Of course, such an approach would require a personnel appraisal system that would identify each organizational member's strengths.

MANAGERIAL MOTIVATION STRATEGIES
AND TYPE OF ORGANIZATION

The effectiveness of these various managerial motivation strategies is likely to differ by type of organization. Approaches that might be effective in the mechanistic organization would not work in the organic organization and vice versa. Although the **fear** approach might be expected to be most effective in mechanistic organizations with employees who have few alternative job opportunities, these employees usually have tenure rights and other protections guaranteed by a union contract. These "rights," are, in fact, probably the results of negative worker reactions to the extensive use of the fear approach by managements in the past. In organic organizations the fear approach would be inconsistent with the value orientations of professionals and may increase their dissatisfaction with the organization to a point where they would look for employment to other organizations with a more compatible work environment.

Reciprocity is probably much more widely used in mechanistic organizations than in organic organizations, especially where supervisors have little power to reward their subordinates differentially for performance. The reciprocity approach may involve an indulgency pattern whereby supervisors allow subordinates to break rules in exchange for meeting certain needs of the supervisor. Obviously the more rules that exist, the greater the possibility of use for this approach, as in the mechanistic organization. Allowing employes to break rules, however, is a real danger in any organization with a strong union. Managerial inconsistency in managing the workforce is likely to be exploited by the union.

The **reinforcement** approach is going to be easier to use in the mechanistic organization than in the organic since it is possible to specify performance requirements in advance and then to reward superior performance as it occurs in this type of organization. The organic organization makes use of more subjective indicators of performance. In addition, in the organic organization even social reinforcements may come primarily from professional peers rather than organizational colleagues. These professional peers may be outside the organization itself, making it difficult for the organization to control these rewards. The organic organization is also likely to make greater use of group work assignments, making it difficult to pinpoint and then reward the contribution of a particular individual. When group rewards are used in such situations, it is often necessary to reward all members of the team equally, as is usually done with professional baseball teams who play in the world series.

Team building involves increasing group cohesiveness. Some research shows that increasing cohesiveness may increase productivity where such attitudes toward the organization are positive but may decrease productivity where such attitudes are negative.[18] It is likely that such attitudes are more positive in the organic than in the mechanistic organization. In addition, the organic organization also usually has a greater need for helping behavior than the mechanistic organization, another reason for the greater likelihood of success for the team building approach in the organic organization as compared to the mechanistic.

Competition works best where work is independent. It may be most useful where there are highly differentiated organizational units organized on a product, not a functional, basis. In a functional organization coordination between units is too important to be endangered by competition, even though competition between groups will increase cohesiveness within each group. It may be effective in the organic organizations where the resulting group cohesiveness may foster the necessary helping behavior between group members.

The **ego-involvement** approach is rated higher by the engineering supervisors in Table 16.1 than by the other types of supervisors. This is not surprising since professionals and specialists are likely to be more personally involved in their work than the externalists and organizationalists. This is partly because the professionals have spent a great deal of time in developing their competencies, and demonstrating this expertise to themselves and others is important to them. This approach also can have effects in very routine work. When persons become more involved, they are more likely to pay attention to detail, reducing error rates, scrap rates, and the like, which may have important effects on costs.

Job design is probably considered by many to be the most fruitful way to improve performance in mechanistic organizations. The work in organic organization may already be rich in intrinsic motivation. Job design strategies focus directly on presumed cause of low performance in bureaucracies—routine and repetitive work. It has been postulated by many writers that increasing variety and challenge in routine work can significantly improve performance. Such research, however, cited earlier, indicates that the positive effects of job design may be confined to those organization members who are concerned about satisfying higher order needs (e.g., achievement, self-esteem, personal fulfillment).

MOTIVATION AND PERFORMANCE

The skills, attitudes, and values of individuals at work interact with group influences, technological constraints, and the leader's managerial style to determine the level of performance. A manager looks at all these influences and tries to determine what he or she can do to get better work results. What can be done depends upon the specific nature of the work the manager supervises, whether it is "human-skill-dominated" or "technology-dominated" work. This is the first thing that a manager must determine because the relationship between motivation to work, performance potential, and performance is very different for human-skill-dominated work than it is for technology-dominated work. In this section we show how this difference comes into play in motivation.

Figure 16.1 shows the general relationship between motivation to work and the different levels of individual performance.[19] In this example we show that *motivation to work* (the horizontal axis) may vary from very low to very high. We illustrate this by giving motivation to work a low value of 1 to a high of 4. A low score means there is little drive to perform and a high score indicates a strong desire to do well.

Performance (the vertical axis), meaning the person's output, also can range from low to high. Low performance, for a salesperson, for example, would mean that he or she met 80 percent of quota; high performance might mean the salesperson exceeds 120 percent of quota.

The level of effort, or how much of one's performance potential is exerted, may vary with the motivational level and is a determinant of the level of performance.

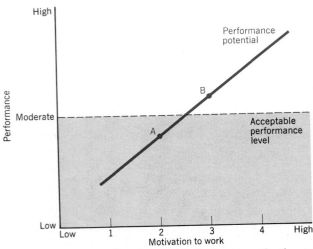

FIGURE 16.1   General relationship between motivation to work, performance and performance potential. (after Reitz, H. J., Behavior in Organizations, Homewood, Illinois, R. D. Irwin, 1981)

The ***performance potential*** is shown as the line in Figure 16.1. If the salesperson works hard, the sales quota will be achieved. If he or she applies less effort, it will not. The dotted line in Figure 16.1 shows what level of performance is acceptable to the management of the company. In other words, anything above a "moderate" performance level is defined as enough performance to satisfy a supervisor.

From Figure 16.1 it is easy to see that this person must have at least a "motivation to work" level of nearly 3. Lower levels, say 2, will not result in enough effort being applied to the job; consequently there will be inadequate performance.

If you are the supervisor of the person shown in Figure 16.1, what you do depends upon whether or not the level of performance is acceptable. Suppose performance is at point A. Is it possible to raise the motivation to work from level 2 to 3? How can it be done? To further complicate matters, the potential performance line represents the ability level of only one person. Another individual may have very different abilities and hence different potential performance.

MOTIVATION IN SKILL-DOMINATED WORK

Consider Mary and Joan, with differences in potential to perform the task of "preparing a budget," as illustrated in Figure 16.2. The "potential performance" line shows that Joan can perform anywhere from a relatively low level to a very high level. Mary's ability is not quite as high as Joan's so her "potential performance" is lower, but she still is quite adequate. How well each performs depends on how motivated each is to work. If both are in the same accounting department, with potential performance as shown, and the required performance standard is "moderate,' Joan's motivation to work must be at level 1 for her to achieve a reasonable standard. For Mary, motivation to work must be slightly above level 2. Mary must

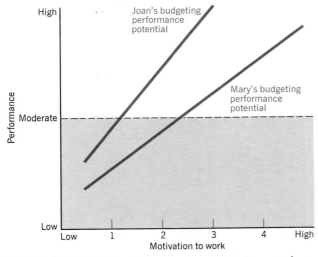

FIGURE 16.2 Relationships between motivation, performance potential, and performance when there are small differences in ability.

have higher motivation to work than Joan to perform acceptably because her skill is lower.

The level of motivation to work for both is a result of a number of sources. For instance, it is partially a result of the internal values and personality orientations of the individuals. Both Joan and Mary may have a "professional" orientation and feel it important to put forth enough effort to meet work requirements. Or the level of work motivation may be partially attributable to the managerial motivation strategy that Joan's and Mary's boss uses, for example, an approach like reciprocity.

If both Joan and Mary, in Figure 16.2, are at motivation to work level 1, then only Joan is performing satisfactorily. If the work motivation of both Joan and Mary increases to level 2, both meet work requirements, though Joan still does more work.

Even if both are at different motivation levels, there is no problem. With Mary at level 2 and Joan at level 1, acceptable performance still occurs. Joan can just do it more easily. There is nothing wrong with that, unless Mary believes she should get more pay because she works harder (i.e., puts out more effort).

Figure 16.3 illustrates a very different problem for the accounting department manager. Between Dick and Betty there is a very large difference in budgeting skills. Therefore there will be large differences in performance, given equal motivational levels. If the "moderate" performance level is the department's standard, then Betty must be at motivation to work level 2. No matter what managerial motivation strategy is used or how much Dick wants to do a good job, he will be unable to achieve an acceptable level of performance. The manager in this case has only a few alternatives. One is to seek a replacement for Dick. A second alternative is for the manager to attempt to increase Dick's budgeting skills with some type of training.

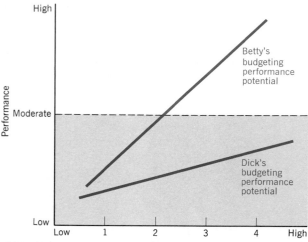

FIGURE 16.3   Relationships between motivation, performance potential, and performance when there are large differences in abilities.

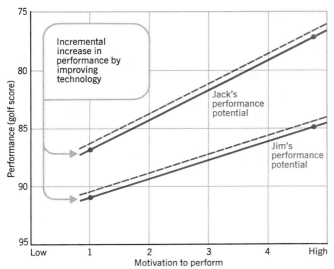

FIGURE 16.4 The effects of technology in skill-dominated work.

Skill-Dominated Work and Technology

When a task is skill dominated, then better technology may have only minimal effects in improving performance. This is shown in Figure 16.4. Let's suppose this graph represents two golfers. Jack is a good golfer and has the potential to score between 87 and 77, depending on how motivated he is to play. Jim is not as good a player, being able to score between 92 and 85. For Jim to beat Jack, Jim must be highly motivated (level 4) and Jack must be at a low level of motivation (level 1). Let's say that Jim obtains a set of new, improved clubs. His performance will improve but probably only slightly. To defeat Jack (assuming Jack has old equipment) Jim must move above level 3, while Jack stays at level 1. If Jack and Jim have the same level of motivation to play, then Jack still always wins, regardless of who has new clubs. Figure 16.4 shows why some athletic teams with players of less skill may upset the teams with better players. The less skilled team may be able to drive their motivation to a higher level than the team with more ability. This brings their performance higher than the better team, which could have a bad day.

MOTIVATION IN TECHNOLOGY-DOMINATED WORK

In technology-dominated work such as assembly lines and computer operations, motivation, performance, and ability fit together differently from human-skill-dominated work. Figure 16.5 shows these relationships for highly technological settings. In Figure 16.5 technology sets an upper and a lower limit on how well Steve and Michel perform. The necessary level of motivation to work must be just enough to get Steve and Michel to activate the equipment. For Michel a motivation to work level of 1+ is necessary. For Steve, a level 2+ motivation to work is

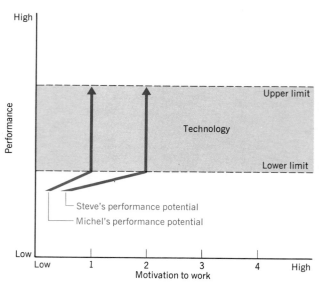

FIGURE 16.5 Motivation, performance potential, and performance in technology-dominated work.

needed. The level of required performance here is easily obtained, though only a low level of motivation is required. Once the equipment is activated, the performance level of all workers becomes the same.

THE ROLE OF MOTIVATION STRATEGIES

Figures 16.1 through 16.5 are useful in visualizing what the role of motivation strategies is in the management of performance. Take the case of Joan and Mary (Figure 16.2). Both may bring a personal motivation level 2+ with them to their position (see Figure 16.1). This motivation to work level may be a result of socialization, training, and experiences such as those outlined in Chapter 5. The accounting department manager, using one or more motivational approaches described in this chapter, seeks to raise their motivation to work to a 3.5 level, as shown in Figure 16.6. If she is successful, it should result in higher individual performance, consequently better departmental results. For example, the accounting department manager may use reciprocity. Suppose Joan and Mary asked their supervisor to be assigned to a management development seminar to be held in Florida in the winter months. She recommends both of them to the personnel department, and they are selected to go. Joan and Mary may feel they should work harder to "repay" for the favor. The reciprocity approach has increased their motivation to work to, say, level 3.5 or higher.

Of course the motivation level that a person has when he or she begins a job may range from low to high. When motivation to work is low, say level 1, the manager seeks to drive it higher. Increasing motivation to work would result in higher performance by Joan and Mary (in Figure 16.2) and for Betty (in Figure 16.3). For Dick, however (Figure 16.3), managerial motivation strategies will not work. A

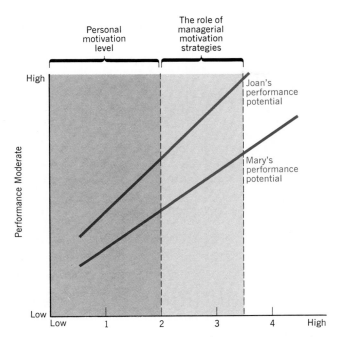

FIGURE 16.6   The role of managerial motivation strategies.

manager might try to raise Dick's skill level by sending him to school to learn budgeting or decide to replace Dick, but the manager should forget about "motivating" him. It just will not work.

What a manager does can affect the motivation to perform. How does this work? The different motivational strategies that managers use affect the expectancies of their subordinates. This requires that the manager be aware of the expectancies that organization members have and the reasons for such expectancies. The supervisor can influence subordinate expectancies ($E \rightarrow P$ and $P \rightarrow O$) by his behavior. He can clarify what he expects of the subordinates when role ambiguity exists. He can attempt to increase the payoffs to subordinates for achieving high performance levels by rewarding high performance. He may be able to build up a subordinate's self-esteem and abilities by appropriate training, support, and work assignments. He can provide facilitation of performance by insuring that supplies and other resources are available at the time and in the form needed, and he can increase the amount of productive time available to an employee through delegation or some other means of more effectively utilizing time.[20]

SATISFACTION—THE RESULT OF PERFORMANCE

Not only does task-oriented effort produce products, but feelings of satisfaction or dissatisfaction may also develop as a result of it. The latter have been called *"intrinsic rewards."* A person may feel good after performing a task. Work may be enjoyable, especially if the person is interested in it. His feelings of self-esteem may be enhanced when a person is doing something that is believed to be worthwhile. *"Extrinsic rewards"* are rewards that are controlled by others, such as pay, promotion, and recognition. Work activity may also lead to such rewards. These rewards are the incentives that are available if reinforcement motivational strategies are used.

When the individual finds work intrinsically and/or extrinsically rewarding, job satisfaction may increase. Conversely, if work is drudgery, with no rewards, dissatisfaction may increase. In general, it is now believed that satisfaction follows performance when the performance results in outcomes valued by the person. Therefore, in our model in figure 15.7 we show satisfaction resulting from work influencing the human input factor, especially the individual-need dimension. For example, if a worker high in achievement needs is successful, she is likely not only to be satisfied but also to raise her level of achievement orientation. The converse may also be true.

SUMMARY

In this chapter we have shown how motivation to work, managerial behavior, skills, and technology are related to performance. To improve results the manager must know more than the simple fact that these elements are related; managers must know how they are related.

These relationships are different depending upon whether or not the work setting is human-skill dominated or technology dominated. In later chapters we will be more specific in suggesting which managerial motivational approach is most effective in the different work settings.

Case 16.1 Wood Manufacturing Company

Jack Wood, president of Wood Manufacturing Company, was invited to a seminar at the University of Florida sponsored by the Management Center. While attending the seminar, Wood attended a session devoted to job enrichment, an approach unfamiliar to him. The seminar speakers talked about the benefits to be gained by redesigning the job so that it would be more satisfying and motivating to the worker.

During the discussion period, Jack disagreed with the suggestions of the speakers. "In my plant and in most plants, jobs get more interesting as you advance in the organization. One of the most important incentives we have for getting our employees to improve themselves and learn on the job is the opportunity to qualify for a more challenging and interesting job in the company. If a worker is bored with his job, why doesn't he just work extra hard so he can get a better one? Let's not destroy one of the most important incentives we have left."

1. Do you agree or disagree with Jack's position in this case? Why?
2. Under what circumstances might Jack's position be workable and under what circumstances unworkable?

Woodside Academy*

Woodside Academy is a small (500 students), all-girl, private high school located in the Woodside suburb of Chicago, Illinois. According to the school's philosophy, Woodside strives to provide for average and above average students a college preparatory curriculum that includes rich and varied intellectual opportunities. Flexibility and individualization of curriculum and teaching methods allow the students to share in the responsibility and delight of intellectual discovery and development.

To implement this philosophy, Woodside adopted a flexible, modular schedule in the early 1970s. This schedule consisted of a five-day cycle, with each day comprised of twenty mods, twenty minutes long. A day included both structured time (class time) and unstructured time (which the girls called "free time"). Almost all courses consisted of one large group lecture and two small group discussion sessions in each week. Classes were usually two mods (forty minutes) long.

At the beginning of each quarter, a student received the course syllabus, which outlined course objectives, requirements, and the evaluation system. To obtain a grade of Very Good (A), Good (B), or Satisfactory (C), a student had to fulfill certain objectives. Objectives took the form of tests, projects, papers, book reviews, and in-depth studies.

To pass a course all students had to fulfill the objectives for a Satisfactory (C). Those students desiring a grade of Good (B) or Very Good (A) fulfilled additional objectives. The additional objectives provided the opportunity to study a topic covered in class in more detail or to explore a related topic of interest that was covered in class. Extra work was expected to be turned in on the due date, but there was usually no penalty for turning work in late. Most extra work was turned in during the last week of the quarter.

In this form of the objective system, grades of B or C required a 70 percent score on all tests and a grade of A required a score of 80 percent on all tests. One feature of the Woodside grading system was makeups. Tests that were failed could be taken over again until a satisfactory score of 70 percent was obtained or made up. As was the case with extra work, makeups were usually completed the last week of the quarter.

If a student did not complete the work before the end of the quarter, she received a grade of Incomplete on her report card for that course. As soon as the work was completed, an appropriate grade was issued. This meant that the last week of each quarter was very hectic for both students and faculty, as students hurried to turn in required work and extra work and to make up tests. For many, the first few weeks of the new quarter were equally hectic: carry over work from last quarter was completed and work for the new quarter was begun.

The idea behind a flexible modular schedule was not to create an overload of work at the end of the quarter, but to provide students with unstructured time during the school day in which work on objectives could be completed. Each major department (English, Foreign Languages, Math, Science, Social Studies, and Religion) had its own Media Center where students could study in groups, work independently, meet with teachers to discuss course work, or receive individual help. Each

*We express appreciation to Cristina Marie Giannantonio, who wrote the original version of this case, for permission to use it.

Media Center contained course texts, other relevant books, reference materials, maps, models, filmstrips, and so on. In addition to these departmental media centers, there was a library with additional resources and reading material. The library was a good place to study because no talking was allowed and this rule was enforced, unlike the media centers, which tended to become noisy and rowdy if no teacher was present.

Besides the library and the six media centers, there were only five other areas where students were allowed during the school day: the cafeteria, the gym, the students' lobby, classrooms not being used for structured classes, and outside the building on certain areas of the school grounds.

On a typical day at Woodside, what would a visitor to the school see? The students' lobby and the cafeteria were usually half full of students socializing, talking, playing cards, and so forth. On the other hand, the library and the media centers were typically one-third full. Though the library was always a quiet place to study, the media centers often became quite noisy. Different media centers and sections of media centers became the meeting places for different groups of friends.

After a while, most of the students settled into a routine. The same few students were working toward As and Bs, but most of them were working toward Cs. Usually if a student was doing well in course work, a teacher often nudged her to work toward a higher grade by pointing out the additional objective required for the grade, or by showing her how close she was to completing the work for a higher grade.

In general, most students worked toward the grade they expect to receive for a course. Those that expected a C completed the work for a C and received a grade of C. Those that expected an A completed the work for an A and received a grade of A.

1. Evaluate the reasons for the students' behavior in this situation.
2. What might the school do to change this behavior to that which they feel is more appropriate?
3. What can the teacher (as a leader) do in a situation like this to improve student performance?
4. What do you think is the most important factor that affects a student's performance: the teacher, the modular schedule, or the student? Why?

DISCUSSION QUESTIONS

1. List and discuss the seven motivational strategies. Do you feel each is a viable alternative?
2. Discuss the five characteristics of work that affect motivation and performance.
3. There are problems associated with job enrichment as a motivational strategy. Discuss these as if you were the manager.
4. Why would ego involvement be an effective motivator?
5. What is meant by the performance level of an employee?
6. How important is motivation to a worker's performance? How would technology affect this?
7. Discuss "satisfaction vs. dissatisfaction" in job performance and its importance to you.
8. Review Table 16.1. What combinations of motivational approaches might be most effective in a bank? A factory? Government office? Why do you think so?

9. Item 16.1 discusses job enrichment as a strategy to combat absenteeism. Do you think this strategy will result in long-term benefits? Why or why not?
10. Which of the managerial motivation strategies do you believe would be most successful in dealing with subordinates? Which would you respond to most? Is there a difference between the way you would manage and the way you want to be managed?
11. Have you ever been involved in a "team project" for which a grade was given? What problems did the grader have if individual team members were to be graded on the value of (1) their work; (2) their contribution? How did you feel about the grade received by those who did work hard? About the grade received by those who did not contribute as much?
12. Why do you believe that managers are so concerned with "motivation"?

REFERENCES

1. Carroll, S. J. "Effectiveness ratings of motivational methods by different groups of supervisors." Unpublished study, University of Maryland, 1973.
2. Goode, W. J., and I. Fowler. "Incentive factors in a low morale plant," American Sociological Review, 14 (1949): 619–624.
3. Gouldner, A. "The role of the norm of reciprocity in social stabilization," American Sociological Review, 15 (1960): 161–178.
4. Krasner, L. "Behavior therapy," Annual Review of Psychology, 22 (1971): 483–519.
5. Nash, A. N., and S. J. Carroll. The management of compensation. Monterey, Calif., Wadsworth, 1975.
6. Perham J. C. "Payoff in performance bonuses," Dun's Review, May 1975, p. 68.
7. Nord, W. R. "Beyond the teaching machine: The neglected area of operant conditioning in the theory and practice of management," Organizational Behavior and Human Performance, 5 (1969).
8. Hackman, R. J., and J. L. Suttle. Improving life at work: Behavioral approaches to organizational change, Santa Monica, Calif., Goodyear Publishing Company, 1977.
9. Miner, J. B., and H. P. Dachler, "Personnel attitudes and motivation," Annual Review of Psychology, 24 (1973): 379–402.
10. Miner, J. B. The management process: Theory, research and practice. New York, Macmillan, 1973.
11. Marriott, R. Incentive wage systems. London, Staples Press, 1968.
12. Carroll, S. J. "Two cases of failure in using competition for motivation." Unpublished case study, University of Maryland, 1973.
13. Miller, L. K., and R. L. Hamblin. "Interdependence, differential rewarding, and productivity," American Sociological Review, 28 (1963): 768–777.
14. Sherif, M. "Superordinate goals in the reduction of intergroup conflict," American Journal of Sociology, 63 (1958): 349–356.
15. Hilgard, E. R., R. C. Atkinson, and R. L. Atkinson. Introduction to psychology. New York, Harcourt, Brace, 1971.
16. Korman, A. K. "Self esteem as a variable in vocational choice," Journal of Applied Psychology, 50 (1966): 479
17. Vroom, V. H. Work and motivation. New York, Wiley, 1964.
18. Seashore, S. E. Group cohesiveness in the industrial work group. Survey Research Center, University of Michigan, 1954.
19. Reitz, H. J. *Behavior in Organizations*. Homewood, Illinois: R. D. Irwin Co., 1981.
20. House, R. J. "A path goal theory of leadership effectiveness," Administrative Science Quarterly, 16 (1971): 321–332.

CHAPTER SEVENTEEN

Control: Process and Structure

Item
17.1 CALCAL's first month of operation this year was not an easy one. So many more problems came up than Pat Redwick had anticipated when he and the staff developed the plans for the year. First was the unexpected labor problem. Jerry Old, one of the four production staff, began to talk about unionizing the production department. He had contacted FTU, the Federated Trade Union, and inquired how he could proceed with a union election.

This caused a problem between Jerry and Cecil. Cecil had been with CALCAL and Pat Redwick from the first day Pat began the company. He was an old hand who was adamantly opposed to the union and he argued, it seemed, incessantly with Jerry and the other workers that the union would be of little benefit to them.

Then there was the problem with Victoria Holt, the secretary. Her young son was critically ill. There was grave concern that he had a congenital heart problem that might be fatal. Victoria was away from work for half the month. She kept up with most of her daily work, but Pat knew she had fallen behind on several things, and he was not sure which projects were in trouble.

The last major problem for the month was Striated Chemicals bankruptcy. Striated Chemicals was CALCAL's major supplier of raw materials for electronic components. It had taken Pat the last four years to build a good relationship with the Striated people, and he had been able to count on them as a very dependable supplier. He could not believe that Striated Plastics had gone out of business so quickly. He did not have any hint of problems at Striated. Their sudden bankruptcy caused Pat to scurry around to find another supplier. The sales manager of Striated, who had become a friend of Pat's, helped him work out an arrangement with Fulton Chemical. Fulton filled in the gap nicely, delivering raw materials to CALCAL two days before their inventory from Striated ran out. CALCAL did not miss a production day.

Pat was relieved when the month ended. Problems like these he faced this month would not be likely to occur again. He thought that he had worked these problems out well.

At the end of the month Pat Redwick received the report from the production foreman for the first month's operations (see Figure 17.1). Pat was surprised and disappointed. With the rest of the staff, he worked out the plans rather carefully. The sale forecasts he made, he was certain, were sound. So were the estimated costs that were budgeted.

The Report of Production Operations (Figure 17.1) indicated that CALCAL's level of production was right on target. Pat planned to produce 1,100 units and Peter Gabriel's unit met that goal. But materials costs, direct labor, and variable manufacturing expenses were in excess of the levels planned.

Materials costs were $150 over budget. In planning, CALCAL management estimated that materials cost per unit should be $2.00. They were $2.14.

Direct labor was budgeted for $2,200, or $2.00 per unit. The total direct labor cost for the period was $2,400, or $2.18 per unit.

Variable manufacturing expenses were $1,175, exceeding the total planned expenditure of $1,100 by $75. There was a difference of $.06 per unit, $1.06 actual unit expense compared to $1.00 per unit budgeted expenses.

Pat was concerned. To continue at this rate, Pat estimated his total costs for the 15,000 units would exceed his planned costs. The actual cost of production per unit exceeded planned costs by $.38 ($.14 + $.18 + $.06). This meant that actual total cost would exceed planned costs by $5,700 ($15,000 × $.38). He knew something had to be done.

Pat phoned Pete. "Come see me as soon as you can," he said. "We'll have to talk about an hour or so. We've got to do something to get these costs back in line."

"I can be there in thirty minutes, Pat," replied Gabriel. Peter Gabriel hung the phone receiver on the hook, put on his jacket, picked up his coffee cup, and started toward the front end of the building where Pat's office was located.

FIGURE 17-1 CALCAL Report of Production Operations, Budget vs. Actual, Month 1

	Budget	Actual	Variance
Units (Number)	1,100	1,100	-0-
Materials	$2,200	$2,350	$(150)
Direct labor	2,200	2,400	(200)
Indirect labor	700	700	-0-
Variable manufacturing expenses	1,100	1,175	(75)
Total production costs	$6,200	$6,625	$(425)

He knew Pat would be upset, but so was he. Peter had felt that things were not working smoothly all month long, but he could not quite put his finger on what was wrong. Now, maybe he and Pat could solve the problem.

When Pete walked into Pat's office, he was not even in a chair before Pat said, "We've got real trouble. If we continue the way we've started this month, by the end of the year our costs will be almost $6,000 higher than we have budgeted. Explain this Production Operations Report to me, Gabe."

"You see the variances, Pat. We have problems all over the place," was the answer.

"Look, Gabe, I've got to know why you haven't been able to keep costs under control out in your shop. What are you going to do? What caused this?" Pat was truthfully puzzled. He continued, "I thought we worked things out rather smoothly this month. This report is a surprise to me."

Pete thought for a few seconds. He did not know what he would do to get costs back under control. There were several things that could have led to these problems.

"Pat, the situation with Jerry and the union must be resolved. He and Cecil have been fighting over the FTU and the company. Those two men stand head to head all day. It cuts into production time and, I think, they are simply turning out too much scrap. That could account for the higher materials cost and the increases in direct labor and variable manufacturing expenses," Peter explained.

Gabriel went on. "We've got to do something about it. I'm not certain what the best way to handle it will be. Do you think I should call Jerry in and raise hell with him?"

"There are some labor laws we've got to watch out for. We could have an unfair labor practice on our hands if you're not careful," Pat cautioned Peter.

The door to his office opened, just as he finished. Victoria stood in the doorway. "Am I interrupting a private meeting? I heard you just received the monthly production report, Pat. It's bad, right? I'm sorry I had to take so much time off. Tim was sick you know, and I felt that I had to be with him."

"It's not your fault, Vic," Pat told her. Pete nodded in agreement.

Victoria walked into the office and sat across from Pat. She said, "You know what I think it is? I'll bet our problems are caused by the raw materials we are buying from Fulton Chemical."

"Can't be," said Gabriel. "Striated Plastic people told me, personally, that Fulton is reliable and the materials we have now are perfect substitutes for those we bought from Striated. I think we have a labor problem. It's in my department and I'll solve it."

"I'm with you, Gabe," added Pat. "I think we've got a crew out in the shop that is going to sabotage us. I don't know why they would. Our pay scale is above average and we surely don't press them too hard. I think it's this change in the work ethic. No one wants to work anymore. Everyone wants to be boss—and they want a white collar job. I think Pete will have to tighten up out there."

"I'd go slowly," Victoria warned, "You could be making a big mistake. Why should that crew change overnight? Jerry Old has been fussing about a union for two years. He and Cecil couldn't survive a day on the job if they didn't have each other to fight. You two sit here for a minute. Get some coffee and relax. I'm going to my office to check out an idea. I'll call you in a few minutes."

FIGURE 17.2 Victoria Holt's Worksheet

	Week 1		Week 2		Week 3		Week 4		Total	
	Budget	Actual	Budget	Actual	Budget	Actual	Budget	Actual	Budget	Actual
Production—units	275	275	275	275	275	275	275	275	1,100	1,100
Materials										
Total	$550	$540	$550	$535	$550	$625	$550	$650	$2,200	$2,350
Unit costs	2.00	1.96	2.00	1.94	2.00	2.27	2.00	2.36	2.00	2.14
Direct labor										
Total	$550	$550	$550	$545	$550	$640	$550	$665	$2,200	$2,400
Unit costs	2.00	2.00	2.00	1.98	2.00	2.32	2.00	2.42	2.00	2.18
Variable manufacturing										
Total	$275	$270	$275	$265	$275	$310	$275	$330	$1,000	$1,175
Unit costs	1.00	.98	1.00	.96	1.00	1.13	1.00	1.20	1.00	1.06

Pat and Peter knew that they should trust Victoria's instincts. More than once she had an insight to a problem that neither of them could see. Pat went to the outer office, poured coffee for himself and Pete. While Victoria was gone, the conversation turned to the regular Saturday tennis game that Pat and Peter had played for the last three years.

Twenty minutes later Victoria returned. She handed Pat and Peter a sheet of paper on which she had made some calculations (see Figure 17.2).

"Look at these figures, will you?" Victoria asked.

"What are they?" asked Pat and Pete almost in unison.

"It's a weekly breakdown of costs for the month," Victoria answered. "We've never had a report like this, I suppose because we've never had a problem like we have now. Look what these data show."

"What?" Pat questioned.

"Look, Pat, it's clear as glass. See the trend? Can't you see the sharp increase between the second and third week?" Victoria asked. "Something happened to our operation between the fourteenth and twenty-first of the month. Do you know what it is?"

"That's when you were gone, Victoria. Right?" Gabriel said as he turned and smiled at Pat.

"You've got it, Gabe." Victoria told him. "But that's the week that we started to take delivery from Fulton Chemicals. I think we've got a raw material problem. Something is causing the high scrap rate. Those poor guys out there in production probably have to be very careful. Parts are probably defective all the time, the work is slow. I'll bet that's the problem."

Gabriel wasn't satisfied yet. "I still think Jerry's at the bottom of this thing. He wants us to come down hard on the workers so he can justify the union election he's been crying for."

"Vic's right about Jerry, Gabe." Pat interrupted before Peter could go on. "He has been supporting a union for a long time. And he and Cecil have always fought with each other. I don't think Jerry would undercut us."

Pat reached for the telephone and as he dialed a number, he looked toward Victoria and said, "Thanks, Victoria. I'm glad we didn't jump to the conclusion that Gabe and I were close to. We would have been on the shop's back for more production."

Pat paused, then spoke into the phone. "Hello, Fulton Chemical?"

This case is an example of the managerial process of control, the activity of insuring that actions and events conform to plans. A good deal of a manager's work is control oriented. For example, standards are determined in budgeting, a phase of operational planning. These standards are derived directly from the goals developed in the strategic planning process. Schedules are developed and policies formulated. Events are measured and evaluated. Corrective action is taken when necessary. The control process at CALCAL was set in motion in the strategic plans formulated. Control became more specific in operational planning and budgeting when production budgets, materials budgets, and cash budgets were developed. These budgets include very specific production, cost, and marketing goals for the various units of CALCAL. These goals and standards were communicated to others in the organization. They filtered down from those levels where the goals are originally set to those points where the work is done. The organization structure of CALCAL has control implications. Work assignments, job descriptions, and procedures all define what a person is to do. Figure 17.3 shows how control is related to other parts of the Management Process.

Control begins before an activity begins, it continues as the activity is going on, and some aspects of control occur after an activity is finished.

Preliminary control functions are those that occur before a work activity has begun. Preliminary control functions are
1. Setting standards
2. Scheduling
3. Developing policies and procedures

Concurrent control functions are those that take place after the activity has begun. Concurrent control functions are
1. Measuring performance
2. Evaluating performance
3. Taking corrective action

Figure 17.4 shows how preliminary and concurrent control functions are related to the execution of an activity.

PRELIMINARY CONTROL

The goal of preliminary control is to reduce the need to take corrective actions later. If we can successfully translate plans into objectives and standards, develop effective schedules, and prepare and develop policies that can be clearly communicated and implemented, the chances of things going well later on are substantially improved. In other words, good preparation pays off in the execution of the plan.

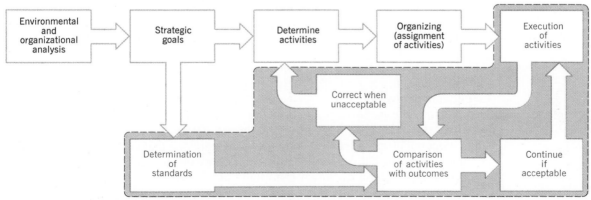

FIGURE 17.3   The relationship of control to other phases of the management processes.

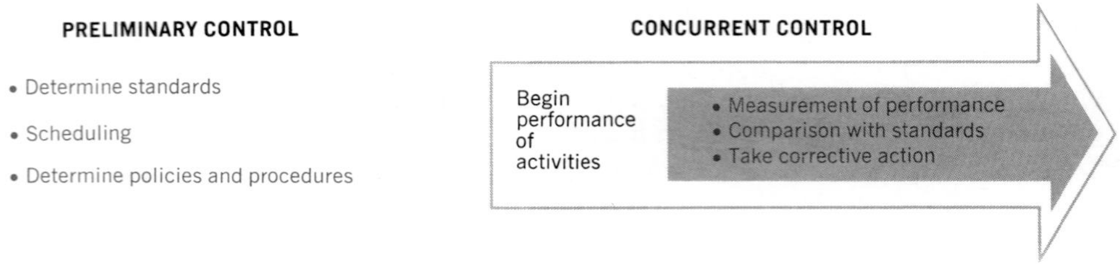

PRELIMINARY CONTROL

- Determine standards

- Scheduling

- Determine policies and procedures

CONCURRENT CONTROL

Begin
performance
of
activities

- Measurement of performance
- Comparison with standards
- Take corrective action

FIGURE 17.4 Preliminary and concurrent control activities as related to the performance of work activities.

SETTING STANDARDS

Everyone sets standards and everyone is measured against standards. We set standards in our personal life, for instance, how much of our income we should spend for food and housing. The federal government sets standards in many areas, ranging from the quality of meat to the average miles per gallon that automobile fleets must attain. Business firms set standards for cost, sales revenues, quality, time required to perform work activities, and so on.

A standard is a quantitative, qualitative, or behavioral index that indicates a desired frequency, desired quantity, or desired type of outcome. These standards are indexes derived from strategic objectives and system objectives. Performance is compared to the standard, or the index, to determine whether corrective action is necessary. When performance falls within acceptable limits of the standard, there is no need for action. For example, a body temperature of 98.6°F is a standard. When a person's body temperature is 98.6°, or very close, we can assume that there are no health problems. Likewise, the president of CALCAL can assume that if the total manufacturing costs for the first month are no more than $6,200 (see Figure 17.1) and if the predicted level of sales occur, then CALCAL's objectives will be attained.

Standards must be linked to and drawn from the objectives. It is hardly worth the time, effort, and cost involved in setting standards unless they contribute to the achievement of goals when they are used. While this may seem obvious, it sometimes actually happens that standards get in the way of effective operations, especially when different organizational units are involved. Consider, for instance, the United States government's environmental standards for the industrial use of high-sulfur coal. The standard effectively prevents electric utilities from using this very abundant energy source because it emits unpardonably high levels of sulfur dioxide, a pollutant. The technology to clean the sulfur dioxide from the coal to meet the clean air standards is very expensive. At the same time, the United States is increasingly dependent on foreign oil supplies, a dependence that could be reduced substantially if more coal were used in place of oil by electric utilities. In this case two objectives and standards drawn from them are in conflict. On the one hand, we want clean air, and on the other hand, we wish to be oil independent.

Another case of how standards can get in way of goal achievement is illustrated by the use of standards to evaluate the performance of interviewers in a state employment agency. A standard was set specifying the number of clients an employment counselor should interview each day. In an attempt to increase agency efficiency, a standard of sixteen clients each day was set for the interviewers. Over the following six months, the average number of clients processed by interviewers increased from twelve to seventeen. The interviewers had exceeded the standards, but this did not mean they were doing a better job. A further analysis of agency records showed that the number of successful job placements was no greater than for the period before the sixteen-interview standard was set. The counselors were seeing more clients, but they were placing them no more effectively than they had in the past. Another standard was developed for the interviewers: percentage of clients who obtained jobs as a result of referrals.

After a time the percentage of placements increased. It was found, however, that many of the positions into which the clients had been placed required skills and experience far below those of the person placed in them. The counselors were sending clients to be interviewed for jobs the counselors were certain the client could get because the client was overqualified. This example shows how each time a standard is set, the result may be different from that which was intended by management.

Types of Standards

Standards can represent either desired levels of output (output standards) or desired ways to carry out a plan or an activity (behavioral standards). **Output standards** generally focus on quantifiable or verifiable measures of quantity, quality, time, or cost against which a particular level of performance can be compared. Time standards, for example, indicate how long an activity should take. We measure how long it takes, say, to assemble a trash can on a bucket assembly line. As long as the elapsed time is less than the standard time, the manager can assume that there is no need for corrective action. Quality standards are output standards that indicate the number or type of tolerable defects. The number of defective units can be counted and compared with the quality standard. Cost standards and sales quotas are other types of output standards.

Those standards that focus on ways to carry out a plan are called **behavioral standards.** Behavioral standards are used when it is not possible to develop output standards for an activity. To use behavioral standards, a manager monitors how a person carries out an activity. For example, suppose we want to evaluate how well a manager develops the potential of those who work for him or her. This is difficult to judge with any good output measures. In this instance we observe whether or not the manager has provided learning opportunities, training programs, and coaching for subordinates.

The assumption underlying behavioral standards is that if a person goes about doing a job in an appropriate way, the goal will be achieved. Behavioral standards may be necessary when an evaluation of performance and a control decision must be made, but the results of the activity being evaluated will not be known for some time in the future.

Establishing Standards

There are several ways to set standards. We can set them based on our past experience, we can set them using the experience of others, or we can create synthetic standards.[1]

A *historical standard* is one based on our own past experience, that is, previous costs, past sales histories, or past production times. The firm's own experience is the basis for setting standards that will be used to evaluate future performance. CALCAL, for example, had collected information about labor costs per hour and the time required to produce one unit from past cost records. After adjusting these data for inflation and productivity changes, CALCAL planners estimate that materials cost in the next year should be $2.00 per unit and direct labor costs should be $2.00 per unit (see Figure 17.1).

Historical standards may be very useful so long as the relationship of one factor of production to others stays fairly constant. For instance, abrupt changes in oil prices have made it difficult to use historical cost standards for pricing electricity by public utilities. The relationship between oil costs and labor costs for electrical power plants is much different from what it was in the past. When managers use historical standards they assume that the conditions that occurred in the past will be similar to those in the future.

The assumption behind the use of historical standards is that if managers control those things which they have learned to be important from their past experience and for which they have developed an acceptable way to measure, the goals of the firm will be attained.

Comparative standards are based on the experiences of others. Comparative standards are set by examining the practices or the results of other organizations, or organizational units, similar to the one in which the standard will be applied. Trade associations generally publish information about the average return on sales, labor costs, advertising expenditures, management salaries, and so on of member firms. A manager may base a standard on such data to evaluate the organization's performance. Comparative standards allow for the assessment of performance of an organization against the performance of other organizations.

Synthetic standards are constructed from "standard data." Standard data are time and/or cost estimates for different predetermined units of work. Using standard data, time and cost standards can be determined even before a task has been performed. Standard data are frequently used by industrial engineers to set operative work standards.

The use of standard data is based on the assumptions that

1. It is possible to divide work into a standard set of activities.
2. A time can be established for these activities.

These assumptions are similar to those of the scientific management approach, particularly the work of the Gilbreths (see Chapter 2). The Gilbreths developed a classification system in which they categorized work activities into basic units, called "therbligs." There are, depending on which variation of this classification system one uses, up to twenty-two therbligs or basic motions. Some therbligs, for example, are

1. Grasp (an object)

2. Select (large, medium, and small object)
3. Position (line up an object)
4. Hold . . .

Standard times are set for each therblig through time and motion studies. To use standard data, we first analyze the work to be done to determine which therbligs constitute the job. After one has determined which therbligs make up a job, it is a simple matter to construct a standard for it. The times for those therbligs are combined. This becomes the "synthetic" standard for that activity. Synthetic standards are often very good first approximations for work standards. They should be modified as experience and conditions warrant.

SCHEDULING

Scheduling is the determination of when activities should begin, how long they should take, and when they should be completed. In scheduling, the rate at which resources are expended is determined. Scheduling is an aspect of control because through schedules we can limit a manager's behavior by authorizing **when** an event or an expenditure should occur.

Production scheduling is an example of the use of scheduling for control. Very elaborate production schedules are used in the manufacturing of automobiles to insure that each subassembly of the car arrives at the required point on the assembly line when it is supposed to be there. Different engines, transmissions, and accessories such as radios and air conditioners must be coordinated with body styles and other accessories to produce the specific car ordered by a customer.

Scheduling is a preliminary control activity because through it we can minimize variations from plans. If our time estimates for an activity are reasonably accurate and resources are available when needed, we can improve overall performance by effective scheduling.

POLICIES AND PROCEDURES

The purpose of policies and procedures is to insure that people in organizations act in ways to attain organizational goals. Policies are general, and procedures specific, guides to action.

Policies link the work to be performed with objectives of the organization by constraining or limiting the decision-making discretion of individuals to the boundaries within which individuals can act to achieve goals. The way that policies act as controls is shown in Figure 17.5. So long as a manager acts within the boundaries of "policy," he or she is working in a way consistent with company goals.

Policies guide the individual to make organizationally acceptable decisions. Policies may cover every operation of a firm. There are product policies, marketing policies, personnel policies, financial policies, and so on. The main function of policy is to control action by giving managers guidelines within which they can act. For example, a large Midwestern department store has a return goods policy that allowed customers to return a purchase with which the customer was not

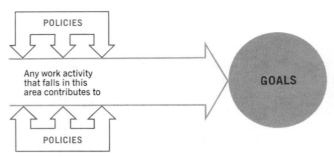

FIGURE 17.5   Policy as a preliminary control function.

satisfied. One customer, unsatisfied with an item supposedly bought ten years ear-lier, sought and obtained a refund. Other department stores have similar return goods policies, but most have a time limit. A store might have an unconditional return policy for goods purchased within the previous ninety days. Those handling customer returns know that they can give a refund or credit for merchandise bought up to ninety days before and that such a refund is consistent with the firm's overall objectives. Policies save the manager's time since employees do not have to ask for a decision about every refund requested. However, having such a policy does not mean that a purchase made over ninety days ago will not be refunded. Requests for deviations from the ninety-day limit will have to be approved by a higher-level manager. In some instances a refund for an item bought before the ninety-day period may be well justified.

Procedures are much more specific than policies. They are preliminary controls because it is assumed that if they are followed, the work will be done correctly. Procedures are often thought of as the "red tape" of bureaucracy, but they are especially useful in that they often insure relatively smooth work operations in very large organizations. Consider how the registration procedure at any large university with, say, 20,000 students controls the enrollment process. Each term these 20,000 students may enroll for an average of four different courses. Courses are scheduled at different times of the day and night. These courses may have very different re-quirements. There must be some systematic way to get these 20,000 students into all these classes in the usually short registration period. Registration procedures serve this purpose. While registration procedures may seem burdensome and cum-bersome to faculty and students, when considered in this light they are very effective organizational devices.

CONCURRENT CONTROL

Concurrent control refers to those aspects of control that take place after the activity that was planned has begun. The three phases of concurrent control are

1. The measurement of performance
2. Evaluating performance
3. Taking corrective action when necessary

Measuring is the act of determining whether or not a characteristic is present, how much of a characteristic is present, how frequently a characteristic occurs, or whether an event has taken place. Giving an examination to a group of students and grading it is measurement; so is administering an intelligence test to an applicant for a position. Timing how long it takes a jogger to run a mile is measurement. Counting the number of bushels of wheat grown on a farm is measurement. So is determining whether or not an advertising department has successfully met a deadline to deliver a program to the marketing department.

Measurement is done through tests, rating scales, simple observation, timing devices, grading scales, or any other method or device that allows us to obtain information in a quantitative form. This does not mean, though, that measurement is always done with finely calibrated devices. Some measurements may be very precise, like jewelers' scales used to weigh gold. Other measurement makes use of much less refined estimators, such as pacing off the distance between two points of land. Some measurement may be relatively simple to accomplish and be done in a relatively objective manner. For example, measuring of the output of a television manufacturing plant may be simply performed at the end of each production period. We count how many TV sets were manufactured. We also measure the presence or the degree of a characteristic in very subjective ways. We can, for instance, determine whether one lawn is more or less green than another lawn.

Through measurement we are seeking to find out whether something is present, how much of it is present, or whether or not something has been done. Managers are interested in measures that will help them judge whether or not subunit and/or the organization goals have been or are likely to be attained. For management purposes, we seek measures that are indicators of how well each of the different organizational subsystems (production, boundary-spanning, external-monitoring, control, and managerial subsystems) perform.

What To Measure

We measure those aspects of performance that have been identified as critical to the achievement of objectives. Some of these areas are identified in strategic planning and operational planning (see Chapters 8 and 9). For example, in developing the various budgets for CALCAL, target expenditures are determined for different types of activities such as direct and indirect labor costs. Production levels are set in the budget. We can then measure those aspects of performance that appear in the budgets. We can determine, for instance, the amount of money actually spent for direct labor (see Figure 17.1) or determine the level of sales at the end of each quarter.

Another form of measurement is to determine whether or not certain important events have occurred. For example, in scheduling a project it is necessary to determine when certain events should occur and how long certain activities should take. We can then ascertain whether or not the event has occurred, or how long it took. In the Space Landing Vehicle project described in length in Chapter 19, we can measure (determine) whether "power system construction" did, in fact, begin nine weeks after the start of the project.

Management by objectives (MBO) also is helpful to a manager in determining what to measure, particularly for management jobs. With MBO, a higher-level executive should focus upon measuring the performance of "special-project" objectives, those goals set in the most critical areas of a subordinate's work. For example, in Chapter 15 we described a foreman's job (shown in figure 15.8), which had the following performance components:

1. Prepare work schedule
2. Order raw materials
3. Dealing with subordinates
4. Running departmental meetings

Suppose that this foreman's manager decides that the first two performance components (i.e., scheduling and ordering) are the most critical facets of the foreman's work. These are the performance components that should be measured and monitored. The first performance component (preparing work schedules) might be measured by verifying that the work schedules are prepared by the foreman. The second performance component (ordering raw material) could be measured by determining the costs of raw materials or, perhaps, whether raw materials deliveries are made on time and the materials are available when needed for the operation.

For most jobs it is impossible to measure all the different facets of performance. It is also probably impossible to measure the important aspects of performance as well as we would like to measure them. A manager must decide which of all the different aspects of a subordinate's performance that can be measured, and should be measured. The manager must also decide which measure of several possible measures of effectiveness should be used to evaluate performance.

To be effective any measurement of performance must meet the following requirements:

1. *Measurement must be related to objectives.* A measurement not linked directly to the organization's strategic and internal systems goals provides irrelevant information. All measurement costs something; therefore, superfluous measurement reduces effectiveness. Superfluous measurement is a particular problem in situations in which data are very easy to gather. For instance, in a firm that makes extensive use of computers, it is very easy to collect vast quantities of information about detailed aspects of work. Managers feel tempted to do so and to use much of these data for evaluation.

2. *Measurement must focus on critical points.* Measurement should provide information that can be used to predict success or failure. This means that a manager must be selective about what to measure, always seeking to assess the most critical aspects of performance. For example, if a manager's problem is to meet a tight production schedule, then he or she should focus on measuring how much time the different phases of a project may take.

3. *Measurement must be reliable and valid.* Reliability and validity are essential properties of good measurement. ***Validity*** means we are measuring what we intend to measure. For instance, suppose that a detailed analysis of the variable manufacturing expenses of $1,175 reported in Figure 17.1 showed that it contained a portion of the cost of CALCAL's lease. Since a lease is generally regarded as a fixed cost, $1,175 is not a valid measure of variable manufacturing costs.

Using invalid information to make decisions may lead to undesirable results. Suppose as a result of the reported variable cost of $1,175, which CALCAL management assumed contained appropriately allocated costs, they took severe action to cut variable expenses. They may eliminate certain machine maintenance services. Because maintenance was not performed, CALCAL might experience future equipment breakdowns. Clearly, invalid information led CALCAL to make an incorrect decision, which will lead to less affective operations.

Reliability refers to the stability of the measurement over time. When the same conditions prevail, the measurement should give the same result. For example, CALCAL planned to sell 1,000 units the first month and 1,200 the second month. Suppose they actually sold those amounts, the report of sale showed 1,050 units for the first month and 1,210 units for the second month. The measurement of sales level is unreliable because of the reported level of sales varies from the actual level.

EVALUATING AGAINST STANDARDS

Evaluation is the act of comparing a measure of performance against a standard. From a control perspective, evaluation is done to determine whether or not it is necessary to take some corrective action. When the performance measure deviates far enough from the standard, some corrective action is likely to be taken to bring performance back into line.

Does Performance Meet Standards?

This is the basic question of evaluation. This is a more involved issue than just seeking a simple "yes" or "no" to the question. It is not necessarily safe to conclude that all is going according to the plan if the performance meets standards. Perhaps the standard was incorrectly set. Suppose quality control inspectors in a food processing plant pass *all* the production as having met quality standards. This should probably be viewed with some skepticism, since it is only common sense to assume that there are some flawed products. We should reexamine the standard to see whether it has been set too low. Perhaps the inspection function is not being performed properly. Maybe the inspectors are making bad judgments, or the inspection equipment does not detect deficiencies that are present.

Suppose performance regularly deviates in an undesirable direction from the standard. The standard may be set too high, as in the case when an instructor gives very difficult mathematics examinations to an introductory class and the resulting grades are very low, leading the instructor to assign failing grades to a large number of students. The quality of the students is not necessarily the reason for the low grade distribution. A deviation of a grade distribution from the instructor's standards for acceptable performance could be caused by:
1. An increasingly high standard
2. Very poor teaching
3. Very poor students

Evaluation Never Tells What The Problem Is

Evaluation only indicates a symptom that exists, revealing that something is not as it should be—for instance, a thermometer that records the body temperature. When a person has a fever of 100°, a diagnosis must be made to determine the cause of the fever. Similarly, when a manager finds that performance does not meet standards, he or she must seek the cause of the deviation. This is shown in the CALCAL illustration in item 17.1. Pat Redwick, CALCAL's president, saw that materials costs, direct labor costs, and variable manufacturing expenses varied significantly from a level that he thought acceptable. He estimated that if the firm continued to operate as it had, actual costs would exceed planned costs by $5,700. In this case, actual performance was far out of line with planned performance when the monthly results were compared against the standard.

TAKING CORRECTIVE ACTION

Corrective action is the last step in control. It involves three steps:

1. Identify the most probable cause of the deviation of the measure from the standard.
2. Select the alternative most likely to eliminate the cause.
3. Implement the solution chosen.

These steps were already discussed in Chapter 7, where we examined several different ways to go about selecting alternatives. Their importance is highlighted in the CALCAL case in item 17.1. Pat Redwick and the production foreman were ready to take some action that would have involved Jerry and Cecil. However, Victoria Holt's analysis suggested another, more likely, cause of the variation from budgeted cost levels. She concluded from her analysis that the supplier was the most likely cause. The corrective action for CALCAL is to take steps to insure that the new supplier, Fulton Chemical, provide raw materials to exact specifications. An approach that may be of use to the manager in this step of control is the Kepner–Tregoe approach to determining the most probable cause of a problem, as discussed in Chapter 7.

ORGANIZATIONAL CONTROL STRUCTURES

An important reason for having an organization is that by bringing the efforts of several people to bear a problem, more effective and efficient results will occur than if each person approached it individually. In organizations we come to depend upon others. Imagine the problems in any large organization if those in it were not relatively certain what others were going to do. The marketing vice president for a computer manufacturer knows (at least believes it to be relatively certain) that salespersons in branch offices all over the country will call on customers and attempt to sell the company's product. In every organization there is effort aimed to insure that the activities of people and the operation of the technology are directed toward common goals.

In organizations we seek to increase the degree of predictability of the behavior and/or the outputs of others. For example, a manager of a printing plant wishes to predict accurately the output (how many pages) that can be produced and what the cost of production will be. The printing manager depends upon workers, other managers, and the clerical staff being at their jobs when they are supposed to be. Likewise, a market research group manager wishes to be certain that when faced with a problem that the methods (behaviors) the staff members use to solve it will result in the most accurate answer. Being able to predict what people will do, or how they will act, with relatively high accuracy makes the management job much less difficult.

Organizations demonstrate observable behavior patterns over a relatively long time span. In fact, it is by the observation of these behavior patterns that we know an organization exists. We can accurately predict much of the behavior in most organizations after observing these behavior patterns for a very short time. Consider the behavior patterns around a college. Traffic is extremely heavy each weekday around a campus shortly before 8:00 A.M. Secretaries, students and professors are hurrying to classrooms and offices. By 8:05 A.M., it becomes remarkably quiet, except for a few stragglers late for class. At 8:50 A.M., the halls are again filled with rushing students and by 9:02 A.M. there is quiet again.

There are stable and predictable patterns for business firms, government agencies, not-for-profit organizations, and social organizations. These behavior patterns develop as a result of several systems that cause and reinforce them. We call these systems the organizational control structure. They are shown in Figure 17.6.

We will examine some of the most prominent facets of the control structure. Some of them have been discussed earlier. Here we will try to point out how they effect control in organizations.

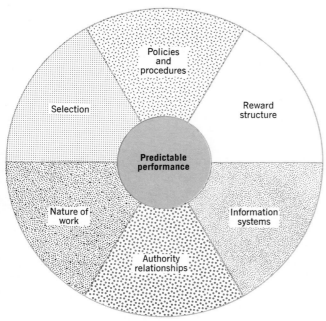

FIGURE 17.6   Components of the control structure.

1. Policies and procedures
2. Rewards structure
3. Information systems
4. Authority relationships
5. Selection
6. The nature of work

The organizational control structure is made up of those components of the organization that constrain and direct the behavior of the members. Control, in the sense that people act in a fairly predictable way, occurs because individuals react to the elements of the control system that have been embedded in the organization. For example, work starts every day at 8:00 A.M. because a decision was made earlier that this would be the case. All kinds of other behavior patterns emerge because starting time is 8:00 A.M. Meetings are not scheduled until 8:30 A.M. or 9:00 A.M. because we want others to have some time to get settled and prepared.

POLICIES AND PROCEDURES

We have already said a good bit about policies and procedures. They are part of the organizational control structure because they govern behavior in an important way. Both policies and procedures are rules. Knowing which rules others are following permits us to predict what they are going to do. Here are two examples of how policies and procedures controls behavior. Earlier in this chapter we cited an instance in which a store has a return goods policy of accepting returns on purchases made within the previous ninety days. With such a policy the person supervising this department knows under what conditions approval must be obtained from higher management. Such approval is necessary only when a customer insists on returning an item purchased over ninety days before. Therefore it will be exceptions to the policy that will cause the return goods supervisor to seek out a superior for help in solving this problem.

The procedure for paying employees also illustrates how behavior patterns may be affected by procedures. In one firm employees are paid on alternate Friday mornings. Each employee comes to the personnel office, usually between 8:00 A.M. and noon, to receive a paycheck. If the plant manager wishes to schedule a meeting, Friday morning is a good choice since virtually everyone will be in on that day, even those who are not scheduled to work. In a similar plant in the same town, the payroll office has arranged with local banks for paychecks to be electronically deposited to each employee's checking or savings account, if the employee wishes. Everyone in the plant participates in this plan. Hardly anyone is in the payroll office on Friday morning except the office staff. This illustration shows how different procedures will result in different behavior patterns of organization members.

REWARD STRUCTURE

The nature of rewards affects behavior since people tend to do those things for which they are rewarded. Organization rewards are payments to persons such as wages, salaries, pay increases, promotions, increased recognition, status, and other social rewards. Rewards may also be permission to use certain organization resources generally limited to a select group, such as access to the company airplane or the executive dining room.

Organizations allocate rewards differentially to members. The basis for this differential allocation is, presumably, the individual's worth to the organization. Worth to the organization is generally a function of how well one performs relative to others in similar jobs, the importance of the job in the organization, and/or the importance of the individual. Therefore, we expect (1) better workers to be more highly paid than those who are not as productive; (2) pay levels to be generally higher in the higher echelons of the organization; and (3) a person who possesses a very critical skill to be more highly paid than one whose skill is not so critical.

There are two general classes of rewards, **general rewards** and **task-specific rewards.** Taken together, the sum of general rewards and task-specific rewards equals the individual's total set of payments for his or her contribution.[2]

General rewards are given to all individuals because of their membership in a particular class. They are given without regard to how well or how poorly a person does a job. General rewards are earned not because of what one does, but because the person is one of a group entitled to them. For example, in most organizations all personnel are entitled to participate in the health insurance plan. All employees receive a permit to park in the company lot. Across-the-board wage increases are another form of general reward.

Task-specific rewards are linked to how well or how poorly a person does a job. They are tied to the level of task performance. A salesperson's commission, based on the level of sales, is a task-specific reward. Piece rate pay systems in manufacturing plants are task-specific pay systems.

To make use of task-specific rewards at least three conditions must exist:
1. They must be clearly linked to the work for which they are given.
2. They must be large enough to be worth the effort.
3. They should be seen as equitable relative to others in the organization.

On the face of it, it seems to make sense for management to try to use task-specific rewards as much as possible. Over time, individuals would be more likely to work harder at their job because rewards (recognition, promotion, and pay) and performance would be highly correlated. If a person wants to earn more or be promoted, all he or she would have to do is produce more.

However, it is very difficult to use task-related rewards in most cases. First, it is often impossible to separate the contribution of one person from others when they all are engaged in highly interdependent work. For example, when a product development group completes the design of a new product, we may not know which person in the group made the greatest contribution. It is virtually impossible to separate the work of one worker on an assembly line from the work of another in order to use task-related rewards.

Second, some tasks have time-delayed outcomes. A time-delayed outcome means that the results of work will not be known (and therefore cannot be assessed for reward purposes) until a future time. However, before the results are known, pay increases and/or promotion decisions about the people involved must be made. For example, the advertising group may complete a marketing program for a new lawn care product in June. The product may be introduced the following February, so as to be available for the spring gardening season. However, management must make pay and promotion decisions for the advertising staff in September, three months after the program is developed and perhaps nine months before the program's effects can be judged.

When task-related rewards cannot be used, then rewards are allocated based on other factors, which are likely to be somewhat subjective. To decide how to reward the head of the advertising group in the example just cited, our judgment would be based on whether or not we believe the group went about designing the program in the "best way," rather than how effective the program is, since the results are not known at the time of our decision.

Over time, personnel will develop behavior patterns that are consistent with the way the reward system actually operates, not with the way that it is believed by management to operate.

INFORMATION SYSTEMS

In its most basic form, an information system consists of a sender, a channel, and a receiver (see Figure 17.7). Control decisions depend upon information transmitted by an information system. Someone must receive data about the actual or predicted level of performance to compare to the standards. The function of an information system is to transmit information from the sender to the receiver so that the receiver can take some action.

The sender observes, or monitors, some activity that is presumably of some interest to the receiver. The sender encodes information about the environment. Encoding involves selecting which facet of the environment should be communicated and then translating this facet into some form (a language) understandable to the receiver. For example, a quality control inspector (the sender) may wish to communicate the number of defective products to a shift supervisor (the receiver). The quality control manager may encode this information by recording the number of defective units and the type of defect. This information is then transmitted through the channel to the receiver. The information channel is the path through which information travels and the mechanisms used to convey it. The quality control information, encoded by the inspector, goes first to the quality control supervisor. It is then recorded and stored in a computer. A report is printed out and delivered to the department supervisor in which the defects were found. The receiver decodes the information (figures out what it means). If these data show that the number of defects are excessive (above standard), the department supervisor should take some action.

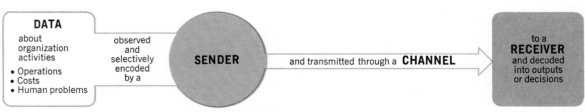

FIGURE 17.7 A simplified information system.

Problems can occur in an information system for several reasons:

1. *The sender encodes the wrong information from the environment and enters it into the system.* This would be the case had the quality control manager entered the number of hours worked by the crew instead of the defect rates.

2. *The channel may be a poor transmitter.* Information can be delayed in a channel. In some cases reports may be too late to take effective action. Suppose, for instance, that the cause of the defective production was substandard raw material. However, by the time the supervisor received the report all the substandard product had been processed. No effective control action could be taken.

3. *Information may get distorted in the channel.* In a channel, data may be handled by several people, they may be combined with other data, or they may be interpreted, and it is this interpretation that is passed on to the ultimate reviewer.

4. *The receiver may decode the information incorrectly.* The receiver may not understand the message and, therefore, cannot use the information correctly since it is unintelligible.

Types of Information

Data found in information systems are of three types. **Production data** characterize the quantity and quality of the organization's output. How many units of production were manufactured? How many clients were serviced? **Financial information** reports revenues and expenditures. Sales values, wages, payments to suppliers, costs of materials fall into this category. **Personnel information** is data about the members of the organization. Level of education, tenure with the company, promotability, and so forth are examples of personnel information.

The Systematic Nature of Information Systems

Because all organizations have some activities that occur regularly—and some organizations have many repetitive activities—information systems will be developed to convey data from the point of performance to (1) managers who must make control decisions, (2) staff units who must process data for regular payments such as taxes and wages, and (3) auditors, who monitor the financial performance of the organization.

Information systems require regular inputs from organization members. Many people spend much of their time obtaining and processing this information. An information system influences behavior patterns because meeting input requirements is a necessary activity for the system to operate effectively.

AUTHORITY STRUCTURE

The structure of authority is part of the control structure because it defines the limits of decision-making activities for an individual. In some organizations decision making is decentralized, that is, decisions are made at the lowest organizational level possible. The philosophy that underlies a **decentralized** authority approach is that the person closest to the point where an activity occurs is generally in the best position to make decisions about the activity. For example, with a decentralized philosophy, a sales supervisor in Figure 17.8 would be responsible for the control decisions. Under a decentralized authority structure, the sales supervisor would set

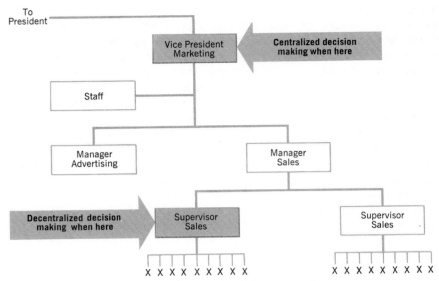

FIGURE 17.8   Centralized and decentralized decision making.

a sales quota for each salesperson, evaluate how well the sales level of each of the selling staff meets the standard, and decide what corrective action should be taken if sales quotas (standards) are not met.

Under **centralized** control, these decisions may be made by the vice president of marketing (see Figure 17.8). Sales quotas may be set by the staff in the vice president's office and communicated to each salesperson through the sales manager and the sales supervisors.

Organizational behavior patterns under centralized authority systems will differ from those under decentralized systems. Under centralized control, lower level managers such as the sales supervisor and sales managers will primarily pass information to higher levels. They will be responsible for collecting information, organizing it, and passing it on to managers at higher levels. The work of a mid-level manager in a centralized authority system will be more routine, involving much more paper shuffling than would the work of a manager at the same level under a decentralized authority structure.

Under decentralization, sales supervisors would be much more active in planning and controlling the activities of the selling staff. Sales supervisors might be assigned a quota for their whole unit. The supervisors under decentralized control would set the goals for each salesperson. This can be contrasted with centralized control, in which individual sales goals might be set at higher organizational levels.

SELECTION

Selection approaches used in an organization can affect the predictability of behavior. Suppose a firm consistently selects young management trainees with high achievement needs. We can expect such a firm to lose many young managers very early in their careers since it is impossible to provide enough advancement opportunities to satisfy the achievement needs of those trainees.

Selection approaches are usually designed to bring into the organization people who will be highly productive, need less supervision, and are not likely to leave. For example, at Massachusetts Mutual Life Insurance Company five key areas are evaluated for each applicant for a salesperson's position: age, aptitude, college background, market contacts of a prospective applicant, and the success pattern on previous jobs.[3] Points are assigned to each of these categories and an applicant is evaluated and a score given in each category. The company seeks to hire applicants with higher scores. Massachusetts Mutual's experience with such a technique has been promising. After three years with the firm, those agents who were rated highest on these five factors produced nearly three times the sales volume as lower-rated employees. The high-scoring applicants are also less likely to leave the company than the low-scoring applicants. Good insurance agents (those who generate a lot of sales) are much easier to manage than poor ones. They are less of a management control problem.

Training programs also have control implications, because through training, a person may improve abilities so that he or she is able to perform more effectively at work. This means less need for direct supervision. Similarly, if some training efforts are successful, members may acquire attitudes and values more likely to lead to compliance with orders and directives from management.

THE NATURE OF WORK

The activities that constitute a person's job are another aspect of the organizational control structure. What a person does, when it must be done, how it is to be done, and with whom it is to be done govern behavior patterns in the work place. There is clear evidence that the job can affect attitudes[4,5] and perceptions[6] as well. The belief that work has such a powerful effect in a person's responsiveness and motivation is a basic assumption of the "job enrichment" approach. Characteristics of the job that affect organization behavior patterns are

1. The degree of autonomy
2. Task interdependence
3. Repetitiveness

Autonomy

Autonomy is the degree of individual freedom that a person has in making choices in the job. In a job with high autonomy, the person controls the work. In a job with low autonomy, the work controls the individual. Autonomy can be affected by the following factors in the work place:

1. Machine control of the work pace
2. Initiation of work activity by others
3. Need for dependable performance

1. *Machine control of the work pace.* When there is a machine control of work, a technological instrument is the main determinant of how a job is to be done. For instance, a secretary uses a typewriter to prepare letters. The secretary's speed and work pace are not influenced substantially by the typewriter. In this instance the work is not machine controlled. This is not true for the worker on an assembly line. Work must be performed when the machine presents it to the worker. An example of a job that is highly machine controlled is that of a spot welder in an auto assembly plant. In describing his job, the spot welder said

> "I stand in one spot, about two- or three-feet area, all night. The only time a person stops is when the line stops. We do about thirty-two jobs per car, per unit. Forty-eight units an hour, eight hours a day. Thirty-two times forty-eight times eight. Figure it out. That's how many times I push that button."[7]

While machine control of the work pace is predominant in many unskilled jobs, there are some instances in which quite complicated tasks are subject to machine control. The manned space probes are examples of this. The astronauts on board space vehicles were very much under the control of the machine in which they were working.

2. *Initiation of work activity by others.* In some jobs a person's work activity is controlled by others. A long-distance telephone operator, for example, responds to requests made by a caller to be connected with another person. The operator's work is initiated by a customer and the way the work is performed is quite specifically structured by the procedures that must be followed to connect the caller with another person.

In some jobs, while work activity may be initiated by others, the person performing the work has a great deal of autonomy in deciding how the work is to be done. For example, an ill person visits a doctor, initiating the doctor's work. But the choice of treatment for the illness is decided by the doctor.

3. *Need for dependable performance.* When it is imperative that a task be performed in a specific way, individual autonomy is limited when possible. For example, in the U.S. space program, astronauts had much of their time in space programmed for them because certain experiments were deemed necessary and mission planners wanted to be certain they were conducted.

Three ways to obtain dependable performance are (1) to insure that the person doing the job is trained so that it is done in the desired manner, (2) to develop procedures and rules that the person must follow, and (3) to substitute technology for individual skill.

Task Interdependence

When tasks are interdependent it means that success in performing the whole job depends upon successfully performing each individual task. Task interdependence is most visible in long-linked technologies such as assembly lines, though it is quite high in other types of work as well.

When tasks are highly interdependent, autonomy is relatively low because others are depending upon the person's performance. Making an error or working slowly causes problems for others who will have to work on the product. As one worker in a manufacturing plant said:

> "If you get behind, you're in the hole. When you get in the hole, you're bumping into the next worker. Man, sometimes you get in the hole and you run down. The next worker up from you, he can't do his job until you get finished. If you're slowin' up, that starts a chain reaction all the way up the line."[7]

Repetitiveness

The work cycle is the time that elapses from the start of a work activity until it starts again. For example, the work cycle for the spot welder in the example above is 1.25 minutes, since he works on forty-eight cars each hour. On the other hand, the work cycle for a professor teaching in a college that has divided the academic year into semesters is sixteen weeks. Each semester the professor begins teaching a new class just as each minute and a quarter the spot welder begins working on another car.

Of course there are some very significant differences between these two jobs, one of the most important being the length of the work cycle. A short work cycle that occurs repetitively requires the person's presence and attention.

CONTROL AND TYPES OF ORGANIZATIONS

The type of organization will significantly affect the control structure and the way that the control process is carried out. Mechanistic organizations will pose different control problems from organic organizations. Some differences in the control structures in the different types of organizations are discussed in this section.

CONTROL STRUCTURE DIFFERENCES

The predominant components of the control structure in a mechanistic organization are the nature of the work, policies and procedures (or formalization), and the authority relationships (see Figure 17.9). In general, in these organizations work is very narrowly defined into specialized and rather simple tasks. Because it is easy to perform this work, it is an easy matter to have someone do it and have it done right.

Policies and procedures, as we have already pointed out, will be quite specific. There will be little individual discretion in how to do the work.

Finally, the third dominant element in the mechanistic organization is the authority structure. We expect that decisions will be very highly centralized in the hands of a few people in the policymaking levels. Very few important decisions will be left to those who perform the work itself.

Figure 17.10 illustrates the dominant features of the control structure in organic organizations. The dominant facets will be selection, the reward structure, and the information system. Selection is particularly important here because in organic organizations the individuals are the most important resource in the sense that they bring the skills to work, rather than having them built into the technology.

The reward structure is critical in that professionals, who will constitute a major part of the population of organic organization, seek rewarding work. To the extent that the reward structure taps the intrinsic motivation of the group, performance will be quite high.

The information system takes on added importance in the organic organization. Much of the work that is done in such an organization has a time-delayed outcome. Therefore, professionals and technicians must have frequent and current information to make changes in the work as it is going on.

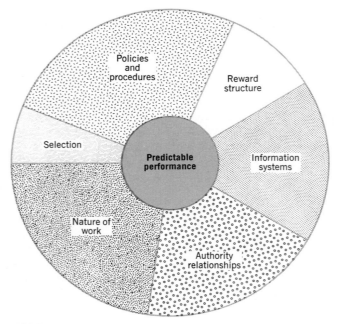

FIGURE 17.9 Components of the control structure in a mechanistic organization.

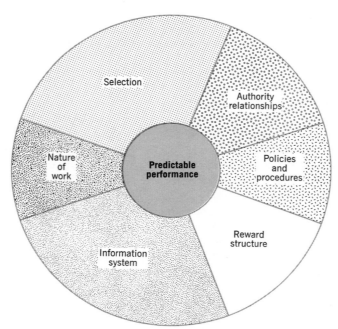

FIGURE 17.10 Components of the control structure in an organic organization.

These two figures (17.9 and 17.10) along with Figure 17.6 illustrate some important points in management process contingency theory. The points are (1) that in *any* organization it is necessary to be able to count on the performance of individuals who contribute to the overall objective, (2) that *all* organizations have a control system, but (3) that the elements in the control system will have a different degree of effect in different organizations.

MANAGERIAL CONTROL IN MECHANISTIC ORGANIZATIONS

In mechanistic organizations, since the strategic goals are essentially unchanging over time, organizationally acceptable measures of performance and ways of doing things will be developed. As time goes on and activities within the organization remain relatively constant, cost and performance measures will be developed that will become the basis for both planning and control.

In mechanistic organizations, goals will be fairly constant over time and can generally be considered as having a great deal of uncertainty. But they take on the characteristic of certainty because we assume that they are certain. We do this, for example, by examining the market environment and deciding that a particular group of customers will continue to demand our product over a fairly long future time period. Suppose that the steel market can be broken down into four general segments, automotive firms, appliance firms, defense firms, and others. Strategically, a steel manufacturer may choose to focus on only one of these. To say that there is absolute certainty in any one market is obviously incorrect, but it is possible to attach a very high probability to the existence of certain markets. This means that the steel firm may set strategic goals for the same market sector for many years. The major problem of the steel firm is to determine how much to produce, not what to produce—for that has already been decided.

Internal System Goals

Suppose that the steel firm has chosen to meet strategic goals by manufacturing a particular set of products for a well-defined market segment. Its customers expect that the firm's products meet certain quality requirements and that an adequate quantity will be produced for their needs.

Strategic goals like this can easily be factored into subgoals for each organizational unit. One subunit of the firm will be assigned the task of producing iron, another of rolling steel plate, another the marketing function, another credit and financial control. These factored subgoals are the internal subsystem objectives that are the specific goals for departments and subunits. These departments know fairly well what they are to do. They are going to do what they have done in the past. For these departments the important thing is to know how much and at what cost.

When strategic goals are relatively constant, as in mechanistic organizations, we assume that a particular method of production (the means to achieving them) has been developed. Fixed, limited-purpose production processes have been devised. It is likely that there is a substantial investment in plant and equipment. In a steel company, for example, the equipment produces only steel. In an automobile company, the production system can only produce cars. There are only limited ways for the firm to operate; it will produce its products in a particular way.

There is little need for extensive participation in goal setting of lower-level managerial personnel for the purpose of finding a better way to produce. The most effective way to use participation of lower-level personnel will be in trying to figure out how to do things that are already being done, but at a lower cost. The purpose of having lower-level staff involved and participating in decision making is either to communicate to them desired performance standards or to increase ego involvement.

The internal system goals in mechanistic organizations will be defined in terms of level of achievement, as opposed to the means of achievement. This is so because the means are already established, and there is little need for changing it.

The Characteristics of Controls

For control purposes, performance measures will be constructed from historical precedent; that is, the firm will have a fairly well-accepted, and predetermined set of control points developed from past experience. For example, it may be determined that marketing activities can be effectively controlled by monitoring the number of orders received. When orders drop below a particular level, added sales or promotional activity will be necessary.

By knowing what to monitor the firm can, using historical data, remain aware of what levels of performance are critical. Forecasts can be made of "order-level activity" from previous years' experience, much as was done in the case of CALCAL, described in Chapter 8.

In addition, desired profitability levels can be set by top management. If the firm desires a 25 percent return on capital, it can determine what the level of production should be, when it should be produced, and what cost should be incurred based on its current cost and revenue structure.

One important characteristic of these performance measures is that they will be objective, in the sense that they can be acceptably—though not perfectly—quantified and measured. Scrap rates, sales per employee, return on investment, number of units produced are all less subject to disagreement than more subjective criteria such as "high quality," "effective sales methods," or "the impact of advertising expenditures."

Top management usually has the most influence in the determination of the performance standards in mechanistic organizations. Since the question is one of what level of achievement is appropriate, and there is usually much experience from which to extrapolate, goal levels will be set by top management with the aid of accounting and production engineering staffs.

Fairly rigid performance standards will be set and the primary method of managing the activities will follow a *management by exception* mode. Management by exception means that only when significant deviations from desired levels occur will they be called to top management's attention for corrective action. Because strategic control points are defined and the desired goal levels are specified in planning, particular points in the operation can be observed, and, if these stay within the control limits, adequate performance can be expected.

When internal subsystem goals are translated into rigid standards there will be close, tight control. Little deviation will be tolerated because a small deviation can magnify into a serious problem. For example, in a firm that manufactures 5 million units per year, if actual costs exceed planned costs by only $.10 per unit, it can mean $500,000 in increased costs.

MANAGERIAL CONTROL IN ORGANIC ORGANIZATIONS

Strategic goals for an organic organization will be subject to constant change. The same general objective of survival is present as for the mechanistic organization, but the way to survive varies. For example, an electronics firm in one time period may be producing a component for a space project, while at another time it may be building components for a computer manufacturer, and at still another time it may be producing a recording device for hospitals.

The product goal in the organic organization is likely to change, since what the firm produces will vary from period to period and consumer requirements in terms of type, quality, and quantity will keep changing. This makes it difficult to factor goals and assign them to departments in similar ways over time. An appliance manufacturer, for example, may produce the exterior of refrigerators and stoves with minor changes in design in the same unit year after year. In an organic organization, however, there may be no set production system, except for the life of a project. When the project changes, the production system is redesigned and the staff reconstituted both in size and in the combination of skills required to satisfy the new conditions.

Internal System Goals

In organic organizations internal systems goals will be defined by both level of achievement and means of achievement. Because each project must be designed differently from previous projects, extensive coordination and cooperation will be required from lower-level personnel in order to find out what they can do, how long it will take, and when it can be done.

When there are several different units involved, one of the primary management tasks is the coordination function. Having personnel at lower levels of the organization involved in these work activities requires their inputs in the form of proposals and design. These inputs must be considered, since these are the people who possess the technical expertise and are likely to be the most competent group to provide this information. In the mechanistic organization, lower-level participation serves a communication function; in the organic organization, these lower-level groups will actually influence the way things are to be done. They will be extremely helpful in project design and in determining how a specific objective should be achieved.

The Characteristics of Controls

In the organic organization the focus of control will be the different projects, since both the level of achievement and the means of achievement will be used as performance standards and these will vary from project to project. It is necessary to define the means of achievement for projects, since in many cases the manager may be unable to determine, during the actual conduct of the project, whether or not costs are at an acceptable level or whether or not the product performs adequately. In a steel plant, for example, performance may be monitored during the production process by quality and cost measures, but in the aerospace industry about all a manager can do is determine whether an activity is completed on time and whether those who performed it have done it in a way that is generally acceptable. You can not determine whether or not a rocket will actually fly until it has flown.

Because middle management and professional groups have the technical expertise, middle- and lower-level management in the organic organization will be more extensively involved in setting both end result and activity goals than in the mechanistic organization. Performance evaluation will be based on these jointly set goals. Of course, top management evaluates and approves the goals, but participative management strategies are more necessary than is usually true in the mechanistic organization.

The primary form of the management subsystem to achieve coordination and control in an organic, dynamic organization will be a project organization (see Chapter 11). Under project management, an executive's influence and authority are much more fluid than in the mechanistic organization, changing with each project.

> Project management—molding the organization around a specific task or project—is the concept that has been developed to deal with situations where production and marketing strategies for new projects do not fit into a purely functional type or organization.

> Authority in project decisions may be indifferent to the order of hierarchical affairs . . . project authority depends heavily on the personality of the project manager and how he sees his role in relation to the environment.[8]

SUMMARY

The management process of control consists of preliminary and concurrent control functions. Preliminary control is (1) setting standards, (2) scheduling, and (3) developing policies and procedures. Concurrent control functions are (1) measuring performance, (2) evaluation of performance, and (3) taking corrective action.

In an overall sense, organization behavior patterns are controlled by the organizational control structure. The organizational control structure is composed of several elements that limit or guide individual and group behavior. Policies and procedures, the reward structure, information systems, authority relationships, selection criteria, and the nature of the work are basic components in the organizational control structure.

Case 17.1 National Appliances Corporation

The Midwestern distribution center of National Appliances Corporation was located in Lansing, Michigan. The center employed thirty-five rank and file workers and seven managers. This distribution center stored and shipped consumer durables manufactured at plant sites located all over the country to retailers in ten Midwestern states. The center was supposed to ship products quickly and store products cheaply.

The distribution center stored more than 300,000 items at one time in an area of over a million square feet. The products were transported around the facilities by means of an elaborate system of conveyer belts. The products were routed to various distribution points in the warehouse or to the proper locations in the railroad loading docks by equipment that read routing instructions on the box with laser beams.

The managers in this facility worked under a system of management by objectives in which most of the goals were very quantified. At the beginning of the year, each manager submitted a list of objectives to a group of staff managers in divisional headquarters located in Armand, New York. These objectives were the individual managers' estimates of possible goal attainment for the next year.

One objective for every manager was adherence to cost budgets. For the budget objective, meeting budgeted costs exactly was considered satisfactory performance. For other objectives, a specific level of performance was specified, which was meant to constitute satisfactory performance.

The manager also had to indicate the relative importance of each objective. This was done by assigning the objective a numerical weight. The staff group at headquarters reviewed the group objectives and had to approve the goals and their relative weights.

Each month during the year, each manager received a computer report on how well each objective was being met. At the end of the year each manager received a final report showing in quantitative terms how well each objective was met.

The level of achievement was then given a score. For example, a satisfactory degree of goal accomplishment resulted in a score of 5, 6, or 7 on that objective, depending on what the manager did to achieve it. When performance exceeded the specified satisfactory degree of accomplishment, a score between 7 and 10, depending on amount of accomplishment and the means used, might be assigned to that activity. The rating score for each objective set was multiplied by the importance weight of the objective to get a total quantitative score for all objectives for each person. This was then related to the size of the pay increase, which might range from 7 percent for satisfactory performance to 12 percent for very superior performance.

1. Evaluate this objective performance appraisal system in light of management task requirements as you have come to understand them.
2. Are there any possible problems with such a system of managerial control?
3. Are the managers in this distribution system likely to favor this system? Why?

Applied Chemistry Research Corporation

Case 17.2

Dana Hare, vice president of Engineering of TECAR Industries, was asked by TECAR's president to visit one of its new acquisitions. TECAR Industries headquarters is in Chicago, Illinois. TECAR manufactured a variety of products in a number of different plants in various regions of the United States. Hare was asked to spend a few days at Applied Chemistry Research Corporation in Baltimore, one of TECAR's newest acquisitions. She was to identify any serious problems at ACRC and recommend solutions to TECAR before the transition of management took place.

Hare visited ACRC in the fall. In obtaining background information about the company, Hare found that ACRC manufactured batteries for pacemakers, missiles, and calculators. The pacemaker batteries provided the bulk of the firm's profits. The company controlled more than 50 percent of the total world market for this type of battery.

Hare visited the production facilities for the manufacture of the batteries used in calculators and similar devices. She commented on the rather slow pace of the operators. The production supervisor, Norm Wingard, replied:

WINGARD: Well, in general, in this company we emphasize quality in the work we do. This is true in all of our manufacturing departments, but especially in the case of the pacemaker and missile batteries.

HARE: What types of production problems, if any, have you been having lately?

WINGARD: Well, lately I have been concerned about our line having to stop because of insufficient materials or components. All incoming material to this plant must be inspected by the receiving department for quality, and they seem to take their own sweet time for doing this. They don't seem to recognize that we must keep these lines going.

Hare next spoke with Joe Marcelle, Receiving Quality Control Manager.

HARE: What are your basic responsibilities?

MARCELLE: My basic responsibilities are to check all incoming materials before they get into production. We receive raw materials such as iodine, raw calcium, and iron powder, various components of the battery that we subcontract out to other manufacturers and also tools that we order for our production process. All of these items must be checked against the standards, specifications, or drawings that we have on file here. We must insure that our specifications are met.

HARE: You include the specifications and drawings in the purchase order?

MARCELLE: Yes, that's right. Of course, sometimes after the vendor receives a purchase order, he will call me back and say that he cannot meet the specifications as they are unrealistic or even impossible. When that happens, I have to contact the engineer ordering the part or component or tool to see if he agrees to a modification in what he wants so that the vendor can comply with the request.

HARE: How do you select your staff?

MARCELLE: I select inspectors on the basis of having a mechanical background and being a good observer. Inspectors must be alert or sensitive to small things. They must be able to spot a small deviation.

HARE: Do you employ both males and females?

MARCELLE: Yes, they are equally good at this job. My biggest problem now is a shortage of people. I need two people. One was transferred recently to another unit. It was a promotion for him. Another employee has been ill a long time. We keep her on payroll and cannot replace her yet. This has created a big problem for me. There is a hiring freeze in effect. What am I going to do?

HARE:	Are your people specialists?
MARCELLE:	Yes, they are. Many different jobs, though, are done by the inspectors but each specializes in certain products.
HARE:	When do you inspect items—as they come in?
MARCELLE:	No, I inspect the hot items first.
HARE:	Which are hot items?
MARCELLE:	Well, those that are critically needed or the production line will stop. At any one time there may be several items, though.
HARE:	Do different people in the organization differ as to what they think is important?
MARCELLE:	Yes, definitely. Each project engineer believes that his job is the most important. They are all after me to do their job ahead of the others.
HARE:	What do you do when this happens?
MARCELLE:	What do you do? Well, I do what my boss says. If there is a dispute between several people on what should be done, I let him decide. It's very difficult for me to try to deal with all these engineers plus the purchasing agent myself. I wish we had an expediter or coordinator around here that would be able to establish priorities on all of these incoming shipments so we would know what to do.
HARE:	Do you frequently reject incoming material?
MARCELLE:	Yes, very often. We are very strict about our specifications and drawings. If the incoming material doesn't meet them, we send it back to the vendor. He then will either have to rework the materials to make them acceptable or do the order over. However, if the order is critical enough we might check each item in the shipment separately instead of using sampling. In that way we usually get enough items to keep production going.
HARE:	When personnel allocates staff to your unit, do they consider this extra work you do in inspecting each item on an individual basis instead of using sampling?
MARCELLE:	No, they don't and that's something that also causes me to get behind schedule. My technicians and inspectors have to do extra work like that. If we have a shipment of 500 items and we take a 10 percent sample and find more than 5 percent of the sample defective, we have a lot of extra work if that item is critical. We have to check 450 individual items one at a time.
HARE:	What if the deviation from the specs is slight? Do you accept this?
MARCELLE:	Not unless the QC manager and the ordering engineer agree to it and sign off on the MRB form. This is the materials review board slip. I don't allow any deviations myself. The drawing is my Bible. I must reject something if it's not exactly in line with the drawing. I'm pressured a lot to lower standards, but I won't do it. We can't do it.
HARE:	Have you always worked here? How long have you been here?
MARCELLE:	I came here twenty years ago. I worked for two big companies

before I took this job. I like this company much better. Here I'm important. Everybody knows me and knows what I do. I like that. Last summer I got an offer for $3,000 more a year and turned it down. Money isn't everything. There are just too many other benefits from working in this kind of company.

Hare then visited the company's purchasing agent, Chuck Holmes. He headed a group of six buyers and clerks. Holmes had been with the company for only one year.

HOLMES: What's my most difficult problem? Getting people in this company to give us the information and drawings we need to order components, materials, and tools from suppliers. People give us incomplete information. I have to nag them to be specific. The vendors must have precise information. I think we have too much emphasis on oral communications in this company. We need more written communications so we can document things.

Another big problem is that everybody wants their order ASAP. We can't rush a vendor. He has a production schedule, too. He must have sufficient lead time to schedule in an order from us. Some guys around here say they need something immediately and then, when you bust your butt to get it for them, it just sits around on the floor for six months. Some guys have cried "wolf" just too many times for me to get excited anymore.

HARE: Any other problems?

HOLMES: Just the difficulty of being a purchasing agent in this company compared to my last job. This is a job shop. We have dozens of projects going on all of the time with many different project managers to deal with. It's not easy to keep track of all of them. We also are a growing company with purchasing orders increasing by leaps and bounds every year. We don't have enough space now and the stuff is put all over the place and sometimes gets lost. Also, you have to know the whole manufacturing process for each type of battery to do your job. This makes it tough.

Another problem is that some of the inspectors are just too fussy. They reject an order whenever there is the slightest deviation from specs. They are not being realistic. I'm the one who has to hold the vendor responsible for what are really minor problems.

HARE: How do you get along with everybody?

HOLMES: Pretty well. What I like about this place is that everybody is really open. Around here we are very informal and you go right over to talk directly to the person you may have a problem with. People speak their minds around here and I like that. You don't have to spend all your time figuring what is it they really want, like in my old job. However, the people in the company don't really understand the outside environment. The world is changing today. Many materials are hard to get now, especially from other countries. People here don't understand the energy crisis. They don't know many things are made from oil. They don't understand that many of our vendors use a lot of oil in their manufacturing process to heat materials. We are going to be facing some difficulties in the future that our managers don't realize. They just look inward. One other thing. Nobody around here ever shows any gratitude when you do a good job. They just get after you when something is late.

Hare talked next to Jeffrey Higgs, the Quality Assurance Manager of the pacemaker battery division.

HARE: What does quality assurance mean as compared to quality control?

HIGGS: What is quality assurance? Well, it's broader than quality control, which is just a matter of policing the production line. It means a guarantee of quality—there are a number of means of getting quality assurance other than police actions. You can motivate the work force, for example, to emphasize quality.

HARE: Do your workers have a quality consciousness?

HIGGS: Yes, they do. I think it's because of the product we make. It's a pacemaker and our workers know somebody's life depends on this device. They think they do important work.

HARE: What are your biggest problems?

HIGGS: My biggest problems? Well, getting along with other managers, I guess. When we reject a production run, the production manager is naturally hostile. He thinks it's a reflection on him. That's not so, of course. There are many reasons why a sample may fail. The basic components or materials may be faulty when we get them. It's impossible for any product to have zero defects. The group I have the most trouble with, though, is the marketing group. They scream at me when an order is rejected and will not get to the customer on time. They say it's my fault as I should have done my inspections earlier in the process. They say I wait too long to test. But I only have so many people. I must use my inspectors in an optimum manner. They don't understand the production process. One marketing manager said once that my behavior was criminal. That really bothered me for a while. But I've gotten used to this sort of thing now.

HARE: So your biggest difficulty is with marketing?

HIGGS: That's right. I think the fact they are located in another building down the road contributes to the difficulties I have with them. Also, they are just too optimistic when dealing with customers. They tell the customers that we don't have quality problems.

HARE: Any other problems?

HIGGS: Well, keeping the production workers motivated is a problem. The work is routine. It's boring. Yet we need good quality.

Also, we sometimes have quality problems because the customers want changes in the product. They want the product put in a smaller package or they want more capacity in the same package. They want more reliability. We have to modify the product all the time to keep up with customer demands. This change can create quality problems.

1. What does this case illustrate about achieving effective control and coordination in organizations?
2. What can be done to improve control and coordination in this company?

DISCUSSION QUESTIONS

1. Preliminary controls can help a company keep costs at a desired level and keep corrective measures to a minimum. What are these controls and how are they enforced?
2. How can a firm establish its own standards?
3. Measuring performance is one phase of concurrent control. How is this done?
4. Evaluating performance is the second phase of concurrent control. Why is this phase more difficult than the others?
5. Explain the difference between general rewards and task-specific rewards. Give examples of each. Which would be more meaningful to you?
6. Explain how an information system functions and what problems can arise with its use.
7. Which structure of authority would you choose—centralized or decentralized? Why?
8. Compare and contrast the control structure in mechanistic and organic organizations.
9. Name the basic components that contribute to organizational control structure. Briefly describe each. Do you think one component is more important than the others? How and why?

REFERENCES

1. Richards, M., and P. Greenlaw. Management decision making. Homewood, Ill., Irwin, 1966.
2. Katz, D., and R. L. Kahn. The social psychology of organization, 2nd ed. New York, John Wiley, 1978.
3. ———. "Spotting a winner in insurance," Business Week, February 12, 1979, p. 122.
4. Leiberman, Seymour. "The effects of changes in roles on the attitudes of role occupants." Human Relations, 9 (1956): 385–402.
5. Rousseau, Denise. "Characteristics of departments, positions, and individuals: Contexts for attitudes and behavior," Administrative Science Quarterly, 23, 4 (December 1978): 521–540.
6. Dearborn, D. C., and H. Simon. "Selective perception," Sociometry, 21 (1958): 140–143.
7. Terkel, S. Working. New York, Avon Books, 1974.
8. Cleland, D. "Understanding project authority," Business Horizons, 10 (Spring 1967): 63–70.

CHAPTER EIGHTEEN

Coordination

How GM Turned Itself Around

. . . The process of running GM had grown considerably more complex since the 1950s. The business environment was still uncertain, and outside constraints had to be taken increasingly into account. The review committee wrestled with the implications of such matters during that summer; toward the end of its assignment, it was augmented by Murphy, who had been nominated to replace Gerstenberg as chairman.

What the committee recommended, in September 1974, was a major reorganization at the top. That reorganization, says Murphy, "expanded importantly the top management group. Looking beyond where we were at the time, we designed it to bring new executives into a higher echelon." Complicated in its details, the reorganization upgraded the responsibilities of the executive vice presidents and added a fourth to the three already existing. The upgrading brought forward four relatively young men, all future prospects for the top, to serve on the board and the executive committee. Since the divisions now answer to top management through those executive vice presidents, the reorganization strengthened lines of authority and communication.

The reorganization also redefined and strengthened the jobs of the president and of the new vice chairman, Richard L. Terrell. Supervision of GM's eight operating staffs had previously been split between the president and the vice chairman;

all were brought together under Terrell. That move freed the new president, Estes, to concentrate more fully on operations—and especially upon overseas operations, which were transferred to him from the vice chairman. Along with Ford and Chrysler, GM is planning a growing number of "world cars"—essentially similar models that can be built in the U.S., Europe, or anywhere else. Though the first of those, the Chevette, was barely on the drawing boards for the U.S. that year, GM reasoned that overseas and domestic work could be more directly and effectively integrated if both divisions reported to Estes.

If the reorganization was a landmark event, it was in some ways less important than another change wrought in 1974—the adoption of the project center, a new concept in engineering management, devised to coordinate the efforts of the five automobile divisions. A GM project center, made up of engineers lent by the divisions, has no exact counterpart elsewhere in the auto industry—and perhaps in all of U.S. industry. NASA used the concept for the space program, and Terrell spotted it there when he was head of the nonautomotive divisions, one of which—Delco Electronics—was a NASA contractor. Sloan himself would have appreciated the concept, for it is right in line with the coordinated-decentralization approach to management.

GM adopted the project-center idea in order to meet the special demands created by the downsizing decision. Coordinating the development of a new body line among the various divisions is a complex undertaking even in normal times. To do what it wanted, the company would have to engineer its cars in a new way, using new design techniques and technologies, during a time when the margins for error and correction would be tighter than usual. Particularly under these circumstances, GM could no longer afford the old problem (by no means unique to GM) of what Estes calls "NIH, not invented here, a kind of disease engineers have." An engineer suffering from NIH resists new ideas that originate outside his bailiwick.

The project center is not a permanent group. Every time a major new effort is planned—a body changeover, say—a project center is formed, and it operates for the duration of the undertaking. Thus the A-body center, which shepherded this year's intermediates through development, ran from late 1975 until this past fall. The X-body center is now at work on next year's front-wheel-drive compacts. All project centers report to a board composed of the chief engineers of the automotive divisions.

Project centers work on parts and engineering problems common to all divisions, such as frames, electrical systems, steering gear, and brakes. Many of these are identical in every division; many others are what GM calls "common family parts"—e.g., shock absorbers—that are basically the same but are calibrated or adjusted to divisional specifications. The project center augments, but does not replace, GM's traditional "lead division" concept, in which one division is assigned primary responsibility for bringing some technical innovation into production.

The project center was probably GM's single most important managerial tool in carrying out that bold decision to downsize. It has eliminated a great deal of redundant effort and has speeded numerous new technologies into production. Its success, however, rests on the same delicate balance between the powers of persuasion and coercion that underlies GM's basic system of coordinated decentralization. "We become masters of diplomacy," says Edward Mertz, assistant chief engineer at Pontiac, who was manager of the now-disbanded A-body project center.

"It's impossible to work closely on a design without influencing it somewhat. But the center can't force a common part on a division." Indeed, many of GM's engineers feel the project-center innovation has actually helped enhance the divisions' individuality, by freeing some of them to work on divisional projects.

Source: From Charles Burek, "How GM Turned Itself Around," Fortune Magazine, pp. 87–100, January 16, 1978. Copyright © 1978. Reprinted with permission.

Coordination, or integration, is the process of developing and maintaining the proper relationships between activities, whether they are physical activities or mental activities. Coordination is important in complex organizations because there are many different activities carried out by many people in a large number of departments. The need for coordination arises any time more than one person or group is responsible for a complete task. When there is any interdependence at all among activities, effective results can occur only when they are coordinated. Managers spend a good portion of their time coordinating. In one study of how 300 managers from several different industrial organizations spent their time, it was shown that approximately 15 percent of their time was spent coordinating, that is, relating and adjusting organizationally interdependent activities and programs.[1]

The problems faced by General Motors (and, of course, other automobile manufacturers) because of downsizing the passenger car are complex and enormous (see item 18.1), leaving aside the tremendous costs involved for retooling the plants. For instance, engine size had to decrease, transmission and axles had to be redesigned, tire sizes would be smaller, body styles and structures would have to be altered, safety problems resulting from the smaller sized cars would have to be solved.

In a company like GM, these problems would be studied in many different divisions and in many different departments. To coordinate the work of all these different units, the project center was created. Item 18.1 indicates the project center was successful in that it "eliminated a great deal of redundant effort, and has speeded new technologies into production."[11]

Coordination has been found related to the effectiveness of organizations and organizational units. Lawrence and Lorsch[2] found that differences in coordination achieved among units of six plastics firms were related to differences in organizational performance. The plastics firms with greater coordination among units were also higher on changes in profits, sales, volume, and new product development in the preceding five-year period than those firms with low coordination. Mahoney and Weitzel found that effective scheduling and coordination with other units was one of seven key factors related to the overall effectiveness of 283 organizational units.[3] Effective coordination with other units is a major contributing factor to the overall success of government departments.[4]

INTERDEPENDENCE—THE NEED TO COORDINATE

Coordination is most important among those organizational members or units where the work is interdependent. The more work of different units or individuals is linked together, the greater the probability of coordination problems occurring. For example, the work of assembly-line workers has to be coordinated quite closely since the product is moved from one specialized worker to another. If workers could

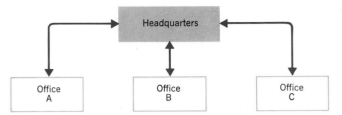

FIGURE 18.1 Pooled interdependence.

produce the complete product or service by themselves, coordination problems decrease considerably, though costs would most likely increase. In most assembly-line operations, the machinery itself is the major coordinating devices. There are other types of interdependence, and the way to achieve coordination depends upon what type exists.

Pooled Interdependence

Pooled interdependence occurs when several units of an organization operate in a fairly autonomous manner, such that what one does is not entirely dependent on the others. The interdependence exists because the success of the whole organization rests on the fairly unique contribution of each of the units. As James Thompson says, "each part renders a discrete contribution to the whole and is supported by the whole"[5] (see Figure 18.1).

An example of pooled interdependence is the consumer lending division of Commercial Credit Corporation. This loan company has several hundred offices scattered throughout the country. Each branch office manager has ties with the headquarters office for resources and control, but not with other branch office managers.

Sequential Interdependence

When work activities must be performed in a particular sequence and the activities are assigned to different units in such a way that a product must begin at point A, go to point B, then to C before it gets to D, there is sequential interdependence.[5] Assembly-line work is characterized by sequential interdependence, as shown in Figure 18.2. An example of sequential interdependence is the procedure for processing requests for travel reimbursements in a state agency. The employee who has returned from a trip submits a request for reimbursement. This is prepared in the agency office. The reimbursement request is then sent to the "travel" section of the accounts payable department. There it is audited and verified. Once it has been verified, it is sent to the state's department of finance, which then issues a check to the traveler in the authorized amount.

FIGURE 18.2 Sequential interdependence.

Reciprocal Interdependence

Mutual dependence between two or more units is called reciprocal interdependence[5] (see Figure 18.3). A simple example of reciprocal interdependence is the registration procedure at some colleges and universities. At a designated time, students must go to the office of the Registrar (Box A). There they are given registration forms and material for the next academic year, which authorizes them to begin enrollment. From there the students take the material (permission to register) to various departments (Box B), where they are advised and placed in courses according to their class standing and course availability. In the department some form of endorsement or formal authorization is received. The student then goes back to the Registrar's office (Box A) where fees are computed and then paid.

Coordination and Interdependence

We have said that coordination is the process of developing and maintaining proper relationships among activities. This is, in reality, exactly what each phase of the management process seeks to contribute toward. Planning is an effort to anticipate problems that might occur between units and solve them early. Organizing, likewise, seeks to insure that people and resources are set in proper relationships to each other. Leading seeks to influence behavior; control attempts to keep things in line.

When there are different types of interdependence, coordination might be sought in different ways. For example, coordination might be achieved through the use of standardized procedures, processes, or products when there is pooled interdependence. In other words, the various branch offices of Commercial Credit are required to use similar procedures for handling loans and making decisions. This allows the headquarters group to know what is going to be done and how it will be done.

When there is sequential interdependence, coordination through planning is likely to be effective. Decisions can be made about what the best sequence of work is, how long it should take, and how much it should cost. Scheduling is a useful process to increase effectiveness of the operations of sequentially interdependent work.

Finally, where reciprocal interdependence exists, the coordination must occur through mutual adjustment. Individuals and groups must be readily able to adapt to and cope with the often unpredictable nature of demands placed on them by other units to get the work done.

Of course, most organizations have several types of interdependence.

> . . . all organizations have pooled interdependence; more complicated organizations have sequential as well as pooled; and the most complex have reciprocal, sequential and pooled.[5]

FIGURE 18.3 Reciprocal interdependence.

This fact leads to the obvious conclusion that many different approaches must be taken to get an effective level of coordination.

HORIZONTAL AND VERTICAL COORDINATION

Both vertical and horizontal coordination is required in organizations. Vertical co-ordination refers to the development of effective and integrated relationships between activities at different organizational levels. The approval of capital expenditures at, say, the vice presidential level that is coordinated with the delivery and acceptance of the capital equipment at the operating level is one example of vertical coordination.

Horizontal coordination is the development of smooth relationships between individuals or groups at the same level. For instance, the flow of timely information from marketing to manufacturing about sales so that manufacturing may develop efficient production schedules is an illustration of horizontal coordination.

CAUSES OF COORDINATION PROBLEMS

Coordination problems arise out of organizational conditions and human problems. Organizational conditions are those problems that occur because different organization units have different sets of activities that must be accomplished, but the activities have different time schedules. Many of the coordination problems of the GM project group (see item 18.1) are of this type. Human factors are those relating to problems that develop between people, groups, and departments.

ORGANIZATIONAL CONDITIONS
AND COORDINATION

Organizational situations that cause coordination problems occur:
1. When organizational subsystems cross departmental boundaries
2. When interdependent activities have different time schedules
3. When there is a substantial geographical distance between departments

1. Cross-departmental subsystems. Some organizational subsystem activities are carried out in different formal departments. For example, in a firm organized in a product basis (see Chapter 11, Figure 11.5) production subsystem activities will be found in each of the major product divisions. This is the case in a manufacturing firm in which some products are manufactured in the consumer products division and others are manufactured in the construction product division. While the products are different, many raw material requirements are the same. However, the two manufacturing managers in the different product divisions could not coordinate their raw materials procurement because each manager is subject to different policies, within each of the respective divisions, that are imposed by the different division vice presidents.

2. Time schedule differences. Unfortunately, most activities in organizations require different amounts of time for completion. In the case of General Motors, engine development takes a different amount of time than does styling. Some activities can be completed very quickly while others take more time. This is like the coordination problem that a chef faces in the preparation of a dinner. The main dish may take three hours to prepare. Salad ingredients may be cleaned and mixed in thirty minutes. Vegetables may take twenty minutes to cook, and the dessert, perhaps, can be prepared and cooked in two hours. The success of a meal depends as much on whether or not the chef can bring the foods to the table at the correct time as it does on the care and competence of preparation.

3. Geographical distance. When the distance between persons involved in interdependent work is too great to allow for frequent face-to-face contact, coordination problems occur. One person may not meet a deadline because he or she is pressured to work on different projects from others who are in closer proximity. The first person cannot complete the project until the work of the second has been completed, so the job gets finished later than it should be.

HUMAN FACTORS AND COORDINATION

Some coordination problems are due to differences between people and between groups rather than organizational problems. Personal feelings can get in the way of good working relationships with others. One group or department may compete with another for resources and/or status.

Relationships between groups and departments can be characterized as cooperative, helpful, synergistic, or as uncooperative, antagonistic, mutually destructive. We should not assume, however, that intergroup cooperation is good and intergroup conflict is bad for an organization. Some conflict is productive when it results in two conflicting objectives being satisfied. For example, there may be substantial disagreement in a firm between the engineering group and the sales group as to whether a product should be designed with an emphasis on quality or on price. Both quality and price must be considered, and the disagreement between the two groups may insure that both factors are considered in the design and production of the product.

On the other hand, two groups may cooperate to the detriment of the organization by jointly opposing needed changes. Or two groups may place such a high value on avoiding disagreement that problems that should surface and be discussed are not.

Many different factors can contribute to poor coordination between groups, leading to unproductive results such as confrontation, maneuvering, and marshalling strength to overcome the other.

1. Competition over resources. Groups can work more easily and group goals can be easier to achieve when they have adequate resources, money, people, or physical assets. When a number of groups are dependent upon limited resources, however, there is likely to be a great deal of competition for resources. This gives rise to hostility and conflict. In addition, groups will want representation in decision making about resource allocation to insure that they are equitably treated.

In a large university on the West Coast, the College of Business Administration was given three new positions by the provost to help cope with increasing enrollments. The dean of the college asked the chairperson of the executive committee to recommend to which departments the new positions should be assigned. This committee was composed of a representative from each of the six departments of the college. They began to determine priorities that would be the governing rules for the assignment of these three positions. One department was accused of creating a shortage in their area because they required too many courses for their undergraduate majors. Another group was told that it taught courses of little relevance to the business student. Another faculty group was accused of such poor faculty selection in the past that it needed the new positions to improve its outside image. They were asked: Why should we subsidize poor selection in the past? The different faculty groups become estranged from each other. Each felt all the others were trying to gain an unreasonable advantage.

2. Status differences and work flow. Poor coordination develops, not only because of the work-flow sequence in an organization, but also because work relationships are such that individuals from a low-status group appear to be telling individuals in a high-status organizational group what to do. Considerable resistance to such pressures may develop in the higher-status groups. The higher-status group may attempt to show its independence and power by delaying to do what is requested, by anger, by ridiculing members of the lower-status group, or by avoiding contact with representatives of the lower-status group. For instance, when draftsmen give suggestions to engineers, when technicians criticize the work of production experts, or when students criticize faculty members, there may be negative feelings generated in the higher-status group member because of what appears to be inappropriate behavior by the lower-status group.

In one manufacturer of sophisticated production equipment, the drafting staff was on the average much older and more experienced than the typical engineer the company employed.[6] Draftsmen often made suggestions to the engineers about the design of a production system that had to be tailored to the customer's particular needs. In spite of the need for creativity in design, engineers often rejected this advice out of hand, feeling that the draftsmen should just draw what the engineers designed. Similarly, in an electronic test equipment manufacturer, new product ideas were developed in R&D, connected to blueprints in the production engineering department, and then sent to the production department. There were always poor relations between production and production engineering. These often led to delays in getting products to market. These delays were, in part, due to the fact that production department perceived production engineering to have very low status in the firm, and production did not like being told what to do.[6]

3. Conflicting objectives. Different groups often have different objectives. These may be conflicting, leading to considerable disagreement between two groups that must coordinate their efforts. For example, a production group responsible for minimizing production costs may emphasize longer and more efficient production runs, disagreeing with a sales group which seeks to have shorter manufacturing runs of several products so that customers have a variety of products from which to choose. Short production runs are more costly than longer ones.

Disagreement is especially likely when the two different groups are rewarded for meeting their assigned objectives rather than the coordinated objectives of the firm. Such conflict between objectives is difficult to avoid because an organization pursues many objectives simultaneously and many of these are contradictory, as in the case of the conflict between marketing and production described above.

Different executives may disagree on the relative importance of different company objectives. Some may stress short-run organization objectives while others may be more concerned with long-run objectives. Such differences in objectives are related to differences in group memberships in the organization, as we have noted in Chapter 6. These, in turn, are related to differences in the problems facing different groups and differences in their values.

4. *Different perceptions, attitudes, and values.* Even though different groups may interact regularly, members of one group may perceive things differently from members of another. One frequent source of disagreement is the tendency of any group to value its own ideas, proposals, and creations more highly than those of other groups. Each of two groups making a proposal tends to overvalue its own work and to undervalue the work of the other group.

Perceptual differences arise from the tendency of an individual to evaluate things in terms of personal experiences. Since organization members have had different experiences, training, and education, they tend to perceive problems and their causes differently.[7] This is especially likely to occur when the problems or possible solutions are ambiguous.

Morse and Lorsch showed how attitudes and values differed between individuals in mechanistic and organic organizational units[8] (see Chapter 4). The managers in organic units differed from those in mechanistic units in that those in organic units

1. Had more tolerance for ambiguity
2. Could deal with more complex problems
3. Preferred autonomy
4. Valued individualism
5. Looked to outside influence groups
6. Had high professional values

5. *Ambiguous authority and work assignments.* When tasks require the work of two or more groups, it may be difficult to pinpoint responsibility or to allocate credit or blame correctly for good or bad performance. For this reason, members of some groups may not wish to undertake joint assignments. A group may attempt to get another to assume responsibility for the unpleasant, difficult, or unfairly rewarded tasks, while it tries to gain control over the more pleasant, easy, or fairly rewarded tasks. Actions such as these lead to conflict between groups.

6. *Domination or influence efforts.* Different units will vary in their status and power in the organization (see Chapter 4). Differences in status and power are related to the demands placed upon the organization by its environment and by the ability of particular groups to cope with these demands. Those groups that can best cope with environmental uncertainty will tend to have the most status and power in an organization. In a study of a manufacturing plant, for example, Crozier[12] found that the maintenance engineers enjoyed unusually high organization influence. This seemed to be so because the factory was highly automated and the main source of uncertainty was that of possible equipment breakdown. The maintenance staff could control equipment breakdowns, so they were highly influential. In another company, the production department dominated the organization for many years. As production policies, procedures, and systems became more routine, however, the marketing department gradually gained in power. In a final test of strength, the head of the marketing unit was made executive vice president while the head of production was appointed to a less important position as facilities planning consultant. But the production units refused to accept fully the higher status of sales until after the older production managers retired and were replaced by new personnel.

There is some research in both organizational and nonorganizational settings that shows what happens ***within*** competing groups and ***between*** them.[9]

Within groups that are threatened, cohesiveness increases. As each group senses threats from others, it becomes more closely knit and seeks greater loyalty from its members. Members close ranks and bury some of their internal differences. The group climate changes from informal, casual, and playful to work and task oriented. Concern for the members' psychological needs declines, while the emphasis on task accomplishment increases. Leadership patterns tend to change from democratic toward autocratic, and the group becomes more willing to tolerate this change. Each group becomes more highly structured and organized. More loyalty and conformity are demanded from members in order to be able to present a solid front.

Between the conflicting groups hostility begins to emerge. Each group begins to see other groups as the enemy. The group begins to experience distortions of perception—it tends to perceive only the best parts of itself, denying its weaknesses, and tends to perceive only the worst parts of the other group, denying its strengths. Each group is likely to develop a negative stereotype of the other ("They don't play fair like we do"). Hostility toward the other group increases, while interaction and communication with it decrease, making it easier to maintain negative stereotypes and more difficult to correct perceptual distortions. If the groups are forced to interact—for example, if they are forced to listen to representatives plead their own and the others' cause—each group is likely to listen more closely to their own representatives than to the representative of the other group, and to find fault with the latter's presentation. In other words, group members tend to hear that which supports their own position and stereotype. The group that emerges the winner in the competitive situation is likely to become more cohesive. The losing group tends toward internal dissension and fault finding with certain of its members.

METHODS OF COORDINATION

A manager must insure that the activities of units at lower organizational levels are integrated and that when conflict exists among these units, the manager must seek to resolve it. Coordination of activities and resolution of conflict are achieved through the activities of the control subsystem (see Chapter 3).

The way to achieve coordination and resolution of conflict must be related to the source of the difficulties. Some approaches are more effective when the problems arise from organizational conditions, and others when the difficulties arise because of human problems.

COORDINATION THROUGH ORGANIZATION

Many coordination problems occur because the different organizational units are responsible for different activities and these activities have different time schedules and/or work requirements. Some of these problems can be avoided by the effective design of the organizational structure. Procedures can be used to coordinate activities. Sometimes redesigning the structure may be a useful approach. In other instances, it may be necessary to use individuals or groups in coordinating roles to achieve effective integration.

Organization Structure

Perhaps the most general and the most powerful coordinating mechanism for activities in a complex organization is the formal organization structure. The work of several units with divergent tasks and personnel with different values can be integrated well when the structure is compatible with the environmental demands of the organization. This was one of the steps taken in General Motors, in addition to the project group (see item 18.1). The number of executive vice presidents was increased from three to four and the responsibility for supervision of the operating staffs was changed.

In mechanistic organizations a good deal of coordination is achieved through the use of many procedures developed over time, a fairly stable authority structure, and the work flow itself, which is often machine paced. In these stable organizations the departments will be clearly defined into separate units, each with assigned tasks to perform. The basic integration of activities will come through the use of coordinating staff units and through policy decisions made by the top management. For example, the ways in which the marketing activities and the production activities are coordinated in a firm like Ford Motor Company are a result of policy decisions made by the firm's top management, implemented through planning and scheduling departments.

In mixed organizations using a matrix form, the specialist assigned to a project performs a major coordinating function. That specialist brings knowledge to the unit about how the technical facets of the unit's work should be carried out so that the work is integrated with that of other parts of the organization.

In organic organizations where projects are constantly changing, there will be a need to coordinate the work of group members actively, often on a daily basis. Since team members are changed as the project changes, the project leader has the major coordination responsibility. Each time a project begins, a new set of work relationships will be developed and these must be coordinated. In project organizations we can expect coordination to be achieved through the personal competence of the project leader, bringing the team together rather than using formally designed project assignments. For example, in an electrical engineering firm, project leaders met daily with team members to discuss each one's progress and the group's progress.

Plans and Procedures

Procedures and plans are another coordinating device. A procedure links work activities of several different people, often in different departments, to accomplish some project. A procedure outlines each step to complete a project and indicates in which department and/or by whom the step would be performed. Figure 18.4 is a work procedure flow diagram. It illustrates how the activities of the warehouse, processing, cooling, casing, and finished goods storage departments are related to each other in a food processing plant making tomato juice. Each arrow designates movement of the product from one activity to another. This flow-process chart

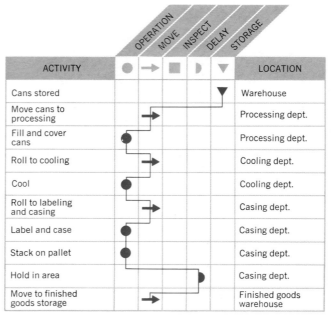

FIGURE 18.4 Manufacturing procedure for a tomato juice processor.

shows a sequence of production activities; cases of empty cans are brought from the warehouse to the processing department, they are filled and moved to a cooling department, labels are put on in another department, then the cans are cased and moved to the storage area. Procedures may be developed for any organization activity such as sales problems, personnel problems, and the other work activities.

System Redesign

When coordination problems are due to the design of the work system, then the system can be restructured and the problem solved. For example, if a problem develops because a lower-status group is initiating action for a group that perceives itself to have higher status, the problem might be alleviated by redesigning the work flow so that the lower-status group does not impose its wishes on the higher-status group. This can be accomplished by transferring certain elements or personnel in the lower-status group to the higher-status group, or by combining the two groups into one.

Suppose there are four units within the personnel department: Personnel Classification, Personnel Evaluation, Administration and Payroll, and Training.[10] Each of these units is responsible for the activities listed in Figure 18.5 when a person is hired. Let us assume that the work flows from Personnel Classification (A) to Personnel Evaluation (B) and from Personnel Evaluation (B) to Administration and Payroll (C) to Training (D), as shown in Figure 18.6. Let us further assume that the relationship between Personnel Evaluation (B) and Administration and Payroll (C) is quite poor. This could be true for a number of reasons such as the quality of work

Unit	Activity
A. Personnel Classification	1. Receive applications 2. Contact references 3. Determine where applicant is needed
B. Personnel Evaluation	1. Evaluate credentials 2. Interview candidates 3. Make selection decision 4. Notify new employee
C. Administration and Payroll	1. Provide new employee with information about company personnel practices 2. Initiate pay and fringe benefits
D. Training	1. Assess training needs of new employee 2. Determine how training will be done

performed by Administration and Payroll (C) depends upon the quality of information received by it from Personnel Evaluation (B) and Administration and Payroll (C) resents this dependency. Or perhaps Administration and Payroll (C) staff consider themselves to be superior to those in Personnel Evaluation (B) but that Personnel Evaluation seems to be giving them orders.

In Example 2 in Figure 18.6, direct contact between the Personnel Evaluation and the Administration and Payroll has been eliminated by placing a liaison, or coordinator, between them. An individual may be assigned to bridge the gap between these two units. In some cases, the coordinator may have informal authority, being able to work out problems through discussion and negotiation. In some organizations the coordinator may have formal authority and be able to employ sanctions against those who are not cooperative. For example, the coordinator may be given a budget and authorized to make certain kinds of decisions, therefore having some control over the resources.

In Example 3, the Personnel Evaluation unit and the Administration and Payroll unit have been combined. This strategy is based on the belief that when individuals are brought together in a group, they are inclined to help fellow group members, as we have discussed in Chapter 6.

In Example 4, a segment of the Administration and Payroll unit has been transferred to the Personnel Evaluation unit. The new staff added to Personnel Evaluation (B) now no longer represent Administration and Payroll but identify with their new group, Personnel Evaluation. Of course, this identification will not be immediate, but it should develop over time. This approach has been used with some success in a chemical company when the chemical engineers were transferred from a research unit to an engineering unit in which other types of engineers worked.[11]

Example 5 illustrates a solution in which interaction between Personnel Evaluation and Administration and Payroll is no longer necessary because Administration and Payroll (C) has duplicated, within itself, some activities performed by Personnel

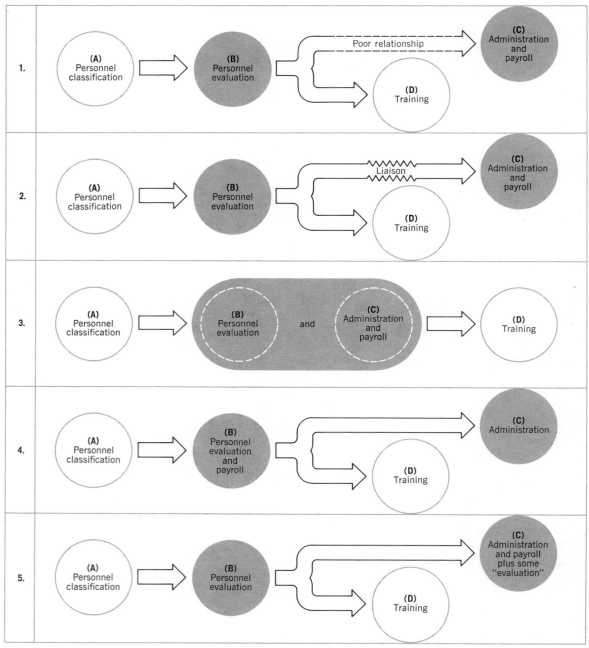

FIGURE 18.6   Different approaches to improving coordination between two problem departments (B and C).

Evaluation. In other words, Administration and Payroll may, in fact, begin to perform some of the evaluation functions itself. This would make it unnecessary to deal with Personnel Evaluation. In many companies this approach evolves naturally when relationships between groups become so unpleasant that there is strong motivation to stop all interaction. This approach can be taken by management consciously in a reorganization program or informally by the parties themselves, provided they can obtain the necessary resources.

Sometimes a procedural change, rather than a change in the structure of organization units, can solve the problem. For example, conflicts between two groups can be the result of one group frustrating another group in the latter's attempts to achieve its objectives. This frustration leads to aggressive feelings and behaviors directed at the first group. In a dress manufacturing company, the marketing group, after receiving orders from customers, found that the credit department often did not allow certain orders to be shipped when the order exceeded the customer's credit lines with the company. The marketing personnel, not knowing a customer's credit standing, had already counted on receiving bonus credit for the sale and were naturally angered by the credit department's rejection. The situation was improved by having the orders sent to the credit department for approval before, rather than after, they were sent to the marketing department.[12]

Coordinating Departments

Many companies use coordinating departments to help achieve coordination among diverse and specialized organization units. Thus, there may be a product scheduling unit in an organization that is responsible for insuring that all necessary activities are carried out by the different units to meet customer delivery dates with products of requisite quality.

The way coordinating staffs operate seems to be linked to organization effectiveness. Coordinating staffs operate across several functions and several units. Their role is to insure that the activities of the several units are well integrated. A study of two firms, called Crown and Rhody, showed how different coordinating orientations affected success.[13] Those in the coordinating unit of Rhody, the more successful organization, tended to be very balanced in the way they considered the problems of those units they coordinated. They were aware of both the short-range problems faced by the marketing and production units and the long-range problems of research. At Crown, the less successful firm, the coordinating unit tended to be much more concerned with short-range marketing problems and showed less concern for the short-range problems of production and the long-range problems of research.

Coordinators seem to be more effective when they make decisions based on competence and knowledge rather than authority, when they are rewarded not for individual performance but for total product responsibilities, and when they have integrative skills. It is also important that they have top management support. Individuals in coordinating roles are more effective when they possess a variety of skills that can be used to bring about coordination and conflict resolution. They may use confrontation approaches that involve placing the facts of a dispute in front of those parties involved and then discussing the matter until a solution is reached. A "smoothing approach" involves avoiding conflicts and disagreements that might threaten harmonious relationships in any way. The "forcing approach" involves the use of power or authority to achieve coordinating goals. The importance of conflict resolution skills is noted in the GM example in item 18.1. As one of the project group members said, "We became masters of diplomacy."

Committees

The committee is another widely used coordinating device. When there is no formally designated unit to handle coordination problems, a committee is often formed to deal with them. A committee can achieve coordination because it brings individuals together from the several units that will be involved in implementing a complex project or plan. For example, the new product planning committee in a food manufacturing firm is composed of representatives from marketing, research and development, production, and finance. This committee meets regularly to discuss the current development stage of different new products. For example, one product is a new meat casserole dish in the early stage of development and another product, pizza, is now ready to be released to the marketing department for advertising and sales planning and to the manufacturing division for the design of the production equipment. Committee members can carry information about the different stages of each product back to their respective departments so that each department can be informed about plans.

Committees can be used to work on long-term coordination problems. The new product planning committee above has been in existence for the past five years and there are no plans to discontinue it. Committees can be used to solve short-term coordination problems. Recently, for example, a major state university formed a committee of several deans, faculty, and administrative staff to coordinate action to reduce energy consumption and costs. The members are to bring conservation ideas to the attention of the committee. They are also to bring suggested approaches to conservation to their respective colleges and staff units.

COORDINATION THROUGH ORGANIZATIONAL DEVELOPMENT (OD)

When coordination problems result from interpersonal and intergroup differences, tinkering with the organizational structure, procedures, and committees may have only a limited effect. The best designed structure is worthless when the people refuse to work together. Some form of systematic effort to change the individuals and groups may be necessary. These systematic efforts at changing people, groups, and organization structure are called ***organizational development (OD).*** Two general OD approaches that could improve coordination are (1) confrontation approaches and (2) development of superordinate goals.

Confrontation Approaches

In some organizations there seems to be a belief that if problems between groups are ignored or suppressed, they go away. There are unwritten norms against raising issues that are particularly troublesome. Usually problems will not go away; they need more than aspirin and rest. One way to resolve conflict is by confrontation— to face up to the conflict and allow each party to express its hopes and its views. In the study of six firms in the plastics industry, it was found that more successful firms used confrontation more extensively than did the less successful firms in dealing with conflict and coordination problems.[2]

Various types of confrontation approaches may be used to achieve coordination and resolve conflict. **Bargaining** is one form of confrontation. There are two types of bargaining: distributive bargaining and integrative bargaining. In **distributive bargaining,** one party's loss is the other's gain. Conflict over the allocation of limited resources is an example of distributive bargaining. The objectives of the conflicting parties are contradictory, and some type of compromise is usually worked out. In **integrative bargaining,** on the other hand, there is a possibility of a solution that will benefit both parties. This is most likely when one group has more than adequate resources and another group not enough, or two groups can reduce costs or increase revenues by sharing.

Team building may be a useful way to improve relationships between two or more groups, especially where perceptual distortion and the negative stereotypes within each group have exaggerated group differences and have provided a justification for the resulting coordination problems. In team building, the problem groups are brought together to discuss the weaknesses in their relationship and to work out a new one. A team-building approach was used with two groups of female professionals who were having coordination problems in a hospital. Both groups were brought to a conference site away from the hospital.[14] The team-building program took two days. On the first day each group met separately to discuss the weaknesses and strengths in its own group as well as its perception of the other group. Then each of the groups selected a spokesperson to communicate this perception to the other group. The groups were then brought together to provide feedback to each other on how they perceived the current relationship between them. The second day began with each group meeting separately to discuss the implications of this feedback. Each group worked out a plan to develop a better relationship between the groups. Then the two groups met together once more and devised a plan to develop an improved relationship with each other.

The initial reaction in both groups after the team-building experience was that there was an improved relationship. Six months later, however, the attitudes of group members regressed toward the old levels. Perhaps because there were no changes in the structure of the organization, the underlying cause of the problem (inequitable treatment of the two groups) remained. Only some of the distorted perceptions were changed. For team building to be effective and relationships to be significantly improved over the long run, there must be a real change in the organization and social system itself.

It is not easy for a manager to use this technique. Generally, most people wish to avoid open conflict, avoid expression of emotions, and not openly show antagonism toward others. Furthermore, the candid expression of feelings and individual perceptions is often seen as quite risky by the parties concerned, since they become vulnerable because of their disclosures. Team building and other confrontations are most likely to be effective when the following conditions exist:[15]

1. Both parties must be motivated to eliminate or minimize the conflict, and it is best if both are motivated to use this approach at the same time.
2. The organizational power of each party should be relatively equal.
3. The dialogue between groups should allow an opportunity for both parties to describe the points of disagreement to express their feelings about them.

4. There should be a time period when the parties can express their similarities and common goals and their desire to manage their disagreements more effectively.
5. The participants must know how to provide interpersonal feedback and reassurance, to understand clearly what the other party wants, and maintain a productive dialogue.

Development of Superordinate Goals

Sometimes relationships between groups can be improved through the establishment of superordinate goals.[16] These are goals that are desired by two or more groups and that can be reached only through the cooperation of the groups. For example, replacing a departmental bonus plan with a plant-wide bonus system may induce the various departments in the plant to work together more effectively. Suppose that managers in a department that manufactures refrigerators are paid a bonus based on reducing manufacturing costs. This may lead to low cooperation and coordination with marketing, which may be trying to service an important customer as well as obtaining cost estimates needed to provide customers with information. Coordination between departments could be improved if the company would shift from a "cost center" bonus system to a "profit center" bonus system in which the amount of sales and the price received influenced the amount of bonus for the manufacturing managers. The new system rewards the production managers as well as sales managers for obtaining new customers and servicing them more effectively.

SUMMARY

Coordination is the development and maintenance of the proper integrative relationships between activities in an organization. Coordination is necessary because so many activities are interdependent, but are performed by different people in the same unit or by several different units. Some coordination problems exist because individuals and groups have goals that contradict those of other units or of the organization itself. Problems also exist because of task interdependence, cross-departmental subsystems, time schedule differences, and geographical distances.

Coordination can be achieved in several ways. A properly designed organization structure can lessen coordination problems; alternatively, systems coordinating committees may be formed. When coordination problems are a result of human, not organizational, problems, organizational development techniques such as confrontation approaches and the use of superordinate goals may improve relationships.

We have indicated that the various organizational types vary in their coordinating difficulties. The greater the task interdependence and the greater the amount of diversity among the different units, the more difficult the coordination. As coordination difficulty rises, greater managerial effort must be devoted to coordination, and the coordinating methods are likely to be complex rather than simple, such as the use of integrators rather than standards and procedures. The organic organization is likely to have more difficult coordinating problems than the mechanistic and must develop a structure and set of managerial systems that recognize these difficulties. The mixed organization has additional coordinating problems because of the diversity in its unit structures and types of personnel employed.

The Belmont County Police Department*

Prior to 1971 the Belmont County Police Department received numerous complaints from various sources regarding the reporting of automobile accidents. Most of the criticism came from the State Division of Motor Vehicles. The DMV was dissatisfied since the County's reporting system made it difficult to file or computerize the reports accurately. Consequently, their accident recording system was very inefficient. DMV believed that the cause of this problem was the lack of uniformity in the reporting systems the various law enforcement agencies used. There was incongruity in accident reporting between the different agencies (state, local, and county police departments) in addition to differences among individual officers within these departments.

Insurance companies, concerned because of claims problems, also voiced complaints to the county police department. Their major contention was that the accident reports were not clear and concise. As a result, it took them a longer time than necessary to process claims, resulting in terrible inefficiencies. Failure to receive payments also led individuals involved in automobile accidents to complain vigorously to the police. Some insurance companies threatened to withhold payment of claims, since the accident reports were not providing the types of information that were necessary to judge the nature of the liability.

The courts were also critical of the reporting practices of the police department. A report prepared by the court declared that the accident reports did not provide adequate evidence as to which party was at fault. Many cases set before the court were dismissed because of the lack of necessary information.

All these complaints led the blame to be focused on the police officers who actually wrote the reports. Obviously, it was felt, they were not doing a good job since these problems were deeply rooted in accident reports prepared by them. The policemen, however, did not believe that it was their fault. There were no clearly stated guidelines, they complained to their superiors, to follow in filling out the accident reports for the two basic types of accidents: (1) those involving only property damage to the motor vehicle, and (2) those involving personal injury as well as property damage. The officers argued that since no rules or guidance was provided for them, they could not be expected to know precisely what to do. Often the reporting officer neglected certain information or accident diagrams simply because he or she was not aware that this information was necessary. Without explicit procedural instructions, each officer filled out what he or she considered the most important and relevant on the vehicle report.

As a solution the Department of Motor Vehicles initiated the State Automated Accident Reporting System (STAARS) in 1971. For all types of accidents involving motor vehicles, one form was required to be used throughout the state. This would unify the reporting methods of the state, local, and county police departments. In addition, each officer received a 160-page manual that provided instructions on how to fill out the form. This, it was thought, solved the problems of (1) lack of guidelines for the police and (2) lack of standardization.

On the form were seventy-two different information items that the officer recording the accident had to obtain. Each of these had to be entered on the form and coded in accordance with the procedures outlined in the manual.

The STAARS system was quite effective, initially. It alleviated many of the problems and complaints about poor reporting that had plagued the police department. Eventually, however, new problems arose, this time within the police units. Too many man-hours were being devoted to filling out these reports. The forms were too cumbersome and elaborate. Regardless of how minor the accident was, each of the seventy-two blocks on the form had to be completed, or else the data could not be recorded in the computer.

The police officers began complaining to their administrators. The officers felt they were working for the benefit of the insurance companies, and that the complexities of the reporting system distracted them from their normal and sometimes more important duties. The heads of different law enforcement groups began complaining to the Department of Motor Vehicles. The police officers were unavailable to answer other important calls, since all they were doing was filling out these forms. As a result, there was a shortage of manpower. Something had to be done.

1. What does this case illustrate about reporting systems in organizations?
2. Why does imposing performance control to solve one problem lead to other problems?
3. What can be done to alleviate the problem that exists now?

*We express our appreciation to Liz Nanni, who wrote the original version of this case, for permission to use it.

Case 18.2 Nancy Kidd*

I am employed by the Mercuto Corporation, located in Pullman, Washington. This company manufactures and sells typewriters, programmable calculators, and small computers. Mercuto has offices in states all over the country with a training center in Seattle, Washington, for management training, sales training, programming, and service training. The Pullman, Washington office employs over fifty persons. The person in charge of the office is the Branch Manager Bob Filley. Under Filley are two line managers. One is Al Hamner, Systems Sales Manager, in charge of five to six computer salesmen and four to five computer programmers. The other manager is Tim Banks, General Line Manager, who is in charge of ten to fifteen typewriter salesmen.

Five years ago I started to work for Mercuto as a computer programmer. I went immediately to the training center in Seattle for six weeks to learn to program a particular machine. At the completion of this training I was told I would need an additional three weeks' training to learn a new language that had been developed for the machine. I returned to Seattle many times over the five years I have been employed with Mercuto, each time to learn a new language or machine and each time to undertake the training in a serious, professional manner.

However, each time a training course was completed, I would return to my branch office full of feelings of accomplishment and professionalism, only to be met with disillusionment and frustration. One reason for this was the lack of appreciation from management for having completed the course. Since the management of the branch was not technically oriented, completing the course was not something that they thought helped them to make sales; instead, it was simply a requirement of the home office in Seattle.

Another cause of these feelings was the lack of opportunity to apply the knowledge on the job that I gained at the training center, since some of the equipment I was trained for was never sold in the Pullman area, and other units were sold so infrequently that only one programmer was necessary for support. It seemed to me, too, that in the learning environment of the classroom there was more respect for professional achievement than there was at the branch.

This isn't surprising, though, when you know how both Filley and Hamner became branch managers. Filley, for example, worked his way up to branch manager by being a successful salesman. During the time he was working his way up with the company, Mercuto's main products were typewriters. Later some programmable calculators were added, most of which were very simple to operate. Hamner became a manager in much the same way as Filley. His stepping stone, however, was his sales record in small computers, as compared to Filley's record in typewriter sales.

The computer salespersons reporting to Hamner are not paid on a commission basis in this company. However, at the end of the month the salesperson with the most sales receives a small plaque with his or her name and the date inscribed on it. In general, all the sales staff enjoy certain privileges, such as keeping track of their own time, coming in to the office on their own schedule, and contacting customers at will.

Although the sales staff were also required to attend classes in Los Angeles to learn the capabilities of the computers, many often took this to be a time to party and socialize. The company policy was that those in sales were to know the machines thoroughly and should be able to do an independent analysis of customer needs, without the aid of the programmers. In fact, the job descriptions for a sales position indicate equal responsibility for software installation as well as hardware installation.

Unfortunately, none of the sales staff were capable of doing this. Instead, the salesperson would get a lead, call on the customer, and promise the customer nearly anything to make a sale. Once a sale was made, a contract was signed, which gave the salesperson credit for the sale. However, the customer was given a customer sign-off sheet. This relieved the customer of any legal obligation until both the hardware and software were delivered and set up to his or her satisfaction. Although the salesperson received sales credit at the time of contract signing, no commission for the sale was paid until the sign-off sheet had been received in the home office.

The sales commissions were often late because the software was not delivered in time. The programmers complained that this happened often because of the inadequate information given them by the sales personnel. Eventually, due to protest from the salesmen about slow deliveries, management decided it would be better if the programmers were entirely responsible for the software needs.

New problems developed. Often the software did not match the hardware sold the customer. In addition, customers continued to call everyday for the programs that the salesmen said would be ready in two weeks. There was always the threat of customer cancellation. New customers were often put off in order to solve the problems of the old customers. There was always an atmosphere of chaos. Mercuto was facing serious financial setbacks as well as internal conflicts.

1. What are the primary causes of coordination problems in Mercuto?
2. What could they do to alleviate such problems?
3. What is the effect of this situation on the job adjustment of Nancy Kidd?
4. How are these job experiences likely to affect Nancy Kidd in the future?

*We express our appreciation to Sandra L. Englar, who wrote the original version of this case, for permission to use it.

DISCUSSION QUESTIONS

1. Two causes of coordination problems are organizational conditions and human problems. List the organizational situations and briefly discuss them.
2. What are the human factors that result in coordination problems? Discuss them.
3. Why must the manager be aware of good and poor coordination?
4. Would coordination procedures be similar in mechanistic and organic organizations? Why or why not?
5. What are some advantages and disadvantages in using coordinating departments? Committees?
6. Coordination through organizational development usually takes either the confrontation approach or the development of superordinate goals. Which approach would you feel most comfortable with and why?
7. Discuss various types of confrontation approaches.
8. How would you initiate the development of superordinate goals?

REFERENCES

1. Mahoney, T., T. Jerdee, and S. Carroll. Development of managerial performance: A research approach. Cincinnati, Ohio, South-Western Publishing, 1963.
2. Lawrence, P. R., and J. W. Lorsch. Organization and environment: Managing differentiation and integration. Graduate School of Business Administration, Harvard University, 1967.
3. Mahoney, T., and W. Weitzel. "Managerial models of organizational effectiveness," Administrative Science Quarterly 14, (1969): 357–365.
4. Paine, F. "Organizational assessment dimensions as related to the overall effectiveness of assessment teams," Proceedings, Eastern Academy of Management vol. 7 (1978): 114–123.
5. Thompson, J. D. Organization in action. New York, McGraw-Hill, 1967.
6. Lawrence, P., and J. Seiler. Organizational behavior and administration: Cases, concepts and research findings. Homewood, Ill., Richard D. Irwin, 1965.
7. Dearborn, D., and H. Simon. "Selective perception," Sociometry, (1958): 140–144.
8. Morse, J., and J. Lorsch. "Beyond theory Y." Harvard Business Review, 48 (1970): 61–68.
9. Schein, E. Organizational psychology. Englewood Cliffs, N.J., Prentice-Hall, 1970.
10. Adapted from Hampton D., C. Summer, and R. Webber. Organizational Behavior and the Practice of Management. Glenview, Ill., Scott-Foresman, 1973.
11. Seiler, J. A. "Diagnosing interdepartmental conflict," Harvard Business Review, 41 (1963): 121–132.
12. Lawrence, P., L. Barnes, and J. Lorsch. Organizational behavior and administration: Cases and readings. Homewood, Ill., Richard D. Irwin, 1976.

13. Lorsch, J., and P. Lawrence. "Organizing for product innovation." Harvard Business Review, 43 (1965): 109–123.

14. Carroll, S. J. Reducing intergroup hostility. Unpublished Case Study, University of Maryland, 1976.

15. Walton, R. E. Interpersonal peacemaking: Confrontations and third party consultations. Reading, Mass., Addison-Wesley, 1969.

16. Sherif, M., and C. Sherif. Groups in harmony and tension. New York, Harper and Row, 1953.

CHAPTER NINETEEN

Planning and Control Techniques

Item
19.1

Pat Redwick, CALCAL Electronics president, is pleased and puzzled at the same time. The board of directors approved the acquisition of ABC Electronics, a firm that manufactures stereos and televisions. Pat thinks this acquisition will fit well with CALCAL. There is a good deal of overlap in the kind of managerial and technical skills required in CALCAL and ABC.

Pat thinks the greatest problem for the newly acquired ABC operation will be in the manufacturing management areas. The manufacturing process at CALCAL is simple—one product and one department. ABC has four departments and manufactures two products. Some departments can work on both stereos and televisions, other departments can work only on one product or the other. For example, the components department that manufactures basic elements can produce 600 TV components and no stereo components, 400 stereo units and no TV units, or some combination of the two. The speaker department can produce 400 TV speakers and no stereo speakers, 500 stereo speakers and no TV speakers, or some combination of the two. The TV assembly department can assemble up to 350 TVs, but it cannot be easily converted to stereo assembly. The stereo assembly unit can put together 350 stereos and cannot be converted to TV assembly. Pat also knows, from the analysis that was done before the acquisition, that the unit profit on TVs is $20 and the profit in stereo units is $40.

He has just called Peter Gabriel, the CALCAL production manager, and asked him, "Gabe, what should we do to make the most money with this new acquisition?"

For the most part, the discussion of managerial processes we have presented has been conceptual in the sense that we have described basic ideas underlying planning, organizing, leading, coordinating, and controlling. In this chapter we introduced some approaches that may be used actually to implement these processes, especially planning and control. Two techniques are presented because, in a sense, they represent ways that planning and control might be approached in the mechanistic and in the organic organization. Basically, we think that mechanistic organizations use planning and control strategies in which certainty is assumed or when probability estimates can be made with some confidence. In organic organizations the manager must operate with approaches that recognize uncertainty. Here are two of many approaches that can be used for planning and control.

A PLANNING AND CONTROL APPROACH IN MECHANISTIC ORGANIZATIONS

When the environment is well-defined, known, and relatively constant—as it is for mechanistic organizations, deterministic techniques can be applied to decision problems. The decision maker assumes that certain costs, conditions, and circumstances can be specified with accuracy. With such an assumption various alternatives can be evaluated, and the one that best achieves the goal can be selected. This is called **decision making under certainty.**

Decision making under risk is also likely to be employed in mechanistic organizations. Often, even though a manager cannot be certain about things, he may be in a position to make a probability estimate about them. As we noted in Chapter 7, this may be because of his past experience, or perhaps because of data that have been collected and analyzed. These two approaches to decision making and resource allocation are the most prevalent in mechanistic organizations.

A high degree of environmental certainty facilitates the use of decision strategies and resource allocation methods that are called "deterministic." In deterministic decisions, chance elements do not exist; that is, the decision maker feels it is a realistic assumption to assume certainty, that certain situations, costs, and other conditions can be specified with accuracy. Starr gives the following example:

> Assume that an expansion in plant capacity is planned. Several strategic and tactical alternatives are considered. The possibilities are narrowed down and discarded until, finally, a single plan of action is accepted. A final plan is detailed as though no worthwhile opportunities for deviating from the plan will occur.[1]

Planning and resource allocation decisions of this type are generally preferred by managers because they offer several advantages, among which Starr[1] notes the following.

1. Simple formal procedures can be used. There is lessened need for coordination between organizational units to develop the plans. Data such as costs and resource capacities are usually available from production units or cost accounting groups, or computer information systems may have information that is easily accessible. This facilitates the development of plans, since this information can be incorporated into existing planning models.

2. Efficient logistical support is possible. Once the most efficient plan is formulated, it is relatively easy to obtain help, support, and coordination from other departments. The final plan can be quickly disseminated throughout the relevant units of an organization to become the basis for planning their activities.

3. *Control is emphasized rather than planning.* With deterministic methods the planning models (e.g., linear programming) have already been developed. These models pinpoint strategic control points and provide the manager with a specification of ***what*** should be monitored, and also with specific amounts, or measures, to be achieved, such as the number of units to produce or the allowable costs that can be incurred without exceeding the limits.

4. *No recognition of uncertainty is required.* It is easy to make a plan when the planner knows what is going to happen. In fact, somewhere along the line in every organization this assumption must ultimately be made in order for operations to continue, even in a volatile environment. For example, an airplane manufacturer must, in designing and building a prototype of a plane that is to be sold to the Defense Department, at some point give the go-ahead, even though the future sales depend on such unknown factors as the performance of the aircraft, approval by the military, and subsequent congressional approval.

LINEAR PROGRAMMING

Of all the techniques suggested for improving decision making that have emerged from the quantitative or operations research approach (see Chapter 2), perhaps the one of greatest utility to managers is linear programming.

Linear programming is a technique that maximizes, or minimizes, some objective function of an organization—such as profit or cost—through the solving of a set of simultaneous linear equations that represent constraints, or limitations, relative to the function. It has a number of applications in decision-making situations where it is possible to define relationships among the factors in the form of linear equations. The complexity and subtleties of this method are extensive, but a simple illustration can show its conceptual underpinnings.

Let us look at the problem Pat Redwick has to solve for ABC Electronics, the new division of CALCAL, which manufactures stereos and TV sets. Its plant has four departments: (1) a speaker assembly group that can build either 500 stereo speakers, 400 TV speakers, or some combination not to exceed either of these levels; (2) a components manufacturing section that can build 600 TV units, 400 stereo units, or some combination; (3) a stereo assembly department that can build 350 stereos per day, but no TV sets; and (4) a TV assembly unit that can build 350 TV sets, but no stereos.

The CALCAL finance group estimates that the profit returned for each TV set is $20 per unit and the profit from a stereo unit is $40. Figure 19.1 summarizes this information.

CALCAL wants to obtain the maximum level of profit from ABC's operation. The capacity of each department represents restrictions, or constraints. The components shop, for instance, can produce 400 stereo components, but not 600. Assembly for TV sets cannot exceed 350 units, although it can be less. It cannot be less than zero, however, since there is no negative production.

ABC Electronics' level of profit is given by the equation:

$$20x + 40y = \text{profit}$$

FIGURE 19.1   ABC Electronics

503

*Planning
and Control
Techniques*

Constraints	TV (x)	Stereo (y)	Linear Equation
Components department	600	400	$2x + 3y \leq 1{,}200$
Speaker department	400	500	$5x + 4y \leq 2{,}000$
TV assembly	350	—	$x \leq 350$
Stereo assembly	—	350	$y \leq 350$
Profit	\$20	\$40	$20x + 40y$

This equation is called the **objective function** or the factor (in this case profit) to be maximized. Objective functions can also be minimized, as in the case where one might seek a least-cost solution. To simplify finding a solution, the departmental capacities given in Figure 19.1 can be represented as linear equations. They can be computed simply. The method for determining a linear equation is given by the following formula

$$\frac{y - y_1}{x - x_1} = \frac{y_2 - y_1}{x_2 - x_1}$$

The equation representing the components constraint can be determined in the following manner:

$$\text{If } y_1 = 0, \text{ then } x_1 = 600$$
$$\text{If } y_2 = 400, \text{ then } x_2 = 0$$

This is so because, the way the problem is stated, if ABC produces 600 TV components (x_1), then it can produce no stereo components (y_1). If ABC produces 400 stereo components (y_2), then it can produce no TV components (x_2). These two points are shown on Figure 19.2 as points N and O. When these values are put into

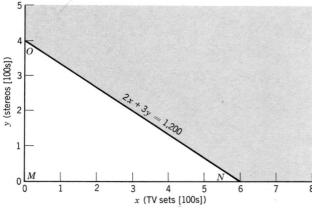

FIGURE 19.2   Components department constraint.

the general equation given above, the specific linear constraint for the components department is found:

$$\frac{y - 0}{x - 600} = \frac{400 - 0}{0 - 600}$$
$$-600y = 400x - 240,000$$
$$-6y = 4x - 2,400$$
$$2x + 3y = 1,200$$

Figure 19.2 shows that ABC can produce any number of components so long as they fall within or along the boundaries of the triangle denoted by *M, N, O*. It cannot produce 800 TV components and zero stereo components. Neither can it produce 400 TV *and* 400 stereo components.

There are other limitations to ABC's level of production. The speaker constraint also acts to reduce the **feasibility area** within which ABC can produce. The linear equation for this department is shown in Figure 19.1:

$$5x + 4y \leqslant 2,000$$

This equation can be derived in the same fashion as that for the components assembly department. Figure 19.3 shows how this constraint limits further the **feasible** production of ABC. It can be seen that the feasibility area in Figure 19.2 is further reduced by the area designated *P, O, Q* in Figure 19.3.

But we have not yet finished considering the limitations that must be taken into account for ABC Electronics. In Figure 19.1 it is also shown that two other departments, TV assembly and stereo assembly, impose constraints. The stereo assembly

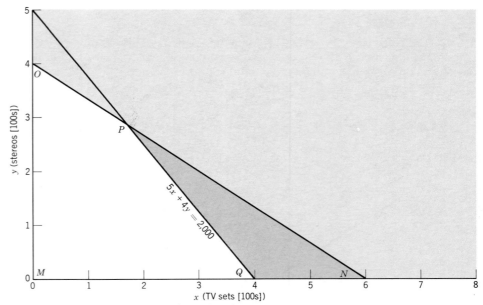

FIGURE 19.3 Components and speaker department constraints.

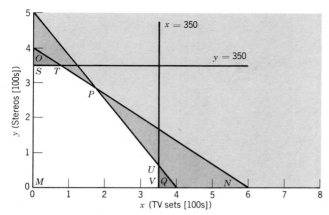

FIGURE 19.4 Components, speaker, TV assembly and stereo assembly constraints.

constraint is given as $y \leq 350$. This means that this department as presently constituted is not set up to assemble TV sets and is capable of assembling up to, but not more than, 350 units of stereo equipment. The departmental constraint is shown on Figure 19.4 along with that of the TV assembly department.

The TV assembly department is also unique, as is the stereo assembly department. Its resources are not transferable; thus, it has a capacity of zero stereo assembly, but up to 350 TV sets. This constraint is given as $x \leq 350$.

This reduces the feasibility area by the amount (O, S, T) to account for the stereo assembly constraint ($y \leq 350$) and (U, V, Q), which eliminates some capacity due to the TV constraint ($x \leq 350$). This gives the feasibility area shown in both Figures 19.4 and 19.5 (M, S, T, P, U, V). ABC can produce any combination of TV sets and stereos that falls within this polygon, or on any of its boundaries.

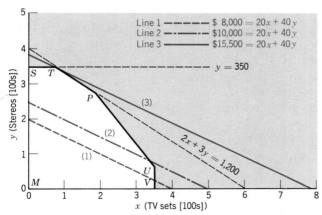

FIGURE 19.5 Maximizing the objective function ($20x + 40y$ = profit).

But we still have not answered the most important question, "How many of each?" The answer to this question is found by considering the relationship of the **objective function,** the function to be maximized, to the feasibility area of production. The objective function, in this case, is a profit relationship and is

$$20x + 40y = \text{profit}$$

Determining the maximum profit level for ABC can be accomplished by examining a family of lines given by the objective function relative to the feasible production capacities. Suppose for example, a profit level of $8,000 is projected. By constructing an **iso profit** line on Figure 19.5, it can be seen that $8,000 can be obtained if ABC produces at any point on line 1, Figure 19.5. An iso profit line is one that any combination of TVs and stereos will result in the same profit. The iso profit line for $8,000 profit can be constructed as follows:

$$20x + 40y = \$8,000$$
When $x = 0$, $y = 200$ and
when $x = 400$, $y = 0$

It can be seen, by examination of Figure 19.5, that there is still a great deal of feasible capacity. If the projected profit is set at $10,000, the iso profit line would be given as line 2 in Figure 19.5, or

$$20x + 40y = \$10,000$$
When $x = 0$, $y = 250$, and
when $x = 500$, $y = 0$

The maximum profit is obtained when the iso profit line reaches a point away from the origin of the graph (M) so that it is still tangent to the feasibility area. This occurs when the line given by the objective function $(20x + 40y)$ passes through point T in the feasibility area, or line 3 on Figure 19.5. It is impossible to produce above the line at this point because that would be **outside** the feasibility area. To produce below the line leaves unused capacity. This point T can be found easily. It is located at the point where the stereo assembly constraint $(y \leqslant 350)$ intersects with the components constraint $(2x + 3y = 1,200)$. This is shown below:

stereo assembly $y \leqslant 350$
components $2x + 3y = 1,200$

This problem is solved by substituting the value of y (350) from our first equation above into the second equation.

$$2x + 3(350) = 1,200$$
$$2x = 1,200 - 1,050$$
$$x = 75 \text{ units}$$

The maximum profit appears, then, when ABC produces 75 TVs and 350 stereos. The amount of profit is

$$\$20 \,(75) + \$40 \,(350) = \text{profit}$$
$$\$1,500 + \$14,000 = \$15,500$$

Is this the maximum level of profit? Consider what happens if ABC produces elsewhere within the feasibility constraints. If it moves back along the constraint, $y \leq 350$, to produce one less TV set (74), the profit is reduced by $20. If it produces one less stereo (349), the profit is reduced by $40. What would the profit be at another point in the feasibility area, say U? This point U is located where the components constraint ($2x + 3y = 1,200$) intersects with the components assembly constraint ($x \leq 350$). Thus, it is located where these equations are equal. To find the number of stereos and TVs at point U, we begin with the two constraints

components $2x + 3y = 1,200$, and
TV assembly $x \leq 350$

Since we now have a value for x, it can be substituted in the components constraint ($2x + 3y = 1,200$) and yield a value for y.

$$2(350) + 3y = 1,200$$
$$3y = 1,200 - 700$$
$$y = 166\tfrac{2}{3}$$

Therefore, point U is located where the production levels would be 350 TV sets and 167 stereos. By substituting these production level values in the objective function, the profit is given as

$$\$20x + \$40y = \text{profit}$$
$$\$20 \,(350) + \$40 \,(167) = \$13,880$$

Thus, ABC obtains maximum profit when it produces at point T.

Assumptions of Linear Programming

Two important assumptions that lie behind this approach are (1) additivity and (2) divisibility. Wagner[2] defines additivity to mean the "total amounts of each input and associated profit are the sums of the inputs and profits for each individual process." Divisibility means for "each activity, the total amounts of each input and the associated profit are strictly proportional to the level of . . . each activity [being] capable of continuous proportional expansion or reduction." He goes on to state that

> The assumptions of divisibility and additivity are equivalent to stating that the underlying mathematical model can be formulated in terms of linear relations. Strictly interpreted, the axioms imply constant returns to scale and preclude the possibility

of economies or diseconomies of scale (in both the technology and profit aspects). Suitable mathematical devices of an advanced nature often make it possible to introduce economies and diseconomies into a modified linear model. In real situations the above two postulates may hold only approximately, but nevertheless well enough, to permit useful application of the linear approach.

Some Other Uses of Linear Programming

The resource allocation problem as shown above in simple form is probably the most frequent illustration of linear programming. The method can be used to determine the most efficient way to allocate production facilities when the objective is to maximize profits or minimize costs. For instance, a plant might have several departments, each with different capacities to produce different combinations of several products. Knowing the true profit contribution of each product can determine how many of each to produce.

A PLANNING AND CONTROL APPROACH
IN ORGANIC ORGANIZATIONS

The manager in the organic organization faces a much less certain decision environment than one in a mechanistic one. In an organic organization, the manager may not be able, or willing, to assign **risk** (or probability) to various states of nature, and he or she therefore is likely to make use of techniques for decision making under conditions of **uncertainty.** In this chapter we will explain in more detail the concepts of decision making under uncertainty, which were introduced in Chapter 7, as well as some specific techniques for making such decisions.

Planning and control in organic organizations must take into account the uncertainties involved. The organic organization must rely on less accurate estimates of project time and costs than the stable firm. In planning and control in the organic organization, the control process can be facilitated by giving managers some idea about what aspects of the project are critical in order to pinpoint strategic control points. These points can then be monitored to see that events are conforming to plan. The following example shows how this can be accomplished using the method known as PERT.

PERT (PROJECT EVALUATION AND
REVIEW TECHNIQUE)

Suppose you are a project manager for the MLZ Aerospace firm. You have just been told that the company is going to embark on the design and construction of a space-landing vehicle. While MLZ has been active in the space program, it has never been involved with a project quite like this. You have virtually no experience with landing vehicles, but the company has successfully produced other equipment that is similar but still substantially different enough so that you, as a manager, feel somewhat uncertain about how long such a project will take.

In cases like this, PERT is a useful planning and control device, since it introduces the concept of probability estimates, which have some utility when planning is done in a relatively uncertain environment. To use PERT for this project, you must:

1. Identify each task required
2. Obtain time estimates for each task
3. Determine the sequencing and relationship of each task to the others

Figure 19.6 shows the basic network design for this project. Each task (or activity) is designated by an arrow (→) and represents some relatively discrete part of the work on the project. Each activity starts and stops with some identifiable event and is designated by a circle (○), so that an activity event chain will look like this, $A \xrightarrow{1} B$, where the activity (1) can be clearly identified by a beginning and an end point. An example might be the activity (1) of **going to work.** It is preceded by the event **leave home** (A) and followed by the event **arrive at work** (B). For each activity, a time estimate is made. For example, you might estimate that, based on past experience, it will take you thirty-five minutes to get to work.

Time Estimates

Network diagrams had been used extensively prior to the development of PERT. The Gantt Chart, for example (mentioned in Chapter 2), is a planning, scheduling, and control device similar to PERT, but is constructed without the use of time probability estimates. The time estimate is the significant component of the PERT approach.

Figure 19.7 lists the activities that you, the project manager, know will be required to complete the space vehicle. Figure 19.8 is a list of events that designate the starting and ending of each of these activities.

Also shown in Figure 19.7 are the time estimates necessary to construct the PERT network. For each activity three time estimates are obtained, the *optimistic, most likely,* and *pessimistic.*

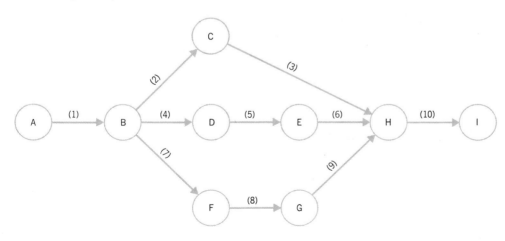

(A), (I)   Denotes events (see Figure 19.8)

(1) , (2)   Denotes activities (see Figure 19.7)

FIGURE 19.6   Basic PERT network for space-landing vehicle project.

FIGURE 19.7   Activity time estimates

Activities	Optimistic (a)	Most Likely (b)	Pessimistic (c)	Activity Time Estimate (Te)
1. Approve specifications	2	2.5	6	3
2. Develop recruiting plans	1	3	5	3
3. Hire work force	3	4.5	9	5
4. Design power system	4	5.5	10	6
5. Build power system	8	11	14	11
6. Test power system	4	6	8	6
7: Design frame	3	4.5	9	5
8. Build frame	9	9.5	13	10
9. Test frame	1	3	5	3
10. Assemble and test vehicle	4	6	8	6

1. *Optimistic time* (a). In the event that the work proceeds without any problems, interferences, or obstacles, what is the least time that the activity would take?

2. *The most likely time* (b). What would the manager expect the activity time to be under normal circumstances? Realistically, how much time is required to complete the activity?

3. *The pessimistic time* (c). What is the maximum time that the activity would require if things go very wrong? Given the worst of conditions, how much time should the project take?

These times are shown in the columns in Figure 19.7. In order to calculate a time estimate for an activity (*Te*), these times are weighed in the following fashion:

$$Te = \frac{a + 4b + c}{6}$$

These weights are values derived from a beta distribution and when used with the three time estimates provide, some planners think, optimum accuracy in estimating.[1]

As the project manager you go to each section chief responsible for the designated activity and ask for each of these time estimates. Suppose you get, from the head of power system design (activity 4) the following time estimates:

a.   Optimistic design time = 4 weeks
b.   Most likely design time = 5.5 weeks
c.   Pessimistic design time = 10 weeks

FIGURE 19.8   Events for space-landing vehicle project

A. Receive specifications	F. Begin frame construction
B. Begin project	G. Begin frame test
C. Begin recruiting	H. Assemble frame and power system
D. Begin power system construction	I. Deliver vehicle
E. Begin power system test	

Using the formula for computing Te, we find that the estimate used in our network is 6 weeks.

$$Te = \frac{4 + 4(5.5) + 10}{6} = \frac{36}{6} = 6 \text{ weeks}$$

By obtaining similar estimates of each of the activities listed in Figure 19.7, the manager constructs the network shown in Figure 19.9. Figure 19.9 is a representation similar to Figure 19.6, but the activity times (Te) have been entered below the arrows.

The Critical Path

By examining Figure 19.9, you can see that there are three main branches, or paths, in this project.

$$
\begin{aligned}
&1.\ A{\rightarrow}B{\rightarrow}C{\rightarrow}H{\rightarrow}I && = 17 \text{ Weeks}\\
&2.\ A{\rightarrow}B{\rightarrow}D{\rightarrow}E{\rightarrow}H{\rightarrow}I && = 32 \text{ Weeks}\\
&3.\ A{\rightarrow}B{\rightarrow}F{\rightarrow}G{\rightarrow}H{\rightarrow}I && = 27 \text{ Weeks}
\end{aligned}
$$

The longest of these is called the **critical path.** Knowing the critical path can be of great help to the manager.

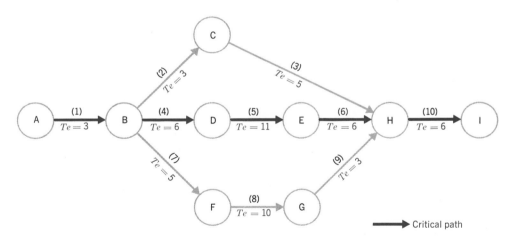

FIGURE 19.9 PERT network for space-landing vehicle project, showing estimated activity times and critical path.

1. **It is the longest path in the project.**
2. **It is the shortest time in which the project can be completed.** If our estimates of time are correct, it will be impossible for MLZ to build the space vehicle in less than thirty-two weeks, as resources are currently allocated.
3. **It identifies strategic control points.** The manager is able to identify which parts of the project should be observed most closely. If activities along the critical path take more time than estimated, then we can be certain that the length of the project time will be extended.

There is, once the project starts, no leeway in time on the critical path. On the other paths, however, there is some leeway. This leeway is called "slack time" and is the amount of time that we have that is, in a sense, noncritical to the project target date. As Figure 19.9 shows, the path *BCH* takes eight weeks and the path *BDEH* takes twenty-three weeks. This means that we have slack time, or leeway as to when event *C* must begin. The total slack time on this path is fifteen weeks.

The knowledge of where slack time exists is important because it identifies pockets of potential resources that conceivably could be diverted to the critical path to shorten it. To compute slack time, two other concepts are needed in PERT.

EARLIEST POSSIBLE TIME (EPT) This is the earliest, or soonest, that an activity can begin. It takes into account the times for all activities in the PERT network that precede it that are linked to it in sequence. In the example, for instance, the earliest possible time for event *C* is six weeks after the project begins. This is so because activities (1) and (2) each take three weeks.

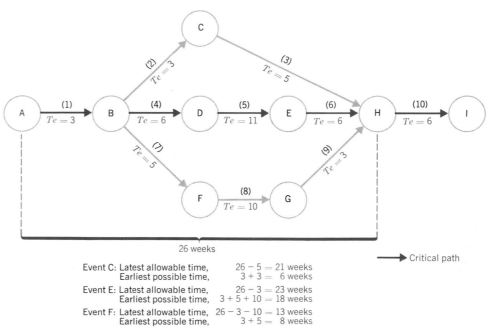

26 weeks

→ Critical path

Event C: Latest allowable time, $26 - 5 = 21$ weeks
        Earliest possible time, $3 + 3 = 6$ weeks

Event E: Latest allowable time, $26 - 3 = 23$ weeks
        Earliest possible time, $3 + 5 + 10 = 18$ weeks

Event F: Latest allowable time, $26 - 3 - 10 = 13$ weeks
        Earliest possible time, $3 + 5 = 8$ weeks

FIGURE 19.10   Slack time computation for space-landing vehicle project.

LATEST ALLOWABLE TIME (LAT) This is the latest time at which an activity can begin in order to meet the time requirements of the critical path. It can be seen from Figure 19.9 that the latest allowable time for event C is five weeks before the event H. Figure 19.10 illustrates these concepts. By computing the time required for path ABDEH on the critical path (twenty-six weeks), and subtracting the time required for activity (3), "hiring the work force," which takes five weeks, the latest allowable time for event C is 21 weeks (26 − 5). In Figure 19.10, latest times (LAT) and earliest times (EPT) are illustrated for both paths in the project other than the critical path.

Figure 19.11 is a summary table in which the slack time (LAT − EPT) is computed for each event in the network. It is constructed in the following manner. The first event (A) is designated as time 0, or the start of the project; the LAT and EPT are the same. The EPT for event B^* is three weeks after the project begins, since this is our estimated project time. The latest allowable time is also three weeks, because event B^* is on the critical path. Each event on the critical path has been identified in Figure 19.11 with an asterisk (*). LAT and EPT for events on the critical path are the same; therefore, there is no slack time for any of them. This is shown by the zero in the "Slack Time" column of Figure 19.11.

The manager can now proceed to compute the EPTs for all events not on the critical path. By beginning at the start of the project and adding the activity time for all activities preceding an event, the EPTs are determined. Event C has an EPT of six weeks after project start. Event F's EPT is eight weeks ($A\xrightarrow{3}B\xrightarrow{5}F$). Event G's EPT is eighteen weeks ($A\xrightarrow{3}B\xrightarrow{5}F\xrightarrow{10}G$).

The latest allowable times are computed by working back along the noncritical paths from a point where they meet an event on the critical path. It has been shown that the LAT and EPT for event H is twenty-six weeks. Since we have made a time estimate of three weeks for activity (9), "Testing the frame," the LAT for event G is three weeks *before* event H, or twenty-three weeks (26 − 3) after the start of the project. The slack time for event G is five weeks.

$$LAT - EPT = slack\ time$$
$$23 - 18 = 5\ weeks$$

FIGURE 19.11 Computation of slack times for events in space-landing vehicle project

Events	Latest Allowable Time (LAT)	Earliest Possible Time (EPT)	Slack Time (LAT − EPT)
A. Receive specifications*	0	0	0
B. Begin project	3	3	0
C. Begin recruiting	21	6	15
D. Begin power system construction*	9	9	0
E. Begin power system test*	20	20	0
F. Begin frame construction	13	8	5
G. Begin frame test	23	18	5
H. Assemble frame and power system*	26	26	0
I. Deliver vehicle*	32	32	0

*Denotes event on critical path.

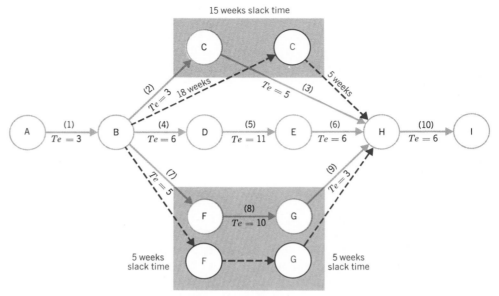

FIGURE 19.12 Slack times for space-landing vehicle project.

Figure 19.12 illustrates the notion of slack time on noncritical paths. Events along them may, in effect, be slid forward to the LATs for events C and G. Events on these paths may start any time after EPT, but begin no later than the LAT. It is, in this sense, that slack time is leeway for the project.

Redesigning the Project

Having gone through the analysis of the project, the manager decides that the project time of thirty-two weeks is unacceptable. The deadline is thirty weeks from project start, not thirty-two. Knowing where slack time exists permits him to shift resources to the critical path, or to move activities off the path.

Faced with the dilemma of a deadline that cannot be met with the current plan, one possibility would be to move events off the critical path. If, for instance, the path *BCH* comprised some activities other than recruiting, and activity (6) were not dependent on activity (5), one alternative might be to move activity (6) as shown in Figure 19.13. This changes the critical path, as shown, and reduces planned project time to twenty-seven weeks. This is not a likely alternative for MLZ because of the nature of the project, but it is one solution to other network problems.

Perhaps the most realistic alternative for the project manager in this case would be to use some of the slack resources on path *ABFGHI*. Assume that these activities are technical engineering functions performed in different departments. If frame design engineers also have competence in designing power systems, it may be possible to transfer some of these people to the power system design and construction stage. Let us do so and assume that the times for the following activities on the critical path become these:

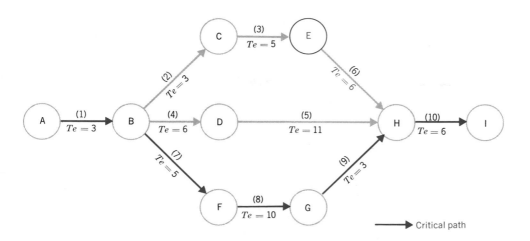

FIGURE 19.13   Revised network with events and activities moved off the critical path to locations where slack exists.

Activity	Te
4. Design power system	4 weeks
5. Build power system	9 weeks
6. Test power system	3 weeks

These reduced activity times have been obtained because resources have been directed to the critical path. The new network is shown in Figure 19.14. The new critical path is *ABFGHI* and is twenty-seven weeks.

SOME APPLICATIONS OF PERT

There have been a number of different applications of the PERT technique to management decision problems. It has been used, for example, in the construction industry for the planning of large-scale projects such as buildings, dams, and roads. It has been used to plan and control major defense projects such as the building of the Polaris submarine. To make an assessment of the costs for a project, instead of time estimates, a manager can use the most likely cost, the least cost, and the highest cost for activities. Then the manager can proceed as described in the time estimate example above.

Perhaps the most important point of this chapter is that the ways to manage in

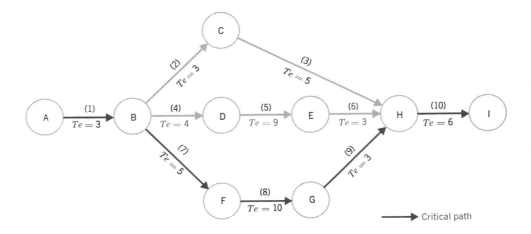

FIGURE 19.14 Revised network showing critical path when resources are shifted from frame division to power system division.

the uncertain environment are different from those in a certain environment. Organic organizations require different techniques than might be useful in the mechanistic organization, but the manager faced with uncertainty should find some comfort in knowing that approaches exist that can be of help to him.

Case
19.1 The Pot Shop

Barbara and Bruce Stetson are both good recreational potters who have recently decided to try their luck at making a living making pots. Together they have designed some unique lamp bases and flower pots, which have always sold well at local art shows. This led them to open up B and B Pots.

Basically, there are two operations at B and B. In the production room, they make the lamp bases and the flower pots. In the kiln room these are baked and hardened.

There are some important differences in the way these two products are made. The lamp bases are more extensively glazed and require a good deal more care than the flower pots. A lamp base takes four hours to make, while a flower pot takes only two hours. Barbara and Bruce, who do all the ceramic work themselves, figure they have a total, together, of forty-eight hours per week during which they can make either lamps or flower pots.

The products also require different times in the kiln. A lamp base takes three hours and the flower pots take four hours. The total available kiln time is eighty hours each week.

Their estimated profit for a lamp is $80 and the estimated profit for a flower pot is $60.

1. At what level of production do the Stetsons maximize profits?
2. What would be the maximum profit if there were some additional constraints as follows:
   a. Their shop has a lamp display rack that will hold only ten lamps and hold no flower pots.
   b. Their shop has a pot display area that holds fifteen pots and no lamps.
   c. The profit for the units are $40 for a lamp and $50 for a pot.

John Webb

Case 19.2

John Webb had a problem. As personnel manager of a plant belonging to the Inert Company, he had the responsibility of implementing a new job evaluation system for rank and file employees in record time. Larry Summer, the plant manager, gave him a deadline to implement the new system. Larry had to be at a meeting scheduled at corporate headquarters in six weeks. He wanted to be able to brag, then, about his plant's new wage system.

The new job evaluation system was already designed. It was to be installed in each of the plant's two product divisions. Each division had its own general manager and the new system was to be presented to each general manager separately by the personnel department. The system was quite simple. Each employee in the plant was to complete a job description questionnaire. In the questionnaire the employee would describe his or her duties and responsibilities. On the basis of these job descriptions, each employee would be assigned a labor grade. This would be done by comparing the information on the job description with the requirements for placement in the grade, as stated in the general grade descriptions that had already been written.

Each of the division's employees was classified as a production employee. There were five grades for the production employees, six grades for the clerical employees, and eight grades for the technical employees. Associated with each grade is a wage rate. This rate had been determined through a wage survey conducted among companies in the local area.

Larry wanted to have wages assigned to all rank and file jobs in the plant by May thirteenth. Since it was now April second, that left just twenty-nine working days to complete the job. John felt that the only way to insure that this date was met was to use PERT.

1. Draw up a list of the events that must occur to complete the assignment in the allocated time.
2. Draw a network to represent the relationships among these events.

DISCUSSION QUESTIONS

1. What are some types of problems for which linear programming is an appropriate approach?

2. Suppose you were an office equipment manufacturer. You produce typewriters and small calculators. Your plant has three departments and the capacities are shown below

	Capacity	
	Typewriters or Calculators	
1. Frame	200	300
2. Circuit and machinery	300	225
3. Assembly	250	200
4. Shipping	150	400

The profit for each of these products is $100 for the typewriters and $75 for the calculators.

(a) What level of production will maximize profit?

(b) What is the equation for the iso profit line?

3. Suppose you had a small plant with three departments. Department A can assemble 400 washers but no dryers. Department B can assemble 500 dryers but no washers. Department C can produce 600 washers or 600 dryers, or some combination not to exceed 600 units. What production levels would yield maximum profit if

(a) Dryers yield $40 unit profit and washers yield $80?

(b) Dryers yield $75 unit profit and washers yield $30?

4. You have worked out the following network for a problem. The numbers between the events (A, B, . . . I) denote the optimistic, most likely and pessimistic time:

(a) Determine the critical path for the project.

(b) Which path has the most slack time?

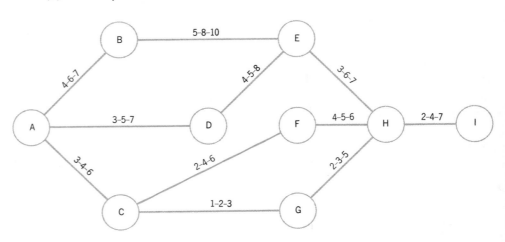

5. Construct a PERT network for a project you are planning, say a vacation with a friend. Where is the slack time? What is the critical path?
6. What is slack time? Where does it occur?
7. "The critical path is the longest activity path in a project. It is the shortest period of time in which the project can be completed." Comment.
8. What help to a manager is it to know the critical path?

REFERENCES

1. Starr, M. Management: A modern approach. New York, Harcourt, Brace, Jovanovich, 1971.
2. Wagner, H. Principles of operations research. Englewood Cliffs, N.J., Prentice-Hall, 1969.

Management and the Future

In this book we have discussed what management structures and systems we might expect to find in an organization if it is to be productive and survive. Structures and systems must be compatible with differences in organizational environments and the differences in individuals who make them up.

   We would be remiss if we did not end this book by pointing out some of the possible future developments that could influence organizational members. We do this because such future changes will influence the effectiveness of alternative organizational structures or management systems.

   It is always hazardous to predict the future. Nevertheless, we identify for our readers some of the geopolitical, economic, technological, and social factors that we think may have significant effects on management in the future.

CHAPTER TWENTY

Organizations and Their Goals: Present and Future

Can the Corporation Survive?

Item
20.1

The American free-enterprise system is in mortal danger of extinction unless cor-porate managers, in their enlightened self-interest, face the reality that their sole task is no longer to maximize profits for their stockholders, maintains Courtney C. Brown, Dean Emeritus of Columbia University's Graduate School of Business.

In Beyond the Bottom Line (Macmillan Publishing Co., Inc., New York) . . . Brown argues that in the long-run interest of shareholders, today's managers must also take into account the views of such constituencies as customers, employees and the general public. These groups expect the modern corporation to deal with such goals as environmental purity, plant safety, and equal opportunity, among others, as well as the basic one of profits. If business had dealt with these problems years ago, it might not be faced with such a welter of government regulations, Brown contends. It is up to the board of directors, which must be drawn from a wider range of talents and sectors of society than is today's typical board, to set the new tone.

Brown, seventy-four, is a director of CBS, Inc., Union Pacific Corp., and As-sociated Dry Goods Corp. He has also served as a director of Exxon, Inc., Borden, Inc., and American Standard Inc. In this interview with Executive Editor Gerald R. Rosen, Brown discusses how corporations can cope with the new demands being made on them and why it would be perilous for business to ignore these realities.

Organizations
and Their
Goals:
Present
and Future

523

The title of your new book is Beyond the Bottom Line. *What do you mean by that phrase in terms of the responsibilities of today's chief executive officer?*

As you know, maximizing the bottom line has been the single most important—if not the only—consideration in the whole corporate decision-making process. The book concerns itself with what happens to the corporation and the structure of the company when management decisions are concerned with issues beyond just making profits for stockholders.

Isn't management's sole responsibility to maximize profits?

There are many very serious scholars as well as businessmen who would say that should be its only concern; Milton Friedman is perhaps the most conspicuous. The point that I'm making in the book is that management has no alternative but to bring into the orbit of its decision-making considerations that extend beyond the bottom line. It must think of other constituencies besides stockholders.

Today, corporate law concerns itself primarily with stockholders and stockholder interest. And while corporate management has made many speeches about having numerous constituencies, the fact of the matter is that this hasn't been recognized either in law or very extensively in business decision-making.

Isn't the corporate manager literally an employee of the stockholders, and therefore shouldn't that be his sole constituency?

That is the situation with respect to corporate law today.

And you think that's wrong or ill-advised or impractical?

Well, I would modify it only gradually and carefully, but it's already being modified by legislation that compels management to recognize the needs and requirements of other constituencies. These include the racial and sexual mix of its personnel, safety conditions in the plant, and the impact of its factories on the community's air and water. In other words, there have been a large number of restraints placed upon management through government regulatory procedures that have already begun to modify this single constituency assumption of corporate law.

Would it be in business' interest to participate more in the legislative process and try to get some of these laws changed? Or do you think that's impractical?

I think it would be in business' interest to undertake a redefinition of purpose that would include other constituencies and do the things that are now required voluntarily rather than be compelled to do so. One of the reasons we have gotten an almost malignant growth of government regulation is that business has been too slow to accept the expectations that the public has placed upon it.

Do you think that the nation might not have such tight environmental laws if business had done some cleaning up on its own?

I'm sure of it. As a matter of fact, I think business made a serious error in failing to foresee the environmental problem. It should have petitioned the government to legislate in sensible ways rather than have Washington impose regulations.

Are there any other problems that you would cite along that line?

Equal employment opportunity and plant safety come immediately to mind, and there are certainly others. Business has a major role to play in the conditioning of life in our society and should be a leader in the development of attitudes and policies that serve the public in a most effective way. In this manner, I think it can adapt itself to society's changing values and recapture the credibility of the public.

Do you think it lacks that credibility now?
I'm afraid so.

Can you think of some additional area in which business is likely to be faced with punitive legislation?
The whole field of affirmative action is a place where business can do a great deal right now without additional federal compulsions. If it doesn't, even more regulations are inevitable.

You said before that business has been rather laggard in coming to grips with some of these social problems. Can you think of any companies that have done an outstanding job?
Oh, yes. Dayton Hudson, The Bank of America, and Connecticut General Insurance Company have all done a fine job in the equal opportunity area. Texas Instruments has been outstanding in the environmental area, and there are many others.
I want to emphasize that the whole concept of social responsibility goes beyond simply reacting to these emerging attitudes of the public, as expressed in legislation or through the administrative agencies of government.
Management must develop a different attitude. Whether a particular policy is good should not be related entirely to its effect upon the bottom line, but whether it's good for the public. I think management must take the view that what is good for the public will, in the long run, be good for the company and for American business.

The chief executive officer works for a board of directors to whom he must justify his actions. Would it help him to meet the public responsibilities you cite if some directors represented constituencies besides stockholders—such as labor, customers, or the general public?
I do not believe that public directors are desirable, nor do I believe that directors should represent a specific constituency. When a person goes on the board of a corporation, he or she represents the company and the company's interest. I think that intelligent directors will from time to time sponsor a specific program favoring a given constituency, but if for instance you had a labor representative on the board of directors, there would frequently be a conflict between the company's interest and that of the workers. I would say that a board of directors with a variety of backgrounds, whose members had track records in different communities of our society, is the most desirable.

Do the boards of most of our major corporations reflect that kind of diversity?
Not yet. But they're beginning to in a very tentative and cautious way.

In the main, what kinds of people are they lacking?

Well, it's easier to answer you by saying what kinds of people they do have. They have lawyers, bankers, chief executive officers of other corporations, and a scattering now of academics, blacks and women. But I don't think they have gone nearly so far as they will ultimately want to go and must go to achieve a diversity of points of view and interests.

Are you maintaining that if they don't go that route they may be faced with legislation requiring them to?

It would be very awkward. And most undesirable. While there is no great push for legislation right now, such things can't be ruled out. I hope that the boards themselves will see the importance of getting a diversity before that happens.

If the directors solely represent the interests of the company, isn't it difficult for the chief executive not to emphasize the maximizing of profits in his decision-making?

The first step is to give the board more authority, and that entails insuring that the chief executive is not also chairman of the board. If the chief executive is the president, it should be his job to maximize the bottom line, and that of the board to set down other goals and considerations. The board—not the chief executive—must take the longer view and reconcile the needs of society with those of the corporation.

How about the whole nature of the American corporate system? Is that going to be very different fifteen or twenty years from now? Is government going to be more and more intrusive?

Government will play a larger role if business doesn't modify and adjust and accept the importance of the new values that are beginning to assert themselves in society. The failure of business to change will bring on continued government encroachment and ultimately strangulation.

If, on the other hand, business does adjust itself to the emerging society, and to the kind of mixture of values that seem to be important, I think we could see a retrenchment of government.

Of course, business isn't entirely innocent in this process. When industries or companies are facing trouble, they often run to Washington for help. Don't you think this creates a dangerous precedent?

It certainly does. Very dangerous. Competition is a task master that protects the public. But there are penalties as well as rewards in a competitive society. If we are to have a free competitive society, business must accept the penalties of failure.

Would you then have opposed the Lockheed loan of a few years ago?

I don't think Lockheed is a private company. Its major—almost its only—customer is the United States government. So that was a different situation.

How about trigger prices for steel or import quotas for textiles and other devices to protect certain industries?

Any time business asks the government for relief, either by some modification of the competitive edge or through a subsidy, it is playing a very dangerous game as far as the future of the private enterprise system is concerned.

You refer to competition quite frequently in this discussion. What about our antitrust laws? Are they doing a good job in maintaining competition?

I think the answer is "yes and no." I don't want to be ambiguous, but I think the answer is "yes" in that they have been able to maintain workable competition in most markets. I think the answer is "no" when you look at the mass of administrative rulings and judicial opinions that think of preserving competition, not in terms of open markets but in terms of protecting competitors.

Could you cite an example?

Take Eastman Kodak and its Instamatic. It has a new camera that would be beneficial to the public. The company put the camera on the market and hurt some of its competitors. In an initial ruling, a Federal District Court imposed an $87 million penalty on Kodak for damaging its competitors, which was ultimately reversed in the Court of Appeals. It was a ridiculous antitrust ruling in which a company put a product on the market that benefited consumers and then was hit by the courts for damaging its competitors. The antitrust laws have become a means of protecting companies from competition.

How about the IBM case, which has dragged on for ten years?

That's unbelievable to me. As far as its mix of products is concerned, IBM isn't the same company it was ten years ago. It has done a tremendous job for the public in terms of lowering the cost of computer time. But by serving the public so well, IBM has hurt its competitors, and that's apparently what the antitrust action is all about.

You indicate in your book that labor as well as business should be subject to the antitrust laws. Would you elaborate on that a bit?

That ties into the problem of inflation. There has been a tremendous amount of discussion about inflation, but none of it is very conclusive. No one has been able to put his finger on the single most important cause of it. It is most commonly attributed to budget deficits and an easy monetary policy. I'm inclined to think that may be a result rather than the cause.

The inflationary spiral stems from the power of organized labor that began to build with the passage of the Wagner Act in 1935 (the unions were already exempt from the antitrust laws under the Clayton Act of 1914). The evidence suggests very strongly that we unbalanced the bargaining table. Most of the collective bargaining since the 1940s has resulted in wage settlements in excess of productivity increases.

Could management have been tougher in resisting these demands?

Since management has been concerned only with its own bottom line, it had no incentive to resist these wage demands. Most companies knew they could pass the cost along in higher prices, and the government would then accommodate the inflationary impact through deficits and easy money. This has been the case whether the Administration was Democratic or Republican. In the past twenty-five years, the federal government has run only four budgetary surpluses.

Should a responsible chief executive draw the line with labor and refuse to give wage increases in excess of productivity increases?

Under the present emphasis on bottom-line considerations, he wouldn't be a chief executive very long. But I think the public is beginning to sense that something is out of gear, that there is a built-in generator of inflation in the structural arrangements that we have in our society.

Still, labor wouldn't like being subject to the antitrust laws.

I'm not sure, since we've given labor a monopolistic position and you can't blame labor for abusing it. I'm sure business would do it under the same circumstances.

How do you see the corporate system evolving by the year 2000? Do you think it's going to be very different than it is today?

It depends on the emergence and crystallization of public attitudes on the one hand and business reaction on the other. Amitai Etzioni, a sociologist at Columbia University, has developed a theory that every great society has to have a single purpose. And there's no doubt about the purpose of the United States for the 100 years prior to the 1950s: it was to increase material well-being through economic growth. Then we began to be more concerned with such things as the disadvantaged and the environment, even questioning the Puritan ethic of work and saving.

Now the United States is in the midst of making up its mind as to which of these should take priority. My own hunch is that we will not make up our mind and neither will become a single priority. We're going to try and get a mixture of some of the old values of material well-being and growth and some of the more ameliorating, egalitarian, compassionate attitudes.

Throughout this book we have emphasized the goal of survival for an organization. We have indicated that organizations, to survive, must be able to adapt to environmental demands. Since the environments facing different organizations vary, the subgoals which organizations need to achieve the strategic survival goal will vary. In certain environments meeting cost objectives through the use of management systems designed to maximize efficiency is critical. In other environments cost considerations are less important than quality or performance goals. Of course, these subgoals are the means for achieving profit goals, which are related to the survival goal in business organizations. In nonbusiness organizations survival may be related to the attainment of other goals such as political acceptance.

The goals of organizations today are more complex than they were in the past. This is especially true of business organizations where many social goals have been imposed on industrial organizations by government and society. These problems are discussed in item 20.1. The simpler goal of profit can no longer be pursued to the exclusion of others as it was in the past. The survival goal of a business organization appears to require the consideration of many more factors today than in previous years. It is not only government that is pressuring business organizations; technology, international developments, and changing societal expectations are also factors that must be predicted if organizations are to survive over the long run. Our economic history provides tens of thousands of examples of organizations—some large and some small—that could not adapt and perished. At the present time some of the largest business enterprises in the world are so threatened as to have an uncertain future.

Throughout this book we have emphasized the importance of organizational structures and systems being compatible with the tasks and responsibilities imposed on organizations by elements in their outside environments. We have paid particular attention to the technological and market environments of the firm but have pointed out that other environments also create important pressures for organizations. For some organizations, political environment may be far more important than technological and market environments in shaping managerial policies and systems.

Of course, we must not forget that all environments of an organization are not necessarily independent. Changes in one environment can create changes in other environments. Some of the more important current and future shifts in environmental pressures that must be considered in developing and choosing from among the alternative organizational structures and systems are described in this book.

CHANGES IN THE SIZE OF ORGANIZATIONS

Perhaps the first factor that will be relevant to future managerial concerns is the sheer size of organizations. We can expect organizations in the future to be larger than they are today.[1] In 1947 the largest 200 corporations in the United States produced 30 percent of the value added to manufacturing output, but by 1970 the top 200 produced 43 percent of the value added.[2] Greater size, of course, suggests greater formalization. Whether such organizations will need greater differentiation in their own structures to meet increased environmental pressures is a question for future analysis.

While the merger fever of the late 1960s and early 1970s will probably not be rekindled, we expect that already large firms, like ITT and Gulf and Western, will continue to acquire profitable small firms. Most likely these acquisitions will result in greater diversification of the "business" a firm is in. While this has some effect of hedging risks, it certainly can also lead to serious managerial problems, much like those we described as common in the mixed-type organization.

INCREASED FOREIGN COMPETITION

United States firms will be facing increased foreign competition. At the present time, a significantly higher proportion of the automobiles, sewing machines, binoculars, musical instruments, electrical motors, television sets and radios, clothing and shoes, bicycles, motorcycles, and other products that are sold in this country are made by foreign manufacturers than was the case a few years ago. The high quality of these goods, as well as effective price competition, have made foreign competition difficult to cope with. Some feel that the quality of imported goods is higher than that of those produced domestically.[3] Many domestic industries have been seriously affected by outside competition in recent years. The U.S. automobile industry, as an example, has suffered significant economic losses. Foreign competitors often have very efficient modern plants, built since the Second World War, and they have taken very quickly to modern management methods developed chiefly in the United States in the past twenty years. Their labor forces are highly motivated and often willing to work at low wages.

Increased foreign competition requires that domestic producers pay more attention to costs and technological improvements and, where the technology is volatile, more specialists and more market research techniques and activities are needed. Such competition also increasingly involves the government because the economic actions of large firms or industries may have a significant impact on national policy, imports and exports, foreign-exchange relationships, and currency reevaluations, all of which play a significant role in prices in the product or factor markets.

Foreign competition is taking a different form as well. No longer are goods produced outside the U.S. and shipped here. The tendency in recent times has been for foreign firms to expand operations by building plants and locating branches in the United States. Volkswagen, Honda, and several Japanese electronics firms have begun manufacturing operations in the United States. This is partially due to foreign exchange rates, which make it more profitable for these firms to build in the U.S. than on their own soil. It is also due to the concern by foreign manufacturers that a "protectionist" trade philosophy will develop and lead to stiff tariffs in the U.S. Having manufacturing facilities here will minimize this problem.

GROWTH OF THE MULTINATIONAL ORGANIZATION

In the past two decades, large firms all over the world have opened operations in other countries or have entered into joint ventures or licensing arrangements with firms in other countries. Virtually every large business enterprise in the United States has overseas operations at present. One major toolmaker, for example, has plants in England, Panama, Spain, Greece, France, Italy, Japan, Mexico, Germany, and Australia. In the past few years, Japanese firms have opened several plants in the United States as well as in other countries. A firm in Taiwan has formed relationships with dozens of firms from other countries. The large oil companies have their operations widely dispersed over the world.

There are many reasons for this expansion. Transportation costs for many products are simply too high to ship them long distances and still sell them at a competitive price. New foreign markets are not perhaps as saturated with certain products as domestic markets, making it possible to sell the product more readily at a higher price than in the domestic market.

Foreign operations obviously create much more environmental uncertainty than do domestic operations. Market forces as well as government actions must be predicted, and this may be difficult in countries without a stable political structure or mature economy. The growing trend toward the nationalization of foreign industries in some countries is also a threat.

Cultural differences and differences in needs and values of local employees suggest the need for different leadership and decision strategies. Some observers feel, for example, that the ability of middle managers or foremen in underdeveloped countries may be lower than that of the typical American manager. If true, this would necessitate more centralization in decision-making in such operations.

531

*Organizations
and Their
Goals:
Present
and Future*

SHIFTS IN PUBLIC POLICY

Governmental regulation will have a different cast in the future. Past public policy was aimed, it seems, at maintaining competition (restraining monopolistic tendencies) and regulating certain industries in which it was believed that competition would reduce the social benefits, such as airlines, transportation, and public utilities. In the future there will be three major areas that will receive a good deal of attention.

1. *Increased environmental regulation.* The 1980s should be a period when government policy and regulatory controls to protect the environment will increase. This means that firms can expect more pressure to reduce the negative effects of emissions, chemical waste, and dangerous substances. Many of these regulations are with us now, in the form of upper limits that must not be exceeded. Pollution controls are one example. The disposal of nuclear waste is another.

Some of the new government regulations will be very restrictive and have serious economic consequences, particularly in the short run. The limitation on dumping chemical wastes from steel production into rivers and streams has seriously affected the steel producing area of northeastern Ohio. Cities such as Youngstown and Akron are faced with plant closings because steel companies believe it less costly to relocate facilities in other areas rather than to renovate antiquated plants.

Some regulations, however, might be more advantageous than restrictive. Emission control pollutants discharged into the air have been a particular problem for firms using coal. In the past, EPA regulations were written so that they set rather tight emission controls for each smokestack. A recent ruling allows a state to consider the emissions for a plant as a whole unit when assessing environmental impacts. Under this rule, plants must control total emissions, rather than one type. They may be able to burn more coal and reduce dust, for instance.

2. *Tendency toward deregulation.* The experience of deregulating the airlines will be an impetus to further efforts to remove governmental restraints in some industries. The result of airline deregulation has been somewhat mixed. Bakersfield, California, and Ithaca, New York, are two cities that had a reduction in service when airlines became free to make some decisions about which routes would be served. However, there have been some very substantial reductions in certain classes of fares. Discount fares, though somewhat restrictive, have reduced the cost of air travel as much as 40 percent. This makes air service available to many more of those who wish to travel. The net balance so far seems to have been struck in favor of deregulation.

Similar deregulation has been suggested for the trucking industry, though at this time it has not come to pass. De facto deregulation will occur in some facets of the communication industry, especially television and radio. It is now possible for individuals to acquire antennae that will receive signals broadcast by commercial networks through satellites. Private, non-network affiliated television stations already sell their programming to cable TV services all over the country. WTBS, in Atlanta, is received by cable services in every part of the United States. Certainly such a technological change will have important effects on the management of major networks.

3. *Inflation-driven monetary and fiscal policy*. The high levels of inflation are likely to continue during the 1980s. Fiscal and monetary policy will be oriented toward bringing about some substantial reduction in inflation, though it will probably not be succcessful. The federal government will probably continue to hold interest rates high, hoping to curb consumer spending to some degree by restricting credit. High interest rates will also have a restraining effect on capital investment.

Fiscal policy will be continually difficult to manage. There may be a greater reluctance to support social welfare programs than in the "Great Society" days of the 1960s. Fiscal conservatism will become much more fashionable.

In the United States at the present time, Congress enacts 1,000 new laws a year.[4] Of course, not all involve regulation, but many do. In addition, federal regulatory agencies issue some 9,000 regulations and resolutions each year. The various states and municipalities also pass many regulations. Since such regulations can eliminate existing products, profits, or organizations themselves, it is necessary for business organizations to learn how to ***predict*** them. There are a number of different methods for doing this.[4]

One approach is to identify those countries that are pacesetters in government regulation. Countries such as Sweden and Germany typically adopt regulations of business before the United States. Within the United States, states such as California and New York are pacesetters in terms of regulations.

Another is to examine current public opinion on various issues since eventually legislation is passed to mirror that public opinion. In fact there tends to be a certain sequence for government regulations.[4] It seems to start with certain problems emerging as a result of disastrous events. The victims of the event complain. Their cause is taken up by champions and then by the intellectual segment of the nation. Publicity is given the issue by the mass media. This is often followed by new regulations. These regulations are appealed through the court system for several years, and, if vindicated, executive branch enforcement of the regulation may take place after several years of developing standards and investigative procedures.

Another current, and popular, approach for predicting various events of the future such as new laws and regulations is the Delphi Technique. This approach was first described in an article published by Helmer and Rescher in 1959.[5] This technique involves obtaining the forecasts of experts on a subject independently by questionnaire to avoid the stifling or suppression of ideas often found in committee deliberations. After each expert is polled independently, their responses are summarized and presented to all of them before the experts are asked to make further forecasts. This process may continue for several rounds. Some research has indicated that such forecasts are often superior to those obtained by other methods.[6]

TECHNOLOGICAL CHANGE

Technology has advanced extremely rapidly in recent years, and this trend can be expected to continue. To keep abreast of such advances, firms obviously need large numbers of highly specialized professionals with knowledge of such changes and their significance for marketing and production methods. Some industries, especially electronics and computers, seem in the state of constant change. These industries have been significantly affected by developments in microelectronics. Extremely small electronic devices such as calculators are now being made and sold. In the future very small computers will be available to people in their homes and for use in a variety of products. New electronic devices will make it possible to make significant savings in energy use. The office of the future will be much influenced by these developments. The typewriter of yesteryear will disappear.

Even traditional products can change significantly in size and performance. Power drills, for example, can be made small enough to fit into a worker's back pocket. The 1980s promise a revolution in communications. The use of satellites and cable television allow a person access to information and events almost anywhere in the world instantaneously. There is also a biological revolution occurring. Developments in the fields of genetics may make it possible to increase food production greatly and to eliminate some present diseases.

Of significance to the business firm is the time required for ideas to be converted to products. Figure 20.1 shows the relationship of basic research to the development, distribution, and eventual death of a product. Basic research, of course, is not carried out to produce specific new products, but typically produces new concepts, ideas, or modifications of existing models or theories. In the applied research stage, the new idea is tested in terms of its specific product application, and technological advantages are considered for the first time, while in the product development stage, the product is developed, evaluated, and subjected to cost analysis.

Research and development expenditures in the United States have steadily increased on an absolute basis every year and are significantly higher than in any other country in the world. However, research and development expenditures are

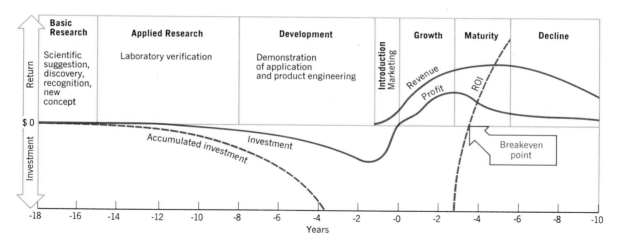

The product life cycle represents the history of a commodity or service from the time of its initial conception to its ultimate withdrawal from the market because of inadequate profit margin. There are four distinct phases of the life cycle after the initial introduction to the market: introduction, growth, maturity, and decline. Profit during these phases may be defined as the margin realized after both fixed and variable costs have been covered. The return on investment (ROI) does not begin until breakeven on the total accumulated investment is realized. The position of the breakeven point is determined by the effectiveness of management in controlling the investment prior to market introduction and in providing a correct pricing policy thereafter. (*Source:* McLoughlin, W. G. *Fundamentals of Research Management.* New York: American Management Association, 1970, p. 17.)

FIGURE 20.1   Product Life Cycle

not rising as fast as gross national product. In Europe and Japan, on the other hand, the percentage of national income devoted to research and development is rising, a development that has worried a number of analysts,[7,8] though it should be noted that Japan and European nations started at a very low base rate. U.S. firms often have access to technological developments from other countries, however, through joint ventures, licensing agreements, or imitation, and the reverse is also true.

Clearly, the fact that other nations are investing more heavily in research and development accelerates product change, making the technological environment of firms ever more volatile. Some of the nations that formerly imported technology, such as Japan, are now exporting it, particularly to the less developed nations.[9]

There is some disagreement among authorities over how long it takes a new concept or idea to be developed into a marketable product. Some say the period averages from fourteen to nineteen years,[10] but others believe that the time has shortened recently. Ayres believes both that the lead time has shortened and that new technological processes saturate an industry much more rapidly than was the case a few years ago.[11] Thus, today it is more important than ever for an industrial organization to be able to discern new technological and scientific developments quickly and to convert them to products or new technology.

The energy crisis will have an important effect on research and development. Instead of spending for new product and new technology development, which is critical for economic growth, it is likely that many of the development dollars will go to energy research. This will divert funds from growth-oriented R & D to energy development.

CHANGES IN DEMOGRAPHIC CHARACTERISTICS

The study of demography, or the science of populations, has never been a popular field in colleges and universites. Yet it is a very important subject. Many of the difficulties that societies periodically experience can be traced to demographic changes. Such demographic changes are often not particularly noticeable and, even if they are, their implications are often not appreciated. This is especially true when the changes in population characteristics are not in an orderly progression. Sudden and volatile shifts in population characteristics create the most turbulence.

An example of such a problem is the so-called baby boom of the years after World War II. By the mid-1950s there were over four million births a year.[12] This had been preceded by a very low birth rate in the 1930s before World War II. The "baby boom" fizzled out in the early 1960s and was followed by the "baby bust," or a declining birth rate.[13] In 1976 there were only about three million births. This huge surplus of individuals preceded and followed by a smaller number has created certain social problems for the United States. This is because social institutions have had to adjust to this large group.

It is difficult to cut back on the resources assembled to handle this large group. The society's attempts to handle the baby boom have been likened to a boa constrictor digesting a melon.[12] As the large group moves through various age levels, the number of school rooms and teachers rises dramatically, and then quickly falls. Empty schoolhouses are being sold by municipalities across the country and college enrollment is declining. The baby boom group is now competing for jobs, thereby

535
*Organizations
and Their
Goals:
Present
and Future*

creating some unemployment. This group later will expect the younger working population to support them with pensions in their years of retirement. After the year 2000, the proportion of producing workers will decline but will somehow have to pay the enormous retirement incomes of the larger older segment of the population at that time.

As the baby boom group moves through the various age categories, the sales of products needed by different age groups will change. Sales of diapers go down, and jeans go up. Then automobile and new home purchases increase, and finally, after 2000, the increased sales will affect pharmaceuticals and travel agencies.

Political attitudes also change as a large group moves through life, becoming more conservative with increasing age. The crime rates go down as the proportion of the population made up of younger people declines. Since a large proportion of the baby boom group have higher levels of education than in the past, the educational requirements of various jobs may increase. It may be necessary to have some college education to obtain a clerk's job. High school dropouts may have great difficulty in finding any jobs at all.

A management problem of some importance will be the difficulty of managing a very large workforce with a small group of senior managers born during the baby dearth in the 1930s.[12] This will have some serious effects on the managerial job and the age distribution of managers. Raising the mandatory retirement age may also be very functional for society for the next two decades, given these types of problems.

Of course as the large group moves through various age levels, there may then be a labor shortage facing organizations as the baby bust group enters the work force in the late 1980s. This may increase labor costs significantly at the time and may accelerate the shift to more machine-intensive technologies such as the use of robots on the assembly line.

Some predict another baby boom in the 1980s.[14] It has been projected that baby births in 1985 will be higher than in any previous year in history. The effects of this will be the same as for the baby boom of the postwar years. The trends for the various age groups in the future are shown in Table 20.1.

CHANGING COMPOSITION OF THE LABOR FORCE

The relative proportions of different occupational groups in the U.S. labor force has changed over the years, and this is perhaps not surprising in the light of both technological and social change. Presently, the number of professional and technical workers is increasing more rapidly than other categories. The number of service, clerical, and sales workers is also increasing more rapidly than such occupational groups as craftsmen, foremen, and factory workers. The average educational level of a United States employee is above twelve years of school, and white-collar workers now constitute 50 percent of the labor force. This, of course, has implications for the effectiveness of different management approaches.

A newer phenomenon is the working wife.[14] The female labor workforce is growing at least twice as fast as the growth in the female population. By 1985 more than half of all married women will be in the labor force. Part of the reason for this is economic, with such working wives providing about 30 percent of total family income. However, a large proportion of women enter the labor force for the psy-

TABLE 20.1   Trends in age groups in the 1980s

Age Category	Projected Trends
0–4	Although they have been contracting since 1960, between 1980 and 1985 *they will grow almost four times as fast* as the average for the whole population.
5–15	They realized great growth during and since the 1950s and were one-fourth of the population in 1970. *They will decline relatively* and account for less than 20 percent of the population in 1985.
18–24	They are currently expanding and represent the age category of first marriage and first child for many Americans. *They will decline relatively* during the 1980s.
25–34	They young marrieds *will continue to realize the greatest growth rate of all groups* through 1980. They are expected to grow by 46 percent over the decade of the 1970s.
35–44	The early middle-agers have high income, high home ownership, and teenagers at home. *They will expand at a rate of four times that of the general population* from 1980 to 1985.
45–54	The middle-age group is the one which enjoys the highest income and rate of savings. *It has been contracting* since 1970 and will continue to do so during the 1980s but will expand greatly in the 1990s.
55–64	The late middle-agers and younger senior citizens have high savings and buying power. They are empty nesters and *will grow at about the same rate as the general population* during the 1980s.
65 and over	The senior citizens present a growth market. Their incomes are lower than those of other adult population segments. The growth rate through 1985 is expected to *be twice that of the population rate,* and the proportion of women in this category is increasing.

Source: Lazer, W. "The 1980s and beyond: A perspective," *MSU Business Topics*, 25 (1977): 21–35.

chological rewards that such work can provide them. The increase in working wives has obviously created changes in family living patterns that influence not only consumption habits but also may create different work and social values among the population.

INCREASED EMPLOYMENT OF THE DISADVANTAGED WORKER

Pressures have increased upon every organization to employ more disadvantaged workers. In considering this question, we should examine the socialization that has affected the attitudes and positions of persons who are disadvantaged in the U.S. labor force. Usually, the disadvantaged are defined as those ethnic, racial, or other groups who historically have not enjoyed the same educational and social opportunities as other Americans. Because of this long history of reduced participation in U.S. society, the disadvantaged often have low levels of self-esteem.[15] Such persons tend to have a short-run perspective and do not expect future benefits to result from what they are currently doing.[16] As personal frustrations increase, they become less optimistic and less motivated to find a job or to exert effort on a job.[17] Lack of success at work contributes further to reduced self-esteem and a feeling of irrelevance.[18]

Money may not be an effective incentive for such groups because their paychecks often are spoken for in advance by creditors, relatives, or friends. They are often expected to share whatever they have with those close to them and thus cannot fully utilize the fruits of their own labor.[19]

The disadvantaged groups in the 1980s will not be exactly the same as those in the 1970s. Immigration into the U.S. has increased since 1968 and, to the extent that those who enter the United States are not highly skilled and easily absorbed into the mainstream of economic life, problems will exist for them. We should *not* expect, though, the employment problems of blacks, hispanics, American Indians, and others to disappear in the 1980s. Many of the problems today, for example, high unemployment of teenagers and underemployment, will continue in the 1980s.

The employment of disadvantaged workers unquestionably constitutes a contribution to the community and an appropriate exercise of corporate responsibility. It calls for a number of adjustments. Perhaps special confidence-building programs and greater job security might work, since they would address themselves to some of the primary problems involved. Special training programs have been launched in a number of companies,[20] and some positive results have been obtained when the proper "supportive" climate has been established.[21]

Special training is needed, not only for the disadvantaged employees themselves, but for the personnel who will carry out programs for the disadvantaged, since those people seem most resistant to changing company procedures or policies in order to meet the special needs of the disadvantaged.[22] Also, such training is needed because supervisory supportiveness and personal counseling along with peer supportiveness have been found to improve the likelihood that such individuals will adjust successfully to the organization. To keep the hard-core unemployed working, emphasis must be placed on organizational factors such as pay, job security, and promotional opportunities.[23]

INCREASED EMPLOYMENT OF MINORITY GROUP MEMBERS IN HIGHER-LEVEL MANAGEMENT POSITIONS

There is evidence of discrimination against blacks and other minorities and women in compensation and promotion.[24,25,26,27,28] Government and private groups in the past have placed substantial pressures on organizations to eliminate such discriminatory practices. Initially, conciliation procedures were used, but these have not been effective, and more stringent procedures are now used.[29]

The number of blacks and women in management and professional positions has slowly increased, but there is still resistance to their employment in such positions. Part of the bias lies in sexual and racial stereotypes, which result in negative evaluations by incumbent managers.[30] It does not appear that such stereotypes are disappearing quickly.[31] Some research shows that even female managers are likely to favor males over females in promotion, selection, and placement decisions.[32] There is also evidence that blacks and females have difficulties not experienced by white males in performing their roles.[33,34,35]

There is evidence of a change in perspective, however. In one study of the factors preferred in job applicants, it was found that persons making selection decisions tended to choose those who had qualifications that closely matched job requirements. Male applicants were *not* preferred over female applicants.[36] Another study found little evidence for bias against female scientists. When salaries of women and men with similar training and similar work records were compared, there were no meaningful differences.[37] Those are hopeful signs since the number of women in the workforce is increasing, as is the number of women in professions such as teaching, law, and medicine.

There is no empirical justification for such general discrimination at work. Research has shown that there is a great deal of overlap among the white male group and female, black, and other minorities on various abilities, and there are no differences in personality factors, values, and job satisfactions between white males and minority group members that cannot be accounted for by variations in social situations.[38] The evidence continues to mount that the same behaviors found to be related to success for white males are also related to managerial success for minority group members.[39,40] There also appears to be no differences in the job satisfaction and performances of groups supervised by blacks and women as compared to the job satisfaction and performance of groups supervised by white males.[41] This seems to be true even when the members of such groups are of a different race or sex than their supervisor.[41]

There are some average differences in values and motives of males and females, but these differences may simply reflect tendencies for men and women to fulfill various sex roles imposed by the culture.[38] It is also possible that organizations are forcing women managers to adopt the male role stereotype.[32] Perhaps, as we discussed in Chapter 5, individuals are often forced to adapt to the organization's value system.

CHANGING SOCIETAL VALUES

There is growing evidence that the younger age groups in society have different values than similar groups in the past, particularly those values that are unrelated to the world of work. As compared to previous generations, today's high school students put less emphasis on security and promotions and more on autonomy and interesting work. They are also less accepting of authority today than in the past.[42] The same seems to be true of older individuals.

Some experts believe that there is a trend toward humanistic values and away from materialistic values among the general public.[43] These humanistic values are manifested in increasing public favor for the rights of others to be different, and for the government assuming various social responsibilities.

There also appears to be some antitechnology sentiment present in the nation. Opinions differ on the permanence of this trend. One view says that technology and science will continue to advance and that reactions against their products (nuclear plants, genetic engineering, etc.) mark a normal process of social adjustment to significant and rapid technological change.[44] This view indicates that such resistance has been common at various times in the past but has always passed. The other view indicates that individuals have in fact changed their values signficantly toward more individual growth and the pursuit of leisure.[44] Heilbroner expresses this pro-spiritualistic and anti-materialistic position:[45]

> For surely the business system has lived up to or exceeded the fondest hopes of its protagonists with respect to its productive virtuosity. What prodigies of material achievment the contemporary American enjoys as he drives over plains where his forebears trekked! What miracles of engineering does he not command to wash his clothes and his dishes, clean his teeth, shine his shoes, tell the time to the nearest tenth of a second, detect his incipient cancers, converse with friends in distant cities! Is he not only healthier and longer-lived than his forefathers, but better informed, better entertained—in a word, ''better off' in nearly every measurable dimension?
>
> But does not this recital reveal what has not been gained as well as what has been gained? Is the contemporary American a better as well as a richer citizen than his antecedents? Is he more at peace with his children, his parents, himself? Is he wiser as well as more informed; happier as well as more pampered; sturdier and more self-reliant as well as better fed, housed, clothed, transported? To ask these questions, rhetorical though they be, is, I think, to express a hollowness at the center of a business civilization—a hollowness from which the pursuit of material goods diverts our attention for a time, but that in the end insistently asserts itself.

Business executives themselves predict a shift in national ideology in the United States by 1985.[46] Among 1,800 executives surveyed, there was a preference for the traditional U.S. emphasis on individual rights and responsibility. The vast majority, however, predicted a new dominant ideology by 1985 that will stress rights stemming from the group and the use of property according to the goals of the community. If these studies reflect a coming permanent shift in values, contemporary management strategies must change. This is because such a value shift will be reflected in public policy in the economic sphere as well as the social. Societal values influence the political system, which in turn attempts to bend the economic sphere to its objectives.

CHANGES IN ECONOMIC FACTORS

As is typically the case, there is a difference in opinion as to what is in store for the world in the next several decades. There are optimists and pessimists. Some feel that the standard of living of the United States will be lower in the future because of slow economic growth and because of high inflation. They feel that this will happen with an increase in the low productivity service sectors of the economy and the decline in the high-growth manufacturing sectors. Heilbroner even sees the demise of our present capitalistic system after perhaps another fifty years. He feels that the present capitalistic system will decline as national economic planning increases in response to inflation and continuing economic downturns.[45]

Some take exception to Heilbroner's predictions. They feel that the present economic system in the Western nations will not change appreciably over the next several decades.[44] There are many other fairly optimistic forecasts with respect to the likely future state of the U.S. economy. They feel that the high inflation and low productivity of the early 1980s is perhaps an aberration rather than a harbinger of the future. They feel we are still making progress. As Lazer points out:[14]

> . . . Even with higher inflation rates, there has been a substantial increase in the real incomes of American families, and, on the average, they are much more affluent than in the 1960s. . . . Over the next decade this trend will continue. We are, in fact, fast becoming a nation of upper-middle-income families.

Similarly, the Edison Electric Institute brought together more than twenty nationally known consultants to study the future of economic growth in the United States.[44] The final report represented over eighteen months of research and analysis. They predict different rates of growth depending on the economic policies adopted by the government. They concluded that there is a trade-off between economic growth and environmental needs. Assuming that a moderate growth rate is chosen, rather than a high rate, so that environmental needs can be met, the average growth rate of gross national product in real terms should average a little over 3.5 percent a year for the next twenty-five years. They point out that even under policies designed to curtail growth, the average increase in gross national product would be 2.3 percent over the next twenty-five years.

The authors of the report see shortages of capital, rather than shortages of energy or raw materials, as the primary constraint to economic growth in the next twenty-five years. Others are not so sanguine about future raw material availability, pointing out that by the year 2000 the United States will have to import more than 90 percent of seven basic minerals needed in the economy.[47]

Although many are optimistic about the long-run future of the U.S. economy, some are more pessimistic when discussing the economic situation in other parts of the world. Most see little improvement in the gap between the national incomes of the developed and the developing nations. According to some figures, 80 percent of the world's population now creates only 15 percent of the world's annual product.[47] Given present trends, by the turn of the century 85 percent of the world's population will generate about 12 percent of the world's annual product.

Part of the cause of the economic difficulties of the poorer countries can be attributed to their population problems. The birth rate of the developing countries is much higher than in the developed countries. The world's population in 1960 was three billion people. It is projected to be more than six billion by the year 2000. Some feel that it will be impossible to feed this many people, as Figure 20.2 indicates.[47]

Two reports from the Club of Rome have attracted a great deal of attention all over the world. The first report, called *The Limits of Growth,* was published in 1972 and predicted the collapse of the world around the year 2000.[48] This collapse would be caused by the exhaustion of the resources of the world, coupled with an increase in population that cannot be fed. The report was based on a computer simulation of the world as it responds to population, food production, industrial production, nonrenewable resources, and pollution. The first report indicated that to avoid economic collapse, future population or economic growth should be curtailed.

The first report was followed by a second report, *Mankind at the Turning Point,* written by different authors.[49] This second report indicated that the very underdeveloped nations would suffer a profound crisis in the future and the developed

541
*Organizations
and Their
Goals:
Present
and Future*

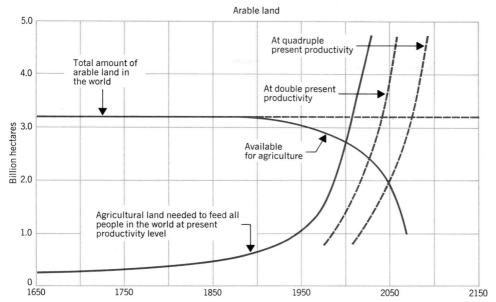

FIGURE 20.2   Historical patterns of changes in land use. (*Source:* Meadows, Donella H., et al., *The Limits of Growth*. New York: Universe Books, 1972.)

nations would suffer severe economic crises due to insufficient resources in the future. An actual collapse of the world, however, was not predicted.

It does appear from all these reports on the economic future that many very serious problems face the world in the next few decades. An expanding world population and a decreasing supply of critical nonrenewable resources seem to be the most important causes of these future difficulties. A decline in the economic growth rate in the developed nations and a decrease in the population rate in the developing nations would appear to be necessary to avoid serious future economic crises. Good management, in the sense of achieving more with much fewer resources, appears to be absolutely mandatory in the future. Capital will have to be allocated very cautiously. Finding enough jobs for all may be a problem after a future baby boom.

CHANGING IDEAS ABOUT SOCIAL RESPONSIBILITY

In recent years the term ***social responsibility*** has been defined in many different ways and used in research studies to cover many types of behaviors.[50] To study the relationship of the degree of social responsibility of business organizations to performance, some researchers have simply accepted Moskowitz's list of companies that were unusually high or unusually low in corporate social responsibility.[51] Companies rated high on social responsibility were compared to companies rated low on this dimension with ambiguous results.[52]

Other studies seem to show that a moderate, rather than a high or low, score on the social responsibility factor is related to higher organizational performance,

TABLE 20.2 Performance scores as a function of social
responsibility category

	Social Responsibility Level		
	Low	Medium	High
Sturdivant & Ginter	0.69[a]	1.26	1.18
Bragdon & Marlin	9.6[b]	11.9	10.3
Bowman & Haire	10.2[b]	16.1	12.3

Source: From Aldag, R.J., and Bartol, K.M. "Empirical studies of
corporate social performance and policy: A survey of problems and
results," in Preston, L., (ed.), *Research in corporate social performance and policy,* 1 (1978): 165–200.

[a]Average economic performance, in terms of growth in earnings per
share, relative to industry.
[b]Median percent return on equity.

as indicated in Table 20.2. In these studies the measures of social responsibility
focused on such things as pollution control, attitudes toward minorities, perceptions
of the poor, and the amount of attention given to social responsibility in the annual
report.[52]

Why might moderate scores on the social responsibility measure rather than
more extreme scores be related to economic performance? A moderate score may
reflect a management that is appropriately balanced between economic pressures
and social pressures on the organization.[52] A moderate position on such issues may
also result in the most consensus among the managers in the organization. Previous
work on organizational effectiveness indicates that management goal consensus is
related to an organization's success.[53]

SUMMARY

In this chapter we have outlined briefly some of the major conditions that will affect
organizational structure and management systems in the future. Other factors—the
effects of pollution, for example—are perhaps too evident from the information we
receive daily to warrant discussion here, but the discerning reader will see their
relevance to our theme.

The various environmental changes taking place today will have consequences
that can hardly be predicted with accuracy but that can be analyzed to some degree
in the light of the contingency framework set forth in this book. Clearly, certain of
the changes will contribute to increased stability of certain types of organizations;
for example, increases in sheer size may in many cases result in increasingly stable
organizations, and whether this will be an advantage or a disadvantage, in view of
changing social values, is something that remains to be seen. Certainly, managers
will find it necessary continually to reassess the relationship of their organization
structures and its goals to the values of the various publics, internal and external,
with which it interacts. One assumption might be that increasing environmental
pressures of the kind outlined in this chapter will result overall in substantially
greater differentiation among organizational subunits with respect to structure, personnel, and the way the managerial process is carried out.

543
*Organizations
and Their
Goals:
Present
and Future*

The applied behavioral sciences will become increasingly important in management, since human resource problems in organizations will be more complex. The tremendous increase in the literature of applied behavioral science and a similar increase in management training and consulting programs are also indicative of this trend. The trends will continue, and knowledge in the behavioral area, as well as other areas of management, can be expected to increase as greater resources are committed to its development. This will mean that certain portions of this book—and others like it—will quickly become dated. Advances in management techniques will be required to sustain and increase managerial effectiveness. For these reasons, we expect to meet many of our readers again.

The Female Professor

A few years ago, Alan House, Chairman of the Department of Economics of Mid-Atlantic University recruited Dr. Barbara Washington as assistant professor. Professor Washington was, and still is, the only female member of the department. Dr. House was very pleased. He had long sought a qualified female faculty member. He believed that women students in economics courses should have an appropriate role model with whom to identify.

In the next several years Dr. Washington was asked to serve on countless university, college, and department committees. She was a member of the Academic Senate, the governing body of the university. She was frequently asked to speak on women's issues. Many female students on campus sought her out as an advisor.

Dr. Washington soon began to think of her sex as a real disadvantage. Afraid to be labeled as uncooperative, she continued her extensive university service.

Dr. Washington was approaching the time when she had to be considered by the tenure and promotion committee for the rank of associate professor. Such a promotion automatically carried tenure at the university. Professor House, in examining Dr. Washington's record over the past few years, saw immediately that it contained fewer articles, papers, and other research activities than the standards the committee had held when considering promotions. Dr. House was concerned that Dr. Washington would not be granted tenure. Dr. House wondered what he should do about the situation.

1. What problems in minority hiring does this case illustrate?
2. What should be done in this case? Why?
3. What are the implications of this problem for managers, whether in universities, industry, or government?

Deer Bows, Incorporated

In the mid-1940s John Philbrick returned to his home in northern Wisconsin from service in the Marine Corps during World War II. John lived in a small town, population 2,000, in the lake area and loved the woods and the water that were close by. He spent his leisure time in the woods, and became particularly good at using a bow and arrow for hunting. He gained a reputation as a huntsman and soon began to serve as a guide for downstate hunters who came to the area. He interested many of them in bow hunting and eventually specialized in guiding only bow hunters during the season.

As time passed, John began to make bows when he was not working as a guide and sold them to hunters. Eventually, he was spending all his time making bows and had little time to hunt.

Ernest Murphy, a local banker who was a hunting enthusiast, thought that John should begin to manufacture bows and arrows in larger quantities. He agreed to finance John in starting Deer Bows, Incorporated.

John began slowly, but by the late 1950s he had 200 employees working in the company. John's reputation spread nationwide, and soon Deer Bows became the preferred equipment for serious bow hunters. Sales grew and finally stabilized at around $7,000,000, and John felt very successful.

An important factor to John was the relationship that Deer Bows had with the community. Deer Bows was by far the largest employer in the whole area, which had very little industry and relied on tourism for its economic well-being.

During the mid-1960s and into the early 1970s, Deer Bows experienced another rapid increase in sales. This was due to the increased interest in outdoor sports and because of more active use of leisure time. By 1973 Deer's sales were around $15,000,000, and there were 300 employees working in the plant.

In 1974 John was approached by a large sporting goods manufacturer, Balata Balls, and was offered a very high price for the company. He wasn't interested in selling it, but he was growing older and felt that it was time for him to begin phasing out of the business. He accepted the offer, though he agreed to remain as chairman of the board.

Balata brought in their own top management team, but they retained all the old employees. Everything seemed to be going well until 1976. It was at that time that Deer Bows experienced its first labor problems. The workforce, unionized by the BOW, went on strike. The strike was long and bitter. John felt betrayed by his employees—and the community—that he thought he had served as well as they had served him.

The effect of the wage increase that the BOW won was startling. Hourly wage rates were very high and profits were down. It was then that Bob Foley, the president, began seriously to consider relocating the plant.

Balata and Deer retained a site location consultant to investigate places that might provide a more hospitable climate for the plant. The location study took eighteen months.

In July 1978 the consulting firm recommended three sites for the location of Deer Bows: (1) Valdosta, Georgia, (2) Tallahassee, Florida, and (3) Fernandina, South Carolina. All these locations had, according to the consultants,

1. Relatively low taxes
2. A very abundant labor force
3. Negative attitudes toward unions
4. Warm climate
5. A good rapport with business
6. Wage rates 30 percent under those Deer was currently paying

The management team of Deer Bows visited each one of these cities. They spent two weeks in each, looking at factors such as living conditions, schools, and other community factors.

Eventually the word had leaked out back in Wisconsin that Deer might move. The townspeople were concerned. City, county, and state politicians began making overtures to Deer about ways to provide the company with an incentive not to move. Citizen groups were organized, resolutions passed in the legislature, and the governor even called Bob Foley.

By then, Foley, Philbrick, and the rest of the executive group had decided to move to Florida. In 1980 the plant was in operation at a site just outside Tallahassee, Florida. The Tallahassee Chamber of Commerce was ecstatic. There were 350 new jobs, a new industry, and "some just plain nice people who came to town."

1. What are the long-run effects of such a move on Tallahassee? The small Wisconsin town? Deer Bows?
2. Is this case illustrative of a trend to move industry to the "sun belt"? What does such a trend mean for the northeastern and midwestern U.S.? For the southern states?
3. Are there ethical implications for Deer? The BOW union? For the states that lured Deer away?

DISCUSSION QUESTIONS

1. Why do we expect organizations to grow considerably in the future?
2. How does the growth of foreign industry affect U.S. corporations?
3. How might multinational organizations benefit the world population?
4. How might government policy change in the future regarding industry?
5. Explain how monetary and fiscal policy can affect both U.S. and foreign industry?
6. What significance does rapid technological change have on our future industries?
7. How do you think the labor force will be affected in the future? More employment? More unemployment?
8. What are the effects of changing demographic characteristics of the workforce?

REFERENCES

1. Bennis, W. G. "Toward a truly scientific management: The concept of organizational health," in J. Ghorpade (ed.), Assessment of organizational effectiveness: Issues, analysis, readings. Santa Monica, Calif., Goodyear Publishing, 1971
2. Burek, C. G. "The intricate 'politics' of the corporation," Fortune, 91 (1975): 109–112.
3. Rowan, R. "Better made in Japan" Washington Post (April 24, 1980): p. 19
4. Molitor, G. T. T. Issues Management, a meeting of the National Association of Manufacturers, National Public Affairs Conference of National Association of Manufacturers, January 1980.
5. Helmer, O., and N. Rescher "On the epistemology of the inexact sciences," Management Science, 6 (1959): 25–52.
6. Campbell, R. M. A methodological study of the utilization of experts in business forecasting. Ph.D. Dissertation, University of California, Los Angeles, 1966.

7. Dean, R. C., Jr. "Why is U.S. technological prominence withering?" in Twenty-Seventh National Conference on the Administration of Research. Denver Research Institute: University of Denver, September 1973.

8. Boretsky, M. "U.S. technology—trend and policy issues," in Twenty-Seventh National Conference on the Administration of Research. Denver Research Institute: University of Denver, September 1973.

9. Ozawa, I. "Transfer of technology from Japan to developing countries." Unitar Research Report No. 7. United Nations Institute for Training and Research, 1973.

10. McLoughlin, W. G. Fundamentals of research management. New York, American Management Association, 1970.

11. Ayres, R. U., Technological forecasting and long-range planning. New York, McGraw-Hill, 1969.

12. "Americans Change," Business Week (February 20, 1978): 84–90.

13. "Labor's big swing from surplus to shortage," Business Week (February 20, 1978): 75–77.

14. Lazer, W. "The 1980s and beyond: A perspective. MSU Business Topics, 25 (1977): 21–35.

15. Ausubel, D. P., and P. Ausubel. "Ego development among segregated Negro children," in A. Ferman, J. L. Kornbluh and J. A. Miller (eds), Negros and jobs. Ann Arbor, Mich., University of Michigan Press, 1969.

16. Coleman, J. S. Equality of educational opportunity. U.S. Department of Health Education and Welfare; Office of Education; and U.S. Government Printing Office, Washington, D.C., 1966.

17. Means, J. E. "Fair employment practices legislation and enforcement in the United States," International Labor Review, 93 (1966): 211–247.

18. Liebow, E. Talley's corner; A study of streetcorner men. Boston, Little, Brown, 1967.

19. Davis, A. "The motivation of the underprivileged worker," in W. S. Whyte, (ed.), Industry and society. New York, McGraw-Hill, 1964.

20. Doeringer, P. B., Programs to employ the disadvantaged. Englewood Cliffs, N.J., Prentice-Hall, 1969.

21. Friedlander, F., and S. Greenberg. "Work climate as related to the performance and retention of hardcore unemployed workers, Proceedings of the 77th Annual Convention, American Psychological Association, 1969.

22. Goeke, J. R., and C. S. Weymar. "Barriers to hiring the blacks," Harvard Business Review, 47 (1969): 144–152.

23. Goodman, P. S., and D. Salipante. "Organizational rewards and retention of the hard-core unemployed." Journal of Applied Psychology, 61 (1976): 12–21.

24. Garfinkle, S. "Occupations of women and black workers, 1962–74," Monthly Labor Review, 98 (1975): 25–35.

25. Hauser, R., and D. Featherman. "White-nonwhite differentials in occupational mobility among men in the United States, 1962–1972." Demography, 25 (1974): 247–266.

26. Commerce Clearing House. Employment practices guide. Washington, D.C., 1972.

27. Cates, J. N. "Sex and salary," American Psychologist, 28 (1973): 929.

28. Equal Employment Opportunity Commission, Promise vs. performance. An Equal Employment Opportunity Commission report, Washington, D.C., 1972.

29. Adams, A. V. "Toward fair employment and the EEPC: A study of compliance procedures under Title VII of the Civil Rights Act of 1964. EEOC Contract 70-15," Equal Employment Opportunity Commission. Washington, D.C., 1972.

30. Rosen, B., and T. H. Jerdee. "Sex stereotyping in executive suite," Harvard Business Review, 52 (1974): 133–142.

31. Haefner, J. E. "Sources of discrimination among employees: A survey investigation," Journal of Applied Psychology, 62 (1977): 265–270.

547

*Organizations
and Their
Goals:
Present
and Future*

32. Schein, V. E. "Relationships between sex role stereotypes and requisite management characteristics among female managers," Journal of Applied Psychology, 60 (1975): 340.

33. Jones, E. W. "What it's like to be a black manager," Harvard Business Review, 51 (1973): 108–116.

34. Kanter, R. Men and women of the corporation. Englewood Cliffs, N.J., Prentice-Hall, 1978.

35. Hennig, M. and A. Jardim. The managerial women. New York, Doubleday, 1977.

36. Renwick, P., and H. Tosi. "The effects of sex, marital status and educational background on selection decisions." Academy of Management Journal, 12 (1978): 92–103.

37. Ferber, M. A., and H. M. Lowry. "The sex differential in earnings: A reappraisal," Industrial and Labor Relations Review, 29 (1976): 377–387.

38. Tyler, L. Individual differences: abilities and motivational directions. Englewood Cliffs, N.J., Prentice-Hall, 1974.

39. Huck, J. R., and D. W. Bray. "Management assessment center evaluations and subsequent job performance of white and black females," Personnel Psychology, 29 (1976): 13–30.

40. Miner, J. B. Theories of organizational behavior. New York, The Dryden Press, 1980.

41. Bartol, K. M., C. L. Evans, and M. T. Stith. "Black versus white leaders: A comparative review of the literature," Academy of Management Review, 3 (1978): 293–304.

42. Bachman, J. G., and L. D. Johnson. "The Freshmen, 1979," Psychology Today, 13 (September 1979): 79–87.

43. Bell, D. Work and its discontents. New York, League for Industrial Democracy, 1970.

44. Edison Electric Institute. Economic growth in the future. New York, McGraw-Hill, 1976.

45. Heilbroner, R. L. Business civilization in decline. New York, W. W. Norton & Co., 1976.

46. Martin, W. F., and G. C. Lodge. "Our society in 1985—Business may not like it," Harvard Business Review, 53 (1975): 143–150.

47. Gordon, T. J. "A view of the world in 2000," In W. H. Newman (ed.), Managers for the year 2000. Englewood Cliffs, N.J., Prentice-Hall, 1978.

48. Meadows, D., J. Randers, and W. Behsey. The limits of growth. New York, Signet, 1972.

49. Meservoic, M., and E. D. Pestel. Mankind at the turning point. New York, E. P. Dutton, 1974.

50. Aldag, R. J., and K. M. Bartol. "Empirical studies of corporate social performance and policy: A survey of problems and results," in L. Preston (ed.), Research in corporate social performance and policy, 1 (1978): 165–200.

51. Moskowitz, M. "Profiles in corporate responsibility," Business and Society Review, 13 (1975): 28–42.

52. Aldag, R. J., and K. M. Bartol. "Empirical studies of corporate social performance and policy: A survey of problems and results," in L. Preston (ed.), Research in corporate social performance and policy, 1 (1978), 165–200.

53. Child, J. "Organizational design and performance: Contingency theory and beyond," Organization and Administrative Sciences, 1 (1977), 169–183.

GLOSSARY

A

Acceptance When referring to a characteristic of an objective, acceptance is the degree to which a person who is expected to carry out the plan will be willing to put forth the necessary efforts to do so. (See Q/A objectives, A/Q objectives, and A = Q objectives.)

Accountability Accountability is reporting to another person, usually a superior, about how well one has met his or her work responsibilities.

Action plans Action plans spell out the means, or ways, to reach goals or objectives. The action plan should summarize what is to be done. For complex activities an action plan should be broken down into subprograms that rep-

resent the best alternative that would achieve the goal.

Activity In PERT, an activity is some relatively discrete part of the work on a project. Each activity starts and stops with some identifiable event. (See Event, PERT.)

Additivity An assumption in linear programming. Additivity means that the total amounts of each input and associated profit are the sums of the inputs and profits for each individual process. (See Divisibility, Linear programming.)

Administration Administration means the use of prerogatives, techniques, and rights associated with one's position in an organization, such as making decisions and giving directions in order to get others to work toward organization objectives. Administrative

tools are organizational factors such as budgets, procedures, compensation systems, plans, and other control mechanisms. When such factors are used to obtain compliance, compliance is obtained through administration. (See Leadership.)

Administrative man In decision theory, a view of individuals that suggests that a person has limited knowledge of alternatives and consequences, and he or she makes guesses about the likelihood of certain events occurring in the future. (See also Bounded rationality, Satisficing.)

Administrative skill Administrative skill is the ability to make decisions and conceptualize relationships in an organization directed toward overall goal achievement, rather then toward maximizing return to some specific subunit.

Administrative theory   An approach to studying management that focuses on analyzing the basic tasks of managers. Administrative theorists differ from scientific management advocates primarily in the fact that they look at the work of managers, while scientific management looks at the work of operative employees.

A/Q objectives   A type of objective in which acceptance requirements by the subordinate are more important than the quality requirements. (See Q/A objectives, Acceptance, and A = Q objectives.)

A = Q objectives   A type of objective in which the acceptance requirements by the subordinates are of equal importance as the quality requirements. (See Q/A objectives, Acceptance, and A/Q objectives.)

Attitude   An attitude is an individual's feelings and beliefs about other persons, objects, events, and activities. Attitudes can be positive or negative and reflect some preference, like, or dislike toward the object.

Attitude change goals (development)   Development goals are aimed at changing attitudes. They may be targeted at either individuals or groups.

Authority   Authority is the right of decision and command over others and resources. This right always includes physical facilities, such as plant equipment and tools. When a person has managerial responsibility, it is necessary that the right cover decisions about others, the exercise of some command over subordinates, and the way the subordinates use resources.

Authority, formal   Formal authority is a right of decision and command a person derives from the position held. These decision rights are delegated from higher organization levels. It is the amount of designated discretion that an individual has in determining who gets what and how resources are used.

Authority structure   Different positions in organizations may have different degrees of authority and responsibility. The authority structure refers to how authority is distributed in an organization and how the positions are related to each other with respect to authority.

Automation   Automation is the substitution of machine energy for human energy. A tool is automated when the force that drives it comes from some source other than a person.

Autonomy   In reference to work, autonomy is the degree of individual freedom that a person has in making job choices. In jobs with high autonomy, the person controls the work. In jobs with low autonomy, the work system or supervisors control the individual.

B

Behavioral approach   This approach to management is concerned with attempts to understand how human psychological processes, such as motivation and attitude, interact with work activities to affect performance in organizations.

Boundary-spanning subsystems   These organization subsystems carry on transactions with individuals or organizations in the external environment, procuring inputs, disposing of outputs, or

assisting in these functions. The basic activity itself is performed within the organization. These activities connect the organization with outside units.

Bounded rationality   Bounded rationality refers to an individual's limitation in decision making. One's capacity for solving complex problems is limited to the alternatives of which he or she is aware. In addition, the manager makes decisions on the basis of perceptions of the situation, and this may or may not be what the situation actually is. Bounded rationality refers to the fact that the ability to make a rational decision (selection of the best alternative) is limited by the number of alternatives known by a person. (See satisficing.)

Brainstorming   This is a technique for generating alternatives to problems in which individuals gather in a group setting and generate as many ideas as possible without criticizing anybody else's ideas.

Breakeven analysis   Breakeven analysis shows the relationship between fixed costs, variable costs, and sales volume so that it is possible to determine a breakeven point. The breakeven point is that point where sales and costs are equal. A profit occurs when sales are above the breakeven point. Losses occur below the breakeven point.

Budgets   Budgets are projected levels of activities, revenues, and expenditures that are targets or goals that, if achieved, will result in the desired level of organizational performance and profitability.

Budgeted income statement   This projected statement shows future gross income from sales, minus the cost of goods sold, labor charges, depreciation, and other expenses. It shows what the estimated income will be for each budget period.

Budgeted balance sheet This shows the projected impact of operations on the assets and liabilities of a firm for the planning period.

Buffering Buffering is protecting the internal operations of the production subsystem by sealing them off from external forces. This can be done by creating some sort of ''buffer,'' such as having an inventory of raw materials to permit steady production despite variability in the flow of input of raw materials. (See Smoothing.)

C

Capability, production Production capability refers to whether the firm has, or has access to, the appropriate technical and human resources, with the skill to produce current or planned products.

Capacity, production Capacity refers to the availability of production resources that can be used for manufacturing the product or delivering the service.

Capital budgeting Capital budgeting is a process of assessing the value of future expenditures and/or returns for several alternatives to determine which is the most desirable in the long run. (See Net present value.)

Career adjustment The balance that exists between the different facets of a person's life structure, that is, work, family, peers, and other loved ones. (See Life structure.)

Career progression planning A job rotation system in which a sequence of moves is planned as the individual moves up the hierarchy of the organization. For example, a person may have an initial job in manufacturing, then he or she may move to a higher level position in another department, say, personnel, after which a move may be made to another unit, say, marketing.

Career socialization The influence on values, beliefs and attitudes that occurs during the educational experience of individuals who choose occupations for which specialized training is required is career socialization. (See Socialization.)

Cascading of objectives The cascading process is one that transmits strategic goals set at the highest organization levels, through each level, to the lowest operative level. In doing so, these goals become a more specific work assignment.

Cash budgets Cash budgets show the timing of cash in and out of an organization. Such a budget helps a manager estimate whether or not there will be excess cash or shortages during a particular operating period.

Centralization (decentralization) This term refers to the way that authority is distributed among positions in an organization. The more decisions are made at higher levels of the organization, the greater the centralization of decision making. When decisions (authority) are dispersed throughout the lower organizational levels, the decision making is said to be decentralized.

Charisma A term used to denote the influence of a particular kind of leader. Charismatic leaders exert referent power and command the loyalty and commitments of their followers, not because they have a particular skill or a position, but because their followers respond to them as individuals. (See Power, referent.)

Changing Changing in the development process is the act of altering the state of the target of development. Changing involves two steps: unfreezing and changing. (See Unfreezing, Development process.)

Climate, work Work climate is the ambience that exists within the work group. It is the degree of trust that subordinates have in the leader, the level of group cohesiveness, the general satisfactoriness of the leader in group relationships, and the congruence between individual and organizational needs and values.

Clinical skills Clinical skills refer to an individual's ability to evaluate problem situations in which the data about the problem are not easily organized or categorized. The data about the problem are not easily quantified and subject to formula. Subjective individual evaluation is an important facet of clinical skill.

Cluster chain A form of grapevine pattern in which information is passed from one person to several others, but then the information flow continues only from one of these individuals to others. (See Grapevine, Liaison individuals.)

Cohesiveness Cohesiveness refers to the hold a group has on its members. It is the ability of the group to maintain itself, or to continue to exist, when it is subject to pressures or stress.

Committees These are contrived

groups that generally work on problem-solving, investigating, reporting, idea development, and, perhaps, decision making.

Communication Communication occurs when information, transmitted from one source to another, is understood by the recipient.

Compensatory (noncompensatory) criterion In decision making, when there are compensatory criteria, then high scores on one criterion can offset low scores on another. When criteria are noncompensatory, then high scores on one will not be offset by high scores on another.

Competition A motivation strategy in which individuals or groups compete against each other for a reward. (See Motivation strategies.)

Comprehensive managerial planning Comprehensive managerial planning involves the development of a whole family of formal plans, including long-range plans and short-range plans.

Concurrent control Concurrent control functions are those that take place after an activity has begun. Concurrent control functions are measuring performance, evaluating performance, and taking corrective action. (See Control.)

Conditional values (CV) A conditional value is the payoff that one can expect if a particular strategy is chosen and a particular state of nature occurs.

Conference method (developmental method) This is a group-centered method of development in which the participants interact with the conference leader. They engage in discussions to develop ideas that can lead to greater understanding of what is being taught.

Confrontation approaches In confrontation approaches, parties to conflict are brought together and the differences between them are aired in each other's presence.

Consequences Consequences are stimuli that are associated with a response (verbal, physical, or psychological). Associating a consequence with a response alters the likelihood of the response occurring. (See Response, Evoked set, Stimuli, Reinforcement.)

Consideration This term refers to a leadership style, or behavior. Consideration is the extent to which the leader works in a relationship with subordinates characterized by mutual trust, respect for their ideas, and concern for their feelings. Leaders who engage in this behavior have good rapport and two-way communication with subordinates. (See Initiating structure.)

Contingency theories This is an approach to management in which the appropriate organizational structure and management processes are defined as being contingent upon the environment. Contingency theories generally present alternative forms of organization and management strategies that would be appropriate for different types of organization. Contingency theories exist for several areas of management, such as organization structure, leadership, performance appraisal, decision making, and control.

Control (as a management process) Control is the activity of insuring that action and events conform to plans. There are two stages in control: Preliminary control

functions (those that occur before a work activity has begun) and concurrent control functions (those that take place after an activity has begun). (See Preliminary control, Concurrent control.)

Control structure (organizational) The organizational control structure is made up of those components of the organization that constrain and direct the behavior of members. Some elements of the control structure are policies and procedures, the reward structure, information systems, authority relationships, selection, and the nature of work.

Control subsystems Control subsystems seek to smooth out the operations of the other organizational subsystems (production, boundary spanning, external monitoring, and managerial) and to monitor their internal operation. Control subsystems seek to ensure the effective operation of the entire subsystems by increasing the level of predictability of the other subsystems.

Cooptation Cooptation is one process by which organizations adapt to the environment. It is the process of absorbing external groups into the organization, generally into the policymaking and decision structure.

Coordination Coordination is a process of developing and maintaining the proper relationships between activities, whether they are physical activities or mental. (See Integration.)

Coordination, horizontal Horizontal coordination is the development of smooth relationships between individuals or groups at the same organizational level.

Coordination, vertical Vertical

coordination refers to the development of effective and integrated relationships between activities at different organizational levels.

Cost centers A cost center is an organizational unit to which it is possible to associate only the costs that it incurs in its operation. When it is difficult to associate revenue with the unit but costs can be allocated to it, a cost center can be established and the unit evaluated on the level of costs that it incurs.

Critical path In PERT the critical path is the longest path, or chain, of activities in a project. It represents the minimum time in which a project can be completed.

D

Decentralization (See Centralization.)

Decisions, Nonprogrammed This is a problem situation in which it is necessary to design new solutions because there are no readily available solutions of acceptable quality.

Decisions, Programmed A programmed decision is one that is made when the alternatives are presented to the decision maker and the most appropriate one is selected, given the specific dimensions of the problem. The alternatives and their consequences are worked out in advance.

Decisions, rational A rational decision is the selection of the best alternative. The implication of this definition is that all possible alternatives are evaluated.

Decision Theory This set of concepts seeks to guide one to the best choice. In a decision theory approach, the decision makers are required to determine which objectives are important so that each alternative may be compared against the objective.

Decision making Decision making is the act of choosing from among alternatives and coming to a conclusion about what should be done in a particular situation.

Decision process The decision process consists of five steps: recognizing a problem, diagnosing causes of problems, generating alternatives, selecting alternatives, and implementing decisions.

Decisions under certainty In decision making under certainty, the decision maker knows the state of nature before the choice is made and can therefore calculate the consequences for each alternative. In decisions under certainty, it is not necessary to estimate probabilities of states of nature.

Decisions under risk A decision under risk is one that is made when the decision maker does not know for certain which of several states of nature will occur, but is willing to assign a probability to each of the states of nature that may occur.

Decision under uncertainty Decisions under uncertainty are made when the decision maker is unable or unwilling to make a probability estimate of the occurrence of different states of nature. In these kinds of decisions, the personality of the decision maker plays a very influential role.

Delegation Delegation is the act of assigning authority and responsibility for a particular task to a subordinate.

Departments A formal group comprised of individuals who have similar work roles or interdependent work roles is called a department. A department is created when subsystem activities are differentiated and reorganized around work similarities and/or work interdependence. Departments are formal groups, generally supervisory units, that provide administrative convenience and have relative permanence.

Developmental goals (knowledge and ability) Knowledge and ability goals are generally targeted at individuals. Knowledge change refers to efforts to increase the level of information a person has. Ability change efforts are aimed at improving how well a person can do certain things or how a person might solve problems.

Development process A series of steps or phases that seem to be involved in successful change efforts constitutes the development process. It includes three basic stages: (1) diagnosis, (2) change, (3) maintenance.

Development targets Development targets are the objects of human resource development. Development targets refer to the level at which development is focused: the individual, the group, or the organization.

Diagnosis Diagnosis is a process of trying to determine whether or not conditions are present that will allow organization change efforts to be successful. (See Development process.)

Differentiation Differentiation is a process by which the subsystem activities of an organization are segregated, unbundled, and rearranged into smaller units, generally some form of departments. (See Integration.)

Differentiation, horizontal This refers to the number of different units that occur as a result of the differentiation process at a particular level of the organization.

Differentiation, vertical This refers to the number of major organizational levels created when hierarchy is introduced through the differentiation process.

Divisibility An assumption in linear programming, divisibility means that for each activity, the total amounts of each input and the associated profit are strictly proportional to the level of each activity, being capable of continuous proportional expansion or reduction. (See Additivity, Linear Programming.)

Domain The domain is the general technological and market sectors that an organization will operate within or, to say it another way, those environmental sectors to which the company must adapt. (See Mission.)

E

Earliest possible time (EPT) In PERT the earliest time that an activity can begin takes into account the times for all activities in a PERT network that precede an activity and that are linked to it in sequence. (See Time estimates, Latest allowable time.)

Economic man In the decision-making literature, economic man is a view of man in which the individual is assumed to have full knowledge of all alternatives, of the consequences of each alternative, and of the probability of occurrence of various conditions affecting the decision.

Effort→performance expectancy The E→P expectancy refers to the person's expectation about the relationship of his or her effort expenditures to the attainment of certain performance levels. It refers to the amount of effort likely to lead to a particular level of performance. (See Expectancy, Expectancy theory.)

Ego involvement A managerial motivation strategy in which an attempt is made to increase the person's involvement with the work of the organization. This is often accomplished by allowing the individual to participate in the establishment of performance goals. (See Motivation strategies.)

Emergent behavior Emergent behavior is behavior that actually occurs in a group or organization. It goes far beyond the required organization behavior specifications. (See Required behavior.)

Employee-centered supervision The employee-centered supervisor is one who is concerned about subordinates' feelings and attempts to create an atmosphere of mutual trust and respect. Employee-centered supervisors tend to engage in general direction, providing subordinates with goals to be achieved rather than attempting to tell them how to achieve them. (See Production-centered supervision.)

Environmental complexity Environmental complexity refers to the number of organizations in the relevant environment. As the number of elements of the relevant environment increases, environmental complexity is high. When there are few external elements in the environment, environmental complexity is low.

Environment, organization The environment of an organization is made up of other organizations and sectors of the society that affect it. These external units provide inputs, make use of outputs, exert pressure for decisions, and, in general, deal in some important way with the organization.

Environment, relevant The relevant environment of an organization is made up of groups or institutions beyond its boundaries that make immediate use of inputs, exert significant pressures on decisions, or make use of the organization's output. Any external force able to generate sufficient pressure to lead to changes within organizations is defined as part of the relevant environment.

Equity theory This approach to understanding motivation is part of a broader theory called exchange theory. Equity theory focuses on the motivational effects of perceived imbalances in exchanges between individuals and groups or among individuals themselves. Equity theory predicts the performance and attitudinal consequences of feelings that individuals have of being underrewarded or overrewarded for work. Equity theory takes into account how individuals feel about their work outputs relative to their work inputs and how the ratio of these two factors compares to the inputs and outputs of others.

Event In PERT an event is a relatively clearly identifiable point that represents the beginning and ending of an activity. (See Activity, PERT.)

Evoked set When stimuli act on an individual, not all the attitudes, values, and behavioral alternatives are affected. A cue evokes only the particular set of factors that the individual associates with the cue. The set it brings forth is called the evoked set. (See Stimuli, Reinforcement theory.)

Expectancy An expectancy is a probability estimate about how likely a particular amount of effort one exerts is to lead to some result. (See Expectancy theory, Valences.)

Expectancy theory This motivation theory attempts to predict an individual's motivation to work by considering his or her expectancies and valences. An expectancy is a belief that the amount of effort a person puts forth in work will lead to specific results. Valences are satisfactions that a person *anticipates* will occur when the result is obtained. (See Expectancies, Valences.)

Expected value Expected value is calculated by multiplying the payoff (conditional value) of an event by the probabilities that it may occur. Expected values may be thought of as the average value (or loss) one would incur while making a particular decision a large number of times.

Explicit costs Costs that can be assessed or verified because they are formalized or accounted for in the control or information system are explicit costs.

External monitoring subsystems These are activities in the organization designed to sense changes in the organization's relevant environment.

F

Feasibility Area In linear programming, the feasibility area refers to the organization's capacity to produce after all constraints and limitations are taken into account. As each constraint is considered, the feasibility area is generally reduced.

Fixed costs These are costs that are fairly constant and remain the same regardless of the level of activity (production) of an organization. It should be noted that all costs change over time, but for the purpose of breakeven analysis, it is generally assumed that for the planning period there will be only minor variations in these costs and that they are, for all practical purposes, fixed.

Formal authority system This defines, in a systematic, formal, usually written way, who reports to whom and the nature of the reporting relationship. (See Authority, Responsibility.)

Formalization Formalization refers to the existence of prescribed rules, policies, job descriptions, and other documents that specify work and other organizational relationships. High formalization exists in an organization when it makes considerable use of written policies, procedures, methods, and rules. There is low formalization in an organization when it makes less use of rules, policies, etc.

Functional authority Functional authority is the right of decision and command that a person outside a chain of command has over some very specific activities (or functions) of someone in the chain of command.

Functional organization In the functional form of organization the major characteristic of the important organizational units is that they contain the activity of a single related business activity, such as marketing, production, or personnel. The functional form of organization has department units that closely parallel the organization's subsystems of production, boundary-spanning, and external-monitoring activities.

G

Goal-directed behavior Behavior is goal directed in the sense that individuals act in response to a "need" that is aroused and the person, feeling some tension, acts to reduce the tension.

Goals (See Objectives.)

Goals, individual Individual goals are those of particular persons or identified subgroups. These goals are end states that the individuals expect the organization to provide to them.

Goals, internal system These are objectives of the subunits of the system. They are related to the strategic objectives in that every unit must provide some output to other organizational units. These outputs, at the required level, are internal system goals.

Goals, market share Market share goals specify toward what particular group of clients or customers the product or service is aimed, as well as the proportion of the total market that the organization believes it can obtain.

Goals, organization effectiveness These goals are aimed at improving the overall level of performance of the total organization. They are complex goals to achieve and require that the organization structure be congruent with the environment and, second, that individuals in the organization have an adequate skill level to perform as well as the willingness to do so.

Goals, personal development These are objectives with increased human potential as an end. They focus on improving skills and abilities, changing attitudes, or improving interpersonal relationships.

Goals, product Product goals state the desired character of the output, whether a product or service.

Goals, productivity Productivity goals measure the efficiency with which resources are used. Productivity is the output obtained relative to inputs used.

Goals, profitability Profitability goals are those that reflect the desired financial returns that should be obtained on sales or investments.

Goals, strategic Strategic goals are those organizational goals that are related to meeting the survival needs of an organization as imposed by the external environment. They are derived to meet the requirements or demands of the environment, and they serve as a standard against which organizational activities will be evaluated to determine whether those activities are effective.

Grapevine The grapevine is the information channel through which rumor flows. (See Cluster chain.)

Group effects model This model explains the impact of groups and group processes. It contains three classes of variables; group characteristics, individual factors, and group outcomes. Group characteristics are norms, roles, status, information flow, and group structure. Individual factors are job satisfaction, perceptions, performance, and role conflict and ambiguity. Group outcomes are productivity and cohesiveness.

Group effectiveness Group effectiveness refers to the ability of a group to achieve its goals, whatever they may be.

Groups Collections of individuals who come together for some purpose are groups. The purpose may be some common personal objective or a more enduring objective. In groups, individuals interact regularly with one another; they are psychologically aware of each other and perceive themselves to be a group. Two key concepts in the definition of groups are identification and interaction. (See Identification, Interaction.)

Groups, extra-organizational These are groups outside the organization to which individuals belong. A structure of the external group is determined by its members, independent of the work organization.

Groups, formal These are groups in which several people interact predictably; the interaction is generally specified in written documents. The two predominant characteristics of a formal group are that (1) membership is usually determined by an official in the organization and (2) the major interaction patterns are determined, defined, and specified by officials or others in the organization.

Groups, internal friendship These groups form within an organization because the members find it relatively pleasant and satisfying to interact with each other.

Groups, nonformal These fairly persistent relationships among individuals are not defined or specified by officials and managers in a work organization, but they still affect members in their work roles.

Groups, reference An individual looks to a reference group for guidance in determining appropriate behavior and attitudes. Reference groups have an important effect on how people act and feel.

Groups, system People who interact regularly as part of their job assignments with others from other departments constitute system groups. The interaction occurs because the individuals all perform an activity in the same organizational subsystem. System groups are characterized by cross-departmental interaction. (See subsystems.)

Groups, temporary work A special group formed to solve a particular problem or to work on a project for a specified period of time is called a temporary work group.

Growth stage During this stage, an organization begins to increase in size and resources. Initial stages of growth may be very rapid, with growth occurring at an increasing rate. In latter periods of the growth stage, the rate of growth begins to slow down and occurs at a decreasing rate.

H

Hawthorne experiment This classic study in organization behavior was conducted at the Hawthorne Plant at Western Electric beginning in 1927. The experiment was a major impetus in the development of the study of human factors in management and the use of humanistic approaches to managing workers.

Human relations skill Human relations skill is the capacity to work with people and motivate them in such a way that they want to perform well.

Human resource approach The human resource approach assumes that the job or the task itself is a primary source of satisfaction and motivation for individuals. Therefore, tasks should be designed in such a way that individuals have an opportunity to satisfy their higher-level needs in the work itself.

Human resource audit This is a systematic analysis of the strengths and weaknesses of the human assets in an organization. In a human resource audit, information about the current performance and the potential, or promotability, of each individual is obtained.

Human resource development Human resource development is the set of activities in an organization that are designed to improve the skills and abilities and affect the attitudes of those who are already working in an organization.

Human resource inventory chart This is a graphic representation containing the type of information obtained in a human resource audit. It shows the current structure of positions in the firm as well as future changes. It indicates who is currently in the position, potential replacements for each position, and the current state of readiness of each candidate. (See Human resource inventory.)

Human resource planning Human resource planning focuses primarily on human factors in the organization. It involves two steps: forecasting needs and auditing the capacities of the current personnel.

Human - skill - dominated work This is work in which machinery and equipment take on less importance. Basically, the level of accomplishment is a function of what the human being can do with only minimal tools and equipment.

Hygiene factors These are factors in Herzberg's motivation theory. When hygiene factors are present on the job, they are not related to better performance. But when they are absent, there is dissatisfaction. Hygiene factors refer to the *context* in which work is done. Factors such as technical supervision, salary, working conditions, status, and company policy are hygiene factors. (See Two-factor theory, Motivating factors.)

I

Identification When persons identify they consider themselves, along with others, to be part of a group. It means that a person recognizes a commonality with others. (See Groups.)

Implicit costs Implicit costs are rather difficult to determine because no particular dollar value is attached to them, but they nevertheless represent real costs to the organization.

Indifferent orientation A person who is indifferent is one whose work view is dominated by the wish to be away from work, doing something else. Indifferents generally prefer leisure over work or involvement with extra-work organizations rather than the one in which they earn their livelihood.

Industrial Revolution A period beginning in the 1700s and continuing through the middle 1800s during which manufacturing and commerce grew particularly rapidly, especially in Western countries. The Industrial Revolution was triggered by the ability to harness power so that machines, rather than men, could do the work.

Industry structure This refers to the number of firms, their size, and output in a particular industry. It also has reference to how the sales of the firms that make up an industry are distributed among them.

Influence Influence is a process or series of actions that one initiates intended to get another person to do something. (See Leadership.)

Information network This is the pattern of information flow among members of a group or organization.

Information system An information system consists of a sender, a channel, and a receiver. Information, or data, flows from the sender through the channel to the receiver.

Initiating structure A leader behavior or style in which a leader is more apt to define and structure the leadership role as well as those of subordinates toward goal attainment. Individuals who are high in initiating structure play an active role in directing group activities, communicating information, scheduling, and trying out new ideas. (See Consideration.)

Integration Integration is the process of linking separate departmental units together, tying them with each other in order to achieve organization coordination. (See Differentiation.)

Interaction Interaction is a process that occurs when one person's behavior affects the second person's behavior and the second person responds in some way to the first. (See Groups.)

Interdependence Interdependence is the degree to which work of different units or individuals is linked together.

Interdependence, pooled Pooled interdependence occurs when several units of an organization operate in a fairly autonomous manner such that what one does is not entirely dependent upon others. Each part of the organization, however, renders a measurable contribution to the whole organization and is supported by the whole.

Interdependence, reciprocal Reciprocal interdependence is mutual interdependence. This means that activity A and activity B both affect each other.

Interdependence, sequential This is a form of interdependence in which work activities must be performed in a particular sequence. Activities are assigned to units or segments in such a way that a product (or activity) must begin at point A, go to point B, and then to C before it gets to D.

Intergroup cooperation goals These goals focus on developing smooth and effective working relationships between different groups. Intergroup cooperation goals may be developed for either group or organization targets.

Intervention This is a development process in which an effort is made to identify the causes of a problem by gathering information from those involved in the problem. Data are then fed back to the participants and a solution is worked out with them, usually with the aid of a consultant.

Innovation Innovation is a new and different way to do something. It may take the form of a new product or an old product that may acquire a new market. Innovation may take the form of new production techniques or new distribution techniques.

Iso Profit Line An iso profit line is a linear equation. Any point on the iso profit line represents a combination of factors (e.g., production of different units or products) that will yield the same profit. In a linear programming the maximum profit is obtained when the iso profit line reaches a point away from the origin so that it is still tangent to the feasibility area.

J

Job enrichment This managerial motivation strategy emphasizes motivating the worker through the task of job itself. Work is assigned to individuals so that they have the opportunity to complete an identifiable task from beginning to end. They are then held responsible for successful completion of the task. The motivational effect of job enrichment flows from the opportunity for personal achievement, challenge, and recognition.

Job facet A job facet is an identifiable aspect of work and the work situation. Pay, recognition from supervisors, working conditions, relationships with peers, and so on are job facets.

Job rotation A developmental method in which the individual is systematically moved from one position to another is called job rotation. The purpose of these moves is to allow the person to learn something about each of the positions as well as the purpose and function of various organizational units relative to each other.

Job satisfaction Job satisfaction is a generalized attitude toward work. It is evoked by the configuration of feeling that exists because specific facets of the job situation (working conditions, pay, etc.) are linked together and associated with work.

Job shop A method of production in which the various activities, equipment, or machines can be rearranged, when necessary, to perform the activities in a number of different sequences to produce the products. The sequencing of operations will vary from project to project in a job shop. (See Technology, intensive.)

K

Key Skill analysis Key skill analysis is the determination of what critical skills are necessary to succeed in a particular organizational environment.

L

Latest allowable time In PERT, the latest time at which an activity can begin in order to meet the time requirements of the critical path is the least allowable time. (See Earliest possible time, Time estimates.)

LBDQ (Leader behavior description questionnaire) This is a psychometric scale that measures leader behavior. It measures several different facets of leader behavior, but most notably it assesses the level of leader initiating structure and consideration. (See Initiating structure, consideration.)

Leader–member relations Leader–member relations is one of the variables in Fiedler's contingency theory of leadership. It refers to the amount of trust in the group and how well the leader is liked. (See Leadership, contingency theory.)

Leadership Leadership is the process of influencing others to act in the way desired by the person who is making the influence attempt. The essence of organizational leadership is the influential increment over and above mechanical compliance of others with routine organizational directives. (See Influence, Motivation.)

Leadership, autocratic This is a leadership style in which the leader makes all the decisions and allows the subordinates no influence in decision making.

Leadership, laissez-faire (free rein) In this leadership style the subordinates, as individuals or as a group, have complete autonomy to make a decision.

Leadership, participative (democratic) Individuals who use this style of leadership consult with their subordinates on appropriate matters. They allow the subordinates some influence in the decision-making process.

Leadership theory, behavioral The behavioral approach to leadership looks upon it as a series of acts, or a behavioral repertoire, intended to help a group achieve its objective. From this perspective, leadership is seen as acting out a series of behaviors that could vary depending on the group's need for greater task effectiveness, member satisfaction, and cohesiveness.

Leadership theory, contingency A contingency theory of leadership is one that takes into account situational factors such as the nature of the work and the characteristics of the subordinate. In such a theory, the leader behavior that is most appropriate depends upon work characteristics and subordinate characteristics. Two rather well-known contingency theories of leadership are that proposed by Fiedler and path-goal theory.

Leadership theory, trait The underlying premise of the trait approach to leadership is that leadership is an attribute of personality,

that a certain identifiable trait or collection of traits makes a person effective as a leader. The trait approach to leadership sought to identity these characteristics. (See Leadership theory, behavioral, and Leadership theory, contingency.)

Leading Leading is the managerial process of motivating and influencing others to obtain compliance from them so that they contribute to the achievement of organizational goals.

Lectures As a development method, perhaps the most common form of training is lectures. In a lecture a person competent in a topic area presents a set of concepts or ideas to the group. Lectures are an "instructor-centered" method of learning.

Liaison individuals Those persons in a grapevine who pass on information to others.

Life structure Life structure is the way the work, family, peer, and other relationships of an individual are interwoven. (See Career adjustment.)

Line authority The chain of command that results from the differentiation of production, boundary-spanning, and external-monitoring subsystems is the line organization. Line authority is the right that the manager has to allocate resources and assign tasks to personnel in the unit for which he or she is responsible. It is associated with line organization activities.

Line organization Line organization is that set of organizational activities that are related directly to the differentiation of production, boundary-spanning, and external-monitoring subsystems. This is the *line* organization, and per-

sonnel performing these activities are said to be performing in the "line."

Linear programming This is a mathematical programming approach in which maximization or minimization of some objective function is attained through the solving of a set of simultaneous equations. These simultaneous equations represent constraints, or limitations, relative to the objective function. (See Objective function.)

LPC A leadership measure in Fiedler's contingency theory of leadership, LPC refers to the "*least preferred co-worker*." A manager is asked to describe the co-worker with whom he or she least likes to work. (See Leadership theory; LPC, high; LPC, low.)

LPC, high This is a people-centered leadership style in which the leader is oriented toward the feelings and the relationships in the work group, with a tendency to be permissive. (See Leadership, theory, contingency; LPC.)

LPC, low This is a task-centered style of leadership in which the leader has a tendency to be directive and controlling. (See Leadership theory, contingency; LPC.)

M

Management by exception In management by exception, only major deviation from standards or plans are brought to the attention of the superior.

Management by objectives (MBO) In this system a superior and a subordinate attempt to reach consensus about (1) what goals the subordinate will attempt to achieve, (2) the plan or means by which these goals should be accomplished, and (3) how goal progress will be measured. This approach requires that there be regular performance reviews. (See Work planning.)

Management process contingency theory This is a theory that takes into account variations in the structure of the organization and the type of personnel, as well as prescribing the appropriate management processes to be effective with such differences.

Management science The application of quantitative methods and operations research techniques to management problems. It uses any scientific, mathematical, or logical means to cope with problems. It differs from scientific management in that management science focuses primarily on decision making and planning while scientific management analyzes the structure of work. Management science is essentially a quantitative approach to management that seeks to produce rational decisions. (See Scientific management.)

Managerial processes These activities of planning, organizing, leading, and controlling are carried out in the performance of managerial responsibility.

Managerial subsystems These are organized activities for dealing with the coordination of subsystems and the adjustment of the total system to the environment. The managerial subsystem is concerned with solving general policy issues, the determination of organization structure, the interpretation of market information, and strategic organization decisions.

Managers Managers are individuals in organizations who are in positions that have at least two characteristics: they make decisions about how other people, primarily subordinates, use resources: they are responsible to a higher-level superior for the supervision of subordinates.

Marginal costs These are costs incurred when a decision is made. They refer to the additional costs incurred because of the addition of another unit of production.

Market-dominated mixed organization (MD-mixed) This is a form of organization in which the marketing subsystem interacts with a volatile external market segment leading to an organic structure in the marketing and distribution system. On the other hand the technological environment is relatively predictable leading to mechanistic production and engineering activities. (See Mixed organization.)

Market environment The market environment is that sector of a society or subset of other specific organizations that make use of the commodity, product, value, or service that an organization produces. Basically, clients and customers are the major factor in the market environment, though it is necessary to consider the firm's competitors and their actions since they may have an effect on demand.

Market saturation This is a condition in which demand for the product diminishes to a point where the product or service is primarily a replacement market. Growth in sales comes from replacement and not new consumers. Sales increases then are largely attributable only to changes in population level.

Materials purchases budget This budget shows the amount of raw material that must be maintained to meet production plans. It is particularly useful because it shows variations in raw materials inventory levels.

Matrix organization Matrix organization is a form of structure in which technical specialists are assigned to more stable functional or product teams to bring the specialist's expertise to the organization. In a matrix organization each member of the team is subject to orders from a project manager and from the manager of the department to which he or she is assigned.

Maximax approach (See Optimistic criterion.)

Maximin approach (See Pessimistic criterion.)

Mechanistic organization The mechanistic organization develops in response to a stable market and stable technology. It uses standard production methods and has well-defined and fixed channels of distribution. Tasks in it change slowly. Authority/responsibility relationships are specified. This organization is relatively rigid and hierarchical. It is commonly called a bureaucratic organization.

Mid-career blues Individual feelings of dissatisfaction about work and other facets of life that occur around the age of forty are called mid-career blues. (See Life structure.)

Middle management Middle managers supervise both managers and operative employees. They tend to do more planning than managers at lower levels and have the primary responsibility of translating broad organizational objectives into specific product or service plans.

Mission (See Domain.)

Mixed organization This type of organization has subsystems that interact with environments with different degrees of uncertainty. For example, one segment of the organization may be affected by a stable environment while another may be interacting with a volatile environment. There are two types of mixed organizations, technology-dominated mixed (TD-mixed) and market-dominated mixed (MD-mixed). (See Technology-dominated mixed and market-dominated mixed organizations.)

Model A model is an abstraction of reality. It is an attempt to portray, in some miniature fashion, a particular state. There are physical models, qualitative models, and mathematical models.

Models, mathematical In a mathematical model the relationships between features or characteristics of the subject of interest are represented by numbers and mathematical relationships.

Models, physical In physical models a miniature version of the real object is developed—for example, the use of scale models of planes used in testing.

Models, qualitative In qualitative models a phenomenon is explained using everyday language and sometimes symbols.

Most likely time In PERT the most realistic estimate of the time an activity might take under normal circumstances is most likely time. (See Optimistic time, Pessimistic time.)

Motivating factors Motivating factors are one of two sets of factors in Herzberg's two-factor theory.

They are also called satisfiers. When they are present, high job satisfaction and willingness to work harder exist. They may induce more effort. If they are absent, the absence will not produce dissatisfaction. Motivating factors are work facets such as responsibility, achievement, advancement, and the work itself. Motivators are job content factors, a characteristic of the job itself. (See Hygiene factors, Two-factor theory.)

Motivating potential Motivating potential refers to the degree to which a job has the capacity to induce the individual to perform. Characteristics of the job that affect motivating potential are meaningfulness, responsibility, and knowledge of results. Jobs high in these factors have high motivating potential. (See Job enrichment.)

Motivation (as a management activity) As a management activity, the term refers to attempts to motivate or to attempt to influence a person or group to behave in a particular way. Used in this way, motivation is a synonym for leadership.

Motivation (the psychological meaning) The psychological meaning of motivation refers to a person's psychological drive state, which causes the person to behave in certain ways. It is a psychological state of tension that induces behavior.

Motivation strategies The different approaches that may be used by managers to increase an individual's drive to perform better are called motivation strategies. Motivation strategies are fear or threat, reciprocity, reinforcement, job enrichment, team building,

competition, and ego involvement.

Motives (See Needs.)

"Must" objectives These objectives specify the minimum outcomes or states that a decision must attain. Unless an alternative satisfies all "must" objectives, the problem will not be considered solved. (See "Want" objectives.)

N

Needs Preferred goal states that an individual strives to achieve are needs. These become the basis for goal-directed behavior of the person. (See Motives.)

Needs, achievement Achievement needs refer to the individual's desire to do work better, advance a career, or accomplish important things. Individuals high in achievement needs prefer situations in which they have individual responsibility for accomplishment, where a specific feedback is provided, or where their goals are clear and of moderate difficulty.

Needs, affiliation Affiliation needs refer to the individual's concern about his or her relationship with others. Individuals high in affiliation needs seek out jobs or activities in which there is an opportunity for friendly interaction and helping behavior.

Needs, avoid failure Some people are motivated, not by a need to achieve, but rather by a need to avoid failure. Such individuals attempt to avoid circumstances in which they might fail.

Needs, ego The human desire to be respected by others and the need for a positive self-image are ego needs.

Needs, higher order Basically psychological and sociological, higher-order needs are social, ego, and self-actualization. They are met in different ways by different individuals. (See Social needs, Ego needs, Self-actualization.)

Needs, physiological These are basic individual requirements for survival, such as food, shelter, and physical well-being.

Needs, power This refers to the individual's need to influence or control others. Individuals high in power needs prefer positions that allow them to exercise influence and seek high position because of the power associated with it.

Needs, primary These are basically the physiological and security needs of individuals. They are also called "lower-level" needs. (See Physiological needs, Security needs.)

Needs, security The human need to ensure that physiological needs will continue to be met is called security needs. These include protection against the loss of shelter, food, and other basic requirements, as well as the desire to live in a stable and predictable environment.

Needs, self-actualization This is the individual need to do what he or she is fitted for. Self-actualization needs are directed at the individual's desire to satisfy or meet his or her potential.

Needs, social The human need to interact with others and have some social acceptance and approval is a social need.

Negotiable goals These represent activities and/or goals in which the responsible executive is willing to modify his or her position, paying close attention to inputs from subordinates.

Net present value (NPV) A method of capital budgeting in which the cost of capital, generally, is used to discount the future stream of cash flows from an investment. The present value of these cash flows is obtained, then compared to the cost of the project. If the net present value is greater than the outlay, then the investment should be made. If there are several alternatives, then the alternative with the greatest net present value should be selected, if only one investment can be made.

Non-negotiable goals A non-negotiable goal is one in which the responsible executive requires that subordinates take a specific approach to solving a problem or carrying out an activity. In these cases, the lower-level personnel have no discretion.

Nonreinforcement This occurs when either positive or negative consequences that have been associated with a particular behavior by a person are withdrawn. As the contingency is not associated with a response, the frequency of the action diminishes. (See Reinforcement, Consequences.)

Norm A norm is an expectation that one person has about what another person should do. Norms are rules, of a sort, and standards that govern the conduct of group members. Norms are ideas that others have about how another person "should" behave.

Norms, peripheral Peripheral norms are important within an organization. Compliance with them may be desired, but it is not essential in order to maintain one's membership in an organization.

Norms, pivotal Pivotal norms are the most important norms, those which must be accepted by all organizational members.

O

Objective function An objective function is the factor to be maximized or minimized in linear programming.

Objectives An objective, or goal, is a desired end state, some place you want to be in the future, something you want to have or a condition you wish to exist. (See Goals.)

Objectives of development These are the kinds of changes that are sought by the development process. The following goals may be objectives of development: ability and knowledge change, attitude change, increasing intergroup cooperation, and increasing organization effectiveness. (See Development targets.)

Objectives, routine Routine objectives represent the normal requirements of the job, the kind of activity typically found in a job description.

Objectives, special project These are objectives that, for some reason or another, have taken on special importance. This may occur because of emergency, changes in priorities, or management decisions.

Off-the-job development methods With these techniques the learning environment is away from the work setting. Usually off-the-job methods occur in classroom situations.

On-the-job development methods These are developmental techniques in which the individual's work experience is designed to achieve the goal of improving competence and skill within the organization. The job is used as the developmental vehicle, and the person is placed in jobs in such a fashion as to make them learning experiences.

Open systems A view of organizations that sees them as an element in a more complex environment. The organization as an open system must adapt to the environment, either evolving into a form that will function in its environment or designing and shaping such a form.

Operative employees These individuals in an organization are actually involved in or perform the work of the organization, making the product or providing the service, rather than planning or managing the work.

Opportunity costs These are costs incurred when we commit resources to one strategy. When we do so, we cannot use them for another strategy; therefore, we have given up an "opportunity."

Optimistic criterion Under conditions of uncertainty, the decision maker may feel fortunate. The decision maker, using this criterion, selects the strategy that has the greatest payoff. This approach is also called the "Maximax" approach. (See Maximax approach.)

Optimistic time In PERT, a time estimate that represents the amount of time that an activity will take if the work proceeds without any problems, interferences, or obstacles is the optimistic time. It is the least time that the activity might take. (See Most likely time, Pessimistic time.)

Organic organization This type of organization is found where the market and the technological sectors are volatile. It is an organization in which the structure, relationships, and jobs are loosely defined in order to ease the prob-

lem of adapting to a rapidly changing environment.

Organization A group of people working together to achieve an objective, or set of objectives, is an organization.

Organization climate The way in which an organization's practices and procedures are perceived by the members, and the relationship of these perceptions to the individual's ways of thinking about the organization and the subsequent behavior that occurs, is the organization climate.

Organization development Organization development is any systematic effort at changing people, groups, and organizations.

Organization Planning Organization planning is projecting what the organization will look like in the future, taking into account data developed from strategic plans, such as long-range building or capital expansion projects. It is an attempt to forecast the "ideal" organization structure in the future.

Organization system An organization system is a set of interrelated subsystems that absorbs inputs from some systems and transforms them into outputs that are used by other systems. Subsystems are related groups of similar activities within the organization that must be performed to meet its objectives. (See Subsystems.)

Organizational behavior This is a narrow view of human behavior in organizations that has a major focus on the individual and individual processes. It is commonly called the "micro-approach" to management.

Organizational theory The focus of analysis in this discipline is

the organization as a whole. It tends to be built on concepts that help one understand how elements within an organization are related to each other. It is commonly called the "macro-approach" to management.

Organizationalist Organizationalists are persons who are highly committed to the work organization. They tend to be highly loyal to it. Their self-concept is tied to work. The organizationalist is committed to where he or she works, rather than to what he or she does. (See Orientation toward work.)

Organizing Organizing is the managerial process that includes designing the organization's structure, attracting people to the organization, and creating conditions and systems that ensure that they work to achieve the strategic and internal system goals.

Orientations toward work These are views that individuals have about work and work organizations. They reflect the individual's values and desires about the particular kind of involvement with work organizations and what the person expects from the work organization. (See Organizationalist, Professional orientation, Indifferent orientation.)

P

Participation Participation refers to the degree of influence a person has in a decision about something that is normally beyond the formal authority in his or her job. Participation means sharing of power.

Participation, pseudo An attempt to make subordinates believe that they have participated in decision making. This is a process in which subordinates are asked to make contributions, suggestions, set objectives, and develop plans. After any of these have been done, the manager ignores the recommendations and implements a decision he or she had already made.

Path-goal theory Path-goal theory is a contingency theory of leadership that asserts that the leader obtains good performance from the work unit by making sure that the subordinates know what they have to do (the path) to be rewarded for good performance (the goal) and by reducing barriers to effective performance. Path-goal theory is an approach to studying leadership that seeks to explain leader behavior using concepts of expectancy theories of motivation. (See Leadership theory, Contingency.)

Payoff matrix A payoff matrix is a way to represent a decision problem. A payoff matrix is constructed with the states of nature being the columns, the available strategies or alternatives the rows, and the payoff (or conditional value) for each strategy at a given state of nature at the point where the row and column intersect. (See State of nature, Expected value, Conditional value.)

Perception Perception is the manner in which we organize the information about the world as we observe it.

Performance component Performance component is a unique subset of a job that is different from other subsets. Different performance components require different skills and abilities and may be affected differently by the individual's motivation. Each performance component may have a different mix of technological and human input factors so that achieving successful results of a performance component may be quite complicated.

Performance objective A performance objective is derived directly from the job assignment of an individual. It covers work areas, such as the continuation of recurring or routine activities, problem solving, or the creation of innovative ideas, products, or services.

Performance→outcome expectancy This is another type (P → O) expectancy and refers to the individual's expectations about the relationship between achieving a particular performance level and the attainment of certain outcomes. For example, an employee may feel that if he or she consistently attains a particular high performance level, there is a high probability that fatigue will occur, a moderate probability that others will become angry with the person, and so forth.

Personality Personality is the unique pattern of psychological and behavior characteristics of a person. The characteristics that make up personality are: (1) skills, ability, and knowledge; (2) attitudes; (3) values; (4) needs or motives. Individuals have different combinations and levels of these characteristics, which accounts for differences in personality.

Pessimistic criterion A decision rule that can be applied under conditions of uncertainty. The decision maker adopts a pessimistic attitude, that the worst is likely to happen. Knowing the states of nature, the alternatives and the conditional values, the decision maker selects the strategy that yields the greatest amount under the worst conditions. This approach is also called "Maximin." (See Maximin approach.)

Pessimistic time In PERT the maximum time that an activity would require if things go very badly is pessimistic time. (See Optimistic time, Most likely time.)

Phase plans Phase plans are a part of organizational planning. They are intermediate plans or steps necessary to achieve the desired organizational structure on a sound and practical basis.

Placement Placement is the process of determining the appropriate organizational position, role, or field in which to place a selected individual.

Planning Planning is a managerial process of determining what human and technological resources are required to reach a goal, when these resources will be needed, and at what rate they will be used. Planning is future oriented and may concentrate on the long run or the short run.

Planning, strategic Strategic planning, often used interchangeably with long-range planning, refers to those plans that take into account the more distant future. Strategic planning considers where the organization should be relative to its environment.

Policies Policies are general decision rules to be followed by managers. They are designed to guide behavior and decisions made at lower levels within the boundaries of the mission and domain statement. They reflect the direction that top management believes decisions should take. (See Strategy.)

Position A position is a cluster of related roles performed by an individual in a group. An individual may be involved in role relationships with several different people. Together all these role relationships determine the position. (See Role.)

Power Power is a force one uses to obtain compliance from others. The force is activated in the influence process. The use of power is leadership.

Power bases Power bases are the conditions, characteristics, or circumstances that are the source of influence. Power bases may be organizational or individual.

Power, legitimate This is a form of power in which the person subjected to the power believes that it is proper for the other person to influence him or her. So long as the requests, commands, directives, and suggestions of a superior fall within the boundaries of the psychological contract, they will be complied with.

Power, organizationally based Organizationally based power is influence that an individual has that is based on the fact that the person is in a particular organizational position. Organizationally based power may arise from formal authority or the location of a position in the organization. Formal authority resides in the position, not the person in it, in the sense that once the individual leaves that job he or she loses the power base.

Power, position Position power is equivalent to formal authority. It refers to the amount of discretion that a leader has, i.e., whether the leader has a right to reward, sanction, evaluate, or promote those

who work for him. (See Leadership theory, contingency.)

Power, referent Referent power is based largely on the attraction exerted by an individual over another person or a group. The stronger the attraction, the stronger the power. Persons who exercise this kind of power are called charismatic leaders. (See Power, organizationally based.)

Power, skill and expertise When an individual has the capacity to influence others because he or she has more skill or knowledge in a particular area, the skill and expertise become the base of power. This type of power is very specific to the type of problem that one faces and to the person with the skill. It is not easily transferred, as is organizationally based power. (See Power, organizationally based.)

Preliminary control These are control activities that occur before a work activity has begun. Preliminary control functions are setting standards, scheduling, and developing policies and procedures. (See Control.)

Principles of management Guides for designing and managing an organization are called principles of management. Principles are theoretical statements that prescribe the most effective way of planning, organizing, leading, and controlling work in an organization.

Probability Probability refers to the frequency of occurrence of a particular event.

Probability, a priori An a priori probability is one that can be determined because something is known about the possible outcomes as a function of the situation

itself. For example, the a priori probability of tossing a head is .5 because there are two sides of a coin and only one side can come up. Thus, the probability of a head (or a tail) is 1/2.

Probability, empirical An empirical probability is one derived from experience with an event. For example, a firm may find that three out of four employees hired stay with a company for at least five years. The probability, then of one staying with the firm is .75. The empirical probability can be determined only by knowing the circumstances.

Probability, subjective A subjective probability is one's best estimate of the likelihood of an event occurring. Subjective probabilities are educated guesses based on one's experience, intuition, and feelings.

Problems A problem exists when there is some relatively important difference between what is (or will be) happening in a particular situation and what should be happening. In this case something must be done to solve the problem.

Procedure A procedure outlines each step in an activity required to complete a project. Generally, it indicates who or which department is responsible for that step, along with the responsibility for preceding and subsequent activities. Procedures link the work activities of several different people, often in different departments, with each other to accomplish a project.

Process maintenance In the process-maintenance phase of development, the conditions that support the desired behavior or attitudes must be put in place, if they are not already there. The organization structure, groups that make up the organization, and the managers of those exposed to development must reinforce the change efforts made. (See Developmental process.)

Product life cycle The product life cycle reflects the periods of growth, maturity, and decline in the demand for a particular product.

Product market analysis Product/market analysis is an assessment of such factors as the quality image, the availability of dealers, dealer service organizations, and other product characteristics on which a firm can capitalize. It may show the manner in which management conceptualizes the product, as well as the stage of the product life cycle in which different products may be.

Product organization In a product organization, the major form of departmentation is to have units organize around different products or services. In product organizations, each major unit will contain subsystem activities of production, boundary spanning, etc. Individuals from diverse backgrounds, like marketing, engineering, and manufacturing, are brought together and placed in a unit to produce and distribute a particular product.

Production budget The production budget shows the number of units of production to be manufactured and how much of the production will be held in inventory. Typically, the production budget is broken down into operating periods, such as quarters, weeks, days, and, in some cases, even hours.

Production-centered supervision A production-centered supervisor is one who is primarily concerned with achieving high levels of production and views subordinates merely as instruments for doing this. (See Employee-centered supervision.)

Production subsystem A technological process, a complex of physical objects, procedures, and knowledge by which a certain output is produced to be distributed to the market, client, or user is a production subsystem. This subsystem is the technical core of the organization.

Productivity The ratio of outputs obtained relative to inputs used to obtain them is productivity. Productivity is typically expressed as a ratio such as sales per employee or units produced per worker.

Productivity, group The outcome that a group produces results from task performance. Productivity refers to the task-oriented output of the group.

Professional orientation This view is one characterized by a strong set of values oriented toward the career or the work itself, not the organization. The professional is more concerned with what he or she does, not with the organization in which it is done. (See Orientations toward work.)

Profit centers Profit centers are organizational units to which large portions of both revenues and costs can be allocated. This permits the determination of the profitability of each of these units. (See Cost centers.)

Profit impact of marketing strategies (PIMS) PIMS is a planning approach that attempts to analyze strategies by subdividing the organization into strategic business units (SBUs) and determining the consequence of specific strategies for profitability and/or cash flow in the short run and in the long run. In this approach, each of these units must identify its mission, strengths and weaknesses, likely competitive developments, trends, and strategy. These are then integrated and compared to the overall corporate strategy to see how they fit together.

Programmed instruction In this technique of development, concepts are presented to learners, and then a series of diagnostic questions are asked. Only when all the questions are answered correctly does the learner move on to the next concept. If the questions are answered incorrectly, the learner is directed to additional material on the subject.

Project evaluation and review technique (PERT) PERT is a planning and control device that is a form of network analysis. In PERT a network design for a project is constructed that links each task and activity. A basic characteristic of PERT is that it takes probability time estimates into account to determine activity times.

Project organization In this type of organization, a group of individuals with talents and skills required to meet the demands of a specific project is formed, usually with a relatively short time horizon. Projects are generally unique; no two are the same. Therefore, when projects change, the members of the organization are shifted to other projects.

Psychological contract The psychological contract is an expression of the relationship that develops between an individual and an organization. The individual has a variety of expectations about the organization and the organization has a variety of expectations about the individual. These not only cover how much work is to be done for the pay to be received, but also includes the whole pattern of rights, privileges, and obligation between the individual and the organization. (See Real boundaries, Public boundaries.)

Psychological success Feelings of self-esteem that individuals have when they are successful in an occupational field constitute psychological success. Typically, when a person experiences high psychological success, motivation and occupational involvement increases.

Public boundaries The public boundaries of the psychological contract encompass those aspects of an individual's work that he or she wishes others, especially the superior, to believe he or she will perform as part of the job. Usually, these are agreed-upon work activities between the superior and subordinate. (See Psychological contract, Real boundaries.)

Punishment Punishment is the application of a negative consequence or the withholding of a desirable one. (See Reinforcement.)

Q

Q/A objectives This is an objective dominated by the quality aspect. Acceptance of this objective by subordinates is of little consequence because, generally, they will concur in it for any number of reasons. (See A/Q objectives, and A = Q objectives, and Acceptance.)

Quality When referring to the quality of an objective, this means that the objective, if achieved, will increase the probability that the organization's level of effectiveness will increase. (See Acceptance, Q/A objectives, A/Q objectives, and A = Q Objectives.)

R

Rational criterion An approach to making decisions under uncertainty that is based on the notion that if it is not possible to make a reasonably accurate estimate of the probability of one particular state of nature occurring, there is no cause to believe that another state of nature is more likely to occur than another. It can, therefore, be reasonably assumed that all states of nature are equally likely to occur. Using the rational criterion, the decision maker assigns equal probability to all states of nature. It is then possible to compute expected values.

Real boundaries (psychological contract) The real boundaries of the psychological contract define the limits beyond which a person is unwilling to act within the organization. In most cases the real boundaries of the psychological contract are far more inclusive than the public boundaries. (See Public boundaries.)

Reciprocity Reciprocity is a motivation strategy that operates on the "norm of reciprocity." This norm states that what one is given will be repaid in approximate equivalence. Individuals who receive benefits from others feel guilty if they have a chance to reciprocate and do not do so. The psychological contract is based on the concept of reciprocity. (See Motivation strategies.)

Recruitment Recruitment is a process of attracting applicants to work for the organization.

Regret criterion In this approach to making decisions, it is assumed that once a decision maker makes a choice and knows the results, he or she might have been better off having done something else. A regret criterion is based on the idea that the decision maker should attempt to minimize the regret which may be experienced because one alternative is selected over another.

Reliability Reliability refers to a character of measurement or standard. Reliability means the degree to which the measure is stable over time.

Reinforcement Reinforcement is a type of consequence that is associated with a response. Reinforcement increases the probability of a response occurring. (See Consequence.)

Reinforcement, negative Negative reinforcement occurs when undesirable (or negative) consequences are withdrawn or withheld. With the negative reinforcement, the probability of engaging in the behavior that avoids the undesirable consequence is increased. (See Reinforcement.)

Reinforcement, positive Positive reinforcement is the application of desirable consequence to a behavior. A positive reinforcement increases the probability of the response occurring. (See Reinforcement.)

Reinforcement schedule A reinforcement schedule is the frequency and rate with which various contingencies (rewards and punishments) are associated with a particular response. This schedule affects the speed with which responses are learned or behavior changed.

Reinforcement theory This approach to motivation explains behavior in terms of the consequences that are associated with individual's responses to stimuli.

Required behavior This refers to those behavioral requirements that are established for, and expected of, organization members. It is an organizational requirement. (See Emergent behavior.)

Response Response, part of the evoked set, is the individual's reaction to the stimulus. It may be behavior or it may be an emotional reaction. (See Evoked set, Stimulus, Reinforcement theory.)

Responsibility Responsibility is an obligation a person has to perform the assigned organization tasks in a satisfactory way.

Responsibility center A responsibility center is an organizational subunit that is evaluated by the degree to which it is able to achieve cost and/or revenue goals that can be assigned to that unit because it is fairly self-contained and integrated within itself. In this instance, the subunit must be separated clearly enough from the rest of the firm so that the cost it incurs, or the revenue it generates, can be reasonably accounted for and associated with it. (See Profit centers, Cost centers.)

Rewards, general General rewards are those which are given to all individuals in an organization because of their membership in it or in some particular class of the organization. General rewards

are given without regard to how well or how poorly a person does a job. (See Rewards, task specific.)

Rewards, task specific These are rewards linked to how well or how poorly a person does a job. They are tied to the level of task performance. (See Rewards, general.)

Robber barons A term applied to owners of large firms in the United States during the period between 1860 and 1900. These men were accused of having little concern for the common good and of attempting to do little except amass personal wealth and power.

Role Roles are behavioral sequences of an individual's interactions with others. Roles are composed of groups of related norms. Basically, a role refers to a behavioral relationship between one individual and another. (See Position.)

Role ambiguity A situation in which individuals are not clear as to what the role requirements are, that is, they may not know precisely what to do.

Role ambiguity, social/emotional This occurs when a person is unclear about how others evaluate him or her.

Role ambiguity, task A person experiences task ambiguity when he or she is uncertain about what behavior or task requirements are expected.

Role conflict Role conflict occurs when a person is subjected to inconsistent demands with respect to his or her role behavior.

Role conflict, interrole This type of conflict occurs when a person outside the role set imposes demands that cause problems within it.

Role conflict, intersender This is caused by inconsistent demands

made from different individuals within the role set.

Role conflict, intrasender This results from inconsistent demands made on an individual coming from the same source.

Role conflict, personal This condition occurs when the role demands on a person are inconsistent with the individual's own value system.

Role playing Role playing is an experiential, student-centered method of instruction. In role playing the student (learner) is asked to act as another person. In a role-playing situation, each person receives a set of facts and then is instructed to represent his or her role as outlined in the instructions. After a period of time, the role playing is stopped and the event is analyzed. Role playing seems especially useful in developing interpersonal skills and for instructing in problem solving.

Role set The group of other individuals with whom a particular person, in a role, interacts very frequently.

Rumor A rumor is information disseminated through nonformal or unofficial organizational information networks.

S

Satisficing Satisficing is a decision strategy in which one searches for an alternative that achieves some minimal level of satisfaction for the desired objectives. This is the alternative usually selected. In satisficing, the decision maker does not identify all possible alternatives but rather stops in the search for alternatives when one or two are found that seem to be adequate, given the objectives and expectations. (See Bounded rationality.)

Scheduling Scheduling is the determination of when activities should begin, how long they should take, and when they should be completed. In scheduling, the rate at which resources are expended is determined. Scheduling is a preliminary control function.

Scientific management This movement, commonly attributed to Frederick Taylor, attempted to bring research and logic to the analysis and design of work. Scientific management, for the most part, addressed itself to analyzing the work at the operative level of the organization. It advocated the use of the scientific method to be applied to work problems. (See Management science.)

Selection Selection is the process of making a determination of which applicant will be offered employment.

Sensitivity training Sensitivity training is a form of development in which the nature of interpersonal relationships is explored. Individuals are brought together in groups with little or no structure. With the help of a leader, individuals are placed in an ambiguous situation and must work out their own group structure and relationships. The objectives of sensitivity training are achieved when individuals become more accepting of feedback about themselves from others, more candid about expressing their own feelings, more trusting, more spontaneous, more flexible, more sincere, and more willing to face up to conflict in personal problems.

Simulation (business games) Simulation is an attempt to create a learning situation that approximates the real world. In simulation, the learner is faced with a series of decisions to be made. When the decisions are made, they are analyzed for their appropriateness. Often, simulation decisions are fed into computer models and their effects shown.

Slack resources Slack resources are unused capacities, either technical or human, of an organization.

Slack time In PERT slack time occurs on paths, or chains, of events other than the critical path. It is the amount of time that is, in a sense, noncritical to the project completion date. Slack time represents pockets of potential resources that may conceivably be diverted to the critical path to shorten it. Slack time is computed by determining the difference between the latest allowable time and the earliest possible time for an event. (See Earliest possible time, Latest allowable time.)

Smoothing Smoothing is an attempt to minimize severe fluctuations of the environment by offering inducements to those who use services during "troughs" or charging premiums to those who contribute to "peaking."

Social facilitation Social facilitation occurs when an individual's level of performance is increased by the presence of others.

Social inhibition Social inhibition occurs when the presence of others inhibits or diminishes an individual's performance.

Socialization The process by which a society, a culture, or other institutions condition the attitudes, values, and behavior of individuals is called socialization.

Socialization, organizational A process of learning the organizational-preferred values and ways of doing things after one takes a position in an organization. Organizational socialization is the process by which the person adapts to work and the work organization. (See Socialization.)

Solution-minded An individual state of mind that, during the process of problem solving, leads individuals to jump to premature conclusions about the causes of a problem. This leads them rapidly into the next stage of decision making: searching for alternatives.

Span of control The span of control is the number of subordinates that report to a particular manager.

Specialists Individuals with very high skill levels in a particular kind of work are specialists. A specialist is generally extensively trained in a narrow area of competence.

Stable environment The stable environment is one in which changes are relatively small, occurring in limited increments with a minimal impact on the structures, processes, and output of an organization. This environment is characterized by a very high level of predictability. (See Volatile environment.)

Staff authority This refers to the relationship between individuals in line organizations and in staff units. Staff authority is advisory, which means that the staff recommends actions or alternative actions to the appropriate line manager. The line manager then makes the decision about whether or not to implement the staff advice.

Staff departments Staff departments are units that provide support to the rest of the organization.

Their primary objective is to help support the line or primary activities. The role of staff should, in general, be advisory or supportive in relationship to these units.

Staffing Staffing is a process of providing needed human resources to the organization. It includes the activities of recruitment, selection, and placement.

Standard A standard is a quantitative, qualitative, or behavioral index that indicates the desired frequency, desired quantity, or desired type of outcome.

Standard, explicit An explicit standard is an objective, obvious, and usually quantitatively expressed criterion against which a comparison is made to determine whether a situation is acceptable or needs some corrective action.

Standards, behavioral These standards focus on ways individuals carry out an activity. Behavioral standards are used when it is not possible to develop output standards for an activity. In using behavioral standards, a manager monitors how a person goes about doing a job rather than the output. (See Standards, output.)

Standards, comparative These standards are set by examining the practices or the results of other organizations, or organizational units, similar to the one in which the standard will be applied.

Standards, historical Historical standards are based on previous cost, past sales history, or past production time. The organization's own experience is the basis for setting historical standards, which are used to evaluate future performance.

Standards, output Output standards generally focus on quantifiable or verifiable aspects of qual-ity, quantity, time, or cost against which a particular level of performance can be compared. (See Standards, behavioral.)

Standards, subjective A subjective standard is a feeling of what should be, rather than an explicit standard.

Standards, synthetic Synthetic standards are constructed from "standard data." Standard data are time and/or cost estimates for different predetermined units of work. Using standard data, time and cost estimates can be determined before a task has been performed and measured.

State of nature The state of nature is the environment, beyond the control of the decision maker, in which the choice will be implemented and which will determine the success or failure of the decision.

Status Status refers to the hierarchical ranking of roles in a group or organization such that some roles may be said to be "higher than" or "superior to" others. Status distinctions are usually a function of skill, wealth, power, or popularity.

Stimulus (cue) A stimulus is a factor or a condition that triggers a response. Stimuli or cues are those aspects of the environment that have a significant impact on behavior in the next time interval. (See Reinforcement theory.)

Strategy Strategy is the overall master plan of how to provide goods and services within the bounds of the mission and domain. Strategies are conceptual ideas about how to achieve these strategic objectives. (See Mission.)

Strategy congruence Strategy congruence refers to the degree to which there is a "fit" between cur-rent activities and planned activities.

Structure, group Group structure refers to the predictability of norms, roles, networks, and status and how these factors are related to each other. When interaction patterns within a group are easily predictable, there is said to be high group structure. When interaction patterns are less predictable and are not quite so clear, there is low group structure.

Subsystems Subsystems are related groups of activities within the organization that must be performed to meet the organization's objectives.

Subsystems, cross-departmental This is the case in which a subsystem activity (say, production or boundary spanning) is carried out in different formal departments, such as in the manufacturing department and in the marketing department.

Sunk cost principle A resource is worth, not what it cost in the past, but what it will bring in the future. Past investments, and expenditures are history and must be forgotten, written off, and discarded if they have no earning capacity, no matter what their book value is.

Supervisory management Managing at the lowest organizational level is supervisory management. A supervisor usually has responsibility for operative employees or specialists, but not other managers.

Synectics Synectics is an approach to generating alternatives to problems in which the decision maker is required to make analogies from some unrelated field to the problem at hand to find effective solutions to problems.

T

Task cluster   This term is used to refer to a group of jobs that have similarity of task content, and are different from other groups.

Task interdependence   When tasks are interdependent it means that success in performing the whole job depends on successfully performing each individual task.

Task structure   Task structure refers to the extent to which a job is well defined. High task structure refers to well-defined jobs in which each aspect is spelled out. Low task structure is present when job requirements are unclear and ambiguous. (See Leadership theory, contingency.)

Team building (development process)   Team building is a process by which problem groups are brought together to discuss the weaknesses in their relationship and to work out a new one. Team building is a particular kind of confrontation approach in which a group leader attempts to minimize problems by constructing an agenda that provides each group an opportunity to express problems, consider the problems of the other group, and then discuss and evaluate these differences before developing a solution.

Team building (motivation strategy)   This is a motivation strategy in which effort is made to foster the formation of cohesive work groups that adopt the norm of high performance. The idea underlying this approach is that groups with a high standard of performance will pressure individual members to perform at a higher level.

Technical skill   Technical skill is the specialized knowledge a person needs to perform the major functions and tasks associated with the position.

Technological environment   The technological environment includes the machines, procedures, and knowledge used to produce products or services. It also includes the scientific or technical knowledge on which the production system is based.

Technological factors   Technological factors are the tools, machines, facilities, and equipment that a person uses in performing a task. Work may make use of very limited technological factors, such as in human-skill-dominated activities. On the other hand, some work is dominated by technology. (See Automation.)

Technologies, intensive   In this production system, many different techniques are used to produce the product or service, but these techniques are selected and combined into different sequences based on the product, project, or object itself. Job shop manufacturing is an example of an intensive technology. (See Production subsystem.)

Technology, long-linked   This is a work system in which there is serial or sequential interdependence of tasks, such that Task B can be performed only after Task A is completed, while Task C requires both A and B to be finished. (See Production subsystem.)

Technology, mediating   In this production subsystem, activities are designed to link clients, or customers who are or who wish to be interdependent. (See Production subsystem.)

Technology - dominated mixed organization (TD-mixed)   This is an organization for which the technological environment is highly volatile, while the market environ-ment is relatively stable. The TD-mixed organization has one major part of its structure interacting with the stable market, leading to a mechanistic structure in the marketing sector. The adaptive subsystem of a TD-mixed organization interacts with a highly volatile technological environment, leading to a more organic structure within the adaptive system. (See Mixed organization.)

Technology - dominated work   With technology-dominated work, machinery of some sort controls the pace, capacity, and quality of an individual's output. (See Human-skill-dominated work.)

Theory X   This approach to management is based on the assumption that human beings are lazy, their personal goals run counter to the organization's, and, therefore, a person has to be controlled externally. Theory X advocates close supervision and guidance, so that high performance will be obtained.

Theory Y   This approach to management is based on the assumption of trust in the individual. It assumes that a person is mature, self-motivated, and self-controlled. Advocates of Theory Y believe there is little need for a rigid organization or interpersonal controls.

Time-delayed outcome   A time-delayed outcome means that the results of work will not be known, and therefore cannot be assessed for control purposes, until a future time.

Time estimates   For PERT, a time estimate is a judgment of the time required for an activity to be completed. To obtain a time estimate (te), three estimated times are obtained. The optimistic (o), the most likely (ml), and the pessimistic (p). The time estimate is determined by the following formula:

$$te = \frac{o + 4ml + p}{6}$$

(See PERT, Optimistic time, Most likely time, and Pessimistic time.)

Time Horizon The period of time into the future for which a plan or forecast is made is the time horizon.

Top management Top management includes those managers at the highest level of the organization who have the responsibility of making decisions about organizational objectives and how to get there. Top managers generally focus on policy questions.

Total costs The sum of fixed costs plus total variable costs equal total costs.

Two-factor theory A motivation theory proposed by Herzberg, this theory proposes that two specific sets of factors affect the individual at work. One set of factors is labeled *hygiene*. The second set is called *motivating*. Hygiene factors are associated with dissatisfaction with work, but their presence does not cause satisfaction. Motivators, on the other hand, do not induce dissatisfaction if they are not present, but their existence in the work setting induces higher motivation and performance. (See Hygiene factors, Motivating factors.)

U

Unfreezing Unfreezing is the first step in the change process. In unfreezing, attempts are made to motivate the target person, group, or organization before the actual change or intervention is introduced. Common to the unfreezing stage is the removal of social support for the individual for the old behavior or attitudes. (See Changing.)

Unity of command Unity of command is a managerial principle that states that a person should have only one superior to whom he or she is accountable in an organization.

V

Valence Valences are anticipated satisfactions that will result from work outcomes. Different outcomes have different valences for individuals. Valences are individual's estimates of the future pleasantness or unpleasantness of an outcome. (See Expectancy theory, Expectancy.)

Validity Validity is a characteristic of measurement or standard that refers to whether or not the measure assesses what it is intended to measure.

Values Values are deeply ingrained, general beliefs about what a person considers good or bad, important or unimportant. Values serve as a means or a standard for evaluating things and events. Values are the base from which attitudes emerge, perceptions develop, and behavior occurs.

Values, intended These values are important to a manager, but do not necessarily fit the work situation. Usually a person's experience leads him or her to conclude that while these values are important, they are often not organizationally rewarded. Some intended values are rationality, patriotism, and freedom.

Values, low behavior relevance These are values that are unlikely to affect a manager's work behavior directly but may be important in other dimensions of life. Values such as equality, material comfort, and external conformity have low behavior relevance to work.

Values, operative Those values that have the most direct influence on the work behavior of managers. Operative managerial values are achievement and success, activity and work, practicality and pragmatism.

Variable costs These costs vary or change as the production level changes. They are costs incurred each time an additional unit is produced and/or sold.

Vertical loading Vertical loading refers to a form of job enrichment. It means that instead of merely assigning a person more different activities, the job should be expanded vertically in the organizational hierarchy. Vertical loading means including some responsibility for deciding how to do a job and when to do it. It increases the amount of autonomy on a job. (See Job enrichment.)

Volatile environment This environment is turbulent and unstable with more intense changes than in the stable environment. Changes are likely to be rapid and random, and prediction of these changes is very difficult. (See Stable environment.)

Vroom-Yetton model of leadership This is a contingency theory of leadership, based on the work of Norman Maier. It is a normative or prescriptive model of leadership because it describes how managers should act or behave. The leader behaviors in this theory may range from autocractic to participative. The appropriate leadership style is contingent upon seven characteristics: (1) the quality characteristics of the problem; (2) the amount of information a decision maker has; (3) the problem structure; (4) the importance of subordinates' acceptance; (5) whether or not the decision is within the psychological contract; (6) subordinate motivation to achieve goals; and (7) potential subordinate disagreement. (See Contingency theories of leadership.)

W

"Want" objectives In decision making these objectives are states or outcomes that are not necessarily critical for alternatives to meet, but they are desirable. A decision maker will select an alternative that, after meeting the "must" objectives, satisfies the most "wants." (See "Must" objectives.)

Wealth of Nations, The This is an important book on economic philosophy written by Adam Smith. It introduced a new economic philosophy that spurred a change in thinking that allowed the Industrial Revolution to occur as it did. It basically argued that individuals, acting in their own self-interest, would make decisions to enhance the wealth of a nation better than these decisions could be made by a king.

Work cycle The work cycle is the time that elapses from the start of a work activity until it starts again.

Work ethic (also called Protestant ethic) A value or a belief that to work is good and that everyone should want to work. The work ethic emerges when socialization experiences lead individuals to believe that they should be involved in and highly committed to their work.

Work Planning (management by objectives, MBO) (See Management by objectives.)

NAME INDEX

Aas, D., 382
Adams, A. V., 546
Adams, J. S., 396, 412
Aiken, M., 294
Aldag, R. J., 542, 547
Alderfer, C. P., 121
Allport, G. W., 151
Alvares, K., 382
Anderson, R. C., 348
Ansoff, H. I., 211
Argyris, C., 35, 40
Arvey, R. D., 121
Aryeh, K., 122
Atkinson, J. W., 412
Atkinson, R. C., 441
Atkinson, R. L., 441
Ausubel, D. P., 546
Ausubel, P., 456
Ayoub, E., 386, 387
Ayres, R. U., 534, 546

Bachman, J. G., 547
Bakeman, R., 412
Bakerman, R., 151
Banas, P. A., 121
Bandura, A., 343, 350
Barnard, C., 21, 25, 28, 33, 34, 40, 354, 382
Barnes, L., 498
Bartol, K. M., 542, 547
Behsey, W., 547
Bell, C. H., 348
Bell, D., 25, 40, 547
Bell, R. W., 296
Bendix, R., 40
Bennis, W. G., 545

Bissell, G., 19
Blake, R. R., 338, 348
Blau, P., 250, 255
Blauner, R., 91
Bolda, R. A., 342, 349
Bond, B. W., 349
Boretsky, M., 546
Bowers, D. L., 374
Boyd, J. B., 350
Bradley, O. T., 297
Bray, D. W., 547
Brigham, E., 216, 231
Briscoe, D., 122
Brown, C. C., 523
Bucy, J. F., 323
Bunker, D. R., 350
Burek, C. G., 479, 545
Burnham, D. C., 256
Burns, T., 21, 37, 48, 60, 91, 151
Butler, E. D., 349
Butler, J. L., 349
Buxton, C. E., 348

Campbell, J. P., 184, 350
Campbell, R. M., 545
Capwell, D. F., 121
Carey, A., 40
Carroll, S. J., 10, 121, 226, 231, 255, 294, 348, 350, 367, 382, 411, 412, 417, 429, 441, 498, 499
Castore, G. F., 349
Cates, J. N., 546
Cavanaugh, G., 121
Chesser, R. J., 350
Child, J., 294, 547

SUBJECT INDEX